Psychology

James D. Laird

Nicholas S. Thompson

CLARK UNIVERSITY

HOUGHTON MIFFLIN COMPANY Boston Toronto

Dallas   Geneva, Illinois   Palo Alto   Princeton, New Jersey

Senior sponsoring editor: Michael DeRocco
Senior project editor: Carol Newman
Assistant design manager: Karen Rappaport
Production coordinator: Frances Sharperson
Senior manufacturing coordinator: Marie Barnes
Marketing manager: Diane McOscar

Anatomical illustrations by Lena Lyons

Charts and graphs by Network Graphics

Illustrations by Steven Moore on pages 56, 60, 75, 82, 91, 98, 99, 101, 109, 115, 129, 153, 162, 163, 173, 204, 214, 220, 221, 248, 274, 275, 276, 278, and 334

Photo research by Photosearch, Inc. New York City

Credits

Cover: Oskar Schlemmer, *Mädchenkopf in Farbiger Karierung,* 1932. Private collection, © 1991, the Oskar Schlemmer family estate, Badenweiler, Germany. Photoarchive C. Raman Schlemmer, Oggebbio, Italy.

(Credits continue following references.)

Printed in the U.S.A.

Library of Congress Catalog Card Number: 91-71977

ISBN: 0-395-47090-0

ABCDEFGHIJ-VH-954321

Brief Contents

Contents

10 Emotion and Stress   266

11 The Origins of Development   296

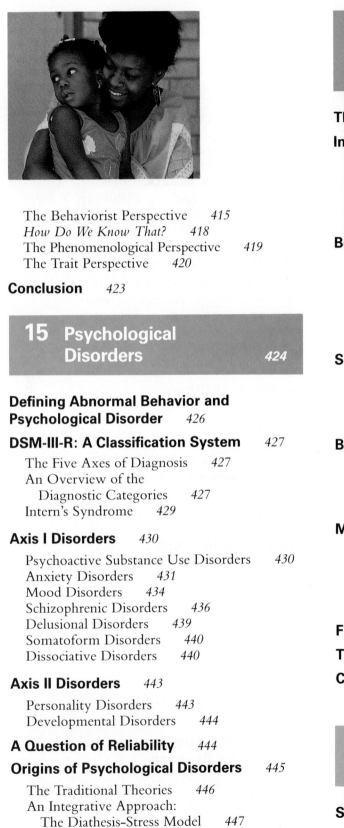

Preface

Some years ago, a volume entitled *The Book of Lists* reached the top of the best-seller lists. Hundreds of thousands of readers (we were two of them) enjoyed such curiosities as the ten funniest names for cities and the ten worst movies of all time.

A book of lists is fine for a rainy day's pursuit of interesting trivia; but an introductory college text, designed to give readers their first coherent picture of a field of study, must avoid the book-of-lists approach. To do otherwise gives students the misimpression that science is about "facts" or "key concepts" when the field's practitioners know it is about far more.

Too often we have been offered introductory texts that provided a biopsychology list, a sensation list, and so on, without actively engaging students in a thoughtful inquiry into the field. Whatever else we may have achieved with this book, we believe we have not added merely another item to the list of books of lists.

Coverage of Psychology

The dynamic nature of psychology, its capacity for change as it accommodates fresh ideas, is what most excites us about the field. We have sought to explain the discoveries psychology has made while acknowledging that many aspects of human behavior remain the subject of debate. We treat controversies and contradictory findings as a positive quality that energizes researchers and thrusts our science forward. Indeed, although our book contains many well-verified research results, we have strived to present the specific, if often incomplete, findings of our science as the outcomes of systematic attempts at problem solving. Thus, for example, Chapter 8 introduces research on teaching sign language to apes as a response to inadequately supported assumptions about animals' linguistic ability. Chapter 14 presents Freudian theory by tracking Freud's attempt to answer intriguing questions and resolve conflicting evidence about the human personality.

In trying to represent the wide range of problems and solutions that psychology encompasses we examine several topics that some other books overlook. Notable features of coverage include:

- Integration of the comparative and evolutionary perspectives wherever appropriate—for example, in Chapter 3 when we discuss the range of sounds humans can hear, in Chapter 5 when we discuss sleep, and in Chapter 11 when we consider the relative helplessness of the human infant.
- In Chapter 4 on perception, discussion of both the traditional constructionist model and the Gibsonian ecological approach.
- In Chapter 10 on emotion and stress, coverage of the relationship between emotion and cognition.
- In Chapter 13 on psychological assessment, substantive consideration of racial, cultural, and gender issues in the study of intelligence.
- In Chapter 15 on abnormal behavior, consideration of behavioral genetics as an influence on both depression and schizophrenia.

The text covers all the main topics in introductory psychology in a sequence that has become fairly standard. To accommodate instructors who wish to teach in a different sequence we have, to the greatest extent possible, designed each chapter to stand alone.

Narrative Approach

We have strived to adhere to the following principles in writing our book:

- Speak candidly to the student as if he or she were seated across a table.
- Draw from our own experiences to create vignettes that connect scientific psychology to everyday life. (Each chapter begins with a vignette that illustrates a principle important to that chapter, and other vignettes are sprinkled throughout the text.)
- Provide abundant illustrative examples. (In our experience as teachers, this proves especially helpful in discussing such topics as sensation and perception.)
- Use questions frequently, both to provoke curiosity and to anticipate the points at which students would naturally be curious. (This narrative technique is compatible in spirit with two critical-thinking features in the book, which we describe below.)
- To keep the student mindful throughout the book that psychologists employ the logic and methods of science, pepper the narrative with succinct descriptions of how research studies have been conducted. (This we have done in every chapter.)

In pursuing these principles we have reviewed, revised, and argued over each other's chapters in every draft. The result, we trust, is an integrated book that flows like a good novel or a good lecture.

Features That Promote Critical Thinking

During the past decade we have recognized an increasing need to help students—especially first-year students—learn how to think analytically. In our experience, the most effective way to achieve this is by gently prodding and inspiring students to tap the vein of their own curiosity and intelligence. We both believe that thinking is not just work but fun as well.

From that perspective we have created two critical-thinking features for the book, *Puzzle It Out!* and *How Do We Know That?* At least one specimen of each appears in every chapter except Chapter 1.

Each *Puzzle It Out!* presents a kind of riddle about human behavior. If a student has studied the preceding chapter text carefully, he or she should be able to provide an approach to solving the riddle. Although a suggested response to each *Puzzle It Out!* appears in the accompanying *Instructor's Resource Manual,* we submit that deriving the precisely correct answers is not the point. The point is to encourage the thoughtful application and synthesis of text material. We have both found that puzzles such as these provoke rich and exciting classroom discussions, as well.

An essential component of critical thinking in psychology involves an understanding of the means psychologists use to gather and interpret information. The purpose of *How Do We Know That?* is to encourage students to "think along with psychologists." Some students have a knack for inquiring about virtually any theoretical assertion or research finding, "How did the psychologist know that?" *How Do We Know That?* enables us to promote such inquisitiveness in *every* reader, and in the process, to explain the logic, as well as the methods, of research psychologists. We ask students to think along with Roger Sperry, Stanley Schachter, and other researchers as they devise ways of learning about human behavior.

Other Pedagogical Features

We have built a number of learning aids into the book, some to help students stay on track as they read, others to promote retention and mastery of the material. Every chapter includes:

- A chapter outline.
- *Gateways,* a chapter introduction that both explains why psychologists study the chapter topic and notes other topics to which the chapter at hand is directly relevant.
- Key terms placed in boldface type and defined in the margin as well as in the text narrative the first time they appear.
- *Recap,* a summary of each major section in each chapter. These are presented concisely in small units of information. Because they help the student to review information in more frequent chunks, we believe these *Recaps* improve upon the standard chapter summary.
- Unusually substantive captions to figures, photographs, and many of the tables. Rather than simply reiterate the text, these captions expand and elaborate on it.

Ancillaries That Accompany the Text

A wide range of ancillary items is available to adopters of the text, including a *Test Bank,* an *Instructor's Resource Manual,* and a *Study Guide,* all of which are unified by the same set of learning objectives.

Test Bank (by Gary G. Bothe and Susan J. Bothe, Pensacola Junior College)

The *Test Bank* contains over 2,400 multiple-choice questions (130 to 135 per chapter plus 30 on statistics). For each question the following is provided: the correct answer; the text page on which the answer can be found; the learning objective to which the question corresponds; and the type of knowledge that the question tests—"F/C" for facts and concepts, and "App" for applications.

Instructor's Resource Manual (by Richard L. Leavy, Ohio Wesleyan University)

The *Instructor's Resource Manual* contains a complete set of lecture outlines and learning objectives. Lecture topics, demonstrations, handouts, classroom exercises, and audiovisual resources complete the package, providing instructors with a wide array of materials that can be adapted to large or small sections of the introductory course.

Unique to this manual is the presentation in every chapter of two topics—gender differences and alcohol use—as a lecture idea, a classroom activity, or both. These topics were chosen because they are notably relevant to students' lives, have been extensively researched, and are broad enough to be linked to virtually every topic in psychology. Moreover, examining topics from different vantage points provides instructors with yet another way to demonstrate the interconnectedness of psychology's subfields.

Study Guide (by Richard L. Leavy, Ohio Wesleyan University)

The *Study Guide* is an interactive learning tool designed to maximize students' involvement with the course material. Each chapter contains a detailed outline, the same learning objectives that appear in the *Instructor's Resource Manual,* and a fill-in-the-blank quiz of key terms. Also provided in each chapter are thirty multiple-choice questions, testing both factual and applied knowledge. An answer key tells students not only which response is correct but also why each of the other choices is incorrect. Inclusion of text page numbers points students to the corresponding sections of the text.

Computer Ancillaries

The *Test Bank, Instructor's Resource Manual,* and *Study Guide* are also available to adopters on disk for use on microcomputers.

- The computerized *Test Bank* allows instructors to generate exams and to integrate their own test items with those on disk.
- The detailed lecture outlines that appear in the *Instructor's Resource Manual* are available on disk in a generic ASCII-code version. This format allows instructors to use standard word-processing software to integrate their own lecture notes and ideas into the text lectures.
- The computerized *Study Guide* is an interactive program that gives students feedback on incorrect as well as on correct answers.

These additional software items are also available to adopters:

- *Psychabilities*, a new package of computer simulations created by Sarah Ransdell, New College of the University of South Florida. *Psychabilities* illustrates intriguing psychological phenomena and allows students to participate in experiments. Specially designed to serve instructors in the lecture hall as well as the individual student in the computer lab, these simulations are accompanied by an instructor's guide.
- *Flash Card,* an ancillary that helps students to master the technical vocabulary of psychology.

Transparencies

Also offered to adopters is a set of 140 transparencies, most in color. One hundred images are from the text, forty from other sources.

Videocassettes

A range of videocassettes containing films on topics in psychology is available to adopters who order a minimum number of new texts.

Acknowledgments

A text of this size and complexity is inevitably a team effort. Reviewers of the manuscript have been an invaluable part of that team. To the following reviewers, who evaluated all or parts of various drafts, we extend our thanks.

James R. Averill, University of Massachusetts, Amherst
Terry D. Blumenthal, Wake Forest University
Galen Bodenhausen, Michigan State University
Gary G. Bothe, Pensacola Junior College
Susan J. Bothe, Pensacola Junior College
John Broida, University of Southern Maine
Gary P. Brown, Kellogg Community College
George A. Cicala, University of Delaware
Keith Clayton, Vanderbilt University
Bob Crowder, Yale University
Ken DeBono, Union College
Wendy Idson Domjan, University of Texas, Austin
Carol M. Donnelly, Purdue University
Robert A. Frank, University of Cincinnati
Philip E. Freedman, University of Illinois, Chicago
Mauricio Gaborit, St. Louis University
Todd W. Gaffaney, Cerritos College
Marian Gibney, Phoenix College
Carol B. Giesen, St. Mary's College
Sherryl H. Goodman, Emory University
Peter C. Gram, Pensacola Junior College
Diane F. Halpern, California State University, San Bernardino
Richard H. Haude, University of Akron
B.R. Hergenhahn, Hamline University
Deborah Holmes, Loyola University of Chicago
Timothy D. Johnston, University of North Carolina, Greensboro
Cindy B. Kennedy, Sinclair Community College
Mike Knight, University of Central Oklahoma
G. Daniel Lassiter, Ohio University
Richard L. Leavy, Ohio Wesleyan University
T.C. Lewandowski, Delaware County College
Inez B. Livingston, Eastern Illinois University
Alan Marks, Berry College
Donald H. McBurney, University of Pittsburgh
Teri L. Nicoll-Johnson, Modesto Junior College
Kenneth W. Nikels, Kearney State College
Thomas C. Patton, Graceland College
Camille M. Quinn, Tulsa Junior College
William J. Ray, Pennsylvania State University
Samuel B. Rhodes, Franklin College
Deborah R. Richardson, Florida Atlantic University
Frank C. Savage, DeAnza College
Jonathan W. Schooler, University of Pittsburgh
Kathryn Schwarz, Scottsdale Community College
Daniel Shaw, University of Pittsburgh
William D. Siegfried, Jr., University of North Carolina, Charlotte
Linda Spear, State University of New York, Binghamton
Joseph J. Tecce, Boston College
Wayne Van Zomeren, Northwest Missouri State University
Benjamin Wallace, Cleveland State University

Paul J. Wellman, Texas A & M University
Ward M. Winton, College of St. Thomas
Ric Wynn, County College of Morris

For sharing their expertise in publishing, we wish to thank a number of people at Houghton Mifflin Company. Our sponsoring editor, Mike DeRocco, helped and encouraged us at every stage of the project, from before we had imagined the book to the writing of the last word. Our developmental editors—Nancy Fleming, who nursed us through the first painful steps, and Barbara Pitnof—had a major impact on the manuscript and taught us much. The book benefited greatly from the skills of its production editor, Carol Newman, who cheerfully insisted that we finish on time and made it possible for us to do so.

Scanning through the Clark University psychology department's roster of colleagues, staff, graduate students, and undergraduate assistants, we are hard pressed to find anyone who did not render us substantial aid while this book was in development; we must, however, single out Josh Searle and Sara Gay, who helped us greatly in our research. Our families, too, played a crucial role, supplying critical commentary, ideas, and boundless patience and understanding. We are grateful to them all.

To the Student

We are pleased to be playing a part in your introductory psychology course, and we welcome you to a field of study that we find endlessly fascinating.

We have included in this book a number of features designed to help you master and enjoy the material. You'll encounter an explanation of these features in the first chapter, on page 23.

We've also included in Chapter 7, on memory, a description of a learning system widely used to enhance the study of any written material—the SQ3R system. You might wish to turn to that description, on pages 204–205, before you begin this textbook.

Both of us are interested in knowing how well this book meets students' needs, and we'd appreciate your sharing your opinions with us. You can write to us at the Department of Psychology, Clark University, Worcester, MA 01610.

Psychology

To our wives, Nan Laird and Penny Thompson, who did more than their share.

Chapter 1

Psychology: The Science of Behavior and Experience

1

Gateways Some years ago, a U.S. Senator bitterly criticized federal funding for psychological research on romantic love. He doubted psychologists could ever understand anything as mysterious as love. Even if they could, he didn't want to know their conclusions, fearing they would rob love of its wonder. The same pair of questions—Can we understand? Should we try?—can be asked about all of psychology.

The weight of this book in your hands implies the answer to the first question. Psychologists have indeed discovered a great deal about human behavior. In the chapters to come, you will read about research on how people gather and retain information, what forces drive us to act, and why each of us acts differently from the others. You will learn what psychologists have discovered about how society shapes us

and how we develop through the life span. You will even find out a little about romantic love. Psychologists are a long way from having all the answers but have made remarkable progress.

As to the second question: Does our knowledge destroy some essential human magic? Does the science of love tarnish its luster, as the Senator feared? We think you will discover the answer is "No," just as under-

standing great cooking doesn't make food less delectable. Knowing more about ourselves and others is sometimes useful and always interesting.

Psychologist George Kelly (1955) once said that we are all psychologists, and in a way he was right. We spend a great deal of time trying to understand why people act and feel the way they do. And like psychologists, we use various methods to explain other people's behavior. We see a behavior, we invent explanations for that behavior, and then we "test" our explanations by watching what the individual does.

Imagine it's your first day back on campus. You see an old friend, and wave and call her name. She stops and looks in your direction, then turns away and goes into a building. If you're like most people, you're going to wonder why she ignored you. Is she mad because you didn't write all summer? Or maybe she just didn't see you. Maybe she wasn't wearing her contact lenses. The next time you see her, you'll watch carefully for some clue about her feelings. Is she friendly now? Does she ask you about your summer? If not, perhaps she's angry because you didn't write. But suppose she squints a little as you come near and then seems to recognize you all of a sudden. Even before she tells you she's lost her contacts, you're pretty sure that's why she didn't speak to you the other day.

This process—observing a behavior, coming up with an explanation for that behavior, and then testing the explanation with more observation—is almost automatic. It's simply your common sense at work, helping you understand the way people act and feel. In many ways it's very much like the process psychologists use. They, too, observe people's actions, develop explanations for those actions, and then test their explanations with further observation.

Of course, there are important differences between psychology and common sense. Those differences have to do with the methods psychologists use to make observations and with the kinds of explanations their observations lead them to. Those differences are what makes psychology a science.

Psychology, the Science

Psychology is the science of behavior and experience. By **science** we mean a discipline that uses systematic observation or experimentation to describe, explain, and predict events in the world. **Behavior** is any activity that can be observed—what we do, what we say, even how our bodies respond to elements in the environment. **Experience** is our feelings, our thoughts, our perceptions.

Psychology is the study of the things we do and feel: how we behave toward our friends and enemies, our children and parents; how we feel about our lives—our fears, hopes, loves, hatreds, joys, griefs; how we perceive the world around us; how we come to be the way we are—optimistic or pessimistic, impulsive or careful, easygoing or intense, sociable or solitary; why our behavior and feelings change from day to day, even from minute to minute.

Just about now you're probably wondering how personal relationships are studied, how thoughts and feelings are measured. The question of how scientific methods are applied to behavior and experience is fundamental to psychology,

Psychology The science of behavior and experience.

Science A discipline that uses systematic observation and experimentation to describe, explain, and predict events in the world.

Behavior Any activity that can be observed.

Experience Feelings, thoughts, and perceptions.

3

and we discuss it at length in this chapter. We explore the similarities and differences between the science of psychology and the common-sense methods all people use to understand themselves and others in the environment. We trace the development of psychology the science. And we describe the methods psychologists use to examine behavior and experience.

The Scientific Method

When psychologists make observations, they follow formal procedures—procedures that are much more systematic than the ones we use every day to understand behavior and experience. These procedures, taken as a whole, are what we mean by the **scientific method.** They help make observations more objective, precise, and reliable.

- Scientific observations should be *objective*—that is, impartial. They should not reflect the observer's personal feelings, prejudices, or expectations.
- Scientific observations should be *precise*. Scientists aren't satisfied to say that someone is "a little scared" or "very hungry." They strive to devise a means of measuring just how scared or hungry that person is.
- Scientific observations should be *reliable*. This means that they can be repeated by the same observer and others following the same procedures.

Precise measurement and description of human activities is a concern not only of psychologists but to others as well. This illustration is an example of a notation system developed by choreographers to describe the movements of dancers. Psychologists have adapted this system to study other kinds of movements, including those of animals.

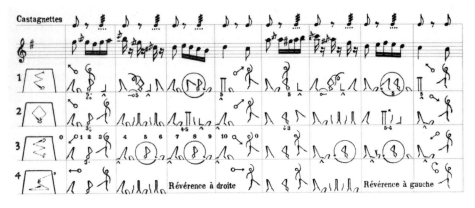

Source: Tufte, 1990.

Theories

Scientific method   The procedures that help make observations more objective, precise, and reliable.

Theory   A general explanation of how things work based on a number of systematic observations.

Hypothesis   An expectation, based on a theory, of how something will behave under specific circumstances.

Operational definition   A description of particular procedures and measurements used in an experiment, which define the concepts being studied.

Scientists use a formal method to make their observations; they also use a formal method to explain their observations. A **theory** is a general explanation of how things work based on a number of systematic observations. Theories are used to generate **hypotheses,** expectations of how things will behave under specific circumstances. For example, the idea that organisms need a minimum amount of sleep to function well is a theory. The expectation that students who stay up all night studying for a psychology exam will earn lower grades than students who get a good night's sleep is a hypothesis.

Theories are *explicit.* They are defined in a way that allows others to examine and test them. This means that every term used in a theory must have an **operational definition,** a description of particular procedures and measurements used in an experiment. For the purpose of the experiment, these procedures define the concepts being studied. In other words, an operational definition is a "recipe" that spells out the ingredients and steps necessary to produce a certain phenomenon. For example, if you wanted to study the effect of hypnosis on memory, you would describe exactly what you would do to produce a "hypnotic state," how you would know if you had succeeded, and how you would measure memory.

Theories are also *general*. Common-sense explanations tend to be specific: "Joe is angry because his car wouldn't start this morning," or "My cousin did well on her SATs because her side of the family always did have the brains." But theories have to apply to as many circumstances and individuals as possible. Sigmund Freud's theories purport to explain the behavior and experience of people in different historical times and cultures. (Whether they do a good job is open to question, as you'll see in future chapters.) B. F. Skinner, the famous behavioral psychologist, called his work *The Behavior of Organisms* (1938) because he believed the theories contained within it were as applicable to pigeons and rats as to people.

Finally, theories are *coherent*. In everyday life, people don't necessarily worry about how their ideas relate to one another. "Absence makes the heart grow fonder" we say when a summer separation seems to strengthen the feelings of a couple we know. "Out of sight, out of mind" we say the following year, when the same couple breaks up after vacation. We don't try to explain why one old saying applies one year and another the next.

Scientists are not this casual. When they find an inconsistency, they work hard to resolve it. For example, in Chapter 3 we describe two different theories that explain how we hear sounds of different pitch (*pitch* is the placement of sound on the musical scale). Our modern understanding of hearing is based on both theories: one explains how people hear low-pitched sounds; the other explains how people hear high-pitched sounds; and a combination of the two explains how people hear intermediate-pitched sounds. Inconsistencies in one theory led to the development of the other, and inconsistencies in the other theory led to the combination theory.

Studying Psychology

The relationship of psychology to the things you do every day makes it different from other subjects you've studied—easier in some ways, harder in others. It's easier because psychology's relevance to your everyday life makes it particularly interesting. For example, if you're active in a club or interested in politics, you have probably noticed that groups of intelligent people often make terrible decisions. You may have your own ideas about why this happens. If so, you won't be surprised to learn that a theory called *groupthink* was devised by psychologist Irving Janis (1983) to explain the problems of group decision making. An understanding of this kind of connection between psychology and everyday events can help you see why psychologists took up a particular line of research and how the results of that research can be put to practical use. Janis's theory, for example, is studied not only by psychologists but also by political scientists, business managers, and others who make their living working with groups of people.

But sometimes the relevance of psychology to everyday life can get in the way of your understanding. You bring to the study of psychology all of the common-sense explanations you've developed or adopted through the years. Some of them are supported by scientific findings; others aren't. *Counterintuitive findings* are findings that violate common sense. Throughout this book we discuss the results of experiments that will challenge your beliefs about behavior and experience (see Figure 1.1). You are going to learn new and surprising things.

Separating psychology from common-sense explanations of behavior and experience is one of the most difficult tasks faced by psychologists. And the problem is not a new one. They've been tackling it for more than a century.

Figure 1.1
Some Counterintuitive
Research Results

Here are some examples of research findings that challenge the
ways in which we tend to see
things. All of them are discussed
in later chapters of this book.

- In a sense, the two halves of the brain have separate personalities. (Chapter 2)
- Some children who are missing large portions of their brains are high achievers in school. (Chapter 2)
- When you mix red and green lights, you don't get a reddish-green or a greenish-red. You get a bright yellow. (Chapter 3)
- When we are sleeping most deeply, our brains are as active as when we are wide awake. (Chapter 5)
- You can get a person who has not been hypnotized to perform almost any task that someone under hypnosis would. All you have to do is ask. (Chapter 5)
- Most punishment has little effect on learning. (Chapter 8)

- At least sometimes, feeling happy doesn't make you smile. Instead, smiling makes you happy. (Chapter 10)
- Newborns actually mimic the facial expressions of those around them. (Chapter 11)
- Most of us pass through adolescence with a minimum of fuss. (Chapter 12)
- Most elderly people are healthy, happy, and independent. (Chapter 12)
- We sometimes don't know what we believe until we hear ourselves say something about a subject. (Chapter 17)
- In certain circumstances, most of us willingly do things that we believe are causing severe pain to another person even though that person is not threatening us. (Chapter 18)

Recap

- Psychology is the science of behavior and experience.

- A science is a discipline that uses systematic observation and experimentation to describe, explain, and predict events in the world.

- Every day we make observations about our own behavior and the behavior of others, invent explanations of those observations, and test those explanations by making more observations.

- The difference between psychology and common sense has to do with the methods that psychologists use to make observations and the kinds of explanations they come up with.

- The scientific method strives to make observations objective, precise, and reliable.

- A theory is a general explanation of how things work based on a number of systematic observations.

- Scientific theories are explicit, general, and coherent.

- Research findings often challenge common-sense explanations of behavior and experience.

A History of Psychology

Psychology is a young science, little more than a century old. Its birth as a science was delayed, perhaps for centuries, because early educators, philosophers, and church leaders believed so strongly in their own explanations of the way people act, think, and feel that they did not recognize a need for the systematic study of behavior and experience.

Here we look at the history of psychology, which we divide into four periods:

- The prepsychology period (before 1859), in which philosophers and theologians dominated discussions of human experience and behavior
- The birth of psychology (the late 1800s), a period in which physiologists, philosophers, and others invented and gave a name to what we now know as the science of psychology
- The period of schools (1880s to 1960s) in which radically different approaches to psychology were developed and advocated
- Contemporary psychology (1960s to the present), a period dominated by practical applications and interest in narrow areas of study

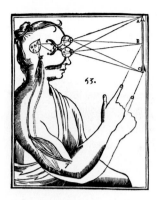

Figure 1.2
Cartesian Dualism

Descartes believed that mind and body are two separate spheres that communicate through a gland in the brain. The mind forms a thought ("move your arm"), and the body responds (the arm moves).

The Prepsychology Period

The science of psychology is little more than a hundred years old (Peters & Mace, 1967). At the time psychology was founded, chemistry had been a scientific discipline for more than a century, physics for at least two centuries, and astronomy for three. Why was a science of psychology so long in coming? And why did scientists suddenly become interested in psychology during the last decades of the nineteenth century?

A key to the answer can be found in the work of René Descartes (1596–1650), a seventeenth-century French philosopher who, in 1641, divided the world into two spheres: mind and body (see Figure 1.2). According to Descartes, elements in the sphere of the mind—religion and spiritualism—should be accepted on faith. Here church doctrine and authority prevail. But everything in the sphere of matter, everything physical, is open to question. Here scientists can doubt at will, creating their own doctrines and systems of authority. The idea that different principles guide the spiritual and physical worlds is called **Cartesian dualism.**

Cartesian dualism had a dramatic liberating effect on most sciences beginning in the seventeenth century. In physics and astronomy, scientists described the principle of gravity and the workings of the solar system. In biology, important advances were made in the understanding of anatomy and physiology. And in chemistry, scientists began to unravel the basic processes that underlie chemical reactions.

Armed with their successes, scientists began to "poach" on the sphere of the mind, on subjects that Descartes had designated as "religious turf." Philosophers began to describe the laws of human society. Physiologists began to study the operation of the human nervous system. And, most important, geologists and biologists began to examine the anatomy of living creatures and the fossils of ancient ones for evidence of human origins.

In 1859, Charles Darwin published *The Origin of Species*. He claimed that people, like other creatures, are the product not of a single act of creation but, rather, of an eon-long mechanical process he called *natural selection*. By replacing the Bible's account of creation, Darwin opened the door for scientists to examine every aspect of life, even the human mind.

Charles Darwin's theory of evolution emphasized the continuity between animal and human development, and implied that the psychological activities of human beings could be studied scientifically. Darwin himself participated in the emerging scientific study of psychology by writing a massive work on emotions.

The Infant Psychology

So, in the late nineteenth century, more and more scientists began to apply the scientific method to mental processes. Physicist Gustav Fechner, for example, tried to measure the human experience of light by relating his subjects' reactions to different intensities of light. Dutch physiologist F. C. Donders developed a

Cartesian dualism René Descartes's belief that mind and body operate under different principles and should be studied by different specialists.

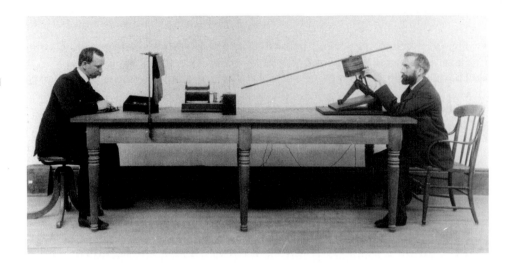

The pendulum chronograph was an elaborate mechanism used for measuring reaction times. It was developed at Clark University and displayed at the 1893 World's Columbian Exposition.

Wilhelm Wundt, one of the earliest psychologists, built the first psychology laboratory in 1879. He conducted research in areas ranging from memory and consciousness to cross-cultural comparisons.

mechanism to measure the speed of thought (Leahy, 1987). And two German physiologists, Hermann von Helmholtz and Ewald Hering, developed theories of how the eye turns the physical energy of light into the experience of color.

Most psychologists trace the birth of psychology to Wilhelm Wundt (1832–1920) and the laboratory he opened in 1879 in Leipzig, Germany (Hilgard, 1987). Wundt and his colleagues were not content to sit back in their armchairs and think about the mind; they wanted to study it, to experiment with it. For example, in an attempt to find out how many ideas people can remember at the same time, Wundt showed groups of letters to his subjects and then asked them to list as many as they could recall. His answer—four to six letters—has been confirmed by contemporary studies (Leahy, 1987).

The Period of Schools

By the end of the nineteenth century, dozens of scientists and philosophers had turned from other projects to the systematic observation of behavior and experience. Many of these people banded together in groups that shared assumptions about the most important questions to be studied and the most appropriate methods of studying them. These groups were called *schools,* although their members often worked at many different universities (see Figure 1.3).

Figure 1.3
School Timeline

This figure illustrates the prime periods during which the various schools of psychology were most influential. Cognitive psychology is still evolving, with many psychologists adopting a cognitive behavioral approach to both theory and treatment.

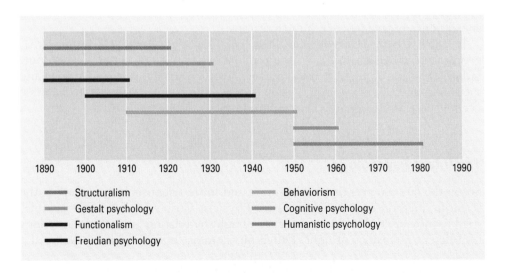

	Structuralism		Behaviorism
	Gestalt psychology		Cognitive psychology
	Functionalism		Humanistic psychology
	Freudian psychology		

Structuralism   **Structuralism** focused on *consciousness,* the awareness of feelings, thoughts, and perceptions. The founder of this school was one of Wundt's students, E. B. Titchener (1867–1927). Titchener believed that experiences could be broken down into elements, just as water can be broken down into hydrogen and oxygen. Using a method called **introspection,** he and his students identified 32,820 elements of color, 11,600 elements of hearing, and 44,435 elements of general sensation (Boring, 1942). It's not surprising that even psychologists within the structuralist tradition questioned the complexity of its method and the accuracy of its results.

Gestalt Psychology   Structuralism was analytical; it attempted to explain complex experiences by breaking them down into simpler ones. For example, taste was not a general sensation; it was a mixture of flavor qualities (sweetness, bitterness, sourness, saltiness). Adherents of **Gestalt psychology** did not agree. Psychologists like Kurt Koffka (1886–1941), Wolfgang Köhler (1887–1967), and Max Wertheimer (1880–1943) argued that the whole is a basic sensation in and of itself. (*Gestalt* is the German word for "whole" or "form.") Music, not the individual notes, is the experience. The image, not the lines used by the artist to create it, is the experience. To demonstrate Gestalt principles, psychologists used images like Figure 1.4, which showed that we first and most strongly experience the whole circle, not its parts (the x's).

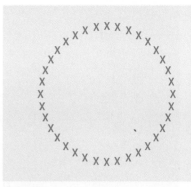

Figure 1.4
Gestalt Principles

When we look at this image we see a circle, not individual groups of Xs. Gestalt psychologists used images like this to demonstrate that we perceive forms as a whole, not by adding up their individual elements.

According to functionalists, animals (including people) are born with *instincts*—tendencies to behave in certain ways. Our instincts trigger responses to different stimuli that allow us to survive in our environment. The maternal instinct, for example, makes this mare respond to her baby's cry by nursing it.

Structuralism A school of psychology that analyzed experience by breaking it down into basic elements; associated with the work of E. B. Tichner.

Introspection The procedure of confronting subjects with a stimulus and then asking them to describe their experience of it in detail; a method used by the structuralists.

Gestalt psychology A school of psychology that believed the whole, not its parts, is the fundamental experience.

Functionalism A school of psychology that believed behavior is governed by instincts that help the individual adapt to the environment; associated with the work of William James.

Functionalism   William James (1842–1910), an anatomist, established a psychology laboratory at Harvard in 1897. His *Principles of Psychology* (1890) was the basic text for a generation of psychology students. In it he laid out the principles of **functionalism.** Drawing on Darwin, James believed that human consciousness has been shaped by evolution and that human behavior is governed by *instincts*—tendencies to behave in particular ways that help the species adapt to and survive in its environment. Like the structuralists, the functionalists focused on experience and consciousness. But the functionalists were concerned with how consciousness functioned to help human beings to survive.

Freud believed that much of our adult behavior reflects the unconscious influences of childhood events. For example, he argued that the *Mona Lisa,* painted by Leonardo DaVinci when he was in his fifties, expressed his early sexual attachment to his mother.

Behaviorism   A school of psychology that believes the study of psychology must be limited to the study of observable activity; associated with the work of John Watson, E. L. Thorndike, and B. F. Skinner.

Humanistic psychology   A school of psychology that believes that people control their own actions and thoughts; associated with the work of Carl Rogers and Abraham Maslow.

Cognitive psychology   A school of psychology that emphasizes the mental processes by which people and animals come to understand the world.

Freudian Psychology   Sigmund Freud (1856–1939) was a physician in Vienna when he came across several patients who complained of physical ailments—paralysis of an arm or leg, for example—but did not seem to have anything physically wrong with them. Freud theorized that his patients' behavior was being affected by childhood experiences that they could no longer remember, that their behavior reflected an ongoing conflict between the impulses and needs of the unconscious mind and the constraints that learning places on the conscious mind.

The problem for Freud was how to study the unconscious mind. Over time he developed the process of *psychoanalysis,* using free association to uncover the source of people's behavior and feelings. First he'd ask his patients to lie down on a couch and say whatever came to mind as they talked about their dreams or symptoms. He found patterns in these apparently random thoughts—the evidence of the unconscious mind—that helped him explain why patients acted or felt the way they did.

Behaviorism   For these early schools of psychology, the subject matter of psychology was principally human experience. **Behaviorists** argued that psychologists should focus on what could be directly observed—people's behavior, and the situation in which they behave.

John Watson (1878–1958), E. L. Thorndike (1874–1947), B. F. Skinner (1904–1990), and other behaviorists insisted that observation was a critical part of the scientific method, and that scientific observation must be objective, precise, and reliable. Because thoughts and feelings cannot be seen or measured, they argued, such things can't be studied scientifically.

Behaviorists strongly resisted the idea that instincts control behavior. They believed that behavior is shaped primarily by influences in the environment. And they studied the learning of behavior in animals, looking for principles that could be extended to people.

Humanistic Psychology   Between them, Freudian psychology and behaviorism dominated psychology throughout the first half of the twentieth century. Despite their profound differences, the two schools shared the belief that behavior is determined by something other than conscious decision making, that free will is an illusion.

In the 1950s, **humanistic psychology** took issue with these assumptions. Humanistic psychologists—among them, Carl Rogers (1905–1987) and Abraham Maslow (1908–1970)—argued that people can decide the direction of their lives, that they are free to become whatever they are capable of becoming, and that what they think and feel shapes their behavior. Whereas Freud talked about aggression, these psychologists referred to the basic goodness in people and believed that that goodness is what motivates them.

Cognitive Psychology   The behaviorists' refusal to study mental processes produced its own reaction. Some psychologists maintained that behaviorism did not fully explain how animals in general and the human animal in particular go about learning. They argued that people and animals do not just react to their environment; rather, they think about it and come to understand it. At a time when computer engineers and programmers were studying how machines "think," these psychologists wondered why behaviorists were so reluctant to study the thought processes in people and animals.

Cognitive psychology emphasizes the mental processes by which people come to understand the world (Leahy, 1987). The analogy to computers is important to cognitive psychologists. They believe that sensation and perception—the processes by which the brain examines, screens, and analyzes incoming stimuli to find meaning in them—are forms of *information processing*. To cognitive psychologists, asking whether a behavior is instinctive or learned is like asking if it's built into the brain or programmed by everyday experience.

Modern Eclectic Approaches   *Eclectic* means choosing the best parts of different theories. That's the word we use to describe psychology today. With the realization that no single school was "right" came the realization that each approach has strengths and weaknesses. Instead of allying themselves with all the methods and ideas of one particular school, psychologists began to identify with the study of a particular phenomenon, a particular method for studying that phenomenon, or a particular theory for explaining it. Today psychologists tend to group themselves by subject matter, in a list that reads very much like the chapter titles in this text.

The Work Psychologists Do

Contemporary psychologists perform a wide range of tasks in the modern world. They work with patients, they consult, they do research, and they teach.

Clinical psychologists are usually found in health care settings—hospitals, private clinics, youth guidance centers. In these settings, they help the individual, the couple, or the family sort out emotional problems. These problems can range from mild difficulties in daily living to severe disturbances. Clinical psychologists are like psychiatrists in that they treat clients, helping them understand and change their behavior. Unlike psychiatrists who have received medical training, psychologists cannot prescribe drugs. Most clinical psychologists divide their time between testing and diagnosing problems, and treating them.

Counseling psychologists, too, work with patients, often in educational settings. But the problems they see tend to be less serious than those clinical psychologists come up against (There are plenty of exceptions, of course.).

A large number of psychologists work as consultants or staff members in schools (educational psychologists), community organizations (community

Clinical psychologists diagnose and treat psychological disorders. One common kind of treatment, for headaches, for example, is to measure muscle tensions so that the sufferer can learn to control the tension and prevent the headaches.

Industrial psychologists often study the ways that people and machines interact in an effort to improve the effectiveness of the interactions and to make them as pleasant as possible. Computer and software design is one area where psychologists have played a large role.

psychologists), and government and industry (organizational and industrial psychologists). They use their knowledge to help solve the practical problems of the organizations for which they work. They test students or prospective employees to determine where they fit best. They help design work environments that are more efficient and pleasant for workers. They work on product packaging, to make it more attractive. They measure and evaluate the side effects of new drugs in development.

And there are psychologists in colleges, universities, and institutes, whose work is to teach or do research in specific areas of psychology:

- Physiological psychologists relate activity in the central nervous system to behavior and experience.
- Sensory and perceptual psychologists examine how our senses process information from the outside world.
- Comparative psychologists study the behavior and social life of animals, looking for principles of behavior that extend across different species.
- Cognitive psychologists study how people remember and organize information and how they think.
- Developmental psychologists study the changes that take place in the thoughts, feelings, and behavior of people as they age.
- Personality psychologists study the differences between people. They often design tests that reveal individual traits and study the relationship between these traits and what people actually do.
- Social psychologists study the ways in which individuals and groups interact and influence one another, and the effects of their interactions on behavior and thinking.

By any objective standard, psychology is a vigorous discipline, particularly in the United States (Rosenzweig, 1984). In 1987, there were almost 200,000 psychologists in this country (Goodstein, 1988). In institutions of higher learning, roughly one faculty member in every twenty and one graduate student in every ten are psychologists. Moreover, one undergraduate in every seven is majoring in psychology. And these figures underestimate the influence of psychology. For example, they don't include related disciplines—psychiatry, education, and psychiatric social work. In short, psychologists and the products of their work are everywhere.

Recap

- Before psychology became a science, educators, philosophers, and theologians dominated discussions of human experience and behavior.

- By questioning the Bible's version of creation, Charles Darwin opened the door for the scientific study of behavior and experience.

- We trace the birth of the science of psychology to 1879 and the work of Wilhelm Wundt.

- From the 1880s to the 1960s, psychologists tended to adopt a school of thought, each with its own methods and focus.

- Contemporary psychologists tend to concentrate on a specific phenomenon, method for studying that phenomenon, or theory for explaining it.

The Research Process

All science is an attempt to describe and explain objects and events in the real world. We observe something, propose theories to explain it, and then test our theories. Because the focus of science is something in the real world, the basic test of any scientific proposition is very simple: observation. We look to see whether things happen the way the theories claim they should.

Of course, testing psychological propositions isn't quite this simple. The world is complicated; and sometimes it's difficult to understand exactly what we're seeing. Also, we all tend to grow very attached to our own ideas, a tendency that colors our observations. To make observations easier to interpret and less susceptible to bias, psychologists have developed formal research methods.

To give you an idea of the problems psychologists face and how they solve them, let's look at a familiar example. Lots of students say that they do poorly on the SATs and other tests because they're anxious. What do you think? Does anxiety lower test performance? Certainly the idea seems plausible; but to be sure that it's true, you have to test it carefully.

Before we talk about the methods used to test this theory, a word about terminology. Psychologists refer to things like anxiety and SAT scores as **variables** because they can vary in amount. Different people get different SAT scores, and also differ in how anxious they are. What you're interested in, then, is the *relationship* between these two variables.

Naturalistic Observation

You could begin by quietly watching how people behave as they take the SATs, identifying those who seem nervous, and then finding out about their test scores. **Naturalistic observation** has some real advantages—in particular, the fact that it allows you to see what people actually do in a real-life situation. But in this case you also come across one of its weaknesses. You are interested in anxiety, and that's not always easy to observe, especially in people you don't know well. Some people don't show their anxiety; others who seem nervous actually aren't. In general, naturalistic observation works well when you're interested in what people are doing; it doesn't really tell you what people are thinking and feeling.

Observing in natural situations lets us see a phenomenon as it really is. But we can't always tell what's going on. For example, this woman is taking a test. But what is she really feeling? Is she anxious or calm?

Formal Observation

The nature of the problem you're working with largely determines the kinds of observations you make. Because one of your variables is anxiety, and because you can't measure anxiety by simply standing at the back of a classroom and watching students take the SATs, you have to use formal observation. You're still observing a real-life situation, but you're intervening in that situation to the extent that you choose your subjects and ask them to describe their level of anxiety. More formal observational methods present us with a series of issues.

Sampling   The first set of questions to be answered concerns who you will observe—how many people, what sorts of people, and how you'll select them.

How many people?   Suppose you want to know if baseballs float. You just have to watch one sink into a pond, and you have your answer. Because baseballs are all pretty much the same, you can be pretty sure that what one does,

Variable In an experiment, a characteristic that can change.

Naturalistic observation Watching subjects in a real-life situation to see how they behave.

another is going to do too. But suppose you ask a friend if he was anxious when he took the SATs and, then, how well he did. If he says that he was anxious and that he did poorly, can you conclude that anxiety interferes with test performance? Of course not. People aren't baseballs; they're all very different. Knowing how one person responds in a situation doesn't tell you how others would respond in the same situation. To test your proposition, then, you have to study a *group* of test takers.

Notice that your decision here is based on an assumption: that people are different. This assumption is shared by informal and formal theories of psychology. You have to make certain assumptions about the phenomenon you want to study so that you know where to begin. Of course, these assumptions may be wrong. In fact, one function of research is to point out mistakes in theory.

Whom do you compare them with?   What if you find a group of students who all say they were anxious when they took the SATs and who all did poorly on the test? Can you conclude that anxiety reduces test performance? Not yet. It could be that everyone who took the SATs was anxious about the test, even those who did well on it. In order to conclude anything about the relationship between anxiety and performance, then, you need to observe at least two groups: one that claims to have been anxious and one that does not.

This is an important point about psychological research: it always involves a comparison between at least two sets of observations. Usually the comparison is between two groups of subjects or between the same subjects at different times. When we administer a treatment to one group, and do nothing to another, we call the untreated comparison group the *control group*.

Sometimes psychologists conduct a **case study,** a detailed examination of a single individual. Even this involves comparison. You understand and learn from a case study because you implicitly compare the behavior of the individual you're studying with your understanding of how people in general behave. Psychologists find case studies especially important in examining abnormal behavior. As you'll see in later chapters, case studies have helped enormously to shed light on psychological disorders.

How do you select people?   For your study of the effect of anxiety on test performance, you need to compare two groups of people: a group that was anxious about taking the SATs and a group that was not. Then you can see how each group actually did on the test.

How do you go about creating these two groups? You could ask everyone who took the SATs last year whether or not they were anxious about the test. But this isn't feasible, of course, because so many students took the test. The problem here is a common one in psychological research. It's almost impossible to study all of the people of interest, to study an entire **population.** Because you can't study everyone, you have to work with a **sample** of the population.

If you are going to draw conclusions about a population from observing a sample, you must be confident that the sample is like the population in all important ways. This kind of sample is called a **representative sample;** it represents the population. The process of applying conclusions reached from a sample to the larger population is called **generalizing.**

Choosing a sampling method is one of the critical steps in designing a research plan, because that method determines how confidently you can generalize. The ideal sampling method is random. The members in a **random sample** are selected purely by chance, so that every member of the population has an equal chance of being included. So, if you randomly select a sample from all the people who took the SATs last year, you could argue that your sample differs from the population only by small, chance variations.

Case study The detailed examination of a single person or instance of a psychological phenomenon.

Population All of the people or animals to which a theory applies.

Sample The small part of a population that is studied in order to collect information about the whole population.

Representative sample A sample whose characteristics are similar to those of the population from which it is drawn.

Generalizing Drawing conclusions about a whole population from the study of a representative sample.

Random sample A sample whose members are selected purely by chance, so that every member of the population has an equal chance of being included.

And Now a Word from President . . .
Thomas Dewey?

The importance of a random sample was brought home in the 1948 presidential election. Polls across the nation showed the Republican candidate, Thomas Dewey, way out in front of his Democratic opponent, Harry Truman. The *Chicago Daily Tribune* was so sure of the outcome that its newspapers trumpeting Dewey's election were on the newsstands before the vote was counted. Of course, Dewey lost; and Truman laughed all the way to the White House.

In a postmortem that's lasted more than forty years, many explanations have been proposed for this pollsters' nightmare. One has to do with the representativeness of their sample. It seems the preelection polling was done by phone. And in the 1940s, a lot more Republicans than Democrats had phones.

The pollsters learned the hard way. You can't generalize from a sample that's not representative.

Even gathering a random sample can be an enormous job. For your study, you'd have to travel to every place in the country where the SATs were administered this year—a costly and time-consuming process.

Fortunately, a true random sample is not necessary for most kinds of research. You might not be comfortable limiting yourself to the study of students in one high school, but a sample of students from, say, a dozen schools in the state would probably do the trick. At work here is another assumption: that certain basic processes are the same in all kinds of people. What you discover about students' anxiety and their test performance in Massachusetts or Missouri or Montana probably also applies to students in other states. So your theory—and the assumptions it's based on—help define the size and breadth of your sample.

Measurement   Once you have decided *whom* to observe, the next question is *how*. You need to measure as precisely as possible and as accurately.

Quantifying Psychological Variables   You could simply ask your subjects how anxious they were. But if one person says "very" and another says "lots," who was more anxious? Both were probably more anxious than someone who says "some," but how much more anxious were they? Of course, you could ignore these differences and just compare all three to the students who say "not at all"; but in that instance you might be throwing away important information.

This is why psychologists work hard at devising specific measures of psychological variables. One kind of measure is the **rating scale.** For example, a rating scale that measures anxiety might ask subjects to judge their level of anxiety on a scale from 0 to 10, with 0 meaning "not at all" and 10 meaning "terrified." Once we quantify psychological variables, it's much easier to compare subjects.

Rating scales have weaknesses as well as strengths. For example, they are effective only with people who have a pretty good intuitive grasp of numbers and rankings. Young children and others who are not familiar with elementary arithmetic simply aren't capable of rating themselves. Another problem is that rating scales limit subjects' responses to just a few alternatives. When you use a rating scale, you won't hear how a subject's heart pounded or blood raced or hands trembled when she opened the test booklet; nor can the subject tell you how he finally learned to cope with his anxiety.

Every measure you could use involves a trade-off of some kind. So you have to decide which measure or combination of measures is best for your particular purpose. Sometimes psychologists use rating scales; at other times they ask subjects to describe their experiences in their own words; and at still other times they simply observe their subjects' behavior. Or they might use a combination of these and the other measures we talk about in later chapters.

The properties of measurement   Any time you design a measure, you must be sure that it measures what you want it to, that it has a high degree of **validity.** Suppose you decide to use a rating scale in your study of anxiety and test performance. Can you assume that your subjects' ratings are valid? Perhaps not. We know, for example, that many people are reluctant to report feeling anxious. Some don't even recognize their own anxiety. In fact, any measure that asks subjects to describe their feelings may not accurately reflect their true emotional state.

A second important property of any measure is its **reliability.** A measure may be valid, in the sense that it measures what was intended, but still not very useful because it is too prone to error. For example, if you watch people's faces while they take a test, you'd probably be measuring a real reflection of anxiety. But because of all the problems involved in understanding strangers' facial expressions, you'd probably make a lot of mistakes. And the more mistakes you make, the less reliable the measure.

Establishing the validity and reliability of a measure can be a complicated process. We discuss that process in detail in Chapter 13. For now, just remember that the degree to which your measures are valid and reliable is a critical component of your research method. One practical solution is to use a measusre for which validity and reliability have already been established by previous research. Fortunately in this case many studies have demonstrated that rating scales are reasonably valid and reliable in this kind of situation.

Rating scale An instrument used to measure a psychological variable, usually through the assignment of numerical values.

Validity The degree to which a measure relates to the factor it is supposed to be measuring.

Reliability The degree to which a measurement is error free, estimated by the degree to which measurements are repeatable.

Experimentation

You've gathered a sample; you've designed and administered a rating scale that you believe is valid and reliable; and you've collected your subjects' scores on the SATs. Now suppose that you find that high levels of anxiety generally go hand in hand with low SAT scores. Does this confirm your original hypothesis, that anxiety interferes with test performance?

Puzzle It Out!

Psychologists spend a great deal of time designing measures that are valid and reliable. Look over the following list of measures of anxiety. Which one do you think is the best? Why?

- The number of cubic centimeters of water consumed by the subject while taking an exam
- The number of wrong answers on an exam
- The subject's answer to the question "How anxious are you?" asked as the exam is handed out
- The subject's answer to the question "How anxious were you?" asked as the exam grades are handed back
- The subject's answer to the question "How many hours did you study for the exam?"

Maybe not. It could be that those students who received low scores on the SATs were anxious because they knew they were doing poorly on the test. This would mean that poor performance caused the anxiety, not the other way around. If two variables are related in the real world, we often cannot be sure which is the cause and which the effect.

Another possibility is that neither caused the other. Instead a third variable may be responsible for the relationship. For example, taller people tend to have shorter hair. This doesn't mean that your hair grows less as you grow taller, or that cutting your hair makes your legs grow. Instead the relationship is a product of two other variables, gender and social custom. Men are, on average, taller and in our society, wear their hair shorter.

In research, any relationship found between anxiety and test performance could be the product of a third variable—say, age (see Figure 1.5). Maybe younger students are less confident and less well prepared. Or perhaps some other factor is at work here. Whenever you collect measurements from the real world, you face the problem that the real world is very complicated. Even when you find the relationship you expect to find, you can't be sure what it means.

Correlation is the degree to which two variables are related. When a substantial correlation is found between two variables—such as anxiety and test perfor-

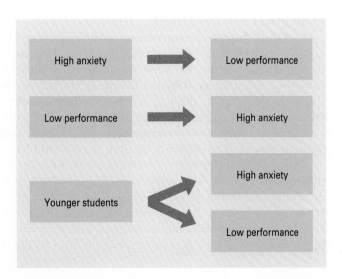

Figure 1.5
Relationship and Correlation

If you find that high anxiety is related to performance, you still don't know which caused the other, or if they are both caused by a third factor, such as age.

mance—we tend to assume that one caused the other. But this may not be true. Correlation does not necessarily mean causation.

The formal experiment is one way to clear up the uncertainty about what causes what. In an **experiment,** the scientist intentionally manipulates one or more variables and then observes the effects of that manipulation on other variables.

Suppose that instead of measuring anxiety, you manipulate it. For example, you might take two random samples of the population. One, the **experimental group,** you expose to the factor you're studying: anxiety. The other, the **control group,** is your comparison group; these subjects are not treated.

How do you make the experimental group anxious without affecting the control group? One idea is to insert an anxiety-producing message in the tests you hand out to the experimental group. Something like this, in bold letters, would probably do the trick:

> THANK YOU FOR PARTICIPATING IN THIS EXPERIMENT. ALTHOUGH THIS EXAMINATION WON'T AFFECT YOUR GRADE, IT WILL SERVE AS AN IMPORTANT INDICATION OF YOUR FUTURE SUCCESS IN LIFE. BE SURE TO DO YOUR BEST!

If the experimental group does not do as well on the test as the control group, you can say with confidence that anxiety lowers test performance. How do you know? First of all, your random sample controls for other variables that might affect test performance. Second, by manipulating your subjects' level of anxiety before the test is administered, you know that the anxiety is not a product of test performance but a factor in that performance. In short, you know what caused what.

There are two kinds of variables in an experiment. **Independent variables** are controlled by the researcher. If the anxiety-producing message makes some people anxious, then the level of anxiety is an independent variable. In principle, the value of an independent variable is *independent* of everything except what the experimenter does. **Dependent variables** are the variables you expect to be affected by the independent variables. In this case, the subjects' scores on the SATs are dependent variables: you assume that they *depend* on the subjects' level of anxiety.

Experiments have a second advantage over observations in the real world. Sometimes it's a lot more convenient to observe subjects in an experimental setting. You can run an anxiety-test performance experiment at any time in just about any place. You don't have to wait for the next time the SATs are being administered or travel to the different schools where students are taking the test.

And sometimes experimentation is the only way you can study a phenomenon. An example: Large numbers of psychologists are busy studying the factors that may lead nations to wage war, especially nuclear war (see, for example, *Journal of Social Issues,* 1988). Obviously it's impossible for these scientists to study nuclear war in the real world. So they use experimental models to examine cooperation, conflict, and other phenomena. Of course, they have to be very careful when they generalize their findings to international relations. But without this kind of experimentation, they would have no findings at all.

Although experiments are more convenient and clarify causal relationships, they do so at a cost. The subjects in your experiment would know that they're not really taking the SATs. Moreover, the anxiety generated by a note in a test booklet may be very different from that generated by an actual testing situation. By creating an experimental condition, you may have changed the situation so much that you cannot generalize your findings to the real world.

Experiment   An observational context in which the psychologist manipulates the amount or presence of one or more variables and then observes the effects on other variables.

Experimental group   In an experiment, subjects who are exposed to the variable being manipulated.

Control group   In an experiment, a comparison group that is not exposed to the variable being manipulated.

Independent variable   A variable that the experimenter manipulates.

Dependent variable   A variable that is expected to change as a function of an independent variable.

The Research Program

One thing should be clear from our discussion: The research process is a series of compromises; it is a process of choosing among alternative methods, each with its own advantages and disadvantages. No single method, in and of itself, is better than any other. In fact, the real unit of progress in psychology, as in other sciences, is the *research program*. In its ideal form, that program combines the work of a number of researchers using a variety of methods all exploring somewhat different aspects of the same basic experimental question, so that the strengths of one method offset the weaknesses of others.

A research program might begin with naturalistic observations, then more formal observations, all designed to generate a theory. Next, a series of experiments might be carried out to test the implications of and further develop the theory. Finally, a series of real-life studies might be used to see whether the theory does what it should—explain or predict events in the real world. These studies also reflect back on and change the theory, leading to more observations and more refinements of the theory as knowledge expands.

This book is filled with descriptions of research—of theories, the methods of testing theories, and the ways in which findings are interpreted. In different chapters different methods dominate, because the constraints of a particular problem often dictate the method used. In research on perception, for example, that method is almost always the formal experiment: In contrast developmental psychologists rely much more on observation than experiments.

What about the effect of anxiety on test performance? We talk about this subject in detail in Chapter 10, but the general conclusion is that the actual effects of anxiety on all kinds of performance depend both on the nature of the task and on the individual. When the task is as complex as taking the SATs, anxiety often interferes with performance. But there are some people who actually perform better in a testing situation when they're anxious.

The type of research being conducted and the various stages of a research program may dictate the different methods used. For example, research on children's development often uses observation and relatively unstructured questioning and discussion.

The Ethical Dimension

The ethical dimension is one way in which psychological research differs from research in the natural sciences. Physicists who study subatomic particles and geologists who study rocks don't have to worry about harming their subjects. But because psychologists study human beings and other living organisms, they have to think about the consequences of their research for their subjects.

The American Psychological Association and the U.S. Public Health Service have issued guidelines governing the use of people and animals in psychological research. And organizations doing psychological research must maintain a review board that examines every proposed research plan and makes sure the subjects are protected. All psychologists who use human subjects are obligated to

- protect them from physical or psychological harm.
- keep their records confidential.
- stress that participation is entirely voluntary and that subjects may leave the experiment at any time for any reason.
- explain the procedures of the experiment before it begins and secure each subject's written agreement to participate.

The last guideline in the list requires *informed consent*. This guideline creates special difficulties for psychologists. Although everyone agrees that informed consent about experimental procedures is essential, the problem is that a subject who is fully informed about the *purpose* of an experiment is likely to bias the results. Some human beings are endlessly accommodating where science is involved, so they try to meet the expectations of the experimenter when they know what those expectations are. They do this without realizing it, even when they've been asked not to. On the other hand, some people attempt to "outsmart" an experimenter, by doing the opposite of what they believe the experiment is seeking to demonstrate.

To solve this problem, psychologists have worked out a compromise. So that subjects can make an informed decision about whether to participate in an experiment, they are told at the beginning about the actual procedures that are going to be used. But they are not informed until after the experiment about possible outcomes or the theory being tested. In your anxiety-test performance experiment, for instance, you would tell your subjects that they are going to participate in a test situation and that they might find that situation distressing. Only subjects who agreed with these conditions would participate. But you would not tell them that only some of the subjects are going to see an anxiety-producing message in their test booklets, or that these subjects are not expected to do as well on the test as the rest of the subjects.

Even research with animals is regulated. The American Psychological Association requires that psychologists take care of their animals. And research that involves medical procedures must be done in such a way that animal subjects do not suffer. Most animal laboratories are registered with the federal government and are inspected regularly to make sure that the subjects are maintained under humane conditions.

In the last few years, considerable controversy has emerged about the use of animals in psychological research. Although claims of extreme mistreatment are not accurate (Coile & Miller, 1984), animals are sometimes exposed to electric shocks or allowed to go hungry over a period of time. The shocks are not more intense than those administered to human volunteers; nor are the animals kept at a level of body weight below that which many human beings choose to maintain. But, of course, the animals have not chosen to participate.

There is no question that the use of animals in psychological research has increased knowledge and helped reduce human suffering. But there is a question as to whether reducing human suffering justifies inflicting suffering on animals. Of course, everyone who eats meat, uses cosmetics, or consults a doctor has made that decision. But even for those who feel that people are more important than animals, there remains the ethical obligation to be sure that laboratory animals experience no more discomfort than is absolutely required by the research.

Some kinds of research would be impractical or unethical if conducted with human subjects. So psychologists sometimes study the behavior of animals instead. How confidently we can apply the results of animal studies to humans depends on how similar we think the experimental animals and human beings are.

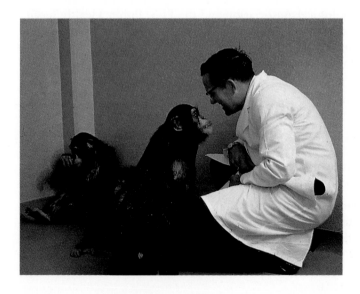

Recap

- The basic test of any scientific proposition is observation.

- To make observations easier to interpret and less susceptible to bias, psychologists have developed systematic research methods.

- Naturalistic observation allows you to see what people actually do in real-life situations, but it doesn't tell you what people are thinking and feeling.

- Formal observation is carried out in the real world, but it involves a certain amount of intervention on the part of the researcher.

- Psychological research always involves a comparison between at least two sets of observations.

- The process of applying conclusions reached from a sample to the larger population is called generalizing. Scientists can generalize only to the extent that their sample is representative.

- A good measure of any variable should measure what it is designed to measure (validity) with as much accuracy as possible (reliability).

- In the real world, a relationship between two variables is expressed as a correlation; but a correlation does not mean that one variable *caused* the other.

- In an experiment, the scientist intentionally manipulates one or more variables and then observes the effects of that manipulation on other variables.

- Although experiments clarify causal relationships, they limit the applicability of research findings to the real world.

- The real unit of progress in psychology is the research program, a program that combines the work of a number of researchers using a variety of methods.

- Theories are not etched in stone; they are constantly being redefined in light of new research.

- The contraints of a particular problem often dictate the method used to study that problem.

- Psychologists, because they study human beings and other living organisms, have a special responsibility to consider the effects of their research on their subjects.

Science and Behavioral Control

Many people are frightened by the science of psychology. Something in us rejects the possibility that human beings can be understood, predicted, and, ultimately, controlled. We do not want to be thought of as predictable, much less controllable, because we believe we are free, in the deepest sense, to act as we will.

Psychologists already know a great deal about human behavior, and their knowledge is expanding rapidly. Does this knowledge threaten our freedom to act? We believe profoundly that it does not. In fact, we believe that knowledge increases our freedom, that in a very real sense the truth makes us free.

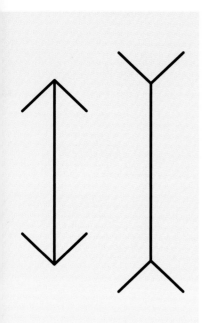

Look at the two lines on the left. Which is longer? Obviously, the line on the right. But this is an optical illusion. (We discuss the perceptual processes that generate this illusion in Chapter 4.) Actually the lines are exactly the same length. If you don't believe us, take a ruler and measure them. Once you know it's an illusion that depends on the direction of the arrows at the ends of the lines, you can begin to control it. Although the lines still "look" different, you "know" the truth. Now you have two ways of responding to the lines: you can respond to the way they look, or you can respond to the way they actually are. The choice is yours.

This is a very simple example, but it shows that knowing about psychological processes doesn't necessarily reduce our choices. On the contrary, it increases them. As long as we just respond to events in the world, our choices are limited. But once we understand why something is the way it is or how our behavior affects other people, we can choose our responses and design new ones as we need them. By learning about psychology, then, we don't forfeit freedom; we increase it.

The Plan of This Book

Human beings can be looked at in many ways—as biological organisms, animals, members of the human species; as individuals; as members of families and social groups; as workers. Every way of looking at human behavior is a source of theories that explain how people act and what they experience. If you are trying to understand why you behave the way you do, it can help to understand something about yourself as an organism. At other times, it can help to understand the pressures your family and social group exert on you and how you affect them.

We continue this book with a chapter on the nervous system. All of the stimuli that generate our sensations and perceptions—all the information we receive from the world—are transmitted to the brain through a network of nerve cells. Then we examine sensation, perception, consciousness, and learning—processes and states of being that are basic to all animals. In fact, much of what we know about them comes from studies of rats and monkeys.

Next we turn to memory and thought and other forms of complex learning in which language plays a prominent role. Here you'll learn skills that can help you study for your courses in general and for this course in particular.

From a focus on thinking, we turn to feeling. We talk about hunger and other biological motives, and about the social motives that push us to achieve. And we discuss emotions and the consequences of stress.

In the chapters on development we describe the physical, cognitive, moral, and social changes that people undergo as they grow older. We consider the nature of those changes and the relative impact on human development of heredity and the environment.

Next we turn to the differences among people, describing what those differences are and explaining how they evolve. Why are some people more energetic than others? More creative? Why do some people worry all the time? We also examine psychological disorders—extreme differences that interfere with normal functioning—and the ways in which those disorders are treated.

Finally, we look at the way society shapes people—how they're affected by those around them, both intentionally and unintentionally. We talk about social pressure and ways to respond to that pressure—to withstand it or to adapt to it.

Every chapter in this book contains special features to increase your enjoyment and understanding of psychology.

- Each begins either with a short description of one of our own experiences or with an observation that helps clarify the material you're about to read.
- Another feature (making its first appearance in Chapter 2) is called *How Do We Know That?* It describes methodological problems and the ways in which psychologists address them. Aside from offering insight into the way psychologists go about solving problems, this feature reinforces the point that psychologists derive information by means of *science,* not through mere guesswork or opinion.
- In addition, you'll find at least one *Puzzle It Out!* in each chapter. This feature presents problems that we find intriguing. Some are whimsical (How did Ben Franklin's alarm clock work?); some more serious (How would you design a test for deafness?). But all of them should get you to analyze and think critically about the material you're studying.
- Now and again you'll also find an insight into the subject we're discussing, a paragraph or two of special interest that we've highlighted for you.

Some of the elements in the text are study aids.

- Chapter outlines present the structure of each chapter—the topics you're going to read about and study, and the order in which they are being presented. The outlines act as maps for each chapter and serve as guides through their content.
- A short introductory lead-in called *Gateways* is found at the top of the first page of each chapter. This feature explains (1) why psychologists study the topic of that particular chapter and (2) how that chapter's topic relates to other topics you're studying. By pointing out these relationships, we hope to help you see and think about the *interconnectedness* of psychology's subfields.
- Key terms, shown in boldface in the text, are defined briefly in the margins of the pages where they appear. Reinforcing the key terms by placing them in the margins will help you master the language of psychology by giving you an instant review of the terminology as it is introduced.
- Figures, photos, and tables are study aids, too. They convey basic information that's better shown than said, including information that's likely to show up on your instructors' exams.
- Finally, at the end of the text you will find both a glossary that alphabetically lists the key terms found in the text's margins and a statistics appendix that presents some of the basic mathematics necessary to understand psychological research and its results.

Conclusion

You bring to psychology a wealth of experience, the thoughts and feelings that are uniquely yours. Through the years, you've used those thoughts and feelings to make sense of the world around you. That's exactly what psychologists do. Only their methods and the form their explanations take are different. Understanding these differences should increase your understanding of yourself and others. This is a critical step in learning to take greater control of your behavior—the surest and perhaps only path to a more productive and satisfying life.

Chapter 2

The Biological Bases of Behavior

Limb, Louisa Chase, 1981

2

Gateways Why must we know something about the brain if we want to study emotions such as joy or anger, or varieties in the human personality, or the causes of abnormal behavior? A basic familiarity with the brain and nervous system is essential to understanding all of these, and much else in psychology as well. To understand emotions (the subject of Chapter 10), we must understand the workings of the autonomic nervous system. Many differences in temperament (Chapters 12 and 14)—whether you are timid or daring, for example—seem to depend on variations in the functioning of the nervous system. Similarly, as you will discover in Chapter 15, many psychological disorders appear to be products of a combination of childhood experiences, stress responses to one's surroundings, and biological factors. To understand disorders, you need to take into account all of these influences.

You will find references to the brain and nervous system in many of the succeeding chapters. In this chapter, we prepare you for these later discussions as well as providing information that is fascinating in its own right.

I was just out of graduate school, teaching the physiological psychology course at a small college. A neurologist friend, Dr. Jonathan Ward, had offered to give my students an hour-long demonstration of human neuroanatomy. We were milling around the room when he walked through the doorway carrying a briefcase and a large brown plastic bag. The students stepped back, as if in reaction to something dangerous at the bottom of the bag.

Preparing the seminar room as an impromptu surgical theater, Jon asked the students to spread some plastic sheeting on the table, where it was soon joined by a stainless steel tray and a few surgical instruments. He took off his jacket, rolled up the sleeves of his shirt, and snapped on a pair of surgical gloves. Reaching into the plastic bag, he lifted out a human brain, white and intricately surfaced, and placed it on the tray. Tentatively, the students approached the table. Looking around and clearing his throat, Jon started: "Okay. We don't have much time, so listen up. The nervous system includes the brain, the spinal cord, and the nerves that connect to the muscles, glands, and sense organs. This, obviously, is a brain."

Working quickly with a scalpel and some other instruments, Jon cut into the brain, pointing out the different structures and describing their functions. After what seemed a very short time, he paused. "Well, I think we have the basics. I've left a few details for the professor here to fill in. Any questions?"

At first nobody had any. Together we stared at the pieces of tissue that not long ago had governed the actions, feelings, and experiences of a unique human being. We were momentarily struck dumb.

Seeing a human brain for the first time can be an unnerving experience, perhaps because of the peculiar relationship each of us has with our brain. On the one hand, your brain is hidden away and unknown to you. On the other hand, it's an intimate, personal part of you, the part that makes you *you*. It affects everything you do and feel—your behaviors, your thoughts, your emotions, your memories, your plans. In a way, you cannot really understand yourself until you understand the influence of the brain and the rest of the nervous system on behavior and experience.

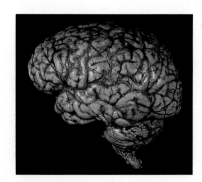

The human brain is an immensely complex structure, with its many parts folded together so that they fit into the tight confines of the skull.

A Communication Network

The **nervous system** consists of the spinal cord, the brain, and all the nerves that connect these structures to the muscles, glands, and sense organs. It is a complex web of fibers that gathers and integrates information from the senses and uses that information to control the muscles and glands. The **central nervous system,** the portion of the web enclosed within the spine and skull, is made up of the spinal cord and brain. The **peripheral nervous system** connects the central nervous system to the rest of the body, as can be seen in Figure 2.1.

Nervous system The spinal cord, the brain, and the nerves that connect these structures to the muscles, glands, and sense organs.

Central nervous system The spinal cord and brain.

Peripheral nervous system The portion of the nervous system that connects the spinal cord and brain to the rest of the body.

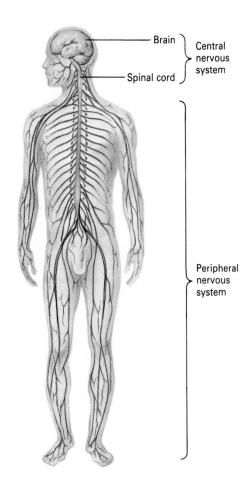

Figure 2.1
The Human Nervous System

The human nervous system consists of two parts. The central nervous system is made up of the brain and the spinal cord; the peripheral nervous system includes all of the nerves that connect the brain and spinal cord to other parts of the body.

All parts of the nervous system are made up of **nerves** and supporting tissues. Nerves are bundles of fibers that carry information throughout the system. Information flows through the nervous system in the form of electrochemical impulses.

We start our examination of the nervous system with a look at the methods used by scientists to explore that system. An enormous amount of information about the nervous system has been gathered in your lifetime. New research tools, particularly those using computers, have dramatically increased our understanding of how the nervous system works.

Next we look at the basic elements of the system, the individual nerve cells. Then we examine the major systems and subsystems into which those cells are organized.

Finally, we turn to the question that most interests psychologists: How do the characteristics and activities of the nervous system relate to human behavior and experience?

Studying the Nervous System

Until about one hundred years ago, the nervous system was very much a mystery. Scientists knew that critical structures and processes were at work, affecting people's behaviors and feelings; but they were missing important information about those structures and processes. Today, our knowledge of the nervous system is increasing rapidly, thanks to new scientific tools.

Nerves Bundles of nerve fibers that carry information throughout the nervous system.

The study of the components and processes of the nervous system is called **neuroscience.** Neuroscientists from physiology, anatomy, chemistry, as well as psychology have contributed to our understanding of how the nervous system works. Within psychology, *physiological psychologists* study how conditions in the nervous system relate to behavior and experience.

Anatomical Methods

At the end of the nineteenth century, scientists still believed that the brain was an undifferentiated mass of tissue. Then Camillo Golgi (1906/1967), an Italian physician, developed a silver nitrate stain. Examining stained tissue under a microscope, Golgi and a Spanish neurologist, Santiago Ramon y Cajal (1906/1967), found that the nervous system is actually an intricate network of individual cells.

Since the 1950s, new tools have increased our understanding of neuroanatomy. Electron microscopes, devices that direct a beam of electrons at a tissue sample, are hundreds of times more powerful than light microscopes. Using such devices, scientists can examine the structure of nerve cells and their connections in fine detail.

Scientists are also using new techniques to trace nerve connections within the brain. For example, when a substance called horseradish peroxidase is injected into nerve tissue, the cells in the tissue carry the chemical back to their cell bodies, leaving traces that researchers can follow.

Technological advances have set the immune system to work as well, mapping the source of the chemicals that play a part in the movement of nerve impulses. The immune system naturally produces antibodies, substances that target certain chemicals in the body. By combining cells, scientists have discovered a way to induce the body to produce *monoclonal antibodies,* "pure" antibodies that search out one specific chemical. They treat the antibodies to make them radioactive and then track them as they move through the body in search of their target chemical. The resulting "map" shows where the chemical is located in the body (Shepard, 1987).

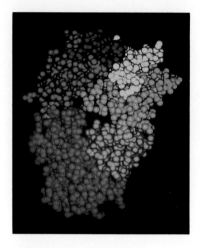

Artificially created monoclonal antibodies seek out target chemicals in the body. When large clusters of the antibodies have accumulated, the location of the target chemicals in the body can be identified. In this case, identification of the target chemicals took place by exposing the antibodies to light, which made the antibodies floresce.

Lesion Studies

Lesion studies are another important source of information about the organization of the nervous system. A **lesion** is an area of tissue that has been damaged accidentally or surgically. Depending on where a lesion is located, it can cause a **deficit**—a specific loss of ability to perceive certain stimuli (light, sound, smell) or to do certain tasks (walking, speaking, remembering). By studying lesions and deficits, scientists learn a great deal about the organization of the nervous system and the ways in which it functions.

One famous lesion study was carried out by French physician Paul Broca in the 1860s. Broca (1865) studied a group of stroke patients who had lost the ability to speak, although they had no difficulty understanding the speech of others. After these patients died, brain autopsies showed that in every case the stroke had damaged a small region on the left side of the brain, near the temple, now known as *Broca's area* (see p. 55). Broca concluded that this part of the brain is essential for the normal production of speech (Damasio & Geschwind, 1984), a finding confirmed by other studies (Ojemann, 1983). Broca's research was indeed a breakthrough in our understanding of language.

Neuroscience The study of the components and processes of the nervous system.

Lesion An area of tissue that has been damaged.

Deficit A specific loss of ability.

Electrical Stimulation and Monitoring

Another way to discover how a part of the nervous system functions is to goad it into action using an *electrode,* a metal probe that delivers tiny electrical shocks. Nerve cells generate very small electrical currents; this is how they move information through the system. With electrodes, scientists are able to stimulate nerve cells to generate impulses.

In the latter part of the nineteenth century, Gustav Fritsch and Eduard Hitzig discovered that by stimulating various portions of a dog's brain with electrodes they were able to make the animal's limbs move (Finger & Stein, 1982). Movement varied according to the position of the electrodes. For example, one placement moved a rear leg; another, a front leg. Fritsch and Hitzig concluded that these sites must be involved in the normal control of specific movements.

Scientists can also learn about the functions of the nervous system by "listening in" to electrical activity in the brain. In 1929 Hans Berger, an Austrian psychiatrist, discovered that sensitive electrodes placed on the scalp could monitor and record electrical activity in the brain. His invention, the **electroencephalograph,** has helped us to learn a great deal about sleep, attention, emotion, seizures, and other phenomena. Using the electroencephalograph, shown in Figure 2.2, researchers have found that different parts of the brain show different patterns of activity, and that the electrical activity of the entire brain varies in predictable ways as the person connected to the machine becomes more or less alert.

Figure 2.2
Electroencephalogram

The firing of neurons in the brain creates tiny electrical currents. The cumulative activity of many neurons can be measured by the EEG. When a region of the brain is active, the neurons fire rapidly, with each neuron performing its own separate task. The result is a low-amplitude, high-frequency pattern, called a *beta wave* (photo on the left). When the brain area is resting, the neurons tend to fire together, producing higher-amplitude, lower-frequency *alpha waves* (photo on the right).

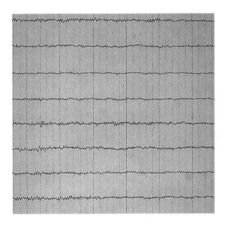 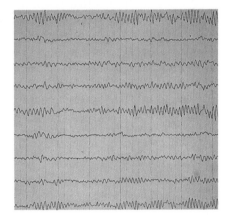

The electroencephalograph monitors and records the activity of billions of cells, but it discloses very little about individual cells. To study individual cells, neuroscientists turn to *microelectrodes,* electrodes that are so small and sensitive that they can stimulate and record the activity of a single nerve cell. In a famous early study using microelectrodes, James Olds discovered "pleasure centers" in the brain (Olds & Milner, 1954). He showed that animals would do work (press a lever repeatedly, for example) to receive small amounts of electrical stimulation to an area of the brain just a few millimeters in diameter (Yeomans, 1988).

Computer-Assisted Techniques

Electroencephalograph   A device that monitors and records electrical activity in the brain on a moving paper chart or computer screen.

Many of the methods we've been describing carry a price—tissue damage. Fortunately, the recent development of compact high-powered computers and radioactive tracers has allowed scientists to examine the living nervous system without damaging it.

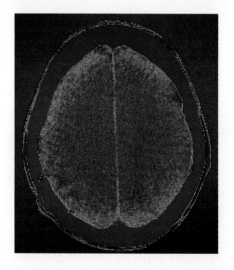 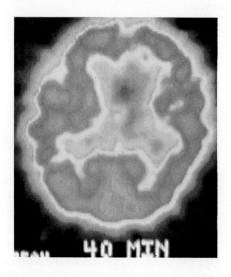

Figure 2.3
Computer Imaging

Various imaging techniques permit researchers to examine the structure and activity of the brain in living, active people. The basic CAT scan (photo on the left) uses a computer's interpretation of X-rays to form an image of a particular "slice" of the brain. The PET scan (photo on the right) uses radioactively labeled glucose to show the areas of the brain that are most active.

A basic tool is **computerized axial tomography (CAT).** A computer-driven X-ray camera maps the *structure* of internal organs in three dimensions, producing an image called a *CAT scan.* A similar technique, **positron emission tomography (PET),** maps the *activity* of internal organs. The patient is given radioactive glucose, which is absorbed into the active areas of the brain. Those areas glow brightly on the *PET scan,* as can be seen in Figure 2.3. Even more precise measures of activity are possible with **magnetic resonance imaging (MRI),** which uses magnetic fields to trace the detailed structure of brain tissue (see Figure 2.4).

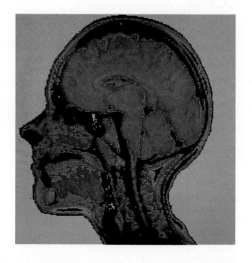

Figure 2.4
Magnetic Resonance Imaging

The MRI uses magnetic fields to induce electrical changes in the atoms of the brain. These electrical changes can be detected and used to map the structure of the brain in extremely fine detail.

Computerized axial tomography (CAT) A process that uses a computer-driven X-ray machine to map the structure of internal organs.

Positron emission tomography (PET) A process that uses a computer-driven X-ray machine and radioactive tracers to study the activity of internal organs.

Magnetic resonance imaging (MRI) A process that uses the brain's magnetic fields to trace the cellular activity and chemical makeup of brain tissue.

Recap

- Physiological psychologists study how the characteristics and activities of the nervous system relate to behavior and experience.

- Among the tools and techniques neuroscientists use to study the human nervous system are anatomical methods, lesion studies, electrical stimulation and monitoring, and computerized methods that record the structure and activity of living tissue.

Nucleus
Dendrites
Cell body
Axon
Myelin sheath

Axon terminals

Figure 2.5
A Myelinated Neuron

A common neuron of the sort found most often in the motor system. Note that the cell body has many branching dendrites and a single very long axon. The axon can often be hundreds of times as long as the cell body is wide. The myelin sheath covering the axon speeds up the rate of transmission of the nerve impulse.

Neuron A nerve cell that carries information in the form of electrochemical impulses.

Glial cell A nerve cell that supports and protects neurons.

Dendrite In a neuron, a fiber that carries information toward the cell body.

Axon In a neuron, a fiber that carries information away from the cell body.

Myelin A shiny white fatty substance, often coating the outside of axons, that speeds conduction.

Axon terminal A fine fiber at the end of an axon that connects the neuron to a muscle, gland, or other neuron.

Neurons

The human nervous system is remarkably complex. It controls our movements; it processes and transmits information about sights, sounds, and smells; it allows us to think, to remember, to make decisions. Yet despite its complexity, the nervous system is made up of just two basic kinds of cells: neurons and glial cells.

Neurons carry information in the form of electrochemical impulses. They are the principal actors in the nervous system. **Glial cells,** or *glia,* are the supporting cast. They tend to be smaller than neurons but much more numerous. Glia support and protect, helping repair damaged neurons and releasing important chemicals that may nourish the neurons around them. Neuroscientists believe glia also help govern the overall level of activity of the neurons around them (Kimelberg, 1988).

The Structure of Neurons

Neurons are the great communicators, moving information through our bodies at hundreds of miles an hour. To understand how they function, we need to look at the parts of the neuron and the way those parts communicate with other cells in the body.

Parts of the Neuron   A neuron has three basic parts: a cell body, dendrites, and an axon. These parts are shown in Figure 2.5.

- The cell body, or *soma,* contains the nucleus of the cell. It maintains the chemical balance in the neuron and can be stimulated directly by other neurons.
- The **dendrites** are fibers connected to the cell body. They generally carry information from other neurons into the cell body.
- The **axon** also is connected to the cell body. It carries information away from the soma, out toward other cells. Many axons are covered with **myelin,** a shiny white fatty substance that speeds conduction. At the far end of most axons are tiny branches that end in **axon terminals,** which connect the neuron to muscles, glands, or other neurons.

Types of Neurons   Neurons come in an extraordinary range of shapes and sizes (see Figure 2.6). *Sensory neurons* transport information (for example, smells, light, or pain) from the sense organs to the spinal cord and brain. Their dendrites come together in a single long fiber that connects directly with the axon.

Motor neurons carry information from the brain and spinal cord to muscles and glands. They have many short, thin dendrites leading into the cell body and a single long axon leading away. The axon of a motor neuron can be thousands of times as long as the diameter of its cell body. An example is the motor neuron that stimulates the muscles in your big toe. Its cell body is in the spinal cord, and its axon runs all the way down to your toe!

Interneurons sit like fat spiders in a web of their own fibers. They carry impulses from sensory neurons to motor neurons. Because their primary job is to connect other nerve cells, their axon and dendrites have thousands—even hundreds of thousands—of branches leading off in every direction.

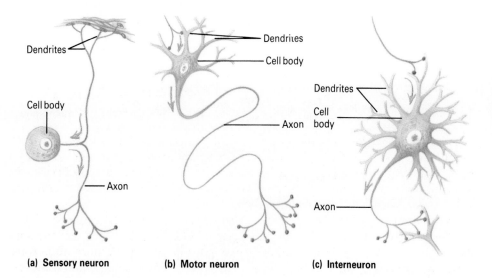

Dendrites

Cell body

Axon

(a) Sensory neuron

Dendrites

Cell body

Axon

(b) Motor neuron

Dendrites

Cell body

Axon

(c) Interneuron

Figure 2.6
Types of Neurons

Three common types of neurons are the (a) sensory neuron, (b) motor neuron, and (c) interneuron. The arrows indicate the direction in which a nerve impulse travels through these neurons.

Moving Information

The nervous system collects sensory information and carries it to the brain. The brain integrates the information and then signals our muscles and glands to respond to that information. The information going to and coming from the brain is in the form of electrochemical impulses. Those impulses flow through the nervous system by moving within and between neurons.

Within Neurons   Remember that information flows into a neuron through its dendrites or by direct stimulation of the cell body. Before that information can be passed on to another neuron, it must move through the transmitting cell—from the dendrites to the cell body, down the axon, to the axon terminals. This movement occurs through an electrochemical process that travels the length of the neuron in a series of mini-events much like a row of dominoes falling. In this process, called *firing,* chemicals move into and out of the nerve cell.

Other understand how the neuron fires, we first need to look at its normal "resting" state. Like all cells, the neuron is surrounded by a *membrane,* a thin barrier of fats and proteins that separates the inside of the cell from its environment. Dissolved in fluid on both sides of the membrane are electrically charged particles called *ions.* Three kinds of ions—sodium, potassium, and proteins—play a major role in the electrical balance of the membrane.

Look at Figure 2.7. It shows the relative concentration of sodium and potassium ions in the resting neuron. Although both kinds of ions are found inside and outside the cell membrane, the concentration of potassium ions is greater

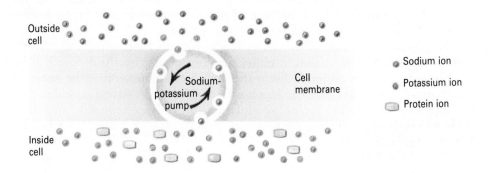

Outside cell

Sodium-potassium pump

Cell membrane

Inside cell

Sodium ion

Potassium ion

Protein ion

Figure 2.7
The Sodium-Potassium Pump

The sodium-potassium pump maintains the electrical balance of the cell membrane by actively transporting potassium ions into the cell and sodium ions out of the cell. The large protein ions are trapped inside the cell.

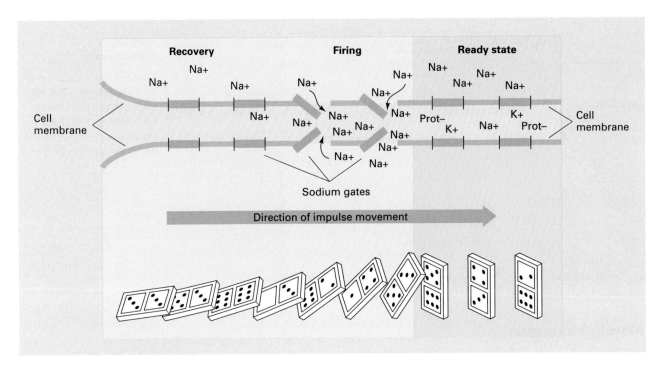

Figure 2.8
The Action Potential

On the right, the neuron is in the ready state, with a strong electrical difference between the inside and outside of the membrane. This charge is produced primarily by the excess of negatively charged protein molecules (Prot⁻) on the inside, and the excess of positively charged sodium molecules (Na⁺) on the outside. The nerve impulse begins with one of the sodium gates opening. The Na⁺ molecules rush in, rapidly reducing the electrical difference. This electrical change causes nearby gates to open, too, which produces an effect similar to dominoes knocking each other over, with the nerve impulse traveling down the axon as a succession of opened sodium gates. Once the sodium rush is over, the gates close and the sodium is pumped out, so that the neuron is ready to fire again.

Action potential The electrochemical impulse that travels down a neuron.

inside whereas the concentration of sodium ions is greater outside. This difference is produced by the *sodium-potassium pump*. This mechanism in the cell membrane moves potassium ions into the neuron and sodium ions out. The large protein ions are trapped inside the cell.

Both sodium and potassium ions are positively charged; the protein ions are negatively charged. As a result of the concentration of these and other ions on either side of the cell membrane, a negative charge builds up inside the cell and a positive charge builds up outside the cell. At this point the membrane is *polarized,* a state it maintains as long as it's at rest.

When a neuron is stimulated by another neuron or a sensory cell, this balance suddenly shifts. Small channels in the membrane that are closed when the cell is at rest fly open, and the positively charged sodium ions diffuse into the neuron, moving from an area of high concentration (outside the cell) to one of low concentration (inside the cell). As these ions move into the cell, the electrical balance of the cell membrane changes (that is, the membrane *depolarizes*), forcing open the channels in neighboring parts of the membrane and setting off a chain reaction of such openings that travels the length of the neuron. This electrochemical reaction is very fast: an impulse travels at speeds of up to 200 miles an hour, passing any particular point within a few millionths of a second and reaching the end of even the longest axon in a few hundredths of a second. This electrochemical impulse is called an **action potential** (see Figure 2.8).

After an impulse passes, the neuron cannot be stimulated again until the membrane *repolarizes,* largely because of the actions of the sodium-potassium pump. This process takes just a fraction of a second.

The neuron follows the *all-or-none principle.* A neuron either conducts an impulse or it doesn't. Like a gun, it either fires or doesn't fire. And once it fires, the progress of every impulse down the length of the neuron is the same. A weak stimulus does not give rise to a weak impulse, and a strong stimulus does not intensify an impulse. Intense stimulation can cause a neuron to fire more often by triggering it during the recovery period. However these impulses are not more intense.

Between Neurons Information in the form of an electrochemical impulse has now arrived at the axon terminals. How does it move on to the next neuron? The axon of one neuron delivers an impulse to the dendrites of another neuron at a **synapse,** the junction between two neurons. The two neurons don't actually touch. The **synaptic cleft,** a tiny gap measuring only about two-millionths of an inch, separates the sending (presynaptic) neuron from the receiving (postsynaptic) neuron. Not all neurons synapse with other neurons, however. Motor neurons, for example, synapse with the muscles that control movement.

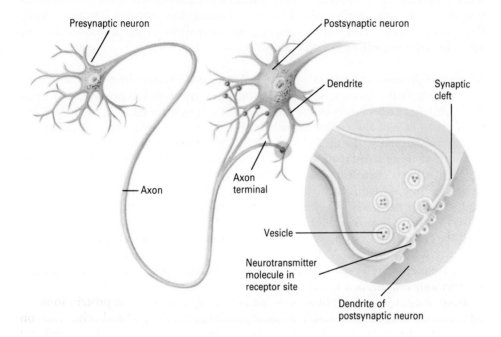

Figure 2.9
Synapse

The synaptic cleft is extremely narrow, even narrower than the cell membrane. So although chemical diffusion is a slow process, the neurotransmitter molecules have only a very short way to go.

At the tip of each axon terminal is a button-shaped knob. When a nerve impulse reaches the knob, the knob releases a **neurotransmitter,** a chemical manufactured by the neuron and stored in sacs called *vesicles*. The neurotransmitter molecules cross the synaptic cleft and bind with receptor sites on the cell membrane of the postsynaptic neuron, changing the electrical balance of that membrane. A synapse can be seen in Figure 2.9.

Neurotransmitters are not all the same. Each neurotransmitter has its own molecular shape, which fits its receptor site the way a key fits a lock (see Figure 2.10). The effect of a neurotransmitter on the postsynaptic neuron varies. Some neurotransmitters are *excitatory*. Working together, they depolarize the cell membrane of the postsynaptic neuron, generating an action potential in that neuron. Other neurotransmitters are *inhibitory*. By increasing the negative charge inside the cell membrane, they inhibit an action potential. Still other neurotransmitters, while not excitatory or inhibitory themselves, cause the release of other chemicals that are (Cooper, Bloom & Roth, 1986).

The movement of information within a neuron is very different from the movement of information between neurons. Remember that a neuron either fires or doesn't fire; firing is an all-or-nothing process. The generation of an action potential in a postsynaptic neuron depends on the balance of excitatory and inhibitory influences. Stimulation here is a kind of committee decision, made by many participants.

Synapse The junction between two neurons.

Synaptic cleft The submicroscopic space that separates the axon terminals of a presynaptic neuron from the dendrites of a postsynaptic neuron.

Neurotransmitter A chemical produced by the presynaptic neuron that moves across the synaptic cleft and binds to receptor sites on the postsynaptic neuron.

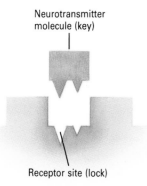

Neurotransmitter
molecule (key)

Receptor site (lock)

Figure 2.10
Lock and Key

Neurotransmitters are complex molecules with individual shapes. Receptor sites on the postsynaptic neuron "fit" and respond to specific transmitters.

Neurotransmitter Systems

A few decades ago, neuroscientists thought the number of neurotransmitters was limited. Today, more than 200 possible neurotransmitters have been identified (Snyder, 1984). Through some evolutionary process, chemicals that play a role in, for example, digestion and the regulation of blood pressure have begun to function as neurotransmitters (Venter et al., 1988). We describe several important neurotransmitters in Table 2.1.

A neuron usually secretes just one neurotransmitter (O'Donohue et al., 1985). Neurons that secrete the same neurotransmitter tend to be organized into systems, and these systems seem to perform certain kinds of functions—controlling muscles or maintaining a general level of arousal, for example. By modifying the action of one neurotransmitter system, chemicals in the bloodstream can affect broad dimensions of behavior.

Drugs and Neurotransmitters   At the synapse, neurotransmitters diffuse across the synaptic cleft. As they move from the presynaptic to the postsynaptic neuron, substances circulating in the bloodstream can modify their effect. How? By taking the place of the neurotransmitter, blocking its receptor site, or attaching to it and changing its form.

Some of these substances occur naturally in the body. For example, glands and glia secrete chemicals that circulate in the bloodstream or brain and can affect synaptic transmission (Kimelberg, 1988; Panksepp, 1986). Others are introduced into the body in order to treat disease. Consider the example of Parkinson's disease, a progressive disorder of the central nervous system. Patients with Parkinson's do not produce enough of a neurotransmitter called *dopamine,* which is why they have difficulty controlling their movements. To treat the disease, patients are given L-dopa, which is the substance from which the cells produce dopamine.

Table 2.1
Neurotransmitters and Their Effects

Whether a neurotransmitter excites or inhibits a postsynaptic neuron is a function of the chemical itself and the properties of the neuron. For example, norepinephrine tends to be excitatory in the cells of the peripheral nervous system and inhibitory in the cells of the brain and spinal cord.

Neurotransmitter	Source and Function
Acetylcholine (ACh)	One of the most widespread neurotransmitters. Occurs in systems that control the muscles and in circuits related to attention and memory.
Dopamine	Concentrated in small areas of the brain, ne of which is involved in the control of the muscles. In excess, dopamine can cause hallucinations.
Endorphins	Found in the brain and spinal cord. Suppresses pain.
Gamma aminobutyric acid (GABA)	Widely distributed in the brain. Works against other neurotransmitters, particularly dopamine.
Norepinephrine	Occurs widely in the central nervous system. May increase arousal and alertness, and regulates mood.
Serotonin	Occurs in the brain. Works more or less in opposition to norepinephrine, suppressing activity and causing sleep.

Many of the drugs used to treat psychological disorders also work on neurotransmitter systems. For example drugs that block the production of dopamine are used in the treatment of hallucinations. And Valium and Librium, two common tranquilizers, work by increasing the effectiveness of GABA.

What about street drugs? Any chemicals introduced into the body can affect the functioning of the nervous system. Many illegal drugs, including cocaine and amphetamines, inhibit or activate specific neurotransmitters and consequently affect behavior. If taken over time and in large enough quantities, cocaine and amphetamines cause hallucinations, change perceptions, and disrupt normal thought processes. We will discuss the effects of street drugs in Chapter 5 on consciousness and the role of drug treatments for psychological disorders in Chapter 15.

Neurons Working Together

The structure of neurons explains the appearance of various parts of the nervous system. The axons of neurons are often bound together in thick bundles. Because the axons are generally sheathed in myelin, the white fatty substance that speeds conduction, we call the bundles *white matter*. Glia and the dendrites, cell bodies, and unmyelinated axons of neurons are darker. This darker tissue is called *gray matter*.

White and gray matter function differently. White matter is found in places within the nervous system where information flows over relatively long distances. Gray matter is found in the integrative centers of the nervous system, where different channels of information come together and influence one another. The distribution of white and gray matter tells us where basic functions are performed and allow us to see clearly how clumps of neurons form larger structures within the nervous system.

Recap

- The nervous system is made up of two basic kinds of cells: neurons carry information in the form of electrochemical impulses (action potentials) throughout the body; glia help them function.

- A neuron has three basic parts: dendrites, a cell body, and an axon.

- The action potential moves information within the neuron, from its dendrites to its axon terminals.

- Neurotransmitter molecules diffuse across the synaptic cleft, carrying information from the presynaptic neuron to the postsynaptic neuron.

- The effect of a neurotransmitter depends on the chemical itself and the properties of the postsynaptic neuron.

- The myelinated axons of neurons—white matter—carry information from the sense organs to the central nervous system, and from the central nervous system to the muscles and glands.

- Information is collected and processed in the gray matter.

The Divisions of the Nervous System

It is important to understand the structure of nerve cells and the electrochemical process that moves information through and between them. But to comprehend how the nervous system generates human behavior and emotion, we have to stand back and take a broad view of that system, its structures, and its functions.

The human nervous system is divided into two main parts: the *central nervous system,* which includes the brain and spinal cord, and the *peripheral nervous system,* which includes all the other nerves (see Figures 2.11 and 2.1). Our discussion starts at the periphery and moves inward, toward the brain.

Figure 2.11
Divisions of the Nervous System

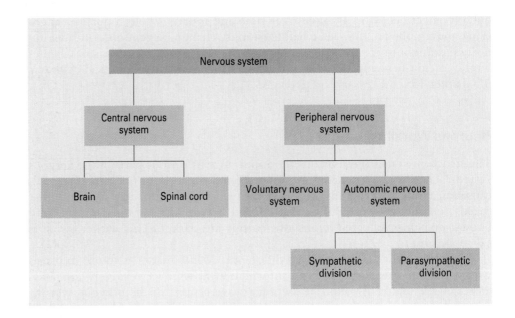

The Peripheral Nervous System

Look at your hand. Inside it's a web of nerve fibers, starting at your fingertips and gathering together in larger and larger bundles in a path toward the brain. These nerves are part of the peripheral nervous system. They send messages to the brain that help you understand your world (perhaps you feel the book slipping in your hand) and receive messages that tell your muscles to act (tighten your hand to keep the book from falling). The peripheral nervous system includes all the nerves that connect sense organs, muscles, and glands to the central nervous system.

The Central Nervous System

The central nervous system is encased within the bony structures of the spinal column and skull. It consists of the spinal cord and the brain.

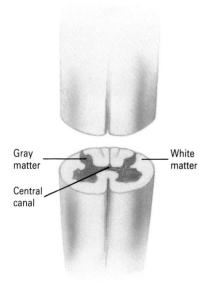

Gray matter

White matter

Central canal

Figure 2.12
Cross Section of the Spinal Cord

The gray area in the center consists of cell bodies and synapses, where spinal reflexes may occur. The white surrounding area consists of myelinated axons sending impulses up and down the spinal column.

The Spinal Cord   If you traced the nerves from your fingertips, you would find that they disappear into the spinal column, somewhere in the neck. Here they become part of the spinal cord and join the central nervous system.

The spinal cord is a cylindrical structure surrounded by a ring of bone. The bone protects the structure, as do the membranes that cover the spinal cord and continue up to the brain. Adding more protection is the *cerebrospinal fluid,* a clear watery fluid that circulates around the spinal cord and brain, cushioning them. The length of the spinal cord is divided into segments. A pair of nerves feed into and out of each segment. Inside the spinal cord, as shown in Figure 2.12 columns of gray matter form a butterfly shape in cross section; they are surrounded by columns of white matter.

Nerves from the peripheral nervous system enter the spinal cord at different locations, generally at a point as near as possible to the body part they serve. Nerves from the arms, for example, enter the spinal cord in the neck region; nerves from the legs enter at the bottom of the spine. By locating a damaged segment, physicians can often predict the effects of spinal cord injuries. A person with damage to the lower spinal cord, for example, may lose feeling and motion in the legs but may retain full use of the arms.

The spinal cord also performs simple processing on information that comes in from the peripheral nervous system. This processing takes the form of **reflexes,** automatic responses. We talk about spinal reflexes on page 47.

The Brain People often compare the brain to a computer. They think of a "machine" that's been designed and manufactured in a single organized process. But the brain is not a machine; it's the product of millions of years of evolution and decades of individual experience. A particular structure in the brain may occupy a particular place simply because that's where it was in an earlier, more primitive brain—the kind of brain a snake or a frog has. A computer engineer can throw out an old design and start over; evolution has to build on what's already there. As a result, the organization of the brain is extremely complex.

On the next few pages, we look at the structure of the brain from three perspectives: a view from behind (Figure 2.13), a view from below (Figure 2.14), and a view inside (Figure 2.15). Please study the illustrations and captions closely.

Reflex An automatic response, originating within the spinal cord.

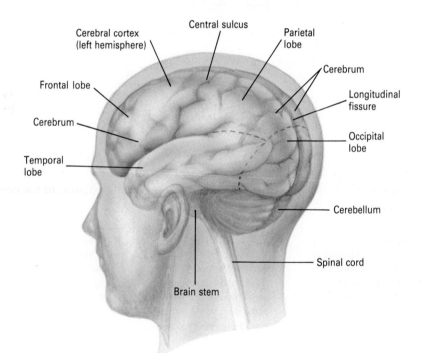

Figure 2.13
The Brain: A View from Behind

You are looking at the brain from behind and to the side.

- The great oatmeal-colored rind of wrinkled tissue is the **cerebral cortex,** six layers of gray matter that cover the top of the brain. It is part of the **cerebrum**.
- The bulges on the surface of the cortex are called *gyri* (singular: *gyrus*). The deep grooves between the gyri are called *fissures*; the shallower grooves, *sulci* (singular: *sulcus*).

- The **longitudinal fissure** runs down the center of the brain from front to back. It divides the cerebrum into right and left halves, the **cerebral hemispheres.**
- Inside the longitudinal fissure is a mass of white matter. This is the **corpus callosum,** which consists of the nerve fibers that transmit impulses from one cerebral hemisphere to the other.

- The longitudinal fissure divides the brain lengthwise into hemispheres; other fissures and sulci divide the brain horizontally into four *lobes.*
- The deep **central sulcus** separates the **frontal lobe** from the **parietal lobe.**
- A sulcus that is not very well defined separates the parietal lobe from the **occipital lobe** at the back of each hemisphere.
- And another sulcus divides the frontal lobe from the **temporal lobe,** at the lower side of each hemisphere.

Figure 2.14
The Brain: A View from Below

The cerebral cortex is the most prominent part of the human brain, wrapping around and obscuring other structures, particularly when you are looking down on the brain. If you turn the brain over, you see a veritable forest of nerve stumps. Among them are several of the "oldest" (in an evolutionary sense) parts of the brain, the parts that are most like structures in other animals' brains.

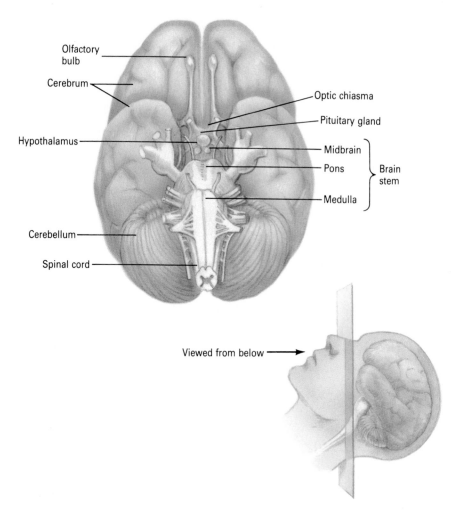

Olfactory bulb
Cerebrum
Hypothalamus
Cerebellum
Spinal cord
Optic chiasma
Pituitary gland
Midbrain
Pons   Brain stem
Medulla

Viewed from below

- The **cerebellum** is the finely wrinkled structure located toward the back of the brain. Like the cerebrum, the cerebellum has two hemispheres. They coordinate movement and help us maintain balance.
- The **brain stem** is the part of the brain just above the spinal cord. It's made up of three structures: the medulla oblongata, the pons, and the midbrain.
- The most prominent structure on the lower surface of the brain is the **medulla oblongata,** the lower part of the brain stem. The medulla carries information from the spinal cord to various parts of the brain and back again. It also controls heart rate, the rate of respiration, and the diameter of blood vessels.

- The **pons** (Latin for "bridge") crosses over the pyramidal tracts and connects the two sides of the cerebellum with each other and with the rest of the brain. Along with the medulla, the pons helps control breathing.
- Sitting behind the pons is the **midbrain,** which connects the upper and lower parts of the brain with the spinal cord (see also Figure 2.15a).
- The **hypothalamus** (literally, "under room") is a tiny structure located just ahead of the midbrain. It is part of the *limbic system,* the system that helps control emotional behavior and memory. The hypothalamus monitors the body's internal environment, receives information from the sense organs about the external environment, and controls hunger and thirst.

- The **pituitary gland** is the pea-like structure that hangs from the base of the hypothalamus. Along with the hypothalamus, the pituitary governs many of the body's automatic functions. Its secretions help control and coordinate almost every system in the body.
- Behind the pituitary is an X-shaped structure called the **optic chiasma** (ki-AZ-ma; Greek for "cross"), which is formed by the intersection of the two large optic nerves leading from the eyes.
- The two structures that look like caterpillars jutting out from the temporal lobes are the **olfactory bulbs.** The olfactory (smell-detecting) nerves originate in the olfactory bulbs.

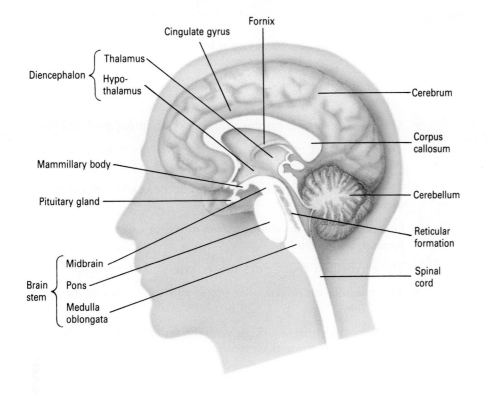

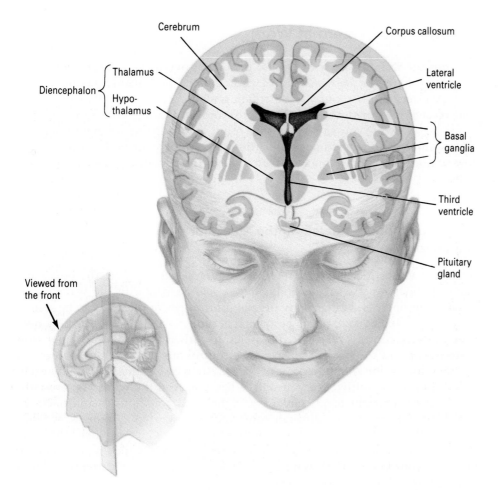

Figure 2.15
The Brain: A View Inside

Inside the brain, hidden away above the hypothalamus and among the folds of the cerebral cortex, are several other important structures. (a) Here you're looking at a midsagittal section, a vertical section down the midline of the brain. (b) In this drawing you're looking at a frontal section of the brain.

- The **thalamus** is actually two masses of gray matter, each at the core of a cerebral hemisphere. It relays (from the medulla to the cerebrum) all sensory impulses except smell, and interprets pain, temperature, and pressure. With the hypothalamus, the thalamus forms the **diencephalon.**

- Near the thalamus, wrapped in the folds of the cortex, are the **basal ganglia,** patches of gray matter that help smooth the actions we make with our muscles.

- The **ventricles** are cavities in the brain through which the cerebrospinal fluid flows. The ventricles come together at the center of the brain and form a channel that runs down into the spinal cord.

- Near the midline of each hemisphere, wrapped around the corpus callosum and the ventricles, are a group of structures known collectively as the **limbic system.** These structures, among them the hypothalamus, help control emotional behavior and memory.

- Starting in the spinal cord and running the length of the brain stem to the thalamus are pockets of gray matter, interconnected cells that form the **reticular formation.** The reticular formation governs overall levels of brain activity, including levels of consciousness and attention.

Recap

- The peripheral nervous system lies outside the spine and skull; the central nervous system lies within them.

- The peripheral nervous system carries messages to and from the central nervous system.

- The central nervous system consists of the spinal cord and brain.

- The spinal cord relays information between the peripheral nervous system and the brain, and processes simple reflex responses.

- The cerebral cortex, the gray matter in the cerebrum, covers the top surface of the brain.

- Fissures and sulci divide the cortex into four lobes: frontal, temporal, parietal, and occipital.

- The cerebellum coordinates movements and helps maintain balance.

- The medulla oblongata, the pons, and the midbrain make up the brain stem.

- The hypothalamus, working with the pituitary gland, governs many of the body's automatic responses.

- The thalamus, two masses of gray matter buried deep in the cerebral hemispheres, processes sensory information.

The Nervous System at Work

The intricate web of nerves wired into the brain governs your interactions with the world. Its *motor functions* control your muscles and glands, taking you to faraway places and keeping you functioning while you're there. Its *sensory functions* receive information from your sense organs, letting you hear music to dance to, allowing you to see the first robin in spring. Its *integrative functions* process information moving to and from all parts of your body, coordinating new sensory data with your experience and helping you to respond appropriately.

Motor Functions: Controlling the Muscular and Endocrine Systems

We have two distinct kinds of muscles: *striated muscles* connect the bones and move the major parts of the body; *smooth muscles* make up the walls of the glands, intestines, and other body organs. Both types of muscles can be seen in Figure 2.16. One portion of the peripheral nervous system, the **voluntary nervous system,** controls the striated muscles; the other, the **autonomic nervous system,** controls the smooth muscles. We control our striated muscles more or less consciously, but the autonomic nervous system essentially operates by itself.

You can see the difference yourself. When you read the word *Go,* tense the muscles in your right hand. *Go!* Easy, right? You consciously controlled the muscles in your right hand through your voluntary nervous system. Now when you read the word *Go,* make your forehead perspire. *Go!* Any luck? Probably not. Because your autonomic nervous system controls your sweat glands; it monitors your body temperature even when you aren't paying attention, but it doesn't respond to conscious intentions.

Voluntary nervous system The part of the peripheral nervous system that controls striated muscles.

Autonomic nervous system The part of the peripheral nervous system that controls the smooth muscles in the body's organs and glands.

 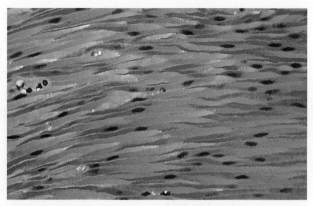

The Voluntary Nervous System: Controlling the Muscles   When you decide to move your arm or leg, the command travels in just two giant steps from the motor area of the cerebral cortex to a synapse in the spinal cord, and then to the muscles in your arm or leg.

Neuroscientists have mapped the motor area of the cortex to show the specific region that controls each group of striated muscles. The total area devoted to a specific muscle group is a function of the type of movement necessary in a given part of the body. The more precise the movement, the greater the area devoted to the muscle group (see Figure 2.17). This is why the muscles that control the thumb and fingers, for example, occupy much more of the motor area than do the muscles that control the trunk or toes.

Figure 2.16
Muscle Tissues

Muscles like the skeletal muscles that move our limbs look striped under a microscope and are called *striated* muscles (photo on the left). Muscles that are found in our digestive system look smooth under a microscope and are called *smooth* muscles (photo on the right).

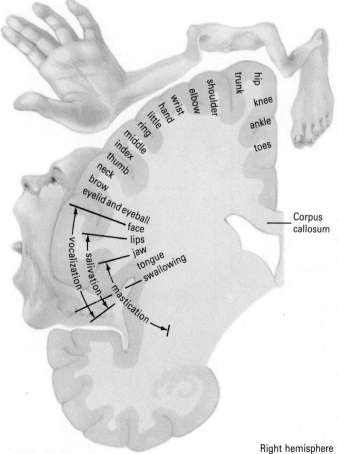

Source: Penfield & Rasmussen, 1978.

Right hemisphere

Figure 2.17
Motor Cortex

Each region of the motor cortex controls movements of a different part of the body. The size of the controlling area is a function of the degree of precision in the control, so that the proportionately largest areas are devoted to the hands and tongue, and relatively little area is devoted to the body.

There is a motor area in each hemisphere of the cortex. The area in the right hemisphere controls muscle groups on the left side of the body; the area in the left hemisphere controls the muscles on the right side of the body. Most motor neurons cross from one side to the other in the medulla before they continue on toward the muscles. In general, the right side of the brain controls the left side of the body, whereas the left side of the brain controls the right side of the body. You'll see this pattern again in the way the brain handles incoming sensory data.

The Autonomic Nervous System: Controlling Smooth Muscles and Glands

The autonomic nervous system regulates functions like digestion and temperature to maintain **homeostasis,** the critical balance in the body's internal environment. It also controls emotional responses (fear, anger) and motivations (hunger, thirst). When your heart skips a beat and the hair rises on the back of your neck at a horror movie, your autonomic nervous system is at work.

The autonomic nervous system has two parts: the **sympathetic division** and the **parasympathetic division.** Both divisions control the activities of a wide range of organs, but they exert different and often opposite effects. In general, what one system excites, the other inhibits. For example, the sympathetic nervous system dilates (enlarges) the pupils of the eyes, increases heart rate, and quiets the intestines. The parasympathetic system constricts the pupils, reduces

Figure 2.18
Autonomic Nervous System

The autonomic nervous system controls a wide variety of bodily functions including eating and digestion and emotional responses.

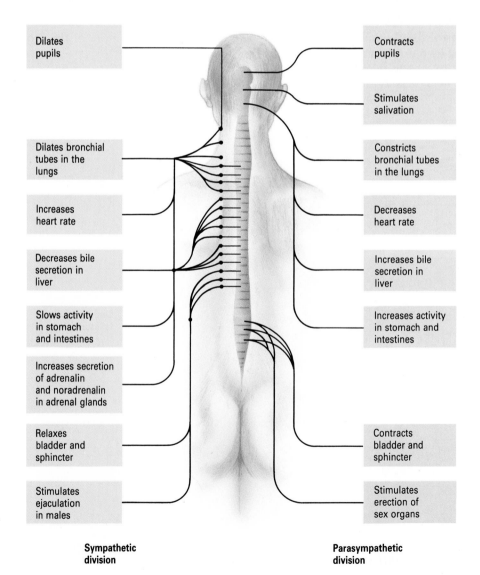

Dilates pupils

Contracts pupils

Stimulates salivation

Dilates bronchial tubes in the lungs

Constricts bronchial tubes in the lungs

Increases heart rate

Decreases heart rate

Decreases bile secretion in liver

Increases bile secretion in liver

Slows activity in stomach and intestines

Increases activity in stomach and intestines

Increases secretion of adrenalin and noradrenalin in adrenal glands

Relaxes bladder and sphincter

Contracts bladder and sphincter

Stimulates ejaculation in males

Stimulates erection of sex organs

Sympathetic division

Parasympathetic division

Homeostasis The relative stability of the body's internal environment.

Sympathetic division The part of the autonomic nervous system that generally mobilizes the body for vigorous action.

Parasympathetic division The part of the autonomic nervous system that generally conserves energy.

heart rate, and activates the intestines. In general, the sympathetic system mobilizes the body for vigorous action, whereas the parasympathetic division conserves energy and governs the ordinary maintenance functions of the body.

The organization of the two divisions reflects their different functions (see Figure 2.18). After leaving the spinal cord, sympathetic neurons form a chain that runs parallel to the spinal cord on either side of it, linking the neurons together. Accordingly, events that affect one part of the system usually affect many other parts. As parasympathetic neurons are not linked, however, control in the parasympathetic division is maintained on an organ-by-organ basis.

The control centers in the brain for the autonomic nervous system are widely distributed. The brain stem and the hypothalamus and other parts of the limbic system all seem to play an important role in coordinating autonomic activities. One of the most important functions of the autonomic nervous system is controlling the **endocrine glands,** which are shown in Figure 2.19. These glands secrete chemical messengers called **hormones** into the bloodstream. Because hormones are carried through the bloodstream to every cell of the body, endocrine glands have broad effects on one another and on other organs.

Like neurotransmitters, individual hormones affect a specific bodily process. But unlike neurotransmitters, which are released into the synaptic cleft, hormones are released into the bloodstream, where they circulate through the body and have the potential to affect billions of neurons and other cells. Given their form of release, hormones work slower but have a much broader and longer-lasting effect than do neurotransmitters.

The most powerful endocrine gland is the *pituitary* (see Figure 2.14). This "master gland" secretes potent hormones that have profound effects on growth, sexual reproduction, and stress. The pituitary gland has two parts. The first, the

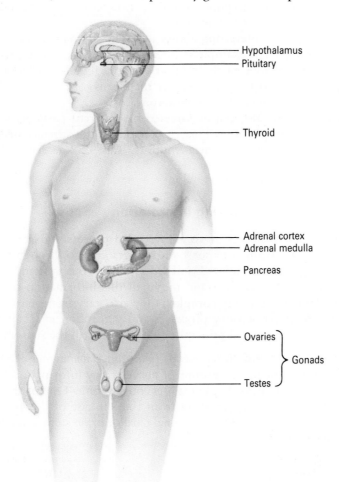

Hypothalamus
Pituitary

Thyroid

Adrenal cortex
Adrenal medulla
Pancreas

Ovaries
Gonads
Testes

Figure 2.19
The Endocrine Glands

The endocrine glands generate chemicals that are circulated through the body by the bloodstream and affect a wide variety of biological and behavioral processes.

Endocrine gland A gland that delivers its secretions directly to the bloodstream.

Hormone A substance secreted into the bloodstream by an endocrine gland that has broad effects on physiology.

anterior lobe, produces hormones that control the activities of muscles and other endocrine glands (the sex glands, the thyroid, and the adrenal glands). The second, the *posterior lobe,* stores and releases hormones made in the hypothalamus.

The **thyroid gland** lies just below the larynx or voice box. This gland stores hormones and releases them slowly over a period of time. These hormones regulate metabolism, growth and development, and the activity of the nervous system.

The **adrenal glands** sit like hats on top of and attached to the kidneys. Each adrenal gland is actually two glands, the inner *cortex* and the outer *medulla.*

The adrenal cortex releases hormones that play a major role in long-term reactions to stress. The adrenal medulla secretes two hormones, *adrenaline* (sometimes called *epinephrine)* and *noradrenaline* (sometimes called *norepinephrine).* Do you remember the last time you were very frightened? You probably didn't know it, but your adrenal glands were mobilizing your body for action—raising your blood pressure, increasing your heart rate, constricting your blood vessels, and releasing sugar from your liver into your bloodstream.

The **pancreas** lies behind and slightly below the stomach. In its role as an endocrine gland, the pancreas produces *insulin,* which controls the utilization of sugar by the body's cells, and *glucagon,* which increases the level of sugar in the blood.

The **gonads**—the testes in males and the ovaries in females—produce sperm and eggs. They also secrete a number of hormones, including *testosterone,* the *estrogens,* and *progesterone.* These hormones are responsible for the development and maintenance of the physical characteristics we associate with males and females. The estrogens and progesterone also help coordinate the female's menstrual cycle. A small amount of these hormones is secreted by the adrenal glands in both sexes, such that every male carries a little bit of the estrogens and every female carries a little bit of testosterone.

Hormones have the interesting ability to carry different messages under different circumstances. An example is luteinizing hormone (LH), which is produced in the anterior lobe of the pituitary. In the female, LH works with the estrogens to trigger ovulation and prepare the uterus for pregnancy. In the male, LH stimulates the production of testosterone.

The same hormone also can be secreted by different parts of the body. Remember that norepinephrine, which is secreted by the adrenal medulla, is also one of the most important neurotransmitters. Table 2.2 describes the effects of several important hormones.

Sensory Functions: Gathering Information

The great network of nerves in your body also processes a seemingly infinite number of messages from your sense organs. As you go through the day, your eyes, ears, nose, skin, and joints bombard your nervous system with information. The connections that sort and move all this information from receiving organ to the brain are not only complex; they also vary from sense to sense. We talk in depth about the sensory processes and perception in Chapters 3 and 4. Here we describe the general principles that apply to all the sensory functions.

Each side of the body sends sensory nerves to the corresponding side of the spinal cord. For each sense, two nerves or groups of nerves carry information from the peripheral nervous system to the central nervous system. One of these nerves or groups of nerves carries information from the left side of the body, the other from the right. The nerves enter the spinal cord or brain stem at the level nearest the organ they serve.

Thyroid gland   A gland that secretes hormones that regulate the body's metabolism, growth and development, and the activity of the nervous system.

Adrenal glands   A pair of endocrine glands that secrete hormones involved in long- and short-term reactions to stress.

Pancreas   The gland that produces insulin and glucagon.

Gonads   The male and female sex glands (testes and ovaries, respectively).

Table 2.2
Principal Hormones: Their
Sources and Effects

Hormone	Source	Effect
Adrenaline (epinephrine)	Adrenal medulla	Raises blood pressure, increases heart rate, constricts blood vessels, releases sugar into bloodstream
Adrenocorticotropic hormone (ACTH)	Anterior pituitary	Controls secretion of stress-related hormones in adrenal cortex
Estrogens	Ovaries	Develops and maintains female physical characteristics
Glucagon	Pancreas	Affects levels of alertness and energy
Insulin	Pancreas	Controls utilization of sugar
Luteinizing hormone (LH)	Anterior pituitary	Prepares uterus for pregnancy; stimulates production of testosterone in testes
Noradrenaline (norepinephrine)	Adrenal medulla	Raises blood pressure, increases heart rate, constricts blood vessels, releases sugar into bloodstream
Progesterone	Ovaries	Keeps uterus in readiness for pregnancy, affects menstrual cramping, elevates body temperature
Testosterone	Testes	Develops and maintains male physical characteristics
Thyroxin	Thyroid	Controls growth and metabolism

Most sensory tracts cross to the side opposite their point of entry. As sensory neurons enter the central nervous system, most cross over to the opposite side. Thus, as previously noted, information about the left side of the body is relayed to the right side of the brain, and information about the right side of the body is relayed to the left side of the brain.

The neurons that carry information from the eyes are a special case. Because each eye sees to both the left and right side of the body, the crossing over in the visual system must be much more complex. After leaving the eyes, the optic nerves turn toward the midline of the brain where they form a kind of cross, called the **optic chiasm.** A casual examination of the optic chiasm suggests that fibers from the right eye are crossing over to the left side of the brain and vice versa. But in fact something more complicated is happening. Fibers from the right side of the right eye's visual field are crossing over to the left side of the brain, but fibers from the left side of the right eye's visual field continue to the right side of the brain without crossing over. A similar thing happens to the fibers arising from the left eye. This curious arrangement assures that objects seen to the right of the body are represented in the left side of the cortex whereas objects seen to the left of the body are represented in the right side of the cortex. Figure 2.20 illustrates this process.

Most sensory pathways synapse as soon as they enter the central nervous system, then synapse again in the thalamus. Sensory neurons synapse initially in the gray matter of the spinal cord or brain. The next synapse in most sensory channels is the thalamus, an egg-shaped mass above the midbrain. The sensory areas of the thalamus relay sensory impulses directly to the cerebral cortex.

Each sensory pathway has a portion of cortex dedicated to it. A portion of the cerebral cortex called a *primary projection area* is devoted exclusively to each sense (see Figure 2.21). The area related to vision is at the back of the brain, in the occipital lobe. Hearing is located at the side of the brain, in the temporal lobe.

Optic chiasm Point at the midline of the brain where the optic nerves cross over to the opposite side of the brain.

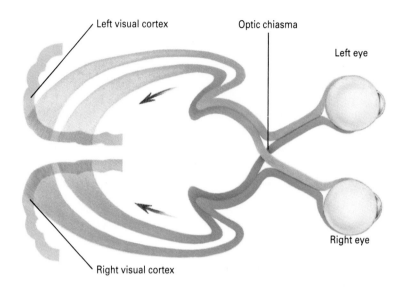

Figure 2.20
Pathway of the Nerves from the Eyes

Both eyes see the same scene, but each eye sends half of the scenic information to one half of the brain, while the other half of each eye sends the information to the other half of the brain. The red parts of this figure represent one half of the information, and the blue parts represent the other half. Notice that a complete picture of what is in front of a person's eyes requires the integration of information from both hemispheres.

Smell also is located in the temporal lobe. Taste is in the parietal lobe. Touch, pain, and sensations from the muscles and joints are represented in a band across the top and side of the brain, where the frontal lobe meets the parietal lobe. Near the primary projection areas are secondary projection areas, where sensory information is processed further.

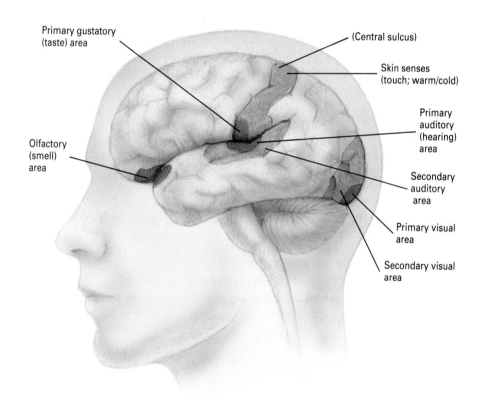

Figure 2.21
Sensory Areas of the Cortex

Each of the various sensory systems sends neurons to a particular part of the cortex. Surrounding these *primary projection areas* are *secondary association areas,* in which the sensory information is further elaborated.

The sensory areas of the cortex are organized much like the motor areas. In general, the space devoted to a specific organ is a function of the number of receptors in that organ, not of the size of the organ (see Figure 2.22). For example, the space devoted to the lips and thumb reflects their high sensitivity.

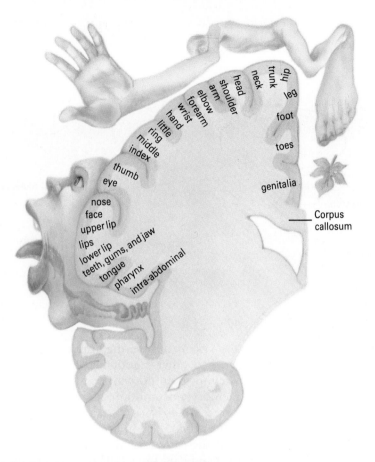

Source: Penfield & Rasmussen, 1978.   Right hemisphere

Figure 2.22
A Map of the Sensory Cortex

The different parts of the body send sensory information to different parts of the somatosensory cortex. The amount of area devoted to a part of the body is proportional to the sensitivity of the skin senses in that body part. Notice that although both the motor cortex and the somatosensory cortex are like maps of the body, the maps differ. For example, although there is a sensory region for the abdominal cavity, there is no corresponding motor area, because we can't move our stomachs or livers.

Integrative Functions: Coordinating Information

If you've ever written a term paper or done a laboratory project, you know that gathering information is only half the job. Until you integrate all your facts, you have a tough time coming to a conclusion. The nervous system, too, must integrate information from various sources and then coordinate its responses. Integrative functions are carried out in the gray matter, from spinal cord to cerebral cortex. As we move up through the nervous system, the process becomes more and more complex.

Integration in the Spinal Cord   A *spinal reflex* is a behavior that does not require the intervention of the brain. Instead, a motor response to a sensory stimulus is coordinated by the spinal cord. The withdrawal reflex is a spinal reflex. When you touch something hot, you immediately withdraw your hand, before sensory information can reach the brain. A sensory neuron in your hand sends a message to the spinal cord. An interneuron in the spinal cord relays that message to a motor neuron, which carries a message back to the muscles in your hand, telling them to pull back. Figure 2.23 shows the spinal reflex.

Integration in the Brain   The reticular formation, or reticular activating system, is an area of gray matter that extends from the spinal cord through the brain stem into the diencephalon (see Figure 2.15). The reticular formation influences the activity level of the cerebral cortex; that is, it influences the organism's general level of alertness.

Figure 2.23
A Spinal Reflex: Withdrawal

A spinal reflex is the smallest possible loop from sensation to response. When a pain neuron reaches the spinal cord, it synapses with a motor neuron to produce withdrawal, before the signals have begun to travel upwards toward the brain. (In most cases of actual withdrawal of a hand from a painful stimulus, many thousands of neurons are involved, but in principle the sequence could proceed as diagrammed.)

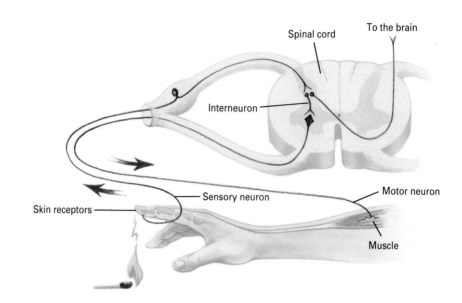

Moving up the central nervous system a little, the limbic system plays a role in the integration of fear, anger, and other emotional responses. The system includes the *amygdala,* which is involved in motivation and emotion; the *hippocampus,* which plays a part in memory and emotion; and portions of the hypothalamus and thalamus (see Figure 2.24).

Damage to or stimulation of the limbic system can have very specific effects on emotional behavior. In one of the earliest demonstrations of these effects, two neurologists, Heinrich Kluver and Paul Bucy (1939), removed the temporal lobe (and therefore the amygdala) of a monkey. The monkey became extraordinarily docile, showed no fear or aggression, was unable to distinguish between edible and nonedible objects, and became sexually overactive.

Figure 2.24
The Limbic System

The limbic system is a group of highly interconnected brain structures that lie underneath the cerebral hemispheres. The limbic system structures appear to be heavily involved in emotional and motivational responses and in memory.

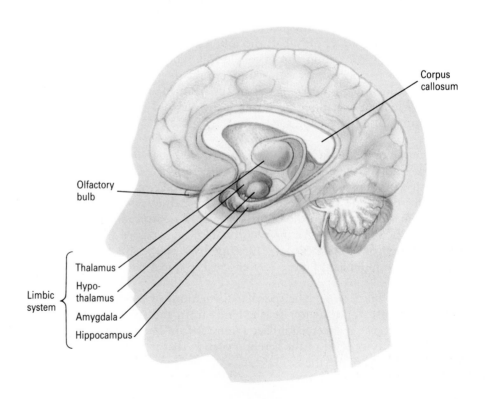

Studies of animals also show the role of the hippocampus. By stimulating one part of the structure in a cat, researchers were able to produce flight behaviors: the cat tried to bolt. When they stimulated other parts of the cat's hippocampus, the animal exhibited defensive threat behaviors, raising its fur, hissing, and snarling (de Molina & Hunsperger, 1959). Lesion studies of the hippocampus have demonstrated its effect on memory. In one such study, patients with lesions in the hippocampus were unable to turn short-term memories into long-term memories (Kupferman, 1985a). This failure is a symptom of Korsakoff's syndrome, a condition that sometimes accompanies chronic alcoholism.

The nervous system performs its most complicated integration in the *cerebral cortex*. Here perceptions are integrated, memories are stored, and actions are planned. Now, we'll focus on the functions of the cerebral cortex.

Recap

- Working together, the parts of the nervous system carry out motor functions, sensory functions, and integrative functions.

- The voluntary nervous system controls striated muscles; the autonomic nervous system controls smooth muscles.

- Specific areas in the cerebral cortex control specific groups of muscles.

- The autonomic nervous system maintains homeostasis in the body.

- The sympathetic division of the autonomic nervous system mobilizes the body for action; the parasympathetic division conserves energy and coordinates the digestive processes.

- Endocrine glands, which are controlled by the autonomic nervous system, secrete hormones into the bloodstream.

- Although hormones are transmitted more slowly than neurotransmitters, their effects are much broader and longer lasting.

- The nervous system carries information from the sense organs through the spinal cord and the thalamus to the sensory areas of the brain.

- Integration is a function of the gray matter in the spinal cord and brain.

The Cerebral Cortex: The Great Integrator

Complex integration—perception, memory, learning, and planning—takes place primarily in the cerebral cortex. For more than a century, neuroscientists have searched for clues to help them understand how the different parts of the cortex work together and with other parts of the nervous system to coordinate behavior and experience.

Understanding the Human Cortex

The human cortex, more than any other part of the brain, seems to define us as humans. Laboratory studies of cats may help us understand the amygdala, but no other animal has quite the same kind of cortex that we do.

How Do We Know That?

As we noted earlier, one source of information about brain function is the effect of damage to the brain. When a deficit seems to be the product of an injury, it's always tempting to assume that the damaged area is a "center" for the control of the lost function. But neuroscientists have become increasingly leery of the center concept for most of the cerebral cortex. The fact that a lesion eliminates a function may mean many different things (Finger & Stein, 1982). Instead of being the place where the function is actually controlled, the damaged part of the cortex could be

- Part of a sensory system carrying information necessary for that function.
- Part of a motor system carrying instructions from the cortex to the muscles and glands.
- Part of a system that excites the cortex, so that any processing is possible.
- A connection linking different systems that together control the function.
- Entirely unrelated to the function. (Lesions irritate the brain and generate abnormal electrical and physiological activity around them. A lesion could simply be interfering with the normal functioning of the cortex in some way.)

Neuroscientists are understandably cautious about interpreting the findings of lesion studies as evidence that functions are assigned to particular areas of the cortex. At times, they've drawn the wrong conclusion. In the 1950s, having discovered that animals with lesions in the hypothalamus stopped eating, scientists concluded that a particular part of the hypothalamus was a "hunger center." More recent research revealed that this structure was in fact just a small part of a much larger eating control system that involves many parts of the brain and other organs of the body (Rolls, 1986).

What is true for the hypothalamus is almost certainly true for the cortex as well. The cortex is even more complex than the hypothalamus. Each cortical region is assumed to contribute to many functions, and each function is assumed to rely on many regions. In light of these interrelationships, we can begin to understand how any one part of the cortex contributes to the functioning of the whole only after we've examined it with a number of techniques under a number of different circumstances.

How do we get information about the human cortex? Obviously we can't cut into a living person to manipulate the brain. Studies of accident or stroke victims give us some clues, but lesion studies are limited in terms of what they can teach us. Brain autopsies, like those performed by Broca, and electrical stimulation studies of patients undergoing surgery also contribute to our knowledge, but they too are limited by many of the same factors that limit the usefulness of lesion studies. As a result of these difficulties, we are still unclear how the cortex functions.

In fact, research on the functions of the cortex seems to indicate two very different, contradictory hypotheses:

- *Cortical functions are localized* According to this view, the cortex is made up of regions that, like stations in an assembly line, are the sites of distinct and highly specialized tasks. These tasks are permanently assigned to areas of the cortex and cannot be assumed by other regions.

- *Cortical functions are distributed* The distributed-function hypothesis says that the cortex is a single integrated system, adaptable to damage or stress. Functions are widely distributed over the surface of the cortex, and different regions can perform different tasks on different occasions.

Before we look at how contemporary psychologists are trying to resolve this contradiction, let's review the research that supports each hypothesis.

Evidence for Localization   There is widespread agreement on certain facts that seem to support the concept of localization.

The cortex is divided into anatomically distinct areas.   When Golgi and Cajal (1967/1906) looked through their microscopes at stained cortical tissue, they found that the cortex was divided into six layers, as can be seen in Figure 2.25. In different parts of the cortex, the thickness of the layers varies. Thus the cortex can easily be divided into different regions based on the structure of these layers (Brodal, 1981).

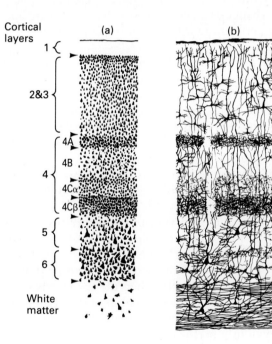

Figure 2.25
Layers of Cortex

The cortex consists of six layers of cells that can be distinguished by the different ways in which they are organized. Some layers connect primarily up and down to other cells near them in other layers, while other layers connect primarily with regions some distance away in the brain. In different parts of the brain, the patterns of layers are different, indicating that the parts of the brain are organized in different ways. Part (a) shows layers stained to emphasize cell bodies. Part (b) shows same layers stained to emphasize entire cells.

Moreover, layers of these different regions are "wired" in different patterns: some layers connect a cortical region to other parts of the cortex; some to the thalamus; and some to lower parts of the brain and spinal cord.

Cortical lesions often produce specific deficits.   Remember that damage to certain regions in the cortex can produce very specific losses. People or animals with lesions in a sensory area, for example, show deficits in the affected sense.

Lesions outside the primary motor and sensory areas also can produce specific deficits. Damage to a small part of the cortex along the border between the occipital and temporal lobes may leave the victim unable to recognize familiar faces (Damasio, 1985). One child with this condition could not recognize her own mother's face, although she knew her mother and other people readily by their voices (Young & Ellis, 1989).

Other lesions can produce difficulties in speaking or comprehending speech. These specific losses, too, suggest that certain abilities are localized in specific areas.

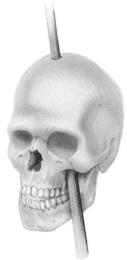

Medical literature contains many cases of people who recovered from devastating injuries to the cortex, but the most infamous case is that of Phineas Gage, who had an iron bar driven through his skull in a blasting accident. After the accident, Gage recovered his ability to walk and talk but displayed a dramatic change in personality. Disruptive and unpredictable, he lost his job with the railroad and ended up a featured attraction in a carnival sideshow.

Stimulation of the cortex often produces highly specific responses. Surgeons attempting to locate a brain tumor can gently stimulate the cortical surface and observe the patient's responses. As patients are fully awake during the procedure (which is painless because there are no sensory neurons in the brain), they can discuss their reactions.

Canadian neurosurgeon Wilder Penfield used cortical stimulation to demonstrate many specific relationships. For instance, stimulation in the motor area often produces muscle twitches or movements. In certain sensory areas, the response might be a flash of light, a sound, or a tingling feeling in some part of the body. Stimulation in other areas produces more complex experiences like memories of past events (Penfield & Rasmussen, 1957).

There is a very specific relationship between a person's behavior and experience and the activity in particular parts of the cortex. Earlier in this chapter we discussed the revolution the computer has started in the study of the brain. We can now see that different specific parts of the cortex are active when the person is doing different things. Researchers have even been able to watch patterns of brain activity change as a person moves from thinking about performing an action to actually performing it (see Figure 2.26) (Sargent, 1987).

Evidence for Distributed Functions

Case studies of the recovery of functions that had been lost after the cerebral cortex was damaged are the most important evidence for distribution. If cortical functions are localized (that is, if specific areas of the cortex are permanently assigned to specific tasks) damage to a particular cortical area should leave a person or an animal permanently unable to perform those tasks. In cases of recovery of function, there is no permanent deficit. An initial loss occurs, but in time the ability to perform the task returns.

Here only two possibilities exist: either the damaged cortical tissue has repaired itself, or other tissues have taken over the lost functions. Because the central nervous system rarely repairs itself, some neuroscientists think that recovery of function must mean that other tissues are taking over the lost functions. If they are, the principle of localization does not apply.

In fact, hundreds of studies demonstrate that animals who are properly treated often recover from what seems to be devastating damage to their nervous systems, particularly when the damage is done in small steps (see Figure 2.27). When the damage to a region of the brain occurs in a series of small steps, apparently other parts of the brain can gradually take over the functions that were previously performed by that part.

Figure 2.26
Localization of Function in the Living Brain

Different areas of the brain are active during different kinds of activities, as these PET scans make clear. Greatest brain activity is indicated by the red color.

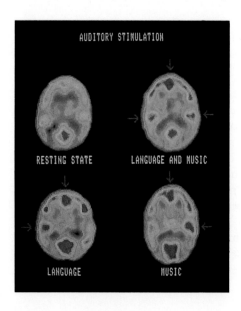

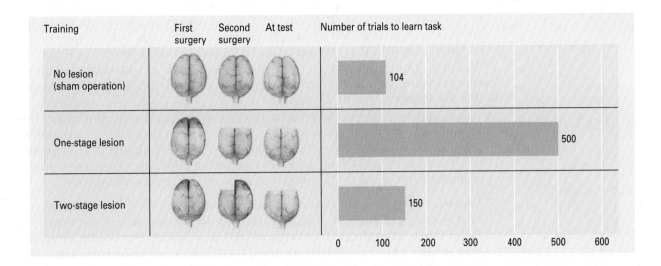

Training	First surgery	Second surgery	At test	Number of trials to learn task
No lesion (sham operation)				104
One-stage lesion				500
Two-stage lesion				150

Figure 2.27
The Effects of One- and Two-Stage Lesions on Learning

To study the effects of gradual damage to the cortex, researchers used three groups of rats. The first group had sham operations: the subjects were anesthetized and their skulls were cut open, but their brains were not touched. Rats in the one-stage lesion group had both frontal lobes removed in a single operation. Rats in the two-stage lesion group underwent two separate operations. Although rats in the two-stage group did not do as well as the control group in learning a task, they did much better than the subjects in the one-stage group (Finger & Stein, 1969)

Research on certain rare medical conditions suggests that people also can recover lost brain functions, particularly if the damage is inflicted early in life. Some children are born with only one functioning hemisphere. To help them survive, surgeons remove the nonfunctioning half of the brain when the children are infants. Although these children are missing one entire cerebral hemisphere, researchers have found only small intellectual differences between them and children with two hemispheres. These differences are so small, in fact, that they often can be detected only with sophisticated measurement procedures (Nass, Peterson & Koch, 1989). Apparently, as each of these young people grows, the brain reorganizes itself, and the remaining hemisphere takes over the functions that would have been performed by the hemisphere that was removed (Nass, 1984; Brizzilara et al., 1984).

A Third Perspective: Distributed Parallel Systems   Contemporary psychology offers a third perspective, *distributed parallel processing,* which draws on both localization and distributed function theories.

From localization, this hypothesis adopts the idea that the cortex is clearly organized into very specific areas and that these areas have very sharp boundaries (Kaas, 1987). However, not all aspects of a function are performed in one area, and not all cortexes are organized in exactly the same way. From distributed function theory, distributed parallel processing borrows the idea that cortical organization is dynamic and depends on the individual's patterns of use and experience.

Neuroscientists now believe that the cortex is localized in some respects and distributed in others. Most functions are represented in many parts of the brain, and several parts of the brain often work together on different aspects of a single problem (Mountcastle, 1978).

Cortical Lateralization

If you read popular magazines or watch television, you probably have seen or heard some reference to right brain–left brain differences. There are people who believe that each of us has two brains (the right hemisphere and the left hemisphere), and that a different side of our being is represented in each. Although the popular version of this bit of psychology is oversimplified, it is true that the two hemispheres sometimes play different roles in different tasks.

The integration of our experience and behavior seems to take place in many closely coordinated regions of the cortex. Often the two sides of the cortex do similar work, each side operating as a sort of control panel for the opposite side of the body. Remember that many motor and sensory impulses starting on the left side of your body are eventually processed in the right side of your brain, and that many impulses starting on the right side of your body are processed in the left side of your brain. In other words, the cortex is *bilaterally symmetrical:* corresponding parts of the left and right sides of the cortex often play the same role for opposite parts of the body.

But sometimes the corresponding sides of the cortex do different work. Remember that the cortex often relies on various parts of the brain to carry out its tasks, and that several parts of the brain can be working simultaneously on different aspects of a problem. Instead of performing the same task, these corresponding parts of the two hemispheres perform *different but related* tasks.

Language   Psychologists have known for a very long time that language is a **lateralized function,** a function performed by just one side of the brain. As earlier noted, Paul Broca discovered in 1865 that a small area on the left of the frontal lobe, what we call **Broca's area,** is essential to the normal production of speech. Patients with lesions in this area suffer from *expressive aphasia;* they understand speech but cannot produce it.

A few years later, Broca's colleague Carl Wernicke identified an area of the brain that apparently is necessary for understanding speech. **Wernicke's area** is located on the same side of the brain as Broca's area, in the temporal lobe. Damage to Wernicke's area is characteristic of patients with *receptive aphasia:* they can speak readily but have difficulty understanding the speech of others.

Wernicke theorized that a person could have normal speech function only if both Broca's area and Wernicke's area are intact and, equally important, if the connection between the two areas is intact. He predicted the discovery of a form of aphasia that would arise when brain damage interrupted the nerves connecting the two areas. This condition, known as *conduction aphasia,* was later identified. People with conduction aphasia can both speak and understand speech, but they have a problem connecting the two abilities: they have difficulty repeating what they hear; and although they speak fluently, they speak incorrectly, aware that they are making mistakes but helpless to fix them (Kandel, 1985; Mayeux & Kandel, 1985). Figure 2.28 shows the cortical regions in which damage leads to one or another form of aphasia.

Both Broca's area and Wernicke's area are on the left side of the brain. Studies tell us that the rhythm and intonation of speech and the interpretation of these components of speech seem to be dependent on two areas on the right side of the brain. The area that governs the rhythm and intonation of speech is in the right hemisphere, in a position corresponding to Broca's area on the left (Ross, 1981, 1984; Heilman, Scholes & Watson, 1975). And the area that governs the interpretation of the emotional aspects of speech is on the right side of the cortex, in a position corresponding to the location of Wernicke's area on the left. The corresponding parts of the two hemispheres perform different but related tasks. (Despite the symmetry, however, the area devoted to communication is larger in the left hemisphere than in the right [Geschwind & Levitsky, 1968].)

Split-Brain Experiments   Psychologist Roger Sperry (1968) performed a series of experiments that dramatically demonstrates the relationship between the brain's two hemispheres. Sperry worked with a small population of patients whose corpus callosum—the major connection between the two cerebral hemispheres—had been surgically severed to prevent the spread of severe epileptic seizures from one hemisphere to the other.

Sperry and his colleagues saw in these patients an unusual opportunity to study the mental abilities of the two hemispheres. They set out to design experimental procedures that would allow them to "communicate" with one hemisphere of their subjects' "split brains" without communicating with the other (Kupferman, 1985b).

Lateralized function   An activity that is performed by just one side of the brain.

Broca's area   A small area in the left frontal lobe of the brain that is necessary for the production of speech.

Wernicke's area   A small area in the left temporal lobe that is necessary for understanding speech.

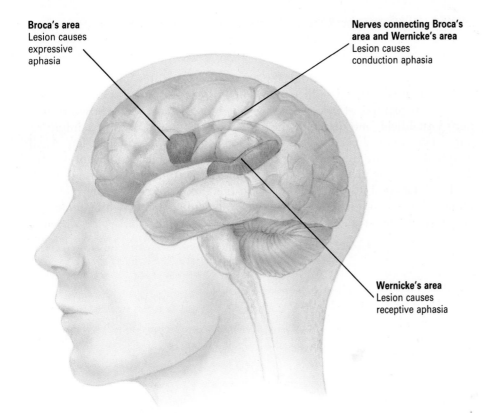

Broca's area
Lesion causes expressive aphasia

Nerves connecting Broca's area and Wernicke's area
Lesion causes conduction aphasia

Wernicke's area
Lesion causes receptive aphasia

Figure 2.28
Language Functions and the Cortex

Damage to Broca's area in the left hemisphere causes expressive aphasia, in which a person has difficulty speaking. Damage to Wernicke's area causes receptive aphasia, in which the person has difficulty understanding speech. And damage to the connections between these two areas cause conduction aphasia, in which the person can both speak and understand, but cannot combine the two. Such a person cannot, for example, repeat the speech of another.

To solve this problem, Sperry's group used what they knew about the way nerves in the eyes are "wired" to present visual images to their subjects' right and left hemispheres. The subjects were asked to look at a point in the middle of a screen. While their gaze was fixed on this point, a picture was projected very briefly to the right or left of the point. The exposure time was long enough to allow the subjects to recognize the picture but not long enough to allow them to move their eyes to look directly at the image. Remember that because of the complicated divisions in the optic chiasm, information from the left side of each eye goes to the left side of the brain, while information from the right side of each eye goes to the right side of the brain. Because the subjects could not shift their gaze, the information on each side of the picture went to only one side of the brain.

With their apparatus, Sperry and his colleagues could direct different information to the right and left hemispheres. For example, they could show their subjects a picture of a dog in the right visual field and a picture of a cat in the left visual field (see Figure 2.29). When asked what they saw, most split-brain subjects said they had seen a dog. Although images of both the cat and the dog were reaching the cortex, only the dog image was being relayed to the left side of the cortex, the side that could answer the researchers' question verbally. But if asked to point with their left hand (controlled by the brain's right side) to a picture of what they had seen, subjects would point to the cat.

The experiments Sperry and his associates conducted on split-brain patients have increased our understanding of how the two hemispheres function. For instance, Sperry found that although the left brain is more competent at speaking, the right brain is better at solving spatial problems. Split-brain subjects who were asked to arrange blocks in a pattern found themselves unable to complete with their right hand a pattern that they could complete easily with their left. Sperry describes a poignant scene in which a patient's left hand tried to come to the aid of his helpless right hand as it struggled to solve a difficult spatial problem (Gazzaniga & Sperry, 1967).

Puzzle It Out!

In a series of experiments, Roger Sperry directed pictures with emotional content to subjects' left and right visual fields. In one test, for instance, he showed his subjects pictures of naked people. When the pictures were shown to the right visual field (and therefore the left side of the brain), a subject might report seeing a naked person. When the pictures were shown to the left visual field (and therefore the right side of the brain), the subject could not describe the content of the picture but would indicate by grinning or laughing that he or she understood its emotional implications (Sperry, 1968). If the split-brain subjects knew enough about the picture to be embarrassed, why couldn't they explain their embarrassment?

"Look at the dot in the middle of the screen."

"Point with your left hand to the picture and tell me what you saw."

Figure 2.29
Sperry's Split-Brain Experiment

A split-brain subject can only answer questions that relate to information presented to the right visual field (or hand). Information presented to the left visual field (or hand)—and so to the right hemisphere—is not available for verbal processing.

The popular press interprets split-brain research as evidence that each of us has two brains—one creative and emotional, the other verbal and analytical—and that each of them is struggling for control. As we've seen, there is some separation between the two hemispheres in the control of verbal and nonverbal expression. But neuroscientists generally emphasize the unity of the brain, reminding us that in all but extraordinary circumstances, there is no conflict between the hemispheres (Harth, 1982; Sergent, 1987). Most complex functions require large areas of both sides of the cortex for their execution.

An example: You meet a friend and the two of you say hello to each other. Think about what's involved in this simple exchange. First, the nerves in your ears pick up the sound of your friend's voice, sending a message to one auditory area in the cortex, and then to another. From the secondary auditory area, an impulse is transmitted to Wernicke's area, on the left temporal lobe. Here the sounds are interpreted and your reply is turned into neural impulses that are passed over the nerve cells that connect Wernicke's area with Broca's area. From Broca's area, commands go out to the motor areas in both hemispheres, directing your speaking apparatus to speak. Meanwhile, the right side of your brain is making its own contribution. Opposite Wernicke's area, a portion of your cortex is interpreting the speed and intonation of your friend's speech. Opposite Broca's area, a portion of your cortex is determining the speed and intonation of your response. Without even considering the parts of the brain that decide what you're going to say, we've identified eight cortical areas involved in responding to a question as simple as "How was your weekend?"

Recap

- Complicated integration takes place primarily in the cerebral cortex.

- The findings of research on the functions of the cortex seem to support two contradictory views: that cortical functions are localized and that cortical functions are distributed.

- Strong evidence of localization can be found in anatomical, lesion, stimulation, and recording studies.

- Recovery of function is evidence of distribution.

- Distributed parallel processing helps explain the contradiction between localization and distribution.

- Although the cortex is bilaterally symmetrical in many areas, some functions, particularly those related to language, seem to be lateralized, such that the two sides of the cortex play different but complementary roles.

Conclusion

Knowledge about the nervous system is central to psychology. Whether you are interested in social behavior, personality, mental illness, child development, or learning, knowing how the nervous system works is essential. Does that mean that everything in psychology may some day be explained by brain activity? Philosophers have thought a lot about this question, and even though the issue isn't settled, the best answer seems to be no.

The reason is that, although brain activity is involved in all human behavior, brain functions alone are rarely sufficient to explain that behavior. The contributions and the limits of physiology become clearer if we compare the brain to a car. Both are mechanisms that make actions possible. The brain is the mechanism for thought and feeling, the automobile for driving.

Clearly, if you want to understand driving, you have to understand how cars work. If you want to know why cars can't go much faster than 120 miles per hour, you need to know something about the way motors and transmissions work. In the same way, if you want to understand why people sweat and shake when they're angry, you need to know about the autonomic nervous system.

But it is also important to recognize what you will *not* know. No amount of knowledge about the principles of automobile design will explain why cars that can travel 120 miles per hour rarely go more than 65 miles per hour. To understand that, you need to know about traffic laws, not engineering. Similarly, to understand anger, you need to know about the autonomic nervous system. But to know why a person gets angry when you insult his favorite baseball team, you need to know about his social group, not his physiology. Clearly, there are kinds of questions that cannot be answered by looking at a person's brain.

Human behavior is complex. Although some behavior can be explained by brain functioning alone, most can't be. But the more we know about the brain, the better, if only because we can identify when we should worry about issues of brain function and when we shouldn't.

Chapter 3

Sensation

My Sweet Rose, John William Waterhouse, c1880

3

Gateways Almost everything we know, feel, think, or do is a result of experience. A basic part of that experience involves information that comes from our senses. To understand human beings, then, we need to understand the mechanisms by which our senses put us in touch with ourselves and our surroundings.

This chapter is half of a pair with the next, perception. Both chapters deal with how we ex-tract information from the world. This chapter is concerned mainly with the ways that information about the world is translated into the only language the nervous system understands—the language of nerve impulses. Chapter 4 on perception examines different but equally complex processes, those that elaborate sensory information and turn it into a picture of the world. Further discussions of how we gather and interpret information about ourselves and the world around us appear in Chapter 5 on consciousness, Chapter 10 on emotion, and Chapters 17 and 18 on social psychology.

Imagine, a science fiction story in which a mad scientist has captured a brain and put it in a vat. Imagine, further that the mad scientist has devilishly contrived to keep the brain alive and healthy by supplying it with nutrients and oxygen. Imagine finally that he fiendishly tickles the cut-off nerve endings of the brain so as to imitate the stimulation of the nerves that would occur if the brain was in an active, aware human being. What would the brain know?

The brain would have no choice but to believe that it was still in a person, living the life of a person. In fact, each of us has no way of knowing that we are *not* such a brain in a vat. Everything we see around us, every sound we hear, could simply be the result of the mad scientist stimulating our nerves. When we look, he stimulates our vision nerves so that we see; when we listen, he stimulates our hearing nerves so that we hear. When we command our hands or feet to move, he stimulates the nerves cut off from our muscles so that we think we move. In our science fiction story, the whole world of our experience could be caused by the activities of the mad scientist.

The brain in the vat may be nothing more than a fantasy designed to scare you. But something terrifyingly reminiscent of the experiences of the brain-in-the-vat actually does occur. It is known as a *phantom limb*. People who have had an arm or a leg amputated often experience feelings—even severe pain—that seem to be taking place in the missing limb.

How do we explain these feelings? The answer to this question helps explain how our senses translate the world into sound, color, smell, taste, and touch. Even though the limb is missing, the nerves that connected it to the brain are alive and functioning. And when the severed ends of those nerves are stimulated—by touch, a change in temperature, or infection, for example—they send messages to the brain. The brain translates those messages into **sensations.** Since these are the nerves that used to carry pain messages to the brain, the brain can only interpret these nerve impulses as a feeling of pain in a limb that doesn't exist.

The phenomenon of phantom limb demonstrates a basic principle of sensation—that everything we know about the world and our bodies is a product of activity in the nerves leading toward the brain. To understand how we know about the world, we need to understand how our sense organs collect information; how that information is transformed into nerve impulses, the only language the brain understands; and how nerve impulses are transmitted to the brain (see Figure 3.1).

The Sensory Processes

Each sensory system gathers information about a different aspect of the physical or chemical environment. Our **senses**—hearing, vision, smell, taste, touch, balance, and motion—are the products of the different sensory systems. Although the sensory systems are different in many ways, they still share some important features.

Sensation An awareness of conditions inside and outside the body.

Sense A type of awareness produced by a sensory system, such as vision, hearing, and touch.

59

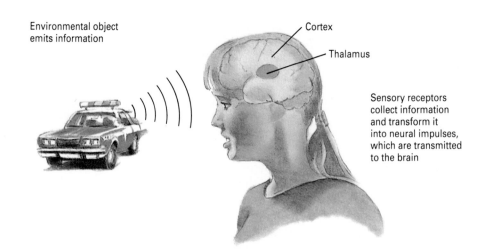

Figure 3.1
The Sensory Processes

Each sense gathers information about the physical or chemical environment, codes that information as a pattern of neural impulses and sends it on to the brain, which coordinates a response. The sight of the on-rushing car and the sound of the blaring siren are coded by the sensory structures of this person's eyes and ears as nerve impulses head toward the visual and auditory parts of her brain.

Environmental object emits information

Cortex

Thalamus

Sensory receptors collect information and transform it into neural impulses, which are transmitted to the brain

Collecting and Translating Information from the Environment

The structure of the external sense organs reflects their special functions. The fleshy folds of the outer ear collect sound; the lens on the eye focuses the light, and the passageways of the nose gather the airborne chemicals that we call odors. Each organ also has its own *receptors,* specialized nerve cells that translate information from the environment and body into nerve impulses.

In sensory receptor cells, the nerve impulse begins when an environmental stimulus—some form of energy or a chemical substance—comes in contact with the cell membrane. Through the process of **transduction,** that energy or substance is converted into a nerve impulse.

How does transduction work? Think for a minute about a thermometer. A thermometer is a transducer; it transduces the energy of heat into the physical movement of mercury. As the temperature rises, so does the mercury in the tube. Sensors in street lights are transducers, too. They transduce daylight into the electrical energy that automatically switches street lights on at dusk and off at dawn. Sensory receptors work in much the same way, converting the energy of heat or light or some other stimulus into nerve impulses.

Transduction occurs in two basic ways:

1. Mechanical distortion of the receptor's cell membrane triggers an action potential. The most obvious example of mechanical transduction is the sense of touch. Pressure on your skin distorts nerve cells lying beneath the skin, opening sodium channels along their membranes and triggering a nerve impulse. Mechanical changes also initiate nerve impulses in the sense organs that govern hearing, balance, and motion.
2. The stimulus produces a chemical that functions like a neurotransmitter, triggering an action potential in the receptor cell. Chemical changes generate nerve impulses in the sense organs that control vision, smell, and taste.

Coding Sensory Information

Transduction The process of converting a physical or chemical stimulus into a nerve impulse.

Coding The process of translating sensory information into patterns of nerve activity that allow the brain to distinguish among the properties of a stimulus.

Pressure on your skin is a mechanical distortion that triggers a nerve impulse. That pressure could be gentle, a pat or a stroke; or it could be hard, a slap or a pinch. The nerve impulses that carry sensory information to the brain must relate systematically to variations in the properties of the stimulus. This process—the translation of sensory information into patterns of nerve activity that allow the brain to distinguish among the properties of a stimulus—is called **coding.** Coding translates the pressure on your hand into a specific pattern of nerve activity that helps the brain distinguish between a pat and a slap. It also, for instance, translates the movement of receptor cells in the ear into a specific pattern of nerve activity that helps the brain distinguish between the noise of a jackhammer and a baby's cry.

Recap

- Sensory processes gather information from the environment and the body, translate that information into nerve impulses, code the information, and carry it to the sensory cortex.

- Each sensory system is highly specialized, responding to a specific physical or chemical stimulus with specialized receptor cells.

- Transduction is the process of translating physical or chemical stimuli into nerve impulses.

- Coding translates the properties of a specific stimulus into specific patterns of nerve activity that help the brain identify the stimulus.

Hearing

Everything that moves creates waves in the air. When we drive a car, throw a ball, or say hi to a friend, we're making waves in the air. If those waves are the right size and speed, we experience them as sound.

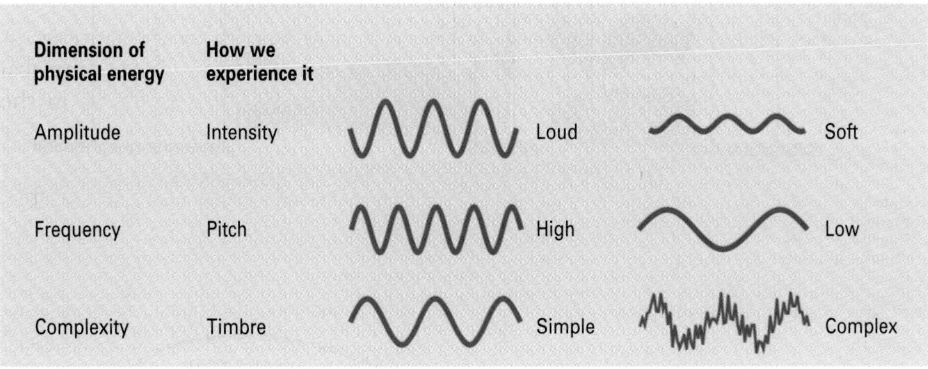

Dimension of physical energy	How we experience it				
Amplitude	Intensity	∿∿∿	Loud	∿	Soft
Frequency	Pitch	∿∿∿	High	∿	Low
Complexity	Timbre	∿∿	Simple	⋎⋏⋎	Complex

Figure 3.2
Sound Waves

Each of the properties of a sound—its intensity, pitch, and timber—relates to a specific property of the sound waves that make the sound. High-amplitude waves are loud sounds, frequent waves are high-pitched sounds, and irregular waves are complex sounds.

Unlike water, air has no upper surface. The waves we hear are not bulges on a surface but, rather, increases and decreases in the density of air. The changing patterns of density of air determine the dimensions of sound—its intensity, pitch, and timbre.

Intensity is the level of sound, its loudness. We measure intensity by assessing the **amplitude** of a sound wave in decibels (dB). Bigger waves produce louder sounds; smaller waves, softer sounds. Normal conversation measures about 45 dB; a vacuum cleaner, about 75 dB. At around 115 dB, sound becomes painful.

Pitch is the placement of sound on the musical scale, its "highness" or "lowness." Pitch is determined by the **frequency** of a sound wave, the number of times the wave crests each second (see Figure 3.2). Faster, higher-frequency waves produce high sounds; slower, lower-frequency waves produce low sounds. Frequency is measured in hertz (Hz). A wave that crests once each second measures 1 Hz; a wave that crests one hundred times a second measures 100 Hz.

Intensity The level or loudness of sound; related to the energy of sound.

Amplitude The energy of a sound wave, usually measured in decibels.

Pitch The placement of sound on the musical scale; related to the frequency of sound.

Frequency The number of wave crests in a unit of time, it determines pitch.

Most sounds in the real world are a mixture of many different frequencies. And the complexity of these frequencies determines the **timbre** of sound—its depth and tone. Every sound has a *fundamental frequency,* usually the most intense frequency, which determines its pitch. The other frequencies that combine to make sound are called *overtones.* Overtones add depth to the sensation of sound.

Timbre is what gives each sound its distinctive character. For example, although both men and women can sing the same notes, their voices sound "different." That difference is a product of the overtones surrounding the fundamental frequency.

Sound Waves

The human ear cannot hear all the waves of pressure in the air. Our range of hearing extends from about 20 Hz, the throbbing sound made by the largest

Figure 3.3
The Human Voice and Hearing

This sound spectrograph or *voiceprint* depicts the frequencies of the sounds as someone says "Santa Claus." Notice that the sounds of the "s" are relatively high, but most of the other sounds are confined to a relatively narrow region between 100 and 4,000 Hz—the middle range where speech can be distinguished best.

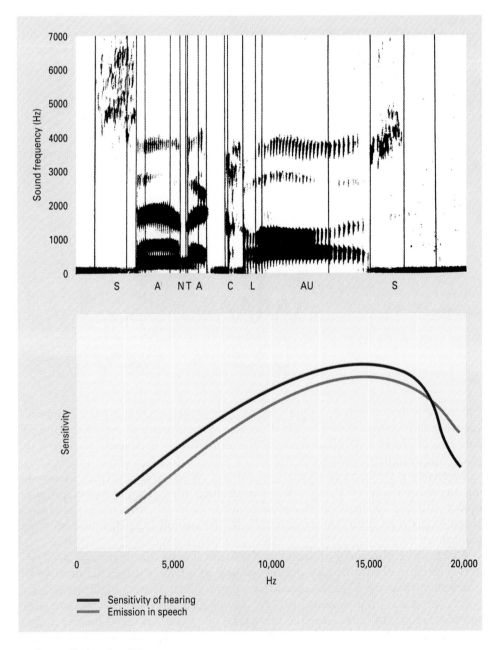

Timbre The tone and depth of sound; related to the complexity of sound frequencies.

Source: After Lenneberg, 1967.

pipes of a cathedral organ, to about 20,000 Hz, the sound made by one of those whistles that only dogs are supposed to be able to hear. (My dog may hear more of that sound than I do, but I always hear some of it and it hurts my ears!)

The range in which we hear best is also the range in which we tend to speak. As shown in Figure 3.3, the human voice usually operates in the lower half of the scale, mostly from 100 to 4,000 Hz. Why this range rather than some other? Humans have trouble hearing the precise beginnings and endings of low sounds, and high sounds do not travel well over long distances. If we spoke in a lower range, we would have to speak more slowly, saying less in a given time. If we spoke in a higher range, we would have a harder time being understood at a distance. The pitch we use to hear and speak is the product of an evolutionary compromise between the need to speak relatively quickly and the need to be heard over distances.

The Ear

The organ that allows us to hear is the ear. As shown in Figure 3.4, it is made up of three parts: the outer ear, the middle ear, and the inner ear. Each part performs a different function.

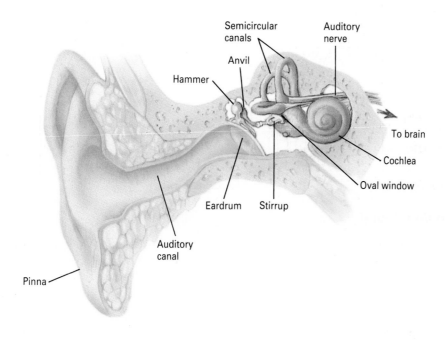

Figure 3.4
The Ear

The structures of the ear are divided into three important groupings, each with an important function. The outer ear, including the pinna and the auditory canal, gathers sound energy and focuses it on the eardrum. The middle ear, including the eardrum and the ossicles, transmits the sound energy to the inner ear. The structures of the inner ear include the semicircular canals, which are part of the system that helps us maintain our balance and the cochlea, which analyzes sound energy and codes it as patterns of neural activity for transmission to the brain.

The **outer ear** consists of the *pinna,* the fleshy folds we think of as the ear; the *auditory canal,* a passageway into the skull; and the *eardrum,* a thin transparent membrane. The pinna and auditory canal gather sound waves and focus them on the eardrum.

The **middle ear** consists of the *ossicles,* three small bones—the hammer, anvil, and stirrup—that are attached to the eardrum. These bones transform the vibrations of air molecules into mechanical vibrations before passing them on to the inner ear (von Békésy & Rosenblith, 1951).

How does this transformation work? The ossicles are sandwiched between two membranes—the eardrum and the *oval window.* When sound waves reach the eardrum, the membrane vibrates. This vibration moves the ossicles, which pick up and amplify the vibration. The third bone of the ossicles moves the oval window, which separates the middle ear from the inner ear.

Outer ear The pinna, auditory canal, and eardrum; the part of the ear that collects and focuses sound.

Middle ear The ossicles; the part of the ear that conducts sound from the outer ear to the inner ear.

The **inner ear** contains the cochlea, where sound is translated into nerve impulses. The **cochlea** (KO-kle-a) houses the receptor cells that translate the physical energy of sound into nerve activity. The inner ear also contains an unrelated structure, the **semicircular canals** that help us maintain balance.

Transduction in the Ear

The cochlea is a coiled bony tube filled with fluid (see Figure 3.5). The tube is divided lengthwise by several membranes, among them the basilar membrane. Running along the surface of the basilar membrane are **auditory hair cells,** the receptor cells for sound. When the oval window vibrates, it creates waves in the fluid, which move the basilar membrane. The vibrations of the membrane bend the hairs on the receptor cells, distorting the cell membranes and generating a nerve impulse (Santos-Sacchi, 1988).

Figure 3.5
The Cochlea: Coiled and Uncoiled

The transduction of sound energy into neural activity takes place at the basilar membrane, a thin sheath of tissue that lies coiled in the cochlea. Embedded in the membrane are the actual auditory receptors—hair cells that are stimulated as sound energy vibrates the basilar membrane.

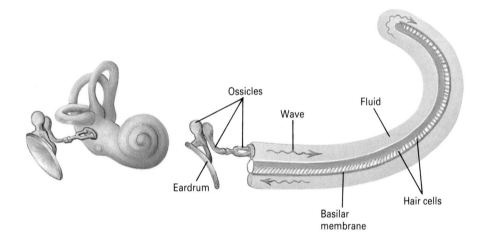

(a) Coiled cochlea   **(b) Uncoiled cochlea**

Coding Sound

How do the hair cells communicate information to the brain? We know that the more intense the sound, the more hair cells are firing and firing faster. The brain identifies the level of sound, then, by the rate at which these receptors fire and by the number firing.

What about pitch? How do the hair cells tell the brain that the notes being played on a piano are low notes or high notes? Physiologists have been arguing about this question since the nineteenth century. Modern research indicates that the answer combines parts of two conflicting theories: frequency theory and place theory.

According to **frequency theory,** hair cells faithfully reproduce the frequency of sound in the nerve impulses they send to the brain. As the basilar membrane vibrates, the hair cells are stimulated at the same rate. So if you are listening to sound at 80 Hz, the hair cells in your ear send impulses toward your brain at 80 Hz.

Frequency theory explains how we hear low-pitched sounds; it doesn't easily explain how we hear high-pitched sounds. Remember that humans can hear sounds ranging from 20 Hz to 20,000 Hz. But the nerve cells in our ears cannot fire at rates faster than 1,000 Hz. If frequency theory is correct, we should not be able to hear sounds higher than 1,000 Hz.

What if the hair cells in the cochlea team up to send messages to the brain? Could that explain how we hear high-pitched sounds? Frequency theorists think

Inner ear The cochlea; the part of the ear that transduces physical energy into nerve impulses.

Cochlea The structure in the inner ear that houses the receptor cells for sound.

Semicircular canals A structure in the inner ear that helps maintain balance.

Auditory hair cells The receptor cells for sound; they run along the surface of the basilar membrane.

Frequency theory The theory that the hair cells in the cochlea reproduce the frequency of sound waves in the nerve impulses they generate.

so. They suggest that hair cells fire in volleys, that groups of such cells work in teams (Wever, 1949). If each of 20 cells fires at 100 Hz, together they fire at a rate of 2,000 Hz. See Figure 3.6 for an illustration of frequency theory.

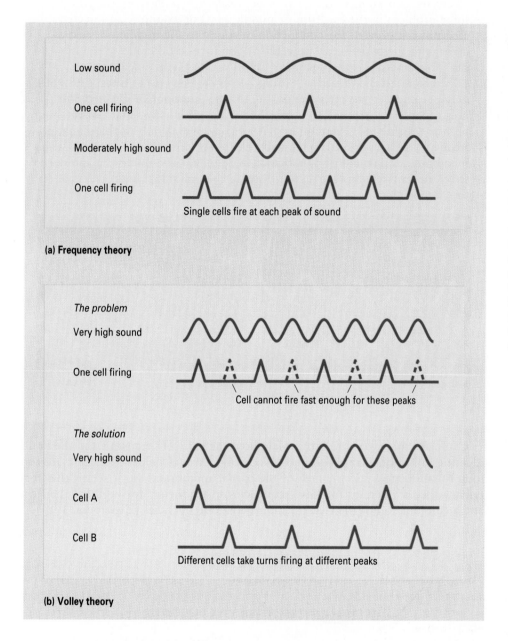

Figure 3.6
Frequency Theory and Pitch

According to frequency theory, a sound's pitch is coded by receptors that fire at the same frequency as the sound itself. For low sounds, the receptors fire slowly; for moderately high sounds, they fire more rapidly. The theory has a problem (part a) explaining our ability to hear very high pitched sounds, because receptors cannot fire fast enough to keep up with the frequency of such sounds. Frequency theory solves this problem by offering the volley theory (part b). According to the volley theory, more than one receptor cell cooperates to represent a high frequency sound.

This explanation makes sense, but it is limited by research that shows groups of neurons firing at frequencies of only up to about 600 Hz (Tong et al., 1982). Apparently neurons, even working in teams, cannot fire quickly enough to reproduce higher frequencies. Some other mechanism must therefore be at work generating high-pitched sounds.

Place theory describes that mechanism (von Békésy, 1960). According to this theory, the brain identifies pitch by the location of activity in the basilar membrane. For every frequency of vibration of the oval window, one point along the basilar membrane is affected more than any other. At that point, the membrane vibrates harder, stimulating the hair cells there (see Figure 3.7). These cells fire; the cells on other parts of the membrane do not.

Place theory The theory that different frequencies target specific areas on the basilar membrane.

Deafness

There are two kinds of deafness. One, *conduction deafness,* is caused by some problem in the eardrum or middle ear. For example, an infected eardrum can prevent the conduction of sound to the middle ear, just as damage to the ossicles can prevent the conduction of sound to the inner ear. This kind of deafness is most readily treated with a hearing aid.

A second kind of deafness is called *nerve deafness.* A common cause of nerve deafness is prolonged exposure to very loud noise—the level of noise people are exposed to when they work with heavy machinery or play in a rock band. Remember place theory, which tells us that higher-frequency sounds stimulate the hair cells of specific regions of the basilar membrane. If a sound of a particular frequency is too intense, it can destroy the hair cells in that region, leaving the individual unable to hear that frequency.

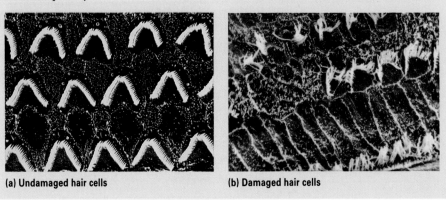

(a) Undamaged hair cells   **(b) Damaged hair cells**

Can place theory be used to explain how the hair cells transmit and the brain identifies all frequencies of sound? No. Sound waves below 1,000 Hz are too long to stimulate a specific area of the basilar membrane. So it seems that frequency theory operates for low frequencies, place theory for high frequencies, and a combination of the two for intermediate frequencies (Zwislocki, 1981).

Figure 3.7
Place Theory and Pitch

This simplified drawing of an un-coiled cochlea shows how place theorists think pitch is encoded. High-pitched, high-frequency, short wavelengths distort the basilar membrane near the oval window, whereas low-pitched, low-frequency, long wavelengths distort the basilar membrane near its far end. Hair cells in each location carry the message to the brain that a high-frequency or a low-frequency sound has been sensed.

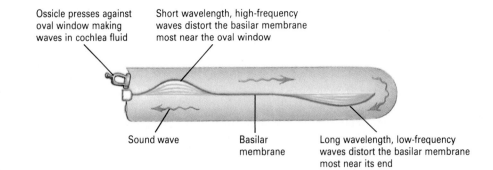

Ossicle presses against oval window making waves in cochlea fluid

Short wavelength, high-frequency waves distort the basilar membrane most near the oval window

Sound wave

Basilar membrane

Long wavelength, low-frequency waves distort the basilar membrane most near its end

Transmitting Information to the Brain

Each hair cell synapses with a neuron in the auditory nerve. The impulses generated by the hair cells travel along that nerve, moving through the medulla oblongata, the midbrain, the thalamus, and on to the auditory centers of the cortex in the temporal lobe (see Figure 2.21). These impulses carry information about the amplitude, frequency, and complexity of sound waves. The brain converts that information into the sensation we call sound.

Recap

- Sound is the product of vibrations in the air.

- The amplitude, frequency, and complexity of sound waves determine the intensity, pitch, and timbre of sound.

- The pinna and auditory canal focus sound waves on the eardrum.

- When the eardrum vibrates, it moves the ossicles, which vibrate against the oval window.

- The vibration of the oval window creates waves in the fluid-filled cochlea.

- These waves move the basilar membrane, which in turn bends the hair cells, the receptor cells for hearing.

- The movement of the hair cells generates a nerve impulse, which travels through the auditory nerve to the brain.

- A combination of frequency theory and place theory explains how hair cells communicate information to the brain about the frequency of sound.

Vision

We are bathed in electromagnetic radiation—energy from the sun, from the earth, from all the things around us. Light is a form of electromagnetic radiation. It is the very small portion of that radiation that we can see with our eyes.

The photo on the left is a silver-weed blossom seen in visible light. The photo on the right is the same flower seen in ultraviolet light. The dark area in the center is the "nectar guide" seen only by insects, who can see light in the ultraviolet range.

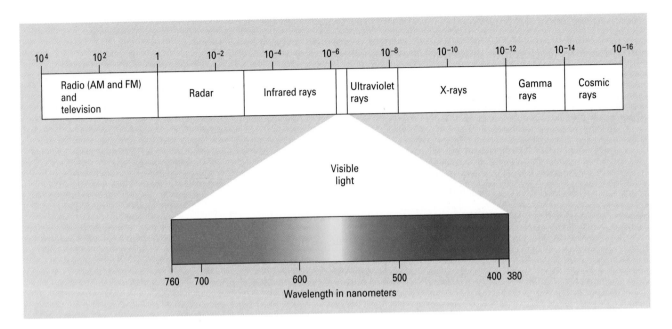

Visible
light

760   700   600   500   400 380
Wavelength in nanometers

Figure 3.8
Visible Radiation

The light we see is only a tiny part of the enormous range of radiation that falls on us every minute of the day. Visible radiation has wavelengths between 380 and 760 nanometers. A nanometer (abbreviated nm) is a billionth of a meter. For comparison, the waves that bring TV to our antennas are billions of times longer than light waves. At the other end of the range, X-rays used to photograph our bones are thousands of times shorter.

Visible Radiation

We identify different forms of radiation by wavelength. Although you can't see short- and long-wave radiation, you're familiar with many of its applications. X-rays are a form of very short-wave radiation; longer waves of radiation are used to cook food in microwave ovens and to broadcast radio and television programs.

As show in Figure 3.8, *visible radiation*—light—falls in a very narrow range, from around 380 nanometers to 760 nanometers. (A nanometer equals one-billionth of a meter.) At 380 nanometers, light appears as a very dark purple. At 760 nanometers, it's a deep red.

Wavelengths that are shorter than visible light are called *ultraviolet light*. Ultraviolet light provides much of the energy that plants use to grow. Although you can't see ultraviolet light, you experience its effects on your body whenever you get a tan or a sunburn.

Wavelengths that are longer than visible light are called *infrared light*. You can't see infrared light either, but you can feel its warmth on your skin. Infrared light from the sun and earth supports metabolism in plants and animals.

The Eye

Cornea Part of the eye; a transparent membrane that covers and protects the iris.

Iris The band of muscle that controls the amount of light that enters the eye.

Pupil The transparent opening through which light enters the eye.

Lens The round clear fibrous material that adjusts the focus of light on the retina.

The eye is the sensory organ that collects information that allows us to see. It is here that light energy is converted to nerve impulses.

Shown in Figure 3.9 is the **cornea,** the shiny transparent membrane on the outside of the eye. The cornea protects the eye. Behind it is the colored **iris.** This circular band of muscle controls the size of the **pupil,** the opening through which light enters the eye. Just behind the iris and pupil is a tough, clear, round piece of tissue called the **lens.** The lens helps focus light on the receptors at the back of the eye. Within the eyeball, open spaces in front of the lens are filled with a watery fluid called the *aqueous humor.* The cavity behind the lens is filled with the *vitreous humor,* a transparent jellylike substance. Both the aqueous humor and the vitreous humor help focus light in the eye and retain the eye's shape.

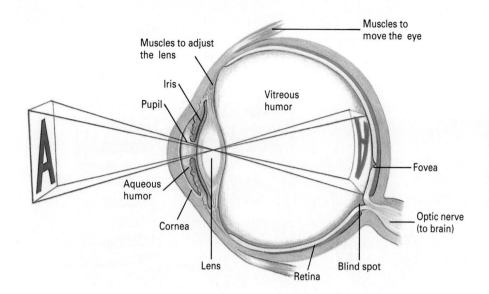

Figure 3.9
The Eye

The structures of the eye include those that gather and focus light—the cornea, the aqueous humor, the pupil, the lens, and the vitreous humor; the retina, the structure that translates light into neural impulses; and the optic nerve, the structure that transmits these neural impulses to the brain.

At the back of the eye is the **retina,** which consists of three thin layers of light-sensitive tissue. Located in the retina are the receptor cells that translate images and colors into nerve impulses.

Seeing

The eye serves two functions: It focuses light and then transduces the light energy into nerve activity.

Focusing Light   The curve of the cornea focuses the light near the retinal surface, and the lens then provides the fine adjustments in focus. The lens is a flexible structure, the shape and curve of which are determined by the contraction and relaxation of the smooth muscles around it. When we are looking at things close up, the muscles contract, shortening and thickening the lens, increasing its curve. When we are looking at things at a distance, the muscles relax, flattening the lens. This process, which is called **accommodation,** changes the degree of refraction to help focus images on the retina.

The images focused on the retina are not exactly the images we see. They are inverted and reversed, as shown in Figure 3.9. Light reflected off the top of an object we are looking at is focused on the bottom of the retina. And light reflected off the bottom of the object is focused on the top of the retina. In the same way, light reflected from one side of the object strikes the opposite side of the retina.

If the image on our retina is upside down, how do we see the world right side up? Actually, no one "sees" the inverted image; it's simply a source of information. From the moment that light strikes the retina, our sensory system begins analyzing it and extracting information from it about the world. That information is not a picture in the sense that the image on the back of the retina is. Rather, it's data feeding into an information processing system, a system that can operate in any orientation.

Analyzing the Retinal Image   The retina is an area of tissue on the back wall of the eye. There are three layers of nerve cells here: ganglion cells, bipolar cells, and photoreceptors (see Figure 3.10). Light passes through the ganglion cells

Retina The thin layers of light-sensitive tissue at the back of the eye.

Accommodation In vision, the process of changing the shape of the lens to bring objects into focus on the retina.

Figure 3.10
Detail of the Retina

The retina has three layers: (1) the photoreceptor layer where rods and cones convert light to nervous system activity, (2) the bipolar level, which interconnects the receptors with each other and with the ganglion cells, and (3) the ganglion cell layer, whose fibers transmit information from the other two layers over the optic nerve to the brain. Notice how richly interconnected are the cells in the retina, so interconnected in fact that every ganglion cell is influenced by many, perhaps hundreds of receptors.

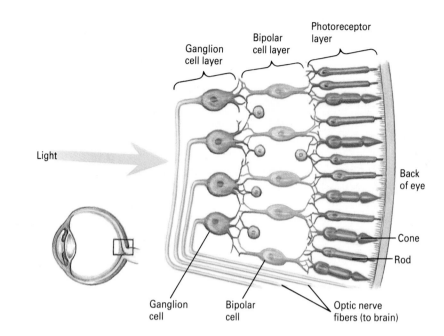

and bipolar cells to the photoreceptor cells. It is this inner layer of cells, the farthest from the light, that is light-sensitive. Here the energy of light is converted into nerve activity.

From the photoreceptor cells, nerve impulses move through the bipolar cells, the dense network of nerve cells that connects the photoreceptors to the ganglion cells. The ganglion cells gather information from the bipolar cells and send that information to the brain. The axons of the ganglion cells actually cross the surface of the retina and leave the eye in an area called the *blind spot*. At the blind spot, the axons form the optic nerve. That spot is blind because the optic nerve leaves no room for receptor cells at the point it leaves the retina (see Figure 3.11).

Figure 3.11

The blind spot is where the ganglion cell neurons exit the eye on their way to the brain, displacing the receptors. To find your own blind spot, cover your left eye and look at the + with your right. If you move the book nearer and farther from your eye, you will see the ball disappear as the image falls on your blind spot. Why don't we experience the blind spot as a hole in our vision? Because the brain has no cells that correspond to the missing piece of the visual field, it has no way of knowing what it is missing.

There are two kinds of photoreceptor cells: cones and rods. Their names reflect their distinctive shapes. **Cones** are responsible for color vision. They operate only in bright light. There are three types of cones, each sensitive to a different range of wavelength. **Rods** allow us to see in dim light. All rods are of one type and are sensitive to the same wavelengths of light.

The retina has two distinct regions—the fovea and the periphery—which differ in the kind of photoreceptors they contain and in the ways the photoreceptors are connected to the other layers of the retina. In the **fovea**, only one or a few photoreceptor cells, mostly cones, gather light for each ganglion cell, so that a ganglion cell will fire only if that cone is stimulated. As a result, foveal ganglion cells have good **acuity**, that is, they "see" the visual field in fine detail. But, vision in the fovea is poor in low levels of illumination. The **periphery**

Puzzle It Out!

Have you ever bumped your head hard and "seen stars"? A shock to the eyes, or to the parts of the brain that receive information from the eyes, can cause visual phenomena.

The great nineteenth century German physiologist Johannes Müller once served as an expert witness in a case of assault. During the course of the attack, which took place on a pitch dark night, the victim had been struck on the head. Müller was called to testify for the defense because the victim claimed to have seen his attacker in the flash of light generated by the blow to his head.

If you had been Müller, how would you have testified (Shepherd, 1988)?

is the much larger area that surrounds the fovea. In the periphery, most of the receptors are rods, and a great many rods gather light for each ganglion cell, resulting in better vision in dim light, but poor acuity.

Different types of cones have differential sensitivity to different wavelengths of light, so the fovea is involved in color vision. The periphery, whose many rods all have the same range of sensitivity, are not involved in color vision.

Transduction in the Eye

In the visual system, transduction is a chemical process. The cones and rods in the retina contain light-sensitive pigments. Light falling on these pigments causes them to break down into smaller molecules. This chemical change triggers a nerve impulse.

You can experience evidence of these chemical changes. Look for a moment at a white light and then look away. The dark blotch in your visual field is a **negative afterimage.** By looking at the light, you break down the pigment in some of the cells in your retina. Although the retina constantly replenishes its supply of pigments, it cannot always replenish pigment as quickly as the eye uses it. When you look away from the light, the cells no longer have a full supply of pigment, so they respond less vigorously than the cells around them.

Cones The photoreceptor cells that are responsible for color vision.

Rods The photoreceptor cells that are responsible for vision in dim light.

Fovea A small dip in the center of the retina where few receptors gather light for each ganglion cell; receptors are mostly cones.

Acuity The ability to see the visual field in fine detail.

Periphery Area in the retina surrounding the fovea where a great many receptors gather light for a single ganglion cell; the receptors are mostly rods.

Negative afterimage The reverse visual image seen after examining a bright stimulus.

In bright light, vision is based primarily on the activity of the cones in the fovea, which permit lots of fine detail and distinctions between colors. But because there are too few cones to function effectively in low-light conditions, the rods in the periphery take over. The result is less ability to distinguish details and colors.

The human eye has enormous powers of **adaptation.** It's constantly adjusting to the brightness of light. When light is bright, the retina becomes less sensitive; when light dims, the retina becomes more sensitive.

Adaptation takes time. When you walk from a brightly lit lobby into a darkened theater, you can't see anything at first. After a minute or two, you begin to see shapes. Within an hour, you can see almost as clearly in the dark as you can see in the light. In that time, your retinas have adapted, becoming hundreds of thousands of times more sensitive (McBurney & Collings, 1984).

The images sent back by satellites, like the one on the left of Jupiter, must be computer enhanced, like the photo on the right, to reveal the details that were hidden by the fuzzy transmission. Similarly, the images in the eye are enhanced by the processing that begins in the retina.

Processing in the Retina

Sensory systems, like corporations, have levels of management. At various points, information is collected, compared, combined, and elaborated on its way to the brain. In the visual system, the retina is the first of these points.

You know that the retina has three layers. Cones and rods—the innermost layer—are receptors; they are sensitive to light and react to wavelengths. Bipolar cells—the middle layer—carry information from the receptor cells to the ganglion cells. From this outermost layer of cells, information is transmitted to the brain.

Before ganglion cells send visual information to the brain, the retina processes that information. If your brain constructed a view of the world based directly on the information collected by the cones and rods, things would look vague and fuzzy. Why? Because in some ways the eye is a crude instrument. Film on its surface and impurities in the aqueous humor, the lens, and the vitreous humor blur light on its way to the retina. Adding to the fuzziness is the structure of the retina itself, given that light must pass through ganglion cells and bipolar cells before reaching the light-sensitive cones and rods (Walsh, Charman, & Howland, 1984).

We know that the retina corrects visual information because it sometimes overcorrects such information, making us see things that are not actually there. Look at Figure 3.12(a). Moving from right to left, each gray stripe is slightly lighter. The color of each band is solid; there's no variation within the bands, only between them. But when you look at the bands, doesn't each band seem darker where it meets its lighter neighbor, and lighter where it meets its darker neighbor? This illusion is a product of *contour enhancement.* The ganglion cells in the retina are increasing the contrast between light and dark at the edge of each stripe. Contour enhancement also produces the shimmering gray spots in the dramatic illusion known as the Hermann grid (see Figure 3.12b).

Adaptation   The process of adjusting to a stimulus; in the case of the eye, to the brightness of light.

How Do We Know That?

How do we know what ganglion cells are capable of doing? How do we know, for example, that they're responsible for contour enhancement? Using a microelectrode, sensory physiologists are able to record the activity of a single ganglion cell. This technique allows them to map the cell's *receptive field*, the area in the visual field to which the cell is sensitive (see Figure 3.A).

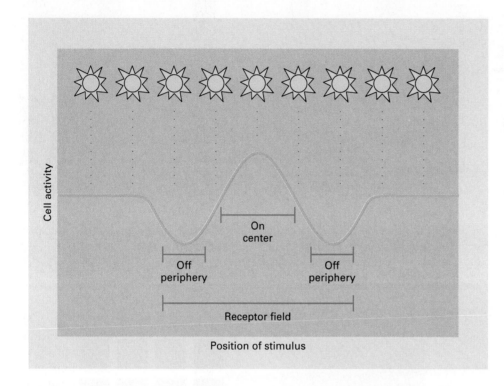

Position of stimulus

Figure 3.A
Mapping a Receptive Field

By probing the retina with pinpricks of light and recording from the visual nerve, scientists can reveal the receptor field of the cell—the part of the visual field to which the cell responds. In many cells, the receptive field has two parts: a center to which the cell responds by *increasing* its activity and a surround to which it responds by *decreasing* its activity.

What they've found is that the receptive field of many ganglion cells consists of two parts: a circle in the middle, called the *center*; and an outside ring, called the *surround*. The way in which light hits these areas affects activity in the ganglion cell. When light falls on the center, the cell becomes more active. When light falls on the surround, the cell becomes less active. The stimulus that most excites this kind of ganglion cell, then, is a pinpoint of light that falls *only* on the center. This pinpoint generates much more activity in the cell than light that illuminates the entire receptive field.

How would a ganglion cell respond if a boundary between light and dark fell across its receptive field? If the boundary fell such that a portion of the surround was in the dark, and the center and the rest of the surround were in the light, then the exciting effect of the light on the center would be the same as if the entire field were in the light. But the depressing effect of the light on the surround would be *less* because part of the surround would be in the dark. This means that a cell with a receptive field mostly but not entirely in the light would respond *more* vigorously than a cell with a receptive field entirely in the light. It also means that a cell with a receptive field entirely in the dark would respond more vigorously than a cell whose surround is partially lit (see Figure 3.B).

(Continued on next page)

Figure 3.B
Activity of Ganglion Cells

Ganglion cell receptor fields may be partly responsible for contour enhancement. Notice that if a shadow falls across a line of typical ganglion cells, they will enhance the contour all by themselves. The cells with their centers in the light but near the shadow will respond more vigorously than fully lighted cells; whereas the cells with their centers in the shadow but near the light will respond less vigorously than cells completely in the dark.

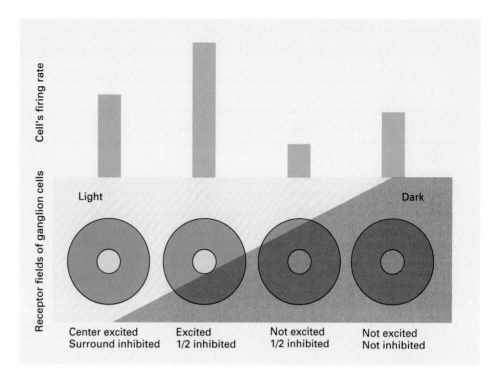

In short, lighted areas near an edge of dark appear brighter, and dark areas near a bright area appear darker. The result is that differences between the dark and light regions are emphasized.

Figure 3.12
Mach Bands and the Hermann Grid

Sharp contours, such as the edges of things like buildings or cliffs, often give us information. Not surprisingly, therefore, our eyes are designed to pick these boundaries out. This characteristic of our visual system is called *contour enhancement*. In part (a) the gray stripes form the illusion known as Mach bands. Notice that near the boundaries between darker and lighter stripes, the lighter stripe appears lighter and the darker stripe appears darker, enhancing the apparent difference between them. In part (b) contour enhancement also contributes to the shimmering spots that you see at the intersection of the white lines in the figure known as the Hermann grid.

(a) Mach bands   (b) Hermann grid

Color

Light, like sound, has three dimensions: brightness, saturation, and hue. **Brightness** is the intensity of light. Like the intensity of sound, it's determined by the amplitude of light waves. **Saturation** has to do with the purity of color—the number of wavelengths that combine to create a specific color. The fewer that number, the purer the color. In the same way that the complexity of sound waves determines timbre, the complexity of light waves determines saturation.

Hue is the psychological experience of color as distinct from the physical stimulus. Each hue is produced by a specific wavelength of light. If somebody were to shine a light with a wavelength of 400 nanometers (the physical stimulus) in your eye, you would see a deep blue (the psychological experience, or hue). A light of 700 nanometers would make you see red.

In the range of wavelengths that runs from about 0.10 nanometers (ultraviolet light) to about 10,000 nanometers (near infrared light), we see only a small band—between 380 and 760 nanometers. Within this band, we can distinguish more than 200 wavelengths. Our visual system experiences each of these wavelengths as a distinct hue (Coren, Porac & Ward, 1984).

Color Mixing   How do we see color? The theoretical answers to this question, begin with the facts about color mixing. Suppose you have a sheet of white paper in front of you and you want to color it yellow. You can do this in two ways. One way is to *add* to the light reflected by the paper by shining colored lights on the paper. If you shine a red light on the paper, it looks red. If you shine a green light on the paper, it looks green. If you shine both red and green lights on the paper, you see a beautiful yellow. When you mix lights, yellow is the *sum* of red and green light. In *additive mixing,* red plus green equals yellow.

But anyone who has ever owned a paint set knows that mixing red and green paints never gives rise to yellow. What you get more closely resembles mud. A different set of principles applies to the color mixing you do with paints and crayons, which is called *subtractive mixing.* The pigments in paints and crayons act as filters, absorbing all wavelengths *except* the color of the paint or crayon.

This means that red paint contains a pigment that absorbs all wavelengths except those that correspond to red. And green paint contains a pigment that absorbs all wavelengths except those that correspond to green. Together the two pigments absorb almost all wavelengths, because the green pigment also absorbs red wavelengths and the red pigment also absorbs green wavelengths. When you mix the two pigments, so many wavelengths are subtracted from the light reflected back to your eyes that you see only a dull muddy mess. Figure 3.13 illustrates the effects of additive and subtractive color mixing.

Theories of Color Vision   The two classic theories of color vision start with the facts of additive and subtractive color mixing. Tricolor theory and opponent-process theory each offer an explanation. And each is correct in part.

Brightness The intensity of light; related to the amplitude of lightwaves.

Saturation The purity of color; related to the number of wavelengths that combine to create a specific color.

Hue The psychological experience of color; related to the wavelength of light.

Figure 3.13
Additive and Subtractive Color Mixing

When blue, red, and green light are shone together, the colors are added together to make white (part a). When we overlap filters, more and more light is subtracted until no light passes through, and the filters appear black (part b). The pigments of paints are filters, and mixing paint colors gives a subtractive, rather than an additive, color mix.

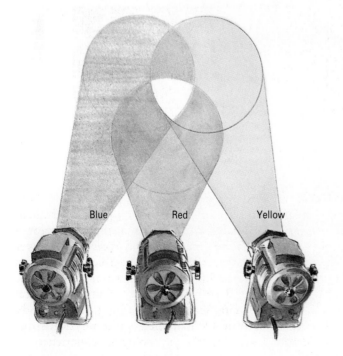

Blue   Red   Yellow

(a) Additive color mixing

(b) Subtractive color mixing

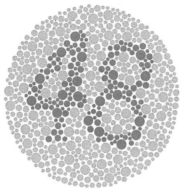

Ever wonder if you have red/green color deficiency? If you can see the number 48 in the circle above, you probably don't. A color blind person would not see the dots that form the numbers as distinct from the rest of the dots.

Tricolor theory was the work of a nineteenth-century physiologist, Hermann von Helmholtz. Simply stated, tricolor theory maintains that we experience color because we have three types of receptor systems: one that responds to red wavelengths, another to green, and a third to blue. Yellow, and every other color, is the product of some combination of activity in the three types of receptors.

Additive mixing supports tricolor theory. All the hues we see in response to different wavelengths can be reproduced in the laboratory by mixing three pure lights: red, green, and blue. Red light mixed with green light produces yellow. Red light mixed with blue light produces violet. If every color can be produced by blending red, green, and blue, then the whole range of colors could be generated from activity in just three color systems, each particularly sensitive to just one color.

But tricolor theory does not explain other aspects of our experience of color. Consider red-green color blindness, for instance. Tricolor theory explains this deficiency by suggesting that people who cannot distinguish between red and green do not have red and green systems. But if all colors are a mixture of red, green, and blue, then people who are unable to see red and green should also be unable to see yellow—the product of simultaneous activity in the red and green cones. In fact, people who are red-green color blind see yellow wavelengths just fine.

It is also the case that when we mix certain colored lights together, they seem to cancel each other out. The end product is white or gray, not another color. These pairs of colors are called *complementary hues,* as shown in Figure 3.14. For example, blue and yellow are complementary hues, as are red and green. The concept of complementary hues suggests that red and green are not independent but opposite experiences.

Figure 3.14
Color Wheel

The hues opposite each other on the wheel, when mixed, cancel each other out and produce gray. Notice that the red that mixes with the green to produce gray is a deep red, not the orange-red that mixes with the green to produce yellow.

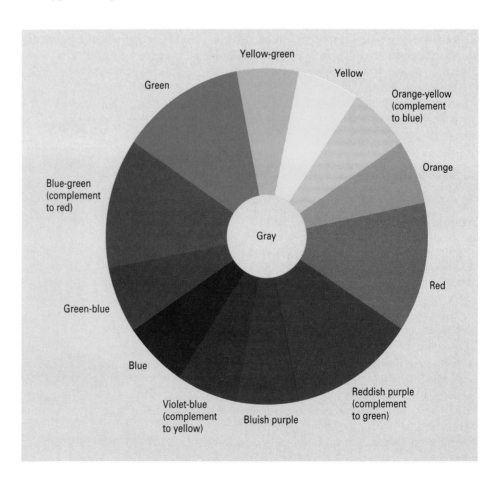

Tricolor theory Hermann von Helmholtz's theory that all color experience is the product of activity in red, yellow, and blue color systems.

The study of negative afterimages provides more evidence that certain colors are opposite experiences. Remember what happens when you stare at a bright white light for a few seconds and then look away? You see a dark image. A similar outcome occurs after you stare at a colored light for a few seconds. When you look away, you see an afterimage in a complementary hue. If you've been looking at a green light, you see a red afterimage. If you've been looking at a yellow light, you see a blue afterimage. You can experience a color afterimage yourself by staring at the flag in Figure 3.15.

Ewald Hering, a contemporary of Helmholtz, used **opponent-process theory** to explain these phenomena. He believed that all color experience derives from the activity of three systems: a red-green system, a blue-yellow system, and a black-white system. The colors in each system are *opponents*. Red is the opponent of green; blue is the opponent of yellow; black is the opponent of white. The color receptors can see one of the opponent colors at a particular spot, but not both. Why does the green, black, and yellow flag produce a red, white, and blue afterimage? Because once you remove the stimulus of (look away from) one opponent color, you automatically activate the other.

Our current understanding of color vision is based on both tricolor and opponent-process theories (Figure 3.16 compares the three theories.). Tricolor theory explains activity at the level of the cones. Each type of cone is sensitive to different wavelengths. (It's tempting to suppose that the three types of cones might be Helmholtz's three receptor systems: red, green, and blue. But this is not the case. The three types of cones do not respond *only* to wavelengths corresponding to red, green, and blue. Although each has a wavelength to which it is most sensitive, all three respond to light of almost any wavelength.) At the level of the ganglion cells, where the cells seem to be organized in opponent systems, opponent-process theory pertains.

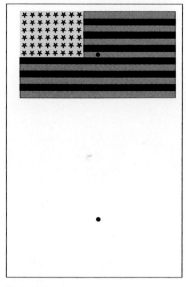

Figure 3.15
Color Afterimages

Look carefully at the black dot in the center of the flag for at least 30 seconds. Now, look at the dot in the white space just below. What do you see?

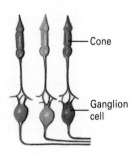

(a) Helmholtz's tricolor theory

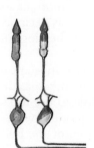

(b) Hering's opponent-process theory

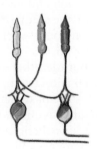

(c) Current understanding

Figure 3.16
Theories of Color Vision

The two classical theories and the current resolution differ in their understanding of the kind of receptors and how they are wired to the ganglion cells. According to Helmholtz, there are independent red, green, and blue cone circuits. According to Hering, there are only two independent color systems—a red/green opponent system and a blue/yellow opponent system. The current view holds that there are yellow, green, and blue cones attached to red/green and yellow/blue opponent ganglion cells.

Transmission to the Brain

The product of all the processing that goes on in the retina is electrical activity in the optic nerve. That nerve connects the back of the eye to the optic chiasm. Here the fibers from the inside half of each eye cross over to the opposite side of the brain (see Figure 2.20). In other words, all of the fibers carrying information about the right side of the visual field end up on the left side of the brain, and all of the fibers carrying information about the left side of the visual field end up on the right side of the brain. (Remember that the image projected on each retina is an inverted mirror image of what we see.)

From the optic chiasm, sensory information in the form of nerve impulses is carried to the thalamus and on to the visual cortex at the very back of the occipital lobes. Many of the cells in this area of the cortex function as **feature detectors,** inasmuch as they respond to specific shapes and edges in that sensory information (Livingstone & Hubel, 1987). From these cells the brain assembles the images we see.

Opponent-process theory Ewald Hering's theory that all color experience derives from the activity of three pairs of color systems.

Feature detectors Cells in the visual cortex that respond to specific elements in the sensory impulses transmitted from the eyes.

Recap

- The eyes respond to a narrow segment of the range of electromagnetic radiation.

- The cornea, aqueous humor, lens, and vitreous humor help focus light on the retina.

- Light passes through the two outer layers of the retina (the ganglion cells and bipolar cells) to the inner layer (the photoreceptor cells), where it's converted to nerve impulses. These impulses move through the bipolar cells to the ganglion cells, which transmit the impulses through the optic nerve to the brain.

- Cones, the photoreceptor cells that allow us to see color and fine detail, are concentrated in the fovea.

- Rods help us see in dim light and are concentrated in the periphery.

- A combination of tricolor theory and opponent-process theory explains how we see color.

- The retina processes the information collected by the receptor cells and sends it through the fibers of the ganglion cells to the optic nerve, the optic chiasm, the thalamus, and on to the visual cortex in the occipital lobes of the brain.

The Other Senses

Audition and vision are our most important sources of information. Partly because the study of these two senses has occupied a central place in the history of psychology, we know more about hearing and vision than we do about the other senses.

But the other senses are equally important to our well-being. Our senses of smell and taste help us decide whether a substance is food or poison. Without the sense of touch, we'd be unable to use tools. Without our sense of pain, we could be wounded or burned and not be aware of it. And without the vestibular and kinesthetic senses, which monitor the body's balance and movement, just walking up a flight of stairs would be impossible.

The Chemical Senses: Smell and Taste

Smell (olfaction) and taste (gustation) are called *chemical senses* because our noses and tongues respond directly to the presence of chemicals in the air we breathe and in the foods we eat.

Functions   Many animals rely on chemical stimuli for information—to identify food, to warn themselves of enemies, and to locate and identify other species members. Humans, too, use smell and taste to gather information, but in a more limited way. Our chemical senses seem to serve two primary functions: evaluating food for consumption and communicating social information.

Like most creatures, we have to decide what to eat and what not to eat. Our senses of smell and taste help us make those decisions. Although we tend to think of flavor as an aspect of taste, flavor is primarily a product of a food's odor. Think back to the last time you had a cold. Your food didn't have any taste. Because your nose was stuffed up, the smell of the food couldn't get through to your olfactory receptors.

In many animals, a poor sense of smell can prove fatal. Like humans, rats are confronted daily by potential nutrients and potential poisons. Once they've eaten poisoned food and have been sick, laboratory rats quickly learn not to eat that food again, even when several hours elapse between the eating and the illness (Garcia, Hankins & Rusniak, 1974). Apparently they use their memory of the taste and smell of the poisoned food to avoid it.

You may not think of smell and taste as nutrition and poison sensors because you live in a world of presorted and prepackaged food. The food industry works hard to separate foods from poisons, and to get the former to us and keep the latter away from us. Still, we do sometimes come across poisonous or tainted foodstuffs—rhubarb leaves and spoiled milk, for example. Even if our parents hadn't told us not to eat these substances, we would probably avoid them. The sensory receptors in our noses and tongues would detect the poisons in these foods and warn us that they smell "foul" or taste "sour."

The sense of smell also serves a social function. Male dogs and cats, for example, use scent to mark their territories, thereby announcing their presence and gender to other members of their species. An odor that communicates a social message is called a **pheromone.**

Odors do not play the central role for humans that they play for many mammals, but even humans may produce odors that announce their gender. In several studies, blindfolded subjects have successfully identified an individual's gender just by smelling his or her skin, breath, or clothing, even when perfume and other obvious cues have been eliminated (Wallace, 1977; Doty et al., 1982; Russel, 1976). In fact, some research suggests that human pheromones exist and that we find them attractive (Engen, 1982).

Transforming Chemical Stimuli into Nerve Impulses   We know that smell and taste depend on receptors in the nose and mouth, and that smell is by far the more complex and sensitive of the two senses. But the way in which a specific chemical is translated into a nerve impulse is still an area of active research.

Smell   Olfactory receptors are located in a region of the nose called the *nasal epithelium,* as seen in Figure 3.17. Each receptor cell has a single dendrite that projects microscopic hairs into the mucous membrane lining the nose. As we breathe in, chemical substances dissolve in the mucous coating on the membrane. The hairs react to those substances, stimulating the olfactory cells.

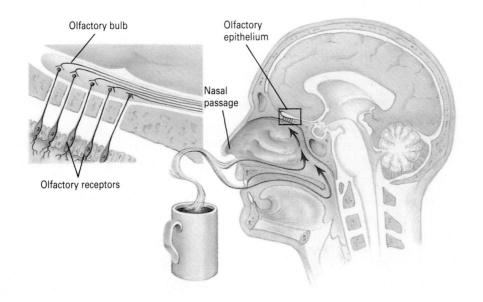

**Figure 3.17
The Nose**

The structures of our sense of smell include the nasal passages that gather and direct odorants to the olfactory epithelium. Here, hair cells analyze the odorant. The information they gather about chemicals in the air is passed directly to the olfactory bulbs, a part of the brain in the under surface of the frontal lobes.

Pheromone An odor that communicates a social message.

Unlike the cones in the retina, the receptors in the nose do not seem to respond to specific stimuli; accordingly, we have no list of "primary" odors. Instead, each receptor in the nose responds to a wide variety of chemicals, with some receptors more sensitive to some substances than to others (Getchell, 1986). We do know that the nose you're smelling with today is not the same nose you smelled with last year: the olfactory receptors are replaced every couple of months (Castellucci, 1985).

The axons of the hair cells travel through the olfactory nerves to the *olfactory bulbs,* two masses of gray matter at the base of the brain (see Figure 2.14). From here, the impulses are carried to the olfactory area of the cerebral cortex and to parts of the limbic system, where they are interpreted as smell.

Taste   Taste buds are located in the tongue and throat. The little bumps on your tongue are not your taste buds. They are called *papillae* (puh-pill-ee), and they house the taste buds.

The taste buds are microscopic structures, shaped something like onions. You can see what one looks like in Figure 3.18(b). Each taste bud has from four to twenty *gustatory cells,* the receptor cells for taste. And each of those cells has a single hair that projects to the surface through an opening called a *taste pore.* These hairs respond to taste stimuli by initiating nerve impulses.

There are four basic taste sensations: sweet, salt, bitter, and sour. And, as Figure 3.18(a) shows different regions of the tongue are more sensitive to each of them. For example, the front of the tongue is most sensitive to sweet substances. Each common taste seems to be related to some important property of food. Sensing sweetness lets us search out sugar, an important body food. Sensing saltiness allows us to find food rich in sodium chloride, which plays a key role in the transmission of nerve impulses within nerve cells. Bitterness may help us determine whether food is poisonous. And sourness helps us determine acidity.

Figure 3.18
The Tongue and Taste

The tongue contains the important structures of our taste sense, the taste buds. Different parts of the tongue contain taste buds most sensitive to different flavors—sweet for the tip of the tongue, sour for the front sides, sour for the rear sides, and bitter for the back. The taste buds are found in the minute crevices in the tongue that surround the tiny bumps on the tongue called papillae. Each bud contains several receptors called gustatory cells, which send fibers to the brain.

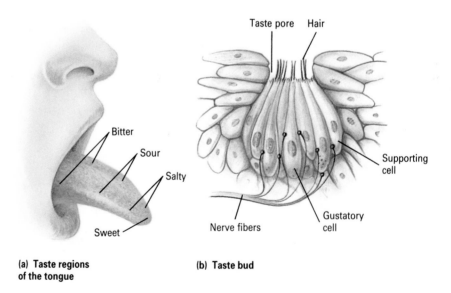

(a) **Taste regions of the tongue**

(b) **Taste bud**

In recent years, the concept of four primary taste sensations has been challenged by the discovery that different cultures disagree about the number of primary tastes. Some Native Americans and some inhabitants of the Pacific Islands recognize fewer than the four primary tastes listed earlier. The Japanese recognize a fifth, which they call *umami* (Yamaguchi, 1979). This seems to be the taste of amino acids, the building blocks of protein.

Does our sensitivity to several tastes mean that each taste has its own receptors? We know that different receptors on the tongue respond differently to the various tastes (Sato, 1986). But there may be more than one kind of receptor for each of the basic tastes (Teeter & Brand, 1987). People can discriminate between two different sugars (beet and cane sugar, for example), even though both are sweet. And there is evidence that individual receptors respond to several substances but most strongly to one (Faurion, 1988).

The nerve impulse generated by the receptor cells travels from the tongue to the medulla to the thalamus and on to the parietal lobes of the cortex. Here the brain, in discriminating taste, must compare the input from many kinds of receptors instead of relying on just one.

The Skin Senses: Touch, Temperature, and Pain

The senses hearing, vision, and smell are like long-distance phone calls. They bring us information about events that are often at a distance from our bodies. But the stimuli for the skin senses—touch, temperature, and pain—involve events at or just below the body's surface.

If we had asked you at the beginning of this chapter to name your sense organs, you might have forgotten your skin. The largest organ in your body, your skin responds to a wide range of stimuli: temperature, touch, vibration, pressure, and stretch. Not all areas of the skin are equally sensitive, however. Most sensitive are the fingers and palms and the soles of the feet. In these areas we find both a greater variety and a larger number of receptor cells.

Transforming Environmental Stimuli into Nerve Impulses   We know that human skin contains a variety of receptors. Some of these are depicted in Figure 3.19. Just how these receptors generate so many different sensations is not quite so clear, however. Some research traces specific skin sensations (changes in pressure, for example) to activity in particular receptors. Other evidence indicates that certain receptors serve more than one function.

Pacinian corpuscles are a good example of receptors that respond to specific sensations. If you were to quickly (but gently!) jiggle the skin on your cheek, for instance, you would distort the Pacinian corpuscles there. This distortion generates a nerve impulse (Lowenstein & Skalak, 1966). Pacinian corpuscles respond to vibration, but not to simple pressure.

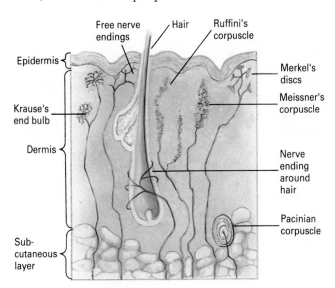

Figure 3.19
The Skin

The skin has many different sensory structures that are related to different sorts of feeling. Free nerve endings are related to pain; Krause's end bulbs, Meissner's corpuscles, and Pacinian corpuscles are related to different degrees of pressure on the skin.

Hot
water

Cold
water

What counts as hot or cold depends on what other hot or cold things are being experienced at the same time. The person who is gripping this coil of warm and cold water pipes will experience a hot pipe. Apparently the nervous system reads the combination of the sharpness of the cold with the warmth as heat.

Pain is produced by other skin receptors known as *free nerve endings* (so called because the ends have no specialized structures). Free nerve endings are attached to two kinds of neurons: larger myelinated neurons, which are related to quicker pain; and very small unmyelinated neurons, which are involved in slow deep pain (Casey, 1982). Remember that myelin (discussed in Chapter 2) speeds the transmission of nerve impulses.

Think back to the last time you hit your thumb with a hammer. First you felt immediate pain; then you experienced more pain that came slowly enough that you could anticipate it. You may have said to yourself, "Oh, that's *going to* hurt!" and then it *did* hurt. The first sensation came from the larger neurons, the second from the small unmyelinated ones.

Free nerve endings play a role in other sensations as well. The cornea of the eye, a specialized kind of skin, is sensitive to temperature and pressure as well as to pain; yet it has just one kind of receptor, free nerve endings. These receptors may allow us to experience various sensations—feelings of heat, pressure, or pain—by translating differing kinds of stimulation into specific patterns of nerve activity.

The question of how skin sensations are coded is still being studied. Regardless of whether there are specific sensors for specific stimuli, interpretation of the activity of these sensors depends on other sensations that are being activated at the same time. Receptors in the skin appear to influence one another; so if you stimulate one point on the skin, neighboring points become relatively less sensitive (von Békésy, 1967).

You've seen this principle in action. When you bump your shin and rub it, the pain lessens. When you rub the area around an itchy bug bite, the itching often stops, even if you never scratch the bite directly (Hagbarth, 1983).

The neurons that carry information from skin receptors form nerves that enter the spinal cord. All the nerves from a particular area enter the spinal cord at the same point. There they synapse with the dendrites of the neurons that communicate with the sensory centers of the brain.

In the spinal cord, sensory information can be modified or even censored. Some nerve impulses may or may not cross the synapse and continue to the brain, depending on the activity of other nerves synapsing in the same region.

After synapsing in the spinal cord, the nerves carrying information from the skin senses synapse in the thalamus and continue on to the sensory cortex in the parietal lobes. Even in the brain, where they form a precise if dramatically distorted map of the body (see Figure 2.22), the fibers remain organized by their site of origin.

The Pain Gate   Why are stimuli that are painful under some circumstances experienced as mere pressure under others—or simply not experienced at all? The answer, according to **gate theory,** is that some neurons in the spinal cord function like a gate (Melzack & Wall, 1982). When the gate is open, information from pain receptors is passed along to the brain. When the gate is closed, the information is blocked. Figure 3.20 shows how the gate theory supposedly works.

The pain gate can be closed in two ways. One is through the competition of other sensory influences. If, along with stimulation from the pain receptors, several different kinds of information enter the spinal cord at the same time, these other kinds of information close the gate, preventing the pain information from being relayed to the brain (Watkins & Mayer, 1982). This is why rubbing that bump on your shin helps ease the pain. The rubbing sends vigorous pressure messages to the spinal cord, where they compete with the pain messages. If you're lucky, the pressure messages close the pain gate.

Gate theory The theory that neurons in the spinal cord can block the transmission of pain to the brain.

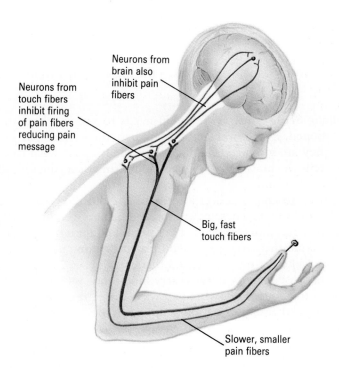

Neurons from brain also inhibit pain fibers

Neurons from touch fibers inhibit firing of pain fibers reducing pain message

Big, fast touch fibers

Slower, smaller pain fibers

Figure 3.20
The Pain Gate

Before you can feel pain from a pin prick, a nerve impulse has to pass from the free nerve ending in your finger into your spinal cord and synapse with a neuron that connects to the brain. This pathway can be blocked in two ways. Inhibitory impulses may descend from the brain. For example, you might be so tired or so worried about something else you don't even notice the pin prick. Or, inhibitory impulses can come from other sensory input. For example, rubbing the pricked area might make the pain go away.

The pain gate can also be closed by messages coming down from the brain (Terman et al., 1984). Researchers have located circuits in the spinal cord that, when stimulated, release neurotransmitters that prevent the transfer of information from incoming sensory cells to the cells reporting to the brain (Mayer & Liebeskind, 1974). These blocking agents are called *enkephalins*. Chemically they are very like both the pain-killing drug morphine and the endorphins, a group of neurotransmitters we talked about in Chapter 2.

The Body Senses: Balance and Motion

Some senses collect information about the state of the body itself. Balance is experienced through the **vestibular sense;** and motion, through the **kinesthetic sense.** Receptors in our vestibular organs and in our muscles and joints report the position and motion of our bodies.

The body senses also help us to differentiate between motion within the body and motion in the world. Every time you move your head, for example, the images on your retina change. By itself, your visual system has no way of knowing whether those changes are a product of your movement or of movement in the world around you. But your body senses are able to tell you that the world isn't spinning, that you're just turning your head.

The Vestibular Sense   The vestibular organs are responsible for our sense of balance. For creatures teetering on the ends of two long legs, remaining vertical is crucial. Unless the motion of the top part of our bodies is precisely adjusted to the motions of our legs, we can't walk. In order to retain our balance, we must be able to detect acceleration in each of three dimensions (up-down, forward-back, and right-left) as well as the acceleration of gravity.

Our sense of balance originates in the **semicircular canals,** three curved tubes just above the cochlea in the inner ear. As shown in Figure 3.21, each canal is oriented in one of the three dimensions—up-down, forward-back, and right-left. These canals contain hair cells that respond to motions of the fluids in the canals as our heads shift position.

Vestibular sense The sense of balance; it provides information about the body's general movements.

Kinesthetic sense The sense of motion; it tells you where parts of your body are in relation to each other.

Semicircular canals The vestibular organ, consisting of three curved tubes located just above the cochlea in the inner ear.

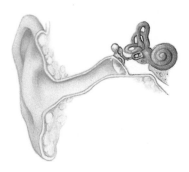

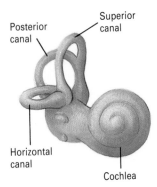

Posterior canal

Superior canal

Horizontal canal

Cochlea

Figure 3.21
The Vestibular Organ

The semicircular canals, part of the inner ear, are responsible for our sense of balance. The three fluid-filled canals are perpendicular to each other so each is sensitive to acceleration in one of the three planes: front-back, up-down, and right-left. Hair cells inside the canals sense the motion of the fluid and send nerve impulses to the brain.

Impulses travel from the hair cells in the semicircular canals to the medulla and the cerebellum. The cerebellum monitors those impulses and feeds them to the motor areas of the cerebral cortex. Here they are translated into messages for the skeletal muscles, messages that tell the muscles how to move in order to maintain balance.

The Kinesthetic Sense   Just as the brain needs to know where the head and body are positioned, it also needs to know where the various parts of the body are and how they are moving. The brain tells the muscles what to do; the kinesthetic sense tells the brain what they are doing. In effect, the kinesthetic sense is a feedback mechanism.

The kinesthetic receptors collect information about the position and motion of our muscles and joints. These receptors are free nerve endings, Pacinian corpuscles, and other receptors embedded in muscle and joint tissue. Like receptors in the skin, the kinesthetic receptors send impulses along sensory nerves to the spinal cord. And like the sensory nerves that carry nerve impulses from receptors in the skin, these sensory nerves carry kinesthetic information from a particular region of the body. Following pathways through the medulla, midbrain, and thalamus, kinesthetic information is passed to the motor area of the cortex.

Recap

- Smell (olfaction) and taste (gustation) are chemical senses; they respond directly to the presence of chemicals in the air and food.

- Olfactory receptors are located in the nasal epithelium.

- Gustatory cells—the receptors for taste—are clustered in taste buds.

- Sensitivity to taste varies from one region of the tongue to another.

- Sensory information is collected by special receptors and free nerve endings in the skin.

- According to gate theory, neurons in the spinal cord can block information about pain from moving on to the brain.

- The vestibular sense originates in the semicircular canals.

- Kinesthetic receptors are free nerve endings, Pacinian corpuscles, and other receptors embedded in muscle and joint tissue.

- The kinesthetic sense operates as a feedback mechanism.

How Good Are Our Senses?

Throughout this chapter we've described the way our senses translate physical and chemical stimuli into nerve activity. One area of particular interest to psychologists is the accuracy of that translation. This interest has given rise to *psychophysics,* the specialty of psychology that focuses on the relationship between physical and chemical stimuli and the experiences they evoke.

In their studies, psychophysicists vary the properties of a physical stimulus and ask subjects to record changes in their corresponding experience. In a study of sound, for example, a researcher might vary the intensity of a sound stimulus, asking subjects to indicate when they first hear the sound. Using this kind of procedure, scientists can identify the **absolute threshold** for a particular stimulus. See Table 3.1 for a listing of familiar threshold stimuli.

Absolute threshold   The smallest amount of stimulation that can be noticed.

Table 3.1
Some Familiar Threshold Stimuli

Sense	Absolute Threshold
Hearing	The tick of a watch under quiet conditions at 20 feet
Vision	A candle flame 30 miles away on a dark night
Smell	One drop of perfume diffused in a 3-room apartment
Taste	One teaspoon of sugar in 2 gallons of water
Touch	The wing of a fly falling on your cheek from a distance of 1 centimeter

Source: Adapted from E. Galanter, 1962.

In another variation, a researcher might play two tones and ask the subject to decide whether the tones are the same or different. This kind of experiment identifies the **difference threshold** for a stimulus—the smallest difference a subject can reliably detect between two stimuli.

We are not equally sensitive to all the stimuli we experience. Among colors, for example, yellow light has a lower absolute threshold than deep red light. That is, we may reliably notice a fairly weak stimulus of yellow light but require a stronger stimulus for deep red light. In the same way, high and low sounds—to be noticeable—must be louder than sounds of intermediate pitch.

Just as our absolute sensitivity varies from stimulus to stimulus, our sensitivity to differences between stimuli varies as well. We can detect very small changes in very faint stimuli: the difference threshold for faint sounds is very small. When stimuli are stronger, the difference threshold is larger.

This relationship is called **Weber's law** (named for Ernst Weber, a nineteenth-century physiologist). The law states that the ratio between the difference threshold (the smallest difference you can reliably detect between, say, two sounds) and the intensity of a stimulus (the loudness of a sound, for example) is a constant (a number that has a fixed value).

Weber's law also states that each sense has a different constant. For the intensity of sound, Weber's constant is 0.05; for the brightness of light, it's 0.08. A Weber's constant of 0.05 means that to noticeably increase the intensity of a sound you must increase it by 5 percent, no matter how loud it is already.

Weber's law has many practical applications. For example, the dials on a radio or television that control loudness are calibrated to reflect the differences we hear. And the same constants are used to decrease stimuli without our noticing a change. We don't see the difference between a 100-watt lightbulb and a 95-watt energy-saving lightbulb because the 5 percent difference is less than the 8 percent difference that we reliably notice. In the same way, a manufacturer of packaged soup could respond to consumer demands for less salt by using Weber's law to determine how much salt per serving could be eliminated before a buyer would notice a difference in the taste of the soup.

Weber's law applies to the *intensity* of stimuli. A similar relationship exists between the *frequency* of sound and sensitivity to changes in frequency. We are less sensitive to changes in frequency among high sounds than we are to changes in frequency among low sounds. This differential sensitivity is responsible for a familiar perceptual phenomenon—the musical scale. As you go up the musical scale, you may think you're taking equal steps from note to note. But this is an illusion. In fact, the physical distance between the steps increases steadily as you go up a scale (see Figure 3.22). This means that the physical distance between two high notes may be many times the physical distance between two low notes.

All of our senses also change sensitivity in response to the level of stimulation. They become more sensitive when they have not been stimulated for a time and

Difference threshold The smallest noticeable difference between two stimuli; also called *just noticeable difference threshold*.

Weber's law The ratio between the difference threshold and the intensity of a stimulus is a constant. Different senses have different values for the constant.

Figure 3.22
An Equal Frequency
Difference Piano

On a normal piano each C key is separated from the next by about a foot. This is because all the differences between Cs sound about the same to us. But the physical difference between the highest C and the next to the highest C is 64 times greater than the difference between the lowest C and the next to the lowest C.

less sensitive after they have been intensely stimulated. This process is called *sensory adaptation*.

Our senses vary not only in the short term but also with age. As we get older, they become less sensitive. We lose the ability to hear high-pitched sounds, our vision becomes less acute, and the ability to taste delicate flavors becomes diminished.

How keen are our senses? When our senses are good, they are very good. For example, our auditory hair cells are so sensitive that they pick up the spontaneous motion of molecules in the cochlear fluid. In fact, if our hearing receptors were more sensitive, we wouldn't hear better; we'd simply hear more noise.

Experiments also show that the smallest possible unit of light, a photon, can stimulate a rod to respond; and that as few as seven rods (if they respond) can trigger a nerve impulse that produces a noticeable light experience (Hecht, Shlaer & Pirenne, 1942).

As effective as human hearing and sight may be, many animals do more with these senses than we do. For instance, bats and dolphins make loud high-pitched sounds and then use the echoes from those sounds to navigate around obstacles in their environment. People who are blind develop a form of this sense. Their canes make sharp tapping sounds that bounce cleanly off walls and other large obstacles, helping them judge the location of those obstacles.

Although our eyes are very light sensitive, their acuity—the ability to detect fine details—is not equal to that of many birds' eyes. In birds of prey especially, a fold on the fovea enormously increases the number of cones on which the focused image plays. Estimates indicate that a hawk's day vision is as acute as human vision aided by binoculars.

Where our senses are bad, they are almost absurdly bad. Compared with many of our mammalian cousins, humans possess an extraordinarily primitive sense of smell. The fault is not with the individual chemical receptors; in fact, our olfactory receptors are so sensitive that they can respond to individual molecules of some substances. The problem lies in the number of olfactory receptors. We have far fewer than other animals. A bloodhound's nose has nearly 1 billion receptors compared with our 10 million, and its sensitivity to smell is

Dolphins compensate for the low-light conditions in which they have to navigate through *echolocution.* By emitting high-pitched sounds that bounce off objects around them, dolphins form a "picture" of the world around them.

many thousand times greater than our own (Dodd & Squirrel, 1980). Where we might have difficulty even noticing a scent, a bloodhound would be able to smell and track that scent hours or even days after it was laid down.

Many creatures, moreover, have senses we don't have. Several species of fish have organs for sending and receiving electrical impulses, which they use to "see" one another in murky water. And pigeons have a magnetic sense that helps them navigate. Experiments in which miniature magnets were mounted on pigeons' heads show that the pigeons' ability to navigate was disturbed by the presence of the magnets when other navigational cues (the position of the sun or stars, for example) were not available (Keeton, 1974).

Recap

- The absolute threshold is the smallest amount of stimulation that can be noticed.

- The difference threshold is the smallest noticeable difference between two stimuli.

- People are not equally sensitive to all the stimuli they experience, nor are they equally sensitive to differences between stimuli.

- Weber's law states that the ratio between the difference threshold and the intensity of a stimulus is a different constant for each sense.

- The sensitivity of a given sense can vary in the short term as well as with age.

Conclusion

As you go over the material in this chapter, think of your senses as an hourglass. At the top of the hourglass is the stimulus world in all its complexity; at the bottom, the experienced world in all its complexity. Between the two is a narrow passage through which information about the world must pass to find its way into your experience. That passage represents not only the incoming nerves from the senses to the central nervous system but also the processes that select and code information for transmission through those nerves. The overall process by which this information is decoded and interpreted to generate the experienced world is called *perception.* It is the topic to which we shall now turn in Chapter 4.

Chapter 4　　　　　　Perception

Chair, Jardin de Luxembourg, Paris 10th August 1985, David Hockney, 1985

4

I've been a bird watcher all my life. I don't get up early or travel great distances to make my observations. Instead I do my bird watching from the breakfast table, looking out over the redwood deck on the west side of my house to the grape arbor beyond. Like all bird watchers, I always hope to see a rare species; but given the informal nature of my bird-watching program, I don't expect to see one very often.

So you can imagine my surprise when I saw a 500-pound robin in my garden one warm spring day. I looked up from my bowl of oatmeal and there it was, perched on the grape arbor just 100 feet away, glaring out across the pasture and flicking its tail feathers irritably. It had to weigh at least 500 pounds because it was fully 6 feet long and 4 feet high.

I had less than a second to wonder why this huge bird wasn't crushing the rickety arbor with its weight, when suddenly it was gone. In its place was a normal-sized robin, perched on the deck railing about 12 feet away. The bird chirped twice and flew off to the garden, where it disappeared among the lettuce.

Suddenly I realized the trick my eyes had played on me. From where I sat at the kitchen table, the railing of the deck and the top of the arbor aligned. As I looked up quickly from my breakfast, my brain had assumed that the bird was perched, not on the railing nearby, but on the arbor 100 feet away. Given that assumption, the only reasonable interpretation of the image was that the bird was very large. My 500-pound robin was a perceptual illusion.

The Perceptual Processes

Why do we see things that aren't there? To answer this question, we have to ask another. How does the brain translate sensory information into a coherent picture of the world?

Perception is the process of organizing, interpreting, and integrating sensory information. The perceptual processes take that information and turn it into experience. These processes are not exactly the same as the sensory processes, but they are closely related.

The sensory processes transform stimuli from the environment and the body into nerve impulses. Simultaneously, they organize information so that by the time it reaches the cortex of the brain, it has already been interpreted to a certain extent. But sensory processes are usually tied to a single sense, and they involve little learning. Perceptual processes—the processes that turn sensory information into the world we actually experience—often integrate information from more than one sense and clearly are shaped by learning.

Nineteenth-century psychologists believed that sensations are bits of raw information collected from the environment and that perceptions are interpretations of that information. But the more we learn about sensation and perception, the more we find that the processes of gathering and interpreting information are connected, that they differ mainly in degree and timing.

Perception The process of organizing, interpreting, and integrating sensory information.

89

The Study of Perception: Traditional Theory

Within psychology, there are two schools of thought on how perception should be defined and research on perception undertaken. The first, the traditional perspective, traces its roots to the earliest days of psychology. It claims that the nervous system constructs our perceptions from the bits of information it acquires through the sense organs.

Later in this chapter we talk about a newer theory, a theory that emphasizes the ways in which perception puts us directly in touch with the world around us. That theory initiated a research dialogue that continues today.

Figure 4.1
Cues, Assumptions, and Principles of Inference

In perception, perceptual rules of inference are used to combine cues from the world with assumptions about that world to make the *percept,* the product of the perceptual process.

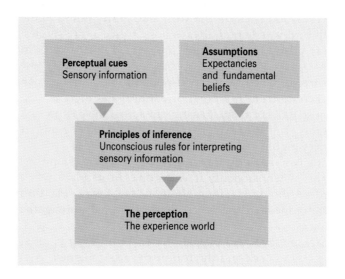

The Constructionist Approach

The traditional theory originated from the work of Hermann von Helmholtz, a nineteenth-century physiologist. (You may recall from Chapter 3 that Helmholtz originated the tricolor theory of vision.) Helmholtz and his followers developed **constructionist theory.** They believed that perceptions are constructed from information gathered by our senses—that our nervous system assembles these fragments of sensory information into experience, much as a child assembles pieces into a model plane. But unlike the process of putting together a model plane, perception, according to Helmholtz, is largely unconscious.

According to constructionist theory, perception is an incredibly fast reasoning process, the product of *unconscious inference* (Helmholtz, 1866/1968). When you leap out of bed each morning, you're behaving as though you know for sure that the floor is going to be there. But that knowledge is actually an inference. You know the floor has always been there before, and you have lots of reasons to suppose it's still there, but you don't *know* it's there. In fact, sometimes when you're away from home, sleeping in a strange bed, you leap out only to find that the floor isn't quite where you "knew" it to be. Your inference was that the floor is the same distance below the bed as it is at home, and you hit the floor with a thump.

Now you may be asking, "What inference? I never inferred anything from my getting out of bed." To that question Helmholtz would have answered, "That's why we say perceptual inferences are unconscious." The inferences you make when you perceive the world are just like the inference you make when you jump out of bed without looking to see if the floor is still there. They are reasonable inferences, and they are usually correct. But you're totally unaware that you're making them.

Constructionist theory The theory that the nervous system assembles fragments of sensory information into human experience.

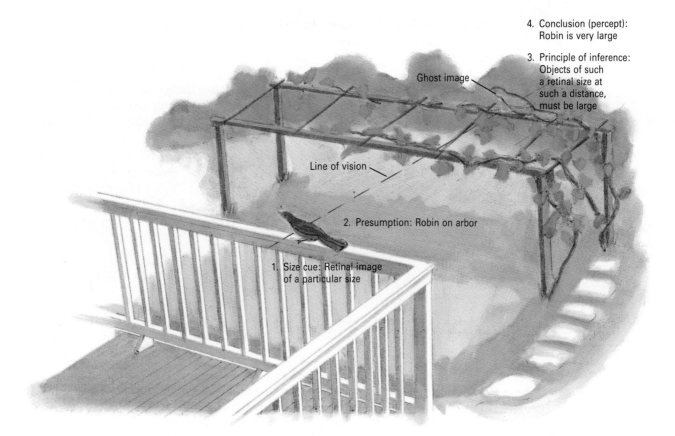

4. Conclusion (percept):
   Robin is very large

3. Principle of inference:
   Objects of such
   a retinal size at
   such a distance,
   must be large

Ghost image

Line of vision

2. Presumption: Robin on arbor

1. Size cue: Retinal image
   of a particular size

Figure 4.2
The 500-pound Robin

The interaction among cues, assumptions, and principles of inference often becomes clear when we misperceive a situation. The illusion of the giant robin was produced when the retinal image of a particular object combined with a faulty distance cue that placed the robin not on the nearby rail but on the distant arbor. The observer's perception combined the distance cue and the faulty assumption about the robin's location with the perceptual rule that for a given size a distant retinal image indicates a larger object than a near one to yield what in this case turned out to be a monstrous avian apparition.

Today, psychologists often speak about *information processing* rather than unconscious inference, and they believe that perception is closely related to the cognitive processes we discuss in Chapter 8. But the basic idea—that raw sensory data are processed and elaborated to construct perceptions—has not changed over time (Gregory, 1981).

Constructionist Methods

Constructionist theory focuses on identifying the cues, assumptions, and principles of inference that generate our perceptions. Figure 4.1 shows how these elements interact to produce perception.

Cues   According to constructionist theory, our perceptions are constructed from **perceptual cues,** bits of information that our senses deliver to the central nervous system. In the case of the 500-pound robin, two important perceptual cues were at work: the size of the robin image on the retina and the alignment of the nearby robin with the distant arbor (see Figure 4.2).

Assumptions   Every perception also relies on assumptions about the world. What was the assumption in the case of the giant robin? That because the robin's body and the top of the arbor were aligned, the robin must be perched on the arbor. Remember, I didn't make this assumption consciously. At no point did I say to myself, "Hey, look at that bird. I assume it's on the grape arbor. It must be a giant bird."

Some of the important assumptions we make about the world are based on our experience. These assumptions are called **expectancies.** Expectancy contributed to my perception of the 500-pound robin because I'd often seen robins

Perceptual cue   An element of sensory information from which perceptions are constructed.

Expectancy   An assumption that is based on experience.

perched on the grape arbor but had never seen one on the railing. The expectation that the robin would be on the arbor influenced my perception of the robin's size.

Expectations are so powerful that we sometimes overlook something we don't expect to see—even though it's there. Irving Biederman and his colleagues asked their subjects to look for certain objects in pictures (see Figure 4.3). The subjects often had difficulty seeing things in places where they didn't expect to see them (Biederman et al., 1981).

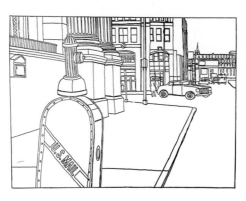 

Figure 4.3
Expectancies and Perception

Expectations can make such a powerful contribution to perception that we may fail to see things because we don't expect to see them. Irving Biederman and his colleagues asked subjects to detect elements in drawings such as these. The subjects were much more likely to overlook elements in unexpected locations such as the fire hydrant on the mailbox or the automobile parked in the motel room.

Other assumptions are so fundamental to perception that they seem to be built into our sensory systems. For example, our visual system "assumes" that only those wavelengths of light between 380 and 760 nanometers are significant, so it doesn't respond to any other wavelengths.

Psychologists can demonstrate that our nervous system makes assumptions about the world by violating those assumptions in experiments. **Illusions**—distorted perceptions—are one product of that violation. They help us understand the cues, assumptions, and principles of inference that underlie our perceptions.

Principles of Inference   Our perceptual system seems to use **principles of inference** to turn cues into perceptions. These guidelines tell the perceptual system how to interpret sensory information. In the robin example, the principle was "the farther away an object is, the bigger it must be to cast a retinal image of a particular size." Combined with the assumption that the robin was on the arbor, this principle led to the conclusion that the robin was very large.

Where do principles of inference come from? Psychologists have been debating this question since the nineteenth century. **Nativists** believe that perceptual principles are part of our biological makeup, that they are present at birth. **Empiricists** believe that we learn those principles through long experience with the environment.

As you will find repeatedly within the field of psychology, the question has no easy answer. Some perceptual principles seem to be innate; others seem to be learned. Still others seem to be partially innate and partially learned. We'll come back to this issue later in the chapter.

Percepts

Psychologists call the product of the perceptual processes, the thing we think we see or feel or hear, the **percept.** Because we are not aware of the inferences our nervous system has been making, we experience percepts as facts. I didn't say to myself, "I have a hunch that might be a giant robin sitting on my grape arbor"; I simply saw a giant robin. Even when a percept was ridiculous, I experienced it as real.

Illusion   A distorted perception of reality.

Principles of inference   Guidelines that tell the perceptual system how to interpret sensory information.

Nativists   Those who believe that perceptual principles are present at birth.

Empiricists   Those who believe that perceptual principles are learned through experience with the environment.

Percept   The product of perception—the thing we see, feel, or hear.

We have a powerful tendency to assume that straight lines in pictures are the edges of rooms and objects that they meet in corners. In his etching, the *Staircase,* M.C. Escher has taken advantage of our assumptions to create an impossible world.

In the next few sections, we'll take a closer look at the perceptual processes by examining three forms of perception: the localization of sound, the perception of brightness, and the perception of depth. Although these three forms are just a small part of the large and complex subject of perception, they allow us to see how cues, assumptions, and principles of inference interact to create our percepts of the world.

Recap

- Perception is the process of organizing, interpreting, and integrating sensory information.

- According to constructionist theory, the nervous system assembles our experience—what we perceive—from the information gathered by our senses.

- Constructionists believe that perception is a very fast reasoning process, the product of unconscious inference.

- Constructionist theory focuses on identifying the cues, assumptions, and principles of inference that generate our perceptions.

- Assumptions that are based on experience are called expectancies.

- Perceptual illusions often reveal the principles of perception.

- Nativists believe that perceptual principles are innate; empiricists believe that they are learned.

- We experience percepts—the things we think we see or feel or hear—as reality.

Localizing Sound

You are standing on the curb of a city street when you hear a siren. You immediately know that a fire truck is coming from the right—even though you didn't expect to hear a siren and didn't know a firehouse was two blocks up the street. You located the direction of the sound using just the sensory information collected by your ears. How?

Cues

Auditory localization is the process of determining the source of a sound using cues provided by the sound itself. Many kinds of cues help us localize sounds, but the most important are loudness cues and time cues (Phillips & Brugge, 1985).

Which Ear Hears the Louder Sound?   One way the auditory system locates sounds is by comparing the intensity—the loudness—of a sound arriving at the right ear with the intensity of the same sound arriving at the left ear. A sound coming from the right enters the right ear directly but takes a more roundabout route to reach the left ear. As a result of this detour, the sound is slightly fainter in your left ear. You perceive that the fire truck is approaching from the right in part because your auditory system detects the very small difference in the level of sound in each ear.

The difference in intensity between the sounds in your two ears is a *sound shadow cue*. As shown in Figure 4.4, the ear farther from the source of the sound is in a sound shadow cast by the head. In our example, the sound shadow cue indicates that the fire truck is coming from the right, not from the left.

**Figure 4.4
Sound Shadow Cue**

One of the two auditory cues that help locate sound is the *sound shadow cue.* The person in the illustration hears the sound of the siren as coming from the right because the sound is louder in the right ear than in the left. The reason for this is that the sound enters the right ear more directly than it enters the left ear.

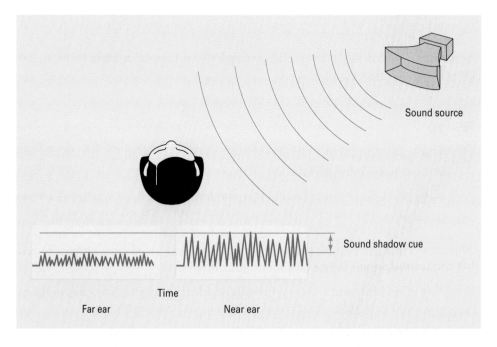

Sound source

Sound shadow cue

Time

Far ear   Near ear

Sound shadow cues also tell us whether a sound is above or below us, or behind or in front of us (Oldfield & Parker, 1984). Here the outer ear seems to play a role. You can test it yourself. Take the top part of each ear and bend it down with your fingers. Then close your eyes. Now have a friend jingle some keys in different positions above, below, and behind you. Don't be surprised if you have a hard time locating the source of the sound.

Auditory localization   The process of determining the source of a sound using cues provided by the sound itself.

Which Ear Hears the Sound First?   Another way the auditory system locates sounds is by determining which ear hears the sound first. Sound travels at a rate of 1,100 feet per second. A sound coming from the right reaches your right ear a few ten-thousandths of a second sooner than it reaches your left ear.

To determine the direction of an approaching fire truck, your auditory system compares the time the sound of the siren arrived in your right ear with the time the sound arrived in your left ear. The product of this comparison is the *arrival time cue,* which is illustrated in Figure 4.5.

The human auditory system needs just a very small difference in arrival time—a few *millionths* of a second—to locate the source of a sound (Durlach & Colburn, 1978). If you were sitting in a dark room with loudspeakers arranged around you in a circle, you could tell whether a sound source was directly ahead or just a few degrees to the right of you by the difference in arrival time.

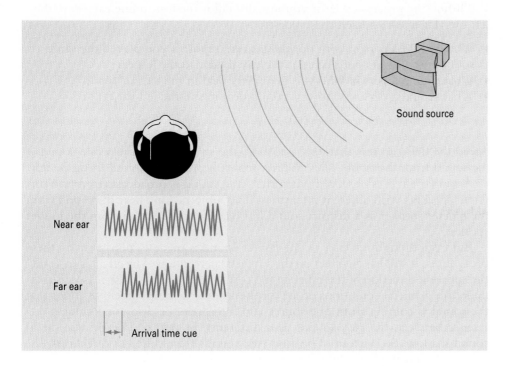

**Figure 4.5
Arrival Time Cue**

The second auditory cue that helps locate sound is the *arrival time cue.* The sound not only reaches the right ear more directly, it reaches it first. The two cues together allow us to accurately assess the location of sounds.

Assumptions

Remember that every perception is based on unconscious assumptions about the world. Our perceptions of sound seem to be based on the assumption that the same sound never arrives at both ears from two different sources.

When a sound reaches one ear a short interval after it reaches the other, your auditory system "assumes" that both sounds actually come from one source and that the second sound is just an echo.

By violating this assumption, Hans Wallach and his colleagues designed a classic experiment that makes sound "disappear" (Wallach, Newman & Rosenzweig, 1949). In the disappearing-sound experiment, Wallach and his coworkers asked subjects to take a seat in a dark room where two loudspeakers were hidden. Then the researchers played the same stimulus—a stream of clicking sounds—through the two speakers, with a slight delay between them. The amount of delay affected what the subjects heard. When the delay was relatively long (more than 0.07 seconds), the subjects heard two sounds, one an echo of the other (Zurek, 1980). For example, when the clicks from the right side arrived 0.07 seconds sooner than the clicks from the left, the subjects heard a sound from the right with an echo from the left. But when the researchers re-

Puzzle It Out!

You're a consulting psychologist. You've been hired by an insurance company to design a test that detects whether people are faking deafness to receive insurance payments they don't deserve. A person who is trying to fake deafness usually reports a hearing loss in just one ear—deafness in both ears is much more difficult to fake.

Your job is to tell the difference between those people who are faking deafness and those who really cannot hear in one ear. You have at your disposal earphones and a tape recorder that can play different sounds to each ear or the same sound more loudly to one ear than the other.

Before you get to work designing a test, here are a couple of hints. First, you'll find the process easier if you initially tailor the test to one ear—say, the left ear. Then ask yourself these questions:

- What would a person with normal hearing report if you played the same sound to both ears but played it slightly louder to the left ear?
- What would a person who was genuinely deaf in the left ear report?
- What would a person who was faking deafness in the left ear report?

duced the delay to less than 0.03 seconds, the subjects heard just one sound— the sound from the right. They did not report hearing any sound from the left.

A similar effect is observed when the same sound is broadcast from two different speakers with different intensities. The subjects don't hear the sound from the quieter speaker as a distinct sound but hear only the sound from the louder speaker.

But even though the later or the fainter sound is made to disappear by these procedures, it still has an effect on the subjects' perception. The effect is to "pull" the apparent direction of the other sound toward the midline. The reason is that, under the artificial conditions of the earphones, the hearing system assumes that the sound is coming from one source and interprets the delay or loudness difference between the two sounds as a difference in arrival time or a result of sound shadow. So, instead of hearing two sounds from different directions, the subjects hear a single sound from an intermediate direction.

Principles of Inference

Several perceptual principles appear to be at work in the process of localizing sound:

- Sound is slightly more intense in the ear that is nearer the source of the sound.
- Sound reaches the nearer ear slightly faster than it reaches the farther ear.
- When the ears hear two different sounds, they hear them distinctly—one sound on the left and one on the right.
- When the same sound arrives at one ear slightly sooner or louder than at the other ear, the "later" or softer sound is not heard.

How do we acquire the principles that allow us to turn shadow cues and arrival time cues into a perception of the location of a sound? Are these principles "in" us at birth? Or do we learn them?

Research in this area is limited by the fact that we can't ask a newborn baby to tell us the source of a sound. By the time a child can speak, he or she has already had time to learn sound-localization cues. But we can study the *orientation movements* of newborns—the movements they make to locate a stimulus source. For example, we can make a loud sound to one side of a baby and see if the baby turns to look in that direction. We know from these kinds of experiments that learning plays an important role in sound localization. The ability of humans and animals to localize sounds improves steadily throughout infancy (Knudsen, 1984).

But we also know that babies are able to orient to sounds almost from the moment they are born (Field et al., 1980; Castillo & Butterworth, 1981). Where does this basic ability come from?

It's possible that the principles of localization are learned in the uterus. Sound and light do penetrate the amniotic fluid. And from an early stage, fetuses do react to external stimuli. But to learn to use sound localization cues, the fetus would have to be able to see or reach out and touch the sources of sound—but this is obviously not the case.

How, then, do we explain the newborn's basic ability to localize sound? It seems that the basic principles of localization develop in the nervous system without any specific prenatal experience. These principles are then elaborated on by experience over the course of infancy.

Recap

- Auditory localization is the process of determining the source of a sound using cues provided by the sound itself.

- The slight difference in intensity between the sound in one ear and that in the other is a sound shadow cue.

- The slight difference in the time it takes for a sound to reach first one ear and then the other is an arrival time cue.

- Psychologists study the orientation movements of newborns to determine the role of early learning in sound localization.

- The basic principles of localization apparently develop in the nervous system without any specific prenatal experience, and then are elaborated on by experience.

Perceiving Brightness

We see most of the objects around us by reflected light. The light, produced by the sun or artificial lights, bounces off the objects to our eyes. The amount of light that reaches our eyes from an object depends on two factors: the amount of light shining on the object and the proportion of light that the object reflects to our eyes.

For instance, imagine that you're at a friend's graduation. She's marching in her robe in the sunshine, and you're sitting in deep shade under a canopy. Looking at her gown, you know without a doubt that it's black. And looking at the graduation program in your hand, you're equally certain that it's white.

Which do you think gives off more light—the black gown or the white program? Most people would say that the program is sending out more light than the gown. But it's not. If you pulled out a light meter and measured the intensity of the light coming from the gown's image and compared it with the intensity of the light coming from the paper's image, you'd see that the black gown in the sunlight is sending much more light to your eyes than the white paper in the shade.

Figure 4.6
Constancies

As you watch your friend walk down the aisle to receive her diploma, it's a wonder that she doesn't change in all sorts of ways. Why doesn't her robe become a brilliant white color when she steps into the sun? Why doesn't she shrink in size as she walks away from you? Why doesn't she become thinner as she turns to walk up the steps of the podium? For that matter, why doesn't the path she is walking on appear to taper, and why does the podium appear like a rectangular box when the image it presents to you doesn't have any square edges at all? The reason is that our perceptual system is able to pick out stable features of the stimulus, even when many of its features are changing or distorted by our perspective.

To understand how black can seem brighter than white, you have to understand constancies. A **constancy** is the perception that an object or a property of an object is not changing even though its image on the retina is changing. Without constancies, things would seem to change color, size, and shape every time they moved from one kind of light to another, moved away from or toward us, or changed their position. Not only would your friend's gown appear to grow lighter as she passed into the sunshine, but she herself would appear to grow smaller as she walked up the aisle and thinner as she turned to walk up the steps to receive her diploma. Without constancies, life would be chaos.

The particular constancy that explains why your friend's gown appears equally bright in sunlight or shade is called *brightness constancy*. Figure 4.6 shows the constancies in action.

Cues

What do we mean when we say that an object is "white" or "black"? As your friend marches toward the podium, she moves from shade to brilliant sunshine. Although the amount of light reflected from the gown increases hundreds of times during that period, you continue to see the gown as black. Why?

Radiation cannot give us information about an object unless it bounces off the object and is deflected to our eyes. Not all of the light that falls on an object carries information back to our eyes; some light is absorbed by the object itself.

To judge the brightness of an object, then, the visual system has to measure the amount of light that the object reflects back to the eyes. We call this measurement *reflectance*.

Reflectance is the amount of light an object reflects relative to the amount of light falling on the object. It's measured on a scale from 0 to 100 percent (see Figure 4.7). An object that does not reflect any light back to the observer's eye has a reflectance of 0 percent. Charcoal is near the low end of the scale, because it reflects very little light. But an object that reflects all the light falling on it back to the observer's eye has reflectance of 100 percent. Snow is at the high end of the reflectance scale. A high proportion of the total light falling on snow is reflected to our eyes.

An object's reflectance does not change. The amount of light falling on the object changes, but the object always reflects the same percentage of that light back to the eyes. Thus the reflectance of charcoal is always low, whether you see it in sunlight or shade; and the reflectance of snow is always high, whether the day is clear or cloudy.

How does the visual system measure reflected light? By making comparisons. One essential cue is the average level of light reflected by all the objects in the visual field. The visual system then compares the amount of light coming from any one object with that average.

Looking at the black gown in the sunshine, your visual system senses that the gown is black because, although the gown is sending out a lot of light, it is sending out much less light than most of the objects immediately around it—only a small proportion of the light it receives. When your friend marches from shade to sunshine, you continue to perceive her gown as black because it continues to send out less light than the objects around it.

Similarly, when you look at the white program in the shade, your visual system senses the paper is white because the paper is reflecting much more light than most of the objects immediately around it—a high proportion of the light it receives.

In short, the visual system gets its cues to brightness from the *relative* amount of light coming from an object. When you look at an object, you are not aware of the total amount of light reflected from it, but you are acutely sensitive to the relative amount of light reflected by that object in comparison to the other objects around it.

Constancy The perception that an object is not changing when its image on the retina is changing.

Figure 4.7
Reflectance

One of the constant features that our visual system seems to be able to pick out is *reflectance*, the proportion of light falling on an object that the object reflects back. Your friend's gown appears black in the sunshine because it reflects so little of the light falling on it. Your commencement program appears white because, even though relatively little light is falling on it, it is reflecting a high proportion of that light back to you.

When an object glows in the dark, it's giving off more light than there is light available—its reflectance is greater than 100 percent. It's easy to understand why a match glows, but why do these shirts glow? The pigments in the shirts' fabric absorb ultraviolet light and send it back as visible light. Because other objects around the shirts don't reflect ultraviolet rays, the shirts give off more light than our visual system can account for. So they appear to glow.

Assumptions

When we estimate an object's brightness, we are making a crucial assumption—that the light falling on the object comes from a single source. In testing this assumption, psychologist A. Gelb produced the illusion that black is white.

When light falls on the visual field, it illuminates the entire field—not only the specific object we are looking at but all the other elements around it as well. We determine the brightness of the object by the relative amount of light it reflects. But what happens when we introduce a second source of light and focus it only on the specific object? That's what Gelb did.

Gelb (1929) illuminated a black disk with a hidden spotlight that shone only on the disk, not on the background (see Figure 4.8). Consequently, the black disk reflected more light than its background. When subjects were asked the color of the disk, they insisted it was white. Gelb then put a piece of white paper in front of the disk, allowing the hidden light to fall both on the disk and on the paper. Now the disk no longer reflected more light than the paper in front of it. The observers immediately saw that the disk was black. But when Gelb removed the paper and again allowed the light to fall only on the disk, the observers saw the disk as white—even though they knew it was black!

Principles of Inference

Gelb's disk and other illusions help us understand the principles that underlie brightness perception:

- If an object reflects more light than other objects around it, it's whiter.
- If an object reflects less light than other objects around it, it's blacker.

Although we've been talking about black and white, the same principles apply to colors. In our discussion of additive and subtractive color mixing in Chapter 3, we said that green paint, for example, absorbs all wavelengths *except* green. So a green object reflects more green light than the objects around it.

When you go shopping to find just the right shade of green sweater, your visual system must gauge the green of the sweater against all the objects in the store. Only then can you decide how "green" a particular sweater is. This ability is known as *object color constancy*.

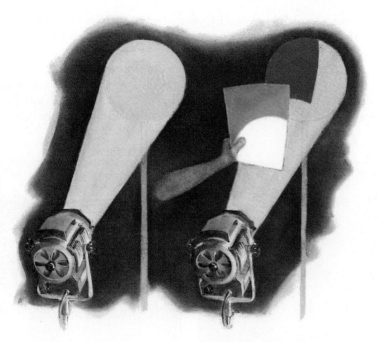

Maintaining color constancy is more complicated than maintaining brightness constancy, because it involves comparisons among the three types of color receptors (Hurlburt & Poggio, 1988). If you choose that "perfect" shade of green sweater in a shop that uses fluorescent lights, you may not think it's quite so perfect when you get it home. Although we have no difficulty identifying colors under various lighting conditions, shades of color can appear different under different conditions (Helson, Judd & Wilson, 1956).

Context also plays a role in color constancy. Look at Figure 4.9. The centers of both circles are the same shade of red. But notice how the dark red background makes the center look pink and how the pink background makes the center look red.

Figure 4.9
Context and Color Constancy

The apparent color of an object, just like its brightness, is dependent on the color of objects around it. Believe it or not, the red centers of these two circles are exactly the same color. The red center in the top circle appears pinker only because it is surrounded by a dark red background.

Recap

- Object brightness constancy is the ability to see an object's brightness as unchanged even when the amount of light falling on it changes.

- Reflectance is a measurement of the light reflected from an object relative to the amount of light falling on the object.

- To estimate the brightness of an object, the visual system compares its brightness with the brightness of other objects in the visual field.

- By violating the assumption that light stems from just one source, researchers can create the illusion that black is white.

- Color constancy, the ability to see objects as having the same color under different illuminations, operates on these same principles.

Depth Perception

Look up from your book a moment, but don't move. Now focus on the doorway leading out of the room. How big is it? How far away is it? How do you even know that this particular opening is a doorway?

Depth perception—the process by which we transform two-dimensional images into a three-dimensional world—is one of the most complex puzzles in the study of perception. This puzzle has two parts. First, we have to explain how we distinguish the object that interests us—the **figure**—from all the other objects and patterns in our visual field—the **ground** (see Figure 4.10). Second, we have to explain how we locate objects in space. To solve this latter part of the puzzle, we have to determine an object's size, distance, and shape.

Figure 4.10
Figure-Ground Perception

What do you see in each of these illustrations—two profiles or a vase? The answer depends on what interests you most—the figure—and what interests you the least—everything else, or the ground.

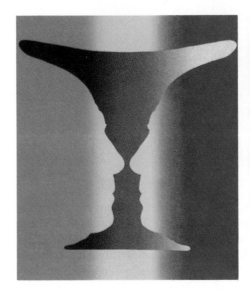

Cues

To perceive objects in space, the visual system uses many different kinds of cues.

Pictorial Cues   When you watch television, even though the screen is two-dimensional, you perceive images on the screen in three dimensions. The cues that add depth to the picture are called *pictorial cues*. Pictorial cues are *monocular cues*: they are apparent even to an observer who lacks sight in one eye. You can test this yourself by turning on the TV and then covering one eye. Even with the eye covered, you should have no problem perceiving depth.

Gestalt cues are a special class of pictorial cues that help us see the different parts of an image as a whole or form. (Remember that *Gestalt* is the German word for "whole.") These cues rely on five principles: proximity, similarity, continuity, closure, and common fate.

1. **Proximity** is the tendency to see objects that are close together in space as a whole. For instance, most people perceive the pattern in Figure 4.11(a) as five groups of circles, not as sixteen different items. This tendency is so strong that we often have trouble perceiving the individual parts of a group (Prinzmetal, 1981).
2. **Similarity** is the tendency to cluster similar objects together and perceive them as forms. Look at Figure 4.11(b). In the first drawing you're more likely to see four rows of similar shapes than four columns of dissimilar shapes; in the second, you're more likely to see columns, not rows (Olson & Attneave, 1970).
   Our visual system also has a tendency to create continuous lines out of broken lines. This tendency is called **continuity.** Continuity explains why

Figure   The part of the visual field that interests the viewer.

Ground   Everything in the visual field except the figure.

Gestalt cues   Perceptual cues that help the individual see the different parts of an image as a whole.

Proximity   A Gestalt cue; the tendency to see items that are clustered in a group as a single element.

Similarity   A Gestalt cue; the tendency to cluster similar objects visually.

Continuity   A Gestalt cue; the tendency to see continuous lines where lines are broken.

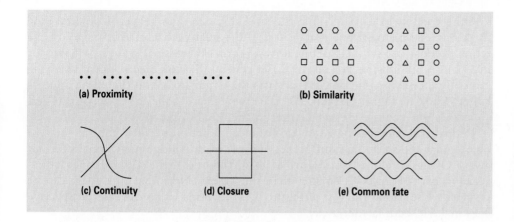

Figure 4.11
Gestalt Cues

Gestalt cues help us see objects as wholes, even when we can't see all of them. The dots in (a) seem to form a group as do the objects in (b). The lines in (c) seem like two continuous lines, rather than two v's with sharp corners. The principle of closure is operating in (d) where the visual system "closes" the open forms. Lines that have the same shape, like the two wavy lines in (e), are also likely to be seen as a group.

we see the pattern of circles in Figure 4.11(c) as two wavy lines that intersect instead of four lines or two V-shaped lines meeting at a point.

3. **Closure** is one of the best-known Gestalt cues. The visual system has a tendency to create solids, ignoring gaps or intruding elements. Accordingly, most people perceive the pattern in Figure 4.11(d) as a rectangle with a line through it, rather than as two halves of a rectangle on either side of a line. As Figure 4.12 shows, closure can exert such a strong influence that we see figures even in the absence of outlines (Kanizsa, 1976).

4. **Common fate** is the tendency of our visual system to group things that behave in the same way. You are more likely to see the top rather than the bottom pair of wavy lines in Figure 4.11(e) as a whole—as a snake, perhaps. In other words, objects that seem to be moving together tend to be seen as one object.

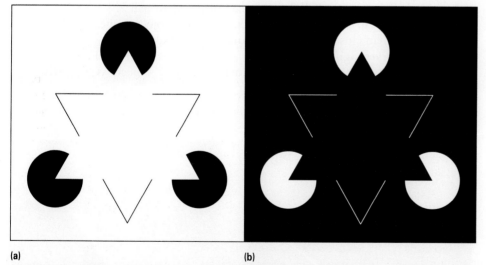

(a)   (b)

Figure 4.12
Closure

Most people who look at these figures see complete sides on the triangles. But, of course, there are no complete sides there. The sides are supplied by your visual system because in nature most objects display closure.

Common fate is a much more dramatic cue in the three-dimensional world of things in motion than in the two-dimensional world of book illustrations. When an object moves against a background, we have no doubt that it is one object (J. Gibson & E. Gibson, 1957). Consider the cheetah in Figure 4.13. So long as the animal remains motionless, its spots—the numerous independent objects—blend into the background. But if the cheetah were to walk away, its spots would move together—like one object—and the animal would be recognized instantly.

Closure   A Gestalt cue; the tendency to see solids where there are gaps or intruding elements.

Common fate   A Gestalt cue; the tendency to group together visually objects that are parallel or that move together.

Figure 4.13
Common Fate

The spots on the cheetah make the form of the cheetah difficult to distinguish against its background. Can you point out some ways in which the spots diminish the cues for "cheetah recognition."

Other cues help us determine the size, distance, and shape of objects. The most obvious pictorial cue is *retinal size,* the relative size of the image on the retina. Retinal size can help define how large an object is. (It was responsible for my giant robin illusion, for instance.) In general, if two objects appear to be the same distance away, the object that casts the larger image on the retina appears larger. Look at Figure 4.14(a). Of the two billiard balls, the one on the left appears larger because it casts a larger image on your retina.

Retinal size can also be a cue to distance. When you know the size of two objects that appear in the same scene, you can readily judge which one is farther away. Of the three balls in Figure 4.14(b), the one at the top appears farthest away in part because it's smaller than the others. Note that this effect can be reversed. The ball at the top of Figure 4.14(c) seems larger because perspective cues make it seem farther away.

Several other cues indicate distance:

- *Linear perspective* is what makes us perceive the image in Figure 4.14(d) as a flat surface that recedes into the distance instead of a geometric shape. Because of the geometry of the visual image, objects appear smaller and closer together as they recede into the distance. Thus, any part of a scene that stretches away from us covers a smaller and smaller visual angle as it gets farther away. Our brains automatically interpret these regular changes in visual angles as distance. As a result, the converging lines in Figure 4.14(d) are seen as parallel lines disappearing into the distance.

- As illustrated in Figure 4.14(e) the closer things are, the easier it is to see their *texture.* Texture cues are particularly powerful in landscapes, where details like leaves and blades of grass get smaller and smaller as they recede into the distance.

- An object that overlaps part of another object is usually perceived to be in front of the other object. This cue is called *interposition.* In Figure 4.14(f), because ball 1 overlaps ball 2, it appears nearer than ball 2.

- *Height in field* can also be a distance cue. Distant objects appear higher in the visual field than close objects, as Figure 4.14(g) makes clear.

- *Atmospheric cues* signal distance, too. As you can see from Figure 4.14(h), distant objects appear hazier and bluer than close objects (Ono, Rivest & Ono, 1986).

The same-sized object covers a progressively smaller visual angle as the object gets farther away, so that parallel lines seem to converge at infinity. This effect produces a powerful sense of distance, as exemplified in this picture, where the road seems to be disappearing toward the horizon.

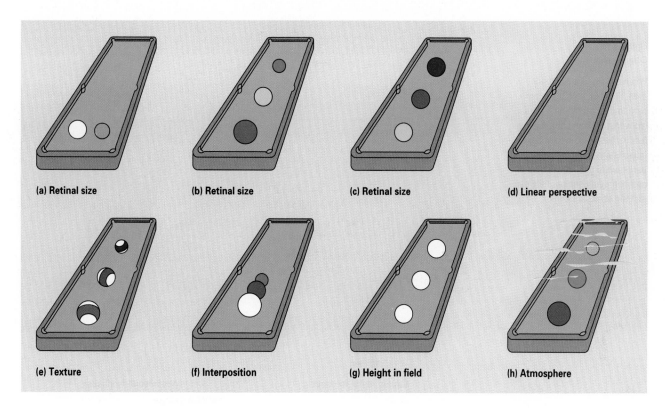

(a) Retinal size   (b) Retinal size   (c) Retinal size   (d) Linear perspective

(e) Texture   (f) Interposition   (g) Height in field   (h) Atmosphere

Figure 4.14
Other Pictorial Cues

In addition to Gestalt cues, many other kinds of cues tell us about the size and distance of objects: retinal size contributes to our estimates of the distance and size of each of the balls in (a), (b) and (c). Atmospheric cues (h), texture cues (e), and the interposition of objects (f) also make a contribution.

Cues from the Eye Muscles Certain muscles in the eye help focus images on the retina through the process of *accommodation* (see Chapter 3). Receptors that record the activity of those muscles are a potential source of distance cues (Wyatt, 1988).

Another possible source of distance cues is feedback from the group of muscles that control the inward rotation, or **convergence,** of the eyes. The nearer the image, the stronger the contraction (see Figure 4.15). Hold your pen at arm's length in your right hand and look directly at the pen with both eyes. Now slowly begin to move your right hand toward the end of your nose, continuing to focus both eyes on the pen. You can feel the muscles in your eyes working hard to direct your eyes inward.

Binocular Disparity Although the distance between your eyes is small, it's large enough that the image projected on your right retina differs slightly from the image projected on the corresponding part of your left retina. This slight difference is a cue for distance called **binocular disparity.**

You can demonstrate binocular disparity yourself. Close your left eye and align your pen with the right edge of the doorway in your room. Now quickly close your right eye and open your left eye. The pen appears to jump to the right of the doorway. Now if you close your left eye and open your right eye again, the pen should align with the right edge of the doorway. The reason the pen seems to move is that the two eyes have somewhat different perspectives. Your brain compares these two views, calculating the relative distance of the objects around you from the differences in the way they look to each eye.

You need special glasses to see a 3-D movie because for this kind of movie, two slightly different images are projected on the screen. (The movie is filmed with two cameras shooting side by side.) Special filters in the glasses let you see one image through your right eye and the other image through your left eye. Your visual system interprets the difference between the two images as depth, even though you're looking at a flat screen.

Convergence The inward rotation of the eyes that keeps both eyes pointed at an image.

Binocular disparity A perceptual cue for distance; the difference in the images projected on the retinas of the eyes.

Figure 4.15
Convergence

When the pen is close to the eyes, the muscles have to work hard to direct the eyes inward (convergence), and proprioceptors in these hard-working eye muscles send lots of impulses back toward the brain. These impulses provide one possible cue that the object is close.

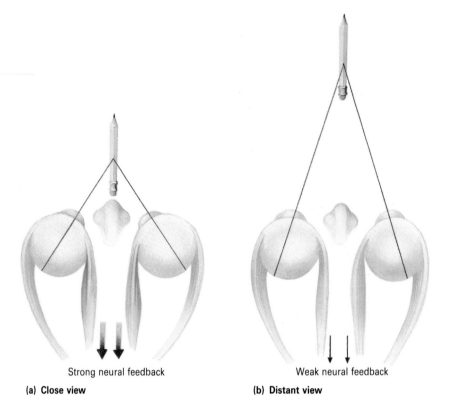

Strong neural feedback

(a) Close view

Weak neural feedback

(b) Distant view

Assumptions

As we've been describing the cues used by the visual system to perceive objects in space, you may have noticed that many assumptions appear to have been built into the process. Each Gestalt principle—proximity, similarity, continuity, closure, and common fate—seems to be based on its own set of assumptions.

Continuity, for example, seems based on the assumption that continuous lines—tree trunks and stream banks—are still there even when they're obscured by other things. Common fate seems to be based on the assumption that if a number of spots move together, they are probably part of the same object—a cheetah.

The assumptions essential to perception are revealed through the study of several classical illusions.

The Ames Room   The Ames room creates one of the most spectacular visual illusions in psychology (Ittleson, 1952). It's a box or even a full-sized room that you look into through a peephole, as depicted in Figure 4.16. From that perspective, the room appears to be square, with square windows, a level floor, and a back wall parallel to the front wall. In one corner is a 6-foot-tall toddler; in another, a dog, much smaller than its actual size. What's going on here?

The mystery unravels when you look at the Ames room from any angle other than the one visible through the peephole. Actually neither the room nor any of the windows is square. The floor, which rises steeply to the right, is much closer to the ceiling in the child's corner than in the dog's corner. And the dog is not beside the boy; it's standing behind him, where the ceiling is much higher.

The Ames room beautifully illustrates the three critical elements in perception: cues, assumptions, and principles of inference. Seen through a peephole (or in a photograph), it provides only pictorial cues—the lines of perspective in the room and the relative sizes of the people. These cues combine to make the

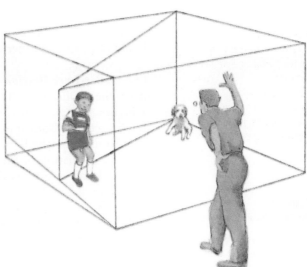

child appear larger than he actually is. So even though we expect toddlers to be larger than their dogs, our visual system concludes that the dog is much smaller than the boy.

This conclusion is based on assumptions that operate in our rectilinear world of skyscrapers and neat city blocks: rooms have right angles; floors and ceilings are perpendicular to walls. But the illusion disappears when we look at the room with both eyes, when *binocular cues*—cues visible only to both eyes together—give us information about the actual shape of the room (Gehringer & Engel, 1986).

The Inside-Out Doghouse   The illusion of the inside-out doghouse demonstrates the assumption that one set of cues is more reliable than another. That is, our perceptual apparatus seems to "trust" one kind of cue more than another. At first glance, the structure in Figure 4.17 appears to be the frame of a doghouse with puppies inside it. But look again. Some parts of the structure that seem to be on the outside are actually on the inside. This illusion is the product of phony continuity, interposition, and perspective cues that have been built into the doghouse. These cues are stronger than the cues that correctly tell us whether the puppies are actually inside or outside the doghouse.

Figure 4.16
The Ames Room

Like many illusions, the Ames room illustrates the elements in perception: cues, assumptions, and principles of inference. Because we assume that the room has right angles we infer from the retinal size cue that the child is much bigger than his dog. As soon as we can see that the angles in the room are not right angles, we realize the boy appears larger only because he is much closer to the camera. When the dog is closer, it appears larger.

Figure 4.17
The Inside-Out Doghouse

Ordinarily cues like perspective cues and interposition cues work together to make a meaningful image. But, in this image, the more you examine its parts, the less sense the image makes. Just what is inside and what is outside of this crazy dog house?

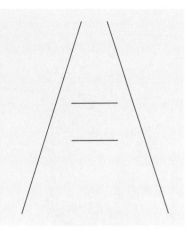

Figure 4.18
The Ponzo Illusion

If the two converging lines were actually parallel lines fading into the distance, as our visual system seems to assume, then the higher horizontal line would be farther away and therefore longer, as it appears to be in this drawing. But, in fact, the two lines are the same length.

Figure 4.19
The Müller-Lyer Illusion

Faulty assumptions about distance may also contribute to the illusion that the right-hand vertical line in (a) is longer than the left-hand one. The angled lines provide false perspective cues that suggest that the left-hand image is nearer—and therefore smaller—than the right. A variation of (a) is shown in (b) where the angles of the lines abutting the vertical lines create two different perspectives: one showing the inside corner of a room and the other showing the outside corner. As shown in (c), the same effect can be produced with circles that use interposition cues to suggest that the left-hand image is nearer than the right-hand one.

The Ponzo Illusion False perspective and height cues help explain the Ponzo illusion, which is illustrated in Figure 4.18. Even though the two horizontal lines are the same length, the higher line seems longer. Why? Because our visual system assumes that the two converging lines are actually parallel lines leading into the distance. Given that assumption, the higher of the two horizontal lines would have to be farther away from the viewer and therefore longer.

The Müller-Lyer Illusion Faulty assumptions about distance may also contribute to the Müller-Lyer illusion, which we discussed briefly in Chapter 1. Look at Figure 4.19(a). Which line is longer? Although the one on top looks longer, they're actually both the same length. (This illusion is so strong that you may want to measure the lines to be sure they are the same.)

One explanation of the Müller-Lyer illusion, as depicted in Figure 4.19(b), is that the brain interprets the inward-pointing arrows as right angles projecting *behind* the plane of the paper and the outward-pointing arrows as right angles projecting *in front of* the plane of the paper. Because the two lines project equal images on the retina, and because the line with the inward-pointing arrows seems farther away, it must be the longer line.

Although this reasoning makes sense, perspective cues do not alone explain the illusion. As Figure 4.19(c) shows, the illusion works nearly as well when we replace the arrows at the end of the lines with circles. A complete explanation of the Müller-Lyer illusion still eludes psychologists.

Principles of Inference

Dozens of principles help us interpret the images around us as objects in three-dimensional space. Here are some of the most important:

- When elements are close together, resemble one another, form smooth lines or closed figures, or have been seen together in the past, we tend to see them as parts of a single object. You saw this principle at work in the discussion of Gestalt cues on pages 102 to 103.
- The larger the image projected to the eye, the closer the object appears. You saw this principle at work in Figure 4.14(a).
- When the form of one object partially conceals the form of another, the overlapping form appears nearer than the other form. We perceive relative distance in this way even when the overlapping form casts a smaller image on the retina. You saw this principle at work in Figure 4.14(f).

Where do the principles that guide spatial perception come from? The same disagreement we saw earlier in regard to hearing occurs here. Some psychologists believe the principles are innate. Others argue that they are based on learning and experience.

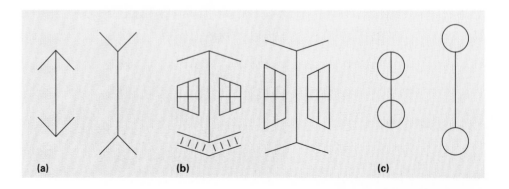

(a)   (b)   (c)

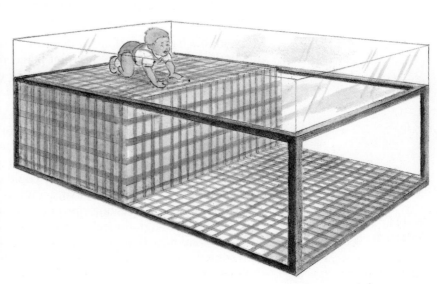

Figure 4.20
The Visual Cliff

Even at this tender age, this youngster interprets the converging pattern of red squares as a cue to depth and cannot be coaxed out onto the plate glass that covers the "visual cliff" that separates him from his mother.

One way to examine the origins of perceptual principles is to study the behavior of very young children for evidence of those principles before the children have had a chance to learn them. In one series of experiments, the researchers used an apparatus called a **visual cliff** (E. Gibson & Walk, 1960). The visual cliff is actually a large piece of plate glass supported from below. Beneath the glass is what appears to be a large step, dropping from table height to floor level. The table top, the face of the step, and the floor below are covered in a red and white checkerboard pattern, so that the drop is obvious. Because the glass extends over the floor area, there is no edge, no "cliff." But as you can see from Figure 4.20, it looks like a dangerous precipice.

To test for evidence of the principles of depth perception, a researcher places a baby who has just learned to crawl on the line between the "shallow" and "deep" ends. Sometimes the researcher simply watches to see whether the baby will crawl out over the "cliff." At other times the mother tries to coax the baby out onto the deep end.

Apparently the principles of depth perception are in place in relatively young children. Babies are reluctant to crawl out on the deep side, even when encouraged to do so. These findings suggest that we don't have to have specific experience with sharp drops to know to avoid them. Comparable research with lambs, chicks, ducklings, and other young animals that can walk within minutes or hours of birth shows that they, too, avoid the deep end of the apparatus almost as soon as they can walk (Walk, 1981).

Another way to explore the origins of spatial perception principles is to see whether people in different cultures experience the same illusions. Earlier we discussed the possibility that the Ames room illusion is created, at least in part, by years of experience with a world of right angles—of buildings and rooms with walls that are perpendicular to floors, and roofs and ceilings that are perpendicular to walls. Perhaps we do learn the assumptions and principles underlying the Müller-Lyer illusion from our experience with straight lines and angles. But what about people who live in worlds that aren't "carpentered"? Do they see the same illusions we do? In a classic experiment, two famous Russian psychologists, A. R. Luria and L. S. Vygotsky, studied villagers in the Soviet republic of Uzbekistan soon after the Russian Revolution. They found that although the Müller-Lyer illusion fooled both educated and illiterate Uzbecks, most other illusions did not (Luria, 1979). In cultures where sharp angles are not

Visual cliff An apparatus used to test depth perception in infants and animals.

How Do We Know That?

Many studies have been done to determine the origin of human capacities, among them the capacity to interpret perceptual cues. As you've seen, psychologists use three basic techniques in their efforts to answer the heredity versus environment question. Each has special advantages and disadvantages.

Human developmental studies   One way to determine whether a tendency is inherited or learned is to look for evidence of its earliest occurrence. That's what Eleanor Gibson did when she wanted to learn the source of the principles that govern depth perception. Because her experiments showed that babies avoided the visual cliff as soon as they could crawl, she concluded that the tendency to avoid sharp drops is innate, not learned.

The problem with drawing this kind of conclusion from research with babies is that although the babies have not had the specific experience in question, they may have had other relevant experiences. For example, infants may learn something about height in their cribs, from raising their heads and abruptly lowering them onto the mattress.

Animal developmental experiments   The ability of developmental studies to rule out the effects of experience increases if psychologists can design experiments that isolate their subjects from possible sources of learning. Obviously researchers cannot isolate human babies from their normal environment; but they can isolate young animals. If an animal responds appropriately to cues despite its isolation since birth, we can be pretty sure that experience is not necessary to the interpretation of cues—at least not in that particular animal.

All research involves compromise. In this case we find the problem of generalizing from experiments with animals to humans. Although findings may settle the question for the animal used in the study, they can't settle the question for human beings. People and animals do not necessarily perceive the world in the same ways.

Cross-cultural studies   Cross-cultural studies are a third way of demonstrating the source of perceptual principles. The assumption is that if people in widely different cultures recognize the same cues, that recognition is more likely to be a product of heredity than of environment. The findings from perceptual studies have been mixed. Where research shows consistent responses across cultures, psychologists interpret the findings to mean that the principles at work in the responses are innate. Where responses are inconsistent, psychologists interpret the findings to mean that the principles involved in the responses are learned.

As you may have guessed, there are problems here, too. First, all people share most genes, but they don't share all genes. Thus it's possible that cross-cultural differences in responses to perceptual illusions could arise from genetic differences among different populations. Second, although the experience of growing up differs from one culture to another, different cultures still offer many common experiences. In every culture babies are fed, cleaned, and cared for. The methods may be different, but the end result is the same. So shared experiences could be the source of similar responses to perceptual illusions in different cultures.

There are two other fundamental problems with cross-cultural research. First, researchers themselves are members of different cultures, which might affect their research methods. And, second, culture can influence the ways in which subjects respond to cues. That is, subjects may fail to demonstrate a perceptual constancy or respond to a perceptual illusion because they don't un-

(Continued on next page)

derstand the way a question is worded, because they feel the researchers expect a particular answer, or simply because they are not motivated to try to understand the question and answer it accurately (Bock, 1980).

Given that every approach to the question of the origin of perceptual principles is limited in some way, no one method is likely to give us an answer. But several forms of experimentation may succeed where a single form fails. This is an example of an overall principle we come back to again and again in this text: the unit of discovery in psychology—in all sciences, for that matter—is not the individual study or even a group of studies. Rather, it is a *literature*— many groups of studies, carried out by many researchers, using a variety of methods that, when taken together, point to a conclusion.

The Zulus live in round houses, in a mostly natural environment, with few built objects. So, they have very little experience with the kinds of verticals and horizontals common to Western experience. One result is the diminished effect of some illusions, like the Müller-Lyer.

common, people tend to see only the round and irregular shapes of plants, clouds, and animals. In a study of Zulu tribe members living in round houses in rural villages, Segall, Campbell, and Herskovits (1966) found evidence of the Müller-Lyer illusion, although the illusion was weaker among the rural villagers than among members of the same tribe who had relocated to Western-style cities.

Recap

- To judge the size, distance, and form of objects in space, the visual system uses pictorial cues, cues from the eye muscles, and cues that are generated by binocular disparity.

- We test the assumptions that underlie perceptual cues by creating illusions.

- Many different principles are at work in our perception of objects in space.

- To determine the origin of those principles, psychologists study very young children and animals, as well as people in different cultures.

The Study of Perception: Ecological Theory

At the beginning of this chapter, we noted that the study of perception is dominated by two schools of thought. We've been concentrating on the traditional school—constructionist theory—in part because much of the research that's been done on perception has been based on that theory. In the 1950s, however, a new theory of perception was proposed. This theory challenged the concept that our perceptions are built on information collected by the sense organs.

The theory was the work of psychologist James Gibson (1950, 1966, 1979). According to Gibson's **ecological theory,** our senses perceive information in the environment directly. Perception is not manufactured; like ripe fruit, we pluck it from the environment.

Unlike constructionist theory, which assumes that perception is indirect, ecological theory argues that perceptual information is directly available in the world around us. It focuses on the way in which perception occurs outside the laboratory and adapts the person or animal to the real world.

The Ecological Approach
Versus the Traditional Approach

Gibson's theory differs from traditional theory in its fundamental concepts, methods, and understanding of the significance of perceptual illusions. See Table 4.1 for a summary of these differences.

Concepts   According to constructionist theory, perception is a form of information processing; by contrast, ecological theory claims that perception is simply the process of picking up information from the environment. This distinction leads to radical differences in the way each theory evaluates the relative contributions of the nervous system and the environment to perception.

Constructionists stress the role of the central nervous system. They believe that the environment gives us only the raw material of perception, the cues from which the percept is constructed through active perceptual processes. But Gibson argued that the environment is so full of information that the perceptual system can perceive the environment directly if it is attuned to the right information. That information takes the form of **environmental invariants,** complex properties of the world that are apparent to any active observer.

Ecological theory further differs from traditional theory in its view of the perceptual apparatus. Whereas traditional theory often explains perception in terms of an image on the retina of a single eye, ecological theory emphasizes the interaction between the whole visual system and the environment (Michaels, 1986). Motion is a vital part of that interaction. According to Gibson, we are constantly in motion: eyes, head, and body are always moving. And as we move, we create an **ambient flow**—a pattern of motion in relation to the objects in our environment. This flow gives us specific information about the size, distance, and shape of those objects.

Imagine you're on a train, looking out the window (see Figure 4.21). Nearby objects seem to flash by in the opposite direction. Objects at a middle distance don't seem to move at all. Faraway objects actually seem to travel along with you. These patterns reflect the ambient flow generated by your motion.

Of course, when a train is moving, the view outside your window changes constantly. But underlying this flux are certain constants. For example, the rate of apparent movement is exactly related to the distance of the object you're seeing. This relationship between distance and the rate of change in the visual scene is an invariant property of the visual world. It is the kind of invariant

Ecological theory   James Gibson's theory that we perceive the world directly through our senses.

Environmental invariants   Complex properties of the world that are apparent to active observers.

Ambient flow   A pattern of motion in relation to objects in the environment that gives the individual information about the size, distance, and shape of those objects.

Question	Constructionist Answer	Ecological Answer
What does the environment contribute to perception?	Cues	Invariants
What is the basic activity of perception?	Information processing	Information pickup
What is the fundamental unit of perception?	An event at the "sensory surface"	A person or an animal relating to its environment
What is the fundamental question that perception theory must answer?	How does the brain construct a coherent picture of the world from the incoherent bits of information provided by the senses?	To which environmental invariants does the person's or animal's behavior relate?
What is the preferred method?	Carefully controlled manipulation of cues in the laboratory	Simple experiments conducted "outdoors under the sky" (J. Gibson, 1985)
What is the value of illusions in helping us understand perception?	They reveal the role of assumptions and principles of inference in constructing reality	They are of little practical value
By what other names is the theory known?	Traditional, indirect	Direct

Table 4.1
The Differences Between Constructionist and Ecological Theories

relationship that Gibson believed our nervous systems are designed to detect. The relationship between your motion and the motion of the objects you see is a constant property of your relationship to your environment—an environmental invariant that allows you to judge the size, distance, and shape of the objects in your visual field.

Figure 4.21
Ambient Flow

Notice that the amount of blurring in the images tells us a lot about how far they are from the moving camera. Gibson believed that this sort of motion is a fundamental cue to distance perception outside the laboratory.

Methods   Constructionist and ecological theories also differ in their methods. Traditional constructionist studies of spatial perception attempt to simplify the experimental situation as much as possible. Experiments are conducted in laboratories, and researchers use instruments that keep subjects from moving or shifting when a stimulus is presented. From this unnatural perspective, subjects peer through small openings or lenses at stimuli that carefully vary a single cue—size, height in the visual field, or binocular disparity, for example. Under these conditions, subjects tend to overestimate near distances and underestimate far ones. How do researchers interpret these findings? As a lack of distance constancy in their subjects.

James Gibson believed that the findings reflect the failure of traditional methodology, not that of the subjects' ability to judge distances. He was a strong advocate of studying perception under natural conditions. In one experiment, Gibson's wife, psychologist Eleanor Gibson, and several colleagues set up a "laboratory" outdoors on the Cornell campus. Using a mobile marker as a stimulus, they asked their subjects to judge when the stimulus was "halfway from here to there." Under these conditions, the subjects gauged distance much more accurately than would have been expected with traditional methods (E. Gibson & Bergman, 1954).

The Role of Illusions   According to constructionist theory, illusions demonstrate the tenuous grasp our perceptual systems have on reality. The dramatic distortions in the Ames room, for example, reveal the extent to which our perceptions of size and distance depend on the assumptions that rooms are square, walls are perpendicular to floors, and ceilings are perpendicular to walls.

According to ecological theory, though, the Ames room demonstrates only that subjects improvise when they are deprived of the natural cues that help them perceive size, distance, and form. (Remember that when subjects look at the Ames room, they usually look through a single peephole, which prevents their use of binocular disparity or movement cues. When subjects can see with both eyes and move about, however, they are rarely fooled by the illusion.) In short, because subjects are forced by the peephole to work with indirect rather than direct cues, they misjudge distance. The product of that misjudgment is the illusion created by the Ames room.

Reconciling the Two Perspectives

Early in his career, Gibson tried to integrate his ideas into the constructionist mainstream. But by the time he died in 1979, he had decided that the two were incompatible. To date, the conflict between traditional and ecological theories has yet to be resolved.

Still, despite their very real differences, the two theories will probably be reconciled eventually. Detailed studies of the neurophysiology of certain perceptual functions seem to indicate that there is room for both theories in our understanding of perception. Let's look at two examples.

Feature Detection: Support for Constructionist Theory   In Chapter 3 we described *feature detectors,* specialized cells in the visual cortex that respond to certain shapes and forms in sensory information. When we look at a cube, for example, some cells in our visual cortex respond to its distinctive features—its angles and lines in various orientations. Our perception of the cube is constructed from the relationship of these elements.

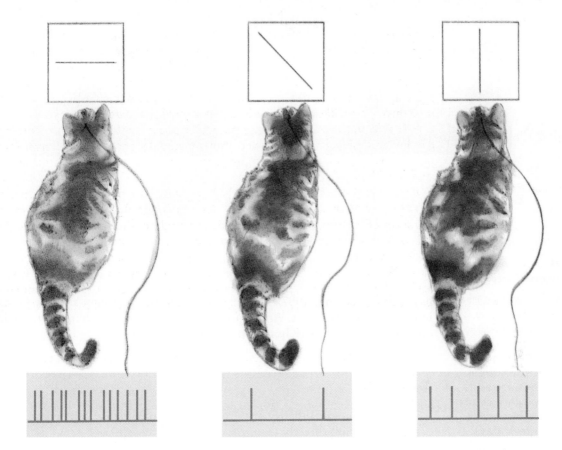

Figure 4.22
Feature Detection

The theory that perception is constructed from bits of sensory information was further supported by Hubel and Wiesel (1979). Their work demonstrated that individual neurons in a cat's brain respond to particular elements in the cat's visual field. For instance, a neuron that responds rapidly when a cat is presented a lighted bar in a horizontal position will respond less rapidly when the bar is in the vertical position and at an intermediate rate for other positions of the bar.

Feature detectors were identified by David Hubel and Torsten Wiesel (1979) through their work on the cortexes of cats. They found that certain columns of cells in the visual cortex respond only to a bar of light in a particular part of the visual field and, as the bar is rotated, that different cells in the column respond in different degrees (see Figure 4.22). They also discovered columns of cells that respond to other features in the visual field—features such as angles, the absence of light, and information about color, shape, and distance (Livingstone & Hubel, 1985).

The research on feature detectors shows the integration of information in the process of perception. Although the ways in which feature detectors function are more intricate than Hermann von Helmholtz would have imagined, they are consistent with his theory that perception is constructed from bits of sensory information.

Spatial Frequency Perception: Support for Ecological Theory   Still other phenomena are more consistent with ecological theory. For example, it seems that parts of the visual system directly perceive complex elements in the visual field. Visual perception begins with an analysis and breakdown of the visual field into *spatial waves,* waves of light and dark (Braddick, 1981). The ability to recognize these waves is called **spatial frequency perception.** As illustrated in Figure 4.23, more closely packed patterns have higher spatial frequencies; less closely packed patterns have lower spatial frequencies.

Spatial frequency perception may be the method utilized by our nervous system to identify the environmental invariants that are important to ecological

Spatial frequency perception
The ability to recognize spatial waves.

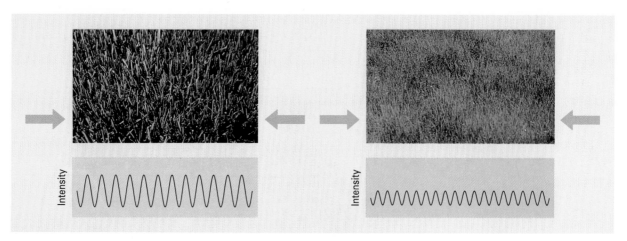

Figure 4.23
Spatial Frequency Perception

The grass in the right-hand photograph, with its fine textures, is characterized by high spatial frequencies. The grass in the left-hand photograph, having a coarse texture, is characterized by comparatively low spatial frequencies. The diagrams show the variations in the intensity of the light across the center of each photograph.

psychologists (Katz, 1987). For example, texture cues may actually be a combination of spatial waves. And figure-ground effects have been shown to depend on spatial frequencies (Klymenko & Weisstein, 1986).

Recap

- Ecological theory argues that the perceptual system perceives information directly from the environment.

- According to ecological theory, perception is not a form of information processing; it is simply the process of picking up information from the environment.

- Environmental invariants are complex properties of the world that are apparent to any active observer.

- Ambient flow—a pattern of motion created in relation to objects in the environment—gives us specific information about the size, distance, and shape of objects.

- James Gibson insisted that traditional methodologies limit the reliability of constructionist findings and strongly advocated studying perception under natural conditions.

- According to ecological theory, illusions are simply the product of the absence of direct perceptual cues.

- Detailed studies of certain perceptual functions seem to indicate that both constructionist and ecological theories contribute to our understanding of perception.

Conclusion

This is the first chapter in which we have focused on the behavior and experience of a whole person. Rather than cells or organs of the body like eyes and amygdalas, we have now turned to what people actually experience about the world. This transition seems to be reflected in the disagreements between the constructionists and the Gibsonians, who seem to stand on either side of the gap. From the perspective of neurons and receptors, millions of tiny bits of information must somehow be combined and interpreted to yield the tiniest piece of human experience. But from the perspective of the whole, perceiving person, what is remarkable is how effortlessly and automatically the facts of the world appear to us.

Both constructionists and Gibsonians agree that the information we collect from the environment becomes our experience of the world. And obviously, once we have acquired information, we may process it further. The issue seems to resolve to a question of how much information the environment provides, and how tuned we are to pick up that information. The Gibsonian research suggests that the information available in the world may be richer, more structured, and better organized than constructionists have believed. Equally clear, not everything we know comes to us "directly," so at some point, something like construction must occur.

And whatever one's perspective, the most remarkable aspect of perception is the incredibly complex quantity of information we can in fact acquire, so quickly and so effortlessly. The physical complexity of the brain at first may seem our most impressive characteristic. Far more impressive, however, is what that physical organism can do, beginning with perceiving the world in which we live.

Chapter 5   Consciousness

Décalcomanie, René Magritte, 1966

Gateways All we know of ourselves and our world is what we are conscious of—even though we recognize that much goes on in life that escapes our awareness.

Modern psychologists have sought to understand consciousness not by proposing grand theories about its essential nature, but by studying facets of its makeup—*states* of consciousness and our movement in and out of these varying states. Psychologists have learned a good deal about how consciousness varies daily between sleep and wakefulness, and how it is affected by drugs, disease, and other influences. They've also learned how these variations affect our abilities.

In this chapter we will discuss topics that relate to other chapters as well. One example is attention, which plays a large part in the preceding chapter on perception. Other examples are hypnosis and drugs, which figure in our later discussions of psychological disorders and their treatment (Chapters 15 and 16).

At a party years ago, a friend of mine boasted that he could hypnotize anybody, no matter how resistant. At that time, I thought hypnosis was a bunch of mumbo jumbo, so I took up his challenge. The "hypnotist" went into the kitchen to "prepare" himself and emerged with a lighted candle on a plate. I was told in a monotonous voice to hold the plate in my left hand and to stare into the candle while making certain gestures with my right hand: "First, make a circle on bottom of the plate. Now make a circle with your hand in the air to your right. Now trace a line on your forehead. Now return to the bottom of the plate." More instructions followed.

After what seemed like a lot of this silly stuff, the candle was taken from my left hand and somebody bruskly grabbed my right and rubbed it with a towel. Then, I was told to wake up my trance. I triumphantly asserted that I had not been hypnotized. Everyone burst into laughter. Somebody held a mirror up in front of my face and, to my horror, I found that my face was covered with black lines and figures. The hypnotist explained that while under a profound hypnotic induction I had painted my own face with soot.

I was bewildered. When the laughing and joking died down, another friend took me aside and quickly explained what had happened. Unbeknown to me, the bottom of the plate had been coated with soot from the candle before the hypnosis session was begun. Because I was paying such close attention to the candle and to the mysterious instructions of the hypnotist, I hadn't noticed the gritty feeling of the bottom of the plate or my hand becoming blacker and blacker as I carried out the hypnotist's instructions.

Had I been hypnotized? Your answer to this question will depend on your understanding of consciousness. Is hypnotism a special kind of awareness? Or is it just a variation in ordinary consciousness—one in which the hypnotized person is very relaxed and pays close attention to the hypnotist. As you will see in this chapter, hypnotism is just one of several mysteries that are easier to understand when you know something about variations in states of consciousness.

The Dimensions of Consciousness

Consciousness is an awareness of one's thoughts, feelings, and surroundings. States of consciousness are constantly shifting in their focus, in their degree, and in their quality.

The *focus of consciousness* is what you're conscious of. You're always aware of some things around you, and more or less aware of others. Right now you're conscious of the words on this page. Are you comfortable in your seat? By asking you this question, we've changed the focus of your consciousness. Suddenly you're thinking about your chair, the ache in your shoulder, the empty can of soda on your desk.

Consciousness is a continuum, ranging from deep sleep at one end, through drowsiness and daydreaming, to close attention at the other. Your *degree of consciousness* is how conscious you are; it is your level of awareness.

Consciousness An awareness of one's thoughts, feelings, and surroundings.

119

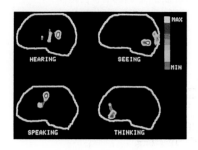

Different areas of the brain are most active when the person is doing different things. You can see this in the PET scan, where the brighter colors indicate greater activity.

The third dimension of consciousness is the *quality of consciousness,* the kind of consciousness you experience. Each day your mind undergoes normal changes in the way it operates: at times you daydream; at other times you're focused on a problem. Drugs or mental illness can produce even more dramatic changes in the quality of consciousness.

Notice that these three dimensions—the focus, degree, and quality of consciousness—are *subjective;* only the individual experiencing them knows what they are. This is why the study of consciousness poses very special problems.

In Chapter 1 we described how psychology evolved from the study of consciousness to the study of behavior. For many decades, consciousness had no place in the science that psychology had become. But in the 1960s, the trend reversed. During that decade, technological advances led to the discovery that activity in the brain is related to states of consciousness. Using PET scans and other devices, researchers can now see the changes in the brain that accompany changes in consciousness (Phelps & Mazziota, 1985). Even more important has been the development of experimental techniques that allow the rigorous study of conscious experience and the states of consciousness examined in this chapter—attention, sleep, dreams.

Attention: The Changing Focus of Consciousness

The focus of your consciousness is constantly shifting. A few minutes ago you were intent on your reading. Then we asked if you were comfortable. That question redirected your consciousness; it focused your attention on something else.

Attention is the mental function that makes you fully aware of an element in your environment. When you're reading, you're paying attention to the words on the page. If you stop to think about the chair you're sitting on or the party this Saturday night, you're refocusing your attention.

Selective Attention

Sensations, thoughts, feelings, memories, objects, events—all compete for your attention. But you are able to focus your attention on just one thing at a time. In a crowded restaurant, you can listen to the friend you're having dinner with, or you can eavesdrop on the conversation at the table next to you. You can't do both at once. At best, you can shift back and forth quickly, but you're bound to miss bits of each conversation in the process. Attention acts like a filter, separating from all the stimuli we could be aware of the single stimulus on which our consciousness is focused (Cherry, 1953).

In general, people don't notice, understand, or remember very much about a stimulus to which they have not been paying attention (Johnston & Dark, 1986). When subjects are given two stimuli at once and told to pay attention to just one of them, they learn very little about the other.

For example, in one study, a group of college undergraduates were asked to watch a short videotape (Neisser, 1979). On the tape, three cartoon images were superimposed: three players in white jerseys passing a basketball around, three players in black jerseys passing a second basketball around, and a woman walking along carrying an umbrella (see Figure 5.1). The subjects were told to press a key each time the players wearing black jerseys passed the ball. After watching the tape, the students were asked if they had noticed anything strange about it.

Attention The mental function that makes the individual fully conscious of an element in the environment.

Figure 5.1
Selective Attention

Subjects asked to watch a video-tape and count the number of times the players in the black jerseys passed the ball never noticed the woman with the umbrella sauntering through the game.

Only a few had noticed the woman with the umbrella; the rest were dumbfounded to see her when the tape was replayed.

But there is a puzzle, here. If we are not aware of the content of unattended stimuli, then how do we ever notice something new? Consider, for example, the opposite side of the *cocktail party effect* mentioned above. At a restaurant, or a party, we have to block out conversations around us in order to understand the person we are with. But if your name is mentioned by someone around you, you will instantly recognize it, and your attention will be directed toward that conversation. The question is, then, how we can ignore other conversations, but yet recognize our name when we hear it mentioned in one of the conversations we're ignoring. The answer seems to be that our attentional processes follow unattended stimuli just enough to discover if they are significant, but not enough to understand them (Shiffrin, 1985).

To demonstrate the impact of unattended stimuli, psychologists James Lackner and M. F. Garrett (1972) played two different messages in their subjects' ears, one in the right ear and one in the left. The subjects were asked to focus on an ambiguous message in one ear—something like "He put out the lantern to signal the attack." They had no way of knowing whether "he" had extinguished the lantern or set it outside on a window sill. In the other ear was either a message that helped clarify the ambiguous statement ("He extinguished the lantern") or a totally unrelated one. The subjects who heard the clarifying message denied hearing it, but that second message influenced their interpretation of the first.

We've been talking about deliberately directing attention to an image or a conversation or a statement—in much the same way that you direct the beam of a flashlight to illuminate what you want to see in a dark room. But sometimes you can't control your attention. Sometimes it's as if someone else is holding the flashlight.

Look at Figure 5.2. Going down the list, quickly name, out loud, the color in which each word is printed. It's not easy, is it? Most people find it almost impossible to keep their attention on the color of the ink instead of on the words themselves. When you see a word, your automatic response is to read it, not to think about the color of the ink it's printed in (Stroop, 1935).

Although we can control the focus of our attention, the stimuli around us often demand attention. The more intense, vivid, or relevant a stimulus, the more likely we are to attend to it.

Figure 5.2
The Stroop Test

Try to read aloud the color of the letters in each word. It's hard because the meaning of the words commands your attention.

BLUE	GREEN
GREEN	RED
PURPLE	ORANGE
GREEN	YELLOW
RED	RED
GRAY	GRAY
BLUE	YELLOW
BLUE	PURPLE

The Functions of Attention

Why are most of us able to focus attention on just one thing at a time? Attention may be a tool that blocks out stimuli that are not immediately relevant. Your attention mechanism sifts through all of the stimuli around you and filters out those that are not important right now. Or it could be that the nervous system simply can't process more than one stream of thought at a time. We know, for instance, that people think better when they pay attention (Broadbent, 1958; Shiffrin & Schneider, 1977). Perhaps the effort of analyzing stimuli into two or more meaningful experiences demands too much mental energy (Kahneman, 1973; Schweickert & Boggs, 1984).

Both of these explanations could be correct. It's possible that people focus their attention on just one object because they choose not to be distracted by other objects *and* because that object is related to a course of action they're planning to take *and* because, having devoted their attention to that object, they've exhausted the cognitive resources they might devote to another.

We all daydream frequently, rehearsing past events and imagining the future. In one study, only 30 percent of students reported that they paid attention in class; most of the others were probably daydreaming.

When Attention Wanders: Daydreams

Sometimes your attention wanders from the task at hand and you daydream. In fact, just about all of us daydream regularly. Jerome Singer (1976) surveyed a group of people ages eighteen to fifty and found that 90 percent of them admitted to daydreaming on a given day.

People daydream in all kinds of places, under all kinds of circumstances. One study of college students found that they actually pay attention to the content of lectures only about a third of the time they're in class (Singer, 1976). The rest of the time they're daydreaming!

What do people daydream about? Usually you relive an event (the argument you had with a friend yesterday) or anticipate an event (a job interview next Thursday). Most people stick pretty close to reality, maybe improving their "lines" a bit. According to Singer, there's very little difference between daydreaming and planning. Your daydream of the upcoming job interview helps prepare you for that interview.

A small number of people seem to go beyond normal daydreaming. These fantasy-prone people were identified by researchers who wanted to know why some people are more easily hypnotized than others (Wilson & Barber, 1981; J. Hilgard, 1979). Fantasy-prone people daydream more than other people do, and their daydreams are very elaborate. Psychologists Steven Lynn and Judith Rhue (1987) found that fantasy-prone subjects score high on tests of vivid mental imagery, absorption in their fantasies, and creativity. They also found that those people tend to recall more physical abuse and punishment at the hands of their parents, and that they were lonelier as children.

Subliminal Perception

In Chapter 3 we talked about *absolute threshold,* the level at which most people report noticing a stimulus. In order to report a stimulus—to say, "Yes, I hear it now"—you have to be conscious of that stimulus. And if you are to be conscious of the stimulus, it has to be of a certain intensity or frequency. But even though you may not be conscious of a stimulus, you still may respond to it. When you fail to report sensing a stimulus but give other evidence that you're aware of it, your response to that stimulus is called **subliminal perception.** Subliminal stimuli are too weak or brief for the individual to be conscious of them, yet they affect behavior.

In one study of subliminal stimuli, three different sets of images were spliced into a videotape (Robles et al., 1987). On one tape the images were humorous (cartoon characters); on another they were threatening (disfigured faces, devils, monsters); on the third they were simply gray frames. The researchers showed each tape to a different group of college students and then used a questionnaire to evaluate each group's level of anxiety. Not one student detected the subliminal images, but each group of students displayed different levels of anxiety (see Figure 5.3). The students who saw the tape with the cartoon characters spliced into it showed the lowest levels of anxiety. Those who saw the tape with the

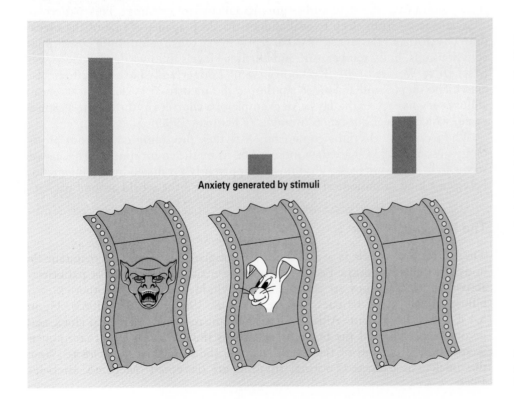

Anxiety generated by stimuli

Figure 5.3
Subliminal Perception

Images like the ones on the left were spliced into three video tapes (the videos were the same, only the images were different) and played to three different groups of subjects. Even though the images were subliminal— none of the subjects reported seeing them—still they influenced the subjects' levels of anxiety, as can be seen in the graphs.

Subliminal perception   The response to a stimulus below the absolute threshold.

threatening images showed the highest levels of anxiety. And those who saw the tape with the gray frames showed intermediate levels of anxiety. Clearly the students had been affected by the subliminal stimuli in the tapes, even though they were not conscious of them.

One interpretation of the research on subliminal perception is that the mind does some preliminary processing on the information that comes from the senses and directs some of this information to our consciousness (Dixon, 1981). We can't process every stimulus to full consciousness. But this mechanism does allow us to respond to stimuli that are particularly important to us in some way.

Recap

- Attention changes the focus of consciousness.

- Attention separates from all the stimuli the individual could be aware of the single stimulus on which consciousness is focused.

- People do not learn very much from stimuli to which they don't pay attention, but those stimuli can affect their behavior.

- When people daydream, they usually relive or anticipate an event.

- Unlike most people, whose daydreams stay close to reality, fantasy-prone people have elaborate, well-developed daydreams.

- The effect of subliminal stimuli is primarily emotional.

Rhythms of Consciousness

Consciousness is constantly changing, not only in focus but also in degree. For most of us, our level of consciousness is lowest in the middle of the night when we're sound asleep, rises when we wake up in the morning, reaches a peak sometime during the day, and begins to fall in late evening. This pattern of consciousness—from sleep to wakefulness to sleep again—is one of the **circadian rhythms,** cycles of activity that repeat every twenty-four hours or so. Like consciousness, body temperature and hormone levels follow a daily cycle as well (Aschoff & Weaver, 1981; Kerkhoff, 1985). Longer and shorter rhythms also exist. The most familiar longer rhythm is the menstrual cycle, which repeats about every twenty-eight days. An example of a shorter rhythm is the alertness cycle, which lasts about ninety minutes (Kleitman, 1982).

Where do these rhythms come from? Are they programmed into our physiology in some way? Or are they imposed on us by the environment? The answer seems to be both. Circadian rhythms are apparently produced by the interaction between a kind of biological clock in our brains and the world around us.

The Biological Clock

The **biological clock** is a name for the mechanism that helps maintain the body's circadian rhythms. People and animals maintain regular daily patterns of activity even when they are isolated from daylight, watches, and other external influences that could be cues to time (Aschoff, 1969; Kleitman, 1963). Figure 5.4 illustrates this point. Although the mechanism of the biological clock may involve other parts of the brain, in mammals the most important component seems to be a portion of the hypothalamus, the *suprachiasmatic nucleus*. When this nucleus is damaged, normal rhythms are disrupted (Meijer & Rietveld, 1989).

Circadian rhythm A cycle of activity that repeats every twenty-four hours or so.

Biological clock The internal mechanism that helps maintain the body's circadian rhythms.

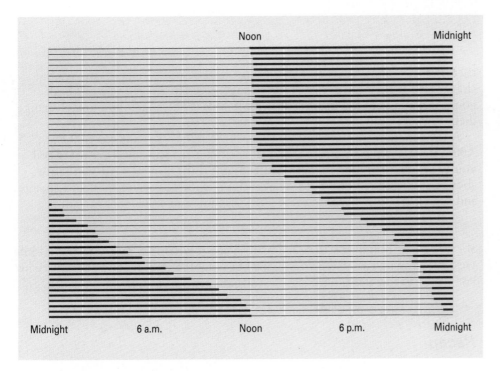

Figure 5.4
Normal and Free-Running Circadian Rhythms in a Laboratory Rat

Each horizontal line represents a day and each vertical line a time. The thickened horizontal bars indicate when the rat was active. As long as the experimenters turned the lights off at noon and on at midnight, the rats kept active in the afternoon and evening. (Rats like the dark!) But when the experimenters maintained a constant dim illumination, the rats went out of synchrony with the 24-hour day and began to drift later and later in the day.

Source: Adapted from Groblewski, Nuñez & Gold, 1980.

Although our biological clocks are fairly regular, they actually operate on a twenty-five-hour cycle. Individuals vary considerably, but deprived of external cues to time, most subjects fall behind "real" time by about an hour a day (Moore-Ede, Czeisler & Richardson, 1983). The same is true of experimental animals kept isolated from daylight. In a particularly dramatic demonstration of this phenomenon, French geologist Michel Siffre (1975) spent six months in a Texas cave, isolated from external time cues (see Figure 5.5). Although his "days" seemed normal to him, Siffre's cycles actually averaged around twenty-eight hours.

Resetting the Clock: The Role of the Environment

The biological clock is "set" to run on a twenty-five-hour day, yet each day it adjusts to a twenty-four-hour day. How? With the help of time cues in the environment (Czeisler et al., 1986). The most important of these cues is light. Patterns of light and dark reset our biological clocks every day. In the absence of the light-dark cycle, the days begin to stretch out, as they did for Siffre in the cave.

Although the biological clock is reset each day, it can be adjusted by only about an hour in any single day (Folkard et al., 1985). Large adjustments—the kind made necessary by a plane trip from New York to California, for example—take several days. During that period, travelers suffer from *jet lag,* a form of stress that occurs when the body's natural rhythm is out of phase with the environment.

It's easier to delay your biological clock than to advance it. Because the biological clock runs on a twenty-five-hour day, your body is already advancing the clock an hour each day just to keep time with the sun. This means that it's easier to adjust to westbound travel than to eastbound travel. Traveling west, you delay your biological clock; traveling east, you have to advance it even more than the one hour that's necessary when you stay in one place (Desir et

Puzzle It Out!

Factories, hospitals, airports—all kinds of organizations operate around the clock. This means that many of the people employed by them work odd hours. To even out the inconveniences of shift work, many employers change their workers' shifts regularly, sometimes as often as once a week.

A local manufacturing plant operates three shifts: 7:00 A.M. to 3:00 P.M., 3:00 P.M. to 11:00 P.M., and 11:00 P.M. to 7:00 A.M. The company has asked you to set up a regular schedule for changing shifts. Given what you know about circadian rhythms, what do you think is the best pattern of shift changes and how often do you think these changes should be made?

al., 1981). Although it's impractical to arrange a trip so that you travel only west, you can at least make your plans knowing that you're going to experience less stress on the westbound leg of your journey.

Figure 5.5
Life in a Cave

Under the watchful electronic eye of scientists from NASA, Michel Siffre spent six months in the depths of a Texas cave. His sole communication with the outside world consisted of brief daily requests to turn the lights on when he began his day and to turn them off when he was ready to go to sleep. Although he exercised regularly and fed himself gourmet astronaut meals, Siffre found the experiment an ordeal. He wrote, "Whether because of confinement, solitude, or both, my mental processes and manual dexterity deteriorated gravely and inexorably toward the end of my stay . . . Now, long after my months in Midnight Cave, I still . . . suffer psychological wounds that I do not understand." (Siffre, 1975)

Beta waves The pattern of brain waves at a frequency of 14 to 30 cycles per second that is characteristic of a high level of activity in the cerebral cortex.

Alpha waves The pattern of brain waves at a frequency of 8 to 13 cycles per second that is characteristic of a state of resting wakefulness.

Recap

- The rhythm of consciousness is a circadian rhythm, a cycle of activity that repeats every twenty-four hours or so.

- The biological clock is a mechanism that helps maintain the body's circadian rhythms.

- In the absence of environmental time cues—particularly a regular pattern of light and dark—the biological clock operates on a twenty-five-hour cycle.

Sleeping and Dreaming

The most prominent circadian rhythm is the pattern of waking and sleeping. Our days are divided between periods of wakefulness and sleep. And within those periods, our level of consciousness is constantly changing.

The Stages of Sleep

In Chapter 2 we described the electroencephalograph, a machine that allows us to monitor the electrical activity of the cerebral cortex. The machine represents those patterns on a paper chart called an *electroencephalogram (EEG)*. When the neurons are busy—that is, when we're actively responding to the stimuli around us—they fire separately, producing on the EEG small, rapid, irregular movements, called **beta waves.** When the neurons are at rest, they tend to fire together, producing larger, more regular movements called **alpha waves.** Using the electroencephalograph and its output, psychologists have identified five stages of sleep.

Quiet Sleep: The First Stages of Sleep EEG recordings reveal that people go through a series of stages of brain activity as they fall asleep. Figure 5.6 shows the electrical activity in the brain as the individual moves from wakefulness into the different stages of sleep.

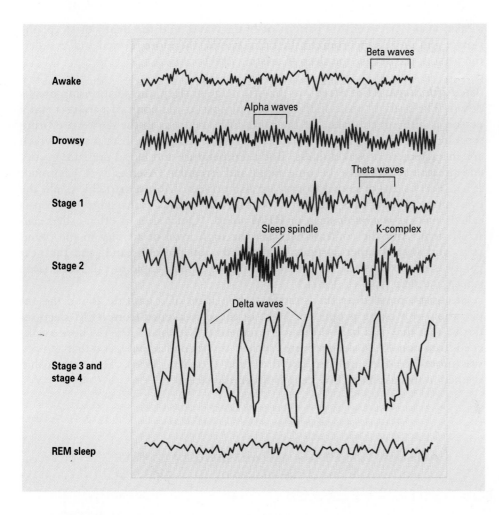

Figure 5.6
Stages of Sleep

Each stage of sleep is recognized
by characteristic waves in the
EEG. Stage 1 by theta waves,
Stage 2 by sleep spindles and
K-complexes, Stage 3 by the ap-
pearance of delta waves, and
Stage 4 by the predominance of
delta waves.

1. *Stage 1: Relaxation* In the first stage of sleep, you're relaxed, with eyes closed. Breathing and heart rate slow, muscles begin to loosen, and body temperature starts to drop. During this stage, alpha waves are replaced by a slightly faster rhythm known as *theta waves*. Stage 1 is a brief transition between sleep and waking lasting about ten minutes.

2. *Stage 2: Drifting off* As you drift off to sleep, your brain waves become more irregular. Among the alpha waves, there are occasional large waves known as **K-complexes** and bursts of rapid activity known as **sleep spindles.** The spindles may be part of a mechanism that lowers your response to stimulation, making sleep easier.

3. *Stage 3: Deepening sleep* As you move into deeper sleep, your respiration and heart rate continue to slow and your muscles further relax. As the neurons in the cortex fire more slowly and in synchrony, the pattern of alpha waves and sleep spindles is increasingly accompanied by slow deep waves called **delta waves.**

4. *Stage 4: Profound sleep* In Stage 4 sleep, more than half of the EEG activity consists of delta waves. By the time you reach this stage, you are not responsive. Sound, touch, and other external stimuli show up on the EEG as brief electrical changes in the brain but make no impression on your consciousness (Williams, Tepas & Morlock, 1962). People awakened from Stage 4 sleep are often confused and disoriented, and report little if any mental activity.

It takes from 30 minutes to about an hour to move through the first four stages of sleep, the stages we call *quiet sleep*. During that time, we generally see

K-complexes Periods of long,
high-amplitude EEG waves that
along with sleep spindles are
characteristic of Stage 2 sleep.

Sleep spindles Short bursts of
high-frequency EEG waves that
are one of two components characteristic of Stage 2 sleep.

Delta waves The pattern of
brain waves at a rate of 1 to 5
cycles per second that first appears in Stage 3 sleep and is
characteristic of Stage 4 sleep.

a relationship between the pattern of brain waves and the depth of sleep: the slower and more synchronized the brain waves, the more relaxed and less alert the person; the deeper the sleep (Carlson, 1991).

The Fifth Stage: REM Sleep   In the fifth stage of sleep, this relationship breaks down. The body is profoundly relaxed, almost to the point of paralysis and a person is difficult to wake. At the same time, neurons in the cortex are firing separately, producing an EEG pattern very like that of the beta waves, which are characteristic of wakefulness. Body temperature and blood pressure go up, and breathing and pulse become rapid and irregular (Aserinsky & Kleitman, 1953). Early signs of sexual arousal are also present. Most remarkable of all, the eyes move rapidly back and forth beneath the eyelids. This stage of sleep is called *rapid eye movement* sleep or **REM sleep.** (Quiet sleep is often called *non-REM sleep*. And the contrast between the high level of activity in the brain, eyes, and several other systems of the body, on the one hand, and the near paralysis of the muscles, on the other, has led some people to call REM sleep *paradoxical sleep* [Jouvet, 1967].)

Scientists, puzzled by this strange combination of responses, found the explanation by waking people up. Most of those awakened from REM sleep reported that they had been dreaming (Dement & Kleitman, 1957). Those awakened from non-REM sleep reported little if any mental activity, and that activity was more like thinking than like dreaming (Foulkes, 1985). The relationship seemed unmistakable: REM sleep is dreaming sleep.

Figure 5.7
A Night's Sleep

Four or five times a night we slip down through the levels of sleep only to return upward again to engage in bouts of REM sleep. These bouts of REM sleep, in which people are very relaxed and difficult to awaken, are accompanied by our most elaborate dreams.

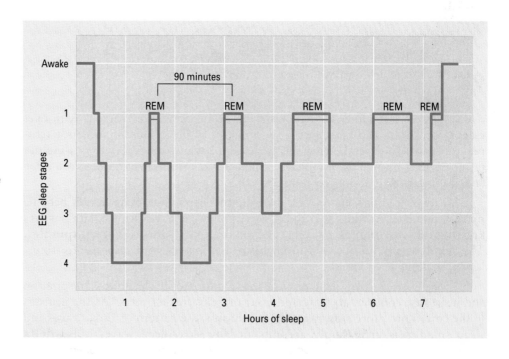

REM sleep   Sleep characterized by rapid eye movement and high levels of activity in the brain and sympathetic nervous system, but very low levels of activity in the muscles; also called *paradoxical sleep.*

Throughout the night you move in and out of the different stages of sleep, entering REM sleep approximately every ninety minutes, as illustrated in Figure 5.7. Between REM periods, you're in one of the stages of quiet sleep. Early in the night, Stages 3 and 4 are most common; later sleep is divided mostly between Stage 2 and REM sleep. See Table 5.1 for a comparison of wakefulness, non-REM sleep, and REM sleep.

Puzzle It Out!

Statesman and inventor Ben Franklin was always finding ingenious things to do with his house key. Tradition has it that Franklin used a key and a washbasin to wake himself up from brief naps. He would doze off in a chair holding the large metal key in his hand. When he'd been asleep for a while, the key would fall out of his hand and tumble into the washbasin, waking him. How did Franklin's "alarm clock" work?

Table 5.1
A Comparison of Wakefulness, Non-REM Sleep, and REM Sleep

Characteristic	Wakefulness	Non-REM Sleep	REM Sleep
EEG	Primarily beta waves	Alpha waves, sleep spindles, delta waves	Primarily beta waves
Eye movement	Present	None, or a few slow movements	Rapid
Body movement	Present	Occasional gross body movements	Muscle twitches in face and limbs
Responsiveness to surroundings	Responsive	Diminished	Greatly diminished; individual difficult to arouse
Thought processes	Fully operational	Dreams infrequent and unstructured	Frequent vivid dreams
Muscle tone	Normal	Reduced	Completely relaxed
Physiological measures	Heart rate and breathing normal; blood pressure uniform; body temperature normal	Heart rate and breathing slow; blood pressure reduced; body temperature low	Heart rate and breathing irregular and rapid; blood pressure highly variable; body temperature unregulated; penis erect; vagina engorged

Source: Adapted from Foulkes, 1966.

Why Do We Sleep?

We spend nearly a third of our lives sleeping. Although people have remained awake for close to nineteen days, laboratory studies indicate that most of us find it difficult to stay awake for more than sixty hours. When we're deprived of sleep, we get cranky and have difficulty concentrating, particularly on boring tasks (Horne, 1985).

Many theories have been offered to explain why we sleep. One suggests that we sleep to replenish our resources. According to this view, sleep is necessary to maintain biological functions. While we're sleeping, body temperature falls and heart rate and respiration slow, almost as though the body is conserving energy. At the same time, the production of proteins increases. These proteins are essential to the repair and maintenance of the body's organs and tissues (Aschoff & Weaver, 1981). Sleep may also play a role in the physical development of children. The hormones that determine the pace of that development are secreted primarily during quiet sleep (Pekkanen, 1982).

Consistent with the "repair" theory of sleep is the finding that vigorous activity increases the amount of time spent sleeping. For example, one study of marathon runners found that they slept about seven hours a night the two nights before a race and about eight and half hours a night the two nights after the race (Shapiro et al., 1981).

But other findings suggest that sleep may not be necessary for biological functioning. Some people seem to survive remarkably well on very little sleep. In one recorded case, a woman regularly slept less than an hour a night, yet functioned normally (Meddis, Pearson & Langford, 1973). And Thomas Edison supposedly slept only three hours a night, which left him a lot of time to be inventive.

Sometimes the nature of their work means that people miss a night's sleep. For example, air traffic controllers often have to work an extra shift when weather conditions are bad. EEGs tell us that when people are very tired, they microsleep—they fall asleep for a few seconds at a time (Webb & Cartwright, 1979). And when people microsleep, their response rates and coordination suffer (Frese & Harwich, 1984). This can mean the difference between life and death if a controller misses something in the complex array of lights on the radar screen.

Virtually the only effect of sleep deprivation is the need to sleep more (Horne, 1985). People who have been deprived of sleep in the laboratory for fifty or sixty hours quickly make up some of that lost sleep by sleeping thirteen to fifteen hours at a stretch. After a few days, their sleep pattern returns to their normal seven or eight hours.

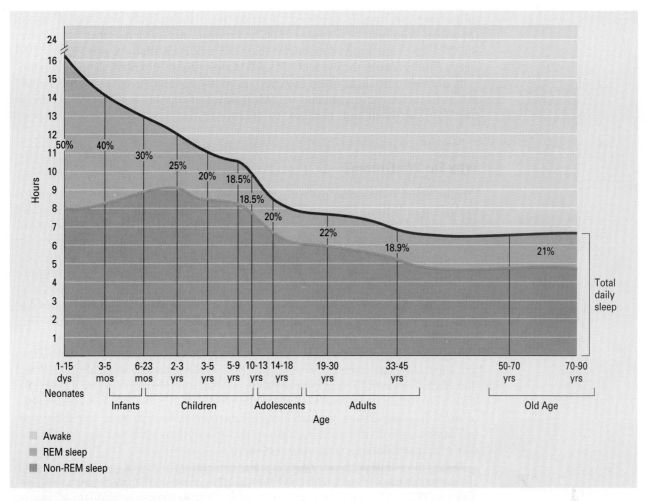

Figure 5.8
Dreaming and Age

One of the reasons that scientists think that dreaming may be important to well-being is that children and young animals do so much of it. As the brain matures in infancy and early childhood, REM sleep declines from 50 percent to 20 percent of total sleeping time.

Another theory suggests that people and other animals sleep to keep out of trouble, to avoid the times of day that they are not equipped to handle (Campbell & Tobler, 1984). Owls, for example, sleep during the day because they aren't "designed" to cope with the hazards of daylight. This theory fits well with the observation that minor sleep deprivation doesn't seem to hurt us. But it doesn't explain why people make up lost sleep. After all, there's no need to avoid danger for an extra two hours tonight because you missed the chance to avoid danger last night.

A final theory is that we sleep in order to dream. Some facts suggest that dreaming might be an important activity. At birth, REM sleep occupies fully 50 percent of all sleeping time, declining rapidly to 20 percent by three to five years and declining further to just under 15 percent in persons over sixty-five (Roffwarg, Munzio & Dement, 1966) (see Figure 5.8). Moreover people and animals who have been deprived of REM sleep seem to make up for lost dreams; they spend more of their total time sleeping in REM sleep. In addition, these makeup sessions are longer and more intense than usual periods of REM sleep, and the eyes move more rapidly during them (Dement, 1960).

But the fact that we compensate for lost REM sleep is not evidence that REM-sleep deprivation harms performance or well-being. We find the same type of compensation among people who have been deprived of non-REM sleep; that is, they tend to make up for it in longer sessions of non-REM sleep.

Other findings are inconsistent. Some researchers claim that REM deprivation diminishes our ability to perform complex mental tasks; others insist that it cures some forms of depression (Vogel, 1975; Vogel et al., 1980). And we know that rats can be deprived of REM sleep indefinitely with no ill effects (Morden, Mitchell, & Dement, 1967). In sum, the evidence that we require REM sleep is no more conclusive than the evidence that we need non-REM sleep. And certainly the evidence for REM sleep doesn't explain sleep in general.

It may be that all of these theories are partly correct. Perhaps sleep evolved as a way to protect organisms at certain times of the day and to give the body time to repair itself and, perhaps, to dream.

Why Do We Dream?

Dreams seem even more puzzling than sleep. Many theories have been offered to explain dreaming. The most important are Freud's psychoanalytic theory and information processing theories.

Freudian Dream Analysis   Sigmund Freud believed that dreams are our way of working through the conflicts we experience in our daily lives. According to Freud, all people have impulses—aggressive and sexual—that are not socially acceptable. Society teaches us to control those impulses when we're awake. When we're sleeping, however, our defenses relax, and those impulses find symbolic expression in our dreams.

Research suggests that aggression is a fairly common theme in dreams. In a pair of studies that spanned two generations of college students, Calvin Hall and his colleagues (1982) analyzed more than fifteen hundred dreams (see Table 5.2). They found that aggression was a very common theme, especially in the dreams of men. In comparison, a much smaller number of dreams were explicitly sexual: about a third of the male students and fewer than a fifth of the female students reported dreams with sexual content.

If dreams are expressions of aggressive and sexual impulses, why aren't they all about aggression or sex? Freud would have answered that even in sleep we disguise the content of our impulses, only indirectly expressing them in our dreams. Thus we have to examine dreams at two levels. First, there's the obvious content of a dream—the characters, the story—what Freud called the **manifest content.** Then, underlying the characters and the story is the **latent content** of the dream, its meaning. Freud believed that every object and event in the manifest dream is a symbol for something that cannot be expressed directly. A dreamer who has hidden sexual impulses might dream about a long conversation. A dreamer who has hidden murderous impulses might dream about a terrible accident, an accident in which he or she plays no part.

Freud believed that if he could decipher the meaning of dreams, he could discover why people behave the way they do. So the analysis of dreams became an important part of his therapy for psychological disorders.

Although Freud's theory might explain the form and content of dreams, it does not explain *why* people dream. Freud was writing on the subject more than fifty years before the discovery of REM sleep and its association with dreaming. He did not know that babies and animals have REM sleep and so presumably dream (Meddis, 1979; Campbell & Tobler, 1984). Obviously babies and animals are not responding to social pressure; they have no reason to hide their natural impulses. There must be other reasons why people and animals dream.

Information Processing Theories   Freud's theory focuses on the emotional content of dreams; information processing theories stress the cognitive content of dreams. One of the latter theories suggests that dreaming is part of the information processing that goes on in the brain. It's a kind of house cleaning, whereby the mind sorts through its files and discards unnecessary information (Crick & Mitchison, 1983).

Manifest content   The parts of a dream—the story, the characters—that the individual recognizes immediately.

Latent content   The underlying meaning of a dream.

Content	1947–1950 Sample		1979–1980 Sample	
	Men	Women	Men	Women
Percentage of aggressive acts per character	0.34	0.24	0.32	0.23
Percentage of aggressive dreams in which the dreamer was the aggressor	0.40	0.33	0.35	0.37
Percentage of aggressive acts that were physical (versus verbal)	0.50	0.34	0.57	0.39
Percentage of friendly acts per character	0.21	0.22	0.16	0.17
Percentage of friendly dreams in which the dreamer was the initiator	0.50	0.47	0.57	0.51
Percentage of dreamers who reported at least one sexual dream	0.38	0.17	0.24	0.10
Percentage of dream characters who were male	0.67	0.48	0.67	0.53
Percentage of familiar characters	0.45	0.58	0.55	0.62
Percentage of dreams with unfortunate events	0.41	0.41	0.36	0.43
Percentage of dreams with clothing references	0.28	0.54	0.10	0.34
Percentage of dreams with weapon references	0.12	0.03	0.15	0.04
Percentage of outdoor dreams	0.51	0.39	0.49	0.37

Source: Adapted from Hall et al., 1982.

Table 5.2
The Content of Dreams

Calvin Hall and his colleagues discovered many interesting differences in the dreams of men and women in our culture. Men are more likely to dream about aggression (particularly physical aggression), other men, sex, the outdoors, and weapons. Women are more likely to dream about people who are familiar and about clothing. Most of these gender differences were observed in both samples, despite the changes in sexual behavior and relationships that took place in the thirty years that intervened between the two studies.

Another theory suggests that dreams help organize information so that we remember it. This theory is supported by research that shows that REM sleep increases during periods of learning (for example, see Block, Hennevin & LeConte, 1977). And several studies demonstrate that subjects who learn material just before they fall asleep are less likely to remember that material the next morning if their REM sleep has been systematically disturbed. In one of those studies, ten pairs of male students volunteered to spend a night sleeping in a laboratory. At 9:00 P.M. each pair of volunteers studied a list of words, several sentences, and a paragraph. During the night, one member of each pair was systematically deprived of REM sleep. The next morning, the students were awakened and asked to write down what they had learned the night before. The REM-deprived students had more difficulty remembering the material (Empson & Clarke, 1970).

It may be that dreams have no function at all. According to this theory, when we're asleep the parts of the brain that handle thought and memory aren't connected to the real world, but they continue to be active. The result is an essentially random succession of thoughts, images, and feelings that takes the form of a dream. The parts of the brain that make sense of our experiences when we're awake make a kind of dream sense out of these experiences when we're asleep (Antrobus, 1991).

Sleep Disorders

You've probably spent at least one night thrashing around in bed, unable to sleep. Maybe you slept late the previous morning? Maybe you were excited about something you'd done during the day. Whatever the cause, wanting to sleep and not being able to is very frustrating.

Occasional disturbances of sleep are nothing to be concerned about. But regular and severe disruptions of sleep are significant and are known as *sleep disorders*. Sleep disorders fall into three categories: insomnia, disorders of REM sleep, and disorders of non-REM sleep.

Insomnia   You have **insomnia** if you are not sleeping enough or if your pattern of sleep leaves you feeling unrested. You may have difficulty falling asleep, or you may find yourself waking up very early in the morning and not being able to go back to sleep.

Some people who complain of insomnia are trying to sleep more than they actually need to. Insomnia is a common complaint among elderly people, who need an average of only five and a half hours of sleep a night (Kelley, 1985). This population is also prone to a form of temporary insomnia caused by schedule changes or travel. The biological clocks of older people take longer to adjust than the clocks of younger people.

Other people actually get enough sleep but don't know that they've slept or underestimate the amount of time they've slept. When measured, their EEG and REM patterns are normal, as is the time they spend sleeping. Yet when they wake up, these people firmly report that they have not been asleep. One explanation of this phenomenon is that while these people are sleeping, they are dreaming that they are awake (Kellerman, 1981).

Anxiety or excitement can also interfere with sleep. Short periods of sleep loss caused by anxiety or excitement are nothing to worry about. If you're going through one of those periods—during exams, perhaps—you can take some consolation from the research that shows that sleep loss does not affect performance in situations in which you are highly motivated.

But a pattern of sleep loss that lasts several weeks can be a serious problem, particularly if it's associated with bad feelings about oneself. Chronic insomnia is one of the symptoms of depression (Kelley, 1985). In this case, the best treatment for insomnia is treatment of the underlying depression.

Insomniacs can be their own worst enemies. Many such people use barbiturates or alcohol to help them sleep. Over time the nervous system adapts to these drugs: if people take them for several nights, they begin to lose the ability to get to sleep without drugs (Kales & Kales, 1984). In addition, although barbiturates and alcohol tend to make people sleepy, they disrupt normal sleep rhythms, especially those of REM sleep.

Insomnia A chronic problem with falling asleep or with the pattern of sleep.

Insomnia can be caused by something as simple as bad sleeping habits. Therapies for sleeplessness train people to avoid doing anything in bed that is inconsistent with sleep—reading, watching television, eating, discussing family problems, or just tossing and turning. If sleep doesn't come within a few minutes, insomniacs learn to get out of bed and do something relaxing until they feel sleepy. Going to bed and getting up at the same time every day are important parts of the treatment.

Disorders of REM Sleep   Perhaps the most bizarre sleep disorder of all is **narcolepsy.** People with narcolepsy may fall asleep at any time—while talking, walking along the street, driving a car. Sometimes they fall into REM sleep, and the near paralysis that characterizes that sleep is evident during the attack. It's not unusual for someone with narcolepsy to suddenly fall to the ground. And many with narcolepsy report dreams so seemingly real that they insist what they were dreaming actually happened.

Narcoleptic attacks are often triggered by an emotional incident, even by laughing. Although the cause of the disorder is not entirely clear, it seems to stem from a neurological abnormality. Narcolepsy is treated with stimulant drugs (Carlson, 1991).

Disorders of Non-REM Sleep   The profound muscle relaxation that is characteristic of REM sleep is absent in non-REM sleep. Accordingly, many of the disorders of non-REM sleep are very dramatic: the sleeper actually gets up and moves around. Such behavior can unnerve an observer more than the sleeper.

People who suffer from *night terrors* wake up screaming in horror, pain, or fear. They show symptoms of terror: perspiration, convulsive shivering, breathlessness, rapid heart rate. When you try to comfort them, they clutch at you. And when you try to find out what frightened them, they just seem confused and disoriented. At most they may describe a vague dream or a feeling of being suffocated. Often it takes several minutes to calm them down and get them back to sleep. The next day they remember nothing about the experience.

Sleepwalking is another disorder of non-REM sleep. Sleepwalkers get out of bed, perform simple tasks (dressing or undressing, going to the bathroom), and then get back into bed. They may talk, but what they say doesn't make sense. Although sleepwalkers sometimes steer through the house successfully, they can have serious accidents. It's better to guide them back to bed or gently awaken them than to let a sleepwalking episode run its course.

Bedwetting is a problem experienced primarily by children and adolescents. It occurs in about one child out of twenty. A bedwetting incident begins with a period of restless sleep, followed by a period of peaceful sleep during which the sleeper wets the bed. The bedwetting itself rarely wakes the sleeper. If allowed to continue to sleep, he or she is likely to incorporate the wet sensation into a dream, thus giving the impression that bedwetting goes hand in hand with dreaming. But if awakened immediately, the bedwetter is confused, disoriented, and unlikely to report any dreaming.

Night terrors, sleepwalking, and bedwetting are alike in several ways (Kelley, 1985). First, they are not accompanied by well-organized dreams. People don't wake in terror or walk in their sleep or wet their beds because of a dream. Second, in the period immediately following the incident, these sleepers are extremely groggy and difficult to awaken. So the disorders seem to be correlated with the very deep sleep of Stage 4. Third, these phenomena are more likely to occur early in the night (when Stage 4 sleep is more common) than to occur later. Finally, all three are phenomena of childhood and young adulthood; they are less common in older populations.

Narcolepsy A disorder in which the individual falls asleep abruptly, in the middle of everyday activities.

Sleep apnea is actually a breathing disorder. Because the sleeper cannot breathe properly, he or she is constantly gasping for breath. In fact, vigorous snoring is a common symptom of the disorder (Weitzman, 1981). In one form of sleep apnea that occurs during REM sleep (when the muscles are profoundly relaxed), the sleeper's throat relaxes too deeply, thereby cutting off the supply of oxygen. As the level of carbon dioxide in the blood starts to rise, the sleeper starts to wake up and the throat muscles tighten up again, restoring the oxygen supply. This pattern may be repeated hundreds of times a night, depriving the victim of one or more stages of sleep. Sleep apnea is a problem for as many as 20 million Americans, mostly elderly men (Palo, 1989).

Sleep apnea may be the cause of *sudden infant death syndrome (SIDS)* (Gould, Lee & Morelock, 1988). Most of us respond to high levels of carbon dioxide in our blood by gasping for breath; the victims of SIDS do not. In the United States, about ten thousand babies die each year from SIDS, and we don't know why. In about half the cases, there's evidence of a viral infection that may suppress the breathing reflex. Other findings point to allergies or structural problems in the breathing mechanism.

Recap

- By monitoring activity in the cerebral cortex, psychologists have identified five stages of sleep.

- The first four stages of sleep—relaxation, drifting off, deepening sleep, and profound sleep—are called quiet sleep.

- The fifth stage of sleep—REM sleep—is characterized by rapid eye movement.

- REM sleep is accompanied by dreaming.

- Throughout the night people move in and out of the different stages of sleep.

- The primary effect of sleep deprivation in adults seems to be the need to sleep more.

- Research suggests that one reason people sleep is to replenish their resources.

- According to Freud, dreams are a way of expressing the aggressive and sexual impulses that society teaches the individual to control.

- Information processing theories of why people dream focus on the physiological process of dreaming.

- Sleep disorders are chronic problems that affect the quality of life.

Hypnosis

If a hypnotist told you to quack like a duck, would you do it? Would you suck your thumb and babble like a baby? Would you lie rigid between two chairs while someone stands on your chest? No? Don't be too sure.

Hypnotism is the process of inducing a state of relaxation in which people seem to behave in ways that they might not otherwise. People who have been hypnotized often report that their actions are involuntary—things that are happening to them, not things that they are doing.

Sleep apnea A breathing disorder that can deprive the individual of sleep.

Hypnotism The process of inducing a state of relaxation in a subject who then can be made to perform suggested behaviors.

The key to hypnotism is *suggestion,* the odd sort of communication used by hypnotists. Instead of issuing a command—"Raise your arm!"—a hypnotist might say, "When I count to three, your arm will rise" or "Your arm is getting very light." This technique is illustrated further below.

> As you become relaxed your body will feel sort of heavy or perhaps numb. You will begin to have this feeling of numbness or heaviness in your legs and feet . . . in your hands and arms . . . throughout your body . . . as though you were settling deep into the chair. The chair is strong; it will hold your heavy body as it feels heavier and heavier. Your eyelids feel heavy, too, heavy and tired. You are beginning to feel drowsy and sleepy. You are breathing freely and deeply, freely and deeply. You are getting more and more sleepy and drowsy. Your eyelids are becoming heavier, more and more tired and heavy. (Weitzenhoffer & Hilgard, 1962)

In responding to hypnotic suggestions, subjects adopt a curiously passive attitude toward their own actions, lifting the arm without feeling that they're in fact responsible for the movement.

There are two kinds of hypnotic suggestions: those that are acted on immediately ("Your arm is getting very light") and those that are acted on when the subject is "awake" ("Tomorrow when you hear a bell ring, you're going to want to quack like a duck"). The latter are called **posthypnotic suggestions.**

Hypnotism was introduced to eighteenth-century science as *mesmerism,* a kind of healing. Its inventor, a Viennese physician named Franz Anton Mesmer, used trances to "cure" his patients. Mesmer claimed the effects were due to "animal magnetism." His explanation was discredited in short order, but his experiments alerted physicians to the possible medical applications of what later came to be known as hypnotism.

Mesmer gathered his patients in groups to administer what he called "animal magnetism" from iron bars and pools of water filled with charged iron filings. Many of Mesmer's patients fell into trances; when they revived, some appeared to be cured of their illnesses.

What Is Hypnosis?

Why do people under hypnosis do things they normally wouldn't do? Are they experiencing a fundamentally different kind of awareness, an altered state of consciousness? Or is hypnosis just a form of ordinary consciousness made to seem special by the ritual that accompanies it?

Posthypnotic suggestion A suggestion made during hypnotism that describes an action to be taken when the subject is no longer hypnotized.

Dissociation: An Altered-State Theory   Psychologist Ernest Hilgard (1986) believes hypnosis is a form of **dissociation,** a state of awareness in which the subject's consciousness is divided into two streams—one that is aware of everything that's going on and one that is focusing on the hypnotist's suggestions. Dissociation theory is an information processing theory because it explains hypnosis in terms of attention and the way the individual processes information about the world.

Hilgard compares dissociation to driving while listening to an interesting radio program. When you get where you're going, you remember the program in more detail than you do the ride. Obviously, because you arrived at your destination safely, you were aware of the road, the other cars, the stop signs, the traffic lights. But those details aren't part of the stream of consciousness that includes your memory of the radio program.

Social-Role Theories   **Social-role theories** stress social expectations and the relationship between hypnotist and subject. According to these theories, the subject is doing what he or she believes is appropriate in the social situation.

Every culture has different expectations of "normal" behavior in different circumstances, and people usually enact that behavior without much thought. Suppose while you were driving and listening to the radio, you came to an intersection where a policeman was conducting traffic. You may not remember much, if anything, about stopping or going at that intersection; you automatically followed the officer's signals. Social role theorists believe that the role of hypnotist elicits this sort of automatic obedience from some subjects. In fact, automatic obedience is very common among the subjects of any experimental procedure (Orne, 1962; Sarbin & Coe, 1972, 1979).

What social role theories are saying is that people do not have to be in a special state of consciousness to behave in the way that subjects of hypnosis do. The situation—not the hypnosis—induces the behavior.

The Research

The rival theories of hypnosis have generated a series of experiments and counterexperiments. In a series of experiments supporting social-role theory, Theodore Barber and his colleagues compared one group of people who had been hypnotized with another group of people who were only pretending to be hypnotized (Barber, Spanos & Chaves, 1974). Both groups were put through standard hypnotic induction and then asked to perform a series of tasks. Observers watched the subjects through a one-way glass window and gave each individual a score indicating the depth of his or her hypnosis based on task performance. Neither the observers nor the hypnotists were able to distinguish between the subjects who were genuinely hypnotized and those who were only pretending. For example, asked to behave like a human board, "awake" subjects are able to lie on two chairs—head on one, feet on the other—and support the weight of a standing person.

The research that was inspired by the altered-state—social-role controversy has not resolved that controversy. But it has clarified a number of hypnotic phenomena.

Susceptibility   Only a minority of people are good subjects for hypnosis. One test developed to ascertain susceptibility is the Stanford Hypnotic Susceptibility Scale, a twelve-item scale that measures the depth of hypnotic trance (Weitzenhoffer & Hilgard, 1962). Items on the scale consist of tasks for the subject to perform. These tasks grow progressively more difficult, from lowering a hand

Dissociation   A state of consciousness in which attention is divided.

Social-role theory   A theory that stresses social expectations and interpersonal relations in explaining a phenomenon.

to ignoring the smell of ammonia or forgetting several test items in response to a posthypnotic suggestion. By counting the number of tasks a subject performs while under hypnosis, the experimenter can assign each subject a Hypnotic Susceptibility score (see Figure 5.9).

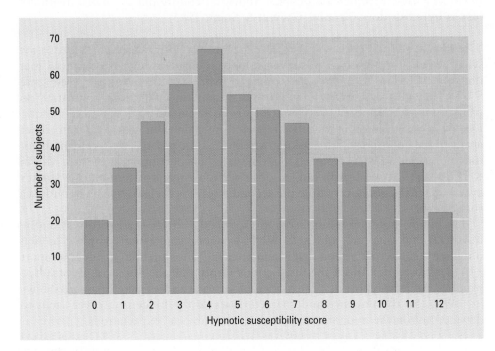

Figure 5.9
Stanford Hypnotic Susceptibility Scale

People vary greatly in hypnotic susceptibility, as can be seen in this graph of Hilgard's experiment. Most people can be hypnotized to some degree, and more than 20 percent are so susceptible that they are able to achieve the highest levels of hypnosis.

When people are tested repeatedly using the scale, their scores are consistent (Morgan, Johnson & Hilgard, 1974). This suggests that susceptibility is a stable characteristic; in other words, an individual's susceptibility to hypnosis is more or less permanent. Highly susceptible people seem to be those who are especially open to imagination and fantasy (Sheehan, 1982; Lynn & Rhue, 1987). Remember that some people have elaborate daydreams; such daydreamers also are highly susceptible to hypnosis. Because social roles are constant for everyone, the fact that people consistently differ in their susceptibility supports the altered-state theory.

Although the ability to be hypnotized is a stable characteristic in some individuals, almost anyone can learn it. Nicholas Spanos (1986) tested this hypothesis on a group of people who were not susceptible to hypnosis. Half the people in the group took part in a training program; the other half, the control group, received no training. The training program focused on removing the fear of and any stigma attached to being hypnotized, and on teaching the subjects to think of their own actions as if they were happening without their will.

The susceptibility scores of people who participated in the training program increased significantly, to the point that they were indistinguishable from those of highly susceptible subjects (Spanos, Lush & Gwynn, 1989). Spanos concluded that hypnotic susceptibility is less a trait than a skill or an attitude that people can learn.

Coping with Pain   Apparently people who have been hypnotized can withstand certain painful stimuli with little or no suffering. In fact, for highly susceptible people, hypnosis is a more effective pain killer than aspirin, tranquilizers, or even morphine (Stern et al., 1981).

As you would expect, social role theorists were eager to show that hypnosis simulators also can withstand greater than normal amounts of pain. In one experiment, the subjects were asked to pretend they were hypnotized and then to hold their arms in a tub of ice water. The ice water rapidly produces a level of pain that surprises anyone who has not experienced it. And yet simulating hypnosis was shown to increase people's ability to endure the ice-water treatment just as hypnosis does (Spanos, Gwynn & Stam, 1983).

The Hidden Observer   In a series of experiments, Hilgard found evidence for what he called the **hidden observer.** Under hypnosis, subjects were told that they would feel no pain when they plunged their hand into ice water (see Figure 5.10). They also were asked to evaluate their pain on a scale ranging from 0 (no pain) to 10 (extreme pain). A control group reported pain within a minute. Deeply hypnotized subjects often reported no pain. But when the researcher changed the question slightly, asking whether "some part of you" is feeling pain, the hypnotized subjects reported that the water *was* hurting them (Knox, Moran & Hilgard, 1974). Hilgard's hidden observer is a stream of consciousness that's aware of what's going on while the second stream is focused on the hypnotist's suggestions.

The hidden observer results seem to support the altered-state theory strongly, but again the issues are confused. When hypnotic suggestions imply a hidden observer ("some part of you that is experiencing this situation"), subjects report a hidden observer. And if the instructions imply that the observer will feel *less* pain, the subjects report that the hidden observer feels less pain (Spanos & Hewitt, 1980). So the presence and characteristics of the hidden observer seem to depend, not on the hypnotic state, but on the subjects' expectations.

Figure 5.10
Hypnosis and Pain

When her arm was plunged into cold water, this hypnotized subject reported that she herself felt no pain. Asked in a different way, however, she could report that some part of her was hurting.

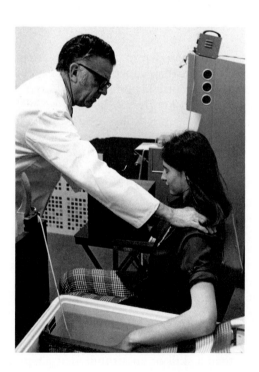

Memory   Under hypnosis, do people remember things they can't remember otherwise? For a long time psychologists thought the answer was yes. Until very recently, in fact, hypnotism was used in courtrooms to help witnesses remember the details of serious crimes. One very famous case involved the kidnapping of a school bus load of children. Under hypnosis, the driver was able to recall the license plate of the kidnappers' car (M. Smith, 1983). But on close

Hidden observer   The dissociated consciousness in a hypnotized subject.

How Do We Know That?

Scientists are always wary of experimental procedures that make it easy for researchers to influence the outcome of an experiment. A particularly dangerous procedure is the interview in which the researcher is looking for a specific response and can continue to probe until it's given. This situation is ripe for the Clever Hans phenomenon.

Clever Hans was a performing horse who was famous for his ability to count. Hans's owner, a Mr. Van Osten, appeared on stage with the horse. In the act, members of the audience asked arithmetic questions, which Van Osten would relay to Hans. Hans would then tap out the answers with his hoof.

His demonstration of equine mathematical talent made Hans a celebrity. Then a psychologist, Oscar Pfungst, demonstrated that Hans could not perform his sums unless the person relaying the questions knew the answers. Hans couldn't do arithmetic, but he was able to read human behavior. Asked to count, he tapped until Van Osten "signaled" that he had reached the correct number. Yet Van Osten had no idea that he was passing this information to Hans. In fact, he was as surprised as anyone to learn that he had been exhibiting his own mathematical abilities, not his horse's.

Parallel effects have been observed in the research on hypnosis. In one apparent demonstration of age regression, hypnotized adult subjects were able to remember which day of the week their fourth birthday fell on. That's pretty impressive considering most four year olds don't even know what day of the week it is today! But close examination showed that the Clever Hans phenomenon was at work. Instead of simply asking the subjects the day of the week, the researcher asked a series of questions: "Was it on a Wednesday?" "Was it on a Thursday?" Of course the researcher knew the correct answers. So the subjects, like Clever Hans, had only to respond to his cues—a certain tone in his voice, a pause—to know when to say yes (O'Connell, Shore & Orne, 1970).

---

examination, what psychologists thought were the effects of hypnosis on memory may well have been the product of imagination, experimenter influence, and relaxation. Let's consider each of these alternative explanations.

Imagination   Perhaps some people manufacture memories to please the hypnotist. Although people who've been hypnotized do call up more memories than people who have not been hypnotized, these "memories" often are of imagined, not real, events. About two-thirds of what we remember under hypnosis is false (Dywan & Bowers, 1983). *Age regression*—a phenomenon whereby subjects, when asked to do so, relive their early childhoods—gives us evidence of the tendency to create memories. Instead of acting like children, these subjects act the way adults *think* children act (Nash, 1987).

People who've been hypnotized often remember things that never happened; they also are unable to distinguish between real memories and their invented ones (Laurence & Perry, 1983).

The influence of the researcher   Apparent feats of memory under hypnosis might also be the product of **experimenter influence.** A researcher who knows the correct answer to a question may unknowingly telegraph that answer to the subject. The risk of unintentional influence is particularly high with hypnotic subjects because they are particularly eager to please and highly attuned to the hypnotist.

Experimenter influence   The unintentional influence that a researcher exerts on a subject's responses.

(a) Subject is hypnotized.

(b) Subject receives posthypnotic suggestion: "When you hear a bell, quack like a duck."

(c) Subject is "woken" up.

(d) Subject acts on suggestion but cannot remember why.

"Quack"

(e) Subject later remembers source of his or her actions after hypnotist orders or gives signal to remember.

Figure 5.11
Source Amnesia

Source amnesia is demonstrated by instructing a subject to do something unexpected on cue after hypnosis has apparently been terminated. When asked, the subject at first cannot remember why he or she is performing the action.

Relaxation Perhaps hypnosis itself doesn't help us remember things, but the relaxation that's part of the process does. In the process of hypnotizing subjects, hypnotists often begin by relaxing them. "You're getting tired." "Your eyes are growing heavy." "You're feeling sleepy." Someone who is relaxed is much more likely to remember a detail, an object, an event, than someone facing police interrogation or cross-examination in a courtroom.

Forgetting Although the effect of hypnosis on remembering is in doubt, there is evidence that hypnosis does affect forgetting (Kihlstrom, 1985). People who've been hypnotized often display **source amnesia.** That is, they carry out posthypnotic suggestions without knowing the source of those suggestions (see Figure 5.11). Hypnotic simulators—people who are just pretending to be hypnotized—do not display the same pattern of forgetting, thus suggesting that source amnesia is a genuine hypnotic phenomenon (Kihlstrom, 1985).

Is source amnesia a failure to memorize the information in the first place or a failure to recall the memory later? The evidence leans toward the latter. People can be given a second posthypnotic suggestion to recall the source of the first when they hear a signal. When that signal sounds, the subjects suddenly remember why they're doing what they're doing (Kihlstrom, 1985). For example, a hypnotist might instruct a subject to laugh when he or she is awakened. Without the second posthypnotic suggestion—"You're going to remember this suggestion when you hear a bell ring"—the subject laughs but doesn't understand why. The second suggestion allows the subject to remember that the hypnotist said to laugh. This ability to remember the instruction indicates that what is lost in source amnesia is *access* to the memory, not the memory itself.

Where We Are Today The competition between the altered-state theory of hypnosis and the social-role theory has produced scores of experiments and the discovery of at least three remarkable phenomena: hypnotic simulation, the hidden observer, and the ability to train people to be good hypnotic subjects.

The theories also seem to have changed over time. Altered-state theories increasingly focus on hypnosis as a cognitive state, whereas social-roles theories increasingly focus on it as an attitude (Spanos, 1986). Because attitudes have strong cognitive components, the differences between the two sets of theories seem less important than they used to.

Meditation

Source amnesia A phenomenon in which subjects perform posthypnotic suggestions but cannot report why.

You've probably seen someone on campus doing it. A man sitting in the sun, legs crossed, eyes closed, hands open on his knees, breathing slowly and deeply, meditating.

Meditation is a deliberate, prolonged, systematic focusing of attention on something. Meditation techniques have been a part of many religions, including Christianity, Judaism, and Islam, for hundreds and thousands of years. The focus of attention and the techniques vary, but in every case the intent is to produce an altered state of consciousness.

In the last twenty years, a number of different meditation techniques that emerged from Eastern religions, especially Hinduism and Zen Buddhism, have become popular in the United States. Perhaps the best known is transcendental meditation (TM), which spread across the country in the 1970s.

People meditate in one of two ways. Some try to empty their minds, to let their minds simply drift where they will. Others focus on a single object. For example, they may repeat a *mantra*—a word or a string of words—over and over again. Mantras seem to be chosen for their droning, hypnotic quality. A common mantra is the word *om* or the phrase *om mani padme hum*. According to its practitioners, a program of daily meditation produces feelings of peace and well-being that extend far beyond the time actually spent meditating.

Seldom does a spiritual movement attract the widespread attention of psychologists. Meditation was an exception. In a study published in 1970, Keith Wallace demonstrated that meditation causes physiological changes—slower heart rate and respiration as well as lower body temperature. These findings offered hope that people with stress-related diseases, like heart disease and high blood pressure, could help themselves by meditating.

Are meditation's effects unique? Probably not. David Holmes and his collaborators compared the physiological effects of meditation with the effects of a simple program of relaxation. In both cases the body's metabolism slowed. In fact, the results were indistinguishable. Apparently the physiological effects of meditation are the same as those of other forms of relaxation (Holmes et al., 1983; Holmes, 1988).

Do these effects have an impact on the individual's health? Some studies suggest that they do. For example, when elderly nursing-home residents were taught transcendental meditation, they functioned at a higher level than did others who were not taught. More important, a larger proportion of the group who'd been taught to meditate were still living at the time of the three-year follow-up (Alexander et al., 1989).

In sum, there seems to be wide agreement among practitioners that meditation does produce changes in consciousness. The implications of these changes for psychological functioning are still being explored.

Recap

- Hypnosis is the process of inducing a state of relaxation during which people behave in ways that they might not otherwise behave.

- Some psychologists believe that hypnosis is an altered state of consciousness, that awareness is divided into two streams.

- According to social role theories, hypnotic subjects are playing a role, doing what they think is appropriate in the social situation.

- The obedience of hypnotic subjects to the hypnotist is similar to the obedience of subjects in any experimental procedure.

- Susceptibility to hypnosis can be learned.

- Hypnotic subjects and hypnosis simulators are able to withstand higher than normal amounts of pain.

Meditation A means of focusing attention to produce an altered state of consciousness.

- The effect of hypnosis on remembering is in doubt, but source amnesia provides evidence that hypnosis does affect forgetting.

- The physiological effects of meditation are the same as the effects of relaxation programs.

Drugs and Consciousness

Many people find it very difficult to resist both street drugs (cocaine, marijuana, LSD, heroin) and legal drugs (tobacco, alcohol, caffeine). Although psychoactive drug use, especially among college students, seems to be declining (see Table 5.3), billions of dollars are still spent each year acquiring drugs. Why?

Table 5.3
Trends in Drug Taking Among College Students

	Percent Who Used in Last Twelve Months							
	1980	1981	1982	1983	1984	1985	1986	1987
Marijuana	51.2	51.3	44.7	45.2	40.7	41.7	40.9	37.0
Inhalants	3.0	2.5	2.5	2.8	2.4	3.1	3.9	3.7
LSD	6.0	4.6	6.3	4.3	3.7	2.2	3.9	4.0
Cocaine	16.8	16.0	17.2	17.3	16.3	17.3	17.1	13.7
"Crack"	NA	NA	NA	NA	NA	NA	1.3	2.0
Heroin	0.4	0.2	0.1	0.0	0.1	0.2	0.1	0.2
Other Opiates	5.1	4.3	3.8	3.8	3.8	2.4	4.0	3.1
Stimulants	22.4	22.2	NA	NA	NA	NA	NA	NA
Sedatives	8.3	8.0	8.0	4.5	3.5	2.5	2.6	1.7
Barbiturates	2.9	2.8	3.2	2.2	1.9	1.3	2.0	1.2
Methaqualone	7.2	6.5	6.6	3.1	2.5	1.4	1.2	0.8
Tranquilizers	6.9	4.8	4.7	4.6	3.5	3.6	4.4	3.8
Alcohol	90.5	92.5	92.2	91.6	90.0	92.0	91.5	90.9

Note: All figures are given in percents. NA indicates data not available.
Source: Johnston, O'Malley & Bachman, 1988.

The Effects of Drugs

Psychoactive drug A substance that affects behavior or experience through its influence on synaptic activity.

Physical dependence The body's inability to function normally in the absence of a drug.

Tolerance The body's increasing adaptation to a drug, such that larger doses are required to produce a constant effect.

Psychological dependence An emotional dependence on a drug.

Psychoactive drugs, as these substances are called, affect behavior or experience through their impact on synaptic activity. They change or mimic the activity of neurotransmitters (which we talked about in Chapter 2) and consequently change the movement of nerve impulses. Psychoactive drugs can and do alter both the level and quality of consciousness.

With regular use, the body adapts to certain drugs; it requires those drugs to function "normally." At this point, the user is **physically dependent** on the drug. With physical dependence comes **tolerance.** As the body adapts to the drug, the user has to take more and more of it to achieve the same effect. And as physical dependence and tolerance grow, so does **psychological dependence.** Getting and taking the drug become the focus of the user's life.

Physical dependence, tolerance, and psychological dependence combine to produce **addiction,** a reliance on the drug to survive and carry on everyday activities. Drug users who try to break out of this spiral of dependency experience **withdrawal.**

The effects of drugs are difficult to describe because they are extremely variable, from person to person and from occasion to occasion in the same person. For example, a dose that is safe for one person under one set of circumstances could be lethal for another person or for the same person under a different set of circumstances. The physical size of the user is one element at work here. Another is that person's level of tolerance. A shot of vodka affects a first-time drinker very differently from the way it affects an alcoholic.

Drugs can also have different effects on the same person at different times, depending on that person's emotional state. We know that fatigue and anxiety, for instance, can replace the euphoria produced by certain drugs with fear.

In addition, people's expectations play a role in their reactions to drugs. For example, many people expect alcohol to reduce sexual inhibitions. One study tested the effects of that expectation on male college students. A first group was served a fruit drink containing alcohol; the other group, the same drink without alcohol. Within each group, half of the students were told their beverage was alcoholic and the other half were told it contained no alcohol.

Which group do you think had the most erotic fantasies and experienced the least embarrassment while waiting to watch an erotic movie? If alcohol consumption was the most important factor at work here, the two groups that drank alcohol should have ranked higher than the two groups that did not drink alcohol. But they didn't. Actual alcohol levels had almost no effect. Instead, the critical factor was what the students believed they had consumed. The students who *thought* they were drinking alcohol had more erotic fantasies and were less embarrassed (Abrams & Wilson, 1983). Clearly, in this case expectations were more important than the actual effects of the drug.

Jim Morrison, lead singer of the rock group, the Doors, died of a drug overdose in 1971. Other public figures who abused drugs and died of overdoses include singer Janis Joplin, actor John Belushi, and basketball star Len Bias.

Addiction Reliance on a substance to carry on everyday activities.

Withdrawal The physical and psychological effects of stopping drug use.

Finally, drug reactions are particularly unreliable in combination. Sometimes a small amount of one drug greatly increases the potency of another. Alcohol and barbiturates interact in this way, apparently because they both interact with GABA (gamma-amino butyric acid), an inhibitory neurotransmitter. Alcohol increases the effectiveness of GABA, and barbiturates increase its production. Taken in combination with alcohol, a safe dosage of barbiturates becomes a devastating overdose.

Varieties of Psychoactive Drugs

There are three major categories of psychoactive drugs: stimulants, which activate the nervous system; depressants, which slow it down; and hallucinogens, which alter the quality of experience.

Stimulants   People take **stimulants** to increase their energy, endurance, and confidence, and to make them feel more alert. Stimulants increase the production of norepinephrine, the neurotransmitter that activates the sympathetic nervous system (Segal, 1985).

Caffeine is the most widely used psychoactive drug. It's a natural ingredient in coffee, tea, and chocolate, and is added to many soft drinks. People use caffeine because it helps them stay awake and gives them a small "high."

Nicotine is the active ingredient in tobacco products. Inhaled or ingested in small doses, nicotine is an effective stimulant. In large doses it's a powerful poison, as many farmers know. Before the invention of modern insecticides, they used extract of tobacco leaves as an agricultural insecticide.

Cocaine is a white powder processed from the coca plant. It is inhaled or smoked. *Crack* is cocaine that has been refined into crystals. It can be smoked or injected. Cocaine, particularly in the form of crack, is a powerful stimulant. Its effects come and go quickly, usually within half an hour. Cocaine apparently achieves its effects by increasing the effectiveness of norepinephrine (Cooper, Bloom & Roth, 1986).

Amphetamines are manufactured stimulants. They are very powerful, and their effects can last for hours. Like other stimulants, amphetamines mimic the effects of frightening or exciting stimuli on the nervous system—by mobilizing the body's metabolic reserves. They arouse the cortex, fight off drowsiness, speed up the heart rate, raise the blood pressure, lower the blood supply to the digestive organs and skin, and increase the blood supply to the brain and muscles. Amphetamines act by directly stimulating norepinephrine receptor sites (Berger & Dunn, 1986).

The hazards of taking stimulants vary not only with the kind of stimulant taken but also with the dosage. Because caffeine and nicotine are usually consumed in small quantities, they are less dangerous than other stimulants. By contrast, cocaine and amphetamines are more risky and produce both physical dependence and tolerance in habitual users.

Even animals can become addicted to stimulants. Experiments have been run in which rats have unlimited access to cocaine by pressing a bar that releases the drug. Although the cocaine causes weight loss and seizures, the rats press the bar almost constantly. More than 90 percent of the rats in these experiments die within thirty days (Bozarth & Wise, 1985).

In humans, the excessive use of stimulants can damage the brain and other organs and lead to extreme fearfulness, nervousness, hallucinations, and even death (Collins, 1985). The effects of crack are especially serious because the vaporized drug reaches the brain very quickly (Cregler & Kaplan, 1986).

Because of its euphoria-producing effects, cocaine has become a popular recreational drug. But users can become both psychologically and physically addicted to cocaine, making it dangerous and harmful.

Stimulants   A class of drugs that increase energy, endurance, and confidence.

Amphetamines   Powerful manufactured stimulants whose effects last for several hours.

Alcohol is so widely used as a social "lubricant," it's hard to think of it as a dangerous psychoactive drug. Yet abuse of alcohol is a far greater societal problem than all the other forms of drug abuse combined.

People who are dependent on cocaine or amphetamines need help to break the addiction. Withdrawal can be very difficult and is often accompanied by depression and listlessness, which in some cases have led to suicide.

Depressants   The effects of **depressants** are the reverse of those of stimulants. Depressants slow the circuits that stimulate the cerebral cortex and the sympathetic nervous system by increasing the effectiveness of inhibitory neurotransmitters. They tend to make the user feel relaxed. But they can also generate a sense of despair and helplessness.

Opiates are derived from the sap of a poppy that grows principally in the Far East. Opium and its derivatives (morphine, heroin, and codeine) simulate the endorphins, the neurotransmitters that suppress pain. They are widely used as painkillers.

Endorphins also control our natural pleasure responses. Opiates give the user a temporary sense of well-being by "short-circuiting" the systems that normally produce pleasure. As a drug-induced high replaces the natural high produced by the body's endorphins, the user becomes psychologically dependent on the opiate and seeks pleasure from drugs rather than work, play, or social interaction.

Because opiates deplete the body's supply of endorphins, withdrawal is accompanied by muscle cramping, pain, and irritability. Ironically, doctors often fight heroin dependence with another opiate, methadone. For reasons we don't understand, methadone and heroin exert the same physical effects but have different psychological effects. Methadone therapy keeps the user physically comfortable while he or she learns to live without the psychological effects of heroin.

Barbiturates are powerful depressants that are prescribed to help patients rest. At one time they were widely used in ordinary sleeping pills—a practice that ceased when scientists found that barbiturates depress respiratory function. They appear to mimic GABA (Nicoll & Madison, 1982).

Also a depressant, **alcohol** is the most widely abused legal psychoactive drug. We don't understand exactly how alcohol affects the brain and other parts of the nervous system. But we do know that it appears to increase the effectiveness of GABA, which generally inhibits the activity of other neurotransmitters (Nestoros, 1980).

Depressants A class of drugs that tend to relax the user.

Opiate A depressant drug derived from or modeled on opium.

Barbiturate A powerful depressant drug that is especially dangerous because of its effect on the respiratory system.

Alcohol A term applied to a variety of beverages containing ethyl alcohol; the most widely abused legal psychoactive drug.

The immediate effects of alcohol are determined by the amount and rate of consumption. Even small amounts of alcohol produce significant deficits in the ability to notice and respond quickly and accurately to stimuli—a changing traffic light, for example. Alcohol also makes the user overestimate his or her skill at simple perceptual and motor tasks.

In small to moderate amounts, alcohol reduces inhibitions (Steele & Southwick, 1985; Steele, Critchlow & Liu, 1985). In large quantities, the drug depresses the functioning of the nervous system at all levels, and the drinker becomes increasingly unresponsive. A large quantity of alcohol consumed in a short period of time can cause coma and death.

Hallucinogens   **Hallucinogens** distort perception. Their effects can be mild (enhancement of colors and sounds) or elaborate (full-scale visions). People who have taken hallucinogens report mystical experiences in which sounds become visible, visual images become audible, and past and present merge. **Hallucinations,** by contrast, are sensory experiences that occur in the absence of sensory stimuli.

Among the hallucinogens are lysergic acid diethylamide (LSD) and mescaline. These drugs are chemically similar to serotonin and norepinephrine, and they interfere with the normal functioning of those neurotransmitters (Jacobs, 1987). LSD attaches to receptor sites for serotonin, putting them temporarily—sometimes permanently—out of action. It also interferes with the action of dopamine (Jacobs & Trulson, 1979).

Most hallucinogens do not induce tolerance or physical dependence. On the contrary, with these drugs *sensitization* can be a problem. Smaller and smaller quantities of hallucinogens may trigger progressively more profound distortions of experience. Most drugs are eliminated from the body in hours, but hallucinogens linger in the user's fat tissue. This buildup intensifies the effects of new doses; it can also cause *flashbacks,* unexpected recurrences of hallucinations.

The most dangerous hallucinogen is phencyclidine hydrochloride (PCP) or "angel dust." PCP attacks the potassium chemistry of the neurons (Herbert, 1983) and has long-term or even permanent effects. (Remember that potassium plays a key role in maintaining the electrical balance on the membrane of the nerve cells.) PCP causes hallucinations; it also can make the user hyperactive, irrationally suspicious, and extremely aggressive. These symptoms, which can occur with just a single dose of PCP, decrease only gradually over a course of days or even weeks. A full 25 percent of the people treated for taking PCP report severe flashbacks long after their exposure to the drug (Luisada & Brown, 1976).

The most widely used illegal psychoactive drug is **marijuana** or its derivatives, hashish and tetrahydrocannabinol (THC). Hashish is distilled from one of the most potent parts of the marijuana plant; THC is the psychoactive ingredient. Marijuana alters the degree or the quality of consciousness, depending on the dosage. Small amounts produce relaxation and euphoria; larger amounts produce mild distortions of time and color perception, and can lead the user to withdraw socially.

Although marijuana users do not seem to develop a dependence on or a tolerance to the drug, the drug does have harmful short-term effects. For example, it impairs perceptual and motor abilities, which makes driving under the influence of marijuana very dangerous.

Hallucinogens A class of drugs that distort perception.

Hallucination A sensory experience that occurs in the absence of a sensory stimulus.

Marijuana The most widely used illegal psychoactive drug.

Recap

- Psychoactive drugs affect behavior and experience, altering both the level and the quality of consciousness.

- Physical dependence, tolerance, and psychological dependence combine to create drug addiction.

- There are three basic types of psychoactive drugs: stimulants, depressants, and hallucinogens.

- Stimulants activate the nervous system.

- Depressants slow down the activity of the nervous system.

- Hallucinogens alter the quality of experience.

Conclusion

As you have been reading, you may have been struck by how many diverse topics came up in a chapter on consciousness. In fact, in this chapter we've talked about states of consciousness—attention, sleep, dreams—and the effects of hypnosis, meditation, and drugs on those states. Running through our discussion is the implication that consciousness is crucially important. Much of what we all think of as distinctively human depends on consciousness, and many of the activities that we enjoy most, for better or worse, are designed to affect our consciousness. It's remarkable, then, that we seem to have so little understanding of exactly what consciousness *is*. The problem may be that we're too close, too immersed in the phenomenon to comprehend it fully. A Chinese proverb says that a fish would be the last animal to discover water. Perhaps because we swim in consciousness, we have a problem studying it.

Chapter 6   Learning

The Piano Lesson, Romare Bearden, 1983

Gateways Although we begin life prepared to become highly complicated people, we start out with little knowledge and few abilities. To a great extent, what each of us becomes will result from learning. Psychologists have studied the processes of learning extensively, in the hope of understanding how our experiences change us, sometimes permanently.

We can recall learning many of the things we know—tying our shoes, for example. Other kinds of learning occur with little or no conscious recognition. This chapter focuses mainly on those kinds of learning. Perhaps because they are not deliberate, they also seem to be the most powerful and the hardest to change.

Understanding the basics of how we learn will help you to appreciate the cognitive and social development of children (which we discuss in Chapters 11 and 12) and the evolution of certain psychological disorders (Chapter 15). And, as you'll see in Chapter 14, the principles of learning underlie a major theory of personality.

I could tell from the way John's old Volkswagen steamed into my driveway that he had something he wanted to talk about. He and I had been sharing occasional rides to work for many years and the half an hour commute was a good time to chew on a problem together. Today he clearly had a problem that wanted chewing.

"You're the psychologist," he asserted almost accusingly, as I climbed into the car. He backed the car out of my driveway with a jolt and accelerated down my street. "What do I do about a five-year-old that won't go to sleep at night?"

"Send her back to the factory!" I said, trying to make a joke.

"No kidding," he said. "I need some help with this one. We're about at our wit's end."

It seems that John's daughter Sara had been behaving strangely during the last few weeks. Normally a good sleeper, Sara had suddenly developed a sleeping problem at bedtime—or rather a teddy bear problem.

It started one night when Sara was cranky and didn't want to go to sleep. To amuse her, John made a big show of putting the teddy bear to bed. He tucked the bear into bed beside her and kissed it good night. Then he had Sara kiss it good night, and then he kissed her good night and off she went to sleep without a fuss. The next night, she wanted him to do it again. The night after that, she wanted him to kiss her stuffed rabbit, too. And, of course, she had to kiss the stuffed rabbit, and the stuffed rabbit had to kiss the teddy bear. Only after all that could John give Sara her good-night kiss.

When about a week later she tried to introduce her frog puppet into the kissing circle, John put his foot down and left the room. Sara wailed bitterly. He left her in her room. Eventually, she seemed to cry herself to sleep. But when he looked in on her later he found her wide awake in her bed, arranging her animals and talking to them. She seemed tense and fretful and was bleary eyed from lack of sleep. So he kissed all the stuffed animals, kissed her, and finally got her off to sleep.

"What am I going to do?" he asked. "Where does it all end?"

Sara had clearly learned a bad habit, but how? And what was John to do about it? Many of the ideas we tried out as we rode to work together were related to the principles of learning described in this chapter. As you read, think about how those principles might be used to help a child get to sleep at night. At the end of the chapter, we'll tell you how John helped Sara with her teddy bear problem.

Learning: A Definition

Learning is an enduring change in behavior produced by experience. It is through experience that you learn to speak French, to drive a car, to bake a cake, to balance your checkbook, to be a good parent. When experience has a long-term effect on the way you behave, you are learning.

Learning An enduring change in behavior that is a product of experience.

Ivan Pavlov was a Russian physiologist who won the Nobel Prize for his work on digestive physiology before he began his pioneering work on learning.

Not all learning is immediately evident. Right now, as you're reading, you're learning about psychology. The learning is going on today, but you probably won't see the change in your behavior until you take an exam or write a paper. Because changes in behavior aren't always immediately apparent, psychologists make a distinction between the acquisition of learning and its performance (Tolman, 1932; Hulse, Fowler & Honig, 1978). **Acquisition** is the process by which experience changes behavioral tendencies; **performance** is the actual expression of those changes in behavior.

The most obvious kind of learning you do is formal learning, through the medium of language. You learn about psychology by reading the words on this page and by listening to your professor's lectures. By studying signs along the street, you learn when the next bus is coming, which days of the week you can park, and whether or not a right turn on red is legal at this intersection.

We talk about language-based learning in later chapters. Here we discuss the forms of learning that do not rely on language, the kinds of learning that go on whether or not we are trying to learn. These basic forms of learning are called *classical conditioning, instrumental conditioning,* and *observational learning.*

Classical Conditioning

The smell of french fries makes your mouth water because in your experience that smell goes along with the salty crunch of the potatoes in your mouth. Eerie music in a movie makes you uneasy because in your experience that kind of music signals that something scary is about to happen. You aren't born knowing that the smell of french fries means good food or that a certain kind of music means cinematic blood and gore. You've been *conditioned* to respond to these stimuli by your experience. **Classical conditioning** is the learning process through which a stimulus that does not initially elicit a particular response is made to do so by pairing it with one that does.

Pavlov's Dogs

Acquisition The process by which experience changes behavioral tendencies.

Performance The demonstration of learning in behavior.

Classical conditioning The process of learning by which a neutral stimulus occurs with a stimulus that evokes a response, so that the neutral stimulus comes to evoke a similar response.

Orienting reflex A response to an unanticipated or new stimulus.

Unconditioned stimulus (UCS) A stimulus that automatically elicits a certain response.

Unconditioned response (UR) A behavior that is automatic.

Conditioned stimulus (CS) A stimulus that elicits a response by being paired with an unconditioned stimulus.

Conditioned response (CR) A response that has been learned.

The identification of classical conditioning was the work of Ivan Pavlov (1927), the great Russian physiologist. When he decided to study the secretions of the salivary glands in response to food, Pavlov had already earned a Nobel prize for his research on how the dog's nervous system controls the secretions of the digestive glands (Ridley, 1987).

Pavlov's methods were precise. To minimize distractions, he conducted his experiments in a special laboratory (see Figure 6.1), and he painstakingly trained the dogs to stand quietly in a special harness. To make accurate measurements, he performed a small operation on each animal so that its saliva flowed directly from the glands into a tube and collected in a specially designed measuring device. Figure 6.2 illustrates the apparatus Pavlov used in his experiments.

Yet despite these elaborate arrangements, Pavlov was frustrated. He found that the dogs were salivating before they were fed—when they heard the researcher coming, or when they saw the container of food. He began to suspect that the dogs were salivating at the "wrong" time because they were associating being fed with different sounds and sights in the laboratory.

To understand the dogs' behavior, Pavlov conducted a series of experiments in which he tried to generate the salivation response by pairing the food stimulus with a neutral stimulus—something that had nothing to do with food, such as the sound of a metronome. When the dogs first heard the metronome, they responded with **orienting reflexes:** they would prick up their ears and look in the direction of the sound. Shortly after the metronome was started, Pavlov would give the dogs a small dose of meat powder. After several pairings of the metronome with the food, the dogs began to salivate as soon as the metronome started clicking—before they were fed.

Figure 6.1
Pavlov's Laboratory

Throughout his studies of conditioning, Pavlov struggled to control the experimental situation. At first he allowed the experimenter in the room with the dogs; then he decided that this arrangement created too much stimulation. Even separating the dogs from the experimenter and the measuring equipment didn't do the job. Ultimately, Pavlov had a fort-like laboratory built, separated from other buildings and designed so that each room in the building was separated from the other rooms by a corridor.

The food was an **unconditioned stimulus (UCS);** it automatically elicited an **unconditioned response (UCR),** salivation. The sound of the metronome was a **conditioned stimulus (CS);** its power to elicit a response was a product of its pairing with the food, an unconditioned stimulus. The salivation it produced was a **conditioned response (CR);** the animals had *learned* to salivate when they heard the clicking of the metronome because they associated the sound with the food. Figure 6.3 shows the development of a salivation response (Anrep, 1920).

Figure 6.2
Pavlov's Apparatus

The dog stood quietly in its loose-fitting harness. Its responses were measured by collecting saliva from its salivary glands, which passed through a tube to control a pen recording on a revolving cylinder.

Figure 6.3
The Acquisition of a Conditioned Salivary Response in a Dog

By the thirtieth pairing of the metronome with food, a salivary response to the metronome was fully developed.

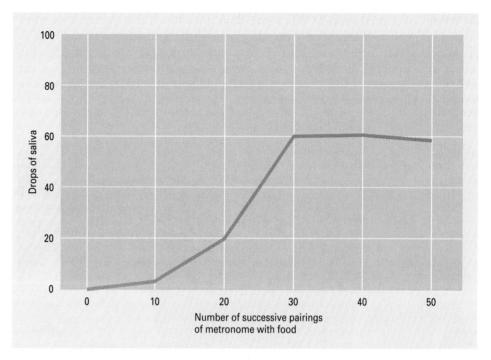

Source: Anrep, 1920.

The Acquisition Process

Pavlov described three steps in the conditioning procedure:

1. Before conditioning, the unconditioned stimulus—in this case, the food—elicits the unconditioned response—in this case, salivation.

Unconditioned stimulus → Unconditioned response
(food)   (salivation)

The neutral stimulus—the sound of the metronome—elicits its own response: the dogs prick up their ears and look in the direction of the sound.

Neutral stimulus   →   Orienting reflexes
(metronome clicking)   (pricking up ears, looking)

2. During conditioning, the neutral stimulus is paired with the unconditioned stimulus: the unconditioned stimulus is presented right after the neutral stimulus. Note that the unconditioned stimulus continues to elicit the unconditioned response.

Neutral stimulus   →   Unconditioned stimulus → Unconditioned response
(metronome clicking)   (food)   (salivation)

As the conditioning progresses, the response to the neutral stimulus—the conditioned stimulus-to-be—grows stronger and faster (Hearst, 1988).
3. After conditioning, the former neutral stimulus becomes a conditioned stimulus and, by itself, elicits the conditioned response.

Conditioned stimulus   →   Conditioned response
(metronome clicking)   (salivation)

Pavlov first described classical conditioning in dogs, but it's a familiar phenomenon among all organisms, including people. Classical conditioning is what makes your stomach rumble before a meal (Rodin, 1981). Certain parts of the digestive process are conditioned to the food situation; they begin before any food actually reaches your stomach. Among them are contractions of the stomach, the secretion of digestive juices, and even the secretion of insulin, the hormone that keeps your blood-sugar level from rising too high after a meal.

The activities of the autonomic nervous system that relate to fear and anxiety are also conditioned. Just walking into a room where you once took a difficult exam can make your palms sweat and your mouth go dry. Many psychologists believe that irrational fears also develop through conditioning, and they use conditioning to treat those fears.

The people who built this bank facade were "banking" on potential customers' conditioned response to imposing buildings with pillars. After all, would you put *your* money in a house trailer?

Classical Conditioning and Drugs

Classical conditioning has even been used to explain drug tolerance—the need to take increasingly larger doses of a drug to get the same effect (Poulos, Hinson & Siegel, 1981). According to one theory, tolerance is a product of the conditioning of opponent processes (Siegel, 1983).

Opponent processes are natural processes that tend to oppose one another (Schull, 1979). If something very exciting happens to you, opponent processes help calm you down. And if you're exhausted, opponent processes give you a lift. The same effects may occur with drugs: the action of stimulants is opposed by natural calming processes; the action of depressants is opposed by natural stimulating processes.

This theory claims that drug tolerance develops from the classical conditioning of the opponent processes to the activity of taking drugs. Let's look at the development of cocaine tolerance, for example. When the user first begins to take the drug, each dose generates a strong stimulating effect, which in turn generates the opponent process, a depressing effect. The person experiences first a high, then a letdown. The conditioned stimulus is the process of taking the drug; the unconditioned stimulus is the high; and the unconditioned response is the opponent process, the letdown that follows the taking of the drug. With repeated use, however, the opponent process moves forward in time, so that it occurs as soon as the drug is taken. Now with each dose, the user experiences both the high and the letdown simultaneously. To get the same high—to combat the simultaneous letdown—the user has to take more of the drug.

The Complexities of Classical Conditioning

Life would be intolerable if every conditioned response you ever learned stayed with you for life. You'd salivate every time you see a baby bottle or cringe in terror every time you see a large dog. But conditioned responses aren't permanent. They can be changed in a variety of ways. Once a conditioned response has been acquired, the experimeter can decide whether or not to present the unconditioned stimulus after the subject has made the response.

Extinction   If the unconditioned stimulus repeatedly fails to follow the conditioned response, the conditioned response gradually disappears (see Figure 6.4). Each time we present the conditioned stimulus (for example, the sound of a metronome) without the unconditioned stimulus (the food), the conditioned response (salivation) grows weaker and slower, and finally disappears. This process is called **extinction.**

Figure 6.4
Extinction and Spontaneous Recovery of a Conditioned Response

If after acquisition the conditioned stimulus is presented alone, the conditioned response gradually extinguishes. If the subject is taken out of the experimental situation for several days, the response spontaneously recovers.

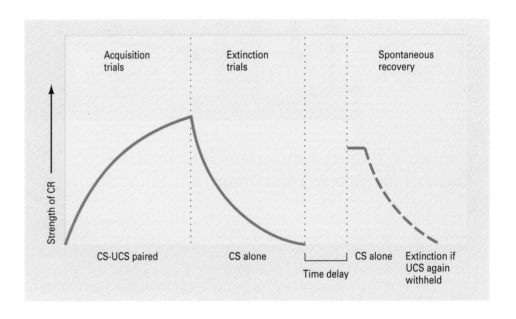

Extinction   The gradual disappearance of a conditioned response once the conditioned stimulus is no longer followed by the unconditioned stimulus or by reinforcement.

Spontaneous recovery   The reappearance, with no additional training, of a conditioned response that has been extinguished.

Higher-order conditioning   Training a subject to respond to a conditioned stimulus by pairing it with the conditioned stimulus from a previous conditioning procedure.

Spontaneous Recovery   Once a conditioned response is extinguished, an animal's responses to the conditioned stimulus are similar to its responses before conditioning took place—except that the conditioned response may suddenly recur without being reconditioned. For instance, if the dog hasn't heard the metronome for a time, it may suddenly salivate to the sound. This phenomenon is called **spontaneous recovery.**

Higher-Order Conditioning   Once a neutral stimulus has become a conditioned stimulus, it can be used as an unconditioned stimulus. For example, once a dog has been classically conditioned to salivate when it hears the clicking of a metronome, the sound of the metronome can be used as an unconditioned stimulus to train the dog to salivate when it hears a buzzer. We simply have to pair the sound of the metronome with the sound of the buzzer. In a short time, the dog will respond to the sound of the buzzer itself. This procedure is known as **higher-order conditioning.**

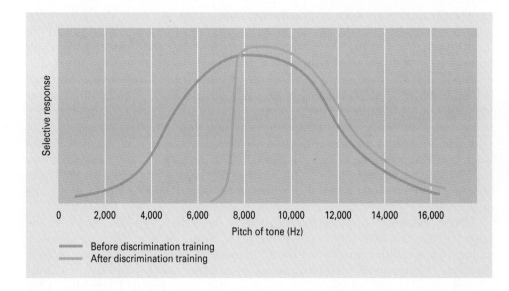

Selective response

Pitch of tone (Hz)

—— Before discrimination training
—— After discrimination training

Figure 6.5
The Relationship Between Discrimination and Generalization

The red curve shows how an animal that has been conditioned to salivate to an 8,000 Hz tone might respond to higher and lower pitched tones. This is a typical generalization gradient. The blue curve shows how an an animal might respond after discrimination training, i.e., after it had been reinforced for salivating to an 8,000 Hz tone but not reinforced for salivating to a 6,000 Hz tone.

Generalization and Discrimination   **Generalization** is the tendency to transfer what you've learned in one situation to a similar situation. In classical conditioning it means that you make the conditioned response not only to the conditioned stimulus but also to other stimuli that are like it. **Discrimination** is the ability to distinguish among similar stimuli by responding to them in different ways. In classical conditioning, discrimination limits generalization. To the extent that you recognize that two stimuli are different, you respond differently to them (see Figure 6.5).

Suppose a friend takes you out to a Greek restaurant and you have a wonderful time. If you find that you begin to salivate whenever you walk into a Greek restaurant, you've generalized among Greek restaurants. Now suppose that you have a couple of bad meals in other Greek restaurants. If you find that you salivate only when you walk into the original restaurant, you've discriminated among Greek restaurants.

Classical Conditioning and Information Processing

Pavlov (1927) insisted that conditioning is automatic, a product of the repeated *contiguity* of the conditioned stimulus with the unconditioned stimulus. (Events are contiguous when they occur closely in time.) He maintained that conditioning is possible only when the conditioned stimulus and the unconditioned stimulus are presented very close in time—say, a half-second apart (Schwartz, 1984). Pavlov's description of the conditioning process as simple and automatic characterized psychologists' perspective of conditioning until the 1960s.

In the last three decades, this perspective on conditioning has been challenged. According to the newer theory, conditioning is not a low-level physiological process like a reflex but, rather, a kind of information processing that alerts the organism to events that have had important consequences in the past (Rescorla, 1988). The individual learns because the conditioned stimulus signals that the unconditioned stimulus is about to occur. To work effectively as a signal, the conditioned stimulus must be more than contiguous with the unconditioned stimulus. It must also be a good predictor of it. When one event is a good predictor of another, the second is *contingent* on the first.

Generalization   The tendency to respond to different stimuli in the same way.

Discrimination   The ability to distinguish among similar stimuli by responding to them in different ways.

The distinction between events that are contiguous and those that are contingent is blurred because the two so often go together. Lightning and thunder are both contiguous and contingent. Not only do lightning and thunder occur close in time to each other, but lightning is a good predictor of thunder.

But things that are contingent are not necessarily contiguous. If you commute a long distance to school, sleeping through your alarm clock and being late for class are not contiguous events; they may occur an hour or more apart. But they are contingent events: every time you oversleep, you're late for class.

Likewise, events that are contiguous are not necessarily contingent. (We call such events *coincidences*.) If you hear a favorite song on the car radio on a day you oversleep, you wouldn't think hearing the song was contingent on oversleeping. Even if it happened more than once, you would assume it was a coincidence.

Recent evidence supports the idea that contingency, not contiguity, is the essential element in conditioning procedures. Some of that evidence shows a failure to learn with contiguous stimuli. In one experiment, for example, Robert Rescorla (1968) conditioned two groups of animals, using a tone as the conditioned stimulus and an electrical shock as the unconditioned stimulus. One group received shocks only when the tone sounded. The other also received shocks when the tone did not sound (see Figure 6.6). Even though the animals received exactly the same number of pairings of tone and shock, those receiving the extra shocks did not learn a conditioned fear response to the tone. Why? Because the conditioned stimulus (the tone), though equally contiguous with the unconditioned stimulus (the shock), did not reliably predict it.

Figure 6.6
Conditioning, Contiguity, and Predictability

Both groups experience the same number of bell-shock pairings, and the bell is always followed by a shock. Thus, if contiguity is the basis of conditioning, both should learn equally. The second group also receives some shocks without the bell, so the bell is not a good predictor of the occurrence of shock. This group does not learn a fear response to the bell, demonstrating that predictability, not contiguity, is the basis of learning.

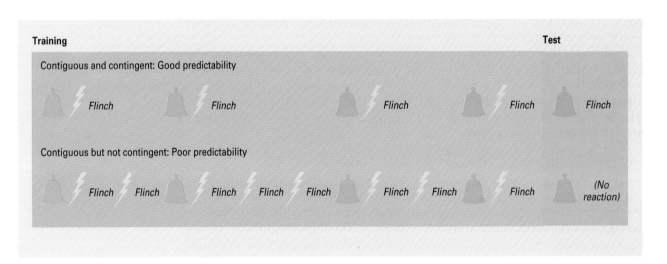

Classical Conditioning and Aversive Stimuli

In his experiments, Rescorla used an electrical shock as the unconditioned stimulus. A shock is an **aversive stimulus**—a stimulus the subject tries to avoid. Aversive conditioning utilizes aversive stimuli. The function of aversive conditioning is to help us learn to avoid things that can hurt us. So you might expect that the process of evolution has made some conditioned responses easier to learn than others and some unconditioned stimuli more effective in certain situations. The question of whether evolution speeds up the conditioning process or influences the effectiveness of certain stimuli was generated by the study of taste aversion.

Aversive stimulus   A stimulus that a subject tries to avoid.

The discovery of taste aversion was a classic example of *serendipity*—a discovery made by accident. While studying radiation sickness in rats, John Garcia and his colleagues (1956) noticed that the rats were not drinking from the plastic water bottles in the radiation chambers. Was aversive conditioning involved? Certain elements of the researchers' work were indeed characteristic of aversive conditioning. The radiation was a kind of unconditioned stimulus; the nausea brought on by the radiation, an unconditioned response; and the radiation chamber and its plastic water bottles, the conditioned stimulus.

But other elements didn't seem to fit. First, the rats stopped drinking the water after just a few exposures to the radiation. Conditioning ordinarily requires repeated pairings of the conditioned stimulus with the unconditioned stimulus. Second, there was a delay of several hours between the exposure to the radiation and the nausea. For most kinds of conditioning, the time between the conditioned stimulus and the unconditioned stimulus must be very short—less than a second. If in fact the rats were being conditioned to avoid the water, the researchers had happened on an extraordinary new kind of conditioning.

To test this idea, Garcia and Robert Koelling performed a series of experiments. Their findings suggested that rats learn to avoid foods that nauseate them, even when there are long delays between the conditioned stimulus (the food) and the unconditioned stimulus (the nausea) (Garcia, Ervin & Koelling, 1966).

Garcia's findings created a storm of controversy among conditioning experts, but they were soon confirmed by other researchers. In time they formed the basis of **preparedness theory,** an evolutionary explanation of conditioning (Seligman, 1971). According to that theory, animals and people more readily acquire and less readily extinguish conditioned responses that relate to biological hazards.

Phobias

A **phobia** is an unreasonable fear that keeps people from performing certain behaviors. The phobic person may be afraid of elevators, of flying, of open spaces, of crowds.

Some phobias are attributed to a single dramatic event in a person's life during which the feared object was paired with some terrifying experience. For example, Levine and Sandeen (1985) describe the case of a construction worker who became terrified of heights—not only the scaffolding on the buildings where he worked but also bridges and airplanes. His terror seemed to stem from a single incident, a fall that left him hanging for several seconds from a beam one hundred feet above the ground. His fear stopped the man from working.

We also know that phobias can be conditioned over time. In an experiment that would never be allowed today with a human subject, John Watson conditioned a fear of rats in a baby (Watson & Rayner, 1920). The child, whom Watson called "Little Albert," was a patient in a hospital where Watson was working. Watson began by having Little Albert get used to petting a tame white rat. Then, each time he presented the rat, an iron bar would start banging behind Little Albert's head. After just seven pairings of rat and banging, the child showed evidence of fear of the rat alone.

Treatment based on extinction can cure phobias. For example, we could take our construction worker someplace high and safe—say the observation deck of a tall building—where he can experience the conditioned stimulus (the height) in the absence of the unconditioned stimulus (a terrifying fall). By repeatedly presenting the conditioned stimulus without the unconditioned stimulus, we should be able to extinguish the conditioned response—the phobia.

Preparedness theory The idea that people are predisposed to acquire and maintain conditioned responses to biological hazards.

Phobia An unreasonable fear that limits the individual's participation in day-to-day activities.

Puzzle It Out!

The third game of the 1989 World Series between the two San Francisco Bay teams, the Oakland Athletics and the San Francisco Giants, was interrupted when a large earthquake shook San Francisco's Candlestick Park. The week before the Series resumed, the San Francisco team practiced in its home stadium, where the next game was going to be played; the Oakland team practiced in Arizona, at its spring training camp. All week long, aftershocks shook the San Francisco stadium, but no new damage was done. The night before the big game, television reporters asked players from both teams whether they were nervous about resuming play in the very stadium where the earthquake took place. Which team do you think was most nervous? Why?

During the third game of the 1989 World Series, a violent earthquake damaged the stadium and killed a number of people in other parts of the city.

Some phobias are more common than others, and many of these are related to biological hazards. Snakes and insects, for instance, are more often the object of phobias than are flowers and birds. Does this fact support preparedness theory? The answer seems to be no. Richard McNally (1987) reviewed the many experiments done to test the idea that we are prepared to develop phobias of biological hazards. He concluded that differences in conditioning using biologically relevant versus biologically irrelevant stimuli are small, nonexistent, or readily explained by other factors.

Recap

- Classical conditioning is the process through which the individual learns to associate a certain response with a certain stimulus.

- By pairing an unconditioned stimulus with a conditioned stimulus, Pavlov was able to elicit a conditioned response.

- Extinction is the process of weakening the conditioned response by presenting the conditioned stimulus without the unconditioned stimulus.

- A neutral stimulus that has become a conditioned stimulus can be used as an unconditioned stimulus.

- In classical conditioning, discrimination limits generalization: to the extent that people recognize that two stimuli are different, they respond differently to them.

- Research shows that the contiguity of the conditioned and unconditioned stimuli may not be as important to learning as their contingency.

- Aversive conditioning helps people learn to avoid things that can hurt them.

- According to preparedness theory, the individual more readily acquires and less readily extinguishes conditioned responses that relate to biological hazards.

- A phobia is an unreasonable fear that limits the individual's participation in day-to-day activities.

Instrumental Conditioning

Through classical conditioning we learn to associate an unconditioned stimulus and response with what was a neutral stimulus. Without consciously thinking about it, we respond to the conditioned stimulus with behavior like that with which we respond to the unconditioned stimulus. Through **instrumental conditioning** we learn to behave in a certain way because we learn to associate certain consequences with our behavior. As I write these words, for instance, my computer scrolls out lines of text. The sense of accomplishment I get from filling the empty screen keeps me going for hours at a time. That sense of accomplishment is a consequence of my behavior; it's a reward that keeps me working. As you read these words, you're also being influenced by the consequences of your actions. There's the reward of learning itself, of better understanding the world around you. And there's the more concrete reward of the grades you get on your quizzes, exams, and papers.

The Development of Instrumental Conditioning

Some years before Pavlov began his experiments on classical conditioning in his laboratory in Moscow, Edward Thorndike, a graduate student at Harvard, was beginning his experiments on instrumental conditioning in a basement in Cambridge (Leahey, 1987). The apparatus he used was a puzzle box, like the one shown in Figure 6.7; his subject was a hungry cat. Thorndike wanted to see whether, if by using what he called *satisfiers,* he could train the cat to work its way out of the box. He identified two satisfiers in the experiment. First, cats don't like being confined. So just getting out of the box was a reward of sorts. The second satisfier was food. Waiting for the cat outside the box was a bowl of food (Thorndike, 1911, 1931).

Thorndike found that in the course of several trials, cats and other animals readily learned to press a lever or turn a latch to escape from a puzzle box and receive their satisfiers. The animals repeated the lever-pressing or latch-turning behaviors because their behaviors were being rewarded. Thorndike discussed the effect of satisfiers on behaviors as the **law of effect.**

Instrumental conditioning
Learning through reinforcement.

Law of effect Responses that are reinforced are more likely to be repeated (learned) than those that are not reinforced.

Figure 6.7
Thorndike's Puzzle Box

Thorndike's puzzle boxes ranged from simple to complex. In the one shown here, the subject pressed a lever to open the box. To open the more complicated boxes, the subject had to perform a sequence of actions.

Because satisfiers seemed to strengthen learning in the experimental situation, in time they came to be called *reinforcers*. And the procedure of giving reinforcers when an animal performed a correct response came to be called **reinforcement.**

Thorndike's techniques were developed and refined by B. F. Skinner (1938). Using an apparatus called a *Skinner box* (see Figure 6.8), Skinner trained rats to press bars and pigeons to peck keys in order to receive food.

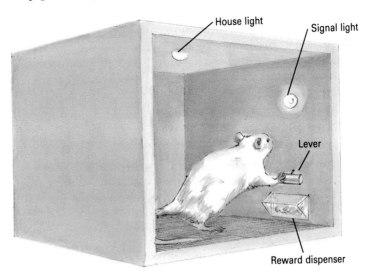

Figure 6.8
A Rat in a Skinner Box

When the rat presses on the lever, food is dispensed. In some versions of Skinnerian training, the signal light may tell the rat when the bar is activated and/or a mild shock may be delivered to the rat's feet through the floor grid.

Reinforcement The process of systematically following a response with a reward in order to increase the frequency of that response.

Operant conditioning A form of instrumental conditioning developed by Skinner that allows the subject to set the pace of learning.

Operant A response that acts on the environment.

Skinner called his learning procedure **operant conditioning.** He defined **operant** as a response that acts on the environment—as a behavior that is *emitted* by the animal, not elicited by the environment (Leahey, 1987). He believed that his experimental conditions more closely approximated those in the natural world in which animals—and people—actually learn than did the constrained conditions used by Pavlov and Thorndike. For example, unlike other conditioning procedures, which were divided into separate trials, Skinner's procedure was ongoing: the animal could respond at any time, thereby setting the pace of its own learning.

How does operant conditioning work? A hungry rat is placed in the Skinner box and allowed to explore it. On one wall of the box is a food cup. Near the cup is a lever that activates an electric apparatus that delivers a food pellet to the cup. At some point while it's exploring, the rat inadvertently trips the lever and receives the food. Once it eats, the rat continues exploring, but now it focuses on the area around the food cup and lever. Once again, it accidentally trips the lever. The process continues until the rat goes directly to the lever after each trip to the food cup.

Operant conditioning can be helped along by a procedure called **shaping** (see Figure 6.9). Instead of waiting for the rat to press the bar accidentally, the experimenter encourages the rat to approach both the bar and the food cup by activating the food-delivery mechanism a few times, giving the rat a few "free" food pellets. As soon as the rat learns that the click of the food-delivery mechanism means that there's food in the cup, shaping begins. First the experimenter provides food every time the rat turns toward the bar, then whenever the rat nears the bar, and finally whenever the rat touches the bar. By reinforcing the rat every time it more closely approximates the right response, the experimenter helps shape the rat's learning.

Figure 6.9
Shaping

By becoming more and more fussy about what responses he or she will reinforce, the experimenter guides the rat to press the bar for food.

The Acquisition Process

Like classical conditioning, instrumental conditioning occurs in three stages:

1. Before reinforcement, the rat responds to the experimental situation with exploratory behaviors such as sniffing and looking around. If we rank the rat's responses from most to least common, sniffing would probably be the most common and bar pressing the least. (The level of bar pressing is low at this stage because it is only very rarely that an untrained animal responds to the strange circumstances of an experiment by pressing a bar.)
2. During reinforcement, the experimenter provides food only when the rat presses the bar.
3. The effect of reinforcement is to change the priority of the rat's responses. After training, bar pressing and the other behaviors that go along with it have replaced exploratory behaviors as the behaviors performed most often by the rat.

Shaping The reinforcement of successive approximations to a desired response.

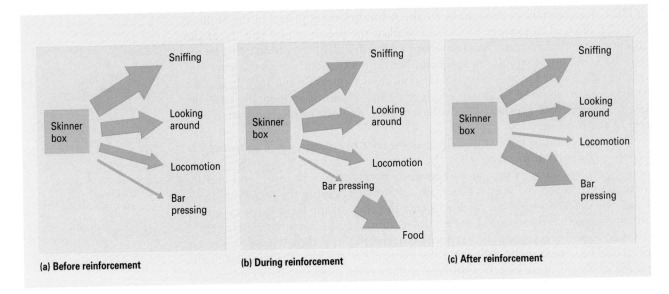

(a) **Before reinforcement**   (b) **During reinforcement**   (c) **After reinforcement**

Figure 6.10
Operant Conditioning

The effect of operant conditioning is to change the priority of the rat's responses. When an untrained rat is placed in a Skinner box it is likely to spend most of its time sniffing, looking and moving around, and pressing the bar, but only rarely. After bar pressing has been reinforced, it soon becomes one of the rat's most frequent behaviors. In this figure, the width of the arrows represents the likelihood of a response—the widest arrow means the response is most likely; the thinnest arrow, least likely.

Figure 6.10 illustrates the three stages of instrumental conditioning.

We keep track of the rat's progress by counting the total number of bar presses the rat makes or by charting changes in the rate at which it responds. Both methods produce a graph called a *learning curve*, which is illustrated in Figure 6.11. The higher or steeper the curve, the faster the animal is learning.

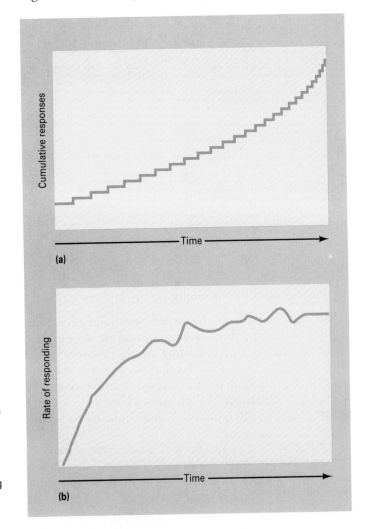

Figure 6.11
Learning Curves

Here are two methods by which operant conditioning data are often presented in the literature. The curve in Part a shows each response as an increase in the height of the trace. The steepness of the curve shows the speed of responding. Notice that the steepness increases as the number of reponses per unit of time increases. This rate of responding is shown directly in the second trace (Part b).

Reinforcement Schedules

A **reinforcement schedule** is the principle that relates the response to its reinforcement. It determines how frequently, consistently, or rapidly the response is reinforced. In our description of instrumental conditioning thus far, we've talked about **continuous reinforcement:** the subject is always reinforced when it responds correctly.

But what happens if we vary the reinforcement schedule? Suppose we go from reinforcing every response to reinforcing no responses? Look at Figure 6.12. With no reinforcement, the animal's rate of bar pressing gradually falls and the relative frequency of alternative responses gradually increases until bar pressing resumes its original position at the bottom of the rat's response hierarchy. The animal is once again less likely to press the bar than to respond in other ways. The conditioned response has been *extinguished*.

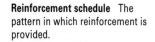

Reinforcement schedule The pattern in which reinforcement is provided.

Continuous reinforcement A pattern of rewarding the subject whenever it responds correctly.

Partial reinforcement A schedule of reinforcement that does not reinforce every response.

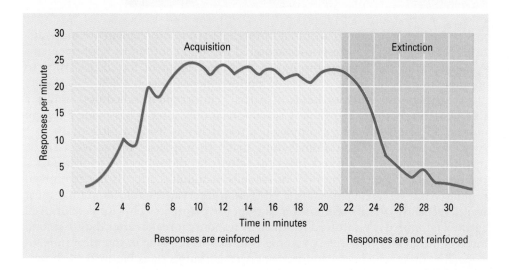

Figure 6.12
The Acquisition and Extinction of an Instrumentally Conditioned Response

When reinforcement is discontinued, extinction takes place and the rat's rate of responding declines rapidly.

Between the extremes of always reinforcing a response and never reinforcing it are patterns of **partial reinforcement,** schedules of reinforcement in which the response is *sometimes* reinforced. Responses that are partially reinforced are harder to learn than responses that are continuously reinforced, as shown in the graph in Figure 6.13. This makes sense when you consider that the subject is simultaneously being reinforced and not reinforced for the same behavior. It also

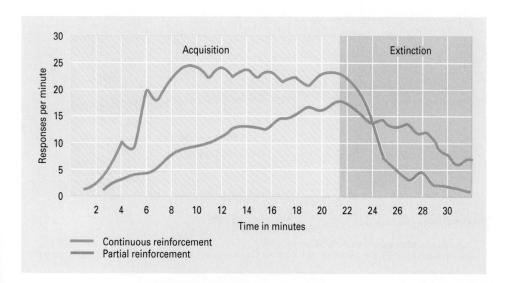

Figure 6.13
Continuous Reinforcement Versus Partial Reinforcement

Partially reinforced responses are harder to learn, but they are also harder to extinguish.

In your interactions with machines you often learn the way a rat does in a Skinner box. If a pay phone doesn't work the first time, how many more times would you try it again? Are you more likely to try it several times if you've used the phone successfully several times before? What if the phone works only sometimes? What kind of reinforcement schedule is that?

makes sense that responses acquired through partial reinforcement are more difficult to extinguish than responses acquired through continuous reinforcement. A subject who has learned through partial reinforcement has also learned to continue to respond in the absence of reinforcement (Amsel, 1962).

Researchers use different kinds of partial reinforcement schedules. Under a **fixed-ratio schedule,** the subject is reinforced only after it has made a certain number of responses. For example, if a researcher is using a ratio of 10 to 1 (what we call *FR 10*), an animal must make 10 responses to receive a single reinforcement. Under a **fixed-interval schedule,** the subject is reinforced for responses made a certain number of seconds or minutes after its last reinforced response. If a researcher is using a 10-second interval (FI 10), an animal must wait 10 seconds after its last reinforced response before its behavior is reinforced again. The animal is reinforced for the first response it makes after the 10-second interval, no matter how many responses it may have made in the meantime.

Each of these schedules has different effects on subjects, as Figure 6.14 shows. An animal on a fixed-ratio schedule cannot accumulate reinforcements as

Figure 6.14
Partial Reinforcement Schedules

Rats respond to ratio reinforcement schedules (fixed and variable) with high and steady rates of reinforcement because these schedules can increase the rate at which reinforcement occurs by increasing the rate of a rat's response. Interval schedules promote lower rates of responding because as long as the rat is responding at a basic rate, no additional responses are rewarded.

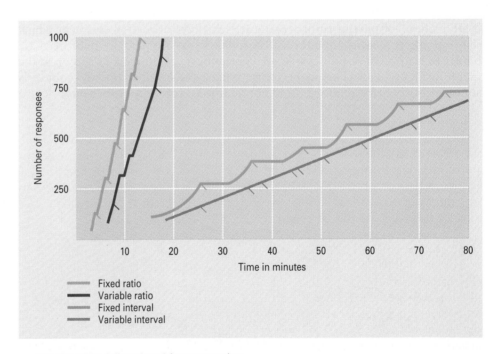

Note: Diagonal lines indicate when reinforcement was given.
Source: Adapted from "Teaching Machines" by B. F. Skinner. Copyright © 1961 by Scientific American Inc. All rights reserved.

Puzzle It Out!

One way to view work is as an instrumentally conditioned behavior in which the reinforcer is a paycheck. Some workers are paid an hourly wage, no matter how much work they do. While others are paid for the job no matter how long it takes. Assuming that principles of reinforcement apply to the workplace, what sorts of work habits would these payment schedules promote?

quickly as an animal on a continuous reinforcement schedule, but it can increase its rate of reinforcement by working faster. Thus fixed-ratio schedules promote higher rates of response. By contrast, an animal working on a fixed-interval schedule cannot increase its rate of reinforcement, regardless of how hard it works. So fixed-interval schedules promote rhythmical bursts of responses that correspond to the length of the interval.

To the repetition and time dimensions of reinforcement schedules we can add a reliability dimension. Fixed reinforcement schedules are very reliable; *variable reinforcement schedules* are reliable only on average. A subject on a fixed-ratio schedule of 10 responses to 1 reinforcement (FR 10) or a fixed-interval schedule of 10 seconds (FI 10) is reinforced for *every* tenth response or for *every* response that occurs after a 10-second interval. By contrast, a subject on a **variable-ratio schedule** of 10 to 1 (VR 10) is reinforced for 1 response in 10 *on average,* and a subject on a **variable-interval schedule** of 10 seconds (VI 10) is reinforced in 10-second intervals *on average*. The actual values vary from reinforcement to reinforcement.

Variable schedules generate faster and steadier responses than do fixed schedules (Skinner, 1961). In the experimental situation, rats behave as though "each bar press may be their lucky bar press." And people aren't much different. The companies that manufacture slot machines design them to pay off under variable ratio schedules because variable schedules keep us pouring in coins at the highest rate of speed.

We've been talking about learning situations in which just one response is reinforced and the animal either makes the response or doesn't. But this kind of black-or-white situation isn't common in real life, even for rats. In everyday life, people and animals choose among many different courses of action whose outcomes are more or less reinforcing. For instance, a student who is taking four courses, working at a part-time job, and maintaining a social life is constantly forced to choose among different courses of action, each with its own consequences.

Researchers have tried to introduce the element of choice in their conditioning experiments by offering their subjects not one but two reinforcement opportunities and seeing which option the animal chooses. The rat might have two bars to press or the pigeon might have two keys to peck, and each bar or key might operate under a different reinforcement schedule. Such experiments explore how the animals allocate their time between the two reinforcers.

The research shows that animals are very skilled at getting the most out of these choice situations. For instance, if offered the choice between two ratio schedules, rats tend to choose the bar with the highest reinforcement rate (Domjan & Burkhard, 1986; Herrnstein, 1958). (Why waste time on the bar that gives you less reinforcement?) And if offered the choice between two interval schedules, rats generally alternate between the two bars, spending time on each bar in proportion to the rate of reinforcement (Herrnstein, 1961). (If you're standing around waiting for the interval on one bar to be over, why not take a whack at the other bar while you wait?)

Fixed-ratio schedule A pattern of reinforcement in which the subject must make a specified number of unreinforced responses for each reinforced response.

Fixed-interval schedule A pattern of reinforcement in which the subject is reinforced for responses made a certain number of seconds or minutes after its last reinforced response.

Variable-ratio schedule An irregular pattern of reinforcement that rewards the subject after a number of unreinforced responses have been made on the average.

Variable-interval schedule An irregular pattern of reinforcement that rewards the subject after a certain period of time has elapsed on the average.

Other Elaborations of Instrumental Conditioning

Using basic operant conditioning as a starting point, learning researchers have discovered many other interesting phenomena of learning.

Secondary Reinforcement   Food is a primary reinforcer; it satisfies a basic biological need. Once we've conditioned a response using a primary reinforcer, we can use the opportunity to perform that response as a reinforcer for another behavior. The response is effective only because of its previous association with a primary reinforcer, so it's called a *secondary reinforcer.*

For example, once a rat has been conditioned to press a bar in a Skinner box, the same rat can be trained to press another bar just for a chance to press the first bar. Because pressing the first bar has been reinforced in the past, the response has itself become a reinforcer and can be used to reinforce a second bar-press response by itself.

The principles of secondary reinforcement underlie token economies. A **token economy** is a system of rewarding behavior with a token of some sort—a poker chip or a ticket, for example—that later can be exchanged for something the individual wants. Token economies are often used in mental hospitals to manage difficult patients (Paul & Lentz, 1977). Patients who behave appropriately are rewarded with tokens that they can exchange for access to television, social events, special food, or other privileges. Here the privileges constitute the primary reinforcer. And the tokens are secondary reinforcers; they derive their power to change behavior from their association with the privileges.

Token economies are an important part of using instrumental conditioning because they allow us to reinforce a behavior immediately after it occurs. And, indeed, reinforcement is usually most effective when it immediately follows a response. It would be impossible to reward a patient with food or a privilege at every step of a sequential activity such as getting dressed. With breaks for candy bars and television, the patient would spend an entire day putting his clothes on. But giving a patient a token for putting on his shirt, another for pulling on his pants, and another for tying his shoelaces is easy. It's also effective because the patient can use the token to choose his own primary reinforcement.

Discriminated Operants   Unlike classical conditioning, operant conditioning doesn't use a specific stimulus to elicit a response. Remember, Skinner believed that behavior is emitted by the animal, not elicited by the environment. But even Skinner acknowledged that the environment plays a role in operant conditioning by providing the context in which learning takes place. For instance, if an animal in a Skinner box is reinforced only when a light flashes, it quickly learns to wait for the light before pressing the bar. A behavior that is conditional on the presence of another stimulus is called a **discriminated operant.**

Like discriminated responses that have been classically conditioned, discriminated operants reveal the degree to which animals generalize and distinguish among different stimuli.

Token economy A system of secondary reinforcement that rewards behavior with tokens that later can be exchanged for something the individual wants.

Discriminated operant A behavior that the subject performs only in the presence of a particular stimulus.

Cognitive Behaviorism

What process is at work in instrumental conditioning? Here, as in classical conditioning, psychologists describe two different processes. Thorndike and Skinner would say that instrumental conditioning is a product of the repeated contiguity of response and reinforcer. Learning occurs because we repeatedly pair response and reinforcer. Instrumental conditioning, then, is a simple, almost mechanical process.

How Do We Know That?

How do psychologists discover whether an animal can tell the difference be-tween two tones? Or between two shades of a color? With people it's easy. All you have to do is ask. But with animals it's harder because they can't tell you what they're hearing or seeing—not in words, anyway.

One method is to vary the stimulus used to instrumentally condition the animals. For example, suppose a pigeon has been instrumentally conditioned to peck a key for food when a yellow light shines on the key. To test the bird's ability to discriminate, we'd project a different colored light—let's say a red light—on the key. To the extent that the pigeon responds less vigorously to the red light than it does to the yellow light, it reveals that it can tell the two lights apart. By increasing the similarity of the two stimuli until the ani-mal responds equally to each stimulus, we can demonstrate which stimuli are so similar that the animal cannot tell them apart (Guttman & Kalish, 1956).

Cognitive behaviorists don't agree. Again, they use an information-process-ing analogy. Instrumental conditioning is a kind of information processing through which animals learn where and how reinforcers are likely to be pro-duced in their environment. Learning occurs, then, not because reinforcement creates a connection between the response and the stimulus in the experimental situation, but because reinforcement teaches the subject which of its actions is likely to be rewarded.

Using rats and mazes, cognitive behaviorists set out to demonstrate that in-strumental conditioning is a cognitive process. Note that a maze is a series of pathways, one or more of which connect the starting point (called the *start box*) with an ending point (called the *goal box*).

One group of experiments trained rats to run a maze by one means and then tested their ability to solve it by some other means. For example, in one study the rats were trained to swim through a maze. Although they had no experience running the maze, the study clearly demonstrated that the rats had learned something about the maze. When they were subsequently placed in the same maze without water, they were quicker to learn to run the maze than were rats that had received no training whatsoever.

A second group of experiments focused on **latent learning,** learning that is not demonstrated immediately. In this case, the researchers hoped to show that rats could learn without being reinforced, thus skewering the argument that the contiguity of response and reinforcement is at the heart of learning. In one of these experiments, several rats were placed in a maze and allowed to explore it without any reinforcement. Later, when food was placed in the goal box, the same rats learned the maze much more quickly than rats that had no experience with it (Tolman & Honzik, 1930b).

A third group of experiments showed evidence of what E. C. Tolman called a **cognitive map,** defined as a mental image of space. According to cognitive behaviorists, rats use their cognitive maps to get around a maze much as we use maps to get around a city.

The researchers in one of these studies designed a maze with three routes to the goal box: a short route, which went directly to the goal box; a medium route, which left the short route at the beginning and rejoined it about halfway to the goal box; and a long route, which left the short route at the beginning and rejoined it at the goal box (see Figure 6.15) (Tolman & Honzik, 1930a). The

Latent learning   Learning that is not demonstrated immediately.

Cognitive map   A mental image of space.

Figure 6.15
Demonstrating Cognitive Maps in Rats

First the rat explores the maze and learns to run from the start box to the goal box over the short path. If the maze is blocked at Block Point 1, the rat learns to take the medium-length path. If the maze is blocked at Block Point 2, the rat returns to the start box. How will it respond during the next trial? If it has a cognitive map of the maze, it should choose the long path—and it does.

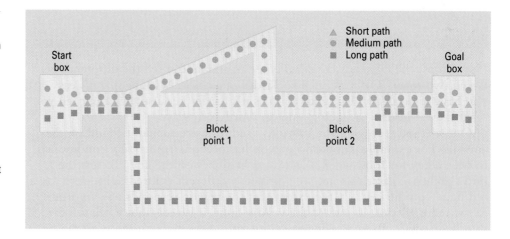

rats quickly learned to choose the short route over the medium route and the medium route over the long route. When only the shortest route was blocked, the rats chose the medium route.

When the experimenters blocked the short route just before the goal box, they, in effect, blocked the medium route, too. If instrumental conditioning is simply a mechanical process, the rats, finding the short route blocked, should have chosen the medium route. But they didn't; they chose the long route. Apparently the rats inferred from their experience with the short route that the medium route was blocked as well.

Over the years, these kinds of experiments forced many traditional behaviorists—psychologists who had supported the mechanical-process explanation of conditioning—to modify their thinking. They began to talk about connections, not between the turning points in a maze and the rats' responses, but between internal representations of those turning points and internal representations of the rats' responses. They didn't extend their explanations to include concepts like understanding and thinking; but by acknowledging the idea of internal representations, they went a long way toward accepting the cognitive theory of how rats run a maze.

Reinforcement Versus Punishment

We've been talking about **positive reinforcement,** the use of something the subject likes—for example, food—to reinforce behavior. But we also can strengthen or weaken a response by using aversive stimuli. **Negative reinforcement** strengthens a response by removing a stimulus that the organism doesn't like—a shock, for example.

To negatively reinforce a response, we remove the aversive stimulus whenever the subject makes the response. A child who must stay in her room until she makes her bed is being negatively reinforced. Every time she makes her bed, the aversive stimulus—being confined to her room—is removed. **Punishment** weakens a response by providing a stimulus the organism finds aversive or by removing one that it wants. In a sense, reinforcement tells the subject what to do; punishment tells the subject what not to do.

To punish a response, we remove a positive stimulus or present an aversive stimulus whenever the subject performs the response. A child who is refused dessert or is told that she must stay in her room today because she failed to make her bed yesterday is being punished for her messiness.

Positive reinforcement A procedure that strengthens learning by giving the subject something it likes.

Negative reinforcement A procedure that strengthens learning by taking away from the subject something it dislikes.

Punishment A procedure that weakens a response by taking away something the subject likes or by giving the subject something it dislikes.

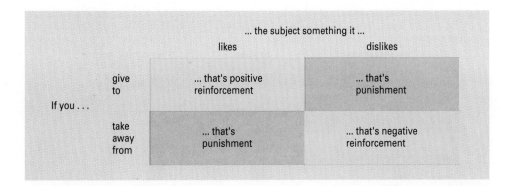

Figure 6.16
The Different Kinds of Reinforce-ment and Punishment

Read this chart like a sentence, from left to right. For instance, "If you . . . give to . . . the subject something it . . . likes . . . that's positive reinforcement."

Negative reinforcement and punishment have opposite effects on behavior. Negative reinforcement, like positive reinforcement, increases the likelihood that a subject will make the same response again in the same circumstances. Punishment decreases the likelihood that a behavior will be repeated. The relationships among the different sorts of reinforcement and punishment are illustrated in Figure 6.16.

Negative Reinforcement   Negative reinforcement is used in two kinds of instrumental procedures: escape conditioning and avoidance conditioning (see Figures 6.17a and 6.17b). In **escape conditioning,** the subject can make a response that stops the aversive stimulus. Suppose we place a rat in a shuttle box, like the one in Figure 6.18, and turn on the electricity in the floor under the rat. The shock makes the rat jump and run about until it leaps over the partition into the other half of the box, where the electricity in the floor is off. If we repeat the procedure, switching the shock between the two halves of the box, the rat quickly learns to leave the "shocking" side of the box as soon as the electricity goes on (Schwartz, 1984).

To turn escape conditioning into **avoidance conditioning,** we would add a light to the experimental situation, using it to signal that a shock is coming. Now the rat can avoid the shock altogether by changing sides of the box whenever the light comes on.

Avoidance conditioning is very resistant to extinction. Rats that have been trained to avoid shock by pressing a bar continue to press the bar in their Skinner boxes indefinitely, long after the shock has been turned off. Why?

The reason may be that once the rats have learned to avoid the shock, they never have a chance to learn that the electricity has been turned off. This may explain why certain phobias last for years. By avoiding the object of their phobias, people don't have the opportunity to experience the object as it really is. For instance, if you're afraid of dogs and avoid them carefully, you never have a chance to experience a happy relationship with one and thus to realize that there is nothing to fear.

Punishment   To punish a response, we present something the subject does not like or take away something the subject does like. To perform a punishment experiment, the experimenter begins by teaching the subject a behavior—say, bar pressing in response to a light. Once the animal is bar pressing reliably when the light comes on, the bar is connected to a shock apparatus. Now, each time the animal presses the bar, it receives a shock. In time the bar-pressing behavior disappears (see Figure 6.17c).

A series of experiments carried out by W. K. Estes and B. F. Skinner (Estes & Skinner, 1941; Estes, 1944) was typical of the early research on punishment. These experiments revealed that punishment doesn't decrease just the frequency of behaviors it is paired with; it decreases the frequency of *all* behaviors—an effect that severely limits its use as a training tool.

Escape conditioning   A form of instrumental aversive conditioning in which the subject's response terminates the aversive stimulation.

Avoidance conditioning   A form of instrumental aversive conditioning in which the subject responds to a neutral stimulus that signals the onset of the aversive stimulus, thereby avoiding the aversive stimulus.

Figure 6.17
Procedures in Escape, Avoidance, and Punishment Training

Each horizontal bar indicates an event: the light or shock being given or the bar being pressed and food being provided. Notice that after avoidance conditioning is successful, the rat rarely experiences shocks. After punishment conditioning, the rat is neither shocked nor fed.

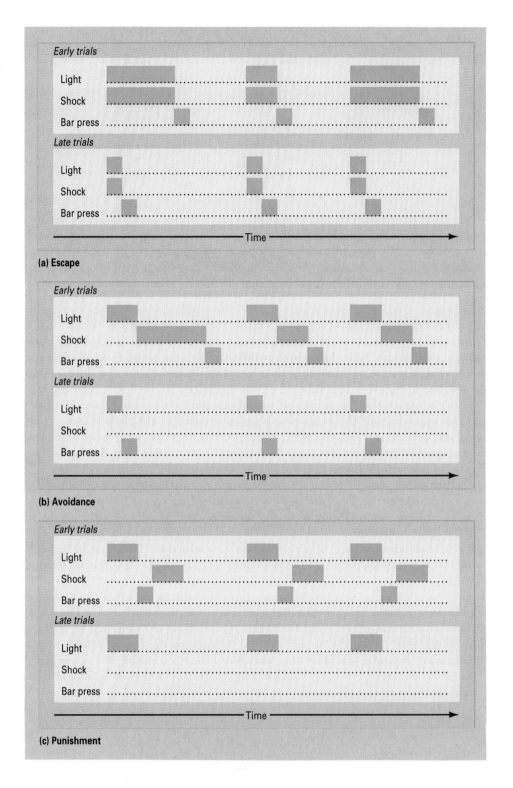

But more recent research shows that punishment can be selective, that it can have a specific effect on unwanted responses. For example, one study tested the effects of punishment on a bar-press-for-food response with three groups of rats (Church & Raymond, 1969). One group, the control group, was not punished. A second group, the noncontingent aversive group, received electrical shocks, but the shocks were not *contingent* on the bar press. That is, the rats were shocked whether or not they pressed the bar. In the third group, the punishment

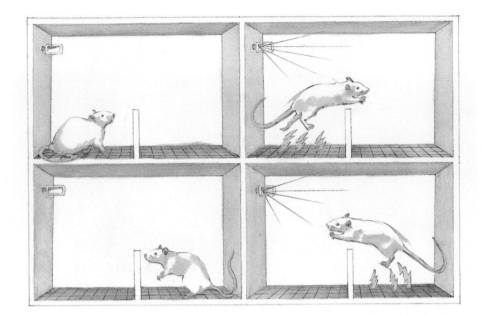

Figure 6.18
A Rat in a Shuttle Box

Avoidance and escape conditioning are often done in an apparatus known as a shuttle box. As the shock is applied first to one side of the cage and then to the other, the rat "shuttles" back and forth between the two sides of the cage.

group, the shocks were contingent on the bar press. Although the experiment showed that both the noncontingent aversive group and the punishment group decreased their bar pressing, the effect of punishment was much more dramatic and long lasting (see Figure 6.19).

Do these findings mean that all psychologists today recommend punishment as a means of correcting children's behavior? No. The conditions that make punishment effective are rarely met in parent-child interactions (Schwartz, 1984). In order to apply what we've learned from studies with animals to child-rearing practices, we would have to fulfill the following conditions:

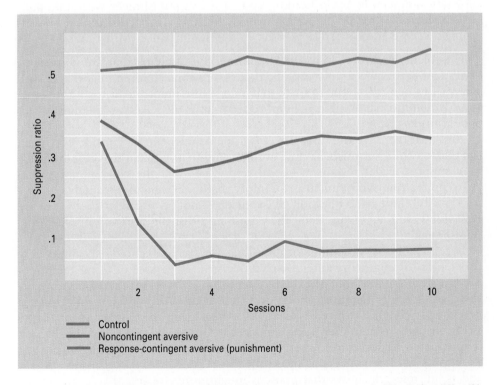

Figure 6.19
The Effect of Punishment on Bar Pressing for Food

Contingent aversive stimulation (punishment) has greater and longer lasting effects on behavior than does noncontingent aversive conditioning.

Source: Russell M. Church, "Response Suppression," in *Punishment and Aversive Behavior,* Campbell/Church eds, ©1969, p. 134. Adapted by permission of Prentice Hall, Englewood Cliffs, New Jersey.

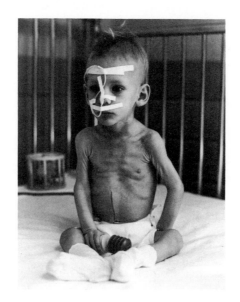 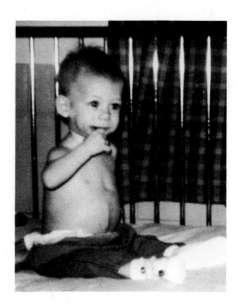

Although there was nothing physically wrong with this baby, he vomited his food after every meal and was rapidly starving to death (Morse & Watson, 1977). After just a few pairings of the electric shock with the vomiting, the vomiting decreased, and the baby began gaining weight. Before you draw the conclusion that physical punishment might have broad use in childrearing, remember that this situation was unusual in two ways. First, the doctors applying the shock were able to punish every instance of vomiting. Second, because the baby's life was in danger, the doctors felt justified in using harsh punishment.

1. *Punishment must be consistent.* A punishment that is administered only occasionally is not effective. Unless we punish children for every instance of the unwanted behavior, we are partially reinforcing that behavior. Instead of weakening the response, then, we're strengthening it. (Remember that a response that has been partially reinforced is very difficult to extinguish.)
2. *Punishment must be swift.* A delay in carrying out a punishment—even one only a few seconds long—makes the punishment much less effective (Kamin, 1959).
3. *Punishment must be harsh.* Leading up to a severe punishment with mild punishments may render all punishment ineffective. To be effective, a punishment should be as harsh as possible in the first instance (Miller, 1960).

Few of us have the ability to administer punishments that are consistent, swift, and harsh. We simply can't be there every time children misbehave. And many of us don't have the heart to deliver a severe punishment for what seems to be a minor infraction. Deeply embedded in us is the idea that the punishment should fit the crime.

And then there are the "side effects" of punishment to be considered. When we spank a child for misbehaving, we do more than weaken that response. We may suppress other responses—good responses—that the child might make. Also, by reacting with violence, we imply that violence is an acceptable behavior. Finally, there's the question of avoidance—not so much of the unwanted behavior as of the person doing the punishing or of the situation in which the punishment takes place.

Recognizing the limitations of punishing children, psychologists and educators tend to strengthen wanted behaviors instead. The idea of using reinforcement instead of punishment extends even into the workplace, where it forms the basis of one of the most widely accepted theories of management. Douglas MacGregor (1960) described two types of managers: the Theory X manager, who constantly corrects workers, ignoring what they do right; and the Theory Y manager, who looks for opportunities to praise workers, ignoring what they do wrong. Which manager is more effective? The Theory Y manager. Again and again, research shows that praise is much more effective than criticism for getting people to work more productively.

Recap

- Through instrumental conditioning, people learn to behave in certain ways because they learn to associate certain consequences with their behavior.

- Instrumental conditioning began with the work of Edward Thorndike, who studied the effect of satisfiers in problem-solving animals.

- B. F. Skinner refined Thorndike's techniques in a procedure he called operant conditioning.

- Through the three-stage process of instrumental conditioning, the frequency of certain behaviors changes. In other words, behaviors that are reinforced are repeated more often than behaviors that are not reinforced.

- Learning is more difficult to acquire under a partial reinforcement schedule, but such learning is also more resistant to extinction.

- Once a response has been conditioned using a primary reinforcer, that response can be used as a secondary reinforcer.

- Discriminated operants reveal the degree to which animals generalize and distinguish among different stimuli.

- Using experiments with rats and mazes, psychologists have shown that instrumental conditioning is a cognitive process.

- The objective of positive and negative reinforcement is to strengthen behavior; the objective of punishment is to weaken behavior.

- Escape conditioning and avoidance conditioning are forms of negative reinforcement.

- Although punishment can be effective in animal studies, the conditions for its effectiveness are rarely met in childrearing or other human interactions.

Learning by Observation

So far we've been talking about learning through direct experience: behavior changes as a consequence of the individual's experience. But is this the only way to learn? Is it possible that we can learn to change our own behavior because we've seen the consequences of someone else's behavior? Do people learn by observation?

Much of the discussion on **observational learning** has focused on the question of whether children learn violent behavior from watching television. The average child watches thousands of hours of television a year and sees hundreds of examples of human cruelty. Is it possible that by letting our children watch this material we are making them more prone to violence and less sensitive to the feelings of others?

At first glance, evidence for the transmission of violence through media models seems persuasive. We're all aware of copycat murders, hijackings, and suicides—all crimes in which the perpetrator follows the model of some earlier crime well publicized or dramatized in the newspapers and on television (Radecki, 1984). If television can have such a compelling effect on adults, shouldn't we expect it to have a similar effect on children?

Observational learning Learning from watching the behavior of others and the consequences of that behavior.

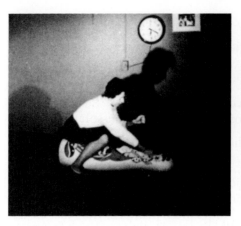

Children frustrated in Bandura's experiment were much more likely to beat the doll if they had seen an adult do so.

Some research does suggest that television violence may be harmful to children. In a classic study, Albert Bandura showed that children can learn aggressive techniques from watching adult models. His experimental procedure had three stages. In the first stage, some children in a playroom were given the opportunity to watch an adult beat up a doll. In the second stage, some of these children were brought one by one into a room full of very interesting toys and allowed to play with them for a short while. In the third stage, the experimenters frustrated the children: they interrupted the children in their play, told them that the toys they were playing with were for other children, and then led the children into a third room, which had fewer toys. One of the toys, though, was the same doll that the children had seen beaten by the adult in the first part of the experiment. Children who had seen the doll beaten in stage one of the experiment and been frustrated in stage three were much more likely to beat up the doll in stage three than children who had not seen the aggressive model or been frustrated. (Bandura, 1973). Bandura's study was followed by several other experiments that seemed to suggest that watching violent acts influenced the aggressive behavior of children.

The comparative evidence is equally suggestive. Numerous long-term studies have shown a relationship between the amount of time a child spends watching violent television and the tendency toward violence later in life. These studies suggest that the more violence on television a person watches as a child, the more likely an individual is to be arrested for violent crimes, to use physical punishment on his or her own children, and to have aggressive children (National Coalition on Television Violence, 1984; Huesmann, Laperspetz & Eron, 1984).

Given the difficulties of doing research with human subjects, these results are open to other interpretations. As with all correlational studies, the long-term studies that "show" that television watching "causes" aggression may be confusing cause and effect. Instead of showing that television watching causes aggression, correlational studies may simply be showing that aggressive children or children from aggressive families choose to watch more aggression on television. Laboratory studies are also ambiguous but in another way. Children are highly sensitive to the context of experiments, and their aggressive behavior in these studies may be due partly to the fact that the experiments seem to give them permission to be aggressive (Josephson, 1987). In other words, the studies may simply be demonstrating that children do what they are implicitly told. After reviewing all the evidence for watching violence on television as a cause of violent behavior in children, psychologist Jonathan Freedman (1984) concluded that despite the plausibility of the hypothesis that television watching causes violence, the hypothesis has not been proven.

Puzzle It Out!

I didn't see John again for several months. But the first time I did see him, I asked immediately about Sara. It seems that after we talked, John came up with a plan. He reasoned that if he was going to change Sara's sleeping habits, he would have to control them. So every evening at eight o'clock, no matter what else was going on, he would put Sara to bed. He gave her one teddy bear, one kiss, and one tucking into bed, and then he settled down in a chair next to her bed to read one of his own books. If Sara was cranky, he simply ignored her and continued reading. If she sat up and started to play with the stuffed animal, he gently put her down again and said, "Go to sleep, Sara." The first night he had to do this several times. But as soon as Sara saw that she couldn't get up, she stopped trying and fell asleep.

After several days, once Sara was falling asleep easily, John began moving the chair away from her bed, until he was reading in the hallway. If he heard her start to get up, he would firmly say the words, "Go to sleep, Sara."

John isn't a psychologist; but as I listened to him describe his solution to Sara's problem, I counted at least five different ways in which he was using basic learning mechanisms. For example, when he refused to respond to her crankiness, he was trying to extinguish a behavior that had been instrumentally reinforced by his attention. What other basic learning mechanisms did John use?

Recap

- Research shows that people learn by watching the behavior of others and the consequences of that behavior.

- Experiments suggest that the more often children watch violent television programs, the more likely they are to be arrested for violent crimes as adults, to use physical punishment on their own children, and to have aggressive children.

- Although the research on observational learning and aggression demonstrates a strong link between watching violence and behaving violently, it does not show cause and effect.

Conclusion

Human beings share with many other animals the ability to be changed by their experiences. The principles of classical conditioning describe how existing responses come to be evoked by new stimuli. This process helps us survive, conditioning us to respond appropriately to stimuli that could help or hurt us. The principles of instrumental conditioning describe how we learn new patterns of behavior in order to get the things we want or to avoid those that threaten us. We can learn even more complex behaviors by observing the activities of others.

We can also be changed by the experiences of others. This kind of learning depends on the medium of language, and it is always more or less self-conscious. In the next few chapters we discuss the mechanisms by which we acquire, retain, and use such knowledge.

Chapter 7   Memory

Double Portrait of the Artist in Time, Helen Lundeberg, 1935

7

Gateways Without your memory—of people in your life, places where you have lived, things you have done—you would not be you. To psychologists, one of the most fascinating aspects of memory is that we don't remember *all* the people, all the places, all the things we've done. Much psychological research has been stimulated by the desire to know why—and how—we remember selectively.

Memory is closely integrated with other psychological processes, such as learning (the topic of Chapter 6). If you ever learned to type, or to ride a bike, you did so partly by storing information in your memory. If that information disappeared, learning would vanish with it.

There are less obvious but still important connections between memory and other psychological phenomena. As you will

see in this chapter, our emotions (the topic of Chapter 10) have a powerful effect on what we remember. And a phenomenon called repression links memory to psychological disorder—a link we examine in this chapter and again in Chapter 15.

George Smith is a burly, energetic man of about fifty-five. He thinks he's twenty-nine. Time stopped for George in the mid-1960s. He can talk to you intelligently about President Kennedy's assassination; he can add, subtract, multiply, and divide; he can carry on a conversation. But if you leave the room and come back again in a few minutes, he won't remember you. And if you showed him his face in a mirror, he'd be horrified at how old he looks.

George is a victim of Korsakoff's syndrome. Chronic alcohol abuse has destroyed small areas of his brain that have to do with memory. He can remember things that happened long ago; and he can remember things that just happened. But he cannot connect the two. The events he experiences now are never going to be a part of his permanent memory; they simply disappear.

We use memory without thinking, effortlessly recalling the name of the boy who sat next to us in fifth grade, the year Columbus discovered America, how to drive a car, to buy milk on the way home. When we think of memory, most of us think of a single large "area" where images of the people and things we've experienced are stored. But the symptoms of Korsakoff's syndrome suggest that there are different kinds of memory—memory systems—and that those systems can function independent of one another.

The Storage and Processing of Information

Memory is a system that allows us to retain what we have learned. Any information-retaining system must perform three tasks, as shown in Figure 7.1:

Figure 7.1
The Memory System

Remembering may be seen as consisting of three stages, encoding, storage and retrieval.

- encoding, the process of choosing the information to be retained and transforming that information into a form that can be saved;
- storage, a means of preserving the information until it's needed; and
- retrieval, the process of finding the information and transforming it back into usable form at some later date.

A notebook is an information-retaining system. When you write information in it, you're *encoding* that information. When you put the notebook on your desk, you're *storing* the information. And, later, when you pick up the notebook and read through it, you're *retrieving* the information.

A computer is a kind of memory system. The keyboard is part (along with your fingers and mind) of the encoding system, the disks are part of the storage mechanism, and the display on the screen is the final stage of retrieval.

We're accustomed to storing information in notebooks and file cabinets, which is why we tend to think of the process in physical terms—saving something concrete in an actual place. But not all information is concrete, and not all systems for storing information involve things you can see or touch. This is especially true of human memory.

In this chapter we talk about memory as a sequence of processes: encoding, storing, and retrieving experiences. This is a logical way to talk about an information-retaining system. But as you read, remember that we are describing a process that we can't see or touch. What we're describing, then, is a theory—a theory that tries to explain how people remember and why they forget.

Encoding

When you take notes in a class, you are encoding information. The process involves several steps. First, you have to choose the information; you don't write down everything the professor says. Then you have to decide how to say what you want to say—the words to use. Finally, you have to decide how to transcribe those words—to print them or to write them.

The process of encoding information in memory is even more complex. Why? Because that information is encoded in a number of memory systems. The best known theory identifies three interconnected systems: sensory memory, working memory, and long-term memory (Atkinson & Shiffrin, 1968). **Sensory memory** is the system that very briefly—for no more than a few seconds—saves all the information gathered by our senses. **Working memory** is the system that helps us remember the information we need to use now, like the topic of the conversation we're having or the phone number we just looked up. And **long-term memory** preserves information over long periods of time. See Figure 7.2 for a breakdown of the encoding process.

Figure 7.2
Encoding Information into Memory

Encoding seems to consist of at least three separate processes or memory stores. Each of these processes contains highly interpreted information, which lasts for progressively longer periods of time (Atkinson & Shiffrin, 1968).

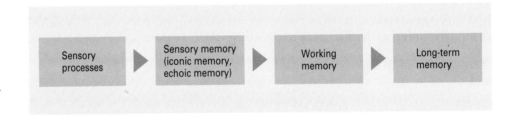

Sensory memory The memory system that briefly preserves perceptual information.

Working memory A memory system, limited in both duration and capacity, that preserves information for processing; also called *short-term memory*.

Long-term memory The memory system that preserves information for long periods of time.

Sensory Memory

The first step in the encoding process involves selecting the information that is going to be retained. To choose that information, you must have all the information available. It's a little like looking over the buffet before deciding what to put on your plate. You gather information through your senses, and you briefly store that information in your sensory memory. It's here that the selection process begins.

Before we think it through, we might assume that we remember everything, that somewhere in the brain is a kind of motion picture with sound (and smell and taste and touch, too!) of everything we've ever experienced. But that's simply impossible, and we *must* select. To understand why, let's look at one possible explanation of how memory might work.

The brain contains something like 200 billion neurons. Let's assume that all are devoted to memory. To preserve your sensory experience, you probably

Puzzle It Out!

Stockade fences. You know the kind, about six feet high with vertical slats. People use them to protect their privacy. And they do the job so long as you're just walking by. Sure, you can see through the small spaces between the slats, but you can't make out the whole picture. What happens, though, if you get in a car and drive past the fence? Now you can see "through" it. Once you're going fast enough, the fence simply darkens everything behind it; it doesn't block out the image. Why? Use what you know about iconic memory to explain how rapid movement changes the effect of the fence.

need one memory neuron for each sensory cell. Consider the eye. There are about a million nerve cells in the optic nerve. If you were to save an image each second, you'd use 1 million neurons a second, 60 million neurons a minute, or 3.6 billion neurons an hour. This means you would have the capacity to save just 55 hours worth of images (200,000,000,000 ÷ 3,600,000,000), and you would not have remembered any information from your other senses.

If you can't store all of your experiences, you have to choose among them. This means that all of your experiences have to be retained for at least as long as it takes to make a selection. This is the function of the sensory registers (G. Loftus, 1983). **Sensory registers** briefly save most or all of the information gathered by your senses, until a selection can be made.

The concept of sensory registers was first demonstrated by a student working for his doctorate in psychology. George Sperling (1960) showed his subjects a group of letters in three rows (see Figure 7.3), flashing the stimulus for less than half a second during each trial. After the stimulus was turned off, the subjects were asked to recall as many of the letters as they could. They were able to report only about half. It seemed they couldn't read all of the letters in the time the stimulus was shown. To check this possibility, Sperling told his subjects which row to report before he flashed the letters. When they knew which row was important, they had no problem reporting the letters perfectly.

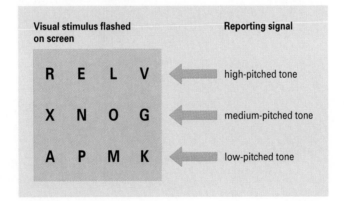

Visual stimulus flashed on screen / **Reporting signal**

R E L V ← high-pitched tone

X N O G ← medium-pitched tone

A P M K ← low-pitched tone

**Figure 7.3
The Sperling Stimuli**

Sperling presented the stimulus array very briefly. After the stimulus was turned off, he indicated to subjects which line they should report by playing tones of different pitches.

Then Sperling tried something new. He came up with a way to tell the subjects which line to report *after* the stimulus was turned off. He would sound a high-, medium-, or low-pitched tone, corresponding to the top, middle, or bottom row of the stimulus. If he flashed the stimulus and then, for example, immediately sounded the medium tone, the subjects were to report the middle

Sensory register A memory system that briefly holds sensory information.

Moving pictures actually present a series of still photographs, each one taken a brief time after the previous one, like this series of cartoon pictures. Because the images remain in iconic memory, we experience smooth, continuous movement, rather than a series of jerky changes.

line. They could do this almost perfectly, whatever the line, even though the stimulus was no longer displayed. Apparently the subjects retained an image of the stimulus after it was turned off, and they could read that image as easily as they could read the stimulus itself.

By varying the time between the end of the stimulus and the sound of the tone, Sperling was able to measure how long the image lasted. His findings are shown in Figure 7.4. If the delay between the stimulus and the tone was as much as 1 second, performance dropped to about 50 percent, the same level as when the subjects were trying to remember all three rows. It seems that the sensory "picture" is retained for less than a second, and then it makes way for new visual images. This kind of visual memory is called **iconic memory** (the Greek word *icon* means "picture"). More recent research suggests that iconic memory actually lasts just a quarter of a second or less (Purdy & Olmstead, 1984; G. Loftus, 1985).

There seem to be sensory registers not only for sight but also for sound (Crowder & Morton, 1969), smell (Richardson & Zucco, 1989), taste, and touch. **Echoic memory** is the sensory register for sound; it briefly stores auditory information. The duration of echoic memory is two to three seconds

Figure 7.4
The Results of Sperling's Experiments

The heavy orange line represents the number of letters that subjects could report if they tried to recall them all. The thinner lines are the letters reported when a sound informed the subjects which line to report. Each line represents a different delay between the end of the stimulus and the time the sound occurred. Notice that subjects could recall only about a third of the letters if they tried to remember them all. But if cued to report a single line, they could do it more accurately, even if the cue came a quarter second after the stimulus ended. Some of the information seemed to remain even after a half of a second.

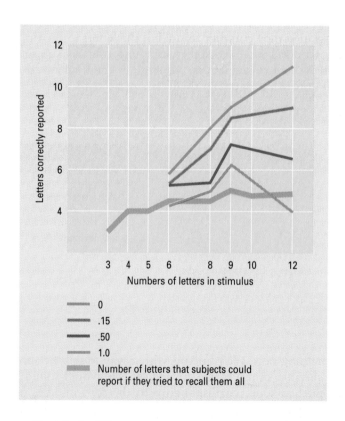

Source: Sperling, 1960.

Eidetic Memory

Apparently we remember our sensory experiences for seconds at most. How, then, do we explain photographic memory? What about the people who can scan a page in a book and repeat it word for word a month or even years later?

The ability to remember over time an exact image of what one has seen is called *eidetic memory*. Does it exist? We know that we all retain a "picture" of our visual experiences for a fraction of a second in iconic memory. The question is whether that picture can be saved for long periods of time.

Some people, especially young children, seem to have a remarkable memory for scenes (Giray, 1985). But true photographic memory turns out to be very rare. Most people who believe they have photographic memories do have very good memories, but they do not retain an exact image of what they've seen (Neisser, 1982). When these people are asked to reproduce a picture, for example, they mention lots of details but they don't include all of the most obvious ones.

And where we do find instances of genuine eidetic memory, it seems to be a special talent, not a characteristic of everyday remembering. In one of the best-known cases, a woman named Elizabeth was able to remember an extremely complex picture, like the one shown here (Stromeyer, 1970). But she remembered it by working at it, using procedures she had developed. She did not, as the popular mythology would have it, just look at the picture and then remember it. Nor did she claim to remember every image she had ever seen.

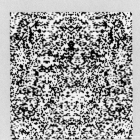 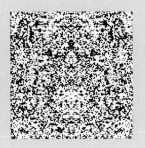

The Julescz figures are pairs of computer-generated patterns of dots. When viewed stereoscopically, with one image in one eye and the other image in the other eye, a three-dimensional effect appears. Elizabeth studied one of these figures for a while and then looked at the other one with just one eye. She was able to experience the three-dimensional effect and report the shape of the figure that appeared, demonstrating that she could indeed remember the first figure photographically.

longer than that of iconic memory. You've noticed your echoic memory working without knowing what it was. Occasionally someone says something you don't quite catch. Just as you ask the person to repeat it, you suddenly realize what was said. While you were getting ready to speak, your analysis of the "echo" continued, until you understood the words.

Working Memory

Sensory registers briefly capture all of our experiences. Only some of those experiences move into working memory; the rest are replaced with a new selection of information. Working memory is really our conscious awareness, our sense of now (James, 1890; Broadbent, 1958; Atkinson & Shiffrin, 1968). In contrast, we are not aware of information in long-term memory until we need it and retrieve it, returning it to working memory.

Iconic memory The sensory register that briefly stores visual images.

Echoic memory The sensory register that briefly stores auditory information.

What's your phone number? Certainly you remember your phone number, but until we asked you what it is, it was stored in your long-term memory. You remembered it, but you weren't aware of it. As you became aware of it, it moved from long-term memory to working memory.

Information seems to move in and out of working memory in relation to what we're doing. When our attention is directed to some information, by a question or the demands of a task, the information moves into working memory. In fact, we call short-term memory *working memory* because of its role in getting cognitive work done (Baddeley, 1983).

Most memory theorists believe that material must be present in working memory before it can find its way into long-term memory and be more or less permanently saved. So working memory is both a memory system and a stage in the encoding process.

The Duration of Working Memory   You look up a phone number, begin to dial it, and then someone or something interrupts you—just for a moment—and you have to look it up all over again. Working memory is brief.

A classic study on the duration of working memory was conducted by Lloyd and Margaret Peterson (1959). They showed their subjects short strings of consonants, such as *GFV* and *RLK,* and then immediately asked them to count backward by 3s from some number like 674. Why? So that the subjects couldn't rehearse the consonants over and over to themselves. Then they asked the subjects to repeat the consonants. Their findings are shown in Figure 7.5. With no counting delay, the subjects remembered the consonants with 80 percent accuracy. But after just twenty seconds of counting backward, most were unable to remember any of the consonant strings. Apparently the duration of working memory is no more than twenty seconds.

Figure 7.5
Length of Retention in Working Memory

The graph shows the accuracy of recalling groups of letters after a short delay spent doing a task that prevented rehearsal.

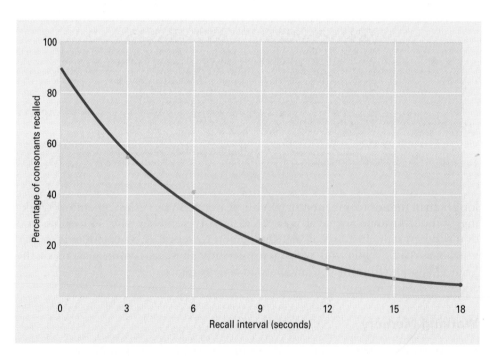

Source: Peterson and Peterson, 1959.

Maintenance rehearsal   Repeating information over and over to retain it in working memory.

Chunking   Organizing random elements into a meaningful whole.

Actually, it may be even briefer. The Petersons' subjects knew that they were going to be asked to remember the groups of letters, so they may have rehearsed them in the seconds before they started counting. To test this possibility, in a later study using similar methodology, the researcher refrained from telling the subjects that they were going to be asked about the letters. After just two seconds, some of the subjects were not able to report the consonant strings (Muter, 1980). It seems that information stays in working memory only as long as it's actively being used. If you aren't using it or don't expect to be using it, it lasts just a few seconds.

The Capacity of Working Memory   Working memory is also restricted in capacity. For most people, the seven digits in a local phone number are about the limit. If we add an area code, we're straining the capacity of our working memory and a foreign number is generally so long we have to write it down. George Miller (1956) reviewed the findings of many studies of memory for numbers, letters, and unrelated words, and concluded that the capacity of working memory is, as he titled his paper, "The Magical Number Seven, Plus or Minus Two."

Long-Term Memory

As noted, working memory is both brief and limited in capacity. During encoding, the role of working memory seems to be analogous to the role of sensory memory. Just as sensory memory stores information that will be processed into working memory, working memory stores information while it is processed for long-term retention.

How does information move from working memory into long-term memory? Two processes—rehearsal and chunking—seem to be at work.

Rehearsal   You've looked up Sam's phone number and dialed it, but the line is busy. How do you remember the number so you can try it again? You repeat it over and over to yourself. This process is called **maintenance rehearsal.** In the short run, maintenance rehearsal preserves the memory by recreating it. After twenty seconds, you aren't remembering the first reading of the phone number; rather, you're remembering the first or second repetition. In the longer run, repetition of any sequence of random stimuli increases your ability to remember them.

The role of rehearsal was first demonstrated formally by Herman Ebbinghaus (1885/1913), who used himself as a subject. Ebbinghaus believed that we create long-term memories by forming associations between elements. To test his theory, he used *nonsense syllables,*—combinations of vowels and consonants, like *GREP* and *BLORT,* that do not form words.

In one experiment Ebbinghaus wrote ten nonsense syllables on cards and, keeping them in the same order, then turned over a card every second. Before he turned over each card, he tried to remember which nonsense syllable was on it. In effect, he was studying the associations he was forming between each nonsense syllable and the one that preceded it. The results shouldn't surprise you. He found that with more repetitions, with more rehearsal, he remembered more of the list for a longer time.

Chunking   Rehearsal works, but it's not the usual way that information moves from working memory into long-term memory. Most of the things we remember are not the subject of rehearsal; instead, we remember them automatically, effortlessly.

How? According to George Miller (1956), the answer is **chunking.** By organizing smaller elements into a larger, meaningful whole, we're able to remember more than the proverbial seven plus or minus two. To understand how chunking works, read the column of numbers in Figure 7.6 slowly, one by one, out loud. Then come back and read the next paragraph.

Herman Ebbinghaus pioneered work on memory by studying his own ability to remember lists of words, numbers, and nonsense syllables.

Figure 7.6
Chunking

Please read the numbers out loud one by one to yourself, and try to remember as many as you can.

1
4
9

2
1
6

2
0
1

7
7
6

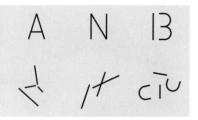

Figure 7.7
Chunking Letters and Symbols

Look briefly at both rows of figures and then go back to the text.

The column consists of twelve digits, which probably exceeds the capacity of your working memory. (It certainly exceeds ours.) In fact, by now you probably can't remember the numbers, unless you happened to organize them into four-digit chunks—1492, 1620, and 1776—all famous dates. If you thought of the numbers as dates, you probably remembered them easily. Chunking reduces the twelve random digits to three dates, well within your memory range. Knowing these dates, you can reconstruct the sequence of individual numbers.

Look at Figure 7.7 for a minute and then read the next sentence. Now take a pencil and paper and write down what you saw. You probably found it easy to reproduce the letters *A, N,* and *B.* But how did you do with the other three symbols?

The latter symbols are actually made up of exactly the same lines and shapes as the letters, but in arrangements that don't form letters. Because the patterns are arbitrary, you have to remember each of the details. In fact, you probably would have difficulty reproducing them now, even if you looked at them again and despite the fact that you know what they are. In contrast, knowing that a symbol looks like an *A* tells you a lot about its organization. You know that the lines at the top meet in a point and that there is a horizontal line between the legs. Your knowledge of the letter means you don't have to remember where each line is; by remembering the whole you can *reconstruct* its parts.

The power of chunking can be seen in the memory abilities of chess masters. After looking at the pieces on a chess board for just five seconds, a chess master can reproduce their positions almost perfectly. Most of us can barely remember the location of a few pieces (De Groot, 1965; Chase & Simon, 1973). It's not that chess masters have amazingly good memories in general; they don't. If the chess pieces are arranged randomly on the board, the masters are no better at remembering them than the rest of us.

What is the difference between chess masters and the rest of us? Apparently chess masters have ways of chunking the positions of pieces on the board so that they can remember the relationships among the pieces. Some of the larger chunks have names like the "Capablanca Bishop's Gambit" and the "Romanian Pawn Defense."

Expert chess players appear to be able to remember extremely well. But, in fact, their memory is only for games in progress, not random assortments of pieces. It also seems to depend on the player's knowledge of many patterns of play that make up chunks in memory.

Chunking increases the capacity and durability of memory, but it can also lead to reconstructive errors. Figure 7.8 shows how. What do you see when you look at the two lines? You probably see the middle figure in the first line as a *B* and the one in the second line as a *13*. Actually the figure is exactly the same in both lines. You see it differently because the surrounding letters or numbers create a context that guides how you define the shape. The actual lines become a part of different chunks. The "loss" in all this is that you probably would not be able to report the space in the figure you see as a *B*. You'd be able to reproduce the shape with reasonable accuracy because you know what *B*s look like, but that's also exactly why you don't notice small deviations from the usual form. (In fact, you've seen this figure before. It's the *B* in Figure 7.7. Did it look like a *13* there? Did you remember the space until we mentioned it here?)

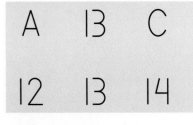

Figure 7.8
Reconstructive Errors

Please read the three letters and the three numbers aloud, and then return to the text.

Chunking as Encoding: Elaborative Rehearsal   In all of our examples of chunking, sets of isolated elements—numbers, letters, or line segments—have been translated into parts of a larger whole. That is, they've been *encoded* into meaningful units, increasing the likelihood that you'll remember them over a period of time. This process is called **elaborative rehearsal.** Elaborative rehearsal is very different from simply repeating something over and over again to yourself. Here you connect the material you want to remember to knowledge you already have.

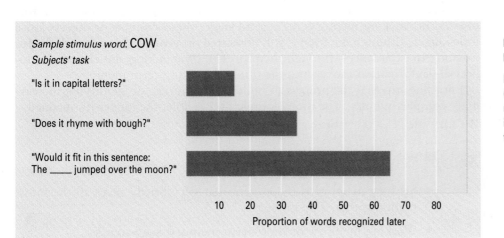

Figure 7.9
Levels of Processing and Recall

Fergus Craik and Endel Tulving (1975) found that the deeper or more meaningful the processing—the easier it is to remember the words.

In a series of studies, Fergus Craik and his colleagues demonstrated the effect of more meaningful processing (Craik & Lockhart, 1972; Craik & Tulving, 1975). In one experiment, the subjects were asked to answer questions about different words (see Figure 7.9). The questions were designed to encourage the subjects to think about the words in increasingly meaningful ways, or as Craik and Lockhart called it, to process the material more deeply.

- In the least meaningful condition, the subjects were asked if the word was written in capital or lowercase letters—a relatively concrete task requiring that the stimulus be processed only to the level of the letters.
- In another condition, the subjects were asked if the word rhymed with a comparison word. This task was a little more meaningful because the subjects now had to think of the stimulus as a word, not just as a collection of letters.
- In the third task, the subjects were asked if the word would fit in a particular sentence. Here they had to think about the meaning of the word, not just about its sound.

Elaborative rehearsal Encoding material into meaningful units by connecting it to what is already known.

After the subjects completed the tasks, they were asked to recall the words they had seen. Not surprisingly, their ability to remember the words increased with how deeply they understood the words they were processing. The *deeper* the processing and understanding, the greater the retention.

Elaborative rehearsal is more effective than maintenance rehearsal. In one demonstration of this superiority, Gordon Bower and Michael Clark (1969) gave their subjects a list of unrelated words to learn. The subjects in one group, encouraged to rehearse the words repeatedly, were able to remember about 13 percent of the words. Those in another group, working with the same words for the same amount of time, were asked to compose stories using the words. This group remembered 93 percent of the words. Clearly, encoding the words in the context of a story was a much better way to remember them.

Encoding: Building Memories

At one time, psychologists believed that the same contents of memory moved along from stage to stage essentially unchanged. But research on the encoding process contradicts this belief.

In the first stage of memory, sensory memory, the stimuli are visual lines and shadows, or their equivalents in other sense modalities. We remember them for seconds at most, just long enough to identify more meaningful combinations of lines and shadows, such as the elements that make up letters or numbers or objects. In working memory, the second stage, these symbols or objects last a little longer, although duration is still measured in seconds. As we attach deeper meaning to experience—through the processes of chunking and elaborative rehearsal—information moves into the third stage, long-term memory.

Encoding, then, is the process of building memories, of identifying increasingly complex wholes. The more complex the whole, the longer it's retained.

Recap

- Sensory memory is the system that very briefly saves all the information gathered by the senses.

- Working memory, or short-term memory, is awareness.

- Long-term memory preserves information over long periods of time.

- The selection process begins in sensory memory, where sensory registers briefly save most or all of the information gathered by the senses.

- Iconic memory is the sensory register for sight; echoic memory, the sensory register for sound.

- Information seems to move in and out of working memory in relation to what the individual is doing.

- Working memory is both a memory system and a stage in the encoding process.

- Both the duration and the capacity of working memory are limited.

- Information moves from working memory into long-term memory through rehearsal and chunking.

- Rehearsal preserves memory by purposefully recreating it.

- Chunking—organizing elements into a meaningful whole—is an automatic process.

- Although chunking increases the capacity and duration of memory, it can also lead to reconstructive errors.

- The ability to remember increases with the meaningfulness of the material that the individual is trying to remember.

- Encoding is the process of identifying increasingly complex wholes.

Storage

Experience is stored very briefly—for a matter of seconds—in sensory memory and then in working memory. In long-term memory, however, it is stored for years. Psychologists have developed two very different, but complementary approaches to explaining long-term memory. One—the *psychological approach*—focuses on the nature of information and the way in which material is organized in memory. The other—the *physiological approach*—focuses on the brain, on the mechanisms through which information is stored and the physical locations where it is kept.

The Organization of Information in Memory

Take a minute to read this paragraph:

> The procedure is actually quite simple. First you arrange things into different groups. Of course, one pile may be sufficient depending on how much there is to do. If you have to go somewhere else due to lack of facilities, that is the next step; otherwise you are pretty well set. It is important not to overdo any particular endeavor. That is, it is better to do too few things at once than too many. In the short run this may not seem important, but complications from doing too many can easily arise. A mistake can be expensive as well. The manipulation of the appropriate mechanisms should be self-explanatory, and we need not dwell on it here. At first the whole procedure will seem complicated. Soon, however, it will become just another facet of life. It is difficult to foresee any end to the necessity for this task in the immediate future, but then one never can tell. (Bransford & Johnson, 1972, p. 722)

What do you think it means? Right now, it probably doesn't mean very much. All you need is a clue, and the meaning of the words will be clear.

The authors of the passage are describing how to wash clothes. Now go back and read the passage again. Suddenly it all makes sense: the sorting, the piles of clothes, using the washing machine. By giving you a framework, a context, we've helped clarify the passage. And within that framework, all of your experience doing laundry adds to the meaning of the words.

Semantic Networks   According to the most popular theories of memory, all of these ideas, or the ones that actually occurred to you, represent a **semantic network** of ideas (Anderson & Bower, 1973; Anderson, 1983). The connections represented by this network establish and constitute the meaning of this story and its parts. In this view, our knowledge is stored in an intricately connected set of ideas or concepts. Figure 7.10 is a model of a part of the network which might exist around washing clothes.

Semantic network A network of ideas relating to a particular subject.

Figure 7.10
A Model Semantic Network

In this model, the lines represent connections between concepts and establish their meanings. The abstract concepts used in the washing story, like "mechanism" and "facility," might have been connected to a variety of more concrete concepts, and so had no clear meaning until those particular connections were established.

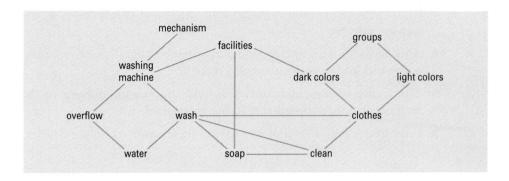

According to the network view, people remember more meaningful experiences better because the connections between different experiences are ways to "get from here to there." To understand how semantic networks function, think of something you know well, such as a job you've had for a while or a hobby you enjoy. Now imagine that you're telling someone about the job or hobby. As you talk, each thing you mention reminds you of something else, and each something else reminds you of another something else. You probably could go on talking for a very long time, moving around and about the general topic. And if you were talking about your job or your hobby on another day, you might start with something different and take a totally different route through your network of knowledge.

Storage as Meaning   A word's connections to other parts of the semantic network help define that word. In fact, we seem to be able to remember the meanings of words better than the words themselves. In one experiment, subjects were asked to read lists of sentences, each of which contained an adjective-noun pair (Light & Carter-Sobell, 1970). The noun in each pair could have more than one meaning. For example, *jar* could mean a container or a bump. The adjectives made clear which meaning was intended. For example, one sentence described a "glass jar," another a "sudden jar." Later, the subjects were given a list of the nouns with new adjectives and asked to indicate which nouns they had seen before. Subjects remembered the words much better when the new adjective preserved the original meaning. For example, subjects who originally saw "glass jar" and then later saw "broken jar" were much more likely to identify *jar* as an old word than those who had first seen "sudden jar." It seems the subjects weren't really remembering the words; they were remembering the concepts or meanings of the words.

Why do we remember the meanings of words better than the words themselves? Because meaning is a kind of higher-order chunk. A single word has relatively few connections to other parts of the network; the concept for which the word stands has many more. For example, it's a lot harder to remember the word *fish* in a list of unrelated words (*hair, profit, upper*) than to remember it in a list of related words (*bird, mammal, insect*). The connections—to kinds of organisms, in this case—help us remember (Summers, Horton & Diehl, 1985).

We've been talking a lot about words, but meaning isn't limited to words. To test the importance of meaning in larger units, John Bransford and Jeffrey Franks (1971) asked their subjects to study a number of short sentences, which, taken together, created a story. For example:

The rock rolled down the mountain.

The rock crushed the hut.

The hut was tiny.

The hut was at the edge of the woods.

After a five-minute delay, the subjects were asked to look at lists of sentences and decide whether the sentences had been part of the original list. Among those sentences were some that combined all the elements of the story. For example:

The rock that rolled down the mountain crushed the tiny hut at the edge of the woods.

The subjects confidently identified this sentence and others like it as parts of the original list, even though they had never seen the sentences. Obviously, the subjects were remembering the basic sense of the story, the *gist* of it—not the individual sentences, much less the individual words.

The same effect was demonstrated by researchers who asked a group of students to record on cards important events in their lives every day for two weeks (Barclay & Decooke, 1988). Then the researchers rewrote the subjects' memories. Some of the new versions described the same event but in completely different words; others used almost the same words but changed them just enough to alter the sense of what had happened. A month later, the subjects were asked to identify which cards contained their original words. They consistently chose the versions that used different words and style but retained the essential meaning. Clearly, what the students remembered was not the details of how they had described the events in their lives but the meaning of the events to them.

These studies also represent another principle we have seen before: memory for details is often reconstructed from a larger chunk. In our example of chess memory, for instance, we saw that the chess masters knew where the individual pieces were because they remembered a chunk, like the "Capablanca Queen's Gambit," and then knew where the pieces had to be. In the Bransford studies, the subjects believed a sentence had been seen before or was one they had written because the sentence contained the higher level meaning that actually was what was remembered.

Our memory processes seem to construct complex, inclusive chunks. Knowledge of these wholes then permits us to reconstruct details that we would otherwise be unable to remember. The other side of that reconstructive process is that we may also misremember details that fit the whole, but are not actually part of the original.

Schemas   As people learn, their newly acquired knowledge is integrated into their existing knowledge. In a classic example of this phenomenon, Frederic Bartlett (1932) asked a group of British subjects to read a Native American folktale. Then he asked them to write down the story, both immediately and at intervals of hours or days. The story contained a number of elements that were not familiar to the subjects. Bartlett found that as time passed between the initial reading of the story and its recall, the story changed. In general, the alien elements were dropped, replaced by elements that were more common to British culture. Bartlett insisted that his subjects were reconstructing the story and, in their reconstructions, were using familiar story forms. The result was that they retained familiar elements and added other familiar elements where they fit.

Bartlett called these familiar story forms **schemas.** A schema is an organizing structure, a framework we impose on our knowledge to help us understand and remember our experiences. According to Bartlett, the subjects came to the story with their own schemas. To make the information in the story fit those schemas, they reconstructed certain details and left others out.

Earlier, we pointed out that more abstract, meaningful processing leads to greater capacity and duration of recall. In this section we have seen that principle extended to include very general sorts of meanings like *gists* and *schemas*. The hierarchy of memory processes is depicted in Table 7.1.

Schema An organizing structure for knowledge.

Table 7.1
Varieties of Memory and Content

Types of Memory	Content	Example	Duration and Capacity
Sensory memory	Lines, shadows, sounds, etc.	A vs ⟩	.25 sec ± unknown, but large
Working memory	Letters, words, and numbers	A vs B, deep vs purple, 725-5708 vs 793-7711	20 sec or less > ± 2 items
Long-term memory	Meaning of words Meaning of sentences (the gist)	Sudden *jar* vs glass *jar* "The hut at the edge of the wood was crushed by a boulder."	Hours or years vs unlimited capacity; both increasing with more meaningful processing
	Schemas	Ghosts don't exist.	

The Nature of Long-Term Memory   We've been talking about the duration of memory and the way in which it's organized. Now we turn to the content of memory.

Declarative versus procedural memory   Through the years, psychologists have identified two very different kinds of long-term memory: **declarative memory,** a memory for facts; and **procedural memory,** a memory for skills (Tulving, 1985). Remembering how to spell *bicycle* is an example of declarative memory; remembering how to ride a bicycle is an example of procedural memory.

We experience the contents of these memories very differently. On the one hand, we are aware of much of our declarative knowledge. If we know a fact or remember an event, we usually know that we remember it. On the other hand, we are seldom aware of our procedural memories. We may be able to ride a bike, but we have no conception of how we do it. We can't express the action in words.

The distinction between declarative and procedural memory is supported by many studies, but the most dramatic evidence comes from observations of people like George Smith, the man with Korsakoff's syndrome we talked about at the beginning of the chapter. If you tell George your name, he won't be able to remember it five minutes from now. He can't remember today's headlines or what he had for lunch or who the current president is.

But George can learn and retain some material as well as anyone. Suppose you try to teach George a new skill, such as how to read mirror-image text. To get an idea of what the task is like, try reading the words in Figure 7.11. At first glance it's hard to make sense of them, but in a few minutes you begin to do better. The ability to read mirror-image text is a skill that can be learned easily with practice. And George could learn this skill as easily as anyone. The thing is that if you tested George tomorrow, he would not remember learning to read the mirror-image text, but he would show just as much skill as anyone who had practiced as much as he did. Although people with Korsakoff's syndrome have pronounced deficits in their memories for factual material, their ability to retain learned skills is not impaired (Cohen & Squire, 1980; Squire, 1986).

Semantic versus episodic memory   Psychologists also make a distinction between two kinds of declarative memory. The things we "know" and can express in words include both general facts ("Mount Whitney is the tallest mountain in the continental United States") and personal experiences ("It rained yesterday," or "I studied French in tenth grade"). The ability to remember general facts is called **semantic memory;** memory for personal experiences is called **episodic memory** (Tulving, 1982).

Declarative memory   Memory for things that can be expressed in words; includes semantic and episodic memory.

Procedural memory   Memory for action and skills.

Semantic memory   Memory for general facts.

Episodic memory   Memory for personal experiences.

It's not really that hard to read this sentence.

Figure 7.11
Mirror Image Reading

See if you can read this text,
which appears as if it is reflected
in a mirror.

The distinction between semantic and episodic memories—like that between declarative and procedural memories—shows up among victims of Korsakoff's syndrome. These people suffer from deficits in both semantic and episodic memory, but the syndrome seems to have a much greater effect on the latter (Mayes, Meudell & Pickering, 1985). For example, in one study, patients were taught a series of general facts—things like "Nairobi is the capital of Kenya." A day later many of the subjects were able to remember the capital of Kenya, but none of them could remember the training session (Glisky, Schacter & Tulving, 1986).

The Physiology of Long-Term Memory

Research on the brain and memory has focused on two questions: how memories are stored in the brain, and where.

How Memories are Stored in the Brain   You retain information in working memory by rehearsing it, by keeping it in your consciousness. But once information is integrated in long-term memory, it lasts without attention for years and years. This difference seems to suggest that different physiological processes are at work in short-term and long-term memory.

In an early version of this hypothesis, Donald Hebb (1949) described working memory as assemblies of neuron loops—that is, as *reverberating circuits* through which a nerve impulse can chase itself around and around (Figure 7.12). Over time, this activity produces change in the neurons themselves or in the synapses, such that each neuron in the loop more readily excites the next. This process, which moves information from working memory to long-term memory, is called **consolidation.** Once the neurons in the loop have changed, constant stimulation is no longer necessary. Only when the information is needed does the circuit become restimulated. The more or less permanent set of changes in the brain that preserve the memory is called the *engram*.

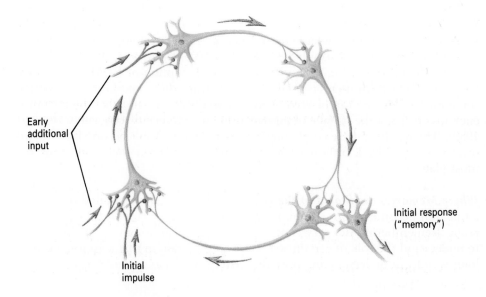

Early additional input

Initial impulse

Initial response ("memory")

**Figure 7.12
Hebb's Reverberating Circuit**

In the early stage, the reverberating circuit of neurons continuously fires. In the later stage, a physiological change in the neurons or at the synapses means that any firing activates the circuit.

Consolidation   A hypothetical process in which short-term memories are transformed into long-term memories.

How Do We Know That?

Like most psychological concepts, memory cannot be observed directly. Instead, we can only observe some relationship between an experience in the past and a behavior in the present. *Memory* is our name for the mechanism that bridges past and present.

If we can't "see" memory, how do we conclude that there is more than one kind of memory? The answer is dissociation. A *dissociation* is any treatment or condition that affects one kind of memory without affecting another. The dissociation between episodic and procedural memory found in people with Korsakoff's syndrome is a particularly dramatic example. These people can't remember learning a skill but do remember the skill itself. They don't remember the experience of learning to play tennis, for example, but they can learn how to play. And every time they step on a tennis court, they are literally surprised that they know how to play.

The dissociation that stems from brain injuries and diseases like Korsakoff's syndrome forms the basis of many theories of human memory (Weiskrantz, 1987). Whether they assume that there are a number of different memory systems (for example, see Tulving, 1985) or different ways in which one system works (for example, see Roediger, Weldon & Challis, 1989), modern theories of memory must explain these separations of function.

Early evidence for consolidation came from experiments with hamsters. First the animals were taught a simple task; then their body temperatures were lowered to the point where all brain activity stopped. When the hamsters were revived, they could still perform the task (Gerard, 1953). Their memory for the task did not depend on continuous brain activity. Apparently, some more or less permanent change had taken place in the animals' brains.

The nature of this change isn't clear, although most scientists assume that it involves the synapse. This could mean a change in the production or function of the chemicals released at the synapse (Rosenzweig, 1984) or a change in the number or efficiency of the synaptic vesicles that store and release neurotransmitter molecules (Desmond & Levy, 1986). In snails and other lower organisms, evidence of these kinds of changes at the synapse has in fact been found (Farley & Alkon, 1985).

If the consolidation hypothesis is true, we should be able to prevent storage in long-term memory by disrupting the brain activity that goes on in working memory. That's exactly what a series of experiments found, using shock and chemical treatments (McGaugh & Herz, 1972; McGaugh, 1983). In fact, it seems that any disruption of brain activity, even the disruption of REM sleep, interferes with long-term memory (Tilley, 1981). But other experiments show that sometimes memories can be recovered. These results suggest that the phenomenon involves not the storage of information but, rather, its retrieval (Crowder, 1989). The result of these conflicting results is that we can't be sure how memories are maintained, although the engram/consolidation theory remains the most plausible.

Where Memories are Stored in the Brain   In Chapter 2 we pointed out that as a function becomes more complex, its location becomes more difficult to pinpoint. Remembering is a very complex activity; and although we are beginning to understand the role of certain structures in the brain in that activity, we are a long way from understanding how the system works as a whole.

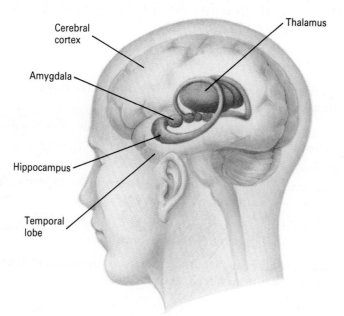

Cerebral
cortex

Thalamus

Amygdala

Hippocampus

Temporal
lobe

Figure 7.13
Parts of the Brain Involved in Memory

The core structures of memory seem to be the thalamus, hippocampus, amygdala, and the temporal lobes of the cortex. But memories with specific sensory content also involve sensory projection areas, and procedural memories seem to involve the cerebellum.

We do know that one important component of the memory system is an area in the middle of the brain that includes the hippocampus, amygdala, and parts of the thalamus (Figure 7.13). This is the region that is most heavily damaged in people with Korsakoff's syndrome. But the specific symptoms of people like George—their ability to remember the distant past and immediate present, but their inability to link the two—suggest that this region is not where memories are stored but where memory processes are coordinated. One possibility is a reverberating circuit of neurons that passes through the hippocampus, amygdala, and thalamus, but that includes many other parts of the brain as well (Squire, 1986).

Consistent with this "distributed" view of memory circuits is evidence that the sensory association areas of the cortex are involved in memory. We know, for example, that if the auditory cortex is damaged, memories for sound are lost (Colombo et al., 1990). And in an intriguing study of visual memories, researchers found that individual neurons near the visual cortex of monkeys responded differently to familiar and unfamiliar faces (Rolls et al., 1989). Of course, most real-life memories involve many senses. This means that many sensory association areas are probably part of the circuit.

The memories that involve sensation are likely to be episodic memories. Because the content of procedural memories is different, and because procedural memories are not disrupted by the injuries that produce amnesia, we would expect different parts of the brain to be involved. And that appears to be the case. Researchers have shown that deficits in procedural memories stem from damage to the cerebellum, the structure that plays a critical role in motor coordination (McCormick & Thompson, 1984).

Recap

- A semantic network is a network of ideas in which knowledge is stored.

- The more meaningful an experience, the easier it is to remember.

- Knowledge of the whole allows the individual to reconstruct details that aren't directly remembered.

- As the individual learns, new knowledge is integrated into existing knowledge.

- A schema is a framework that people use to organize knowledge to help them understand and remember their experiences.

- Declarative memory is memory for facts; procedural memory is memory for skills.

- Research indicates that there are two kinds of declarative memory: general facts are stored in semantic memory, whereas personal experiences are stored in episodic memory.

- Different physiological processes seem to be at work in short-term and long-term memory.

- Consolidation is one possible explanation of how information moves from working memory to long-term memory.

- Research suggests that different parts of the memory function are carried out in different regions of the brain.

Retrieval

Retrieval is the process of finding information that has been encoded and stored in memory, and transforming it back into usable form when it's needed—days, months, or even years later.

Semantic Cues

Quick! What was the name of your third-grade teacher? You probably can't answer that question immediately. But you think you know the name. And with a little "rummaging around," you'll probably come up with it. Right now you're thinking, "She was the one with red hair. Miss . . . definitely Miss, not Mrs. . . . Miss Callahan was first grade. Miss S . . . I'm sure it started with an *S*. Soda? Sober? Sobell. That's it, Miss Sobell!" This kind of experience suggests several properties of retrieval.

This kind of experience reveals much about retrieval. First, retrieval isn't always automatic. Sometimes you have to stop and rummage around to find information. Second, that rummaging around is guided by your semantic networks. Finally, when you think you know something, usually you do. You may not find it immediately, but it's there in long-term memory.

We call this the **tip-of-the-tongue phenomenon.** In one study, subjects were asked to think out loud while they tried to remember the names of not-so-familiar objects—like the small Chinese boat with high ends that's propelled with a pole (Brown & McNeill, 1966). Try it yourself with Figure 7.14. Don't bother with the objects you can name immediately; just think out loud as you try to name the others. After you've finished and have looked at the answers, see if there isn't some logic to your thinking. If you think your third-grade teacher's name starts with an *S*, it probably does. In the study, 57 percent of first-letter guesses are correct. (And Miss Sobell probably also had red hair.)

We see the workings of the semantic networks discussed earlier in the way we locate information in memory. We don't rummage randomly in memory; instead, we follow a path of connections. And we seem to have at least a vague sense of how our semantic networks are organized and how to use them.

Retrieval The process of finding information that has been encoded and stored in memory, and transforming it back into usable form when it's needed.

Tip-of-the-tongue phenomenon A situation in which people know they will be able to remember a fact that at the moment they cannot recall.

1. A waxy, grayish substance formed in the intestines of sperm whales and found floating at sea or washed ashore; used as a fixative in perfume.

2. The cavity into which the intestinal, genital, and urinary tracts open in vertibrates such as fish, reptiles, birds, and some primitive mammals.

3. Favoritism shown or patronage granted by persons in high office to relatives or close friends.

4. A flat-bottomed Oriental skiff propelled usually by two oars.

5. A navigational instrument used for measuring the altitudes of celestial bodies.

Answers: (1) ambergris, (2) cloaca , (3) nepotism , (4) sampan, and (5) sextant.

Figure 7.14
Tip-of-the-Tongue Phenomenon

Here are some uncommon words and their definitions. Try to remember them. Don't spend time on the words you know, but on the others you don't know. Try to verbalize your thoughts about what you're trying to remember as you're trying to remember it.

Note: Definitions taken from the *American Heritage Dictionary,* Second College Edition.

We used a word as an example earlier in this chapter. Do you remember what it was? What if we tell you that it was in a list of organisms? Do you remember it now? The word was *fish*. By telling you that it was an organism, we directed you to a specific semantic network; we defined a category for you to search. We could have given you the same direction by telling you the other words in the list (*bird, mammal, insect*). Using cues to improve memory is called **priming.** An especially effective kind of priming involves knowledge of the larger category that contains the material you want to remember.

Contextual Cues

We remember better when the conditions under which we are trying to retrieve information are similar to the conditions under which we learned the information (Tulving, 1982). By *conditions,* we mean both external and internal environments.

Psychologists often go to great lengths to test a hypothesis; Duncan Godden and Alan Baddeley (1975) went to great depths. Using the members of a university skin diving club as their subjects, they set up an experiment on land and under water. One group studied a list of words on shore; a second group studied the same list submerged in twenty feet of water. Later, when tested on the words (again, on land or under water), those who had learned the words on land remembered them better on land, and those who had learned them in the water remembered them better in the water. Recall is easier when the conditions of learning and retrieval are identical.

This effect is influenced by the nature of the material. When the information is not particularly meaningful, environmental cues help us remember it. But when the material is meaningful, environmental cues are much less important than semantic cues (J. Eich & Birnbaum, 1982). So, although it might be ideal to study for a test in the same room and at the same desk where you're going to take the test, it's not really necessary. By integrating the material into a semantic network, by giving it meaning, you should be able to remember it just fine—even if you study in your own room lying on the bed.

We have noted that the external environment gives us cues that help us remember; the same is true of our internal environment. Take alcohol, for example. People who acquire knowledge while intoxicated are better able to recall that knowledge while intoxicated (Weingartner et al., 1975). The same relationship between memory and what we call *state-dependent cues* has been demonstrated with marijuana and other drugs (E. Eich, 1989).

Priming Using cues to improve memory.

Mood and Memory

Emotional state also can affect memory, as was first observed in people suffering from depression. People who are depressed often dwell on their faults and inadequacies. This tendency has been described both as a symptom of and a contributing factor to chronic depression (Beck et al., 1979). More recently, however, it's been recognized as a direct effect of depression. Depressed people literally cannot remember happy experiences as easily as people who are not depressed can (Clark & Teasdale, 1982).

The effect of depression on memory has led a number of psychologists to examine the general relationship between mood and memory. And in an elaborate variety of studies, they've demonstrated that mood does affect recall (Bower, 1981; Ellis & Ashbrook, 1989). When you're happy, it's easier to remember happy experiences; when you're sad or angry, it's easier to remember sad or angry experiences.

The effect of mood cues is slightly different from that of environmental or state-dependent cues. In this case, the essential match is not between the mood at encoding and the mood at retrieval (Bower & Mayer, 1989); instead, it's the match between the mood at retrieval and the emotional tone of the material itself. We call this phenomenon **mood-congruent memory.** For example, we more easily remember an irritating newspaper editorial when we're angry than when we're happy. And we more easily remember a Woody Allen story when we're happy than when we're angry (Laird et al., 1982). Similar effects have been shown for other emotional states, including sadness and fear (Laird et al., 1989), using a number of different measures of memory (Blaney, 1986).

In sum, recall is better when the conditions at retrieval foster connections to the target material within the network. Matching between the conditions of retrieval and the initial encounter certainly helps. So does matching the emotional state of the rememberer with the emotional quality of the material. Perhaps the most effective way to promote recall is to match the cognitive conditions—to be thinking about the same kind of material. And finally, given the pronounced role of reconstructive processes in remembering, the more relevant the higher level information is, the more easily reconstruction can occur.

Repression

Sigmund Freud popularized the idea that we sometimes don't remember things because remembering them isn't pleasant. To avoid the shame, guilt, or anxiety of remembering, we "push" the memory out of our minds. All of us have had the experience of choosing not to think about something because it made us uncomfortable. You're out with friends, having a good time, and someone mentions an exam you have to take in a couple of days, an exam you're really worried about. You just don't want to think about the exam right now, so you don't. The name for this kind of motivated forgetting is **repression.**

Freud believed that repression is a mechanism that acts on events that are already in memory to prevent retrieval. To demonstrate repression, then, we must show not only that the material has been encoded and stored but also that it would be retrieved if it didn't have unpleasant implications. This objective seems straightforward, but the research has been remarkably confusing and unproductive (Erdelyi & Goldberg, 1979).

Recent studies have explored the personal memories of people who are both highly anxious and highly defensive, a group we would expect to show repressive behavior. And they do. These people report fewer unpleasant memories and, when prompted specifically, take longer to locate those memories (Davis & Schwartz, 1987; Davis, 1987).

Mood-congruent memory A memory whose emotional tone is consistent with the individual's mood at the time of retrieval.

Repression The failure to retrieve the memory in order to avoid the anxiety, shame, or guilt that remembering would cause.

But the fact that certain people report fewer bad memories does not tell us where in the memory system repression is at work. Freud believed that repression disrupts the retrieval process. But others insist that the mechanism operates during the encoding process, that people we call *repressors* are less likely to experience and encode events as unpleasant. There is evidence that supports this view. When confronted with an unpleasant event, most people show the symptoms of elevated physiological arousal like increased heart rate and sweating that indicate unpleasant emotions. But repressors, despite their bodies' responses, deny the unpleasantness and encode the experience as pleasant (Asendorpf & Scherer, 1983).

In sum, repression as a retrieval phenomenon has yet to be demonstrated. Some things that look like repression are probably due to encoding effects. Others may be due to the effects of moods on memory. For instance, the inability to recall unpleasant events when in a happy mood may produce the appearance of defensive repression (Laird et al, 1982). Finally, one of the dominant schemas for memory of our own lives is the self-schema. We have a strong tendency to remember past events in ways that are consistent with our current conception of ourselves (Greenwald, 1980). Sometimes the self-schema introduces distortions that are similar to those implied by the concept of repression.

Eyewitness Testimony and Retrieval

Retrieval processes may affect not only whether we remember something but also how we remember it. Look at the picture of the car in Figure 7.15 on the next page. Now, without looking back at the picture again, answer these questions:

What kind of car is it?

Is it on the right or left side of the road?

Are any other cars visible in the picture?

Is the car stopped at the stop sign?

Is the driver visible?

The point of all but one of these questions was to distract you. The only question that really mattered here had to do with the stop sign. How did you answer that question? If you didn't say to yourself that it was a yield sign, not a stop sign, you (like lots of other people) fell prey to the effect of leading questions on memory. And if we hadn't pointed out the discrepancy to you, later you probably would have remembered a stop sign in the picture. Because the question stated a fact, you probably would have accepted that fact as part of what you saw.

Elizabeth Loftus and her colleagues used experiments like this one to study the accuracy of eyewitness testimony (E. Loftus, Miller & Burns, 1978). In one of those experiments, a group of subjects saw the picture you saw in Figure 7.15; another group saw a similar picture with a stop sign. Then half the subjects in each group were asked whether the car was stopped at the yield sign, and the other half were asked if the car was stopped at the stop sign. Twenty minutes later, the subjects were shown both pictures and asked which they had seen. When the picture and question were consistent, 73 percent of the subjects chose correctly. However, when the picture and question were inconsistent, 59 percent chose the picture that matched the question.

In this experiment, the subjects had two kinds of information about the scene: their visual memories of what was in the picture and their verbal memories of the words used to describe the scene. Apparently the two kinds of memory interacted, and the verbal memory was more powerful.

**Figure 7.15
Eyewitness Test**

Look at the picture for a few moments and then return to the text.

Loftus and her associates have also shown that the way a question is asked can affect how people answer it and how they remember. In one study, Loftus and John Palmer (1974) showed a film of an automobile collision and asked the subjects to estimate the speed of the cars either when they "smashed" or when they "hit." When the question included the word *smash*, the subjects' estimates of the speed were significantly higher than when the word *hit* was used. Smash-condition subjects also were likely to remember that there was broken glass in the film, although in fact none was visible. The word *smash* implies greater impact than *hit*, and apparently the subjects accepted that implication.

These experiments show that information that is part of the retrieval process can influence the memory that's being retrieved. The subjects in these experiments weren't able to distinguish the information implied by the question from the information retrieved from memory, so they combined the two. Moreover, Loftus and her colleagues found that people express as much confidence in these induced memories as in their memories of real events (Cole & Loftus, 1979) and are unable to distinguish between them (Schooler, Gerhard & Loftus, 1986).

These results are frightening because they imply that courtroom testimony may be as much a reflection of lawyers' questions as of the facts. But this is not to say that all witnesses are untrustworthy. There are limits on the extent to which real witnesses accept suggestion (Yuille & Cutshall, 1986). Furthermore, if witnesses are warned, they are much less likely to be affected (Greene, Flynn & Loftus, 1982).

This witness's recall of events may reflect more about the prosecutor's questions than it does about the events themselves.

Recap

- Retrieval is the process of finding information that's been encoded and stored in memory, and transforming it back into usable form.

- Both semantic cues and environmental cues help the individual retrieve information from memory.

- Retrieval is easier when the mood at the time of retrieval matches the emotional tone of the memory.

- Although there is evidence that people repress unpleasant memories, it is not clear whether the mechanism is related to the retrieval process or the encoding process.

- Information that is part of the retrieval process can influence the memory that's being retrieved.

Forgetting

When you can't remember something, you say that you've forgotten it. This implies that the information has been encoded and stored but can't be retrieved.

Actually, forgetting can be a failure at any stage in the process of remembering. Much of what we've forgotten was never encoded. Just because we experience something doesn't mean that we encode it. For example, on a traffic light, is the red light on the top or the bottom? Is it always in the same place? Most people aren't sure, although they've seen thousands of traffic lights. Why? Because for most of us, the information just isn't important enough to be encoded.

Or the problem could be with storage—how long memories last. In one of the very few studies of memory of personal experiences, Marigold Linton (1978) recorded two events each day from her own life over a period of six years. Each month during that time she tested her recall of those events. She discovered that she forgot only about 5 to 6 percent of the original items each year. Furthermore, much of her forgetting was actually confusion. Many of the events that seemed important five years earlier were no longer important or had become routine with repetition and were more easily confused. Also her criterion of accurate recall was a demanding one. She would randomly draw two items from her lists of events and guess which had come first. So she was not remembering what happened; she was trying to remember something more difficult—*when* it happened. Her findings suggest that, once memories are stored, they do last a long time.

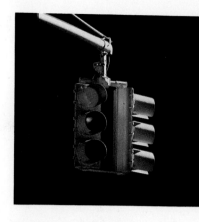

For people who are color blind, the placement of the red light on traffic lights is very important. They don't see the color, just the brightness as the light changes.

Memory and Alzheimer's Disease

In the elderly, memory loss is often a symptom of Alzheimer's disease. Alzheimer's causes a progressive loss of memory so that, in the advanced stages, victims cannot remember such basic details as where they live and who their children are. And eventually they can lose virtually all mental capacity.

Although the nature of the relationship between Alzheimer's and memory is not clear, we do know that one effect of the disease is the degeneration of brain tissue, especially in the hippocampus (Hyman et al., 1984) and in the neurons of the system that produces the neurotransmitter acetylcholine (Whitehouse et al., 1982). Given the importance of the hippocampus in memory processes, the location of the problem is not surprising. However, we don't know at this point whether the memories are actually gone or whether some disruption has occurred in the retrieval mechanism.

Another way to study long-term memories is to ask people to recall events for which the experimenter has some other evidence to use as a standard. For example, Harry Bahrick and his associates asked subjects to remember the people in their high school class, twenty-five years earlier (Bahrick, Bahrick & Witlinger, 1975). Not surprisingly, most were unable to list more than a few names. But when they were shown pictures from their own yearbook, mixed with pictures from other people's yearbooks, they recognized 93 percent of their classmates.

Bahrick (1984) also studied the retention of material learned in school. Specifically, he gave Spanish vocabulary tests to people who had not studied the language for different periods of time. He found that there was considerable loss of memory for the first six years or so but that no loss seemed to occur after that (see Figure 7.16). Even people who were tested fifty years after studying Spanish still remembered substantial amounts of vocabulary and grammar!

Figure 7.16
Recall

Remembering Spanish after years of forgetting. Notice that people forgot about half of what they knew during the first three years or so. But whatever they remembered at that time tended to remain virtually unchanged for another 45 years.

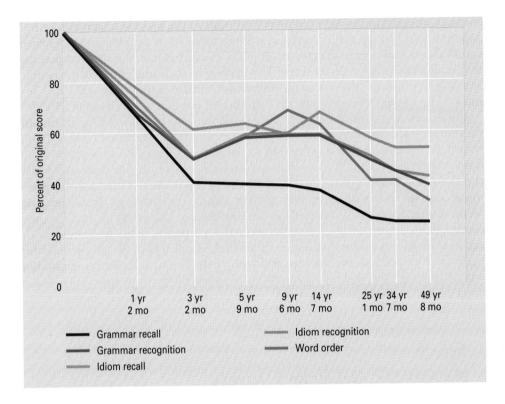

Source: Bahrick, 1984.

If memories can last a lifetime in storage, why do some disappear? One reason is that other memories interfere. Linton's (1978) study gives us several clear examples of this kind of **interference.** Her meeting with an important committee seemed to be a major event when it first happened. Later, after ten more meetings, that first meeting didn't seem so important anymore. In a period of two or three years, Linton was no longer able to remember anything that had happened at the first meeting, or to distinguish that meeting from the fifth or the eighth one. This kind of interference is called **retroactive interference** because later experiences work "backward" to interfere with the memories of earlier experiences.

Proactive interference works in the other direction. Here an earlier memory interferes with the ability to recall a later one. Suppose you learn a list of nonsense syllables. The next day you test yourself to see how many you remember. Then each day you learn another list. It seems reasonable to think that you'd get better and better at learning the list, so that after a while you'd remember the list perfectly the next day. Instead, the exact opposite occurs: you have more and more difficulty remembering the previous day's list. The reason, of course, is that you can't distinguish yesterday's list from the one the day before, or that day's list from the one the day before that (Underwood, 1957). Your memory has become a jumble of nonsense syllables.

These two kinds of interference probably account for most of our forgetting. Both are strongest when the old and new information is most similar. The reason we remember only the most unusual events in our lives may be because these events are the ones that brook no interference from our everyday lives.

Interference The disruption of memory by other memories.

Retroactive interference The disruption of an earlier memory by a later one.

Proactive interference The disruption of a later memory by an earlier one.

Recap

- Forgetting can be a failure at any stage in the process of remembering.
- Much of what people forget was never encoded.

- Once memories are stored, they tend to last for a long time, unless other memories interfere.

- Retroactive interference is the disruption of an earlier memory by a later one; proactive interference is the disruption of a later memory by an earlier one.

- In the retrieval process, forgetting can be a function of mood, repression, or suggestion.

Improving Your Memory

We remember most easily material that is meaningful, material that fits into one of our semantic networks. But suppose the material doesn't fit into an existing network? Suppose we can't find a chunking scheme that works? What do we do then?

One possibility is rehearsal—the use of repetition to move the information into memory. The problem is that maintenance rehearsal is tedious. And there's a problem with proactive interference when we use rehearsal too often. The solution is **mnemonics** (ni-'mon-iks), techniques that have been developed to improve memory—particularly memory for bits of unrelated information.

One mnemonic is the **pegword method.** To use it, you must first learn a series of words to go with numbers, something like "One is a bun, two is a shoe, three is a tree, four is a door." This list is fairly easy to learn because the words rhyme with the numbers. Now, when you want to remember a list of unrelated words, you'd think of some image that combines the pegword and the word you're trying to remember. Suppose you want to remember a grocery list. If the first item on the list is soap, you might imagine a bun covered with soap bubbles. If the second item is apples, you'd picture a shoe stuffed with apples. Later, when you want to retrieve the list, you begin with your pegwords and the combined images come back to you.

Another technique, the **method of loci** ('lo-si), was used by the ancient Romans. A Latin text, *Ad Herennium,* written between 86 and 82 B.C., describes the process (Marx, 1894). First, you think of a location (that's where the technique got its name). Then, for each item you want to remember, you think of a representative image, something that symbolizes that item to you. Finally, you imagine each image in place in the location. For example, to remember your grocery list, you might imagine the floor of your room covered with soap bubbles. The next item is apples, so you picture a giant apple on the chair just to the right of the door. And you continue this way down the list. When you want to retrieve the list, you simply think of your room and the things you left "lying around" it (see Figure 7.17). The more vivid and unusual your images, the easier they are to remember (McDaniel & Einstein, 1986).

Both the pegword method and the method of loci are ways of imposing order on a list of random items. By creating order, you create meaning—and that helps you remember. Also, both of these techniques rely on **imagery,** the representation in thought of a visual scene. We don't know for sure why imagery helps you remember things. One possible explanation is that all concrete images are represented in memory by both words and images—a *dual code.* One part of that code is verbal; that's what you use when you recite a list of words over and over to yourself. The other is visual; and that's what you use when you picture the thing you're trying to remember. Imagery may improve memory, then, by involving both parts of the code rather than just one (Paivio, 1971).

Mnemonics can be helpful, but the best memory aid is a thorough understanding of the material and an appreciation of its relation to your own life.

Mnemonic A technique used to improve memory.

Pegword method A memory aid in which a list of unrelated words is associated with words that have already been memorized.

Method of loci ('lo-si) A memory aid involving the association of a list of unrelated items with images and the mental placement of those images in a familiar location.

Imagery The representation in thought of visual scenes.

Figure 7.17
The Method of Loci

To remember a list of unrelated objects, like a grocery list, first think of a place that you know well, like your room. Then try to form a vivid, unusual image of each object on the list, and then "place" the images in order around the location you are thinking of.

Studying for Remembering: SQ3R

Throughout this chapter we've emphasized the importance of meaning to memory. The more meaningful the experience or the information, the easier it is to remember. To make the material you're studying more meaningful, you have to take an active part in the memory process. Just reading the material isn't enough. You have to connect the new material to your existing schemas; you have to make it meaningful.

When you're reading a textbook, the idea is to think about the material as much as possible, about how it relates to experiences you've had or to things you already know. This concept forms the basis of a study system called *SQ3R*—an acronym that stands for *survey, question, read, recite,* and *review* (Robinson, 1970).

- *Survey* Look at chapter outlines, skim the material, note headings, and read summaries or introductory material for an overview of the material you're going to be studying. You have to know where you're going before you start the trip. This way, when you read something, you'll know the broader context it fits into.
- *Question* Now ask yourself what you should be learning in your reading. Then, as you read, look for answers. Even if your answers are wrong, they can help you recognize what you are actually reading.
- *Read* Go ahead and read. But be aware of the context in which you're reading and the objectives you've set for yourself. Remember, you can think and read at the same time.
- *Recite* Once you've read a chapter (or, in a book like this one, a section), stop and talk about what you've read (yes, out loud!). If you want to take notes on your reading, this is the time to do it. You may find that details that seemed clear before you tried to put them into

(Continued on next page)

words aren't really clear at all. If you have to, go back and reread. This process is very important because it helps you identify what you know and what you don't know.

- *Review* After you've finished a chapter, review everything you've read, looking at how the parts connect with one another and what the overall message of the material is. This task is the complement of the survey task: now you're looking at the overall organization.

Taking an active part in the memory process looks like a lot more work than just sitting down and reading the material. But it really isn't. You more than make up the time you spend surveying and questioning because your comprehension is so much better when you finally start reading. In fact, many of our students report that the system is actually faster because you read more effectively. Furthermore, recitation and review pay big dividends in the amount learned and retained.

Recap

- Mnemonics are techniques that help the individual remember unrelated pieces of information.

- To use the pegword method, the individual associates a list of unrelated words with words that have already been memorized.

- To use the method of loci, the individual places mental images of the items to be remembered around the mental image of a familiar location.

- Both the pegword method and the method of loci rely on imagery, the representation in thought of a visual scene.

- The dual code may explain why imagery helps people remember.

Conclusion

Our memories seem so simple on the surface. Without reflection or effort, we make use of experiences we have collected over a lifetime. Now we can see what an incredible phenomenon human memory really is, what a spectacular feat it is to remember the name of someone you went to school with ten years ago, or the telephone number of a friend, or how to ride a bicycle. At the beginning of this chapter, we suggested a parallel between memory and the process of storing information in a notebook. But if our memories were really like notebooks, consider how large the room full of notebooks would have to be, and how difficult it would be to find the notebook containing the names of grammar school friends, and so on. We are beginning to understand the ways in which memories are constructed and reconstructed, and the complexity of their organization. And each advance in our understanding makes memory seem more remarkable.

Chapter 8

Thought and Language

The Pink Blouse, Henri Matisse, 1922

8

Gateways Human beings are not larger, stronger, or swifter than other species. Instead, we are smarter. Despite all our faults and flaws, we excel at solving problems, understanding the world, and inventing new ways of living. This chapter on thought and language completes the set of topics in cognition that began with perception (Chapter 4), learning (Chapter 6), and memory (Chapter 7). Here we look at the ability that empowers us to achieve these things—thinking. We pay special attention to language, our most powerful tool for thought.

The topic of thinking informs virtually every other chapter in this book. For example, the way people think affects their motivations (discussed in Chapter 9) and how they react emotionally (Chapter 10). There is evidence that thoughts can create psychological disorders as well as cure them (Chapters 15 and 16). And psychologists' attempts to measure thinking abilities is a major topic in Chapter 13 on assessment.

One summer while I was an undergraduate, I worked as a research assistant in Harry Harlow's famous Wisconsin Primate Research Laboratory. I was assigned to help a psychologist who was developing an apparatus to test the limits of monkeys' problem-solving abilities. The arrangement was simple: I would make myself useful, and he would teach me what was going on in the lab.

My first job was soldering wires on a test panel that made it possible for people to try out the problems that the monkeys were going to work on. When I'd finished, it was close to lunch time. My boss asked if I'd like to take a few minutes to try my hand at a simple problem—one that he expected the monkeys to find very easy.

The test panel was a rickety contraption, with wires sticking out in every direction. It had four lighted panels, each with a button underneath it. Projected onto the panels were different-colored shapes—squares, triangles, rectangles, and circles. The object was to push the button under the "right" shape. If you pushed the wrong button, you heard an irritating buzz, and the same shapes would keep appearing until you pressed the right button.

The problem was figuring out which shape was the right one. A pattern was supposed to emerge, but exactly the same shapes never appeared twice. Sometimes the square would be red, sometimes the triangle; sometimes the rectangle flashed in the first panel, sometimes the fourth. I kept trying different combinations of cues—shape, color, and position—but nothing worked consistently. And there was a problem with the apparatus. For some reason, it wasn't projecting all four shapes at exactly the same time. I kept having to wait for all the lights to come on before I made a choice.

All too soon the lab director was at my side, holding his thermos in one hand and his bag lunch in the other, and tapping his foot. "Haven't got it yet?" he asked.

Embarrassed, I said no. "I've tried everything. Are you sure this thing is working? It can't even project the four images at the same time."

The director laughed. "Have you tried 'order'?"

The solution was so simple. The machine wasn't supposed to project the images at the same time. Order was one of the cues! Whichever shape appeared first was the correct one! I was dumbfounded.

"Okay if we go to lunch now?" he asked.

Here I was, about to start my senior year in college, on my way to graduate school in psychology. How did I overlook a solution that a monkey would never have missed? The problem was that I knew too much. Instead of seeing order as a cue, I saw a rickety machine that wasn't working right. Clearly, the experience we bring to a problem affects how we go about solving it.

An Introduction to Thinking

In this chapter we explore the ways people solve problems, how they process and exchange information about the world. Actually, we've talked a lot about information processing in earlier chapters. We've described the physical equipment that gathers information and integrates it. We've discussed the ways in which behavior and thought are changed by experience. And we've talked about the memory systems that record these changes and make them available for future use.

Cognition is the general term psychologists use to describe the psychological activities involved in gathering and using information. **Thinking** is the process that integrates all of the individual's cognitive activities, putting them to work in everyday life. In this chapter we talk about the tools of thought—the concepts, propositions, rules of logic, and images that allow us to manipulate knowledge. We also talk about two distinctive kinds of thinking—problem solving and decision making, and finally creativity.

Language is the medium through which we acquire most of our information, organize it, and communicate it to others. Language and thought are inextricably related in human beings: that we have language affects how we think; and that we think affects the kind of language we use and how we use it. We come back to this relationship at the end of the chapter.

The Tools of Thought

When you think, you use a number of different "tools," among them concepts, propositions, the rules of logic, and images.

Concepts

A **concept** is a category, a way of thinking about objects, events, or people that makes them seem to go together. We experience the world as a collection of things that are like one another—of cars and houses and plants and ball games and work and people and animals. Within these broad groups, there are other, smaller groups—station wagons and convertibles and sedans and sports cars, for example. And even these groups can be broken down further, into Ford station wagons and Chevrolet station wagons and Volvo station wagons—and so on.

Your perception of the similarities and differences among the elements in any group is determined by your interactions with them. All Ford station wagons seem alike until you buy one; then suddenly you realize how different they are. You might head for a car that looks like yours in a parking lot. But up close, you'd never mistake someone else's car for your own.

With every experience, you form new concepts or adjust the ones you have. Concepts are tools that help you organize your experiences into groups of things that you treat as the same for the task at hand. For another task, at another time, you may form new concepts or redraw the lines between same and different in completely new ways.

Defining Concepts   You're always using concepts to think and to communicate, but it's difficult to say exactly *how* you use them. Think about your concept "chair." You've been using this concept for years, but can you say what makes a chair a chair? Most chairs have a horizontal surface that is about the same distance from the floor as your knees. But some chairs are a lot higher. Should a chair have a back? Some chairs don't. Are they really chairs? Obviously it's not that simple to define a concept; and if we have difficulty defining a concept like "chair," what about concepts like "love" and "democracy"?

Psychologists have two different explanations for the way in which concepts come to have meaning. The first relates to **attributes,** the properties of an object. Laboratory research suggests that people form concepts by building a list of characteristics that are typical of examples of the concept (Medin & Smith, 1984).

Cognition   All of the activities involved in gathering and using information.

Thinking   Using and manipulating knowledge to solve problems, make decisions, and create new understanding.

Language   The medium through which knowledge is acquired, organized, and communicated.

Concept   A way of thinking about objects, events, or people that makes them seem to go together.

Attribute   A property or characteristic of an object.

Prototype   The standard used to define a concept.

Suppose that you've never seen or read or heard about cows. You're driving past a field in the country with friends who point out a large, black and white, four-legged object with horns and call it a *cow*. A moment later, they point to a smaller brown four-legged object and say *cow* again. You're left with the sense that there's a family of objects in the world with the name *cow*. Color obviously isn't critical to being a cow because you've already seen a black and white cow as well as a brown cow. So your concept of "cow" at this point is a large object that moves around a field on four legs. A few miles later, you point to a long-legged hornless creature in the field with a black mane and ask if that, too, is a cow. "No," your friends say, "that's a horse." So you add two more attributes—horns and relatively short legs—to your concept "cow." Over time, as your experience with cows grows, your list of the characteristics that distinguish cows from other objects grows: *Cow* A large, horned, four-legged animal, with relatively short legs, that gives milk, moos, eats grass, and is no good for riding. According to the attribute model, you decide how to conceptualize a new experience by running through your lists of concept attributes, checking to see which "fits" best.

The second theory is that you use the best example of a concept—a **prototype**—to form your concepts. The idea of *prototype matching* grew out of two observations about the way people actually use concepts in everyday life. One is that most people can't generate definitions of their concepts as we did just now with the concept "cow." The second is that everyone agrees that some examples fit a concept better than others. Eleanor Rosch (1978) suggested that instead of listing the attributes of each object they come across, people compare the new object to their model of the concept, its prototype. When they're trying to decide if something is a chair, for example, they compare it to their prototype for chair.

Look at Figure 8.1. Which chair is the most typical chair? You probably said the third one because it's what you think of when you think of a chair: it's the most "chairish." You may have difficulty listing the unique attributes that define a chair, but it's relatively easy to pick out the best example of a chair, the chair prototype. And you're not alone. A good deal of research tells us that people agree consistently on the extent to which a particular object or animal or person or idea seems to fit a particular concept (Rosch, 1978).

In fact, both prototypes and attributes probably play a role in how people define concepts. A prototype defines the core meaning of a concept; attributes define the way in which examples of the concept fit. The more an example is like the prototype—the more attributes it shares with the prototype—the better the example fits the concept.

Figure 8.1
The Prototypical Chair

What do you think of when you think of a chair? The first chair that comes to mind for most people will be like the straight-backed chair and probably not like the other two in this figure. The straight-backed chair is most prototypical.

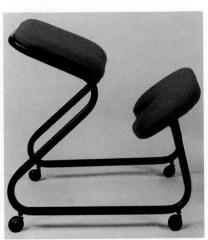

Defining attribute An attribute shared by all members of a concept category.

Characteristic attribute An attribute shared by many but not all members of a concept category.

Certain attributes are more important than others. What we call **defining attributes** are so important that they define membership in the concept group (Smith & Medin, 1981). **Characteristic attributes** fit many but not all members of the concept group. If the defining attributes of birds are having feathers and laying eggs, then other attributes, such as being able to fly and chirping, are characteristic attributes. A "birdish" bird, such as a robin, has both defining and characteristic attributes (see Figure 8.2). A bird that cannot fly or sing, such as a penguin, is still a bird because it has feathers and lays eggs, but it's not a very "good" bird. A long-legged pink bird with a strange beak is a "better" bird than a penguin because at least it flies (Medin & Smith, 1984).

A robin — a "good bird"

Defining attributes
1. has feathers
2. lays eggs

Characteristic attributes
1. sings
2. flys
3. eats worms and bugs
4. small

A penguin — a "poor bird"

Defining attributes
1. has feathers
2. lays eggs

Characteristic attributes
1. doesn't sing
2. doesn't fly
3. eats fish
4. moderately large

A flamingo — a "poor bird"

Defining attributes
1. has feathers
2. lays eggs
3. flys

Characteristic attributes
1. doesn't sing
2. eats plants
3. large
4. has a strange bill

Figure 8.2
The Prototypical Bird

When we think of a bird, the example that comes to mind will be a prototypical bird, like the robin. In contrast to the robin, a "poor" bird has the defining attributes but lacks many or all of the characteristic attributes of birds. An animal that lacks one or more of the defining attributes isn't a bird at all.

Concept Hierarchies Every concept is part of a network of other concepts. When you say that the object hopping on the lawn is a robin, you're not only saying that it has a red breast, eats worms, and corresponds to your prototype "robin." You're also saying that it's a bird, not a mammal or a fish; that it's an animal, not a plant; and that it's an organism, not a rock. The relationships among *robin, bird, animal,* and *organism* represent a hierarchy of concepts, in which each higher level includes those below it (see Figure 8.3).

All concepts are part of hierarchical structures like this one. And all of those structures are probably linked together, too. When you use concepts, you not only assign a particular experience to a particular concept (the hopping thing on the lawn is a robin); you also connect that experience with lots of other experiences that are likewise organized into concepts.

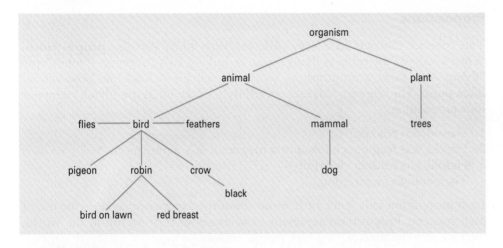

Figure 8.3
A Concept Hierarchy

This theory assumes it takes time to move through the network of relations in a hierarchic structure. Subjects who were asked whether a robin had a red breast answered quickly because "red breast" was connected directly to "robin." Subjects answered more slowly when asked whether a robin had feathers, presumably because "feathers" could only be accessed by first moving to the bird concept (Collins & Quillian, 1969).

Concepts and Words

Most concepts correspond to words, but not all do. Look at the Figure 8.A. Which items go together? You probably answered (a), (c), and (f); and (b), (d), and (e). Why? Because the items in each group seem somehow to "belong" together, and because they're different from the items in the other group. Words, such as *cloudlike* and *geometric*, can be used to describe the concepts you used to group the items, but they aren't necessary. Both concepts are clear without labels, and, in fact, you saw the two groups as distinct before you could describe the difference.

Throughout this chapter we use words to describe concepts and propositions and the rules of logic, because words are the medium we're working with in this book. And most words do refer to concepts. But remember that some concepts, like *cloudlike,* don't need labels.

One more thing. We've been using concrete examples—chairs and cows and birds—in our discussion because they're easy to describe. But lots of concepts deal with actions, such as running and reading, or with abstractions, such as democracy and love.

Figure 8.A
Concepts and Words

Propositions

You connect concepts in a very different way when you use **propositions.** When you say "the robin is flying," you're linking two concepts—"robin" and "flying"—to form a proposition. Sentences contain at least one proposition, often more. The sentence "Harold cheerfully read the interesting book" contains four propositions:

1. Harold was reading.
2. Harold was reading a book (not a magazine or a newspaper).
3. Harold was reading cheerfully.
4. The book was interesting.

Each proposition tells you a little more about the experience, as does the use of each concept. Propositions represent new classes of relationship in the world; they are also the tools with which people reason.

The Rules of Logic

Reasoning is the process of using information you already know to generate new information (Sternberg, 1986). You reason by manipulating and evaluating propositions. The process is guided by certain rules, rules we call **logic.** These rules keep you from making mistakes; they help you reach sound conclusions.

You reason by making *inferences,* by drawing conclusions. Those inferences can be either inductive or deductive. When you draw a conclusion based on your own or others' observations, you're making an **inductive inference.** For example, if you say that college students are young because all of the college students you've seen are young, you're making an inductive inference. Inductive inferences are generalizations based on specific observations.

Deductive inferences move from the general to the specific. Here you take a general rule and, from it, draw a conclusion about a specific case. In philosophy, deductive inferences take the form of syllogisms. A **syllogism** is a sequence of propositions, or *premises,* that leads to a final proposition, or what we call a *conclusion.* Here's a famous syllogism:

All men are mortal.

Socrates is a man.

Therefore, Socrates is mortal.

What we've been describing are the formal rules of logic. These rules define how people *should* make inferences; they don't necessarily define *how* they make inferences. The formal rules of logic outline a reasoning process that can be very different from the process most of us actually follow (Lehman, Lempert & Nisbett, 1988).

Here are two syllogisms. Read them and decide if the conclusions are definitely correct.

Some Cs are Y.

H is C.

Therefore, H is Y.

Some college students are young.

Harold is a college student.

Therefore, Harold is young.

Proposition   An idea that links two or more concepts together by describing a relationship among them.

Reasoning   Generating new information by manipulating old information.

Logic   The rules for manipulating propositions to generate valid inferences.

Inductive inference   A generalization based on specific observations.

Deductive inference   A conclusion about a specific case drawn from a general principle.

Syllogism   A series of premises and the conclusion that follows from them; in philosophy, the form of a deductive inference.

The answer is that H could be Y and Harold could be young, but neither is necessarily true. You probably had to puzzle a bit with the first syllogism, but the second was immediately obvious—despite the fact that the form of both is exactly the same. Why was the second syllogism obvious? Because it connects to things you already know about the world. The first premise in this syllogism says that college students are young; it does not say that *all* college students are young. You are aware of the fact that some college students are not young, so you know right away that you can't conclude for sure that Harold is young.

In experiment after experiment, researchers have demonstrated that people's ability to reason increases as the problem becomes more concrete (Clement & Falmagne, 1986). In fact, some psychologists argue that people reason effectively only when they use very concrete rules that apply to very specific situations (Griggs & Cox, 1982).

Those rules are called **pragmatic inferential rules** (Holland et al., 1986). They are practical translations of the rules of logic, rules that are connected to people's everyday knowledge of the world. And people use these more general rules very successfully, even though they cannot use the equivalent principles of logic (Cheng & Holyoak, 1985).

Images

Words are not the basis of all thought. People also think in **images,** mental representations of visual information.

Try this experiment. Answer the question "Which way do the hands of a clock move?" If you said "clockwise," you're cheating. The question is asking you to explain what *clockwise* means. How's this for an answer? "The hands move so that if they start pointing straight up, they move toward the right, so that they point straight right, then straight down, next around to straight left, and finally back to straight up." Not very helpful, is it? It's much easier and clearer to draw a picture of what you mean, like the arrow in Figure 8.4.

Images as Pictures   In some ways, images are like mental pictures. Obviously we can't see other people's mental pictures. So how do we know how images are used?

The solution to this problem was ingenious. The researchers began with the assumption that if images are like pictures, things that affect how people look at pictures should also affect how people handle images. For instance, if you were holding a picture in your hand, you might rotate it, to see it in different orientations. One experiment was designed to find out if people rotate mental images in the same way. The researchers showed the subjects correctly positioned and reversed *R*s in different orientations—some upright, some upside down, some turned at other angles. The subjects' task was to look at each letter and as quickly as possible decide whether it was right-reading or reversed.

If the subjects had been working with something physical—say, index cards printed with backward and forward *R*s in different orientations—they would have turned each card until the letter was upright and then decided whether it was right-reading or reversed. Obviously, the farther a letter from upright, the longer it would take to turn the card.

If mental images were like drawings, then, we would expect to have to rotate them "mentally" until they were upright. We would also expect it to take longer to perform this mental rotation the farther the *R*s are from upright. This is exactly what the findings show—an almost perfect relationship between how far a stimulus is rotated and how long it takes to decide whether the image is right-reading or reversed (see Figure 8.5) (Shepard & Cooper, 1982).

Figure 8.4
The Concept of "Clockwise"

Although you can describe what you mean by the concept "clockwise," the concept is much better captured by an image like the one in this figure, and best of all by movement.

Pragmatic inferential rules   Principles for making inferences that are similar to the rules of formal logic but are expressed in more concrete language.

Image   A mental representation of visual information.

Figure 8.5
The Relationship Between Degree of Rotation from Vertical and Decision Time

The farther the letter is rotated away from the normal position, the longer it takes people to decide whether it is backward or frontward.

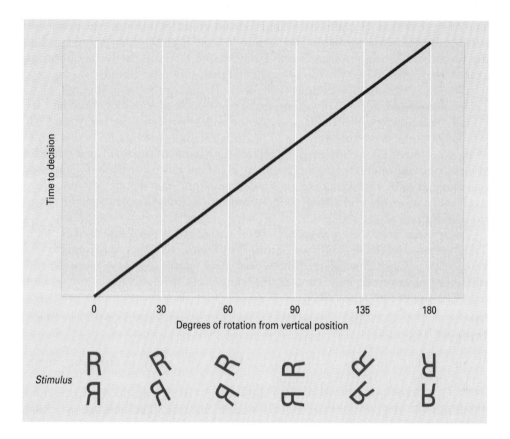

Another study showed that people scan mental images the same way they scan drawings or photographs, focusing their attention first on one part, then on another. It takes longer to scan a larger distance on a real picture; it also takes longer with a mental image. In this experiment, the subjects were shown a picture of a boat (see Figure 8.6). After the picture was removed, they were asked to focus their attention on the motor at the back of the boat. Then they were asked if the boat had either a windshield or an anchor. Subjects took longer to answer the anchor question, as though they had to move their "gaze" farther in order to reach the far end of the boat (Kosslyn, 1980). These findings confirm

Figure 8.6
Using Images

Subjects were asked to look at a picture like this one. When the picture was removed, they were then asked to imagine the boat, focusing their attention on the motor. It took them longer to answer whether the boat had an anchor than whether it had a windshield, suggesting that they were scanning their images of the picture.

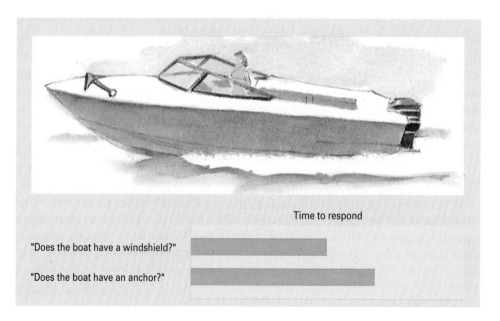

Puzzle It Out!

Which animal is larger? A rabbit or a cow? A rabbit or a cat? Which question took you longer to answer? Using what you know about the role of images in thinking, explain why.

that people manipulate and use mental images in much the same way that they manipulate and use drawings and photographs and other physical images.

Images as Representations   Although images are like pictures in some ways, in other ways they are very different. Your mental pictures are not reproductions of things you've seen. Instead, they seem to be representations of spatial relationships derived from your experience of space. Like memories, images tend to be reconstructed.

The way people use mental maps shows how this reconstruction works. A mental map is a geographical image. When you want to know whether Denver is east or west of Chicago, you "look" at your mental map of the United States and come up with the answer.

Now use your mental map to answer these questions:

- Which is farther north, Seattle or Montreal?
- Which is farther south, Rome or New York?
- Is the Atlantic end of the Panama Canal east or west of the Pacific end?

Most people answer *Montreal, Rome,* and *east.* And most people are wrong (see Figure 8.7).

These mistakes are actually very systematic. They reflect principles of space organization that are generally true but just don't apply to these questions. Canada is north of the United States, so it makes sense to assume that Montreal is farther north than Seattle. Rome is much warmer than New York, so it makes sense to assume that it's farther south. And the Atlantic Ocean is east of the Pacific Ocean, so it makes sense to assume that the Atlantic end of the canal is east of the Pacific end. Apparently people incorporate general geographic principles into their mental maps, and sometimes those principles distort the details in those maps. Although mental maps certainly reflect information that's been picked up from real maps, they also reflect other kinds of information, including people's experience of space and their biases.

Further evidence that mental pictures are not necessarily based on visual experience comes from studies of people who have been blind from birth. We now know that these people manipulate images in the same way that sighted people do (Kerr, 1983) and that they develop mental maps of rooms and other places (Landau, Spelke & Gleitman, 1984).

What the research suggests, then, is that images are representations of spatial relationships, not reproductions of scenes once viewed. They relate to reality in much the same way that a roadmap relates to reality. A roadmap represents the countryside; it's a kind of image of the countryside. But it doesn't look anything at all like what it represents. We could say that a roadmap is an abstract representation of the landscape. It captures certain elements (such as what is left or right of a particular point) at the expense of others (such as cows grazing in a field and houses and backyards). Mental images are abstract representations, too. They take certain—but not all—of the elements from the individual's visual experiences; and to these they add elements that reflect the individual's experience of space and personal biases.

Our mental maps capture some of the spatial relationships of our world, but they are also systematically distorted by our experiences, beliefs, and prejudices.

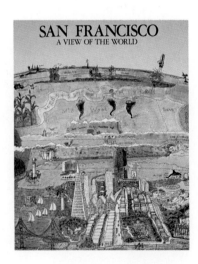

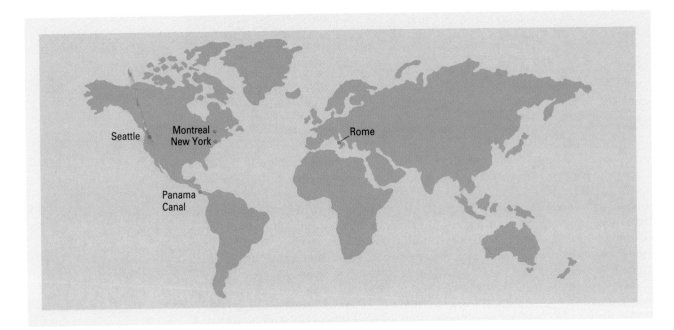

Figure 8.7
Real Maps Versus Mental Maps

Most people think Seattle is north of Montreal, Rome is south of New York, and the Panama Canal runs from east to west. But as these maps reveal, these assumptions are all errors, produced by our knowledge that Canada is north of the United States, Italy is hotter than New York, and that the Atlantic Ocean is east of the Pacific Ocean.

The Importance of Images   What role do images play in people's thinking? In some areas, they're essential. Imagine trying to put together a jigsaw puzzle using someone's verbal description of each piece. But no matter how important images may be, language is the most important medium of thought. This book is an example. We use lots of drawings and photographs to help you understand what we're writing about, but most of what you'll learn from this book is in the form of words.

Recap

- Cognition comprises all of the activities that are part of gathering and using information, including perceiving, thinking, and imagining.

- Thinking is the manipulation of information.

- Language is inextricably related to thought. It is the medium through which people acquire most of their knowledge, organize it, and communicate it to others.

- A concept is a way of thinking about objects, events, or people that makes them seem to go together.

- Apparently people form concepts by matching new examples of the concept with the particularly good examples of concept, called prototypes.

- Prototypes function as models of concepts; attributes define the way in which examples of a concept "fit" the concept.

- All the members of a concept group share its defining attributes; characteristic attributes fit many but not all members of the group.

- Every concept is part of a network of other concepts.

- A proposition is an idea that links two or more concepts together by describing a relationship among them.

- Reasoning is the process of using information that is already known to generate new information.

- Rules of logic guide the reasoning process; they help people reach sound conclusions.

- Inductive inferences move from the specific to the general; deductive inferences, from the general to the specific.

- Pragmatic inferential rules are the practical translations of the rules of logic that people actually use to reason with.

- Images are not so much mental pictures as they are representations of visual experiences, tempered by the individual's experience of space and personal biases.

Problem Solving

If your car stops running, you might not know how to fix it; but you can be pretty sure that there's a reason it's not working and that a mechanic could find the problem and solve it. A **problem** is a question that appears to have an answer, a single correct answer. We may not know how to cure cancer or how the brain stores information, but we have a strong sense that there are solutions to these problems, and that eventually someone will uncover them. *Decisions,* which will be discussed in the next section, are different in that they don't have a clearly correct solution. Decisions are more or less sensible, not right or wrong.

There are three stages in the problem-solving process:

1. formulating the problem;
2. generating a solution; and
3. checking the solution to see if it's correct.

At each stage, different factors operate to affect the outcome.

Formulating the Problem

Before you can solve a problem, you have to define it. This isn't always easy. Often other information, other experience, clouds the issue. When I was a research assistant trying to solve the monkeys' problem, I was so busy paying attention to what I thought was a problem with the apparatus that I ignored order—an essential clue to the solution.

In the laboratory all those years ago, I was distracting myself from the problem; the designers of word problems often create distractions for you. Here's an example:

> You have five brown socks for every four black socks in your drawer. How many socks do you have to get out of the drawer to be sure of having a matching pair?

You probably spent a couple of moments thinking about the ratio of brown socks to black socks before you realized that the ratio doesn't matter. As long as there are just two colors of socks in the drawer, all you need to take out are three socks. If the first two don't match, the third has to match one of them. The sock ratio is irrelevant; it can't help you solve the problem.

Now try this one:

> In a pond there is a single fast-growing lily pad, one foot in diameter. Every day the area covered by the lily pads doubles in size. After twenty days, the pond is completely covered. On what day was the pond half covered?

Problem A question that appears to have an answer.

If you try to start at the beginning of this problem—with a lily pad that's one foot in diameter—you can't solve it. But if you work backward, it's easy. If the plants double in area every day, then the day before the pond was covered, it must have been half covered. So the answer is the nineteenth day.

The reason this problem seems difficult is that we tend to think about natural processes, such as plants growing, from beginning to end. And usually that's a good way to solve a problem. But if you start at the beginning of this problem, you'll never solve it. Why? Because you don't have all the information you need—we never told you the size of the pond. The only way to solve this problem is to work backward.

The way you structure problems is the first step in solving them. Do you remember the story about Archimedes, the ancient Greek who supposedly jumped out of the bathtub and ran down the street, naked, shouting "Eureka!"? It goes like this. The king suspected that his new crown was not made of pure gold, that some silver had been mixed in. So he asked Archimedes to find out. Now Archimedes knew the weights of gold and silver, and if he had known the volume of the material in the crown, he could have solved the king's problem in a minute. But he couldn't figure out how to determine the volume of the ornate crown with all of its nooks and crannies. Of course, he could have melted the crown down, but that probably wouldn't have made the king very happy. Archimedes was stumped. Then, one day as he was getting into his bath, he noticed how the level of the bath water rose on the side of the tub. He realized that the amount of water his body pushed aside was equal to the volume of his body. And it was then that Archimedes leapt out of the tub and ran down the street naked screaming "Eureka!" Subsequently, he filled a bucket to the brim with water, put the crown in the bucket, and measured how much water ran out. That was the volume of the crown!

What Archimedes did was tackle the problem from another perspective. Instead of trying to measure the volume of the crown directly, he measured the amount of water that the crown displaced.

Generating a Solution

Here's an anagram: GYOOLCHYPS. Can you unscramble the letters to make a familiar word? (If you need help, the answer's in the footnote on page 220.) You just generated a solution to a problem. How did you do it? You probably can't explain. This stage of problem solving is the one we know the least about—in large part because we aren't conscious of our thought processes at work.

Algorithms   Suppose we ask you to determine the area of a room that's eight feet by ten feet. You'd probably have little difficulty coming up with the answer (eighty square feet) or an explanation of how you came up with the answer (the area of a rectangle equals the length times the width). You've learned a formula that you can apply to any problem that involves determining the area of a rectangle.

A formula is an example of an **algorithm,** a systematic procedure that produces the solution to a problem. If you follow an algorithm step by step, eventually you're going to come up with the right answer.

You could have used an algorithm to solve the GYOOLCHYPS anagram, systematically trying each letter in turn in each position. And eventually you'd have come up with the solution. Of course, you would have had to work through 3,628,800 combinations, a job that would take a computer more than ten hours to do at the rate of 100 combinations a second!

Algorithm   A systematic procedure that produces the solution to a problem.

The time it can take to run through an algorithm is one drawback to the use of algorithms to solve problems. Another is that not all problems can be solved with algorithms. For example, an algorithm couldn't help you solve the famous riddle of the Sphinx: What goes on four legs in the morning, two legs at noon, and three legs in the twilight? (The answer is a "human being.")

Heuristics   One way to solve problems when an algorithm is going to take too much time or won't work is to use **heuristics,** problem-solving strategies.

You probably used heuristics to solve the GYOOLCHYPS anagram. That is, you took certain rules you know about the English language and about the way people mix things up, and applied them to the scrambled letters. You may have started out by looking at the beginning and end of the anagram to find combinations of letters that crop up frequently in English words. You saw *GY* at the beginning and *PS* at the end. You may also have thought about what is a common mixing strategy, reversing the first and last parts of a word. At this point you were looking at PS _____ GY. This information was probably enough in combination with an important environmental cue—the fact that you're reading a psychology textbook—to give you the answer.

Heuristics are usually easier to use than algorithms, but they don't always solve the problem. Suppose we'd mixed up the letters in the anagram like this:

LYOPCOGYSH

There are common combinations at the beginning and end. But reversing them you get SH _____ LY, which doesn't get you any closer to the solution.

Means-ends Analysis   In order to generate a solution, you have to understand the form the solution should take. Often the form is implicit in the problem statement. When we asked you to unscramble GYOOLCHYPS, we were asking you for a common English word. But there are times when the form of the solution isn't obvious. This is where means-end analysis—a particularly powerful heuristic—comes into play (Newell & Simon, 1972).

Means-end analysis is a procedure for determining the way to arrive at a solution and the form that solution should take. You begin by asking what you want to accomplish, in as concrete a form as possible. Then you describe the means to that end, again in concrete terms. The end is your ultimate goal; the steps that get you there are subgoals. If those steps aren't immediately clear, you define the means to achieve them.

Henry Ford might have used means-end analysis. Ford did not invent the automobile, but he did invent a much more efficient way of manufacturing the automobile. When Ford started out, cars were being made by small groups of people, standing around each car, doing this job and that. There were some real problems with this method. The workers often got in one another's way; they were spending only a small part of their time doing the tasks they were best at; and organizing their work was difficult.

Of course, we don't know how Ford came up with the idea of the assembly line, but chances are he went through a process something like this:

> I want to make cars more quickly. How can I speed up production? More people working on each car. But more workers will get in one another's way. How can I have more people work on each car without getting in one another's way? What if they don't all work at the same time? But if they don't all work at the same time, I won't be producing cars any faster. Suppose I keep everybody busy working on different cars? Suppose I build lots of cars at once? But lots of cars take up a lot of space. If the workers have to walk from car to car, they'll waste time and get tired. What if I have the cars come to them? How would I do that? What if I mount the cars on a big belt that moves them from worker to worker?

Heuristic A problem-solving strategy that is neither systematic nor certain, but that is often efficient.

Means-end analysis A heuristic for determining the way to arrive at a solution and the form of that solution.

With his solution, Ford was on his way to dominating the automobile industry.

The Problems with Problem Solving   Take a few minutes and work the problems in Figure 8.8. How did you do? You probably did fine with the first four problems. But what about the last one? Did it take longer than the others to solve? Were you able to solve it?

Figure 8.8
Luchin's Water Jar Problem

Using jars A, B, and C, measure out the quantities listed in the last column on the right.

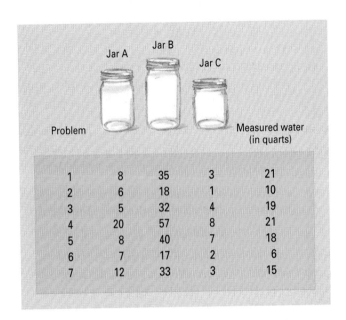

Problem	Jar A	Jar B	Jar C	Measured water (in quarts)
1	8	35	3	21
2	6	18	1	10
3	5	32	4	19
4	20	57	8	21
5	8	40	7	18
6	7	17	2	6
7	12	33	3	15

Why is the last one more difficult than the others? The paradoxical answer is because the others are relatively easy. You probably worked out the formula that solves all of them: $B - A - 2C$. The problem is that the formula doesn't work for Problem 5. But there is a formula that does work for that problem; in fact, the Problem 5 formula is simpler than the formula you used to solve Problems 1 through 4. Try it again, this time assuming that what worked for the other problems *won't* work here. It's simple, isn't it? Just $A - C$. Now look back at Problem 4. You can solve this with the $B - A - 2C$ formula; you can also solve it with the much simpler $A - C$ formula.

The difficulty you had solving Problem 5 and your failure to recognize a simpler solution for Problem 4 were products of **rigidity** (Luchins, 1942). When a particular strategy has worked successfully, people tend to cling to it even when it isn't working. And they certainly don't look for new, more efficient solutions as long as an old one is working. Rigidity may explain why institutions and people who have been successful at one time are less successful as time goes on. They may be persevering with policies that are no longer relevant or effective.

The problem in Figure 8.9 illustrates another kind of interference with problem solving. Can you solve the problem? Here's a hint: Imagine a child on a swing. Any luck? In the original study, the researcher gave the subjects a clue by casually brushing against one of the strings so that it began to swing (Maier, 1930). One solution is to tie the pliers or screwdriver to one of the strings and then set it swinging. After that you'd hold the second string, catching the first one as it swings near.

The reason people have trouble reaching this solution is that they tend to see pliers and screwdrivers as tools, not as weights. And they have a hard time

Rigidity   The unwillingness to give up a problem-solving strategy that no longer works or is not as effective as a new strategy.

The answer to the anagram on p. 218 is PSYCHOLOGY, of course!

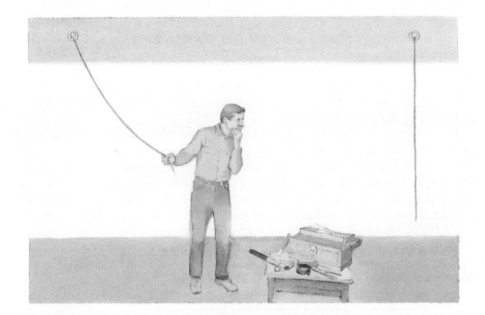

coming up with new uses for familiar objects. The inability to think of a new use for a familiar object is called **functional fixedness** (Duncker, 1945). Functional fixedness, like rigidity, stops people from thinking in new ways, thus interfering with the creativity that is essential for effective problem solving.

By the way, there's another solution to the two-string problem that uses the tape. Do you see it? You would attach the tape to one string, and then spool it out until it reaches the other string. Functional fixedness makes this solution difficult to see, too. Why? Because you usually think of *pieces* of tape, the short bits that you use when you're wrapping a package or sticking a note up on the front door. Here you have to think of it as a long strand, and that's not easy.

Incubation   How do you break the thought habits that interfere with your ability to solve new problems? Sometimes it helps to stop for a while and then come back to a problem. This technique, called **incubation,** was studied using the now-classic problem shown in Figure 8.10 (Silveira, 1971).

The subjects who couldn't solve this problem were given another task to work on. Later, when they returned to the necklace problem, they were more successful. How did you do? Did you get the answer? If not, take a break. Go get something to eat or drink. When you come back, try the problem again—this time making no assumptions. Don't read on until you've worked the problem again.

What's interfering with solving this problem is the assumption that the jeweler has to put the four pieces of chain together. That seems to mean opening and closing four links, which would cost $20. But suppose that the jeweler simply opens the three links on one of the chains, and then uses them to join the three remaining pieces? Now the job can be done for $15 (see Figure 8.11). The point is that the jeweler doesn't have to keep the four lengths of chain intact. (This is another of those problems in which the way it's conceived at the outset interferes with finding the solution.)

Testing the Solution

Obviously, not all solutions turn out to be correct. The final stage of problem solving is testing the solution to see if it is really correct.

Figure 8.10
The Necklace Problem

This is another problem in which the way it's formulated prevents us from finding the solution. Look at Figure 8.11 for an explanation.

Functional fixedness   The inability to think of a new use for a familiar object.

Incubation   Breaking away from a problem for a while before coming back to try to solve it again.

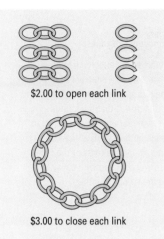

$2.00 to open each link

$3.00 to close each link

Figure 8.11
The Necklace Problem Explained

Because there are four sections to begin with, we tend to think always of four connections. Once we recognize that one of the sections can be completely separated, the solution is obvious.

Insight   Sometimes you just know that the solution to a problem is the right one the moment you find it. That moment of recognition, the sudden sense that "yes, this *is* the answer," is called **insight.** Insight links the solution-generating and solution-testing stages of problem solving. In that flash of recognition, not only do you know the answer, you know that it's the right answer. Presumably this is because we are able to see immediately that the elements of the solution do indeed fit the problem perfectly.

The experience of insight, sometimes called the "Aha!" experience, is pleasant, which is one reason why so many people enjoy crosswords and other kinds of recreational puzzles. Also, the pleasure of insight is probably the major reason that people choose careers in science. Science deals with problems that have solutions (whereas business and politics, for example, involve a much higher proportion of decision making rather than problem solving). If a scientist is lucky, his or her work will be filled with a succession of pleasurable insights.

Some of the earliest and most intriguing research on insight was conducted on chimpanzees by Wolfgang Kohler (1927). Stranded on the Canary Islands at the start of World War I, Kohler set about observing a colony of chimpanzees. In one experiment he hung a banana from a string at the top of a chimp's cage and left a number of wooden crates lying around within the cage. The chimp tried jumping to reach the banana, then climbing the sides of the cage. When neither worked, it stopped and looked around the cage at the banana and at the boxes. Suddenly it began piling the wooden crates on top of one another, until it had a stack high enough that it could easily jump from the top and get the banana. Kohler's chimp seemed in every way to have had an insight into the problem.

Confirmation Bias   Sometimes the solution to a problem isn't that easy to recognize. In such cases, you have to test the solution to be sure that it works. But new problems can emerge during the testing process. There's an example in Figure 8.12.

Figure 8.12
The Vowel Even-Number Cards

All cards have a letter on one side and a number on the other side. *Hypothesis:* "If there is a vowel on one side, there is an even number on the other side." Which cards should you turn over first to check this hypothesis. Check your answer against Figure 8.13.

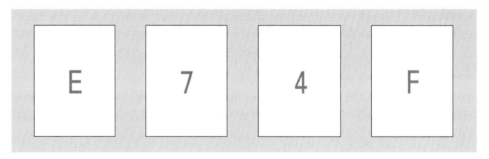

Each of the four cards in the figure has a number on one side and a letter on the other. And the hypothesis you're testing is that if a card has a vowel on one side, it has an even number on the other. Suppose you could turn over the cards to see what's on the other side. Which card or cards would you have to turn over to test the vowel–even number relationship? (You should turn over no more cards than are necessary.)

Most people turn over the *E* card first, which is a good choice. If there's an odd number on the other side, the hypothesis would be wrong. Most people choose the 4 card next, expecting to see a vowel on the back. But notice that if there isn't, it doesn't violate the hypothesis, which says only that *if* there's a vowel on one side, then there's an even number on the other. There also could be an even number with a consonant. In fact, the only observation that violates the hypothesis is a vowel with an odd number on the back. So the card with the *F* is irrelevant because *F* is a consonant. The only other card that should be

Insight   The sudden recognition that a solution is the right solution to a problem.

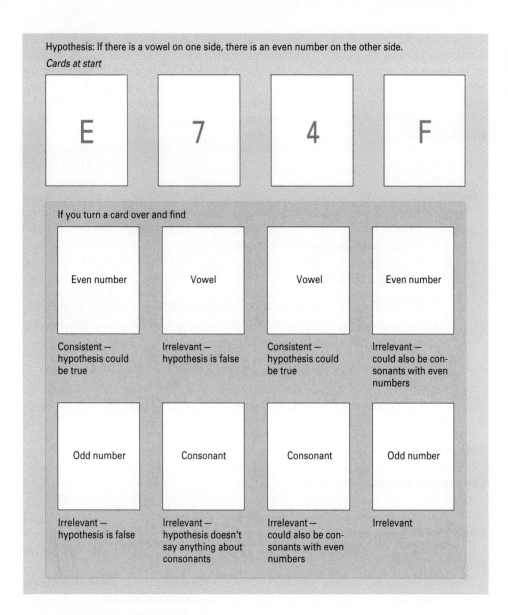

Hypothesis: If there is a vowel on one side, there is an even number on the other side.

Cards at start

| E | 7 | 4 | F |

If you turn a card over and find

| Even number | Vowel | Vowel | Even number |

Consistent — hypothesis could be true

Irrelevant — hypothesis is false

Consistent — hypothesis could be true

Irrelevant — could also be consonants with even numbers

| Odd number | Consonant | Consonant | Odd number |

Irrelevant — hypothesis is false

Irrelevant — hypothesis doesn't say anything about consonants

Irrelevant — could also be consonants with even numbers

Irrelevant

Figure 8.13
The Vowel Even-Numbered Cards Explained

turned over is the 7 because if there's a vowel on the back of that card, the hypothesis is wrong. Figure 8.13 shows the possible alternatives.

As their second choice in this experiment, most people choose the 4, which either fits the hypothesis or is irrelevant, but cannot prove it wrong. And most people don't turn over the 7, which can't prove that the hypothesis is correct but can show that it's wrong. Their choices, then, are likely to collect only the information that fits the hypothesis and to miss information that would prove it wrong.

What we're seeing is an irregularity in the way people test solutions to problems. They do look to see whether a hypothesis is correct, whether it's confirmed. But they are less likely to look carefully to see if it's incorrect. This phenomenon is called **confirmation bias** (Wason & Johnson-Laird, 1972).

Notice that we are not talking about another common human weakness—wanting to believe that we're right—which can lead us to ignore information that is inconsistent with our beliefs and values. On the contrary, confirmation bias can occur even when we're trying to determine the truth. It's just that we tend to look first to see if the data fit the hypothesis, and to overlook opportunities to see if they don't.

Confirmation bias The tendency to pay more attention to information that may confirm a hypothesis than to information that might disprove it.

For example, a manager we know was in the habit of hiring men for a particular job because he believed that men were better at it. He was conscientious, so he checked to make sure that the men he hired were actually performing adequately. And because they were, he felt that the facts supported his hiring policy. He was genuinely surprised when someone pointed out to him that he had never hired a woman to see if she would do equally well. Finally he did—and so did she.

Recap

- A problem is a question that appears to have a single correct answer.

- There are three stages in the problem-solving process: (1) formulating the problem; (2) generating a solution; and (3) checking the solution to see if it's correct.

- Both algorithms and heuristics help generate solutions to problems.

- Rigidity and functional fixedness interfere with the creativity that is essential for effective problem solving.

- Insight links the solution-generating and solution-testing stages of problem solving.

- Confirmation bias makes people more likely to look for confirmation of a hypothesis than for proof that it's wrong.

Decision Making

A problem has a clear-cut answer; a **decision** does not. Which candidate should I vote for? What school should I go to? Which job should I take? Where should I live? These kinds of questions ask you to choose a course of action, not to provide a piece of information.

Because decisions are not clearly right or wrong, they are evaluated differently from solutions. Decisions are reasonable or unreasonable, better or worse, wise or foolish. And often you can't begin to evaluate them until some time after they've been made. It's not surprising, then, that the decision-making process is very different from the problem-solving process.

The Rational Model

We do not, of course, always decide rationally. But by examing how rational decision making might proceed, we can also better understand our less rational moments. You're trying to decide on a major. A decision like this involves weighing different alternatives, balancing positive and negative outcomes. Suppose you're thinking about psychology. You enjoy the courses, but there's a lot of work involved. Also, a career in psychology probably means graduate school, a long hard grind. A major in economics might make it easier to find a job when you graduate, but you don't like the courses. English is interesting but you hate Victorian novels and you're not sure about the job possibilities.

Now you have to "add" the pros and cons, so that you can compare your choices. Some psychologists suggest that you assign points to the various alternatives that represent how you feel about them. For example, you might decide that enjoying the courses in your major is a big plus, worth 50 points. Hard

Decision The choice of a course of action.

work is a minus, so you assign it a negative value—say, −30 points. The cost of graduate school is another minus, also −30 points. In the second column of Table 8.1, we've assigned hypothetical values to each of the pros and cons we've described for each major. By assigning them values, we're *weighting* them. Based on the sum of the weighted values, economics looks like the best choice.

The second factor you have to consider is the likelihood of each outcome. You know you enjoy psychology, so you're pretty sure that you're going to like the courses. But maybe the work won't be hard, or maybe economics won't help you get a job. Each outcome has not only a value but also a probability of happening. In the third column of Table 8.1, we've listed some hypothetical probabilities for each outcome.

Finally, you multiply the values by the probabilities, to estimate the probable value of each alternative. Notice in the fourth column of the table that, once we take the probabilities of each outcome into account, the balance shifts indicating a different decision.

This process may be very different from what you remember yourself doing when you were choosing a major. Even in the middle of the process, few people think about value points or probabilities. But by now it should be clear that you're not always aware of how your psychological processes function. Some psychologists suggest that people actually do weigh the pros and cons and consider the probability of outcomes in making this kind of decision even though they may not be aware of this process (Janis & Mann, 1977).

To test this possibility, a group of psychologists asked couples to estimate the values and probabilities of the outcome of having a baby or not. Using the probable values calculated from these data, the psychologists were able to predict with 70 percent accuracy whether a couple would have a baby in the next two years (Beach, Campbell & Townes, 1979).

Whether you usually analyze your decisions or not, the fact is that this kind of analysis is good. Just doing the exercise—listing the pros and cons, thinking carefully about how much you value each alternative and how likely it is to happen—can improve your decision making (Janis & Wheeler, 1978). At the very least, it reduces the number of regrets you'll have later.

Alternative	Value		Probability		Probable Value
Psychology					
Good courses	+ 50	×	.9	=	+ 45
Hard work	− 30	×	.5	=	− 15
Graduate school	− 30	×	.4	=	− 12
	− 10				+ 18
Economics					
Job search	+ 30	×	.4	=	+ 12
Dislike courses	− 20	×	.9	=	− 18
	+ 10				− 6
English					
Easy courses	+ 10	×	.5	=	+ 5
Dislike Victorian novels	− 20	×	.9	=	− 18
Job search	− 10	×	.4	=	− 4
	− 20				− 17

Table 8.1
A Rational Decision-Making Model

The alternatives, their values, their probabilities, and their probable values.

Probability-Estimating Heuristics

The rational model suggests that there are two critical variables in making a decision: the value of each outcome and the probability of its occurrence. You have to decide for yourself what the values of the outcomes are. But the probabilities are matters of fact. You either will or won't get a job after college, and no amount of wishful thinking is going to change that probability. So you have to estimate how likely you are to get that job.

A scientist would approach the problem systematically surveying recent graduates in each major to see how many had found jobs. Obviously this is a very good way to estimate the probability of finding a job, but it's going to take a lot of time and effort. What do we do when an algorithm is too time consuming? We turn to heuristics. Two of the heuristics that help us estimate probability in different situations are the *representativeness heuristic* and the *availability heuristic*.

The Representativeness Heuristic   You met a student the other day in the cafeteria. He had a crewcut, was about six foot four, weighed at least two hundred pounds, and was eating an enormous meal. He told you that he was majoring in business, and then said he had to leave to go lift weights. Later someone tells you that he is either the school's star halfback or one of fifty students in a drama class. What do you think? What do you think the probability is that you're right?

Most people would say he was the football player. Why? Because he fits everyone's conventional idea of a football player, he's more "representative" of football players than of the students one expects to find in a drama class (Tversky & Kahneman, 1980).

Most people use the **representativeness heuristic** in making judgments about others, even when those judgments conflict with reasonable probabilities. In this example we told you there are fifty students in the drama class, a class any student in the school can take; but there is only one star halfback at any college. So the odds are much better that the student you met was in the drama class. In the absence of any other information, that would certainly have been the better guess.

Here's another example: "Bill is 34 years old. He is intelligent, but unimaginative, compulsive, and generally lifeless. In school, he was strong in mathematics but weak in social studies and humanities" (Tversky & Kahneman, 1983, p. 297).

What's the probability that Bill plays jazz for a hobby? Seems unlikely, doesn't it? Most subjects in an experiment thought so, too. What about the possibility that Bill is an accountant who plays jazz for a hobby? Does that seem more likely? To 87 percent of the subjects in this study, it did (Tversky & Kahneman, 1983). Why? Because Bill fits the conventional idea of an accountant. But consider the actual probabilities. Relatively few people play jazz for a hobby, and only a very few are also accountants. So the condition that Bill is *both* a jazz player and an accountant is much less likely than the condition that he is just a jazz player. Yet people feel more confident about the combined condition than they do about the single condition.

The Availability Heuristic   Do you think that you're more likely to die because of an airplane crash or because of asthma? Which is the more dangerous profession, law enforcement or commercial fishing? It *seems* that airplane crashes and being a police officer are more dangerous, but in fact many more people are killed by the alternatives (Slovic, Fischhoff & Lichtenstein, 1976).

Why is our sense of what is dangerous so different from reality? The answer seems to be another heuristic, the **availability heuristic.** When people are

Representativeness heuristic The tendency to assume that a person or object must be a member of a category if it represents that category especially well.

Availability heuristic The tendency to estimate the frequency of an event by the ease with which it's remembered.

How Do We Know That?

Psychologists are often accused of being more interested in human failure than in human success. After all, they focus on illusions, on errors in memory, on abnormal behavior. In our discussion of heuristics, too, we've certainly concentrated on the problems of using them. By definition, heuristics sometimes don't work. (If they always worked, they'd be algorithms.) Far more often, they help people make sensible decisions where complete information is difficult or impossible to obtain. Why, then, have we spent so much time talking about the problems with heuristics?

The answer is that when heuristics work, we often can't tell how or why. But their failures are extremely instructive. Suppose we ask you which crime is more common, premeditated murder or embezzlement. If you give us the right answer—embezzlement—we are no further along in understanding the decision-making process. But if you respond that murder is more common, we begin to wonder why you've made the mistake. And if we ask a whole series of similar questions and find the same error—overestimating the frequency of vivid crimes—we would begin to realize that something like the availability heuristic is at work. Errors reveal the workings of processes that usually operate just fine (Tversky & Kahneman, 1983).

---

forming an opinion on some subject, they are very strongly influenced by their own experience of that subject. Experience seems a reasonable basis for an opinion, but in fact it tends to distort the decision-making process in at least two ways.

First, our experience is limited. Most of us are lucky enough to have no direct experience of people dying in plane crashes or from asthma. What we use, then, is secondhand experience, gleaned largely from newspapers, radio, and television. We think that plane crashes kill more people than asthma does because plane crashes are news and the media are filled with reports of them. When a police officer is killed in the line of duty, the newspaper headlines scream the story; but when a commercial fisherman disappears over the side of a boat, only family and friends take notice. The available information, then, doesn't necessarily reflect reality.

Second, we don't really use our experience to make probability decisions; we use our *memory* of our experience, a memory that reflects only certain events. It's these "memorable" events that seem more common to us.

Let's go back for a minute to the subject of choosing a major. Suppose that you read somewhere that only 20 percent of the students who major in English find good jobs. The next day you meet some friends who graduated last year with degrees in English. They tell you that they had no trouble finding great jobs in publishing. When it comes time for you to estimate the probability of getting a job as an English major, you're probably going to think it's pretty easy. Why? Because your own experience—listening to your friends—is much more "available" in your memory than the article you read.

By this time it may seem that human beings are incapable of rational thought. But, of course, this isn't the case. After all, we do pretty well in everyday life. And here we see yet another example of the availability heuristic. The evidence of our failures is much more dramatic than the evidence of our successes, so we tend to remember our failures more easily.

Recap

- Decisions do not have clear-cut answers; instead, they prompt the individual to choose a course of action that is neither right nor wrong and that may not be evaluated for some time.

- Rational decision making entails assigning a value and a probability to each alternative, and making a decision based on the probable value of each alternative.

- The use of heuristics can help save time in the decision-making process.

- The representativeness heuristic is the tendency to assume that a person or object must be a member of a category if it represents that category especially well.

- The availability heuristic is the tendency to estimate the frequency of an event by the ease with which it's remembered.

Creativity

In our discussion of thought, we've moved from basic reasoning to problem solving to decision making, from concrete forms of thought to more abstract forms. Now we come to **creativity**—the ability to produce new and useful ideas or to combine information in new and useful ways.

Notice that we use two adjectives in our definition: *new* and *useful*. Innovation is a critical part of creativity; but so is functionality. The product of creativity has to be useful.

Naturally we would like to harness creativity. We would like to become more creative ourselves; or, if that's impossible, we would like to identify conditions that can help children to become more creative as they grow up. At the very least, we would like to be able to identify people who are creative, to work with them and learn from them.

The Nature of Creative People

One way psychologists study creativity is by studying people who are creative. This kind of research has produced a list of attributes that creative people share. For example, we know that most of these people tend to have above-average intelligence. And we know that they are independent, self-accepting, and energetic (Barron & Harrington, 1981).

Yet there are many people who are highly intelligent, independent, self-accepting, and energetic—but not creative. These attributes may help define creative people, but they certainly aren't exclusive to those who are creative.

Tests of Creativity

In the absence of a detailed definition of creativity, tests have been developed to measure creativity. The two most popular of these—the Novel Uses Test (Guilford, 1967) and the Remote Associates Test (Mednick & Mednick, 1967)—are based on the same assumption, that the essential element of creativity is the ability to generate new ideas. Indeed, the tests were designed to provide a context in which new ideas could be produced.

Creativity The ability to come up with new and useful ideas or to combine information in new and useful ways.

Remember the problem about the two strings that are hanging too far apart to be tied together? What that problem asked of you was to think of a new use for an old object. The Novel Uses Test gives you the same task—to think up as many possible uses for a familiar object as you can. For example, one item asks you to think of all the things you could do with a plastic milk container. Both the number of different uses you come up with and their novelty are used as measures of creativity (Guilford, 1967).

One of the items in the Remote Associates Test asks you to think of a word that fits each of three stimulus words. For example, for the words *tug, house,* and *show,* the answer would be *boat* (Mednick & Mednick, 1967).

How effective are these tests at predicting creativity? Not very. What the tests do is predict how well you're going to do on the tests, not how creative you are going to be in real life (Barron & Harrington, 1981).

In the final analysis, tests of creativity may fail because of the nature of creativity itself. Because the word is a noun, standing alone, we tend to think of *creativity* as a property or attribute. But the reality is probably different. First of all, consider the fact that people who are noted for their creativity in one sphere of activity are rarely creative in others. Leonardo da Vinci was a painter, a sculptor, a scientist, an architect, an engineer. He was also an exception. Much more common are people like Einstein, Bach, Edison, and Van Gogh, people whose creativity was confined to one area. Instead of saying that a *person* is creative, perhaps we should be saying that that person's *performance* is creative. Einstein was not creative in general; he was a creative theoretical physicist. Bach was not creative in general; he was a creative composer.

Because the ability of most people to perform creatively is restricted to a particular kind of activity, we would not expect a person who is creative at thinking up unusual uses for a brick or a ball of string to be creative in other ways. Likewise, we can't assume that just because someone is not particularly creative at thinking up new ways to use a brick or a ball of string that the individual is not creative in some other area.

The Circumstances of Creativity

We do know that creativity is affected by the conditions under which people are working. You probably can remember a time when you wrote a paper, painted a picture, or solved a problem almost effortlessly. And you definitely can remember a time when you wanted desperately to do a really good creative job and just couldn't. In fact the more you tried, the worse it got.

One of the most reliable ways to interfere with creativity is to put pressure on someone to be creative (Amabile, 1983). In one demonstration of this effect, two groups of college students were asked to write short poems or make collages. One group was told that its work would be evaluated by experts; the other wasn't. Not surprisingly, the work done by the first group was less creative than the work done by the second group (Amabile, 1983).

Creativity is also affected by the reasons underlying it. The subjects in one study wrote short pieces of fiction after ranking the items on one of two lists of reasons for writing. One of the lists focused on external rewards, such as money and fame; the other focused on internal rewards, the satisfaction of creating something or practicing a craft, for example. When the subjects had been thinking about external rewards, their work was much less creative than when they had been thinking about internal rewards (Amabile, 1985).

Part of our cultural mythology is the image of the artist, writer, or scientist who is out of touch with practical matters, such as making a living. The myth implies that this image is a by-product of the creative temperament, that artists are so wrapped up in their work that they ignore what's going on in the real world. But Theresa Amabile (1983) suggests that we have this backward, that some people can be creative *because* they aren't motivated by external rewards.

Just how external rewards limit creativity isn't clear. One possibility is that they change the emotional climate in which people work, thereby producing pressure, which in turn produces unhappiness. When people are happy, they are much more creative in their use of language, and they perform better on the Remote Associates Test (Isen et al., 1985). They also do better at solving problems like the two-string problem (Isen, Daubman & Nowicki, 1987). In short, happiness seems to foster creativity.

These findings conflict with another part of our mythology about creativity, the belief that artists are tortured, unhappy souls. Of course, some are, and for them perhaps negative feelings don't hinder creativity. But for the majority of us, happiness increases creativity (Isen, Daubman & Nowicki, 1987).

In sum, we aren't sure what makes people creative. But we are beginning to identify some of the conditions that foster creativity. First, there's work for the pleasure of the work itself—not for the promise of rewards or in reaction against the threat of punishment. Second, there is happiness.

Recap

- Creativity is the ability to produce new and useful ideas or to combine information in new and useful ways.

- People who are creative tend to have above-average intelligence and to be independent, self-accepting, and energetic; but many people with these characteristics are not creative.

- Tests of creativity fail largely because people tend to be creative in just one area; thus, doing well or poorly on these tests is not a good predictor of creativity in some other area.

- Creativity is affected both by the conditions under which people work and by their emotional state.

Language

Language is the medium through which you acquire information, organize it into concepts and propositions, and, most important, communicate the information to others. In this section we turn to the last part of this definition, to the central role of language—communication.

The Structure of Language

Language is organized into four different levels, each higher level building on the one below it (see Figure 8.14). At the lowest level are **phonemes,** the sounds used to form spoken words. The next level consists of the particular combinations of phonemes that have meaning in a given language. These units of language are called **morphemes.** Finally, there are the combinations of morphemes into words and words into phrases and sentences.

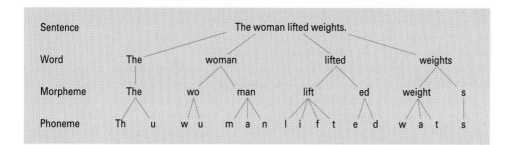

Figure 8.14
The Structure of Language

Language consists of at least four distinguishable levels, each of which consists of elements from the lower level arranged in a particular order.

From Phonemes to Sentences   Human babies babble from the time they are just a few months old. This babbling doesn't seem to require any input from adults; babies who are deaf normally babble at this stage, too. Among a baby's babbling sounds are all of the sounds that carry meaning in any language. Each language selects some of these sounds as phonemes, the constituents of its language. The differences among these sounds are what distinguish different words.

The words *fall, fill,* and *full* differ only in the sound that comes in the middle. Each of those sounds is a phoneme; and each changes the meaning of words in the English language. Some sounds are phonemes in other languages but not in English. For example, we don't use the click sound that's part of certain African languages at all; so the click sound is not an English phoneme. If you make a click sound in the middle of an English word, you aren't changing the meaning of the word.

Other sounds that make important differences in meaning in other languages are treated as the same sound in English. For example, in French there are two *n*-sound phonemes: the word *bon* is pronounced with a shorter, more abrupt *n* sound than *bonne.* Both words mean "good," but the *n* sounds distinguish between the masculine and feminine forms. In English, it doesn't matter if you pronounce *ton* with a short or a long *n* sound; it still means two thousand pounds.

Conversely, some English phonemes are not used in other languages. The Japanese, for example, make no distinction between the *l* sound and the *r* sound, which is why they often use one sound when the English word calls for another.

Notice that English phonemes are something like the spoken equivalent of written letters in the language. But there are differences. English uses forty phonemes and just twenty-six letters. (Other languages have as few as thirty phonemes or as many as fifty.) Some phonemes, like the *ch* sound, are made up of combinations of letters. And some letters, such as *C,* have more than one mean-

Phoneme A sound used to form spoken words that gives the words meaning in a particular language.

Morpheme The smallest meaningful unit of language.

How Do We Know That?

Japanese adults may have difficulty distinguishing between *l* sounds and *r* sounds, but it seems that Japanese infants do not. This finding was the product of a study that used an intriguing method.

Infants suck faster on a pacifier when they hear a sound they are interested in, such as their mother's voice. They also suck faster in response to new sounds. So by measuring the rate of their sucking, we can tell whether or not they're able to distinguish a new sound. Research using the rate-of-sucking measure has confirmed that Japanese babies do hear the difference between the *l* sound and the *r* sound (Eimas, 1971).

If Japanese infants can distinguish between the two sounds, why can't Japanese adults? It may be that, as they get older, they learn that this is not an important difference in their language, and so they learn to ignore it.

ingful sound. For example, how would you pronounce the word *ghoti?* George Bernard Shaw, the English playwright, would have said *fish.* Can you explain why? (The answer's in the footnote on page 234.)

Phonemes are just sounds; morphemes are the smallest combinations of phonemes that have meaning. The words we used as examples earlier—*fall, fill,* and *full*—are morphemes. But not all morphemes are words, and many words contain more than one morpheme. For instance, there are two morphemes in the word *fallen—fall* and *en.* The suffix *-en* is a morpheme because it has meaning in its own right: it conveys the fact that a fall, or the action of any other verb it's attached to, has been completed in the past.

The order in which phonemes are combined into morphemes is crucial. *Tip* and *pit* use the same phonemes but in a different order. Because language is an event that extends over time, the order of its elements is an important source of information. As you move through the structure of language, each higher level of organization consists of elements from the next lower level combined in a specific order through time.

Sentences are combinations of words and phrases. They're used to state propositions, to link two or more concepts together. *Dog see* is a primitive, two-word sentence, the kind children begin to use around the age of two. In this form, the sentence means that the dog is looking at something. *See dog* is also a sentence, but it means something very different.

Syntax   The rules of **syntax** govern the organization of language, the order in which words are used. Each language has its own rules of syntax. In English, for example, one rule says that adjectives precede the nouns they modify. *White house* is right; *house white* is wrong. But in Spanish, *house white (casa blanca)* is the proper form.

By definition, the rules of syntax restrict the use of language; but language is still remarkably versatile. For example, in English we can say the same thing in many different ways. Take the sentence *The brown dog saw the sleeping cat.* Here are some variations on that theme:

The sleeping cat was seen by the brown dog.

The dog, which was brown, saw the cat, which was sleeping.

The cat the brown dog saw was sleeping.

And with a little thought, you can probably come up with several more.

Syntax The rules that govern the order in which words are used in a language.

Because we are competent language users, we know that these sentences say pretty much the same thing. Although the original sentence focuses attention on the dog, and the first variation focuses on the cat, the core meaning in the two sentences is the same. Linguist Noam Chomsky (1972) has described a complex set of syntactic rules to explain our ability to understand the common core of meaning in all of these sentences. He calls this system of rules **transformational grammar.** The rules allow us to transform the *deep structure,* the core meaning, into a variety of *surface structures,* the individual sentences.

One of the striking features of human language is the consistency that characterizes the form of syntactic rules. Most of the principles of transformational grammar are identical in every language system. Chomsky argues that this consistency across languages is strong evidence that the capacity to learn language is determined genetically in human beings. He is saying not that people would speak without being taught but, rather, that people are powerfully predisposed to learn to speak; and that when they do, they follow a number of common principles of language.

The Development of Language

We noted earlier that babies babble, making all of the sounds that serve as phonemes in any language. Between the ages of six and twelve months, babies begin to distinguish among the sounds they make; they begin to repeat more often the phonemes of the language spoken around them and to use other phonemes less (Pye, Ingram & List, 1987). During this stage, babies clearly understand some words and start to use their own first words. Initially those words are just repetitions of selected sounds, like *mama* and *dada.* But they quickly acquire a good-sized vocabulary of single-syllable nouns (*dog, milk*) and verbs (*run, want*). They use these words like sentences. For example, *ball* could mean *I want the ball* or *See the ball* or *Isn't that a nice ball?* We could describe the acquisition of words in the **one-word stage** as the acquisition of concepts.

Two-year-olds have hundreds of words in their vocabulary and already have begun to put these words together in primitive two-word sentences. This stage of language development is called the **two-word stage.** Given the simplicity of the two-word structure, it's remarkable how many different meanings young children can communicate. They can identify an object (*See kitty*), locate it (*Kitty bye-bye*), reject it (*No kitty*), claim it (*My kitty*), describe its behavior (*Kitty ball*) and characteristics (*Nice kitty*), and ask for information about it (*Where kitty?*).

Even at this early stage, children speak with a primitive sort of syntax. They would never say *kitty my* or *kitty where?* And *bye-bye kitty* means something entirely different from *kitty bye-bye* (Maratsos, 1983).

Speech in the two-word stage is **telegraphic speech.** Young children do not use articles (*a, an, the*) in their sentences. Their expressions are clipped, almost like the wording in telegrams (HOME SATURDAY. MEET BUS.). *Want milk* is the way a two-year-old says *I'd like some milk, please.*

The errors they make in speech show us that children at the two-word stage have mastered the basic rules of grammar (Kuczaj, 1978). This is why they say *I runned* instead of *I ran,* or *two mans* instead of *two men.* Obviously they haven't heard these ungrammatical forms from adults, so it's clear that children don't simply parrot what they hear around them.

Over the next three years, children's speech rapidly improves in intelligibility and complexity. Their pronunciation gets better (*poon* becomes *spoon,* for example), and they begin to produce more complex expressions, slowly adding negation (*No want milk*) and articles to their sentences (*I want the ball*). The earlier milestones of language development are shown in Table 8.2.

Transformational grammar According to Chomsky, the syntactic rules that allow the individual to express the core meaning of a sentence (the deep structure) in a variety of forms (the surface structures).

One-word stage The stage of language development at which children use single words.

Two-word stage The stage of language development at which children make two-word utterances.

Telegraphic speech The simple speech — without articles — that is characteristic of the two-word stage.

At the completion of	Vocalization and language
12 weeks	Markedly less crying than at eight weeks; when talked to and nodded at, smiles, followed by squealing-gurgling sounds usually called *cooing*, which is vowel-like in character.
20 weeks	The vowel-like cooing sounds begin to be interspersed with more consonantal-sounds; all vocalizations are very different from the sounds of the mature language of the environment.
6 months	Cooing changing into babbling resembling one-syllable utterances; neither vowels nor consonants have very fixed recurrences; most common utterances sound somewhat like ma, mu, da, or di.
8 months	Continuous repetitions (e.g., "mamama," "baba") becomes frequent; intonation patterns become distinct; utterances can signal emphasis and emotions.
10 months	Appears to wish to imitate sounds, but the imitations are never quite successful; beginning to differentiate between words heard by making differential adjustment.
12 months	Identical sound sequences are replicated with higher relative frequency of occurrence and words (mamma or dadda) are emerging; definite signs of understanding some words and simple commands (show me your eyes).
18 months	Has a definite repertoire of words—more than three, but less than fifty; still much babbling but now of several syllables with intricate intonation pattern; no attempt at communicating information and no frustration for not being understood.

Source: Adapted from Lenneberg, 1967.

By six years of age, basic language development is complete. From this point on, language learning consists primarily of adding new vocabulary and acquiring styles of speech that are appropriate to different situations (for example, speaking more formally with adults than with peers).

The development of language is an incredible accomplishment. In a span of just three or four years, children learn to form relatively long complex sentences that embody the intricate rules of grammar. No less remarkable is the fact that by the time they are grown, they are able to use just 40 phonemes to form about 50,000 morphemes, to make around 150,000 words that can be used to produce an infinite number of sentences.

Animal Language

Do animals use language? In his work, Chomsky (1972) argues that the capacity to learn and use language is genetically determined in human beings. The implication is that we are the only species able to use language. Is this true? We know that nonhuman species communicate. But whether that communication involves language is the subject of ongoing debate.

Consider the honeybee. Beekeepers have known for a long time that when a foraging bee finds an especially good source of nectar (which is used to produce honey), other bees from the hive arrive shortly in great numbers. There was no mystery to the process. It seemed obvious that the other bees follow the foraging bee back to its discovery. But if the foraging bee is trapped as it leaves the hive, the other bees still appear at the source. How do they know where to go?

How did Shaw get *fish* from *ghoti*? He picked up the *gh* sound from *enough*, the *o* sound from *women*, and the *ti* sound from *attention!*

This question intrigued Austrian biologist Karl von Frisch (1974), who spent years studying the honeybee. He found that the foraging bee "tells" the other bees about its find by performing a kind of dance on the surface of the honeycomb (see Figure 8.15). When the food source is relatively close to the hive, the bee simply dances in a circle. When the source is farther away, the bee dances in a sort of figure eight, using its abdominal movements and the speed of the dance to indicate the distance to the source, and the orientation of the dance to indicate its direction.

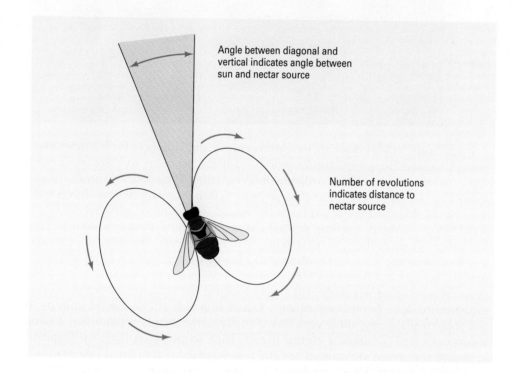

Angle between diagonal and vertical indicates angle between sun and nectar source

Number of revolutions indicates distance to nectar source

Figure 8.15
Bee Language

When the food source is relatively close to the hive, the bee simply dances in a circle. But when the food source is farther away, the bee does a figure eight dance that indicates the direction and nearness of the food source. The rapidity of the dance and the number of times the bee waggles its abdomen indicates the nearness of the food source, and the orientation of the dance indicates its direction.

Is the honeybee's dance language? Not by most definitions. It has just two morphemes, describing distance and direction and no syntactic structures. On the other side of the argument, bees do convey information, and the "language" depends on an arbitrary relationship between a set of behaviors and the information. By "arbitrary relationship" we mean that there isn't a logical or necessary connection between the behaviors and the information; in a sense, the connection is only a convention. For example, the bee could just as easily signal distance by bobbing its head as by wiggling its abdomen. In sum, depending on our criteria, perhaps the honeybee's dance is language, but it's certainly a very limited one.

Apes are a lot smarter than bees, which is why they've been the subject of numerous language experiments. In one of those experiments, psychologists Winthrop and Luella Kellogg (1933) raised a baby chimpanzee side by side with their own son, trying as much as possible to treat chimp and boy in the same ways. Their son learned to talk; the chimp did not. (This experiment came to a sudden end one morning when the son sat down at the breakfast table and emitted a chimpanzee's food bark!)

Another psychologist, Cathy Hayes, and her husband raised a chimp alone so that they could give the animal their undivided attention (Hayes, 1951). Because the chimp never babbled, Hayes had to work especially hard at teaching it phonemes. Despite all her work, the chimp was able to master only three or four words, including *mama* and *papa*. Both Hayes's work and the Kelloggs' seemed to indicate that apes do not have the mental capacity for speech.

Using the keyboard, Lana was not only able to ask for food, water, and companionship but also to ask and answer questions about stimuli presented to her.

It was some years before the research on apes and language took a new direction. Allan and Beatrice Gardner wondered if the problem was that apes don't make word sounds. The Gardners observed that apes don't naturally make sounds like human speech, but they are very skillful at manipulating things with their hands. Maybe they could learn to "speak" with their hands. So the Gardners (1969) set about teaching several chimpanzees how to use American Sign Language. Their findings were striking. After four years, Washoe, the first and best known of the Gardners' chimps, had learned about one hundred and fifty words (Gardner & Gardner, 1971).

Eventually other psychologists began looking for evidence of nonvocal language in the ape. In one experiment, David Premack (1976) taught chimps to put colored plastic symbols on a board to represent words. In another, Duane Rumbaugh (1977) taught a chimp named Lana to press symbols on a special keyboard connected to a computer. The computer then "translated" the symbols into English words. Using nonvocal language, chimpanzees were now learning to use as many as six hundred "words."

The responses discovered by the researchers in these experiments seem to indicate a real understanding of language. When Washoe wants an apple, she makes the sign for an apple. Or she forms a "sentence," signing the two words *give* and *apple*. Once she saw a duck. She didn't know the sign for duck so she combined two signs, *water* and *bird*. For the refrigerator, she coined the compound name *open-eat-drink*. Their ability to create compound words suggests that apes not only understand the concepts behind words but also are capable of generating new concepts and inventing the words to express them.

Furthermore, apes don't just "talk" to people. Washoe and the other chimps in her project now use sign language to communicate among themselves (Fouts, Fouts & Schoenfeld, 1984). They've even taught it to a young chimp (Fouts, Fouts & Van Cantfort, 1989).

There's no question that these findings are remarkable. But it's important to be clear about what the apes can and cannot do. First, although they can learn substantial vocabularies, six hundred words seems to be the record—roughly the vocabulary of a two-year-old (Patterson, Patterson & Brentari, 1987).

Second, although apes do sign meaningful two-word sequences (and occasionally longer sequences), there's a question about their understanding of syntax. Remember that when young children start to use two-word sequences, they almost invariably follow simple rules of syntax. If they want their mother to kick a ball, they say *Mommy kick,* not *Kick Mommy.* (If they say *Kick Mommy,* she'd better watch out!) Do apes understand the distinction between *Mommy kick* and *Kick Mommy?* At least some of the researchers who have spent years teaching chimpanzees to use sign language don't think so (Terrace et al., 1979; Premack, 1986). They insist that the apes just emit strings of signs, and that it's the human observers picking out those signs who are "grammatical."

So, the uncertainty is whether apes using sign language can use language as well as a child at the two-word stage of language. Most researchers seem to agree that apes perform rather like one-word children, and perhaps better. But they definitely do not match the performance of two-year-old children who can understand and use multiword sentences with systematic syntax.

Now we can see why the question of ape language becomes such a matter of definition. We don't for a moment question that baby's first "mama" is also baby's first speech, because we know that in a few months there will be no question. Children go from beings that cannot use language at all, to beings who can use it extremely well. Apes using sign language seem to be able to make part of that journey, but not all of it. We know now that part of the reason they could not begin that development was that they had no symbol system until they were taught sign language. But obviously they had handicaps as well—the most important being that they simply aren't as intelligent as human beings. In fact, if they were just like us except for the ability to make sounds, they probably would have invented sign language long ago.

Recap

- Language exists at several basic levels, from phonemes to sentences.
- Phonemes are the sounds from which spoken words are constructed.
- Morphemes are the smallest meaningful combinations of phonemes.
- Words are morphemes or combinations of morphemes.
- Phrases and sentences express relationships.
- The rules of syntax govern the organization of language.
- The acquisition of words in the one-word stage is essentially the acquisition of concepts, because each word corresponds to a particular concept.
- In the two-word stage, children show a rudimentary understanding of basic syntax.
- Between the ages of two and five, children's speech rapidly improves in intelligibility and complexity.
- By six years of age, basic language development is complete.
- Research with apes indicates that they can develop basic concepts of language, using sign language or other nonvocal language. But their language skills do not match those of a two-year old human.

The Effect of Language on Thought

The primary function of language is communication. But language is also a tool of thought. We think in linguistic forms much of the time. In fact, the early behaviorists believed that all thinking actually was quiet speech. And they didn't change their minds until someone showed that stopping people from moving their tongues and the muscles of the face and throat doesn't stop them from thinking.

This is not to say that speaking and thinking are unrelated. The relationship parallels that between speaking and reading. Most children learn to read by saying the words out loud and then listening to their own speech. At first, therefore, reading consists of speaking the words in the book. If you stop a child from speaking, the child cannot read. In time, however, children begin to read silently, although their lips often move as they do so. Still later, they read without forming the words, without speech. Although reading eventually becomes a distinct activity, its roots lie in speech. In the same way, thought—although different from speech—may be rooted in speech (Vygotsky, 1962).

Language and Perception

If we think in linguistic form, do the properties of our language shape our perception of the world? Benjamin Whorf (1956) believed they do. As evidence he pointed to the Eskimos, who have eleven different words for snow. According to Whorf, the fine distinctions in their language allow Eskimos to make finer distinctions among kinds of snow than people in other cultures, who speak other languages. But which came first—the words or the distinctions?

One answer comes from studies of color names in different language groups. In English we have eleven basic color names; other languages have different numbers of basic color names, some as few as two. If Whorf was right, people with fewer names for colors should perceive fewer differences among colors. But in fact they don't. In a study of the Dani, a preliterate people with just two basic color names, Eleanor Rosch (1973) found that her subjects were able to distinguish among the colors that correspond to our eleven basic color names using nonsense-syllable names. And the Dani made the distinctions among the colors and learned the names Rosch had given the colors as easily as did a group of English-speaking subjects. These findings tell us that language does not affect what we can perceive, that it doesn't limit what we are able to do.

Eskimos aren't the only people with lots of names for snow. Skiers also have all kinds of names for snow, such as "corn snow," "mashed potato," and "blue ice."

Language and Attention

Another version of Whorf's hypothesis is that language affects how we tend to think even if it doesn't completely limit us. Does the fact that we don't have eleven different names for snow mean that we don't pay attention to the different kinds of snow even though we could distinguish them if we tried?

The evidence indicates that although language doesn't affect what we *can* perceive, it does affect what we *do* perceive. According to one recent study, the language that children learn influences what they pay attention to in the world (Bowerman, 1989). For example, in English we make a simple distinction between the concepts "in" and "on." Spanish makes no such distinction. In German, however, there are three different words for "on." One means "on a horizontal surface"; one means "on a vertical surface"; and one means "around" (in the sense that a ring is "on" a finger). To learn how to use these words, German children have to focus on the relationships they describe—relationships that American or Spanish children probably don't even notice. As a result, German children are much more aware of these differences.

As the subject matter becomes more complex, language seems to have an even more powerful effect on thought. In Chapter 7 we described one effect of language on memory. There we talked about how the wording of a question influences the way people remember an experience. When the researcher asked about one car "smashing" into another, the answers were very different from those she got when she asked about one car "hitting" another (Loftus, 1979).

The Issue of Gender

In English there aren't many ways to refer to people without introducing gender. Most of the generic terms for people—words such as *mankind* and *manpower*—actually refer to men. And before the women's movement raised society's consciousness, it was commonplace, when a person's gender was not specified, to use *he* and *his* where a singular pronoun was needed.

In recent years the argument has been made that this kind of usage promotes sexism. Although the masculine forms are supposed to refer to both men and women, most people think of men when they are used (Schneider & Hacker, 1973). And the fact that the labor department studies "manpower statistics," for instance, reinforces the idea that men go to work and women stay at home.

Today most publishers try hard to avoid sexist language. Implicit in their efforts is the assumption that Whorf was right, that language does affect how we think about things.

Recap

- Language is a tool of thought.

- Although language doesn't affect what the individual can perceive, it does affect what the individual does perceive, particularly concepts that are defined in linguistic terms.

Conclusion

Thought and language are the abilities that most specifically distinguish people from animals. We share with many other species our sensory and perceptual capacities, our emotions, and many of our motives. But we differ dramatically in our abilities to think and communicate about the world. We are the thinking and talking species.

We are just beginning to understand these special abilities. The work in artificial intelligence reveals these limits, as well as some impressive successes. As computers have become more powerful, mathematical simulations of human thinking have become possible. For example, an elaborate program for making medical diagnoses has been developed that is more accurate than most physicians. And other programs now exist that allow computers to play chess better than all but the top ten human chess players; indeed, we expect that computers may well beat even the very best chess masters in a few years!

The limits to what computers can do are equally striking. When a computer finally beats those champion chess players, they're going to shrug, get up from their seats, and smile to their friends and family in the crowd. The computer won't be able to do any of those things. And the technology that would allow computers to move or recognize faces is decades or more away.

The computer's limitations highlight the exceptional achievement that human thinking really is. Our thinking actually involves an incredible array of skills, including the abilities to categorize experience into concepts, to construct images that are symbolic representations of physical relationships, to recognize and solve problems, to identify and make decisions, and, most important, to be creative. A computer may well become the best chess player in the world in a few years, but it will be a vastly longer time before a computer can invent a game like chess.

Chapter 9   Motivation

En la Yola, Joaquín Sorolla, 1910

9

Gateways The previous chapters have focused on cognition. In this chapter—as well as the next, on emotion and stress—we bring feelings prominently into the discussion. In the cognition chapters we were concerned mainly with *how* we do things (such as perceive and remember); in these chapters we'll explore *why* we do things.

What moves us to want what we want? Motives have been at the center of many theories of personality, because the question of how individuals differ from one another is often a question of the different things they want. Differences of this sort are discussed in Chapter 14. Motives are also central to much social behavior and are thus examined in

Chapters 17 and 18. We have already discussed motivation in Chatper 6, in considering what motivates learning and how new reinforcers can be created.

In 1982, a young mountain climber, Marty Hoey, slipped out of her climbing harness and fell nearly 6,000 feet down the north face of Mount Everest. Her death ended more than a decade of extraordinary work, sacrifice and risk that would have made her the first American woman to reach the summit of the world's highest mountain. She had endured hundreds of hours of grueling training, climbed dozens of difficult peaks, and exposed herself to the dangers inherent in mountaineering to accomplish this goal. As the expedition's only female member, Marty earned a place in the first summit team through her leadership in establishing a series of camps up the mountain and demonstrated climbing strength. Dedicating the ascent to her memory, the same team returned to Everest in 1984 and were successful (Wickwire, 1991).

Marty Hoey's life was an extraordinary example of human motivation. But if you think for a moment, you'll realize that you may know people like Marty—people who surprise you with the strength of their motivation, people who devote their lives to meeting the goals they've set for themselves. What is this drive, this commitment? And where does it come from?

Marty Hoey on Mt. Everest

What Is Motivation?

Psychologists have many definitions for **motivation** (Kleinginna & Kleinginna, 1981). Common to all is the idea that motivation consists of the psychological factors that energize behavior and determine its direction. Motives vary on a number of dimensions.

Drives and Incentives

If you are like most students, your preparation for examinations is motivated by both drives and incentives. **Drives** are motives that *push* you to behave in certain ways: anxiety about failure drives you to study. **Incentives** are motives that *pull* you toward a certain behavior. We could say that getting an A on a test is an incentive for studying.

Motives come in all different "shapes" and "sizes." Think about all the things you do in a day and the motives they satisfy. You sleep because you're tired; you eat because you're hungry; you wear a sweater because you're cold; you work because you need money; you do a favor for a friend because you care about him; you study because you want to achieve.

Some motives are stronger than others. When two motives conflict, the stronger one determines behavior. When you walk across campus in the pouring rain to get a hamburger, your motive to eat is obviously stronger than your motive to stay dry.

Some motives are intrinsic; others are extrinsic. A behavior is **intrinsically motivated** when the behavior is its own reward. A behavior is **extrinsically motivated** when it is a response to the promise of a reward or the threat of a

Motivation The psychological factors that energize behavior and determine its direction.

Drive An internal stimulus that pushes the organism to behave in certain ways.

Incentive A circumstance or environmental stimulus that pulls the organism to behave in certain ways.

Intrinsic motivation Motivation that is derived from the pleasure of behaving in a certain way.

Extrinsic motivation Motivation that is derived from the consequence of behavior.

241

When a reporter asked Debbie Thomas if she would skate even if she couldn't compete in the Olympics, she smiled and answered yes. She skated, she said because she loved to skate.

punishment. For example, many people enjoy splitting firewood. They find the exercise and the satisfaction intrinsically rewarding. Others make their living cutting and splitting firewood. Characteristically, they don't particularly enjoy their work; they do it for the extrinsic reward of money.

Biological and Social Motives

Motives also differ on how closely they are tied to the biological needs of the organism. Some motives, like hunger, seem entirely at the service of the body, while others, like ambition, seem entirely social.

Biological Motives   The biological needs that direct behavior are an important source of motivation. All organisms, including humans, need a variety of things in order to maintain basic life processes. For instance, we need food for fuel and as a source of crucial nutrients. We need water to move the nutrients around our bodies, to flush out wastes, and to maintain our body temperature. And, of course, we need oxygen for the basic chemical processes that are essential to life.

In the body, **homeostatic mechanisms** maintain physiological variables at necessary levels (Cannon, 1939). These mechanisms operate much like a thermostat, constantly monitoring such things as the temperature of blood or the level of sugar in the blood (see Figure 9.1). When they sense a deviation from normal levels, they trigger corrective action. Biological motives are those that support the body's homeostasis by directing the individual to avoid extreme environments and to ingest the crucial substances that are needed to maintain life.

Social Motives   There is no question that biological needs direct much of human behavior; but social motives also play an important role in that behavior. Many of things you do—practicing piano for hours on end, lending money to a friend, looking for something to do on Saturday night—don't meet biological needs in any obvious way. Rather, these kinds of behaviors reflect the impact of your learning history and the expectations of your family and culture.

All organisms have needs that must be met if they are to survive, including the need for water. If a need is strong enough, the animal will risk great dangers to satisfy it, as this lion is in drinking so near the photographer.

Homeostatic mechanism   A mechanism that regulates the level of a physiological variable.

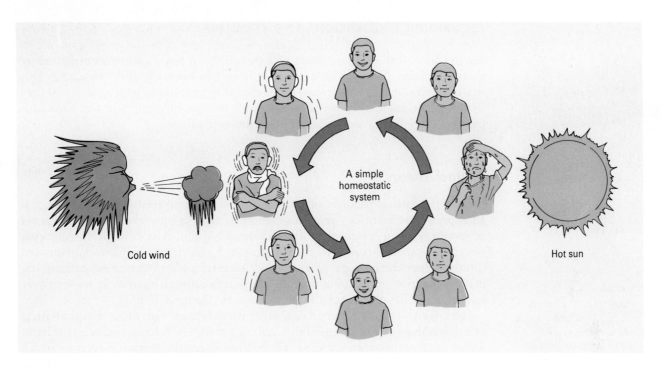

Cold wind

A simple homeostatic system

Hot sun

A Continuum of Motives   Although some motives are biological and others are essentially social, many motives fall somewhere in between, combining factors that are biological and factors that are social. What we have, then, is a kind of continuum of motives.

In this chapter we examine in detail three motives that fall at different points on this continuum. At the biological end is hunger; at the social end is the need to achieve; and situated somewhere between the two is sexual motivation. But before we look at the nature of these motives, we shall examine the theories that attempt to explain motivation.

Figure 9.1
Homeostasis

Homeostatic mechanisms are working constantly to keep your body temperature at 98.6 degrees Fahrenheit. When you're chilled, blood moves away from the surface of your body and your muscles shiver to release heat. When you get overheated, blood rushes toward the skin, and your sweat glands release moisture onto the surface of the body where it evaporates and cools you. On a day when the sun is shining but the air is cool, you may go through this cycle dozens of times.

This swimmer is braving freezing air and water temperatures. How do you think her homeostatic mechanisms are responding?

Explaining Motivation: The Theories

By the time you graduate from college, you will have spent more than three thousand hours listening to lectures, studying in libraries, and working in laboratories; you may have written more than fifty exams and papers; and you may have worked hundreds, perhaps thousands of hours to help pay for your education. Why? Where does your motivation come from?

Instinct Theory

One of the earliest theories of motivation held that all motivations—biological and social—are instincts. **Instincts** are unlearned, innate tendencies to respond in certain ways to certain stimuli (McDougall, 1908). According to instinct theory, people work because of their instinct for security or climb mountains because of their instinct for achievement. In the hands of the most enthusiastic instinct theorists, explaining human behavior became an exercise in making ever longer, more detailed lists of human instincts (Bernard, 1926).

John Watson, B. F. Skinner, and other early behaviorists were sharply critical of instinct theory. They argued that calling a complex behavior—such as achieving or mothering—instinctive says very little about the behavior except that it's innate. And the idea that the tendency to behave in certain ways is inherited was the antithesis of behaviorist theory—which holds that the environment influences behavior.

According to instinct theorists, mothers look after their infants because of their maternal instinct—feelings that direct them to protect, nurse, and clean their babies.

How Do We Know That?

Imagine that one of your classmates wants to do research on why some men don't get married. He designs a survey that includes the question "Are you a bachelor?" He carefully interviews a sample of married and unmarried men from all walks of life, young and old, wealthy and poor, well educated and not so well educated, living in cities and living in the country. He enters the results into a computer, performs the very best statistical analysis, and gets a very dramatic result: without exception, every unmarried male in his survey is a bachelor. Delighted, he comes rushing over to your room to announce his success. "I've found the factor that explains why some men don't get married," he says. "It's because they're bachelors!"

Your classmate has fallen victim to the **naming fallacy.** You can't explain something by using another name for it. Yes, all unmarried men are bachelors. But being a bachelor isn't an explanation for being unmarried; it's simply another name for being unmarried. Although being a bachelor seems a good explanation for being unmarried, it doesn't tell you anything about the behavior.

When offering motivational explanations of behavior, it's easy to make up a motive for every behavior you are trying to explain and thus fall prey to the naming fallacy. For example, why do people explore caves? They must have a spelunking motive. Why do people play baseball? They must have a love of the national pastime. Although these statements may seem like good explanations, they really don't tell us much more than what we knew when we asked the questions.

Motivational explanations aren't the only place where the naming fallacy is a risk. Think how often you have heard people say things like, "Joe has difficulty reading because he has a reading disability," or "Sam does well on tests because he has good test-taking skills," or "Mary couldn't be trusted to say what she meant because she was insincere," or "Ginny is good natured because she has a sunny personality." These explanations don't contribute to our understanding of Joe, Sam, Mary, and Ginny unless they add something beyond a label to explain their behavior.

Sociobiological Theory

A modern version of instinct theory is **sociobiological theory** (Wilson, 1975). According to this theory, a genetic selfishness underlies every human behavior—eating, fighting, socializing, even cooperating. People behave the way they do because, in the course of evolution, the genes governing those behaviors were reproduced in greater numbers than the genes governing their alternatives.

Much of sociobiological theory is devoted to explaining *altruism*—behavior that, at least on the surface, serves the interests of others (Hamilton, 1964). For instance, why do humans (and some animals) amicably share food and other resources? And why do they risk their lives to protect one another? According to sociobiologists, even such unselfish behavior is the result of "selfish genes" (Dawkins, 1976). Altruism is programmed by the genes because it promotes the interests of the genes themselves. What seems to be altruistic behavior in reality is directed at promoting the reproduction of the genes for altruism shared by close relatives.

Instinct An innate tendency to respond to certain stimuli in certain ways.

Naming fallacy A form of disordered logic in which a person tries to explain an event by merely giving it a name.

Sociobiological theory A theory of social behavior that claims that a genetic selfishness underlies all human behaviors, even altruistic behaviors.

This stinging bee will die as a consequence of its stinging, but the genes for stinging will be carried on by the offspring of the hive.

The sociobiological explanation of human motivation has generated an enormous amount of controversy. At the heart of that controversy is the sociobiologists' assumption that complex human behaviors—behaviors that are culturally significant—are largely the product of heredity.

Psychoanalytic Motivation Theory

Freud believed that social motives arise from biological drives through a process called **sublimation.** Freud's list of biological drives included the drive for food, for water, for shelter, for aggression, and for sex. According to Freud, each biological drive is endowed with energy. When a biological drive is frustrated, its energy finds expression in activities that aren't directly related to the original drive. For instance, the energy of a sexual drive may be redirected to a social motive—to achievement in art or dance or literature.

Freud believed that two basic motives—the sex drive and the drive for aggression—are often frustrated because they place the individual in conflict with society in general and with his or her parents in particular. Child-rearing practices repress these biological drives, transferring their energy to new forms of expression. And he believed that these frustrated sexual and aggressive drives motivate most if not all of the individual's day-to-day interactions with other people (Freud, 1923/1962). For example, a husband who's angry with his wife may express that anger by constantly misplacing his wedding ring.

Behaviorist Drive Reduction Theory

Some behaviorists, among them Clark Hull and Kenneth Spence, believed that all learning, and ultimately almost all behavior, takes place through a process called *drive reduction* (Hull, 1943). They claimed that behavior is a response to **drive stimuli,** the unpleasant sensations people feel when their biological needs are not being met. Once those needs are met—by eating or drinking or finding shelter or sexual release—the discomfort goes away and the drive state is reduced.

According to **drive reduction theory,** the process has two important effects. First, it reinforces whatever behaviors were going on just before the drive stimulus was relieved, so that people are more likely to perform these behaviors the next time they experience the drive stimulus. Second, it creates a secondary drive for the circumstances that relieved the original drive stimulus. In other words, circumstances that were once a means to reduce drive levels become incentives themselves.

How does this process create a social motive, such as the need for approval? Let's look at a simple example. Imagine a toddler eating. Every time she takes a bite of food, her father smiles and praises her. The pairing of the praise with the reduction in hunger drive provided by the food creates a secondary drive for the praise. Later the child may draw pictures or put a toy in the toy box just to receive her father's approval. Once praise has become a reinforcer, it too gains the power to turn circumstances—climbing a mountain, writing a textbook, studying all night for an exam—into goals. Through secondary reinforcement, new motives are built, layer by layer, on the foundation of basic needs.

Optimal Arousal Theory

An element that is common to both psychoanalytic and behaviorist drive-reduction theories is the belief in the fundamental importance of biological

Sublimation According to Freud, the process by which the energy of a biological drive is redirected to a social motive.

Drive stimulus The discomfort caused by a biological need that increases the biological drive.

Drive reduction theory The belief that the circumstances surrounding the relief of a biological drive become incentives themselves.

motives to activity. In both theories, biological motives ultimately lie behind everything people do. But certain activities don't seem to have anything to do with biological needs. What biological need is being satisfied when children play in the snow? And what biological need is being satisfied when people pay money to ride a roller coaster?

If the concept of drive reduction is valid, then we should never see people or animals taking part in activities that excite or frighten them, activities that increase drive states. Yet people and animals do in fact spend a substantial portion of their lives exploring the environment and behaving in other ways that don't seem to reduce biological drives (Leuba, 1962; Berlyne, 1971). Why?

One answer comes from **optimal arousal theory** (Duffy, 1957; Hebb, 1955). According to that theory, just as the body needs enough—but not too much—food, water, and heat, so the nervous system needs a moderate amount of stimulation—not too much and not too little. Organisms that are understimulated search out more excitement; organisms that are overstimulated search out less excitement. This creates the *optimal arousal drive*—the need to maintain arousal at the individual's best, or *optimal,* level (see Figure 9.2).

Support for optimal arousal theory comes from sensory deprivation experiments. In a sensory deprivation experiment, the researcher isolates the subjects from as many sources of stimulation as possible. Noise is reduced to a minimum; opaque masks cover the subjects' eyes; special cuffs cover their hands (see Figure 9.3). Despite the fact that their physical needs are being met (subjects are always fed and allowed to go to the bathroom as needed), most subjects cannot tolerate the procedure for more than a day or so. This finding seems to confirm the theory that people need at least some stimulation, even when their other biological drives are being met (Zubec, 1969; Forgays & Belinson, 1986).

Curiosity is one motive that doesn't seem to be related to a biological drive. Studies show that young monkeys spend hours manipulating locks, trying to unlock them, just to satisfy their curiosity. This kind of exploratory behavior in animals raises questions about the idea that all behaviors are motivated by biological drives.

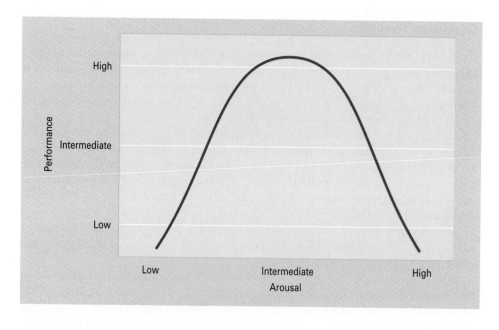

**Figure 9.2
Optimal Arousal**

Moderate levels of arousal are "optimal" in the sense that a moderately aroused person or animal produces the best performance.

Opponent-Process Theory

Optimal arousal theory explains why people search out excitement, but it doesn't explain why people sometimes do things that are terrifying or even painful. It doesn't explain why people sky-dive or climb mountains or drive race cars or run long distances. It doesn't explain why people take risks.

Optimal arousal theory The theory that certain behaviors are motivated by the need to maintain a moderate level of excitement in the nervous system.

Puzzle It Out!

Look again at the picture of the monkeys on page 247. We assume that the monkeys work at opening locks because they find the behavior intrinsically satisfying. But research shows that if the same monkeys are rewarded with food for opening the locks, they soon lose their intrinsic motivation for opening them; they no longer handle the locks in the absence of food (Harlow, 1950). Is this another example of the overjustification effect? If so, does the fact that monkeys also show the overjustification effect mean that monkeys, like people, have cognitive motives? Does that seem impossible to you? Can you think of another reason why the monkeys might lose interest in the locks?

Figure 9.3
Sensory Deprivation Experiments

In sensory deprivation experiments, subjects are isolated from as many sources of stimulation as possible. Although their physical needs are met, most subjects can tolerate this situation for only a day or two.

Overjustification effect   The weakening of an intrinsic motive for a behavior by introducing an extrinsic motive for the behavior.

Richard Solomon (1980) uses *opponent-process theory* to explain risk-taking and pain-inducing behaviors. (We've talked about opponent processes before, in our discussions of color vision and drug tolerance in Chapters 3 and 5, respectively.) According to Solomon, pain and pleasure are opponent processes. The sensation of pain triggers the release of endorphins, the neurotransmitters that dull pain. As long as people are in pain, they experience the effect of the endorphins as a reduction of pain. But once the pain goes away, what was a weak sensation of less pain becomes a rush of pleasure. It is this rush of pleasure that motivates the individual to willingly undergo pain.

Cognitive Theories

Cognitive theories of motivation trace much of human behavior to people's need to make sense of themselves and the world around them. Called on to explain a medical student's hard work or a mountain climber's endurance, cognitive theorists would argue that people take on these kinds of challenges because of what they learn about themselves.

In their studies of motivation, cognitive theorists have tried to influence behavior by giving their subjects information that is inconsistent with the subjects' view of themselves. If you act in a way that is inconsistent with your beliefs about yourself, you may feel discomfort. This feeling is called *cognitive dissonance* and often leads you to change either your behavior or your view of yourself to make the two fit (Festinger, 1957).

An example: You're eating a hot-fudge sundae because you like the taste of ice cream and hot fudge. Now suppose that a psychologist comes along and gives you $10 to eat the sundae.

But now, how are you going to understand your behavior? Is it intrinsically motivated? Are you eating the sundae because you like it? Or is it extrinsically motivated? Are you eating the sundae because you've been paid to eat it? If you accept the money, maybe you don't like hot-fudge sundaes as much as you thought you did. To be consistent with that understanding, you may actually stop eating hot-fudge sundaes unless you're paid to eat them. The psychologist has changed your behavior by changing your understanding of how that behavior is motivated. By giving you an extrinsic reason for eating hot-fudge sundaes, the psychologist has weakened your intrinsic motivation.

This effect—decreasing an intrinsic interest in some activity by supplying an extrinsic motive for the behavior—is called the **overjustification effect.** It's been demonstrated in dozens of studies (Deci & Ryan, 1987). In one such study, two groups of students were given puzzles to solve. The first group worked the puzzles for fun; the second group was paid. Although the students who were paid worked harder at solving the puzzles, the intrinsically motivated students spent more time with the puzzles and came up with more imaginative solutions to them (Condry, 1977). In another study, schoolchildren who were rewarded for drawing pictures with a special set of pens were less likely to draw pictures with those pens on their free time than were children whose first experience with the pens was entirely voluntary (Lepper, Greene & Nisbett, 1973).

These findings raise doubts about the recent trend in colleges and universities of motivating students with grades, honors programs, and other extrinsic rewards—rewards that are likely to diminish students' intrinsic interest in a subject matter (Deci & Ryan, 1987). Educational procedures that promote students' sense of independence—by offering them choices and by giving them feedback on their progress—not only increase intrinsic motivation; they also promote greater cognitive flexibility, better understanding, more self-esteem and trust, better retention of learning, and better physical and psychological health (Deci & Ryan, 1987).

Humanistic Theory: Maslow's Hierarchy of Needs

Abraham Maslow and other humanistic psychologists did not believe that social motives are derived from biological motives. They argued that social motives, like biological motives, are basic human needs. Moreover, they insisted that meeting social needs is essential for human development and that the frustration of these needs, though not deadly in the same sense as starvation, is profoundly damaging to the individual's well-being.

Maslow's theory was based on a **hierarchy of needs** (Maslow, 1970). At the bottom of the hierarchy are the most basic physiological needs—food and water, and then safety needs (see Figure 9.4). Once these needs are met, Maslow believed, people move on to the need to belong and to be loved, and then to the need for esteem. At the top of the hierarchy is the need for **self-actualization,** the need to fully develop one's human capacity to think and feel and understand the world.

Maslow argued that his hierarchy described the relative strength of the various needs. In general, he believed that the chronic failure to satisfy "lower" needs leaves the individual unable to focus on "higher" needs. If people are hungry enough, for example, they may take risks with their safety. And if people are frightened enough, they don't really worry about making new friends.

On the surface, Maslow seems to be implying that people are incapable of altruism. If lower needs must be met before they act to satisfy higher needs, it seems that they would never give a last scrap of food to a loved one or risk their own life for someone else. Yet Maslow was well aware of the human capacity for altruism and good. He argued that lower needs must be met during most of one's life, especially the early years, so that the individual can turn to higher needs. But once the individual has managed to function at higher levels for a period of time, he or she can certainly respond to higher needs and ignore lower needs. Maslow would have pointed out, as his theory predicts, that extreme deprivation in adulthood tends to focus people on their lower needs, such that, for example, some people in Nazi concentration camps stole food from their own children or parents. But equally important to Maslow was the fact that in the same horrible circumstances, some people were still capable of acts of incredible generosity (Frankel, 1959). According to Maslow, these people were those whose lower needs had been met most consistently earlier in their lives.

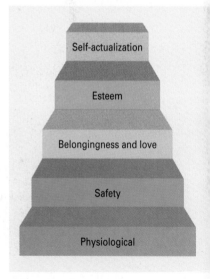

Figure 9.4
Maslow's Hierarchy of Needs

Maslow's hierarchy functions like a staircase. We don't experience higher needs until we have satisfied our more basic needs.

Hierarchy of needs   Maslow's classification of motives.
Self-actualization   Development of the capacity to think, feel, and understand the world.

Recap

- According to instinct theory, all motivations are innate tendencies to respond in certain ways to certain stimuli.

- Sociobiologists believe that human behavior is directed by a genetic selfishness.

- Freud believed that when aggressive or sexual needs are frustrated, their energy may find indirect expression in social activities.

- According to behaviorist drive reduction theory, behavior is a response to drive stimuli.

- Some psychologists explain the need for stimulation in terms of the optimal arousal drive, the need to maintain a certain level of arousal.

- According to opponent-process theory, the rush of pleasure that follows the relief of pain motivates people to undergo pain.

- Cognitive theories of motivation trace much of human behavior to the need to make sense of the self and the world.

- By supplying an extrinsic motive for behavior, psychologists can weaken the intrinsic motive for that behavior. This is called the overjustification effect.

- Maslow believed that there is a hierarchy of needs, and that needs at each level must be satisfied before higher-level needs are.

Hunger and Eating

When you're hungry, specific changes take place in your behavior and experience. You are more sensitive to food—the smell of food, the sound of food cooking, the places you associate with food. And you take action to obtain food. At home, you head for the kitchen and begin to rummage in the refrigerator. Away from home, you find a restaurant and order something to eat. Finally, if these actions are successful, you eat. Once you've eaten, your hunger diminishes for a time and, with it, your awareness of the smells, sounds, and sights related to food. A theory of hunger and eating must explain all of these phenomena.

At the root of hunger is the body's biological need for enough energy to keep your muscles, brain, and other organs functioning vigorously. To examine hunger, we have to look at how the body gathers, stores, and uses energy.

The Energy Account

The energy account the body maintains is like the checking and savings accounts you maintain with your bank. The body maintains an energy "checking account" in your bloodstream for moment-to-moment "income" and "expenses." The currency in this account is *glucose,* a simple sugar. When you eat, the body transforms the food into glucose and deposits it into the bloodstream. When you need energy to work or to keep warm, the body withdraws glucose from the bloodstream and converts it to energy in the body's cells.

The checking account analogy has one important weakness. Unlike the balance in your checking account, your blood glucose "balance" cannot vary widely: if it goes too low for a few minutes or too high for a few hours, you get very sick. So the body maintains its bloodstream glucose very precisely.

Keeping blood sugar within safe limits is no small trick. Energy intake varies from hour to hour. Each time you eat a meal, sugars and other nutrients pour from the intestines into the bloodstream. Energy expenditure also varies from hour to hour. When you go jogging on a cold day, you use two to three times as much food energy as you use lying around watching a football game on television.

The body is able to keep its blood sugar account in balance because it has a "savings account" to deposit into and draw on. If you consume more food energy than you need, your body stores it away in the liver, muscles, and under the skin as starches and fats. If you need more energy than you consume, the body reconverts the fats and starches to glucose.

The process of moving glucose in and out of the bloodstream is coordinated by two hormones that are secreted by the pancreas. *Insulin* promotes the storage of glucose as fats and starches; *glucagon* promotes the reconversion of fats and starches to glucose (see Figure 9.5). This homeostatic process can maintain blood sugar within its required limits for a surprisingly long period of time without any outside help. In fact, without eating at all, human beings can function at close to peak efficiency for a week, and can survive for a month.

Because body fat is the body's savings account, imbalances between energy intake and outgo are reflected as increases and decreases in body weight. For instance, a difference of 240 calories a day—the equivalent of two glasses of milk or a couple handfuls of peanuts—carried over an entire year could mean a weight gain or loss of 23 pounds. Given how small an imbalance is required to gain or lose weight, it's remarkable how stable most individuals' weight remains. Without thinking much at all about what they eat, most people manage to keep more or less the same weight over months, even years.

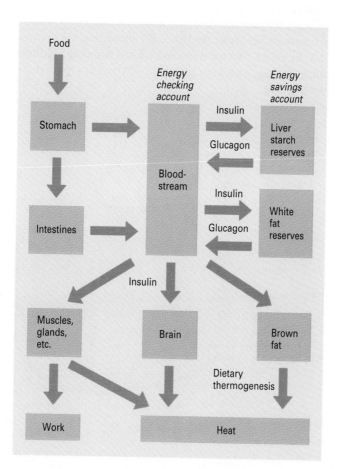

Figure 9.5
Energy Flow and Storage in the Body

Energy "income" comes to the body in the form of food that is converted to glucose. Glucose is used to heat the body and to power the muscles and brain. Excess glucose is converted to fats or starches and stored in the liver or in white fat reserves scattered around the body. When fat reserves are excessive, the body may spill energy in the form of heat given off by the body's brown fat, a process known as *dietary thermogenesis.* The movement of energy around the body is coordinated by two hormones—insulin, which promotes the use and storage of energy, and glucagon, which promotes the retrieval of stored energy reserves.

Apparently the body tries to keep a constant balance in its energy savings account. The value at which an individual's weight stabilizes is called the *set point* (Nisbett, 1972). How does the body balance energy intake and outgo to keep body weight near the set point? The same way any budget is balanced: by adjusting energy income, or energy expenditure, or both.

Controlling Energy Intake

Energy intake is influenced by both physiological and social cues. The body monitors hunger and satiety cues, the internal signs that tell you when to begin eating and when to stop. But external factors such as stress and social expectations also play a role.

Taste Cues from the Mouth and Throat   How a food tastes affects how much of it you eat. Both people and animals begin to eat a food sooner and eat more of it when the food tastes good. But as you eat a food, its flavor diminishes. And once a food loses its flavor, you tend to stop eating (Cabanac, 1971).

Although taste mechanisms limit the consumption of a single food, they don't seem to determine the size of a meal. If a different food is substituted for the one that has lost its flavor, most people continue eating (Mook, Brane & Whitt, 1983). This is probably why you usually have room for dessert!

Cues from the Digestive Organs   As they process food, the digestive organs may generate cues that control our eating. To study the activity of the stomach in relation to hunger, physiologist Walter Cannon asked subjects to swallow a gastric balloon that was connected to a tube that ran up their throats and out their mouths (see Figure 9.6). Then he pumped air down the tube, inflating the balloon. Every movement of the stomach caused a measurable change in the pressure of the air in the tube. By recording these pressure changes, Cannon was able to show that people experience the contractions of the empty stomach as hunger pangs and the distention of the full stomach as satiety (Cannon & Washburn, 1912).

Figure 9.6
Cannon's Apparatus for Measuring Stomach Contractions

Cannon's subjects would swallow a balloon that would then be inflated so that it pressed against the walls of their stomachs. Each stomach contraction would be translated by the tube attached to the balloon as a movement of the needle on the rotating drum.

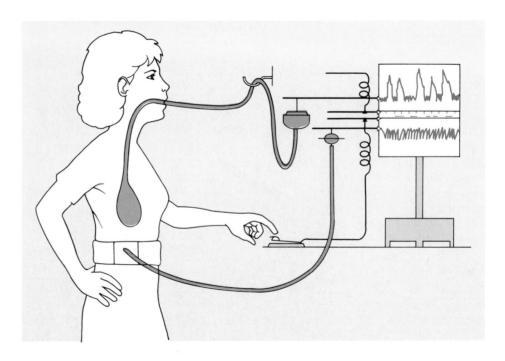

But later experiments would show that stomach contractions are as much an effect of hunger as its cause. Usually people begin to feel hunger pangs when they think they are about to eat (Rodin, 1985). Moreover, people who have had their stomachs surgically removed not only regulate their food intake effectively but also continue to report hunger pangs when they're hungry (Janowitz, 1976).

Cues from the Liver   As soon as digestion begins, the stomach and the small intestines release glucose into the blood, which carries the glucose directly to the liver. One important source of cues that regulate eating may be the glucose receptors in the liver. These receptors respond to changes in the level of glucose by sending messages to the brain. When the levels are low, the receptors seem to "turn hunger on"; when they're high, the receptors turn hunger off (Novin, VanderWeele & Rezek, 1973; Novin et al., 1983).

Cues from the Brain   In 1954, physiological psychologist Eliot Stellar suggested that hunger and other biological motives are controlled by the hypothalamus, a tiny structure deep inside the brain (see Figure 2.14). Stellar believed that the hypothalamus contains one center for initiating each motive and another for terminating it.

Evidence for Stellar's theory came from studies showing that the removal or stimulation of small areas of the hypothalamus has dramatic effects on behavior. For instance, when scientists removed a portion of both sides of the hypothalamus in rats, the animals refused to eat (Anand & Brobeck, 1951). Electrical stimulation of another portion of the hypothalamus stopped hungry rats from eating for as long as the stimulation was continued (Wyrwicka & Dobrzecka, 1960). And when scientists surgically removed this area of the hypothalamus, they produced a rat that didn't know when to stop eating (Brobeck, Tepperman & Long, 1943). Upon being offered food that tasted good, it ate insatiably, growing two to three times its normal weight (see Figure 9.7).

Stellar's hypothalamic theory of motivation in general and hunger motivation in particular has been exceedingly influential. But recent findings contradict that theory. They suggest that the structures in the hypothalamus that seem to operate as centers for the control of hunger and satiety are actually part of a much larger system of energy regulation in which receptors in the liver seem to play a primary role (Carlson, 1991). The system also includes parts of the midbrain, limbic system, and basal ganglia. These structures are connected to the pituitary gland, the taste receptors of the tongue, the pancreas, the digestive tract, and the liver by a web of connections whose complexity we are only beginning to understand.

Figure 9.7
An Obese Rat

A lesion in the ventromedial nucleus of the hypothalamus makes a rat a fussy eater. But if you feed that rat tasty food, it may gain two or three times its original body weight before its weight levels off again.

Social and Other Learned Cues   Not all of the cues that get you to start and stop eating are biological; some are social cues, derived from your interactions with the people around you. Because social cues are not tied to the body's physical needs, responding to them can easily lead to overeating or undereating.

Often behavior is a response to other people's expectations. That is, you eat more than you want to eat to please the chef; and now and again you stop eating when you're still hungry because others are pushing their plates away.

Social stress also affects the way people eat. A weight gain or loss is often a tipoff that a person is anxious or unhappy (American Psychiatric Association, 1987). Indeed, some people eat to relieve their anxiety (Bruch, 1973; Herman et al., 1987). For instance, students who accepted and ate sandwiches during an examination reported that the more they ate, the less anxious they felt about the test (Pines & Gal, 1977). Even rats occasionally eat in response to negative stimulation (their tails being pinched, for example) (Antelman & Rowland, 1981).

Controlling Energy Output

You can also balance the energy budget by regulating your output. The problem with balancing energy by controlling intake is that food is a source of all kinds of nutrients—vitamins, minerals, and proteins. Sometimes, in order to get enough of these crucial substances, the body must take in more energy than it needs. So it must have some process for getting rid of excess calories without storing them as fat.

One way of regulating energy output is through exercise: the more you exercise, the more energy you expend and the more calories you burn. Of course, most of the calories you expend each day are used to maintain basic life processes. This means that only a small amount (about 20 percent) can be worked off through exercise. But regular exercise does have an additional benefit: it increases the rate of metabolism (Thompson et al., 1982). So you get some benefit from the exercise itself, and even more from the change in metabolism.

Another way the body regulates the expenditure of energy is by expending extra heat (Keesey & Powley, 1986). When the supply of energy is high, the body releases large quantities of heat through a special tissue called *brown fat* (Hoyenga & Hoyenga, 1984; Nichols, 1979). Brown fat is not like ordinary fatty tissue whose function is to store energy for lean times. It is a heat-releasing organ found in the back, in the armpits, and around the kidneys whose activities are controlled by the autonomic nervous system. Brown fat almost certainly plays a role in regulating weight by releasing heat when energy is oversupplied and conserving heat when energy is in short supply (Hirsch & Leibel, 1988).

When Eating Goes Awry

Despite all of the body's weight-control processes, many people do have problems with their weight. Some weigh more than is healthy or comfortable; others, much less. When these conditions become chronic or severe, they can be life threatening. Patterns of food consumption and body weight that threaten health are called *eating disorders*. They include anorexia nervosa, bulimia nervosa, and obesity.

Anorexia and Bulimia   The eating disorders known as **anorexia nervosa** and **bulimia nervosa** result in wildly abnormal patterns of weight regulation (American Psychiatric Association, 1980). People suffering from anorexia starve themselves; they refuse to eat. And people suffering from bulimia maintain their body weight at near-normal levels but in an abnormal way. These people alternate *binges* (periods of eating during which they may consume thousands of calories) with *purges* (periods in which they try to get rid of the food by making themselves vomit or by taking strong laxatives).

The causes of anorexia and bulimia are still not clear (Garner & Davis, 1986). Because most of those who suffer from anorexia or bulimia are young women in their teens and twenties, these eating disorders may have something to do with the hormonal changes that accompany puberty. Or they may have something to do with the special demands that society places on women to look like girls (Striegel-Moore, Silberstein & Rodin, 1986). We all have a *body image*—a mental picture of how our body looks. The body image of people with anorexia appears to be seriously distorted. Even after starving themselves to the point where they are little more than skin and bones, anorexics still describe themselves as "too fat."

A third theory points to the low self-esteem characteristic of people with anorexia or bulimia and to feelings that they have no control over their lives. Eating, and especially not eating, may represent the sole area of their lives in which these people feel they have control.

Anorexia nervosa An eating disorder in which the individual starves himself or herself.

Bulimia nervosa An eating disorder in which the individual regulates his or her weight by alternately binging and purging.

Both anorexia and bulimia are dangerous disorders. A shocking percentage of those with anorexia die—by some estimates, as many as 30 percent (Hsu, 1980). And purging leaves the victims of bulimia with an increased susceptibility to infection, as well as to kidney and liver disease.

Treatment for anorexia and bulimia is both medical and psychological (Garner & Isaacs, 1986). The first step is to get the person's weight up to levels where he or she isn't in danger of starving to death. The second step is to deal with the psychological issues that led to the disorder in the first place.

Obesity   The condition of being overweight is called **obesity.** People who are obese maintain their body weight at 25 percent or more above the average body weight for their height and build. In the United States, obesity is widespread: more than 25 percent of all Americans are obese. Obesity is also a serious health risk, increasing the likelihood of diabetes, heart disease, stroke, and death (see Figure 9.8). Moreover, it's a social handicap. Why, then, are so many people overweight? A wide variety of answers to this question have been proposed.

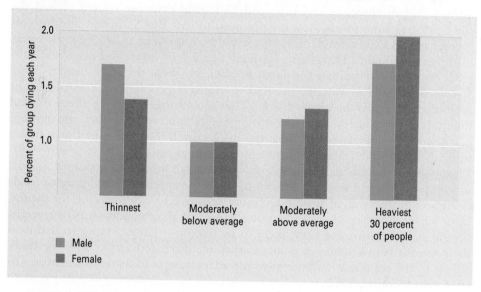

Source: Data from Harris et al. 1988.

Figure 9.8
The Health Risks of Obesity

Note that the probability of death for people over 65 is almost twice as high for the heaviest group compared to the moderately below-average group. The experimenters thought that the increased risk for the thinnest group was due to illness, which made them both thin and likely to die.

Inappropriate set point: A biological theory   As noted earlier, the set point is the value at which an individual's weight stabilizes. According to one explanation of obesity, people who are overweight have an inappropriate set point: their weight stabilizes at a value that is too high (Nisbett, 1972; Rodin, 1981).

If the abnormal set point theory is correct, then we should find that when obese people eat what they want, their weight levels off at some high value and stays there. And, indeed, most overweight people do seem to have a weight value at which they cease to gain weight (Hirsch & Leibel, 1988). Once they've achieved this value, they regulate their weight naturally, matching food input to food needs and releasing heat when they have consumed more food than they need to maintain their set point. When they try to lose weight, however, their bodies may actively conserve energy as though they were being starved (Keesey & Powley, 1986). This makes dieting very difficult.

What determines the level of an individual's set point? Why is it so high in some people? Four facts about obesity are important:

• For those who are obese, weight control is usually a lifelong problem. People who are obese as adults tend to have been overweight as children (Charney et al., 1976).

Obesity The maintenance of body weight at 25 percent or more above the average body weight for the individual's height and build.

- Obesity runs in families. Obese people are likely to have had one or more obese parents.
- Obesity runs in certain cultural groups.
- The babies of obese people show the reduced energy use characteristic of the dieting obese at three months of age, long before they themselves become obese (Roberts et al., 1988).

These findings are consistent with the idea that obesity is somehow transmitted from parents to their children. It's possible that the tendency to conserve energy that is characteristic of people who are overweight is genetic; or it could be caused by over-feeding in infancy (Ravussin et al., 1988).

Oversensitivity to social cues: A social theory   Evidence of the social factors in obesity comes from a series of colorful and ingenious experiments carried out by Stanley Schachter (1968). In one experiment, Schachter and his colleagues designed a procedure to separate social time from biological time. *Social time,* the time on the face of the clock, tells you when you're supposed to eat. *Biological time,* the time since you last ate, tells you when you need to eat. Under normal circumstances, social time and biological time are related. When the clock says it's time to eat, you usually need to eat. But Schachter and his colleagues rigged a special wall clock that could be run fast or slow to suit the needs of their experiment. Then they recruited a group of obese and nonobese subjects, ostensibly to evaluate the flavor of crackers. What the experimenters were actually interested in was the number of crackers people ate. Normal-weight subjects disregarded the phony clocks. They ate more crackers the closer the real time was to the dinner hour. For the overweight subjects, however, the number of crackers eaten depended on what the clock said. If the clock said it was dinner time, they ate more crackers whether it was dinner time or not (see Figure 9.9). Thus it seems that obese people are influenced much more than people of normal weight by external cues—the time of day and the appearance and taste of food.

Although overweight people are more sensitive to external cues for eating, their sensitivity may be a result, not a cause, of their condition. Overweight people in our culture are very likely to be dieting—that is, trying to maintain their weight below their set point. Earlier we discussed above how the body adapts to the set point, and one possible adaptation is to increase sensitivity to food cues (Nisbett, 1972).

Figure 9.9
Schachter's Experiment with Clocks and Crackers

Obese subjects responded to phoney hunger cues provided by the fast clocks by eating more crackers. Nonobese subjects ate fewer crackers, apparently fearing they would "spoil" their dinners.

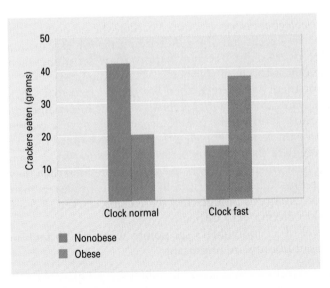

Source: Data from Schacter, 1968.

Table 9.1 summarizes the differences between the biological and social theories. The two theories differ in the factors they blame and in the discoveries their adherents have made.

	Social Theory	Biological Theory
Set point	Normal	Abnormally high
Sensitivity to external cues	Abnormally high	Normal
Sample evidence	Obese people are more influenced by false time cues than are people of normal weight.	People who are obese regulate their food intake normally if allowed to reach a stable weight.

Table 9.1
Obesity: The Social and Biological Theories Compared

Recap

- Hunger is the biological motive that sees to it that the body has enough energy to keep the muscles, brain, and other organs functioning vigorously.

- The body transforms food into glucose and deposits it into the bloodstream. When the individual needs energy, that glucose is withdrawn and converted to energy in the body's cells.

- When a person consumes more food energy than is needed immediately, the body stores it away in the liver and in the body generally as fats and starches. When the energy store is needed, the body reconverts the fats and starches to glucose.

- The set point is the value at which an individual's weight stabilizes.

- The body maintains its set point by adjusting the intake and outgo of energy.

- Patterns of food consumption that threaten health are called eating disorders.

- Anorexia and bulimia may be caused by hormonal changes; or they may be related to distorted body image, lack of self-esteem, and diminished sense of control.

- People who are obese maintain their body weight at 25 percent or more above the average body weight for their height and build.

- According to one explanation of obesity, people who are overweight have an inappropriate set point.

- Another explanation of obesity suggests that obese people are oversensitive to social cues for eating.

Sexual Motivation

Like hunger, sex is often considered a biological motive. But the drive for sex is different from hunger in three important ways.

1. Sex is not related to a physiological deficit. If you don't eat, you die. But nothing bad happens to your body if you don't have sex.
2. Sexual interest is related to the level of testosterone in the body. Testosterone is a hormone produced by both males and females (see Chapter 2). Day-to-day changes in the level of the hormone lead to changes in the amount of sexual interest (Persky et al., 1978).
3. Sex involves an exchange of stimuli and responses between individuals. This kind of exchange is called **courtship.** Even in animals, sex is not the action of one partner on the other but a transaction between the two (see Figure 9.10).

Research on human sexuality has focused on two questions: What happens, behaviorally and physiologically, when people have sexual intercourse? And what factors determine the characteristics people look for in their sexual partner?

Physical Sexuality

It's not easy to study sexual behavior scientifically because people in our culture believe that sex is an intensely private area. In the 1940s and 1950s, Alfred Kinsey and his colleagues used sophisticated interview techniques to document the sexual activities of thousands of Americans (Kinsey, Pomeroy & Martin, 1948; Kinsey et al., 1953). But it was not until the 1960s that human sexual activity was examined in the laboratory. In one of the most remarkable research projects of the last generation, William Masters and Virginia Johnson (1966) studied the physiology of sexual response in some six hundred volunteers on more than ten thousand occasions. Their pioneering work and the studies that have followed demonstrate that human sexual activity is highly variable—so variable, in fact, that any attempt to generalize about it can be misleading.

In their studies, Masters and Johnson identified four different phases of sexual arousal: excitement, plateau, orgasm, and resolution. Each phase is characterized by changes in behavior and physiology, particularly the physiology of the genitals (see Table 9.2 and Figure 9.11). Masters and Johnson found that sexual motivation increases during sexual interaction. As that motivation increases, behavior becomes more and more narrowly directed toward producing and enjoying pleasurable sensations, particularly those coming from the sensitive parts of the body known as **erogenous zones.** After the intense rush of sexual pleasure called **orgasm,** sexual motivation declines for a time (see Figure 9.11). The decline is immediate in males; in females, sexual motivation may be sustained through more than one orgasm. Now the participants become less sensitive to sexual stimuli, and their behavior gradually becomes directed to other concerns. Other motives now assert themselves.

Figure 9.10
Courtship Practices

Animals tend to follow very specific courtship patterns—an exchange of stimuli and responses. The male stickleback fish, for example, performs a zigzag dance that is part of an elaborate courtship ritual. The male hangingfly offers the female an insect he's captured; if she accepts his "gift," they mate. The peacock uses his brightly colored fan to attract a mate. In animals, courtship rituals are characteristic of all members of the species. In humans, they are more variable and characteristic of individuals and social groups, not of the whole species.

Courtship   The exchange of stimuli and responses between two individuals that leads to sexual intercourse.

Erogenous zone   A sensitive part of the body, stimulation of which increases sexual motivation.

Orgasm   The strong rush of sexual pleasure that occurs at the climax of sexual interaction.

Attraction

When it comes to sex, beauty is definitely in the eye of the beholder. All sorts of factors enter into the choice of a sexual partner. Among different cultures, ethnic groups, age groups, social strata, couples, and individuals—even within a given individual on different occasions—we find tremendous variation in the stimuli that lead to sexual interest.

Choosing a Partner   Culture is the most important influence here. A desirable sexual partner in one culture may well be undesirable in another. Even the stimuli that arouse us vary markedly from culture to culture.

	Excitement	Plateau	Orgasm	Resolution
Behavior	Sexual contact begins; sexual feeling increases in erogenous zones.	Sexual sensitivity increases and spreads to other parts of body. Attention progressively focuses on producing and experiencing pleasurable feelings.	A strong rush of sensual pleasure is felt. Involuntary contractions of muscles press participants' bodies together. Participants are momentarily unaware of their surroundings.	Relaxation and drowsiness occur. Further movement may be slightly painful for the male. Sexual feeling rapidly diminishes; awareness broadens.
Physiological reactions	Heart rate, blood pressure, and respiration increase.	Heart rate, blood pressure, and respiration continue to increase.	A storm of activity occurs in the autonomic nervous system. The body may flush and sweat; and blood pressure, heart rate, and breathing rate may double over prearousal levels.	Heart rate, blood pressure, and other physiological measures return to resting levels.
Genitals	Penis becomes erect. Clitoris becomes erect; vagina lengthens and widens. Secretion of lubricating fluids begins.	Further erection occurs in penis and clitoris, and vagina continues to lengthen and widen. Fluid flow increases.	The male's ejaculation propels the sperm deeply into the female's body. Constriction of the outer third of the vagina contains the sperm.	The male's erection is lost; the vagina gradually changes shape, pooling the semen and pressing it against the entry to the cervix.

Table 9.2
The Four Stages of Sexual Arousal

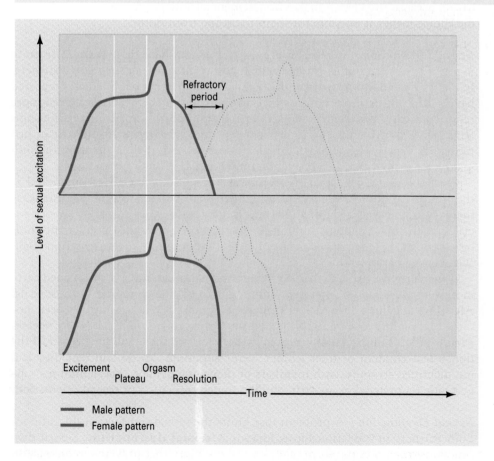

Figure 9.11
The Sexual Response Cycle

Males and females have the same basic pattern of sexual excitation, but there are also some differences. After orgasm, males pass through the refractory period, a span of at least several minutes when they are not sexually excitable. Females, on the other hand, often maintain sexual excitability through more than one orgasm.

Source: Adapted from Masters & Johnson, 1966.

Various studies suggest that both men and women in our culture, are attracted to certain physical characteristics in their sexual and social partners. For example, men prefer women who have relatively high foreheads, large eyes, and small chins (Berry & McArthur, 1987); but women are not attracted to this facial pattern in men. Men prefer women who have medium-sized breasts, legs, and hips (Kleinke & Staneski, 1980; Wiggins, Wiggins & Conger, 1968). Women prefer men who are moderately tall (Graziano, Brothen & Berscheid, 1978), with narrow hips and waist but broad shoulders (Beck, Ward-Hull & McLear, 1976). Both men and women prefer people who are not overweight, although men prefer women to be less skinny than women think they do (Fallon & Rozin, 1985).

Do these findings suggest that the rest of us are out of luck? Not at all. The subjects in these studies made their judgments on the basis of photographs of people they had never met. And, indeed, these are the kinds of judgments that people make about strangers. So physical attractiveness may well play a role in guiding the initial choice of partner. But when people move beyond first acquaintance, other factors—including friendship and love—begin to determine the course of their relationships.

Sexual attraction is also influenced by nonsexual motives. In our society, sex is deeply involved in how we think about ourselves. For some people, sex is symbolic, representing power and achievement, or safety and comfort. Research shows, for instance, that men are influenced in their respect for other men by the attractiveness of their female companions (Sigall & Landy, 1973; Bar-Tal & Saxe, 1976).

Cohen and Friedman (1975) suggest that many of the factors governing adolescents' choice of partner actually have to do with their parents. Adolescents may choose a particular partner because their parents disapprove of the individual or because the choice makes a statement of independence or even because the choice makes it possible for them to escape from home.

Sexual Orientation   So variable are the factors that determine sexual attraction in people that many of us choose people of the same gender for sexual partners. In a survey of adults, 13 percent of all males and 8 percent of all females reported having had one or more homosexual relationships in their lifetime. Even more reported casual homosexual contacts or the desire for homosexual relationships (Brecher, 1984). Of the total number of people who report some sort of homosexual experience, a much smaller number—less than 5 percent for both sexes—are primarily or exclusively homosexual.

Over the years, a host of environmental conditions have been suggested as the "cause" of homosexuality: a domineering mother and a weak or distant father, sexual abuse as a child, adolescent homosexual experiences, even poor social adjustment. Although some have worked their way into popular mythology, none of these factors correlates reliably with homosexual orientation (Bell, Weinberg & Hammersmith, 1983).

Apparently the process that determines sexual orientation is established early in development. In an interview study of almost one thousand homosexuals, Alan Bell and his colleagues (1983) demonstrated a relationship between homosexual preference in adulthood and what they called *childhood gender nonconformity*. Adult homosexuals reported that as children they had done fewer of the things that children of their gender were "supposed" to do and that they had not identified strongly with members of their own gender. These findings suggest either a prenatal or an early-childhood determination of sexual orientation.

Sexual Dysfunction   A problem that limits the sexual satisfaction for either or both partners in a relationship is known as **sexual dysfunction.** Sexual dysfunction often takes the form of a physical disability that prevents intercourse— painful contractions of the vagina, the inability to achieve or maintain an erec-

Sexual dysfunction   A problem that limits the sexual satisfaction for either or both partners in a relationship.

tion, or premature ejaculation, for example. Although these symptoms are physical, they usually stem from psychological sources. The partners may be trying too hard to please each other; or they may be trying to meet some standard of sexual achievement; or they may be frightened because intercourse has been painful before or because they experienced a previous failure to perform. Masters and Johnson (1966) claim that they can successfully treat most patients with these kinds of disabilities by training them to focus on the pleasure that comes from their sexual interactions, not on extraneous motivations or feelings.

Recap

- Unlike biological motives, the sex drive is not related to a physiological deficit; rather, it is related to the level of testosterone in the body.

- Sex involves an exchange of stimuli and responses between individuals that is called courtship.

- Masters and Johnson identified four different phases of sexual arousal: excitement, plateau, orgasm, and resolution.

- Culture is the most important influence in choosing a sexual and social partner.

- Although physical attractiveness may play a role in the initial choice of partner, other factors determine the course of relationships.

- For some people, sex is symbolic, representing power and achievement, or safety and comfort.

- One important study demonstrated a relationship between homosexual preference in adulthood and childhood gender nonconformity, thus suggesting that sexual orientation is established before birth or in early childhood.

- Sexual dysfunction is a problem that limits the sexual satisfaction for either or both partners in a relationship.

Achievement Motivation: Why Do Some People Try So Hard?

Both of the motives we've discussed thus far—hunger and sex—are closely connected to our bodies: hunger to the maintenance of nutrition, sex to the sensations produced in the body during sexual interaction. Society influences and channels these motives, but they have a strong physiological base. In this section we turn to social motives, the motives that seem to stem largely from our culture and our upbringing.

In the 1930s, psychologist Henry Murray (1938) examined twenty-seven social motives using an instrument called the *Thematic Apperception Test (TAT)*. The test asks subjects to make up a story about a series of purposely ambiguous pictures. Murray believed that the subjects' stories would reflect their basic motivations. Why? Because people tend to focus on, and respond to, elements of a situation that are related to their own motives.

Among the social motives Murray identified was the **need for achievement (nAch),** the need to meet challenges and accomplish one's goals. People with a high-level need for achievement told stories about trying to get things done, accomplishing things, and excelling.

Need for achievement (nAch)
The need to meet challenges and to accomplish one's goals.

Murray's student, David McClelland, has spent much of his life studying social motives, particularly the need for achievement. By administering the TAT to people who already had been identified as high achievers, he found that students who do especially well in school score high in the need for achievement, as do successful business executives (McClelland, 1985). Moreover, he established that high levels of the need for achievement precede success. In particular, he showed that students who have a high need for achievement in college go on to challenging jobs with lots of responsibility and risk.

Parenting and the Need for Achievement

McClelland also attempted to identify the developmental background of people with a high need for achievement. He collected evidence indicating that parents' behavior affects their children's need for achievement (McClelland et al., 1958). One study found that the mothers of children with a high need to achieve claimed that they encouraged their children to be independent and to achieve more than did the mothers of children with a low need to achieve (Winterbottom, 1958). Were they telling the truth? Bernard Rosen and Roy D'Andrade (1959) watched parents and their sons in the laboratory while the boys worked at a block-building task. The parents of high-nAch sons set higher goals for their children and were warmer and more affectionate. Moreover, the fathers of high-nAch sons pushed and directed their sons less than the fathers of low-nAch sons; but the mothers of high-nAch children were more inclined to push and direct their children.

More recent research demonstrates that parents with a high need for achievement themselves may start pushing their children in infancy. Remarkably strong correlations have been observed between high parental standards for eating on schedule, for early toilet training, and for neatness, and a high need for achievement in children (McClelland & Pilon, 1983). The more rigorous those standards, the greater the need for achievement.

Task Choice and the Need for Achievement

One indicator of the need for achievement is the individual's willingness to tackle challenging situations. In an experiment carried out by one of McClelland's undergraduate students (Litwin, 1958), student subjects were asked to throw rings at a peg from various distances. Those subjects with a high need for achievement chose to throw the rings from intermediate distances—close enough so that they had a good chance to hit the peg, but far enough away for the task to challenge them. Subjects with a low need for achievement chose to throw from far distances (so far away they couldn't be expected to score) or from close distances (so close they rarely missed). This tendency to choose tasks of moderate difficulty, such as the spelling task illustrated in Figure 9.12, has also been demonstrated among schoolchildren with a high need for achievement (deCharms & Carpenter, 1968).

Why do people with a high need for achievement choose tasks of moderate difficulty? John Atkinson (1957), who worked with McClelland, suggested that moderate-difficulty task choice is a compromise between the subject's assessment of the value of success and the assessment of his or her chances of obtaining success. Subjects choose tasks of moderate difficulty because those tasks yield the best payoff in the long run: they maximize the perception of success. Tossing a ring at a peg from the farthest distance would be a great achievement if it worked, but it wouldn't work very often. So subjects with a high need for achievement avoid long-distance tosses. At the other extreme, tossing a ring from the closest distance is going to meet with regular success, but it wouldn't

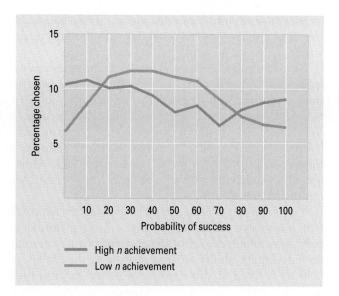

Figure 9.12
Task Choice and Need Achievement

School children with a high need to achieve choose to try to spell moderately difficult words. Children with a low need to achieve are more likely to choose very easy or very difficult words.

represent much of an achievement. So high-nAch subjects avoid the easy tosses as well. Tosses from an intermediate distance have the advantage of succeeding fairly often and representing a fairly high level of achievement, which is why, according to Atkinson, subjects with a high need for achievement choose them (see Table 9.3)

Bernard Weiner used attribution theory to explain task choice. (Attribution theories are ways of making sense of the world.) According to Weiner and his colleagues (1972), we all have different ways of explaining success. People with a high need for achievement believe that success stems from some internal strength over which they have control. They discount the effect of education,

	Approach to the Task	Short Tosses	Intermediate Tosses	Long Tosses
Decision theory	How do I get the best payoff?	I'll get lots of successes but each will have a low value.	A moderate number of successes, each with a moderate value, will give me the best payoff.	Successes will have a high value, but I won't get very many of them.
Attribution theory	How do I confirm my theory that my efforts make a difference?	Successes will be due to the ease of the task; failures, to bad luck.	Successes or failures will be a product of my efforts.	Failures will be due to the difficulty of the task; successes, to good luck.
Diagnosticity theory	How can I diagnose my ability at this game?	Good tosses don't tell me much, and bad ones won't happen often.	Good and bad tosses will give me the best information about my ability.	Bad tosses don't tell me much, and good ones won't happen often.

Table 9.3
Why People with a High Need for Achievement Choose the Moderate Distance in the Ring Toss Game

of friends and family, of coincidence. They believe that success is a product of their capabilities—of the work they are willing to do or the attention they are willing to focus on a task.

According to attribution theory, then, people with a high need for achievement choose tasks of moderate difficulty because these kinds of tasks confirm their understanding of success; that is, they confirm the high nAch subjects' belief that they have the power to affect the outcome of any task they undertake. Very short and very long tosses do not confirm their understanding of success because success in those cases would clearly be the product of external factors— the ease or difficulty of the task, or simply luck. Only by tossing the rings from a moderate distance do they see the effect of their own effort, thereby confirming their basic understanding of success.

Yaacov Trope (1975) offered a third theory. According to Trope, people with a high need for achievement choose tasks of moderate difficulty because those tasks have a high degree of **diagnosticity:** they give the most information about an individual's ability in comparison to the ability of other people. It doesn't help to succeed at short tosses or to fail at long ones because everyone does. And although failing at short tosses or succeeding at long ones would be informational, neither is likely to happen often enough to be reliable. Only tosses from a moderate distance are a reliable source of information about how people with a high need for achievement are performing.

Gender and the Need for Achievement

Many of the early studies of the need for achievement focused on men. During the 1960s, Matina Horner, another of McClelland's students, wondered if the same generalizations were true of women. Horner was struck by the fact that the careers of bright women often seemed to fizzle out, that women seemed to pull back from academic or professional success just as they were about to achieve it. Studies showed that these women had the same need to achieve as their male contemporaries, yet they weren't achieving the same kinds of results. How come?

Horner hypothesized that these young women were afraid of success. She designed an experiment in which male and female subjects had to complete stories for which she provided the first sentences (Horner, 1968). The sentences were designed to elicit the subjects' feelings about achievement. A typical sentence for a male subject was the following:

John has just received the top grade in his medical school class.

A female subject would receive a sentence describing the same circumstances but with a female protagonist:

Anne has just received the top grade in her medical school class.

Just as Horner anticipated, her research suggested that men and women feel very differently about success. Men wrote stories about how John went on to succeed in medical school and became a famous doctor. Women, by contrast, wrote stories in which Anne was thwarted by some twist of fate. Sometimes she lost her boyfriend because of her success. Sometimes she gained the contempt of her classmates for being a "grind." Sometimes she had to set aside her career to care for a family member. Whatever the reason, Anne didn't get the same pleasure from her success that John got from his. To Horner, these results confirmed that bright young women were being crippled by an unreasoned fear of success. And she insisted that if they were less fearful, they would be more successful.

Diagnosticity The capacity of a task to give information about the skills of the person who performs it.

But another reasonable interpretation of the same results was possible. Perhaps the young women were simply reflecting the consequences to women of public success. Perhaps women in our society are so often sanctioned by friends and family and organizations for being too successful that success isn't worth it. What if the fears of success displayed by Horner's subjects were justified?

To explore this idea, Lynn Monahan and her colleagues designed experiments in which both men and women were asked to complete stories about John and Anne. Young men weren't supposed to be afraid of success. If both men and women worked up different kinds of stories for John and Anne, then maybe the stories weren't describing a fear of success so much as an appraisal of the fate of successful women in our society. The results were clear. Both men and women told stories suggesting that Anne's rewards were likely to be less than John's for the same achievement. Both genders agreed that Anne's future would be particularly troubled if her success was achieved in competition with or at the expense of men (Monahan, Kuhn & Shaver, 1974).

Recap

- Social motives stem largely from the individual's culture and upbringing.

- The need for achievement is the need to meet challenges and accomplish one's goals.

- Parents' behavior affects the level of their children's need for achievement.

- People with a high need for achievement choose tasks of moderate difficulty because those tasks yield the best payoff in the long run, confirm their understanding of success, or are the best source of information about their performance.

- Research indicates that women do not fear success; rather, their attitudes toward success reflect society's sanctions against successful women.

Conclusion

In this chapter, we've looked at phenomena as diverse as hunger, sexual motivation, and the need to achieve. In each case, we've seen how complicated are the sources of human motivation. To explain why a person eats on a given occasion, it's not enough to ask how long it's been since that person last ate. We have to know the person's history, culture, even his or her parentage. A similar collage of information must be assembled before we can begin to understand why a person feels sexually aroused at a given time or why a person is working hard to win a particular award. Almost every human motivation is the product of a complex network of factors.

Chapter 10   Emotion and Stress

Whence to Whither (London Transport poster), Cyril Power, c1930

10

Gateways Nothing important happens to us without the accompaniment of emotion. Wouldn't a triumph be hollow without the joy? Could you avoid the oncoming bus without the rush of fear? Emotions make our lives vivid and powerfully shape our actions. The mechanisms that make emotions delightful, useful, and even dangerous are the focus of this chapter.

Sometimes, though, emotions go awry. Prolonged anxiety and stress can destroy our happiness as well as our health. But stress is not the only way that emotions can go wrong. Fear and sadness that become too intense and irrational are at the core of many of the psychological disorders discussed in Chapter 15. We have already examined the impact of emotion on learning in

Chapter 6, and on memory in Chapter 7. And in Chapter 2 we explored the autonomic nervous system, which is central to emotional processes and stress.

I looked at Joan across my desk. It hardly seemed possible that she was the same young woman I'd seen a year ago. Then she was a first-year student, fresh and enthusiastic. It was the end of the fall semester, and she had stopped by with her new boyfriend to get my signature on her spring study card. Her grades were good. She was working ten hours a week in a biology professor's laboratory, and she loved it. She wasn't getting as much sleep as she would have liked, but she was happy.

Now she sat limply in the chair beside my desk, holding a crumpled tissue in one hand and a course-drop form in the other. Her voice was flat and muffled by a terrible cold. Her face seemed thinner than I remembered. Except for her nose, which was red from rubbing, her skin was gray.

Puzzled by the change in her, I asked how things were going. Over the next ten minutes, the whole story spilled out. It had started in September, when her boyfriend was hurt in a motorcycle accident. Because he was a long way from home, the responsibility of helping with the medical decisions had fallen on her shoulders. For a while it had been touch and go, but now his only problems were a bad broken leg and a frustratingly slow recuperation.

Meanwhile, other things had gone wrong. After a summer working in the laboratory, Joan's professor had suggested she run an experiment herself. At first, Joan was delighted. But soon the responsibility—working with the animals seven days a week, no matter what—began to weigh on her.

Between visits to the hospital and her responsibilities in the lab, her grades were suffering. At Thanksgiving dinner, her father had suggested, in front of the whole family, that perhaps she should leave college for a time and return when she could handle the work. She knew he meant well, but his words had made her feel awful. And now it was almost Christmas, and she was failing one of her courses, she had this terrible cold, she hadn't had any sleep for weeks, and she hadn't bought any Christmas presents for anyone!

At this, she burst into tears. I felt my own eyes go hot and wet, and we both fell to rummaging around frantically for tissues—she in her purse, I in my desk drawers. Joan came up with a package of Kleenex and I came up with a napkin from my take-out lunch, but by then the crisis had passed.

I reached across the desk, took the course-drop form, signed it, and passed it back to her. "Things *will* get better," I said. "You've got a lot going for you: you're smart, you're resourceful, you have a boyfriend who loves you, a biology professor who respects you, and a father who's concerned about you. Many students don't have any of those advantages."

I thought for a moment that she was going to burst into tears again, but she didn't. Instead she smiled and said, "I never thought of it like that."

She stood up. Clutching the form and the Kleenex in one hand, she offered me the other hand, and then thanked me.

I saw Joan again near the end of the spring semester. She stopped by my office to have her declaration-of-major form signed. Her grades were back up, and she seemed in good health and spirits. She and her boyfriend had drifted apart, but she was easy about it. The dropped course hadn't proved a problem because the professor she was working with found a way to credit her for her work in the laboratory. That work had gone so well that she is going to report on it at a regional undergraduate research conference next spring. She's planning to major in biology and is thinking about graduate school.

Joan's story reminds me of how complicated is a person's emotional life. I saw her three times, one year apart, and in each of our meetings I found her different. One year she was a bright-eyed enthusiastic freshman, the next year a sad and overwhelmed sophomore, the year after that a steady and determined junior. These differences reached into every corner of her life. They involved both the circumstances presented by the outside world and the way in which she understood those circumstances. They were evident in the actions she was taking, in her gestures and facial expressions, and even in her physiological state and health.

The Components of Emotion

We often think of emotions as basic or primitive, perhaps because our emotional behavior is, in many respects, not very different from that of animals. At the same time, although our emotions may be much like those of animals, they are very complicated, involving many kinds of response. An **emotion** is a complex automatic response to a situation. An emotional response is made up of several elements:

- Emotional action (running away from something we fear, attacking someone who makes us angry)
- Autonomic responses (the pounding heart and sweaty palms that accompany fear)
- Expressive behavior (smiling, scowling)
- Feelings (anger, joy, sorrow)

In this chapter, we discuss each of these elements and then look at how they are related. Next, we examine the ways in which situations generate emotions, the different kinds of emotions, and the source of certain emotions.

Finally, we turn to **stress,** the emotional reaction to elements that disrupt our equilibrium. We talk about the sources of stress, our vulnerability to stress, and ways to cope with it.

Emotional Actions

When you are angry, you are likely to attack. When you are afraid, you run away. When sad, you withdraw, sit motionless, and brood. Each emotion has its characteristic pattern of action (Plutchik, 1980). These patterns change from person to person and with varying circumstances, but the underlying goal of the action is constant. For instance, the attack of an angry person may take a variety of forms; he may say rotten things about the person he is angry with, he may refuse to cooperate with that person, he may try to dominate the other in business or sport, or on rare occasions he may strike out at that person. What unifies these behaviors is the tendency to injure another person in some way. Similarly, a frightened person might physically depart, or perhaps only try to escape being noticed; but whatever the response, it seems designed to avoid a threat.

Some psychologists believe that action tendencies are like the emotional behaviors of animals: innate and common to all members of the species (Buck, 1985; Izard, 1977; Plutchik, 1980; Leventhal & Scherer, 1987). Where do these behaviors come from? Psychologist Robert Plutchik (1980) believes they are a

Emotion A complex automatic response to a situation, composed of emotional action, autonomic responses, expressive behavior and feeling.

Stress The emotional reaction to elements that disrupt our equilibrium.

product of evolution. Plutchik described the *adaptive* functions of a group of basic emotions he believed were essential to our survival (see Table 10.1). For example, people, like all animals, confront danger; to survive, we must escape that danger, and the fear response of running away accomplishes that goal.

Although many action tendencies seem to be products of our evolutionary history, we are all capable of much more complex emotional actions than the simple, adaptive patterns described in this table. For example, when you're angry with a friend, you probably never even think about hitting him or her. You're far more likely to complain about your friend's behavior, or to refuse to do things with that person for a while (Averill, 1983). A punch and a verbal complaint share a basic theme, in that both are attempts to compel the other person to act the way we want. But the distinctions between these two strategies are equally important. One of the essential ways in which we differ from animals is the degree to which our action tendencies are changed by our social experiences (Averill, 1982, 1983). And the variety of culturally influenced emotional reactions is virtually infinite.

Emotion	Function
Fear	Escaping danger, protecting oneself
Anger	Attacking, overcoming barriers and opponents
Joy	Mating, possessing a sexual partner, reproducing
Sadness	Crying for help, coping with loss
Acceptance (trust)	Bonding with a potential mate, forming affiliations
Disgust	Vomiting, rejecting bad substances
Expectancy (interest)	Examining, exploring, finding out about new phenomena
Surprise	Orienting to novel experiences, interrupting ongoing activity

Source: Adapted from Plutchik, 1980.

Table 10.1
Evolutionary Functions Served by Different Emotions According to Plutchik's Theory

Autonomic Responses

Imagine that it's late at night. You're walking along a dark lonely street. Suddenly you hear footsteps behind you. Your heart begins to pound. There's a tightness in your stomach. Your mouth goes dry. All of these responses are produced by your autonomic nervous system.

The autonomic nervous system controls certain automatic functions in the body, such as breathing, heart rate, and digestion (see Chapter 2). Usually we don't notice the effects of this nervous system. But when we're afraid or excited or angry, the sympathetic branch of the autonomic nervous system and the adrenalin that is released from the adrenal glands produce a whole group of changes: we breathe faster, our hearts beat faster, and our mouths go dry. See Figure 10.1 for an illustration.

Physiologist Walter Cannon (1927) described these changes as components of the **fight-or-flight response,** which mobilizes the body's resources for intense action. For example, the flow of blood to the skin is reduced and most internal organs and digestion stops. Instead, the blood is directed to the muscles and the brain, providing more oxygen and fuel for powerful action. At the same time, adrenalin stimulates the release of sugars stored in the liver, giving us the energy to fight or run. The coordination between the autonomic changes and the action patterns makes us more efficient and better able to escape or attack.

Fight-or-flight response The pattern of responses produced by the autonomic nervous system that prepares the organism for intense action.

Figure 10.1
The Autonomic Nervous System

One component of some emotional responses is arousal of the sympathetic functions of the autonomic nervous system. The arousal of these functions prepares the organism for vigorous action.

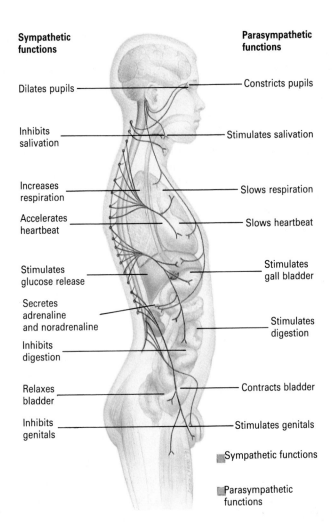

Sympathetic functions

Dilates pupils

Inhibits salivation

Increases respiration

Accelerates heartbeat

Stimulates glucose release

Secretes adrenaline and noradrenaline

Inhibits digestion

Relaxes bladder

Inhibits genitals

Parasympathetic functions

Constricts pupils

Stimulates salivation

Slows respiration

Slows heartbeat

Stimulates gall bladder

Stimulates digestion

Contracts bladder

Stimulates genitals

Sympathetic functions

Parasympathetic functions

Do Lie Detectors Really Work?

The lie detection industry exploits psychology's discoveries about autonomic responses and emotion. Lie detection is based on a series of assumptions about lying. Of course, the liar tries to hide the fact that he or she is lying—for example, by controlling certain emotional responses such as actions and facial expressions. But autonomic responses are very difficult to control. Lie detectors are designed to detect these changes in the autonomic nervous system. They detect the lie by detecting the emotions that go with the lie—that is, by detecting the changes in autonomic arousal that accompany the emotions.

Most lie detectors measure heart rate and the rate of respiration; some also measure *galvanic skin response (GSR)*, a change in the skin's resistance to electric current. The machine transforms these measurements into graphs, consisting of lines on a continuous sheet of paper. Because several such graphs are used during a lie detection test, the machine is called a *polygraph*.

Do lie detectors work? Sometimes, but not well enough to justify their use in most situations. Even experienced operators make mistakes as much as a third of the time (Lykken, 1985), for a variety of reasons. For example, the polygraph operator may not distinguish small "white"

(Continued on next page)

lies from big ones, especially if the subject is nervous about taking the test. In addition, lie detectors do not detect lies; they measure autonomic responses. And these responses may stem from emotions that don't have anything to do with whether a subject is telling the truth. Both of these circumstances may lead the polygraph operator to believe someone is lying when he or she is basically telling the truth.

The problem isn't limited to detecting lies that aren't lies. Some people are able to "fool" the machine, so their lies go undetected. One man who was wrongly jailed as a result of a lie detector test became an expert on how the machines work. He claimed that with just a half-hour's coaching, he was able to help almost 90 percent of his fellow inmates "beat" a lie detector test (Lykken, 1981). Because lie detection is so inaccurate, federal legislation limits the use of polygraphs in most employment screening. Many states also prohibit the use of lie detector results in the courtroom.

If lie detector tests are not reliable, why do people continue to administer them? Some users probably don't know that the tests are often inaccurate or illegal. But for most users, reliability simply doesn't matter. They get the effects they want, even if the tests don't actually work, so long as potential subjects *believe* they work. For example, when the tests were used for job screening, someone with a criminal record for theft wouldn't bother applying for a job in a bank that routinely screened job applicants with a polygraph test. In law enforcement, sometimes just the threat of a lie detector test can lead to a confession. The polygraph is a modern superstition: it compels honesty because people believe it works, not because it really does (Kleinmuntz & Szucko, 1984).

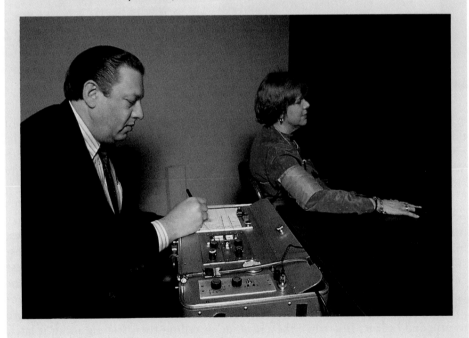

In standard lie detection practice, the subject's heart rate, breathing, and skin conductance are measured, producing a tracing. The operator compares the responses to a test question with responses to comparison questions. If the subject is lying, all of the autonomic responses are expected to change. On average, such changes do occur, but the potential for error in the tester's judgments is unacceptably high.

Expressive Behaviors

Expressive behaviors are the facial expressions, gestures, posture, and other behaviors that show what emotion is occurring in a person. Such behaviors seem to be a means of communication among members of a species.

Expressive behavior A behavior that conveys information about an emotional state.

Among human beings, facial expressions are the primary way of communicating emotion. No species has as wide an array of facial expressions as we do. Charles Darwin (1872) attributed this range of expressions to the fact that we are a very social species. He argued that human facial expressions evolved to help us predict one another's behavior. And he pointed out that other animal species that live in groups—dogs, for example—use expressions in the same way.

Despite the plausibility of Darwin's argument, for a long time most psychologists assumed that facial expressions were learned. Why? Because a number of cultural differences in expressions had been discovered. For example, the Japanese smile when they are being reprimanded, whereas we Westerners tend to look glum.

To test whether facial expressions are different across cultures, psychologists collected pictures of people smiling, frowning, glaring, looking puzzled. Next they constructed stories about what might have happened to the people in the pictures. Then they would show a subject a smiling face, for example, and ask if the person was more likely to have just been told something nice by a friend, to have lost something he or she valued, or to have been insulted (see Figure 10.2). In study after study, across many different cultures, subjects consistently paired the pictures with the right stories (Ekman, Friesen & Ellsworth, 1972; Ekman et al., 1987; Izard, 1971).

Figure 10.2
A Cross-Cultural Test of Expression Recognition

Which of these people has just been insulted, lost something valued, or received something they wanted? Ekman and his colleagues showed pictures like these to people around the world and asked them to match the pictures to events common to all cultures. They found that the same expressions were recognized everywhere.

To make sure that this consistency wasn't due to contact among peoples of different cultures, the experimenters found their way to a preliterate people, the Fore, who lived in a remote area of New Guinea and had very little contact with Western society. The Fore also matched facial expressions and situations easily (Ekman & Friesen, 1971).

If everyone in the world recognizes the same facial expressions, why do some people's expressions seem to mean different things? The answer is simple. Like many innate patterns of behavior, expressions are modified by social influences. In particular, many cultures teach their members that certain kinds of expressions are appropriate in some situations and not appropriate in others. These cultural **display rules** (Ekman, Friesen & Ellsworth, 1972) explain why the Japanese smile when they're being reprimanded. In Japan, people are taught not to display negative emotions in the presence of superiors. So the Japanese learn to grin and bear it. But when they're alone or telling their friends about it later, you can bet they scowl (Matsumoto & Ekman, 1989).

Because facial expressions are essentially the same among all people, they probably are not learned. Evidence that expressions are innate also comes from studies of children who have been blind from birth. These children show the same emotional expressions as do sighted children, and those expressions emerge in the same sequence (Eibl-Eibesfeldt, 1973). Expressions, then, like emotional actions and autonomic responses, are innate responses that are common to the species (Izard, 1990). But, like emotional actions, they can be modified profoundly by cultural influences.

Display rules Cultural norms that govern the expression of different emotions.

Integrating Emotional Behaviors

The three behavioral components of emotion are interrelated. When we're afraid, we turn to run (emotional action); our mouths go dry and our hearts beat faster (autonomic responses); and fear is apparent on our faces (expressive behavior). These three classes of response are all parts of an integrated system, in which each plays a role in relation to the others. For example, in fear the autonomic changes make it possible to run away faster, and the expressive behavior tells others that danger is near.

One sign of the tight connections among the different responses is that if one response changes, the others change too. For example, if you intentionally scowl, trying to make yourself look angry, your autonomic responses also change: your heart rate speeds up, and your skin temperature rises (Ekman, Levenson & Friesen, 1983; Lanzetta, Cartwright-Smith & Kleck, 1976). And studies show that by increasing arousal (for example, by injecting adrenalin in people who are already angry), we increase the intensity of emotional expression (Schachter & Singer, 1962).

Emotional Feelings

Feelings are the conscious experience of emotion. One of the longest-running controversies in psychology centers on the relationship between feelings and the behavioral components of the emotional response. Common sense seems to suggest that feelings produce those other components. In direct contradiction, the James-Lange theory argues that the other responses produce feelings. Another alternative, the Cannon-Bard theory, suggests that the thalamus, a structure in the brain, triggers both feelings and behavioral responses at the same time.

The James-Lange Theory   Psychologist William James initiated the controversy in the late nineteenth century by arguing that the common-sense view of emotion (see Figure 10.3) was wrong:

> Common sense says, we lose our fortune, are sorry and weep; we meet a bear, are frightened and run; we are insulted by a rival, are angry and strike. The hypothesis here to be defended says that this order of sequence is incorrect . . . and the more rational statement is that we feel sorry *because* we cry, angry *because* we strike, afraid *because* we tremble. (James, 1890, p. 449)

James's theory of emotion was something like the joking remark, "How do I know what I think until I hear what I say?" James believed that the experience of an emotion was the perception of the actions, expressions, and autonomic reactions of the emotional episode. His theory came to be called the **James-Lange theory of emotion** because another scientist, Carl Lange, proposed something similar at about the same time.

As Figure 10.4 makes clear, James's theory implies that if you intentionally smile, you will feel happy. James's hypothesis may seem improbable, but before you dismiss it, please try a little experiment. Look away at a wall, or into the distance. Then, try smiling relaxedly in your normal way. Keep smiling long enough so that it feels natural and you don't have to think consciously about what you are doing. Do you notice any difference in how you feel? Now try putting on the angriest look you can. Clenching your fists may help. How does that feel? Many people do feel stirrings of happiness and anger when they perform these expressions. If you did feel these emotions, you have a sense of why James proposed his theory.

Feelings The conscious experience of emotion.

James-Lange theory The theory that feelings are the result, not the cause, of emotional behaviors.

Figure 10.3
**The Common-Sense View
of Emotion**

Common sense says that when
we see something threatening,
such as a bear, the recognition of
the threatening object causes a
feeling of fear. The feeling of fear,
in turn, causes changes in facial
expression, autonomic arousal,
and action.

Figure 10.4
**The James-Lange Theory of
Emotion**

James argued that the perception
of the bear directly causes
changes in expressions and autonomic arousal, and that the perception of these changes produced the feeling of fear.

The Cannon-Bard Theory   The James-Lange theory was almost universally accepted during the first decade or two of this century, until Walter Cannon (1929) (the "fight-or-flight" man) raised some objections to James's theory. Cannon and his associate, Philip Bard, proposed an alternative of their own (see Figure 10.5). Cannon and Bard also disagreed with common sense, in that they did not believe that the feeling of emotion caused the other responses. Instead, they proposed that a central brain process, located in the thalamus, caused the bodily responses, the actions, and the feelings all at the same time.

In arguing for his own theory, Cannon raised a number of objections to James's theory. For example, he observed that the autonomic responses were pretty much the same for all emotions. Whether you were afraid or angry, your heart beat faster, your palms sweat, and so on. Thus, if the feeling of emotion was the feeling of these responses you should have felt only one emotion.

Cannon also pointed out that producing autonomic arousal artificially did not necessarily cause feelings of emotion. When people were injected with adrenalin, they described their feelings as "like an emotion, but not the same" (Maranon, 1924).

The Schachter-Singer Two-Factor Theory   Forty years later, Stanley Schachter proposed a new theory in answer to Cannon's objections—a theory that combined some aspects of the work of both James and Cannon. Schachter and his colleagues (Schachter & Singer, 1962; Schachter & Wheeler, 1962) believed that the adrenalin injections had failed to produce emotions for two reasons. One was that real emotions occur in a particular context, but in the adrenalin studies there was no reason to feel an emotion. The second, related problem was that the subjects in these experiments knew they were being given adrenalin. Since

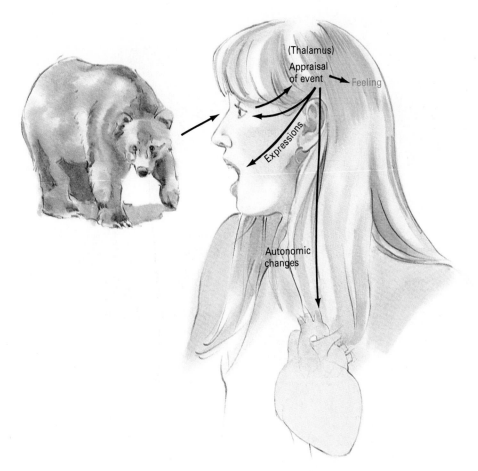

Figure 10.5
The Cannon-Bard Theory of Emotion

Cannon argued that the perception of the bear activated a part of the brain that caused both the feeling of fear and the autonomic and expressive changes.

they knew the source of their arousal, perhaps they didn't interpret its effects as emotional. After all, our hearts beat faster for many reasons, only some of which are emotional.

Schachter's final theory of emotion is called a two-factor (i.e., cognitive-physiological) theory because he believed that one factor, the degree of a person's autonomic arousal, determined the *intensity* of his or her emotional experience, whereas a second factor, the person's understanding or cognitions about the situation, determined the *quality* of that experience (see Figure 10.6). So, whether a person would feel slightly annoyed or enraged would depend on whether that person had been aroused a little or a lot. And whether the person would be angry or happy depended on what was appropriate in that situation. Schachter's theory is a sort of blend, then, considering that the role of arousal in determining the intensity of feelings is just what James proposed, but the role of the situation in determining the kind of feeling more closely resembles Cannon's observation.

Evidence for the Theories

Both the James–Lange theory and Schachter's modification imply that if one could induce a person to perform emotional behaviors, that person would feel the corresponding emotion. In contrast, neither common sense nor Cannon's theory would anticipate the occurrence of this effect. All of the research testing the James–Lange position has examined this general idea. We will describe the research on arousal and expressive behavior separately, beginning with the former because Schachter was the first person to raise this issue seriously.

Figure 10.6
The Schachter-Singer Two-Factor Theory of Emotion

Schachter argued that the perception of the bear caused changes in autonomic arousal, which in turn caused the intensity of the feeling, as James believed. Schachter also held that the quality of the emotion was determined directly by the perception of the bear, as Cannon would have argued.

Misattribution The process by which bodily states produced by one cause lead to feelings as if they were produced by a different cause.

Arousal and Emotional Experience   To test his assumptions about arousal and feelings, Schachter needed to put subjects in emotional situations and then inject them with adrenalin, without their knowledge of its effects. His solution was to tell his subjects that he was testing the effects of a vitamin injection on perception. Actually he injected some of his subjects with adrenalin and others, in a comparison group, with a neutral solution. After they were injected the subjects were led to a waiting room, where a confederate of the experimenter tried to induce the subject to feel either happy or angry. In the happy condition, the confederate acted foolishly, cracking jokes and playing with the materials in the room. In the angry condition, the subjects filled out a very insulting questionnaire; and the confederate also filled it out, all the while modeling anger by mumbling and cursing under his breath (Schachter & Singer, 1962).

Compared to subjects who had received injections of a neutral substance, the adrenalin-injected subjects reported feeling more angry; adrenalin did not, however, increase feelings of happiness. Nonetheless, Schachter and Singer's experimental procedure and results were so intriguing that numerous other studies, manipulating autonomic arousal in a multitude of ways, have followed. When autonomic arousal has been manipulated by drugs, the results have been rather mixed (Reisenzein, 1983); but other follow-up research, using alternative techniques to change arousal, has supported Schachter more consistently (Laird & Bresler, 1990).

In these studies, people are led to "misattribute" their arousal from one source to another. **Misattribution** occurs when someone reacts to arousal from one (nonemotional) source as if it came from a different (emotional) source. In one example of this kind of research, subjects are aroused by the exercise of pedaling a stationary bicycle, until they are breathing hard and their heart is beating rapidly. After a few minutes, they are confronted with a new, emotional situation: someone who is apparently another subject in the experiment insults them. Then, the subjects have a chance to hurt the person who insulted them. Compared to people who have not exercised, the exercise subjects are much more aggressive; they also report feeling much angrier at the other subject. In other experiments, exercise increases the subjects' attraction to a member of the opposite sex (Zillman, 1983). In all of these cases, the subjects seem to interpret the arousal produced by the exercise as if it were produced by the insult or the presence of the attractive other, and they consequently feel more strongly.

In sum, arousal plays a role in the experience of some of the more "excited" emotions, such as anger, fear, and passionate love. However, certain other, "calmer" emotions, such as happiness and sadness, are not affected by arousal changes (Laird & Bresler, 1990). Thus, we can conclude that the theories of both James and Schachter are supported by this evidence.

Expressive Behavior   The evidence that facial expressions may lead to emotional feelings is also consistent with James's theory. If you tried the little exercise we recommended at the beginning of this section, then you have, in effect, been a subject in such an experiment. In these studies, people are induced to adopt facial expressions and then asked how they feel. In general, people do report feeling the emotions their faces are expressing (Adelman & Zajonc, 1989; Laird & Bresler, 1990).

A particularly intriguing method to demonstrate these effects is depicted in Figure 10.7. The researchers asked people to write while holding a pencil in their mouths. There were two pencil positions. As you can see from the photographs, the pencil, when held in the teeth, causes an expression like a smile. But when it is held pursed in the lips, it induces an unhappy expression that has elements of anger and disgust. As James would have predicted, the subjects reported feeling happier during the first expression (Strack, Martin & Stepper, 1988).

Research has shown that the rapid heartbeat and arousal produced by exercise can be mistaken for the excitement of romantic love, which can increase the feelings for an attractive partner.

Figure 10.7
Unobtrusive Manipulation of Facial Expressions

Subjects who held a pen in their teeth, producing an expression like a smile, reported feeling happier than subjects who held the pen in their mouth.

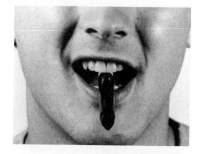

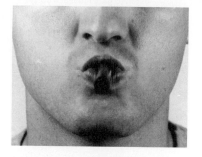

Source: Strack, Martin & Stepper, 1988.

Puzzle It Out!

Dentists commonly add adrenalin to the Novocain they inject in their patients before going to work on their teeth. The reason is that adrenalin constricts blood vessels near the surface of the body (including those in the mouth), thus reducing any bleeding after an extraction. Given the research on the effects of adrenalin on emotions noted in this chapter, what do you think might be the effect on a patient's feelings while in the dentist's chair?

Still other kinds of expressive behavior have been shown to affect feelings. For example, one of the distinctive behaviors of people in love is to gaze into each other's eyes for long spans of time (see Figure 10.8). If James's hypothesis is correct, strangers who gazed into each other's eyes should report feeling attracted to each other. They do (Kellerman, Lewis & Laird, 1989).

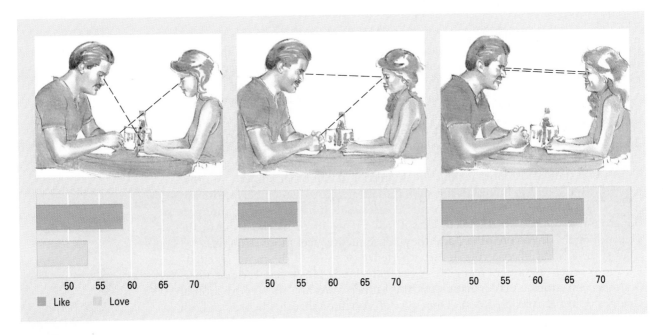

50   55   60   65   70   50   55   60   65   70   50   55   60   65   70

■ Like   ■ Love

Figure 10.8
The Effect of Shared Gaze on Feelings of Love

Opposite-sex strangers were asked to gaze into each other's eyes for two minutes, and then report how they felt about each other. Compared to people who gazed at each other's hands, the shared-gaze people reported significantly greater liking and loving for each other.

In sum, we can say with reasonable confidence that James was correct: if we tremble, we will feel fear, whether or not there is a bear. And if we cry, we will feel sad, whether or not we have lost a fortune. Schachter, too, was correct in believing that arousal would lead to more intense emotional experiences (though not to intensification of *all* emotions). Does this mean that Cannon was wrong? Not necessarily. His major contribution was to propose that specific brain circuits were involved in emotional responses. As we will learn in a few pages, this proposal has been largely confirmed.

So how does emotional experience fit with the other components of the emotional episode? Those other components clearly represent integrated, but relatively primitive, adaptive patterns of action. The experience or feeling of an emotion is the recognition that such a pattern is going on. It is one of the ways in which we know what our own automatic responses to a situation are (Buck,

How Do We Know That?

As a discipline, psychology faces some unique methodological problems. In a sense, we psychologists are our own subjects—beings trying to make sense of everything that happens to us, and then acting in light of that understanding. Often, if our subjects knew what we were trying to accomplish, they would not be able to respond naturally. For example, suppose we told you that we want to test whether you are going to think about ice cream before you read the next paragraph. Now that we've mentioned ice cream, you really can't naturally either think about it or not think about it. If you're thinking about ice cream, it's because we gave you the idea. And if you're not thinking about it, it's because you're deliberately thinking very hard about something else. To avoid this kind of problem, psychologists must often keep their subjects in the dark about what they are doing and why. Sometimes this entails the simple decision not to discuss the objectives of the research; at other times it involves active deception.

Schachter and Singer's (1962) research is a good example of the latter. Their theory explicitly holds that adrenalin affects subjects' feelings only if the subjects do not know that they've been injected with adrenalin or are unaware of adrenalin's effects. The researchers believed that the subjects of earlier experiments did not feel stronger emotions because they knew they were being injected with adrenalin and how they would be affected. To test this possibility, Schachter and Singer examined one condition in which people received adrenalin injections but were told exactly what the effects would be—that their hearts would pound, their faces would flush, and so on. Of all the subjects, these people reported the mildest emotional feelings. Their feelings were less strong even than those of the people injected with the neutral saline solution. Obviously, the subjects' expectations were strongly affected by the outcome of the experiment.

This result demonstrates a serious ethical dilemma, however. On the one hand, a good test of a scientific hypothesis may require that subjects be deceived. But on the other hand, is it ever right to deceive the subjects of a scientific experiment? And if so, under what circumstances?

At one time, psychologists believed that so long as the procedures in an experiment were not harmful, deception was fine. More recently, though, an evolving concern with the ethics of research has led to the conclusion that subjects must give their *informed consent* to all procedures. That is, before agreeing to participate, subjects must be fully informed about all of the procedures they will undergo in an experiment and about their likely effects.

If we wanted to replicate Schachter and Singer's research today, then, we would have to tell our subjects about the potential effects of the injections. And yet, by telling people what the effects of adrenalin will be, we may prevent those effects from occurring. One common solution to this dilemma is to tell subjects correctly about the procedures and their effects, but to keep them in the dark about both the reasons for the procedures and the expected results. Clearly, research on some topics is more complex than in earlier times.

1985; Mandler & Nakamura, 1987). This awareness is probably what most clearly distinguishes human emotional responses from those of animals. Knowing what our automatic response tendencies are permits us to decide whether and how we act on them (Oatley & Johnson-Laird, 1987).

Recap

- Emotional responses combine emotional actions, autonomic responses, expressive behaviors, and feelings.

- Some psychologists believe that the actions we take in emotional situations are a product of evolution.

- One of the ways in which people differ from animals is the degree to which their action tendencies are influenced by social experiences.

- Physiological changes in the body—what Cannon called the *fight-or-flight response*—mobilize the body's resources for intense action.

- The adrenalin released as part of an autonomic response redirects the flow of blood in the body and stimulates the release of sugars stored in the liver.

- Like action tendencies, autonomic responses are adaptive: they have evolved to meet basic survival needs.

- Expressive behaviors are a means of communication among members of a species.

- Facial expressions are innate patterns of behavior, shared by all members of the species. Like other innate patterns of behavior, they can be modified by social influences, particularly cultural display rules.

- The three behavioral components of emotional response are closely related: if we change one of them, the others change too.

- Feelings are the conscious experience of emotion.

- According to the James-Lange theory of emotion, feelings are produced by the behavioral components of the emotional response.

- According to the Cannon-Bard theory of emotion, the thalamus transmits emotional information simultaneously to the cerebral cortex and the autonomic nervous system. In the cortex, that information becomes feeling.

- According to Schachter-Singer's two-factor theory of emotion, arousal governs the intensity of the emotional response; and a second factor, our interpretation of the emotional situation, governs the emotion we feel.

- Studies show that physical arousal increases both the tendency toward misattribution and the intensity of emotion.

- The experience of emotion—in the form of feelings—is the recognition of the patterns of emotional behavior. It is this awareness that most clearly distinguishes the emotional response of humans from that of animals.

Understanding the Emotional Situation

Before we can respond to an emotional situation, we have to understand or appraise it (Arnold, 1960; Lazarus, 1982; Ellsworth & Smith, 1988). If we see a large black blob approaching us, we won't be afraid unless we recognize that it is a bear and understand that bears are dangerous. So cognition—all of the steps involved in collecting and processing information—is a critical part of the process. Our understanding of a situation shapes our emotional response to that situation. And as our understanding changes, so does our response (Lazarus, 1984).

Robert Zajonc (1980, 1984) argues that certain emotional responses occur without cognition. He claims that people sometimes react emotionally to stimuli that they cannot identify or do other "cognitive work" on. In one study, for example, he showed his subjects a large number of Chinese characters. Later they were shown pairs of characters. In each pair, one of the characters had been seen previously; the other was new. When asked to identify which character was one they had seen and which was new, the subjects simply guessed. They couldn't remember the characters they had already seen. But when asked to choose the character they liked better in each pair, they consistently chose the character they had seen before (Zajonc, 1980). They had a feeling of liking for the character (based on their previous exposure to it) even though they did not know they had seen it.

Some of the disagreement about the role of cognition in emotion rests on the definition of cognition. Whereas some psychologists include in that definition all of the processes that have to do with remembering and thinking and making decisions, Zajonc seems to limit cognition to conscious processes. But both sides agree that we cannot respond to a stimulus without interpreting it, and that parts of the interpretive process are so rapid and automatic that we aren't even aware of them (Zajonc, Pietromonaco & Bargh, 1982).

Social Constructions

Remember that the primitive emotional action patterns that we share with animals form the core from which much more complex, uniquely human emotional behaviors have developed. Similarly, the kinds of situations that generate an emotional response are shaped by cultural and social processes. For example, dogs growl only when physically threatened. They don't get angry when a friend is late for the movies or insults them or forgets to call. In fact, the situations that generate most human emotional responses are far removed from the basic situations that generate emotion in animals (Averill, 1983).

When we find ourselves in a basic emotional situation (recall the bear in the woods and the snake in the grass), the processes of defining the situation and shaping our response are relatively straightforward. But when we're angry with a friend because she was late for the movies and we respond by not laughing at the first few jokes she cracks, both the occasion for the anger and the response are the products of our social learning. Nature gave us the reactions we need to deal with bears; but we have to learn and think a lot about the ways to react to a tardy friend.

Recap

- Our understanding of an emotional situation shapes our response to that situation.

- Parts of the interpretive process are so automatic that we aren't even aware of them.

- The kinds of situations that generate an emotional response are shaped by cultural and social processes.

The Brain and Emotion

Obviously, the brain must perform all the processes involved in emotion, appraisal, the activation of bodily responses, and the generation of feeling. Psychologists have wondered for a long time if these processes are located in particular parts of the brain.

In the central nervous system, emotional responses are coordinated by the cerebral cortex and the limbic system. The structures of the limbic system form a ring at the very center of the brain, extending from the frontal lobes through the parietal lobes into the core of the temporal lobes. The limbic system, illustrated in Figure 10.9, consists largely of "old" cortex, which is similar to the brains of many other mammals. This old cortex is contrasted with the new expanses of cortex that occur only in humans. The fact that we share the old cortex with mammals, who also seem to share many of our basic emotional patterns, suggests that this area is especially important in emotional processes.

Research shows that the removal or stimulation of certain structures in the limbic system does have very specific effects on emotional behavior. In Chapter 2, for instance, we described the Kluver-Bucy syndrome, the extraordinary docility found in animals whose amygdala has been damaged. The hippocampus, another structure in the limbic system, seems to integrate emotional responses. In cats, stimulation of one part of the hippocampus produces flight behaviors; stimulation of other parts produces hissing, snarling, and other defensive behaviors (de Molina & Hunsperger, 1959).

What about the cerebral cortex? Whenever we take any action, the whole cortex is involved—particularly the motor centers (Mogenson, 1987). Obviously, then, the cortex is involved in the performance of emotional behaviors. In addition, there seem to be specific relationships between parts of the right side of the brain and the communicative aspects of emotional behavior (Geschwind, 1979). For instance, people with injuries to the right hemisphere are unable to perceive whole objects and patterns (Tucker, 1981) or to recognize faces and identify the emotional expressions on them (Cicone, Wapner & Gardner, 1980). These people also have difficulty speaking and understanding highly emotional speech (Tucker, Watson & Heilman, 1977); in fact, it is hard for them to feel any emotion at all (Tucker, 1984).

Figure 10.9
Brain Structures in the Limbic System Involved in Emotion

The structures in the limbic system that lie just under the cortex seem to be most heavily involved in emotions, although different areas of the cortex are also essential.

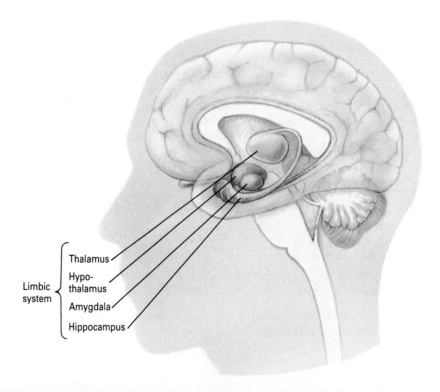

The subjects in much of this research were people whose brains were temporarily or permanently impaired. More recently, however, a number of techniques have been developed that allow us to study brain activity in unimpaired subjects. One involves measuring EEG activity in different areas of the brain during an emotional episode (Davidson, 1987). (Remember that the electroencephalograph measures the electrical activity of large groups of neurons in the brain. "Busy" regions of the brain show EEG patterns that are different from those generated by the same regions in an inactive state.) EEG research reveals that specific areas of both hemispheres of the brain are active in different emotions. For example, when we're happy, the front portion of the right hemisphere is active; when we're angry, the front of the left hemisphere is active.

Recap

- All emotional processes are controlled by the brain.

- In the central nervous system, emotional responses are coordinated by the cerebral cortex and the limbic system.

- Research shows that different areas of the cortex are active in different emotions.

The Varieties of Emotion

Name three emotions. Your list probably includes one or more of these: anger, sadness, fear, and joy. Why? Because just about everyone agrees that these are emotions. But what about boredom? What about enthusiasm? Is the feeling of being ignored or insecure an emotion? Is being hungry an emotion? Most people agree on anger, sadness, fear, and joy. Some believe that boredom and feelings of insecurity are emotions, too (Ortony, Clore & Foss, 1987). But practically no one would call hunger an emotion.

Does this process seem familiar? It calls to mind our discussion in Chapter 8, on thought and language, about how some birds seem to be better examples of the *concept* of birds than others. A robin is more bird-like than a penguin, and anger is more emotion-like than boredom. Anger, sadness, fear, and joy are very good examples—even prototypes—of the concept of emotion. Boredom and enthusiasm may well be emotions, but they are not good examples of emotion.

What accounts for the wide variety of emotions? One possibility is that just a few basic emotions exist, and that many of the other feelings we call *emotions* are simply combinations or variations of those basic emotions. Psychologists who follow this approach have disagreed, however, about which emotions are the basic ones.

There seems to be wide agreement on at least five basic emotions: anger, sadness, fear, joy (or happiness), and disgust (Ekman, 1982). But consensus disappears beyond this point, as (Table 10.2) makes clear. The addition of contempt to the list has been strongly argued, because expressions of contempt are recognized consistently across cultures (Ekman & Friesen, 1986; Izard, 1977). And if we use the cross-cultural criterion, surprise would also be considered a basic emotion (Ekman, Friesen & Ellsworth, 1972; Ekman et al., 1987). Other popular candidates for the list include shame, guilt, and interest (Izard, 1977). And Plutchik (1980) makes an argument for acceptance, or love.

The basic emotions may be the building blocks of other emotions. For example, nostalgia seems to be a mixture of sadness and happiness. And Plutchik

Table 10.2
Some Basic Emotions

Ekman and Friesen	Izard	Plutchik
Joy	Joy	Joy
Anger	Anger	Anger
Sadness	Sadness	Sadness
Fear	Fear	Fear
Disgust	Disgust	Disgust
Surprise	Surprise	Surprise
Contempt	Contempt	—
	Interest	Anticipation (Interest)
	Shame	—
	Guilt	—
		Acceptance (Love)

(1980) argues that contempt is actually a mixture of anger and disgust. Figure 10.10 is a model of Plutchik's ideas about emotion mixing. Unfortunately, no clear method for testing these ideas has emerged.

Several more recent studies have asked people to point out the similarities among emotions. The subjects' judgments are then used to identify clusters of emotions—emotions that seem to belong together. One study (Storms &

Figure 10.10
Plutchik's Emotion Solid

Plutchik identified the emotions in the top circle as the eight basic types, with less intense versions of each emotion lying below it in the solid. He argued that other emotions are formed by combinations of the eight basic types.

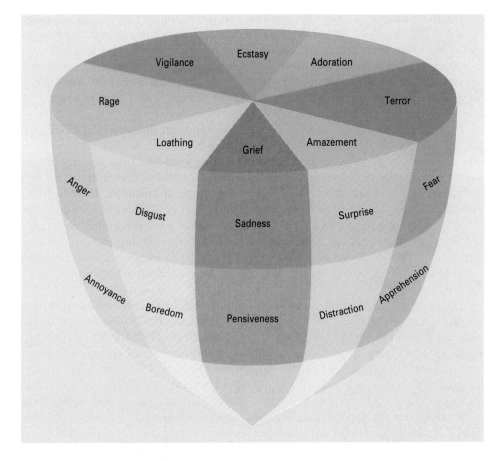

Source: Plutchik, 1980.

Storms, 1987) produced seven major clusters, which are very much like the lists of basic emotions—with some interesting differences. For example, one cluster centers on sadness but includes shame and pain as well. Another includes anger and disgust, as well as hostility—an emotion the researchers distinguish from anger.

The Balance of Positive and Negative Emotions

Look again at Table 10.2. Notice that all of the lists of basic emotions include more negative emotions (such as anger, disgust, and sadness) than positive emotions (joy and love). This imbalance could reflect an imbalance in the real world. But is life so horrible that we need four or five times as many terms to describe feeling bad as we do to describe feeling good? Not really. It's far more likely that psychologists—like newspaper publishers—choose to focus on the "bad" things in life (Averill, 1980).

Our analogy here is a good one. The reason that newspapers print more bad news than good news is not that good things don't happen. Of course they do. It's just that they're so common they simply aren't news. Imagine a paper that reported on every commuter who got home safely yesterday, or on every child who has grown up healthy and happy! In short, happiness isn't news—and it isn't the focus of psychological study—because it's the norm. Most of us, most of the time, feel positive about ourselves and our lives (Taylor & Brown, 1988).

Conversely, negative emotional patterns help us deal with emergencies, the relatively rare events in our lives that require an immediate response. There are many different kinds of emergencies—events that frighten us or disgust us or make us angry or sad—and many different ways of responding to them. But emergencies are not the norm. Most of the time, we "use" just one of our emotions—happiness.

Recap

- Many psychologists believe that there are just a few basic emotions, and that all other emotions are simply combinations of or variations on those basic emotions.

- Most lists of basic emotions include anger, sadness, fear, joy, and disgust.

- The basic emotions (what Plutchik calls the *primary emotions*) are the building blocks of other emotions (the *secondary emotions*).

- Most of us, most of the time, feel positive about ourselves and our lives.

- Negative emotional patterns help us deal with emergencies.

Stress Responses

Many emotions are responses to situations that challenge us to make some response that is important to our well-being. Often our emotions have a homeostatic effect, in that they lead us to take actions which correct the situation that led to the emotion in the first place. For instance, if something threatens us, the emotion of fear may help us to escape. And if a person wrongs us, the emotion of anger may help us to right that wrong. Accordingly, emotions are usually short-lived, because the emotional response quickly restores equilibrium. But what happens when the challenge is sustained, or when many challenges follow in succession? As demonstrated by the incident with Joan, described at the beginning of this chapter, we can sometimes be overwhelmed. The result of this continuing challenge is a series of responses called **stress responses.**

The General Adaptation Syndrome

We are constantly confronted by challenges, by events that we have to cope with in some way. When a challenge occurs, we may be set back briefly; but then we begin to respond. The fight-or-flight response is one way the body mobilizes itself to meet this kind of challenge. In this case, our autonomic responses prepare us to act.

According to Hans Selye (1976), the body's autonomic responses are just the first stage—the *alarm stage*—in what he calls the **general adaptation syndrome (GAS)** (see Figure 10.11). If those responses meet the environmental challenge, adrenalin is no longer pumped into the bloodstream, breathing and heart rate slow, blood returns to the skin and internal organs, and the level of sugar in the blood falls (see Figure 10.12).

Figure 10.11
The General Adaptation Syndrome

Selye observed a consistent pattern of response to many kinds of environmental stressors. First, the capacity to resist the stressor rises, then after awhile, it falls.

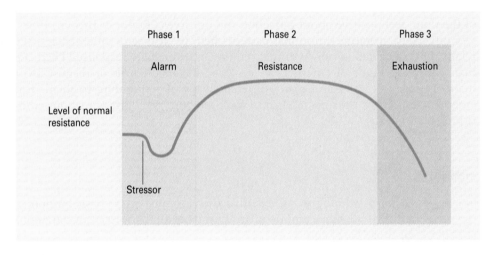

Source: Adapted from Selye, 1976.

If the challenge continues, however, we move into the second stage of the GAS, the *resistance stage*. The body's responses during this stage are very similar to those during the alarm stage, but their intensity is reduced somewhat. For example, the heart beats faster than normal, but not quite as fast as during the alarm stage. It's almost as though the body is reserving its resources, settling in for a long battle.

Of course, we cannot maintain resistance indefinitely. Eventually the body loses its ability to produce adrenalin and the other chemicals that maintain resistance; and eventually the supply of glucose in the liver is depleted (and not replaced because digestion has been reduced as part of the whole response). This is the third stage of the GAS, the *exhaustion stage*. During this stage, the body's resources fall below normal levels.

In several experiments, Selye (1976) demonstrated that animals died if environmental challenges continued after the animals had reached the exhaustion stage. Autopsies revealed that these animals suffered from ulcers and other problems that afflict people. Apparently certain diseases are indeed a product of prolonged environmental challenge.

Stress responses Patterns of responses made by the organism that help to mobilize its resources to deal with an environmental challenge.

General adaptation syndrome (GAS) A pattern of responses to stressful circumstances that consists of the alarm, resistance, and exhaustion stages.

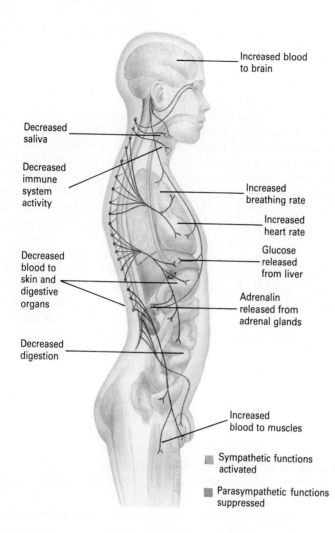

Increased blood to brain

Decreased saliva

Decreased immune system activity

Decreased blood to skin and digestive organs

Decreased digestion

Increased breathing rate

Increased heart rate

Glucose released from liver

Adrenalin released from adrenal glands

Increased blood to muscles

Sympathetic functions activated

Parasympathetic functions suppressed

Figure 10.12
The Resistance Stage of the General Adaptation Syndrome

The stress response affects almost all the systems of the body. Prolonged stress means prolonged disruption of normal functioning for all of these systems, as well as consequent threats to health.

Prolonged challenge produces still other serious physiological changes, especially in the immune system. In such cases, it may well be that the body's resources are being diverted to deal with the external problem that is generating the GAS, instead of with the internal elements such as microbes and viruses that cause disease (Kiecolt-Glaser & Glaser, 1988). We know that the adrenalin and other chemicals that are released during the GAS inhibit the functioning of the immune system (O'Leary, 1990). During the exhaustion stage, then, we are more susceptible to infection (Jemmot & Locke, 1984).

Environmental Challenges

We've been using the word *challenge* where you might have expected to see the word *stress*. In so doing, we want to emphasize that stress is a *response* to an event in the environment, not the event itself. It's also important to remember that some challenges do not produce stress. The stress response is a function of the individual's personality and coping mechanisms.

Selye maintained that any major change in our lives—even a "good"change like starting college or having a baby—can produce a stress response. In developing their Social Readjustment Rating Scale, Thomas Holmes and Richard Rahe (1967) followed Selye's thinking. They asked their subjects to rank forty-three events in terms of *life change units (LCUs),* the degrees of change demanded by each event (see Table 10.3). On their scale, divorce is ranked second. But marriage isn't far behind: it ranks seventh.

To use the scale, begin by noting the events listed there that have happened to you in the last year; then add the LCUs for those events. That total is an indication of the amount of change to which you've had to adapt over the period.

Selye's theory—that any major change produces the stress response—implies that people who receive high scores on the scale should be prone to disease. And they are. Many studies have found that people who score above 150 do tend to have more physical and mental illnesses (Perkins, 1982; Thoits, 1983). However, the relationship between LCUs and illness, while consistent, is not very strong. Many people who have high scores on the scale do not get sick (Krantz, Grunberg & Baum, 1985). One reason may be the inclusion of positive events in the scale. It doesn't seem likely that getting married (50 points) and getting a new job (36 points) that pays a lot more money (38 points) on the basis of an outstanding achievement (28 points) would make you more susceptible to sickness (even given the total of 152 points). Certainly most of us would be willing to take the chance. In any event, more recent research has demonstrated that the negative changes are far better predictors of health risks (Stewart et al., 1986).

Keep in mind, too, that many people who do not undergo major change in their lives are still exposed to a host of little things that can, and do, go wrong. These *hassles,* it turns out, are better predictors of physical and psychological illness than are major traumas (Kanner et al., 1981; Lazarus, 1984; Zika & Chamberlain, 1987). That is, you're more likely to get sick after a day when the alarm didn't go off on time, the hot water wasn't working, the car wouldn't start, you couldn't find a parking place, and you were late for class.

Thus both life events and, to a greater extent, hassles are predictors of physical problems. But neither of these relationships is perfect. Many people who don't seem to be facing big or even little challenges develop stress-related illnesses. And other people who are experiencing intense challenges have no problems. At work here are the differences among people—differences not only in their vulnerability to stressful situations but also in the ways they cope with it.

Table 10.3
The Social Readjustment Rating Scale

Rank	Event	LCU
1	Death of spouse	100
2	Divorce	73
3	Marital separation	65
4	Jail term	63
5	Death of close family member	63
6	Personal injury or illness	53
7	Marriage	50
8	Fired at work	47
9	Marital reconciliation	45
10	Retirement	45
11	Change in health of family member	44
12	Pregnancy	40
13	Sex difficulties	39
14	Gain of new family member	39
15	Business readjustment	39
16	Change in financial state	38
17	Death of close friend	37

(Continued)

18	Change to different line of work	36
19	Change in number of arguments with spouse	35
20	Mortgage over $10,000	31
21	Foreclosure of mortgage or loan	30
22	Change in responsibilities at work	29
23	Son or daughter leaving home	29
24	Trouble with in-laws	29
25	Outstanding personal achievement	28
26	Wife begins or stops work	26
27	Begin or end school	26
28	Change in living conditions	25
29	Revision of personal habits	24
30	Trouble with boss	23
31	Change in work hours or conditions	20
32	Change in residence	20
33	Change in schools	20
34	Change in recreation	19
35	Change in church activities	19
36	Change in social activities	18
37	Mortgage or loan less than $10,000	17
38	Change in sleeping habits	16
39	Change in number of family get-togethers	15
40	Change in eating habits	15
41	Vacation	13
42	Christmas	12
43	Minor violations of the law	11

Table 10.3
The Social Readjustment Rating Scale (*Continued*)

Source: Holmes & Rahe (1967), pp. 213–218.

Vulnerability to Stress

In the 1950s, two cardiologists, Meyer Friedman and Ray Rosenman (1959), noticed that many victims of heart attacks, especially young men, shared certain personality traits. These people had a strong need for accomplishment, a need to compete with and to be recognized by others. They were constantly pushing themselves to meet self-imposed deadlines and increasingly higher standards of success. And they were constantly frustrated by and angry with others. These high-risk people also tended to speak in a characteristic way: emphatically, loudly, and with explosive, rapid speech (Dembrowski & Costa, 1987). Friedman and Rosenman called these aggressive people **Type A personalities.** (Everyone else was called Type B.) Type A people seemed to be living in a state of chronic arousal that affected their immune system and damaged their circulatory system (Rosenman, 1986). Friedman and Rosenman believed that Type A people create their own stress by defining their world in ways that make it continuously challenging. The result is that they are always trying to maintain themselves in the resistance stage of the GAS.

Although many studies have found that Type A personalities have higher levels of heart disease than Type B personalities (see Brand, 1978, for example),

One of the most important indicators of the Type A personality is the individual's speech. Type A people speak emphatically, loudly, and fast (Dembrowski & Costa, 1987).

Type A personality   A type of personality characterized by a chronic state of arousal.

"I DEAL WITH MY EMOTIONS PERFECTLY.
I SUPPRESS THEM."

others have not found a relationship. This inconsistency has led to a reexamination of the Type A personality. Many people who are ambitious, competitive, and under pressure do not seem to be at higher risk for heart disease. Rather, the crucial characteristics seem to be hostility and anger (Chesney & Rosenman, 1985). People who fly into a rage at the drop of a hat, or those who are chronically angry, are at much higher risk of heart disease (Dembrowski & Costa, 1987).

One link between frequent outbursts of hostility or anger and heart disease may be frequent bursts of autonomic arousal. We know that chronic arousal interferes with the metabolism of fats, raising the level of cholesterol in the body and speeding the buildup of plaque in the artery walls. (*Plaque* is a clump of cholesterol and cellular material that can break loose and clog the arteries. In the heart muscle, this kind of clog causes a heart attack.) Other evidence suggests that interference with the immune system can damage artery walls (Krantz, Baum & Singer, 1983). Finally, chronic arousal may produce chronic high blood pressure, a known risk factor for heart disease.

Most public attention has been directed at the relationship between personality and heart disease, probably because heart disease is the most serious health problem in our society. But current theories don't suggest that the effects of hostility and anger are specific. In fact, the chronic arousal produced by hostility and anger makes us susceptible to all kinds of diseases: asthma, rheumatoid arthritis, headaches, and ulcers (Friedman & Booth-Kewley, 1987).

Other emotions—for example, depression and anxiety—have been linked to heart disease as well (Friedman & Booth-Kewley, 1987). It seems that people who generally experience negative emotions are more susceptible to illness (Watson & Pennebaker, 1989).

It's not surprising that people who are chronically angry develop stress-related symptoms. What's less clear is why they keep getting angry. If anger were beginning to hurt, most people would try to do something about it. But Type A people seem to have another attribute that interferes with their ability to change their emotional habits: they seem to be relatively inattentive to their own bodily states. As a result, they may not notice that they're aroused and tense. And their inattention is even worse when they have work to do because they are especially good at focusing their attention on the job and missing information about what that job is doing to their bodies (Scheier, Carver & Mathews, 1983).

The stress response itself limits our ability to recognize emotions. When stressed, we become much less reflective in our thinking, which in turn tends to focus on specific things so that we also become less aware of our emotions (Pennebaker, 1989).

Although anger-prone personalities seem especially likely to create the stress response and fail to recognize its effects, many of these people do not have unusually frequent health problems. One explanation is that something is protecting these people from the effects of their emotions. It could be good genes. Or it might be certain psychological attributes that moderate the effects of stressful situations.

Resisting Stressful Situations

Some years ago, Norman Cousins, a former editor of the *Saturday Review of Books,* learned that he had an incurable fatal disease. His doctors gave up, but Cousins refused to. Instead, he administered his own therapy: laughter. Every day he spent hours reading humorous books, listening to funny records, and watching funny movies (Cousins, 1979). Within a year, he had no symptoms.

Perhaps Cousins was just very lucky. Or it may be that the "Marx Brothers treatment" actually works, that attitude is a critical component in resisting disease. Certainly research indicates that many people are protected from illness by their attitudes, especially their sense of humor (Nezu, Nezu & Blissett, 1988).

A number of other qualities also seem to confer resistance. Underlying all of these qualities is a feeling of competence with which to deal with the challenges in life.

The Hardy Personality   In this connection, Suzanne Kobasa (1982) described the **hardy personality,** a combination of several traits that seem to protect the individual from the physiological effects of stressful events. Kobasa studied groups of business executives in a large corporation, all of whom had faced high levels of stress over the previous year. In her comparison of those who had contracted stress-related diseases with those who had not, she identified three traits shared by members of the healthy group:

- They were committed to, or highly involved in, what they were doing.
- They felt in control of their lives.
- They believed that change is a normal part of life, not a disruption.

Only the first two traits have proved to be good predictors of resistance to stress (Hull, Van Treuren & Virnelli, 1987). People who are committed to their work and who feel in control of their lives are indeed less susceptible to stress-related illness.

These findings are useful but not especially surprising. We would expect people who feel in control to be less affected by challenging events. In the face of a difficult situation, the feeling of being unable to cope certainly makes it seem worse.

Self-efficacy—your belief that you are capable of achieving what you want to achieve—is a related concept. People with a high degree of self-efficacy do tend to be healthier and happier (Bandura, 1988). But the difference between these people and those who feel helpless does not seem to lie in the way they react to uncontrollable events. When people who ordinarily feel in control find themselves in a situation they can't control, they feel just as unhappy and stressed as do people who generally feel they lack control. When the situation is ambiguous, however, people with a high degree of self-efficacy are much less likely to perceive it as uncontrollable (Rhodewalt & Agustsdottir, 1984). Instead, they assume they can handle it.

Optimism   Psychologists Michael Scheier and Charles Carver (1987) recently suggested that people don't have to feel in control so long as they believe that everything will turn out all right. If we think we can handle our problems ourselves, that's good. But relying on luck or God also works.

To test their theory, Scheier and Carver developed a general measure of *optimism,* the confidence that good things are going to happen. Table 10.4 lists some of the items on this scale. The optimism measure seems to predict good health as effectively as measures of hardy personality or self-efficacy. Similarly, a measure of pessimism predicts poor health, even after a delay of thirty-five years (Peterson, Seligman & Vaillant, 1988)!

Extremely Stressful Situations

When we are talking about major life changes or hassles, it seems that individual traits—our personality and attitudes—make us more or less susceptible to stress and stress-related diseases. But personality and attitudes can't protect us from stress when the challenge we face is an earthquake, a tornado, or a flood.

Hardy personality A type of personality consisting of several traits that seem to protect the individual from stress-related illness.

Self-efficacy Belief in one's ability to achieve goals and exert control in life.

Table 10.4
A Measure of Optimism

1. In uncertain times, I usually expect the best.
2. It's easy for me to relax.[a]
3. If something can go wrong for me, it will.[b]
4. I always look on the bright side of things.
5. I'm always optimistic about my future.
6. I enjoy my friends a lot.[a]
7. It's important for me to keep busy.[a]
8. I hardly ever expect things to go my way.[b]
9. Things never work out the way I expect them to.[b]
10. I don't get upset too easily.[a]
11. I'm a believer in the idea that "every cloud has a silver lining."
12. I rarely count on good things happening to me.[b]

Source: Scheier & Carver 1985, pp. 219–247.
[a]These are filler items which are not scored. They are included to disguise the purpose of the scale.
[b]These items are reversed prior to scoring.

People react to disaster in many different ways. Some get angry, others are terrified, still others are numb. At one time psychologists believed that our reactions to a stress-producing event followed a series of steps or stages. Probably the best-known example is Elisabeth Kubler-Ross's (1969) description of the stages of feeling and thought that people go through when they learn they are dying. Despite the plausibility and popularity of Kubler-Ross's model, research suggests that people's responses vary. In fact, some psychologists have concluded that there is no sequence of responses. Some healthy people never feel intense grief, whereas others continue to feel anger, terror, or numbness for long periods of time (Wortman & Silver, 1989).

Those of us who have been lucky enough to escape traumatic stress often underestimate its effects. We expect an immediate intense reaction, but we don't understand the long-term effects. A sad example is the failure of the civilian population to appreciate the impact of the Vietnam war on those who fought it (Brende & Parson, 1985). The extent of that impact is just now becoming apparent. Combat veterans in general are more likely to be arrested and convicted of crimes than are civilians or noncombat soldiers (Yager, Laufer & Gallops, 1984). And some veterans show evidence of **posttraumatic stress disorder:** recurring bouts of anxiety and depression; headaches, dizziness, and intestinal problems; attention disorders; sexual dysfunction; and difficulty interacting socially. A recent study of men who served in Vietnam and their identical twins found that the soldier twins were three times as likely to show the symptoms of posttraumatic stress disorder (Goldberg, 1990).

The impact of traumatic stress on physical health is also clear. For example, in the year after Mount Saint Helens erupted, showering the countryside with debris and ash, the emergency room of a nearby hospital reported 20 percent more admissions than in previous years (Adams & Adams, 1984). Many studies have also demonstrated that divorce or the death of a spouse reduces immune system function and leads to increased likelihood of disease or death (O'Leary, 1990).

Because their civilian friends and relatives could not imagine the horrors of fighting in the Vietnam war, these vets have sought one another's support in dealing with the stress of that experience.

Coping with Stress

Posttraumatic stress disorder
Recurring bouts of anxiety, depression, and other physiological and social disorders resulting from severe trauma.

Every year, more than 2 million people get divorced, 10 thousand people die in automobile accidents, and 62 million are injured (U.S. Bureau of the Census, 1990). If you aren't one of these people, it's very likely that someone you know and care about is. And that means you have to deal with stress.

As evidence that stress is a serious problem in the world today, consider the growth of the stress management industry in recent years. The goal of stress management is to reduce stress when possible and to teach people to handle it when not possible.

Coping Styles   There are two major ways of coping with stress. One family of strategies focuses on the problem that is creating the stress and seeks ways to change the situation. The other focuses on the emotional feelings generated by the stress (Lazarus & Folkman, 1984).

Of the two, *problem-focused coping* is more effective (Suls & Fletcher, 1985). If you're able to change the circumstances, you can do away with all vestiges of the stress, often permanently. Suppose your job is a source of stress. If you change to a different kind of job, you may have solved the problem.

By contrast, *emotion-focused coping* doesn't do anything about the challenges you face; it simply allows you to endure them more easily. If you can't change jobs, perhaps you can learn to live more comfortably with the job you have. A survey of the ways in which people deal with stress in their lives indicated that the second most popular strategy is simply accepting the stress (Stone & Neale, 1984). In this case, individuals are left with an unpleasant situation, but at least they don't add to the stress by demanding that it be changed. The next four most common coping strategies, in order, were distracting oneself, then trying to think of the situation as not so bad after all, followed by expressing one's feelings (presumably to friends rather than, for example, one's boss), and relaxation. Notice that with the exception of problem-focused coping all the other strategies are emotion-focused.

People tend to choose problem-focused solutions when they think a problem is manageable (McCrae, 1984; Scheier, Weintraub & Carver, 1986). And they tend to choose emotion-focused strategies when they believe the problem itself cannot be resolved. Sometimes emotion-focused coping clears the way for problem-focused coping. Once we've dealt with the stress in a given situation, we may find ourselves better able to focus on the problem (Lazarus & Folkman, 1984).

Stress managers use both types of coping strategies, although, understandably, they place more emphasis on emotion-focused strategies. The individual may well be helped by slowing down or changing jobs, but such coping strategies don't sit well with the corporations that hire stress managers to work with their executives.

Relaxation Techniques   Many emotion-focused techniques for stress management are intended to bring about relaxation. The most "high-tech" of these techniques is **biofeedback.** In Chapter 2 we pointed out that people cannot control their autonomic responses. The problem is not an insufficient number of nerves controlling our autonomic responses. Instead, what seems to be missing is sensory information about what is going on in these organs. Unless we know what is happening in our stomachs, we can't change anything. It's rather like trying to drive a car with the windows covered: we have all the controls necessary to take a trip, but in fact we won't get far before we run ourselves off the road.

To make up for this lack of information, psychologists attach instruments that measure heart rate or muscle tension to lights or loudspeakers, so that people can see or hear information that reflects what is going on inside their bodies. Attached to such a mechanism, the person might hear a tone that increases in pitch as their heart rates increase. With this kind of "feedback" about what is going on in their biological systems (hence the term *biofeedback*), the subjects are able to control their heart rates, the activity in their stomachs, the levels of

We can control bodily responses like heart rate, blood pressure, and muscle tension, if we receive information about our responses from biofeedback instruments.

Biofeedback A procedure that allows control of one's own autonomic responses by providing information about them.

tension in different muscles (Blanchard, 1979), and their general arousal levels (Holroyd & Lazarus, 1982).

Biofeedback is used most successfully in the treatment of tension and migraine headaches (Blanchard et al., 1980). Patients are hooked up to an apparatus that gives them feedback about the tension in the muscles of their forehead. From this feedback, they learn to control that tension—and to relieve their headaches—by relaxing their muscles.

Biofeedback requires lots of expensive machinery, without which the beneficial effects may not continue. But similar levels of relaxation can be achieved through **meditation.** In one form—transcendental meditation—the individual sits in a quiet place, closes his or her eyes, and repeats a comfortable sound silently, over and over again. (A favorite is the syllable *om*.) Meditation significantly reduces arousal responses (Benson & Proctor, 1984), although there is some disagreement about whether its effects are really any different from those of ordinary rest.

Another simple relaxation technique focuses on the muscles (Jacobson, 1938). You lie down comfortably and then concentrate on parts of your body, deliberately tensing and then relaxing your muscles one by one. By systematically working from one end of your body to the other, you can relax each muscle group. With practice, you are able to recognize tension and ease it quickly. Progressive muscle relaxation also seems to produce a psychological calm. This kind of relaxation is used in a behavioral therapy technique called *systematic desensitization,* which is described in Chapter 16.

Exercise   In the last few years, exercise has become an extremely popular stress management technique. People report that running and other forms of strenuous exercise are calming. And physical fitness seems to reduce stress responses (Folkins & Sime, 1981).

Do people feel better when they exercise? Or do people exercise because they feel good to begin with? To determine which comes first, Lisa McCann and David Holmes (1984) randomly assigned depressed people to both exercise and control groups. The exercise group showed significant improvement in mood. This improvement may be a product of improvements in the speed with which the adrenalin response rises and, more important, falls after a challenge (Dienstbier et al., 1987).

Exercise, meditation, and relaxation are techniques that you might try yourself, if you are feeling distressed. Although all of these techniques are used by professionals, you can safely and perhaps effectively try them on your own. They certainly do help some people; and if you try them, at the very least you will experience a calm, pleasant interlude. However, if you find that you continue to be seriously distressed, you should consider seeing a therapist.

Recap

- In a way, the emotional response to a challenging situation is a homeostatic mechanism. It restores the balance disrupted by an emotional situation.

- The emotional situation—the imbalance—is usually short-lived. When it continues, it creates stress.

- There are three stages in the general adaptation syndrome: alarm, resistance, and exhaustion.

- The physiological changes that mark the exhaustion stage of the GAS weaken the immune system, thus increasing susceptibility to disease.

Meditation Any of a wide variety of techniques for focusing attention that produces a calming effect on feelings and the body's activities.

- Stress is a response to an event in the environment, not the event itself.

- Any major life change—even a "good" change—can produce a stress response.

- Hassles are better predictors of physical and psychological illness than are major traumas.

- Research shows that certain personality traits (anger, hostility, feeling in control) and attitudes (optimism, pessimism) make the individual more or less vulnerable to stress and stress-related illness.

- The responses to traumatic stress are both varied and enduring.

- Strategies for coping with stress focus either on the problem that is generating the stress or on the emotion itself.

- Relaxation techniques (biofeedback, meditation, progressive muscle relaxation) and exercise are ways of coping with stress.

Conclusion

Everyone feels strongly about emotions. Sometimes they seem to be the curse of human life. The free expression of anger, for instance, can destroy families and careers. Fear and anxiety often narrow and impoverish some people's lives. Sadness and depression reduce others to gray, dull monotony. But emotions can also bring much delight. The joy of success, the warmth of affection for friends and family, the passion of love, are not just the accompaniments of a good life; they are the very definition of a good life. Since we pride ourselves on our civilized distance from our animal forebears, it is striking that these primitive patterns of action are so central to our satisfaction with our lives.

Emotions seem to play this central role because the actions they compel are not just primitive; they are also exceedingly broad. The basic action tendency of anger is to directly confront challenges. For a baboon, this may consist of physical assault on a rival; and if a human is acting primitively, he or she, too, may punch a rival. But humans are likelier to meet challenges with more sophisticated, civilized forms of response. Instead of a physical assault, we compose letters and memos, persuade colleagues, buy and sell, or whatever the appropriate forms might be. What has changed, then, is the civilization of our means, not our ultimate end. Being civilized, then, does not mean being unemotional. To be civilized is to learn more sophisticated reasons for emotion and more sophisticated ways of enacting emotional patterns.

As our means for achieving emotional goals become more indirect and symbolic, new complexities enter our emotional lives. One such complexity arises when our emotional patterns are too prolonged, too indirect, or too poorly recognized. Then emotional reactions can become, in one sense or another, "inappropriate." In this chapter we have discussed just one kind of inappropriate emotional response—the kind that produces chronic stress. But in Chapter 15, where we discuss abnormal behavior, we spend lots of time on inappropriate emotional responses, since much of the work of clinical psychologists and psychiatrists is devoted to trying to make emotions more appropriate.

Chapter 11   The Origins of Development

The Dream as Self Portrait, David Landis Fick, 1976–1982

11

Gateways Recent research has revealed that newborns possess surprising capacities. Nevertheless, compared to other species, humans at birth consist largely of potential. How that potential becomes reality through the processes of development is the subject of this and the next chapter.

A central question about human capacities is how much they owe to the facts of biology—to nature—and how much they owe to the influence of environment—to nurture. In exploring this question, developmental psychologists study a vast range of behaviors examined in other chapters of this book. For example, we have already noted the nature/nurture issue in Chapter 4 on perception, in explaining the difference between the nativist perspective (emphasizing biological makeup) and the empiricist view (emphasizing the environment). The issue reappears in Chapter 6 on learning and Chapter 8 on thought and language. In Chapter 14 we discuss developmental factors in shaping the individual personality and, in Chapter 15, the development of abnormal behaviors.

During the time that my wife and I were awaiting our first child, we were given a beautiful orange kitten. The owner was a woman we met on the street who was taking the kitten to the animal shelter. When we stopped to admire it, she offered it to us. The kitten yowled as the woman passed it to me, and I had to hold it firmly for fear it would bolt and run out into traffic. Quickly, I zippered it into the pouch of my parka where it soon settled down and went to sleep. An hour later, we had it home.

For a while, that kitten was our child and we lavished on it all of the affection that we were preparing to lavish on our new baby. But soon we realized that there was something terribly wrong. The kitten walked strangely and seemed moody and unreliable. Sadly, we agreed that with a new baby coming, we couldn't risk having a sick cat in the house. So the day that my wife went to the hospital to have the baby, I took the beautiful orange kitten to the Animal Shelter and left it.

Three days later, my wife and Becky, our new daughter, came home from the hospital. Feeling a bit woozy after the ride, my wife asked me to come around to her side of the car and take the baby. I took Becky into my hands hesitantly. How different it was holding a baby than it was holding a cat! Animals somehow seem to help you hold them. Holding Becky was like trying to hug a pile of oranges. She seemed barely able to hold herself together, much less help me hold her. Nor was she pleased to be transferred to my awkward grasp. Her face turned a deep red and she began to screech.

I carried her into the house and put her in the cradle in the tiny nursery we had prepared. My wife fussed with her a bit—tried to feed her, covered her up, gave her a pacifier, rocked the cradle for a time, but she was inconsolable. So finally we went and sat in the living room and waited. In time, Becky's crying became less insistent and then suddenly ceased. Had she choked on her pacifier or smothered under her blankets? We crept to the nursery door.

Becky lay face down on the crisp new sheets, her legs gathered under her and her diapered bottom cocked up into the air. The wringled fist of her right hand was pressed to her face. Her eyes were closed so tightly that she seemed to be squinting, as if she were trying hard to remember a distant memory. Where the covers bridged her back, they rose and fell, ever so slightly in a regular rhythm. She was sound asleep.

My wife pulled the nursery door gently shut, and we stood for a moment outside it looking at each other. There was no shelter to which we could take *this* kitten. Our lives were changed forever.

The Process of and Influences on Development: The Debate

Development is the predictable sequence of physical and psychological changes that occur as we age. When we say that people develop, we mean that they change in expected ways as they grow older. "My roommate's got the sophomore blues," "My son's reached the terrible twos," "My grandparents are

Development The regular sequence of physical and psychological changes that we pass through as we age.

297

at the stage of life when they need somebody to look after them a bit"—all of these are statements about development.

Development is such an important part of psychology that we devote two chapters to it. In this chapter we focus on the earliest period of development, beginning before birth and continuing through infancy. In Chapter 12 we focus on development in childhood, adolescence, and adulthood.

The Issues

When psychologists talk about development—throughout the life cycle—two important issues often come up. One has to do with the nature of change as we develop; the other, with the relative influence of heredity and the environment on our development.

Continuity Versus Discontinuity Think about your development since childhood. Are you a completely different person from the ten-year-old "you"? Do you think that your behavior and your thinking abruptly changed when you became a teenager? An adult? Or do you think that you've changed gradually, in subtle ways, and that you're still essentially the same person you were when you were ten?

How do behavior and experience change throughout life? Are there abrupt changes in life when people suddenly adopt the behaviors and attitudes typical of the next phase? Are there periods of stability in our lives, **stages** in which behavior and experience change very little? Are these stages separated by **transitions,** periods of rapid psychological and physical growth in which behavior and experience change suddenly? Are there times in our lives—**sensitive (or critical) periods**—in which certain events have to occur and others must be avoided if we are to develop "normally"?

Psychologists who answer "no" to these questions are called *continuity theorists*. They believe that the same basic processes go on throughout development. Psychologists who answer "yes" are called *discontinuity* or *stage theorists.* They believe that essentially different psychological processes are at work at different times.

Before we continue, a brief caution seems in order. Both stage theorists and continuity theorists recognize and discuss the ages at which developmental events occur. In this chapter we will often describe the average age at which some ability develops. However, you should always keep in mind the fact that these timetables are *only* approximate; that is, healthy children often develop more or less rapidly, and sometimes even reach developmental milestones in a different order than their age peers.

Heredity Versus Environment Although psychologists agree that development is driven by the interplay between genetic and environmental influences, they disagree about the relative importance of these influences. Hereditary influences—what we call *nature*—are a product of the genes passed from parents to offspring. Environmental influences, or *nurture,* stem from the events experienced by those offspring.

Nativism is the theory that genetic factors play the larger role in development. According to nativists, most of the information needed to form a complete human being is available in our genes at conception. The environment simply feeds and shelters us. Nativists attribute the changes that take place during development to **maturation,** developmental processes dictated by our individual biological inheritances.

Empiricism stresses the role of the environment in development. According to empiricists, people are shaped by their families, societies, and the physical environments. Heredity simply gives us the raw materials to work with.

Stage A period in which behavior and experience change very little.

Transition A period in which behavior and experience change abruptly.

Sensitive period A time of special sensitivity in the development of any organism in which certain events must occur or others must be avoided in order for the individual to develop normally.

Maturation The developmental processes that are determined by the individual's biological inheritance.

A Matter of Philosophy

This ongoing debate in developmental psychology can be traced back to a philosophical difference between two great thinkers of the seventeenth and eighteenth centuries. English philosopher John Locke (1632–1704) took a continuity-empiricist position. He thought of development as a gradual process through which the growing individual gains increasing knowledge and experience. Locke described the young child as a *tabula rasa,* a "blank slate" on which the child's parents and teachers must write. And he argued that children should be trained as soon as possible to think and behave like adults.

The discontinuity-nativist position was taken by the French philosopher Jean-Jacques Rousseau (1712–1778). He described development as a process in which the individual's thinking and behavior change profoundly from period to period. According to Rousseau, children are fundamentally different from adults; and trying to teach them to think or behave like adults is to abuse their special nature. Young children have distinct needs and special talents to which their parents and teachers must defer (Grimsley, 1967).

The Stance of Early Psychologists

These different philosophies influenced the thinking of early psychologists. Some took positions in the Lockean tradition. For instance, John Watson, a behaviorist, argued that parents should not encourage their children to do anything that they do not expect them to do for the rest of their lives. In a child-rearing manual written in 1928, Watson cautioned his readers not to cater to their children lest they carry childhood habits and dependencies into adulthood. Watson's thinking probably had enormous influence on how your grandparents were raised (see Figure 11.1).

John Watson
Thumb sucking . . . is an infantile type of reaction which when carried over beyond the age of infancy ends in a pernicious habit almost impossible to break. Indeed, if carried through adolescence in the modified form of nail-biting, cuticle-picking or finger-picking, it becomes practically impossible to break . . .

How can we correct thumb sucking? The answer is, *cure it during the first few days of infancy.* Watch the baby carefully the first few days. Keep the hands away from the mouth as often as you are near the baby in its waking moments. And always, when you put it into its crib for sleep, see that the hands are tucked inside the covers. (Watson, 1928, pp. 138-139)

Margaret Ribble
During the first six months, [sucking] is the infant's most gratifying and all absorbing activity . . . Sucking reaches a maximum intensity about the fourth month of life, and, if it has been fully and agreeably exercised up to this time, its urgency begins to diminish somewhat as the child begins to vocalize, to bite, and to grasp with his hands. (Ribble, 1943/1965, pp. 24-25)

**Figure 11.1
Advice on Thumbsucking**

Psychologists in the traditions of Locke and Rousseau were not shy about offering advice on child-rearing. Watson, the father of behaviorism, assumed that any childish craving had to be nipped in the bud. Ribble, a psychoanalyst, argued that failing to gratify infant needs could lead to unhappy outcomes in childhood and adulthood.

Others took a position more like that of Rousseau. G. Stanley Hall (1904), one of the founders of the American Psychological Association, believed that as we develop we go through stages that reenact the stages of human evolution. Although the relationship to evolution was soon discredited, Hall's work stimulated vigorous study of the stages of development. Hall, Arnold Gesell, and other psychologists formed the child study movement, which devoted itself to charting the milestones of infant and child development. Hall (1904) wrote the first scientific work that described adolescence as a stage of development. And Gesell (1928) wrote a description of child development that identified major stages and indicated when each of these stages could be expected to begin and end.

Another discontinuity theorist with a profound influence on developmental psychology was Sigmund Freud. From his work with patients around the turn of the century, Freud (1938/1900–1914) concluded that every child passes through four stages on the way to adulthood. Freud called these periods of development *psychosexual stages* because during each stage the child fixates on pleasure received from stimulating some part of the body. For example, in the first of these stages, the oral stage, the infant finds gratification in tasting and sucking things. According to Freud, children who are not allowed to gratify the impulses characteristic of these early stages are more likely to display infantile behavior in adulthood. (Freud's stages are described in Chapter 14 on personality.)

Freud's theories had enormous influence on psychologist Margaret Ribble. In her book *The Rights of Infants* (1943/1965), she urged her readers to indulge the special needs of infants for sucking, cuddling, and other forms of comfort.

Here and in Chapter 12 we talk about the work of three other discontinuity theorists: Jean Piaget, who studied cognitive development in infants and children; Lawrence Kohlberg, who studied the development of moral thinking in children and adolescents; and Erik Erikson, who studied the stages of human social development. (Erikson's theory is covered in more detail in the following chapter.)

The Debate Today

Important contributions are still being made to the continuity/discontinuity and nature/nurture debate (Collins & Gunnar, 1990). But the positions taken by modern developmental psychologists are much more subtle than those staked out by Watson and Hall.

Today most psychologists believe that certain developmental processes are continuous or discontinuous depending on how you look at them. For example, many parents' handbooks say that young children cannot be toilet trained until they reach their third year, at which time toilet training is accomplished relatively quickly. So toilet training is an excellent example of a discontinuous process. But underlying this discontinuous process is the continuous development of the child's nervous system. Without this development, the child could not control the muscles of the bowel and bladder in the third year.

We find that this compromise view applies to most issues in the nature/nurture debate. Here most psychologists agree that development is determined not by genes *or* the environment but by genes *and* the environment. For instance, in Chapter 8 we saw that nature (heredity) determines when we learn a language and determines much of the structure of that language (Lenneberg, 1967); but the environment determines which language we are likely to speak, with which accent, and what we are likely to say.

Recap

- Development is the predictable series of physical and psychological changes we go through as we age.

- Theorists differ about whether development is smooth and continuous, or proceeds by a series of "jumps" from one stage to another.

- Theorists also differ about the relative importance of heredity and environment.

- Modern theorists tend to adopt compromises in both controversies, assuming that whether development follows stages or is continuous depends on what one observes. They also assume that every characteristic of the adult is a product of both heredity and environment.

The Genetic Origins of Development

Development begins with conception, the moment when the father's sperm penetrates the mother's ovum and their genetic material is combined. Approximately once a month, an ovum cell matures in one of the female's two ovaries and makes its way down the fallopian tube toward the uterus, a muscular organ deep within the female's body. Sperm cells mature in the male's testicles and, after sexual intercourse, millions of them travel upward through the female's cervix and uterus toward the fallopian tubes. When a single sperm encounters an ovum, the sperm's genetic material is drawn into the ovum's nucleus where it combines with the genetic material of the ovum to produce a new individual.

Forming the Genotype

The **traits** a child inherits from his or her parents are determined at the moment of conception. Controlling every cell in the parents' bodies are minute strands of genetic material called **chromosomes.** The chromosomes are arranged in twenty-three pairs in the nucleus of each cell, as illustrated in Figure 11.2. One of the chromosomes in each pair carries genetic information from the individual's father; the other, information from the individual's mother.

One pair of chromosomes is particularly important because it determines sex. Two kinds of chromosomes can occur in this pair: a longer chromosome, called the X *chromosome,* and a shorter chromosome, called the Y *chromosome.* If you have two X chromosomes, you are female; if you have an X chromosome and a Y chromosome, you are male.

In part, each chromosome consists of an enormous complex molecule called **deoxyribonucleic acid (DNA). Genes,** the basic units of heredity, are segments of the DNA molecule. The particular pattern of your genes constitutes your **genotype,** your genetic makeup. Each gene in your genotype is related to an inherited trait, such as the color of your eyes or your temperament. The expression of your genotype, of all your traits, is called your **phenotype.**

Trait Any observable physical or behavioral characteristic of an individual.

Chromosome A strand of genetic material found in the nucleus of every cell.

Deoxyribonucleic acid (DNA) The large complex molecules that form the chromosomes.

Gene The basic unit of heredity that guides the physical processes of development of the organism.

Genotype The individual's genetic makeup.

Phenotype The actual traits displayed by an individual; how a genotype is expressed in a particular environment.

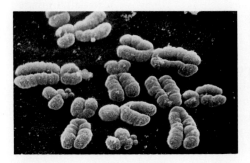
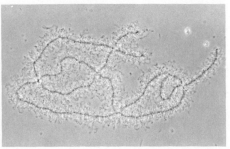

**Figure 11.2
Chromosomes**

Chromosomes are so small that these spectacular pictures were made with beams of electrons. In the left-hand photo, the chromosomes are shown bunched up and lying side by side, as they are when a cell is dividing. In the right-hand photo, they are shown as they are when the cell is functioning—as long thin chains.

You've probably heard people talk about "genes for" a particular trait: a gene for intelligence or a gene for hair color, for example. But genes do not translate into traits as simply as our way of talking about them suggests. Each gene is a template—a kind of blueprint—for a specific protein. DNA directs the manufacture of proteins. And it is these proteins that direct the activities of developing cells.

Some traits are determined by a single gene. For instance, a single gene determines your hairline (see Figure 11.3); another determines whether you can roll your tongue. But most of the traits that psychologists study—temperament, personality, intelligence—are affected by many genes.

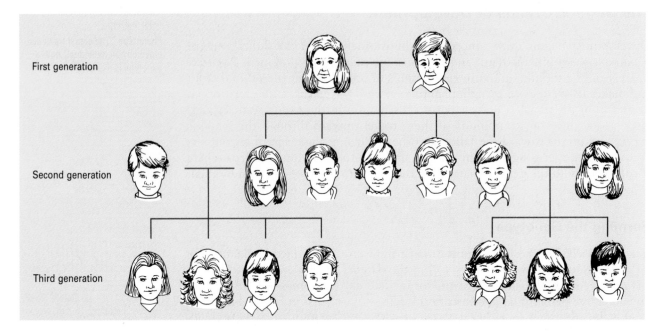

First generation

Second generation

Third generation

Figure 11.3
The Widow's Peak Trait

Your hairline is the product of a single gene. Notice that parents with widow's peaks can have children with or without them. But if neither parent has a widow's peak, then none of the children will have one.

When the ovum and the sperm unite, genes from both parents combine to form the genotype of the offspring. Normally, each offspring receives a unique genotype from his or her parents, because every pairing of ovum and sperm from the parents offers a specific selection of all the genes they carry.

The exception is the case of **identical twins.** Here the fertilized egg, or *zygote,* splits immediately after fertilization. Because identical twins come from the same sperm and the same ovum, they share the exact same genes. **Fraternal twins,** on the other hand, develop when two separate ova are fertilized by two separate sperm at the same time. Although fraternal twins are born together, like ordinary siblings they share only half their genes by descent. Figure 11.4 shows how the two types of twins receive their genotype.

Twins and Twin Studies

Identical twins   Two individuals with exactly the same genotype.

Fraternal twins   Two individuals conceived and born at the same time who do not share the same genotype.

Studies of twins give us the perfect opportunity to disentangle genetic and environmental influences on development. One method compares the traits of identical and fraternal twin pairs. Because identical twins are genetically more similar, the greater similarities we find between them suggest an important role for genes in controlling behavior. For example, the data summarized in Table

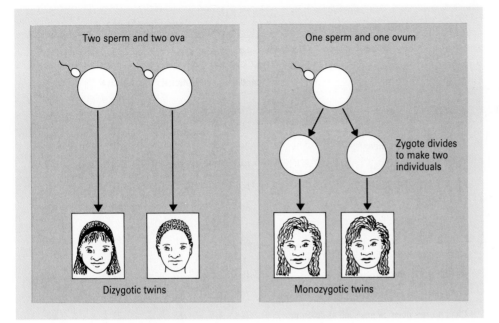

Figure 11.4
Monozygotic and Dizygotic Twins

Identical, or monozygotic, twins are formed when a single egg splits just after fertilization. Fraternal, or dizygotic, twins are formed when two eggs are fertilized by two different sperm.

11.1 suggest that a child's emotionality and activity level are substantially affected by his or her genetic endowment. In contrast, the sociability or impulsivity of the child seems much less determined by heredity. The table presents correlation coefficients that indicate similarity between the twins. The larger the number, the greater the similarity between the twins.

But this inference may be hasty. Remember that identical twins not only share the same genes, but they may also share more similar environments than fraternal twins. Therefore, their similarity could reflect the sameness of their environments. If we are to separate the effects of heredity and environment, then, the best comparison is one between sets of identical twins who've been raised in the same household and sets of identical twins who've been raised in different households. The similarities found under these conditions suggest that heredity is at work, while the differences point to the environment. Identical twins reared apart are remarkably similar on a wide range of temperamental variables, among them adaptability, dominance, assertiveness, self-confidence, conformity, expressiveness, and anxiety (Bouchard, 1984; Buss, Plomin & Willerman, 1973; Rose et al., 1988).

But even these twin studies do not conclusively prove that heredity has an overwhelming influence on human psychology (Hoffman, 1985). Environmental factors may still be at work as well. For example, identical twins who've been raised apart may be alike because they were placed in similar households. It's also possible that the genetic factors that determine similarities may work through the environment. In other words, adult twins who were separated at birth may have the same temperament because, as children, they elicited similar behavior from their caregivers. Finally, we must recognize that identical twins reared apart really do differ from one another in a great many respects, and that each of these differences suggests the importance of environmental variables.

Despite these limitations, studies of identical twins are a powerful tool in the effort to understand the contribution that heredity makes to development. Indeed, much of what we will say in these chapters about the influence of genes on intelligence, personality, and mental illness comes from the study of twins (Scarr & Weinberg, 1983).

Although raised apart, these two identical twins display many similarities in temperament and in the details of their lives. Of course, they also display many differences (Holden, 1980a; Holden 1980b).

Table 11.1
A Comparison of Identical and Fraternal Twins on Several Temperamental Variables

| | Correlations Among | | | |
| | Male Twin Pairs | | Female Twin Pairs | |
Tract	Identical	Fraternal	Identical	Fraternal
Emotionality				
Child cries easily.	.56	.10	.47	.23
Child has a quick temper.	.34	.10	.40	.70
Child gets upset quickly.	.64	.10	.66	.00
Child is easily frightened.	.58	.11	.70	.00
Child is easygoing or happy-go-lucky.	.46	.00	.38	.00
Activity				
Child is off and running as soon as he wakes up in the morning.	.88	.41	.86	.00
Child is always on the go.	.48	.02	.72	.01
Child cannot sit still long.	.76	.25	.65	.27
Child prefers quiet games such as coloring or block play to more active games.	.77	.00	.21	.03
Child fidgets at meals and similar occasions.	.67	.38	.68	.31
Sociability				
Child makes friends easily.	.74	.26	.47	.00
Child likes to be with others.	.61	.27	.29	.05
Child tends to be shy.	.57	.10	.51	.00
Child is independent.	.58	.25	.44	.24
Child prefers to play by himself rather than with others.	.55	.10	.73	.46
Impulsivity				
Learning self-control is difficult for the child.	.75	.55	.83	.69
Child tends to be impulsive.	.81	.00	.68	.39
Child gets bored easily.	.83	.13	.49	.59
Child learns to resist temptation easily.	.72	.35	.70	.52
Child goes from toy to toy quickly.	.82	.44	.83	.62

Source: A.H. Buss, R. Plomin & L. Willerman, "The Inheritance of Temperaments," *Journal of Personality, 41.* Copyright 1973, Duke University Press. Reprinted by permission of the publisher.

Recap

- Development begins at conception.

- The traits that children inherit from their parents are determined at the moment of conception.

- Chromosomes are arranged in twenty-three pairs in the nucleus of every cell in the body. They carry genetic information from the individual's mother and father.

- The genotype is the collection of all the individual's genes; the phenotype is the collection of all the individual's traits.

- Each gene is a blueprint for a specific protein. DNA directs the manufacture of proteins. And the proteins direct the activities of developing cells.

- Identical twins, because they develop from the same fertilized egg, share the same genotype. Fraternal twins, like other siblings, do not.

- Studies of identical twins help us identify the contribution of heredity to development.

The Prenatal Period: Conception to Birth

The thirty-eight weeks between conception and birth are called the **prenatal period.** During this time, the egg develops from a single cell, barely the size of the point of a pin, into a baby, ready to perceive, interact with, and even manipulate the world.

The Phases of Prenatal Development

The prenatal period is usually divided into three phases: the germinal phase, the embryonic phase, and the fetal phase.

The Germinal Phase   The **germinal phase** begins when the egg is fertilized in the Fallopian tubes. For several days after conception, the egg continues to move toward the uterus. As it moves, the cells of the zygote begin to multiply. Roughly seven days after conception, the zygote—now a cluster of about one hundred cells—begins to burrow into the wall of the uterus. Over the next week, tiny rootlike structures reach into the blood vessels in the uterine wall, and the developing zygote begins to draw nutrition from the mother. Implantation marks the end of the germinal phase.

The Embryonic Phase   In the **embryonic phase,** the placenta begins to form and the basic body organs start to develop. During this phase, which lasts about six weeks, the zygote is called an **embryo.**

The **placenta** is the link between mother and developing embryo. It is the structure through which nutrients and oxygen are delivered to the embryo and wastes are removed (see Figure 11.5). It also secretes estrogens and progesterone, hormones that are crucial to maintaining pregnancy.

Throughout the embryonic phase, the limbs, heart, lungs, and other internal organs begin to develop. During this period, the embryo is particularly vulnerable to environmental influences. About a third of all conceptions end in spontaneous abortions, even in healthy, well nourished women (Wilcox et al., 1988). Of these, only 60 percent are caused by genetic abnormalities in the embryo. The rest are caused by environmental factors (Rosenblith & Sims-Knight, 1985). Not all embryos with defects are aborted, however. More than 6 percent of babies are born with defects, and birth defects are responsible for a quarter of infant deaths (Centers for Disease Control, 1989).

Many birth defects are caused by chemicals the mother ingested or by infections she contracted during the child's embryonic phase (Shapiro, Ross & Levine, 1965). Because of the embryo's vulnerability, doctors suspect that defects may be produced by any biologically active chemical that enters the mother's body during pregnancy, particularly during the embryonic phase. A substance that causes physical defects in the embryo is called a **teratogen.** Among the growing list of identified teratogens are alcohol, tobacco, tranquilizers, and

Prenatal period The period of development between conception and birth.

Germinal phase The period of development from conception to the egg's implantation in the uterus.

Embryonic phase The period following implantation, in which the placenta forms and the basic body organs develop.

Embryo The developing human at two to eight weeks following conception.

Placenta The structure through which nutrients and oxygen are delivered to the embryo and wastes are removed.

Teratogen A substance that produces physical defects in the embryo.

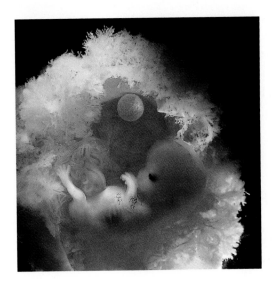

Figure 11.5
The Placenta

The bulk of the placenta develops from a layer of tissue in the uterine wall. The umbilical cord connects the embryo to the placenta.

antihistamines (Holbreich, 1982). Recently Accutane, an anti-acne drug, was found to cause severe birth defects in the children of women who took it, even briefly, during pregnancy (Raymond, 1989). Also implicated in birth defects are viruses that cause rubella, chicken pox, herpes, and other common diseases. Not only can babies be damaged by their mothers' diseases, they can also be infected by them. Some diseases, such as syphilis and AIDS, and some addictions, such as to heroin, can be transmitted from the mother to the developing embryo.

The Fetal Phase   Around eight weeks after conception, the embryo's internal organs are basically developed and many—the heart, the kidneys, and the liver, for example—are beginning to function. At this point, the embryo is called a **fetus,** and the **fetal phase** begins.

The fetus is somewhat less sensitive to harmful chemicals than the embryo, but events during the fetal phase can determine the infant's health at birth. On the one hand, antibodies pass from the mother to the fetus, preparing it to resist the bacteria and viruses it will meet outside the womb. On the other hand, chronic maternal stress, alcohol, tobacco, and heroin have all been shown to seriously diminish the vitality of the fetus and the health of the newborn (Brackbill, McManus & Woodward, 1985).

During the fetal period, we begin to see rudimentary forms of behavior. The fetus starts to move around and to respond to events in its environment. As early as twenty weeks, the mother feels the movements, as the fetus shifts in the uterus. Research with animals suggests that this movement is a form of exercise required by the nervous system and muscles for normal development (Gottlieb, 1976). By thirty weeks, the fetus begins to respond to loud or unusual noises in its mother's environment with strong kicks or lurches.

Not only does the fetus behave; it may also be capable of learning in the final weeks before birth and then remembering what it has learned after it is born. Anthony DeCasper and his colleagues have shown that newborns prefer their mother's voice to a male voice or even that of another female (DeCasper & Fifer, 1980). Even more dramatically, they prefer familiar stories to unfamiliar ones. DeCasper had pregnant women repeatedly read aloud one of three stories (each with a markedly different cadence) during the last months of their pregnancy. Soon after the infants were born, they demonstrated a preference for the story that had been read to them while they were still in their mother's uterus (DeCasper & Spence, 1986).

Fetus   The developing human from about eight weeks after conception to birth.

Fetal phase   The last period of prenatal development—from about eight weeks after conception to birth.

Recap

- The prenatal period—the thirty-eight weeks between conception and birth—is divided into three phases.

- During the germinal phase, which lasts about two weeks, the fertilized egg divides and multiplies as it moves into the uterus.

- The germinal phase ends when the zygote is implanted on the uterine wall.

- During the embryonic phase, which lasts about six weeks, the placenta forms and the major organ systems begin to develop and function.

- The embryo is especially vulnerable to teratogens, substances that cause physical defects.

- During the fetal phase, which lasts about thirty weeks, we see the first signs of behavior.

- In the weeks before birth, the fetus is capable not only of responding to sounds in its mother's environment but also of distinguishing among those sounds.

Infancy

In many ways the human infant is born "too early." Compared with the newborn of other species, the human newborn, or **neonate,** is a remarkably primitive creature. Within a few hours of birth, a young deer is running beside its mother. The human infant does not even begin to walk for a year, and it cannot keep up with a running adult for several years.

The immaturity of the human infant seems to be a product of the conflict in human evolution between the way we walk and the size of our brains. Because human beings walk upright, their pelvises need to be narrow: a wide pelvis greatly diminishes the muscular efficiency of walking upright. However, a narrow pelvis means that the birth canal must also be relatively narrow. At the same time, the human brain is relatively large, which means that the birth canal must be large enough to accommodate the infant's skull. The "compromise" in human evolution, then, has been to bear the infant at a particularly early stage of development, long before the skull has expanded or the brain is fully operational (Leakey & Lewin, 1977).

Yet despite their immaturity, neonates have some very special skills that help them adapt to the external environment. Among those skills are the ability to take in food and to perceive, attract, and interact with their caregivers.

Neonatal Reflexes

The neonate's brain is not well developed. In the cerebral cortex, the neurons are small and largely unconnected. And the nerve cells throughout the central nervous system are almost totally unmyelinated. Remember that myelin, the fatty substance that coats the axons of nerve cells, speeds the transfer of nerve impulses. In the absence of myelin, nerve impulses travel much more slowly.

As a consequence, newborns are incapable of the precise, coordinated actions that even very young children can perform. Their movements are random and not very effective.

Neonate An infant through the first month of life.

Despite the primitive state of the cortex, the neonate displays a variety of simple behavior patterns, called **neonatal reflexes** (see Figure 11.6). These reflexes help the infant survive.

Certain neonatal reflexes help the infant locate food and eat it. When you stroke a baby's cheek, the baby's head turns to meet the touch. This *rooting reflex* brings the infant's lips into contact with breast or bottle. Once contact with the nipple is made, the *sucking reflex* takes over.

Other reflexes seem to be protective in function. The *grasping reflex* allows infants to lock their fingers around anything that's small enough to grasp. The *Moro reflex* is a response to the sensation of falling. When unsupported, neonates fling their arms and legs outward, open their hands and spread their fingers, and then immediately close their fists and rapidly draw their hands together toward the body—motions that help the caregiver gather the infant up (Prechtl, 1982).

Although these patterns of behavior are vital to the infant's survival, they are very primitive compared to the infant's capabilities in just a few months' time. And most of these early behavior patterns disappear after the first few months of life.

Figure 11.6
Neonatal Reflexes

Infants are born with a number of reflexes, two of which are shown here. When a baby feels as if she's falling, she spreads her arms and legs and fingers. This is the Moro reflex (left). The sucking reflex (right) is a baby's lifeline to the world.

 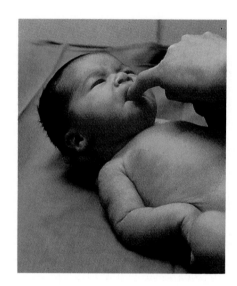

Physical Development

In the first eighteen months of life, the infant gains close to 20 pounds and adds about 10 inches in height. This dramatic physical growth is accompanied by explosive development in the central nervous system.

That development moves outward, from the head and body toward the hands and feet. That is, the infant makes motions first with his arms and legs, then with his hands and feet, before he is able to coordinate movement in his fingers. For example, a six-month-old baby can palm a teething bisquit and press it against his mouth. By a year, he can use a scissor grip to pick up a raisin from a highchair tray, pinning the raisin between the sides of his thumb and forefinger. Only at two years, can he pick the raisin up between the tips of his thumb and forefinger, as we adults would (Rosenblilth & Sims-Knight, 1985) (see Figure 11.7).

Locomotion also develops during the first year. It begins at around three months as a sort of directed wiggling. Placed on a mat with a toy, the infant wiggles toward the toy. At about five months, the infant can remain seated if placed in a sitting position; and at seven months, he can reach a sitting position himself. Soon after that, at around eight months, most infants begin to crawl. And at one year, most begin to walk.

Neonatal reflexes   Patterns of autonomic behavior that are present at birth.

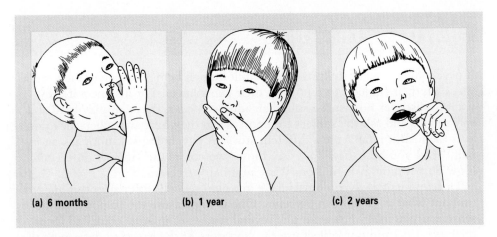

Figure 11.7
Development of Infant's Grip

The infant's grip gradually improves from a palm grip to a precise finger grip over the first two years of life.

(a) 6 months   (b) 1 year   (c) 2 years

The Development of Perception

When we begin to examine infants' perceptual abilities at any stage, we discover a confusing mix of primitive and well-developed characteristics.

Neonatal Perception   Neonatal reflexes reveal excellent sensitivity to touch, especially near the hands and mouth. And we know that the ability to distinguish smells and tastes in foods is developed at birth (Steiner, 1977). Infants react positively or negatively to infant formula to which various flavorants or odorants have been added. For instance, day-old infants will suck more rapidly for formula to which sugar has been added than for plain formula, thereby demonstrating their ability to detect the presence of the sugar.

Hearing, too, is well developed at birth, and it appears to be the newborn's dominant sense (Lewkowicz, 1988). Newborns demonstrate that they can localize sounds by turning their heads to look for the source of a voice. They can recognize familiar voices, and can distinguish the recorded sound of their own crying from that of other newborns (Martin & Clark, 1982). But they are not able to recognize their own image in a mirror for more than a year.

Newborns are able to fix their eyes on objects and follow an object as it moves side to side. And, as Figure 11.8 illustrates, they actually appear to examine objects, concentrating on certain features such as edges or corners. But their visual acuity, the degree of detail in their visual image, is very poor. If newborns were adults, they would be legally blind. They see at 20 feet only about as well as an adult with good vision sees at 200 feet. In fact, a month-old infant cannot recognize her own mother by sight (Bigelow, 1977).

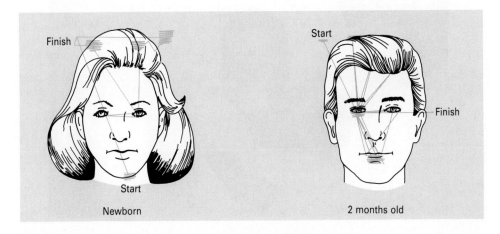

Finish
Start
Start
Finish
Newborn
2 months old

Source: Cohen & Salapatek, 1975.

Figure 11.8
Patterns of Eye Movements in Infants

When newborn infants look at the faces of their caretakers, they focus on the edges of the face. The lines in the left-hand drawing show what the newborn is looking at; the dense zig-zags are places where the newborn paused to focus. Notice that only two months later the infant has shifted his focus to the caretaker's eyes and mouth (right-hand drawing).

How Do We Know That?

If psychologists want to know what adult human beings perceive, they can always ask their subjects to report on their experiences. For instance, if they want to discover how soft a sound an adult can hear, they can play loud and soft sounds and ask the subject to report when they hear and when they don't hear them. But infants are a different story. A psychologist cannot ask an infant, "Did you hear that?" or "Are those two colors the same or different?" How do psychologists find out what an infant perceives?

Developmental psychologists have invented several different techniques to find out what an infant can perceive. One is to measure the response of the sensory organ itself. For example, several studies of infants' ability to focus their eyes on a moving object use the curvature of the lenses to determine the degree of accommodation (Banks, 1982; Haynes, White & Held, 1965; Aslin, 1987). These studies found that accommodation is absent at birth but develops rapidly during the first three months of life. (Recall from Chapter 3 that accommodation is the change in shape that takes place in the eye's lens as a person focuses an object that is moving closer or farther away.)

Another technique focuses on infants' perceptual preferences and thus involves a test of preferential looking, preferential hearing, or even preferential tasting. The basic technique is to offer the infant two stimuli and see which it looks at, listens to, or tastes longer. One general preference that infants have is for new stimuli. For example, infants usually look at a novel stimulus for a longer time than they look at a familiar one. This preference eventually habituates: that is, if the novel stimulus is presented repeatedly, the novelty wears off and the infant stops looking at it (Salapatek & Cohen, 1987).

Some researchers have used infants' fascination with the unfamiliar to determine their concepts of the world. For example, a researcher might show an infant a series of pictures of dogs. Once the infant stops looking at the pictures, the researcher displays a picture of a cat. If looking time increases again, the researcher can assume that the infant has a concept of dogs distinct from his concept of cats.

Some methods for finding out what infants (even newborns) perceive make use of instrumental conditioning (Kuhl, 1987). One, the high-amplitude sucking (HAS) technique, has been widely used to test whether infants can hear differences between speech sounds before they begin to speak themselves or to

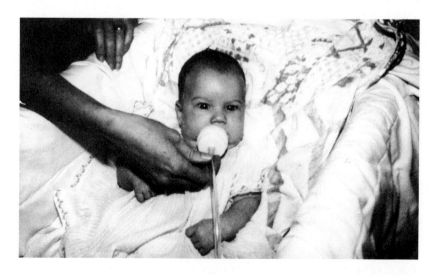

(Continued on next page)

understand speech (Jusczyk, 1985). The infant is given a pacifier that's been wired so that strong sucks produce a recording of a particular speech sound. When the infant has habituated to this speech sound (measured by a decrease in the quantity of high-amplitude sucking), a new sound is presented. If the infant responds to this new sound with an increase in high-amplitude sucking, we can conclude that the infant can discriminate the new sound from the old.

A variation on this technique was used by DeCasper and Spence (1986) in their study described earlier. They showed that newborns can discriminate stories that were read to them a few weeks before they were born from other similar stories.

Another technique, the head turning (HT) technique, is used with older infants (Kuhl, 1985). Here the infant sits on a parent's lap, the experimenter sits to the infant's right, and a reinforcing stimulus—let's say a toy bear tapping a drum—is placed on the infant's left. The infant is presented with a sequence of sounds and is taught that, whenever a new sound occurs, turning his head to the left will activate the bear. For example, the infant might be presented with a sequence of syllables beginning with the *p* sound. In this sequence, the researcher might insert a syllable that begins with a *b* sound. If the infant turns his head when he hears the *b* sound, we can conclude that the infant perceives the *b* sound as a new and different sound.

Using the head turning technique, experimenters have demonstrated that infants are able to distinguish more speech sounds at six months than at one year. In fact, during the second six months of life, infants actually *lose* the ability to discriminate speech sounds that are not a part of the language spoken around them (Werker & Tees, 1984).

Each of these techniques has its drawbacks for revealing whether infants perceive a given stimulus or not (Banks & Dannemiller, 1987). Direct measurement of the sensory apparatus yields an ambiguous positive result. Although such measurement shows that the sense organ is responding to a stimulus, it does not necessarily show that the infant is perceiving the stimulus—that sensory information is reaching the brain and being processed there.

Preference tests and methods that rely on habituation and conditioning give ambiguous negative results because they measure only what infants are interested in, not necessarily what they could perceive if they were interested. So an infant may fail to show a preference because the differences between the stimuli are not interesting, not because they are imperceptible.

This is not a novel problem. Any measure of any psychological variable has both strengths and weaknesses. And the solution is the same here as elsewhere. When several of these different methods are brought to bear on the same problem, as they have been on the problem of infant speech perception, they begin to produce a pattern of converging results that allows us to know with some confidence what an infant does or does not perceive.

Acuity is poor in part because the cones of the baby's retina are not yet fully developed. (Remember that the cones are the receptors in the retina that make use of bright light to see color and fine detail.) Even so, by one month, infants are able to see colors. Experiments using habituation show that one-month-old babies are able to distinguish among wavelengths that they could not differentiate if they were color-blind (Teller & Bornstein, 1987).

Newborn infants respond to some depth cues but not to others. On one hand, they can neither use binocular disparity cues (Aslin & Smith, 1988) nor adjust their lenses to focus on distant objects. Yet, they respond to looming cues; that is, they react more dramatically to images that get larger than to images that get smaller. This finding suggests that they see images that get bigger as getting closer.

In sum, at birth infants possess an array of sensory abilities that matches their abilities to act. Just as their reflexes are directed toward helping them to be held and fed, their sensory abilities help them recognize and appreciate foods, and to respond to nearby adults.

Perceptual Development During Infancy   During the first six months of life, the senses develop very quickly (see Table 11.2). Accommodation, which is virtually nonexistent at birth, reaches adult levels at four months. Acuity also improves rapidly (Banks & Dannemiller, 1987).

**Table 11.2
Milestones of Infant Development**

Months	Motor	Perception/cognition	Social
Newborn to 3 months	Reflexes; can hold head up and roll from front to back by end of period; begins to grasp objects by end of period.	Can distinguish flavors and odors of foods; acuity poor, but some color vision; can fixate and follow moving objects; anticipates pleasurable events by wiggling, etc.; reacts to the disappearance of slowly moving objects. Searches with eyes for source of sound.	Looks at the face of caretaker, smiles only occasionally and reflexively; soon after birth, establishes eye contact, smiles when approached; can recognize own voice and voice of mother.
4 to 6 months	Reflexes inhibited; holds head strongly, sits with slight support, bears some weight on legs, and extends arms and legs toward a surface when held above it; rolls back to front near end of period; able to mouth a teething biscuit.	Acuity and accommodation like adults; anticipates exciting events; repeats an activity that has a pleasurable consequence, e.g., shakes rattle; explores objects with mouth and hands; reacts to disappearance of objects and searches with eyes for source of a sound; locates partially hidden object; anticipates motion of slowly moving object.	Coos or crows in response to a smiling talking adult; cries for attention, coos, chuckles, laughs with pleasure; can tell familiar from unfamiliar people and situations; usually responds well to unfamiliar people and situations.
7 to 9 months	Sits up without assistance, bears large part of weight on legs, stands holding on and pulls self to standing position by furniture; pushes self along floor; makes stepping movements when held in walking position.	Finds object that has been hidden in sight (plays peek-a-boo); anticipates motion of rapidly moving object; looks for family members or pets when named; throws, drops, and retrieves objects.	Shows separation anxiety; explores enthusiastically but may also show uneasiness in new situations; responds to mirror image as if it is a person; shows possessions to others; shouts for attention; babbling begins to have the pattern of adult speech; tests parents' reactions at meal and bedtimes; first words: "Mama, Dada."

(Continued on next page)

9 to 12 months	Stands momentarily and walks holding furniture, creeps on knees and foot; walks holding two hands and then one hand; eats finger foods, may eat some foods from food or cup, but very messily.	Understands "No!"; takes ring stack apart; enjoys looking at pictures in books; unwraps gift.	Sense of humor develops; laughs at incongruous events.
12 to 15 months	Stands alone well and can take a few steps on own; climbs upstairs; begins to establish a pattern of bowel and bladder activity.	Understands pointing; pulls string to retrieve toy out of reach.	Develops independent attitude. Says, "No!" a lot. Tantrums; enjoys imitating adults; shows affection (hugs, etc.); recognizes some people, animals, which are not members of the family; vocabulary of a few words.
16 to 18 months	Walks rapidly; throws ball; carries teddy bear while walking; begins running near end of period.	Identifies self in mirror; identifies body parts (plays "Where's Daddy's nose?); recognizes by name most common objects in environment.	Has vocabulary of 10–15 words; coordinates gestures and speech.

A lot of attention has been devoted to the question of when infants begin to recognize human faces. We know that young infants choose to look at pictures of human faces over bull's-eyes or other simple figures. The conclusion to be drawn from this, according to psychologist Robert Fantz (1961), is that infants innately recognize the human face. But later studies showed that it's the many contrasting features of the human face (hairline, eyebrows, eyes, mouth)—not their arrangement—that interest infants. In fact, one-month-old babies are equally attracted both to disorganized faces and to those that have their features in the right position (Maurer & Barrera, 1981).

True preference for facelike stimuli emerges at two or three months (Dodwell, Humphrey & Muir, 1987). In one study, the researchers showed infants a series of pictures in three different degrees of complexity (Haaf & Brown, 1976). The stimuli were presented in pairs—half facelike, half not (see Figure 11.9). An observer watched the infants from behind a screen and recorded how much time they spent looking at each member of the pair. Both ten- and fifteen-week-old infants preferred looking at the more complex stimuli. In addition, the fifteen-week-old infants showed a preference for the complex facelike stimuli. At both ages, simple scrambled faces were preferred to simple faces.

Table 11.2
Milestones of Infant Development (*continued*)

Figure 11.9
Ordered and Disordered Faces

In Haaf and Brown's study, both ten-week-old and fifteen-week-old infants preferred more complex figures. Only the fifteen-week-old babies showed a strong preference for complex facelike figures. Neither group preferred the simple facelike figure.

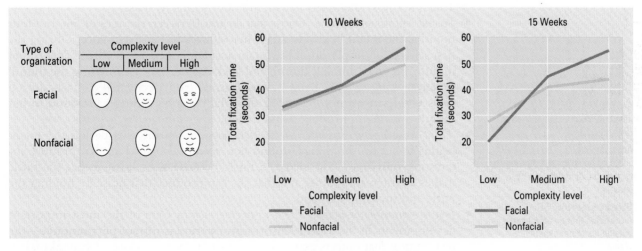

Source: Haaf & Brown, 1976.

Cognitive Development

At birth, infants respond by reflex to the world around them. Over the next eighteen months, they develop the capacity to think about the world. We call changes in the ways infants come to understand their world *cognitive development*.

Piaget's Sensorimotor Stage   Jean Piaget, a Swiss biologist-turned-psychologist, closely chronicled the dramatic changes that result from cognitive development. Piaget (1978) believed that cognitive development is the process of adapting schemas to new experiences or adapting experiences to existing schemas. Schemas are basic ways of approaching and understanding the world. To an infant, for instance, one of the most important schemas is mouthing an object.

The developing child has at her disposal two basic methods for adapting her schemas to the challenges presented by the environment. She can **assimilate** the challenges; that is, she can apply familiar patterns of thought and behavior to the novel situation. Or, she can **accommodate** her schemas to those challenges—that is, change her thinking and behavior to suit the demands of the environment. For instance, presented with a new rattle, a young infant may mouth it, thus assimilating the rattle to its familiar mouthing schema. Or, upon hearing the rattle make a noise, she may move the rattle to produce more sound, thus accommodating her behavior to the new stimuli provided by the rattle. At an older age, a child might know that the family vehicle is called a "car." If the child sees the mail carrier's van and calls it a "car," she has *assimilated* this new experience to the old concept. But once she learns that this new kind of vehicle is called a "truck," she must accommodate her concept of "car" to exclude four-wheeled vehicles that are not designed for carrying people.

Piaget identified four stages of cognitive development. Here we shall talk about the first stage, what he called the *sensorimotor stage*. (We examine the later stages in Chapter 12.) During this stage, which Piaget divided into six periods, the infant gradually comes to distinguish the self from other people and objects in the world.

Like most stage theorists, Piaget felt that the timing of these stages is approximate and varies from individual to individual. He also believed, however, that the stages always occurred in a particular order; that is, the first stage always preceded the second, the second always preceded the third, and so forth.

- *First sensorimotor period: Birth to one month* As we've already seen, the newborn responds to the world reflexively. Touch her cheek, the infant turns her head. Touch her lips, she opens her mouth and begins to suck.
- *Second sensorimotor period: One to four months* Between the ages of one and four months, the infant begins to adapt her reflexes to her experience. During the first sensorimotor period, if the infant accidently brushes her hand against her mouth, she may find her thumb and suck it—thereby assimilating the thumb to her sucking schema. And having learned from accidental contacts during the second sensorimotor period, the infant begins to bring her hand to her mouth—an example of accommodation.
- *Third sensorimotor period: Four to eight months* During this period the infant begins to act on the things around her, to repeat behaviors that produce interesting outcomes. She shakes a rattle because she's learned that the rattle makes an interesting noise and that she can produce that noise by holding the rattle and moving her hand.
- *Fourth sensorimotor period: Eight to twelve months* One of the most important developments in the fourth sensorimotor period is **object permanence**—the recognition that objects exist outside the infant's experience. If you take a ball

Assimilation The process of adapting a new experience to an existing schema.

Accommodation The process of adapting behavior and thinking to meet the demands of a new situation.

Object permanence The infant's recognition that an object exists outside his or her experience with it.

Puzzle It Out!

One of the most popular games you can play with babies is "peekaboo," in which you hide or cover your face and then suddenly reveal yourself. Babies often seem delighted and surprised at your sudden appearance and continue to enjoy your emergence for many repetitions. At what age would you expect babies to find the game boring, and why?

away from a six-month-old, she may cry for a minute but soon forgets all about it. The ball has meaning only when she can touch it or suck it or see it. But by ten months, the infant understands that objects exist whether she is playing with them or not. If you take a ball away from a ten-month-old, she looks for it—usually in the last place where it was found. She sets a goal and follows a primitive plan of action to meet that goal.

- *Fifth sensorimotor period: Twelve to eighteen months* Through the first year of life, the infant's behavior is mostly opportunistic. She stumbles on interesting effects and repeats them; she doesn't try to produce them. In the fifth senso-rimotor period, the infant begins varying her activities to see what effects she can produce in the outside world. She experiments, dropping her spoon from her highchair to hear the noise it makes, or pulling the cat's tail to see what the animal does.

   During this period, the infant learns to follow a sequence of operations. If she watches you hide a ball, she knows to look for it in the place where you hid it, not in the place where she last found it.

- *Sixth sensorimotor period: Eighteen months to two years* During the last period of Piaget's sensorimotor stage, the child comes to understand not only that objects exist outside her perception but also that things can happen to those objects while they are out of sight. The ball isn't necessarily where it was last found; someone else may have moved it. If the ball isn't where she expects it to be, then, the child looks for it elsewhere.

The infant's changing understanding of the world throughout the sensori-motor stage is an example of diminishing egocentrism. At first, the infant makes no distinction between herself and other people and objects in the environment. But gradually, over a period of eighteen to twenty-four months, the infant begins to distinguish herself from the people and things around her. She comes to understand that she, other people, and objects all exist in a world that is larger than the world she controls.

Responding to the Impossible: Challenging Piaget   Recent studies have begun to challenge many of Piaget's findings, in particular his observation that infants don't recognize the permanence of objects until they are eight months old. Renee Baillargeon and her colleagues used "impossible events" to demonstrate that young infants are aware of objects they can't see. An "impossible event" is something that cannot happen if we assume that hidden objects continue to exist. In one experiment, for example, a toy rabbit moved along a track, disappeared behind a screen, and seemed to reappear on the other side (see Figure 11.10). What made the event "impossible" was a cutout in the screen. As the rabbit actually moved behind the screen, it should have been visible through the cutout—but it wasn't. Actually, Baillargeon used two toy rabbits in this procedure: the one that disappeared behind the screen as well as another that appeared a moment later from the other side of the screen. By staring, five-and-

Figure 11.10
An Impossible Event

Even five-and-a-half-month-old infants indicated their surprise by staring when the rabbit seemed to pass behind the screen without its head and ears appearing through the cutout.

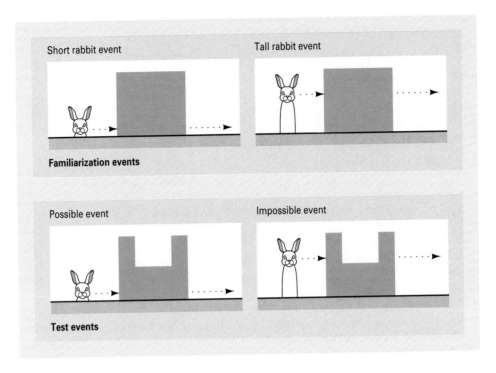

Source: Baillargeon and Graber, 1987.

a-half-month-old infants showed they were surprised that they could not see the rabbit through the window (Baillargeon & Graber, 1987). If infants under the age of eight months had no sense of object permanence, they should not have responded to this kind of impossible event.

It may be that Piaget's description of the order of stages of cognitive development is accurate but that his timetable is not. Experiments like Baillargeon's show that infants do develop concepts such as object permanence at a younger age than Piaget thought possible.

Social Development

Considering their limited repertoire of behaviors, newborns are remarkably skillful at controlling those around them. Soon after birth, they use gurgles and cries to regulate the behavior of their caregivers.

Parents are especially sensitive to the sounds made by their own child, as illustrated in Figure 11.11. For example, they can distinguish their own baby's cries from those of another infant. And mothers are able to tell the difference between anger cries and pain cries in their own infants (Wiesenfeld, Malatesta & DeLoach, 1981).

The Newborn as a Social Being   The first meeting between a baby and his caregivers is an important event. In fact, some psychologists argue that this first meeting sets the tone for the future relationship between infant and caregivers (Klaus & Kennel, 1976). From the infant's first minutes of life, he is treated as an individual, with an individual's personality and needs. In an intriguing study of first meetings between neonates and adults, Judith Dunn (1983) was startled to discover how quickly doctors, nurses, parents, and relatives are prepared to make judgments about whether a newborn is lively or calm, good-natured or bad-tempered, bright or dull, sociable or withdrawn—labels that often stick throughout the child's life. Some parents make these judgments even before

Both the adult and the baby in this picture are smiling. But why? Does the infant have an image of the adult's smile, and is he trying to copy it? Or is it simply that the adult's smile makes the baby happy?

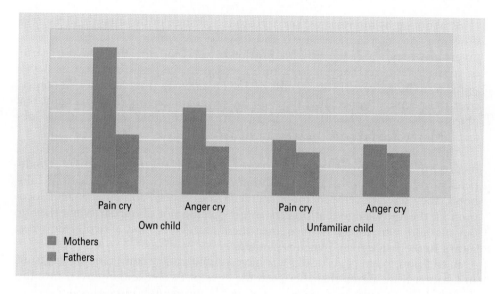

Figure 11.11
Parents' Responses to Pain and Anger Cries of Their Own and an Unfamiliar Infant

Notice that the responses of both mothers and fathers are greater to their own child than to an unfamiliar child. Mothers' responses are more dramatic. Mothers also respond more strongly to their child's cries of pain than of anger.

Source: Weisenfeld, Malatesta & DeLoach, 1981.

their children are born. According to one study, the more difficult mothers expect their child's birth to be, the more temperamental they expect the child to be as an infant (Mebert & Kalinowsky, 1986).

Infants almost immediately become active participants in social interactions. In just a few weeks' time, they recognize and respond to familiar human faces. Moreover, very young infants are capable of making the same facial expressions they see on those around them—smiling, pouting, opening their mouths, even sticking out their tongues. Some psychologists insist that infants actually imitate the facial expressions they see (Meltzoff & Moore, 1977, 1983). Others argue that expressions, like yawning, are "contagious"—that the adult's expression simply stimulates a similar expression in the infant (Over, 1987). Whatever the particular mechanism, the result is a beginning of coordination between the actions of adults and the infant.

Social Development During Infancy   As the infant grows, he undergoes a sequence of predictable changes in his relationships with his caregivers. This process is called *social development*. Communication skills develop rapidly during infancy. By one month, the infant begins to be an active social partner. At this age, he can fixate on his parents' eyes and mouth and respond to their attention with wiggles, smiles, and exuberant crowing. At four months, the infant and his caregivers actually have "conversations," in which each participant speaks or acts and then pauses, waiting for the other's response (Stern, 1977; Trevarthen, 1979).

> PARENT, GENTLY TICKLING BABY: *Are you my big boy?*
> BABY: [*Wiggles.*]
> PARENT: *Are you my big, big boy?*
> BABY: [*A more vigorous wiggle.*]
> PARENT: *Yes, you are! (Stern, 1977)*

In conversations with their babies, parents tend to use an exaggerated, high-pitched, simplified form of speech known as *motherese*. Anne Fernald (1985) has demonstrated that infants prefer motherese to other forms of speech, and that it is the high or variable pitch of motherese that makes it attractive to infants (Fernald & Kuhl, 1987).

At about eight months, we see a profound change in the infant's social relationships. At this point, he forms an exclusive attachment to his primary caregivers and may cry if separated from them. Many infants also become fearful of strangers. These changes seem to be related to the infant's cognitive development, to his increasing awareness of his separateness from and lack of control over the people around him. As soon as the infant begins to understand that objects exist independently, he recognizes that his mother or father is an "object" from which he could be separated.

Although this increasing selectiveness in infants often appears to be like an increase in dependence, it actually prepares them for the new degree of independence characteristic of early childhood. By the time children reach early childhood, they have developed three characteristics crucial for independent locomotion: the knowledge that objects and people do not disappear when they go out of sight, the ability to recognize their caregivers, and a strong desire to return to their caregivers when separated.

In addition, youngsters at this age have a rudimentary command of language. In Chapter 8 we noted that, between the ages of twelve and eighteen months, most babies assemble a vocabulary of single-word utterances through which they can ask for or refuse dozens of objects or activities in their environment. Even so primitive a language capacity enormously increases the range of information that can be exchanged between infant and caregivers.

Figure 11.12
Assessing Young Infants' Temperaments

Pediatrician T. Terry Brazelton designed a scale that assesses young infants' temperament on measures of such characteristics as fussiness and cuddliness. For example, cuddly newborns adapt their bodies to being held. Noncuddly babies go rigid; they seem to resist being held. Using Brazelton's scale and others, several researchers have demonstrated that noncuddly infants elicit a different kind of care from their mothers than do cuddly infants.

This is a summary measure of the infant's response to being held in alert states. There are several components which are scored in response to the baby being held in a cuddled position both vertically on the examiner's shoulder and horizontally against the examiner's chest. The baby's resistance to cuddling should be assessed as well as the ability to relax or mold and cling to the examiner. It is best to give the baby a chance to initiate cuddling. It is only if there is no active participation on the part of the baby or if the baby is unable to relax or mold that the examiner should facilitate cuddling. If the infant does it him- or herself, he or she gets a score of 5 or above.

Scoring

1. Actually resists being held, continuously pushing away, thrashing, or stiffening.

2. Resists being held most but not all of the time.

3. Doesn't resist but doesn't participate either, lies passively in arms and against shoulder (like a sack of meal).

4. Eventually molds into arms, but after a lot of nestling and cuddling by examiner.

5. Usually molds and relaxes when first held.

6. Always molds and relaxes when first held.

7. Always molds, initially nestles head in crook of elbows and neck of examiner.

8. In addition to molding and relaxing, the infant nestles and turns head, leans forward on shoulder, fits feet into cavity of other arm, all of body participates. Always molds initially. Head nestles in crook of elbow and neck. Turns toward body in horizontal and turns forward on shoulder.

9. All of the above, and the baby grasps and clings to the examiner.

Source: Brazelton, 1984.

Temperament **Temperament** comprises the long-term fundamental disposi-tions of a person, such as energy level. Infants, like adults, have very different temperaments (see Figure 11.12). Pediatrician T. Berry Brazelton invented a scale that assesses young infants in the degree of temperamental characteristics such as fussiness and cuddliness. Cuddly newborns adapt their bodies to being held; non-cuddly babies go rigid and appear to resist being held. These differ-ences in infant temperament may affect how they are treated by those around them. Many studies show that infants whose parents believe they are "difficult" receive less effective or attentive care than do infants whose parents believe they are "easy" (Sirignano & Lachman, 1985; Maccoby, Snow & Jacklin, 1984; Crockenberg, 1986).

Over the years, developmental psychologists have tried to demonstrate whether differences in temperament are carried over from infancy to adoles-cence and even into adulthood—whether, for instance, the same people who are irritable babies become irritable children, adolescents, and adults. In a classic study of childhood temperament, researchers asked parents to rate their children every year throughout the first five years. The parents judged their children on a range of variables, among them level of activity, regularity, adaptability, and attention span. Over time, the parents identified stable patterns of temperament in their children (Thomas & Chess, 1977).

It seems, then, that our temperament as infants stays with us into childhood. But does our childhood temperament follow us into adulthood? Here there is less consensus. Long-term studies of temperament in which people were rated by independent observers both as children and as adults produced mixed results. Some aspects of temperament change dramatically from childhood to adult-hood; others show evidence of continuity (Kagan, 1978, 1989; Macfarlane, 1964; Block, 1981).

Recap

- In the first months of life, the infant's responses are reflexive.

- Development in the central nervous system moves outward, from the head and body toward the hands and feet.

- Neonates show a sensitivity to touch, the ability to distinguish smells and tastes in foods, and a well-developed sense of hearing; but color vision, visual acuity, and the ability to respond to certain depth cues do not develop for weeks or even months.

- Piaget believed that cognitive development combines the processes of accommodation and assimilation.

- During the sensorimotor stage—Piaget's first stage of cognitive de-velopment—the infant gradually comes to distinguish the self from other people and objects in the world.

- One of the most important developments during the sensorimotor stage is object permanence—the recognition that objects exist outside the infant's experience.

- Despite their limited behaviors, newborns are remarkably skillful at controlling the people around them.

- Parents are especially sensitive to the sounds their own child makes.

- Communication skills develop rapidly during infancy.

- At about eight months, infants form exclusive attachments to their

Temperament The individual's fundamental disposition.

primary caregivers—a change that seems to be related to infants' increasing awareness of themselves as separate from the people around them.

- Temperament is an individual's fundamental disposition, the way he or she tends to respond to experience.

- Although there is strong evidence that temperament differences persist from infancy into childhood, there is no consensus on the question of whether temperament characteristics persist from childhood into adolescence and adulthood.

Figure 11.13
Konrad Lorenz and His Imprinted Goslings

Ethologist Konrad Lorenz studied animals in their natural environment. He demonstrated that there were sensitive periods during which irreversible learning takes place. Here baby geese follow the first creature they were exposed to the day after they were born.

Attachment   The process by which a bond is formed between infant and primary caregiver; the bond itself.

Imprinting   Learning during a sensitive period.

Attachment

Our description of infant development is largely concerned with the evolving relationship between infants and their caregivers. The central role of this relationship raises an important question: is a deep exclusive relationship with a single caregiver an essential part of growing up happy and socially competent? This issue has become particularly significant in the last two decades because of the dramatic increase in the number of families in which both parents work. Today, in nearly half of all American families, the mother works outside the home while her children are still preschoolers (Scarr, Phillips & McCartney 1989).

The contemporary debate on this issue dates from a report commissioned by the World Health Organization in 1951 from a British psychiatrist, John Bowlby. In this and later writings, Bowlby (1969) argued that human genes require that every infant establish a close relationship with a single caregiver during the first few months of life.

Bowlby was influenced by the work of René Spitz (1945). While working with children in orphanages, Spitz had discovered that children could be well fed and protected but still not thrive because they lacked a strong relationship with one adult. Developing Spitz's ideas, Bowlby called the process of bonding between an infant and a primary caregiver **attachment.** He claimed that if a bond was not formed in the first year between the infant and a primary caregiver, or if the bond was of poor quality, it could not be formed later and the quality of all the infant's future relationships would be threatened.

Bowlby's thinking about attachment was also influenced by ethology, the study of animals' behavior in their natural surroundings. One of the founders of ethology was an Austrian zoologist, Konrad Lorenz. Working with baby geese, Lorenz (1937) identified sensitive periods in their development. One of those periods comes during the day after they are hatched. If a gosling is exposed to its mother during that day, it will follow her just as goslings do in nature. But if a gosling is exposed to some other moving stimulus—say, a dog or a person—the gosling will follow that object instead (see Figure 11.13). Lorenz called this kind of time-dependent learning **Imprinting.** And he believed that what animals learn during a sensitive period cannot be reversed. He observed that geese that had formed an attachment to a human as goslings often sought a human as a mate when they were adults.

Later research showed that many animal species have sensitive periods in which they must identify and bond with their mothers. If they don't, the relationship between mother and offspring does not form properly. For example, if a mother goat does not learn the odor of her kid within a few hours after birth, she rejects it, leaving it to die (Klopfer & Klopfer, 1968).

Bowlby believed that the attachment process in humans is very like the imprinting that Lorenz and others described in animals. He suggested that a child's development could be endangered if both parents return to work before the child is a year old because the shift of caregivers interferes with the infant's formation of a strong bond with a primary caregiver. Notice that, from Bowlby's point of view, even shared caregiving can be unhealthy: if parenting responsibilities are shared equally, the child might not form a primary bond with either parent. If Bowlby had been right, then many of the current generation of children who are being reared with the help of daycare centers or cooperative-care arrangements would be in trouble.

The Psychological Needs of Infant Monkeys

Bowlby's concerns were further supported by some dramatic studies of infant monkeys, conducted by psychologist Harry Harlow and his collaborators (Harlow & Zimmerman, 1959; Harlow & Harlow, 1965). As often happens in science, Harlow's research was inspired both by a common observation and by an uncommon insight into its meaning. In the confined cages of laboratories, mother monkeys often mistreat their babies. Accordingly, scientists in Harlow's time adopted the practice of raising infant monkeys alone in individual cages. Some unknown lab worker had discovered that these isolated babies were more likely to survive if they were given a bit of cloth to cling to. Harlow wondered why a piece of cloth thrown on the bottom of a cage could be so important.

To see just how important the cloth was, he raised some babies with two surrogate "mothers." As Figure 11.14 shows, one consisted of a wire-mesh cylinder wrapped in terry cloth toweling to which the infant could cling. The second mother consisted of a similar cylinder of wire mesh without the towel. In the center of the "chest" of this wire mother, Harlow placed a milk bottle. The baby monkeys were very clear in their preferences. They clung to the terry cloth mother most of the time, except for occasional explorations around the cage and quick trips to the wire mother to satisfy their hunger.

Figure 11.14
The Harlow Experiments

The monkey on the left was raised alone with a wire mesh dummy; the monkey on the right had access to another dummy wrapped in terry cloth. Although the cloth-raised monkeys appeared to develop normally at first, only monkeys raised with other monkeys functioned normally as adults.

Moreover, if the terry cloth mother were removed from the cage, the infant would huddle and rock pitifully in the corner of the cage where the terry cloth mother had been, mourning just as normally reared monkeys do when separated from their real mothers. Thus, in a sense, Harlow was able to demonstrate not only that his infants had a relationship with their surrogate mothers but also that the relationship was based on softness and clinging, not on the satisfaction of being fed.

The behavior of the infants raised on terry cloth contrasted sharply with that of monkeys raised only with wire mothers or without any mother surrogates at all. Those monkeys were sad creatures. Deprived of anything soft to clasp, they clasped themselves pitifully. They were terrorized by new stimulation and spent their days huddling and rocking in the corner of their cages. They seemed not to exerience pain in normal ways and often mutilated themselves with their own teeth. Confronted with other monkeys, they were immobilized with terror.

Harlow argued that his research demonstrated an innate need of monkeys for "contact comfort." A monkey who did not have enough contact comfort in infancy was doomed to become a strange, terrified adult.

Using similar deprivation techniques, Harlow also discovered that monkeys required interaction with other monkeys in childhood if they were to grow into competent, healthy adults. Baby monkeys raised without any opportunity for play with other baby monkeys would grow and thrive physically but, as adults, would have great difficulty in mating and parenting.

Although Harlow worked only with monkeys, his experiments attracted an enormous amount of attention because they seemed to suggest the idea that infants of many species have special needs above and beyond the obvious needs to eat, drink, keep warm, and avoid pain. And the failure to meet those needs at a particular time in life may have devastating effects on the later development of infants.

Of course, Harlow's work does not prove that human babies have the same needs as monkey babies. There are lots of differences between humans and monkeys, not the least of which is that most human parents aren't as fuzzy! But Harlow's findings, like those of Spitz and Bowlby, do suggest that in a highly social species, social interactions in infancy have important consequences for development.

Attachment in Humans

Much of the research on human attachment has focused on the relationship between the infant-mother bond and the child's later transition to nursery school. These studies center on two questions: What kinds of child-rearing practices produce a high-quality attachment at age one? And does the quality of attachment at age one accurately predict whether a child will make a good adjustment to nursery school at age three or four?

To determine the *quality* of attachment—the strength of the bond between infant and primary caregiver—psychologist Mary Ainsworth created a testing procedure called the "strange situation" (Ainsworth & Bell, 1970). At different stages of the procedure, the infant is briefly separated from and reunited with his or her mother, and then briefly introduced to a stranger (see Figure 11.15).

There are three elements here that can distress the infant, particularly when they occur in rapid succession: introduction to an unfamiliar environment, contact with an unfamiliar person, and separation from the caregiver. From her subjects' responses to these elements, Ainsworth identified three levels of infant-mother attachment: secure attachment, and two categories of insecure attachment, avoidant and resistant.

Secure children are confident in their bond with their mother and use her as a base from which to explore the world. They quickly adapt to the new room and begin to examine its resources. They interact with their mothers, often bringing toys over to show them. They are likely to interact with the stranger when she appears. When left alone or with the stranger, most securely attached children are not greatly distressed, apparently assuming that their mothers will be back

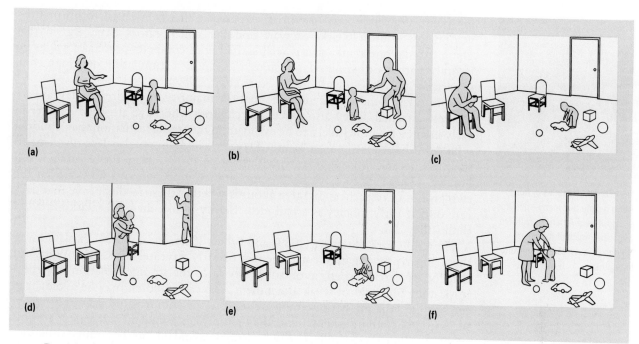

soon. Reunited with their mothers, they are glad to see them and quickly reestablish contact with them. Those who have been distressed are quickly comforted and soon regain interest in the room and toys.

Insecure, avoidant children are more aloof from their mothers; in fact, they almost seem to avoid eye contact with them. They quickly begin to explore the room but, unlike securely attached infants, do not interact with their mothers during this exploration. They are also quick to establish relationships with strangers. And they are not overly distressed when their mothers leave the room, nor do they take much notice of them when they return.

Insecure, resistant children are clingy. They do not readily use the toys in the room and are fearful of the strangers when they enter. They are very distressed when their mothers leave, are not easily comforted upon their return, and do not go back to playing with the toys. Resistant children do not seem to trust the bond with their mothers.

Why do babies differ in their attachments? At least part of the answer, as you would expect, has to do with the way in which their mothers (or other caregivers) act. Ainsworth and others have found that mothers who are affectionate, attentive, and responsive to their infants generate attachments that are more secure (Ainsworth, 1979; Goldsmith & Alansky, 1987).

Does the level of attachment at age one affect later development? Apparently it does. One study shows that infants who are securely attached at fifteen months of age are popular and well adjusted to their peer group two years later. And the same study revealed that children who were ambivalently attached at fifteen months were more likely to be aloof and not well integrated in their play group (Damon, 1983; see also Matas, Arend & Sroufe, 1978).

Parent Care or Daycare?

Studies of the behavior of one-year-old babies in the strange situation imply that a strong attachment between an infant and a particular caretaker might be important to subsequent development. This implication has sparked a lively debate over the wisdom of infant daycare. Jay Belsky and his collaborators (e.g., Belsky & Rovine, 1988) warn that parents who use daycare centers may be depriv-

Figure 11.15
The Strange Situation

The strange situation was developed to test an infant's security of attachment to his or her mother. Infants who explore the room and its toys enthusiastically, who do not become overly distressed when their mothers leave the room, and who reunite quickly with their mothers when they return are regarded as securely attached.

The economic realities of the 1990s dictate that many—perhaps a majority—of American children will spend much of their early childhood in daycare of one sort or another.

ing them of an individual parenting experience that is essential to normal development. Allison Clarke-Stewart and her collaborators have argued that going to a daycare center that is well-staffed with competent caretakers does no harm to parent–offspring relationships and can be a stimulating developmental experience (Clarke-Stewart, 1989; Scarr et al., 1989).

Both sides of the argument agree that the majority of children in daycare are securely attached. They also agree that children who have attended daycare in early infancy are more likely to be avoidant in the strange situation than children who have been cared for at home. Daycare children are also less obedient to their parents and more aggressive with their peers—a pattern the researchers call "bratty." These effects have been demonstrated in dozens of studies. What the two groups of reseachers disagree about is whether these results prove that daycare during early infancy is a bad idea. Belsky thinks they do; Clarke-Stewart thinks they don't.

How do Clarke-Stewart (1989) and others (Scarr et al., 1990) explain away these apparently negative consequences of early daycare? First, they point out that for daycare children, avoidant behavior in the strange situation may be a misleading indicator of weak attachment. Daycare children may be avoidant in the strange situation because they are used to the comings and goings of adults in semipublic environments, and they simply go about their business accordingly. So while these children may be scored "avoidant" in the strange situation, they may in fact be well-attached to their caretakers in their day-to-day lives.

The evidence that daycare-raised children are more "bratty" is also open to other interpretations. In the first place, this effect is not exclusively an effect of daycare in *early* infancy as the Belsky interpretation suggests: children who have come to daycare *late* in infancy also show the same forms of brattiness. Moreover, although irritating to parents, "brattiness" may not necessarily be a sign of maladjustment. Daycare-raised children may simply be more independent and assertive. Finally, daycare advocates point out that early daycare has some clear short-term benefits. Daycare-raised children develop intellectually more rapidly and are more self-confident than home-raised children, although their home-cared peers quickly catch up when they join the daycare children in nursery school and kindergarten.

Because many parents have no choice about whether to work, families should probably concentrate on trying to find the highest-quality daycare arrangements possible. And when they are with their children, parents can provide the attention, affection, and responsiveness that lead to secure attachments in their children.

Recap

- The question of whether a deep exclusive relationship with a single caregiver is an essential part of growing up happy and socially competent is particularly significant today, given the dramatic increase in the number of families in which both parents work.

- According to British psychiatrist John Bowlby, the infant's need to establish a close relationship with a single caregiver during the first few months of life is genetic.

- Bowlby based his findings on studies of children in orphanages and research on imprinting in young animals.

- Harlow's work with young monkeys supports the idea that the human infant's social interactions have important consequences for his or her development.

- The "strange situation" is a procedure used by psychologists to determine the quality of the infant–mother bond.

- Apparently the quality of attachment at age one affects the child's later development.

- Children who have been placed in daycare in early infancy are more likely to be avoidant in strange environments than are children who have been cared for at home; they also tend to be less obedient and more aggressive.

- The proponents of daycare argue that these findings do not necessarily prove that daycare during early infancy is a bad idea.

Conclusion

Compared to most animal species, we humans are born very immature. We come into the world totally unable to survive on our own, and in the first few months we must accomplish much of the physical development that other species have completed before birth. To make up for lost time, we develop explosively during the first few years of life.

In the course of a year or two, infants go from being incompetent organisms to becoming clearly recognizable humans, walking on their hind legs, using their hands cleverly, already better at solving novel problems than any other species, talking a language more complex than any other species can master, and existing in an elaborate complex of social relationships.

Much remains, however, before a child becomes an adult. In the next chapter we trace the rest of this developmental journey.

Chapter 12

The Stages of Development: Childhood Through Adulthood

The Builders, Jacob Lawrence, 1974

12

Gateways   Certain of children's achievements following infancy are most intriguing because we never knew (or tend to forget) that they needed to be achieved. We all know that pouring a glass of milk into a different glass doesn't change the amount of milk, and we may find it difficult to imagine a mind that didn't know that. But our casual assumption of this principle is something we acquired in childhood. Much of the research discussed in this chapter indicates that childhood may be a more alien land than we knew, and the trip to maturity a more remarkable journey than we guessed.

The issues of self and identity are central to childhood and especially adolescence, and we touch on them repeatedly in Chapters 14 and 15 on personality and psychological disorder. The development of social motives and emotional capacities have already been discussed in Chapters 9 and 10. The principles of learning described in Chapter 6, especially observational learning, are central to the understanding of social development in these years.

"I'm thirsty." Jason, my five-year-old, is cranky. We've just arrived home late from a trip, and he should have been in bed hours ago. I lift him from the back seat of the car and carry him through the garage and into the kitchen.

"Me, too!" announces his older sister, Becky. Eight-year-old Becky is still lively. She skips ahead of us and opens the refrigerator door. I set Jason down on a stool at the kitchen table and join her at the open refrigerator.

"Oh, boy," she says brightly. "I'm going to have some orange juice."

"*I* want juice!" Jason whines from the table.

"Okay, okay, coming right up." I reach into the refrigerator and pull out the carton of orange juice. As soon as I lift it, I know I'm in trouble. There's barely enough for the two of them. While Becky pulls a chair up to the kitchen table, I take down two plastic glasses from the cupboard. I pour Becky's glass about two-thirds full.

"I want a whole glass," she says.

"There isn't enough," I say, pouring Jason's glass. The juice reaches just halfway up the side of his glass.

Jason looks at the level of juice in the two glasses for a moment and then bursts into tears. "I want more!" he wails.

I turn to Becky, but she has her hand on her glass. "I'm bigger," she says primly.

"Jason, drink what's there and then I'll get some water for you."

"NOOO," Jason wails, his face red and tears pouring down his cheeks.

In desperation, I reach into the cupboard and pull out a tall thin glass. Setting it down beside Becky's, I transfer the juice from Jason's glass to the narrower one. The level of the juice comes to rest just above the level in Becky's glass. I slide the glass toward Jason.

"There," I say to Jason. "Now you have *more* than Becky. Look!"

Jason's sobs subside. Snuffling, he reaches out a grubby, tear-soaked finger and runs it along the level of the juice in his new glass. "My juice is bigger than your juice, Becky," he says happily.

Becky starts to answer, but I put my finger to my lips. We exchange knowing looks.

Development in Stages

In my efforts to get my two tired children to bed, I used my knowledge about the stages of development in childhood. I knew that at his stage, Jason would see the smaller amount of juice as greater in the thinner glass. I also knew that his older sister would see that she still had more juice than Jason.

In Chapter 11 we said that *stages* are stable periods during which behavior and experience change comparatively little, and that stages are separated by periods of rapid psychological and physical growth called *transitions*. When we say that development proceeds in stages, we're also implying that these quiet and dynamic periods occur in predictable order: people are infants before they are children, children before they are adolescents, and adolescents before they are adults. Developmental stage theories also assume that each stage ordinarily occurs at a predictable time in life. From the day you were born, your progress has been tracked by your doctors and teachers using **developmental norms,** widely published average ages at which children perform obvious and important behaviors, such as walking and talking (Bayley, 1969).

Stage theories are everywhere in psychology. There are stage theories of living, of dying, of grieving, of loving, of learning. In this chapter we examine stage theories of child and adult development. Before we begin, however, a word of caution: although these theories have had tremendous impact on the field of psychology, each has been criticized for failing to capture the development of many or even most people. Human development is an enormously complex process. Our descriptions of the changes that occur in behavior as people grow up describe more or less accurately what happens in the lives of a great many people in our society, but there are many individual variations. As we discussed in Chapter 11, there are even disagreements about whether the idea of stage best captures the progression of development. Some psychologists believe that development is better conceived as a continuous, smooth process. Still, there seems to be general agreement on the broad outlines of development and how children change over time.

The Stage Theories

Much of the research that's been done on development is a response to the theories of three men: Jean Piaget, Lawrence Kohlberg, and Erik Erikson. In the next section we will briefly describe their theories. And in subsequent sections we will return to these theories frequently in our discussion of various specific developmental changes.

Piaget's Stages of Cognitive Development

Although Jean Piaget began his career studying how lake snails adapt to the force of waves, he is most famous for his studies of how children adapt to their environments during the course of development.

Developmental norm The average age at which an important behavior is first performed.

Jean Piaget, a Swiss psychologist, started his career as a biologist, studying the way animals adapt to their environments (Ginsberg & Opper, 1988). His interest in adaptation led to an interest in human cognitive development—in the ways we come to understand the world as we grow older.

Piaget worked with children, often his own. His method was to confront subjects with a puzzling situation and ask them to explain it. For example, upon pouring water back and forth between differently shaped glasses, he found that his young children (like Jason, whom we met in the opening to this chapter) thought the amount changed when the water was poured into a new container. In their responses he recognized a pattern of development, a sequence of stages through which they passed as they came to understand the world around them.

Piaget believed that transitions from one stage to another are spurred by conflicts that arise between children's environment and their schemas, their ways of understanding that environment (Piaget, 1952). Schemas may be as abstract as ways of thinking about a problem or as concrete as specific techniques for solving it. According to Piaget, as children grow, they experience new things that challenge their existing schemas. This conflict creates *disequilibrium,* a sense that something is wrong. Children respond to disequilibrium in two basic ways: accommodation (by adjusting their schemas to the environment) and assimilation (by adapting the new experience to an existing schema).

Piaget believed that cognitive development is an ongoing process of adaptation that moves through four major stages (see Table 12.1). He believed that the adaptations made by the child at one stage solve one set of problems but lead to the challenges that produce the transition to the next stage.

Table 12.1
Piaget's Stages of Cognitive
Development

Stage	Approximate Age	Characteristics
Sensorimotor (Piaget)	Infancy (0 to 2)	Infants' knowledge is centered on their own feelings and actions.
Preoperational (Piaget)	Preschool years (2 to 6)	Children can talk about events that are not taking place at the moment and about people and objects that are not present at the moment. In imaginative play, something stands for something else. But children are still so focused on how they see the world that they have difficulty understanding things from other perspectives.
Concrete operational (Piaget)	Grade school years (6 to 12)	Children's powers of imagination and reasoning expand, allowing them to perform many kinds of logical tasks. But their imagination is limited to manipulations they can actually perform.
Formal operational (Piaget)	Adolescence (13 plus)	Adolescents are capable of abstract thought, of thinking about concepts they have not experienced. And they are able to understand the reasoning process, to separate the logic used to arrive at a solution from the solution itself.
Dialectical reasoning (Riegel)	Adulthood	Thinking in this stage is more open, more flexible. Adults are able to apply the principles of abstract reasoning to the practical issues of living, to integrate conflicting principles in their decison making.

Piaget's four stages describe cognitive development from infancy through adolescence. Other theorists have added a fifth stage, dialectical reasoning, which extends from young adulthood through late adulthood (Riegel, 1973).

Kohlberg's Stages of Moral Reasoning

Psychologist Lawrence Kohlberg (1927–1987) studied the development of moral reasoning, the way in which we think about issues of right and wrong. Kohlberg derived his stage theory of moral development from studies in which he asked his subjects—mostly boys and young men—to comment on moral dilemmas, situations in which a person is forced to decide between conflicting moral principles. Here's an example:

> In Europe, a woman was near death from a special kind of cancer. There was one drug that the doctors thought might save her. It was a form of radium that a druggist in the same town had recently discovered. The drug was expensive to make, but the druggist was charging ten times what the drug cost him to make. He paid $200 for the radium and charged $2,000 for a small dose of the drug. The sick woman's husband, Heinz, went to everyone he knew to borrow the money, but could only get together about $1,000, which was half of what it cost. He told the druggist that his wife was dying and asked him to sell it cheaper or let him pay later. But the druggist said, "No, I discovered the drug and I'm going to make money from it." So Heinz got desperate and considered breaking into the man's store to steal the drug for his wife. Should Heinz steal the radium? [Kohlberg and Gilligan, 1971, pp. 1072–1073]

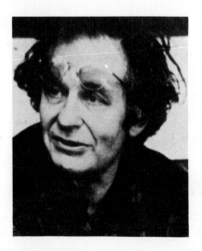

Lawrence Kohlberg pioneered studies in children's moral reasoning.

Psychosocial theory Erikson's theory that at each of various stages of life the individual must resolve a critical issue in his or her relationships to others.

Kohlberg was interested not so much in the decisions his subjects made as in the reasoning they used to reach those decisions. And he found a pattern, a series of consistent changes in the way his subjects reasoned as they grew older.

Kohlberg's theory was tied to Piaget's stages of cognitive development. He believed that as we develop, our moral reasoning reflects our growing awareness of our place in society and the rules that govern society (Kohlberg, 1976). In the *preconventional stage,* the child evaluates moral issues in terms of consequences to the self. In the *conventional stage,* the child's moral reasoning is a response to social expectations. And, finally, in the *postconventional stage,* the adolescent— now capable of abstract thought—evaluates moral issues in terms of moral principles, such as truth and justice (see Table 12.2).

Table 12.2
Kohlberg's Stages of Moral Development

Stage	Age	Characteristics
Preconventional	Early school years	Young children evaluate moral issues in terms of consequences to the self. They will argue, for instance, that you shouldn't steal a cookie because "you might get caught" or because "then there won't be any cookies for your dessert."
Conventional	Middle school years	Older children evaluate moral issues in terms of social expectations and conventions. They will argue that "you shouldn't eat other people's cookies" or that "you shouldn't eat between meals."
Postconventional	Adolescence	Adolescents evaluate moral issues in terms of moral principles. For them the argument is "What happens to the structure of our society if people go around taking cookies whenever they want?"

Erik Erikson's psychosocial theory had a profound effect on how psychologists view social development.

Erikson's Psychosocial Theory

Erik Erikson (1902–present) is a psychoanalyst who was trained in Freud's group in Vienna. As a result, his theory reflects both Freud's ideas and Erikson's own experiences as a psychotherapist for children and as an anthropologist who had studied numerous other cultures. Erikson also studied a number of historical figures, such as Mahatma Gandhi and Martin Luther, to test his ideas about development through the life span.

Erikson's **psychosocial theory** of development was based on Freud's idea that children move through stages in which they have specific impulses. (Freud's theory is presented in Chapter 14 because Freud's influence was greatest in the area of personality and disorders.) According to Freud, if those impulses are not gratified, infantile behaviors are likely to continue into adulthood. Erikson, however, substituted issues for impulses in his theory. He argued that, throughout life, each of us contends with important issues—how to trust ourselves and others, what our identity is, and how we can be intimate with others (see Table 12.3). Erikson believed that these issues were constant throughout life, but that each is particularly relevant at a specific stage of our lives. He also believed that the failure to resolve an issue when it is critical has long-term effects on our self-concept and on our relationships with others (Erikson, 1963).

Table 12.3
Erikson's Stages of Psychosocial Development

Stage	Issue	Favorable Outcome	Unfavorable Outcome
Infancy (first year)	Trust versus mistrust	Confidence in other people	Wariness toward other people
Infancy (second year)	Autonomy versus shame and doubt	Willpower; the ability to take control of one's own actions	Uncertainity about the ability to do things by oneself
Preschool (3 to 5)	Initiative versus guilt	Enthusiasm for new tasks; a tendency to forget failures quickly	Reticence; a tendency to dwell on failures; an uneasiness with independence
School-age (6 to puberty)	Industry versus inferiority	A focus on productivity and competence	Feelings of inferiority; little interest in doing things
Adolescence	Identity versus role confusion	A sense of self; an understanding of one's place in the world	Aimlessness; confusion
Early adulthood	Intimacy versus isolation	Commitment to other people, particularly a mate	Loneliness; a sense of isolation
Middle adulthood	Generativity versus stagnation	Satisfaction with work and family; a sense of community	Self-centeredness
Late adulthood	Integrity versus despair	Pride; a sense of fulfillment	Regret; despair

Source: Adapted from Erikson, 1963, p. 273.

You may have noticed some similarities in the stage theories. To make these similarities clearer, we have presented the theories together in Table 12.4. Notice that there is substantial agreement among the theories: in particular, all four agree that there are major changes around age 2, age 6, and age 13. To some extent, these similarities occurred because the theorists influenced each other. Piaget was quite aware of Freud's work, which was also the inspiration for Erikson; and Kohlberg was deliberately developing Piaget's ideas. Still, the agreement among their theories suggests that the years in question may indeed be times of major change.

Table 12.4
Comparison of Major Stage Theories

Approximate Age	Piaget	Kohlberg	Erikson	Freud
0 to 2	Sensorimotor		Trust	Oral
2 to 4	Preoperational	Preconventional	Autonomy	Anal
5 to 6	↓	↓	Initiative	Phallic
7 to 12	Concrete operations	Conventional	Competence	Latency
13 +	Formal operations	Postconventional	Identity	Genital
			Intimacy	
			Generativity	
			Integrity	

Recap

- Stages theories of development imply that development alternates between periods of quiet and periods of active change, and that these periods occur in predictable order and at predictable times of life.

- Piaget believed that children respond to disequilibrium by adjusting their schemas to the environment (accommodation) and by adapting new experiences to existing schemas (assimilation).

- According to Piaget, cognitive development is an ongoing process of adaptation that moves through four stages: sensorimotor, preoperational, concrete operational, and formal operational.

- In his studies of moral development, Kohlberg asked his subjects to respond to moral dilemmas, situations in which two or more moral principles are in conflict.

- Kohlberg's stages of moral development—preconventional, conventional, and postconventional—are tied to Piaget's stages of cognitive development.

- According to Erikson's psychosocial theory, at different stages of life we have to contend with different issues; and the way in which we resolve those issues affects our later development.

Childhood: Ages Two to Twelve Years

Childhood begins when the child can walk well alone; it ends with puberty. This ten-year span encompasses the preschool years (roughly ages two to six) and the grade school years (roughly ages six to twelve).

Physical Development

During childhood, the explosive physical growth of infancy slows. At about age three, children settle down to a steady growth of 2 to 3 inches in height and 5 or so pounds in weight each year (Lowrey, 1978).

The rapid neurological development of infancy is nearly complete by the beginning of early childhood, with one important exception: at age two, young children have a denser network of cortical connections than they will have as adults (Chugani & Phelps, 1986; Huttenlocher, 1979). During infancy, the brain seems to make many more connections than it needs; during childhood, those that don't get used are "pruned" (see Figure 12.1). As children learn new skills, habits, and information, some pathways in the brain are strengthened while others are eliminated.

(a) At birth

(b) Six years old

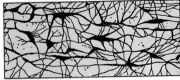
(c) Fourteen years old

Figure 12.1
Cortical Connections

At birth infants' brains are far from fully developed; many more cells and connections appear in the first few years. Later development consists in part of removing unnecessary connections.

Cognitive Development

Cognitive development in early childhood is closely related to language development (see Chapter 8). Between the ages of two and six, vocabulary increases from fifty to more than ten thousand words (Benedict, 1979); sentence structure becomes increasingly complex; and pronunciation improves dramatically.

These developments in language seem closely related to the development of **representational thought.** In early childhood, children begin to talk about events that are not taking place at the moment (yesterday's trip to the zoo, Andrea's birthday party next week) and about people and objects that are not present at the moment (mommy at the office with her briefcase, the swing in Tim's backyard). Closely linked to the acquisition of representational thought is the appearance of *imaginative play,* play in which something like a cardboard box stands for something else, such as a fort or a castle (Bruner, 1973).

Piaget and Childhood Cognition   According to Piaget, children pass through two developmental stages—the first at around two years, the second at around six years. In both stages he found important changes in their ability to perform mental operations. He defined **operations** as "internalized actions that have become reversible" (Piaget, 1936/1977, p. 354)—in other words, actions that children can carry out and reverse entirely in their imagination.

The Preoperational stage   Piaget called the preschool years (roughly ages two to six) the *preoperational stage.* He used the word *preoperational* because, although preschool children have acquired many of the skills that are necessary to later cognitive, linguistic, and social development, they are not yet able to understand things from perspectives other than their own.

To demonstrate his theory, Piaget designed a procedure called the *three-mountain test,* illustrated in Figure 12.2. The child sits in one of four chairs at a small table. On the table are three model mountains, all different sizes. The researcher asks the child to imagine what the mountains look like to a doll sitting on another chair at the table. Preoperational children are not able to work out the view from other perspectives; instead, they insist that the view from the other chairs is the same as the view from where they are sitting.

Figure 12.2
The Three Mountain Task

How would the mountains look to the doll? A preoperational child assumes they look just the same to everyone—the way they seem to the child.

Representational thought   The ability to talk about events or people not taking place or present at the moment.

Operation   An action that a child can carry out and reverse entirely in his or her imagination.

Piaget described the preoperational child's thinking as egocentric because these children are unable to imagine another perspective on the world. To avoid **egocentrism,** they would need to imagine how the view of the world they see before their eyes could be transformed into something different. Piaget pointed out that this is a considerable achievement, which preoperational children have not yet mastered (Piaget, 1952).

Egocentrism also limits the ability of preoperational children to conserve. **Conservation** is the ability to understand that certain properties (amount and number, for example) stay the same despite a change in the appearance, shape, or position of the object (see Figure 12.3). Some of Piaget's most striking observations about children's thinking concerned the failure to conserve. In one demonstration, Piaget showed a child two pieces of clay about the same size. After the child had agreed that they were the same size, Piaget would roll one piece into a long thin shape. Now the child would say that the long piece contained more clay, presumably because it looked longer. Similarly, it was Jason's inability to conserve that made him think he had more juice than Becky when it was poured into a tall, thin glass, and it was Becky's ability to conserve that helped her understand that he didn't.

**Figure 12.3
Conservation**

These are some of the tasks used to test whether children can conserve. In each task, a change in the appearance of the material leads preoperational children to assume that the quantity of material has changed as well.

Form of conservation	Child first sees	Child then sees	Child's response
Liquid amount		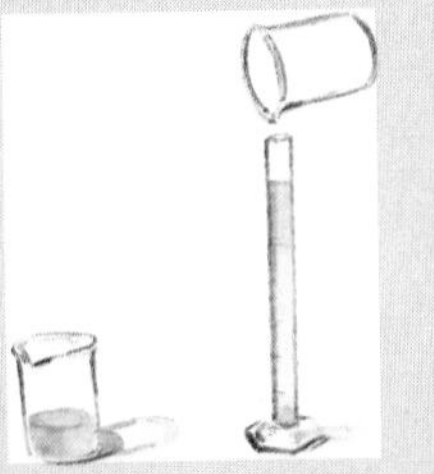	"Which beaker has more water?" Preoperational child chooses the taller thinner beaker. Operational child recognizes that the amount of water has not changed.
Solid amount			"Which shape has more clay?" Preoperational child chooses the longer form. Operational child recognizes that the amount of clay has not changed.
Number			"Which row has more buttons?" Preoperational child chooses the wider row. Operational child recognizes that the number of buttons has not changed.

Piaget pointed out that, in one sense, what children at this stage fail to recognize is that actions such as pouring from one container to another or rolling clay are reversible. That is, if you pour the juice into a taller container, you can also pour it back into the flatter container, and it will look the same again. Something—what we recognize as the volume of the juice—is conserved during these reversible operations.

Concrete operational stage According to Piaget, children move into the *concrete operational stage* at about age six. During this stage they understand that the three mountains look different from different perspectives; that the amount of water doesn't change when it's poured into a different-shaped container; and that the

Egocentrism The inability to see the world from another's perspective.

Conservation The ability to understand that certain properties of an object stay the same despite a change in the shape or position of the object.

quantity of clay remains the same whether the clay is in a ball or rolled. But despite their ability to perform many kinds of logical tasks, children in the concrete operational stage are not capable of abstract thought. Their imaginary manipulations are limited to physical actions that they can actually perform themselves, such as rolling a ball of clay into a snake.

Criticism of Piaget's Theory   According to Piaget's critics, his results may be a consequence of how his child subjects understood the test situation, not a consequence of how they understood the world. These critics have challenged Piaget's conclusions with experiments showing that young children are capable of reasoning correctly when problems are presented to them in the right way (Cohen, 1983; Matthews, 1980). For example, Martin Hughes and Margaret Donaldson (1979) questioned Piaget's findings in the three-mountain test. They argued that children should use their knowledge in a more familiar landscape. Mountains were too unfamiliar a landscape to test most children's awareness of other points of view. So they devised a test in which they asked their subjects to hide a little boy from the prying eyes of three policemen, as shown in Figure 12.4. When the problem of perspective is put this way, even three-year-olds can solve it.

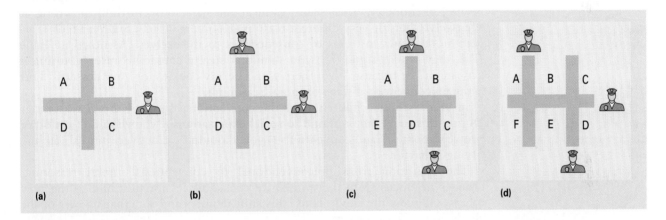

Source: Hughs & Donaldson, 1979.

Figure 12.4
The Three Policeman Test

Martin Hughs and Margaret Donaldson wondered if preschoolers' performance on Piaget's three-mountain test didn't have more to do with their lack of interest in mountains than with their inability to imagine the world from another person's point of view. When asked to find a hiding place "the policemen" couldn't see, most preschoolers chose the correct location.

Other studies show that preoperational children are able to conserve. In the chipped-beaker procedure (a variation on Piaget's water-beaker experiment), an equal amount of water is poured into two identical beakers. Then the researcher "notices" that one of the two beakers is chipped and, looking around, produces a taller, narrower beaker as a substitute. Once the transfer is made, the child is asked if the amounts are changed or still the same. In this case, many younger children recognize that volume has been conserved (Light, Buckingham & Robbins, 1979).

What has changed here is the nature of the substitution. When young children believe that the switch is part of the puzzle, that the experimenter is purposely manipulating the situation, they don't conserve. However, when they think the substitution is not part of the puzzle but the result of chance (a chipped beaker), they do. Perhaps the children think that if the experimenter has gone to the trouble to change something, he or she must want a different answer.

This point was made very effectively in a procedure called the *naughty teddy test* (McGarrigle & Donaldson, 1975). The test is similar to one of Piaget's standard conservation of number tasks, but with one important difference: the child is asked to believe that a mischievous teddy bear, not the researcher, carelessly disorders the materials.

For instance, in one of Piaget's standard conservation tasks the researcher spaces out two rows of buttons to the same length. Then, as the child watches, the researcher moves the buttons in one of the rows closer together. When asked whether the rows still contain the same number of buttons, most preoperational children said no. They believed that the longer row had more buttons, indicating they had failed to conserve number.

In the naughty teddy procedure, the same rows of buttons are used, but then the experimenter moves a teddy bear around the table, "accidentally" pushing the buttons together. Surprisingly, children too young to conserve number in Piaget's task do so readily under the naughty teddy condition.

What do these findings say about Piaget's stages? Obviously they call into question the timing of those stages. But they don't disprove the existence of the stages or the fact that they follow a sequence. Although children may pass through Piaget's stages of cognitive development earlier or later than he claimed, they do indeed pass through them and do so in the order that Piaget described.

The Development of Moral Reasoning

As children's ability to reason develops, so does their understanding of right and wrong, of morality. What seems right at age six may seem right or wrong at age twelve, but for very different reasons (Kohlberg, 1963). Six-year-olds evaluate moral issues in terms of consequences to themselves. As noted in Table 12.2, they would argue that you shouldn't steal a cookie because "you might get caught" or because "then there won't be any cookies for your dessert." This is the preconventional stage of moral reasoning.

In grade school, children enter the conventional stage of moral reasoning. During this stage they respond to social expectations ("you shouldn't eat other people's cookies") and conventions ("you shouldn't eat between meals") in justifying behavior.

The transition from preconventional to conventional moral reasoning changes the focus from the immediate consequences for the child to the way others will view the child. Thus, this shift requires and is perhaps a part of the child's loss of egocentrism.

Social Development

As children become increasingly mobile, they become less dependent on their families and more dependent on their peers and community institutions. The process by which children learn the customs and attitudes of the communities in which they live is called **socialization.**

Childhood corresponds to Erikson's third and fourth stages of psychosocial development (see Table 12.3). In the third stage, the preschool years, children struggle with their increasing independence. The child who manages this third stage well is more likely to become a self-directed individual, one who is capable of confidently initiating projects. But if this third stage goes badly, Erikson argues, the child may suffer from excessive feelings of guilt and indecision.

In the grade school years during Erikson's fourth stage, children typically focus on mastering social and practical skills and learn to measure their own competence against that of their peers. Children who resolve the conflict between industry and inferiority are likely to be productive and feel competent; those who don't are likely to lose interest in accomplishing tasks and to feel inferior.

Socialization The process by which children learn the customs and attitudes of their community.

Patterns of Social Interaction   From their original attachment to their mothers and fathers, children reach out to other members of the family and to their peers. Young children who are regularly in contact with their peers—in daycare centers, nursery schools, play groups, or large families—show a steady increase in the size of their groupings and in the degree of interdependence in their activities (Parten, 1933; Damon, 1983).

This developing interdependence can be seen in the way children play as they grow older. Toddlers engage in solitary or parallel play. In *solitary play,* children play by themselves, interacting with other children only when materials bring them into conflict—when two toddlers want the same toy, for example. Children engaged in *parallel play* seem to enjoy being close to another person. They play beside each other or with the same materials, but without trying to influence each other's play and without exchanging materials. By age four or five we see *associative play,* during which children interact over materials, talking about what they are doing and exchanging materials. Two four-year-olds playing with crayons and paper might pass the crayons back and forth and talk about their pictures, but they aren't likely to work on a drawing together. Indeed, such coordination of activities toward a common task is the hallmark of the later stage known as *cooperative play,* which emerges around age six or seven (Damon, 1983).

As children grow, they tend to seek out friends of the same age and especially gender (Hartup, 1983). Gender-linked differences can also be observed in the way preschoolers play and in the number of friendships they form (Pitcher & Schultz, 1983). Little boys tend to roughhouse, playing in open areas and large groups, with large objects. Little girls tend to play more quietly, in protected areas, with smaller toys and just a few close friends. In their imaginative play, boys pretend that they are superheroes or policemen in scenes that are full of action and conflict. Girls pretend that they are mothers or daughters or nurses or teachers, and the scenes they imagine are more realistic and often drawn from family life (Pitcher & Schultz, 1983).

In parallel play, children play by themselves but enjoy the proximity of others.

Girls' play is quieter, more cooperative, in smaller groups, and more likely built around familiar household situations. Boys' play is more boisterous, more aggressive, often in larger groups, and more likely to involve superheroes or "cops and robbers."

These differences in play patterns foreshadow a lifetime of differences in the social patterns of men and women. Women who interact with men in work settings—including female students at co-ed colleges—often complain that men dominate the setting. In groups, men are more interested in power and dominance; they tease and sometimes disrupt their female colleagues, talk louder, interrupt more, listen less, and are less likely to compromise than are their female counterparts (Maccoby, 1990). The same patterns of behavior are already apparent in four-and-a-half-year olds (Huston, 1985; Block, 1983).

Figure 12.5
Patterns of Play in Early Childhood

At age two, children play side by side but don't actually interact with each other very much. In the next few years, they begin to interact much more, but most of the increase is in playing with the same-sex children. By age five, play groups usually consist of boys or girls but are not mixed.

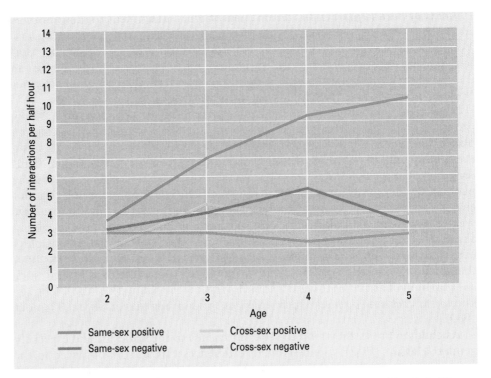

Source: Reprinted by permission of Greenwood Publishing Group, Inc., Westport, CT, from *Boys and Girls at Play* by E.G. Pitcher & L.H. Schultz. Copyright © 1983 by Praeger Publishers.

During early childhood, boys and girls increasingly choose to play in separate groups. Although the overall level of interaction among children rises dramatically between ages three and six, what's really increasing is interaction within gender-based groups (Pitcher & Schultz, 1983; Maccoby & Jacklin, 1987) (see Figure 12.5).

What causes this segregation of the sexes? Eleanor Maccoby (1990) suggests that two factors are at work here. First, most girls don't usually like the rough-and-tumble play that boys seem to engage in naturally. Second, girls often find boys frustrating to play with because boys are more competitive and less likely to mediate conflicts or encourage their playmates. Segregation seems to come about, then, because boys and girls reject each others' styles of interaction.

Why do these different styles show up so early? It's possible that parental influence is responsible. In Chapter 11, we saw how parents begin attributing personality to their children from the first hours of life. And by the time they enter nursery school, children are increasingly capable of understanding and assimilating the things that adults say about them, such as "Johnny's a real boy. He loves to wrestle and get dirty," or "Janie's such a little lady. She loves to wear dresses." With an awareness of gender roles may come increasing segregation.

Another possibility is the influence of testosterone. This hormone, which males produce in larger quantities than females do, appears to increase activity levels and decrease sensitivity to pain. Both of these effects could explain why most boys enjoy rough play and why most girls do not (Moyer, 1983).

Aggression   As children grow older, their aggression becomes more frequent but less physical. Aggression increases in frequency because, as children interact with other children more, they inevitably have more frequent conflicts. At the same time, however, both children's verbal skills and the proportion of verbal to physical aggression increase steadily. The result of these two trends is that the frequency of physical aggression peaks at about four years of age and then declines thereafter (Hartup, 1974; Parke & Slaby, 1983).

Of course, some children are more aggressive than others. One study followed a sample of New York schoolchildren from the third grade into adulthood (Huesmann et al., 1984). The researchers found that children may learn aggression from other family members. Children whose parents and siblings are openly aggressive are more likely to be aggressive themselves, as are children who are unloved or rejected. Physical punishment also influences aggression (Huesmann et al., 1984; Patterson, 1982). It decreases aggression in children who are not aggressive, and it increases aggression in children who are aggressive. These findings suggest that parental behavior reinforces children's behavior.

Apparently children are sensitive to the aggressive models they see around them. What about the models they watch on television? Children watch an average of twenty-six hours of television a week (Nielson Media, 1990). Depicted in much of what they see are acts of violence. Does watching violence on television encourage children to be aggressive?

As we indicated in Chapter 6, dozens of studies have tried to answer this question, but none has done so definitively. Nonexperimental observational studies do link aggressive behavior with violence on television (Rubinstein, 1983). But such studies don't distinguish between cause and effect. They don't tell us whether violence on television causes aggression, or whether children who are aggressive simply choose to watch more violent programs (Friedrich-Cofer & Huston, 1986).

Experimental studies can distinguish between cause and effect. When children are shown films and videotapes that depict aggression, they behave more aggressively; and their behavior in the experimental condition—the form their aggression takes—is modeled on the behavior they've watched (Singer & Singer, 1983a, 1983b). For example, Wendy Josephson (1987) showed second- and third-grade boys videotapes of either athletic action or violent police drama. A few minutes later, the same boys were observed playing floor hockey in a gymnasium. The observers, who did not know which videotape the players had watched, counted the number of times each boy elbowed another boy, pushed him down, hit him with a hockey stick, tripped him, or verbally abused him. Boys who had previously been rated aggressive by their teachers played more aggressively if they saw the violent videotape, but unaggressive boys were less

The more violence a child watches on television, the more violent behavior that child is likely to display, but which is cause and which is effect?

affected. It seems that violence on film can trigger aggression in youngsters, especially if they tend to be aggressive already. But even experimental studies like this one are inconclusive. In the artificial experimental setting, the children might assume that researcher—an authority figure—is sponsoring the aggression depicted in the videotape.

So, although psychologists have shown that watching violence on television is associated with aggression in the nonexperimental setting and that watching videotaped violence causes aggression in the experimental setting, they have yet to provide incontestible evidence that watching violence on television *causes* aggression in the nonexperimental setting (Freedman, 1984, 1986). Still, the National Institute of Mental Health, the American Academy of Pediatrics, and the American Psychological Association have "all concluded that television violence causes aggressive behavior in children" (Zilke, 1988, p. 1831).

Recap

- During childhood, the explosive physical growth of infancy slows.

- The development of representational thought in early childhood is closely related to the development of language.

- In Piaget's preoperational stage, children are not yet able to understand things from other people's perspectives.

- Egocentrism—the inability to see the world from another's perspective—also limits the ability of preoperational children to conserve.

- In the concrete operational stage, children are able to perform many kinds of logical tasks, but they are not yet capable of abstract thought. Their mental manipulations are limited to actions that they can actually perform.

- Research calls into question the timing of Piaget's stages but not the existence of stages of cognitive development and the fact that they follow a sequence.

- As children's ability to reason develops, so does their understanding of right and wrong.

- In the preconventional stage of moral reasoning, children evaluate moral issues in terms of consequences to themselves.

- In the conventional stage of moral reasoning, children respond to social expectations and conventions in justifying behavior.

- Socialization is the process by which children learn the customs and attitudes of the communities in which they live.

- In Erikson's third stage of psychosocial development, children struggle with their increasing independence.

- In the fourth stage of psychosocial development, children typically focus on mastering social and practical skills and learn to measure their own competence against that of their peers.

- There also are gender-linked differences in the way preschoolers play and in the number of friendships they form.

- As children grow, they tend to seek out friends of the same age and gender.

- As children grow older, they become more aggressive; but the form of their aggressiveness changes—from predominantly physical to predominantly verbal.

- Studies seem to indicate that children learn aggression from aggressive models, particularly the members of their families.

- Although psychologists have shown that watching videotaped violence causes aggression in experiments and that watching violence on television is associated with aggression outside of experiments, they have yet to prove conclusively that watching violence on television causes aggression in the nonexperimental setting.

Adolescence The developmental stage between childhood and adulthood.

Puberty The period of physical change that prepares the body for reproduction.

Adolescence

Adolescence, the developmental stage between childhood and adulthood, is a period of important change. The first psychologist to write about the turbulence of adolescence was G. Stanley Hall (1904). Our three stage theorists also believed that adolescence is a critical time. For Piaget it is the time when newly discovered powers of abstraction are first applied to mathematics, ethics, and other areas. For Kohlberg it marks the appearance of the third level of moral reasoning, the stage during which the developing person begins to reason in terms of abstract moral principles such as justice and respect for life. For Erikson it is the period in which the developing individual works out an identity. Those who successfully resolve the issues of adolescence become adults with a firm sense of who they are and what they stand for.

Physical Development

Sometime between the ages of ten and fifteen, the pituitary gland sharply increases its output of the hormones that control the thyroid and sex glands. This phenomenon triggers the onset of **puberty,** the period of physical change that prepares the body for reproduction.

Most cultures attach significance to the onset of puberty, often marking the occasion with elaborate rituals.

During puberty, the individual's rate of growth doubles. Although the growth spurt occurs somewhat earlier in females, it is more dramatic in males. Some young men grow as much as 6 inches in a single year. This explosive growth produces startling changes in the relationships among the parts of the body and, sometimes, clumsy movements until boys have relearned fine motor control.

The *gonadotropins* are the hormones that act on the sex glands—the testes in the male and the ovaries in the female. These hormones trigger the production of testosterone and the estrogens, the hormones that control the development of the reproductive organs. These organs we call the **primary sex characteristics.** The gonadotropins also govern the development of the **secondary sex characteristics:** the female's breasts, the male's deep voice, the distribution of pubic and facial hair, and the shape of the adult body (see Figure 12.6). Under the influence of testosterone, the male's bones become sturdier, his muscles thicker, his chest and shoulders wider. Under the influence of the estrogens, the female's pelvis widens to facilitate childbearing, and she develops a layer of fat under her skin, giving her body a smoother, more rounded appearance.

One to two years after the onset of puberty, the body is capable of reproduction. Sometime after they start menstruating, young women begin to produce fertile eggs. And at about age fourteen, young men begin to produce viable sperm.

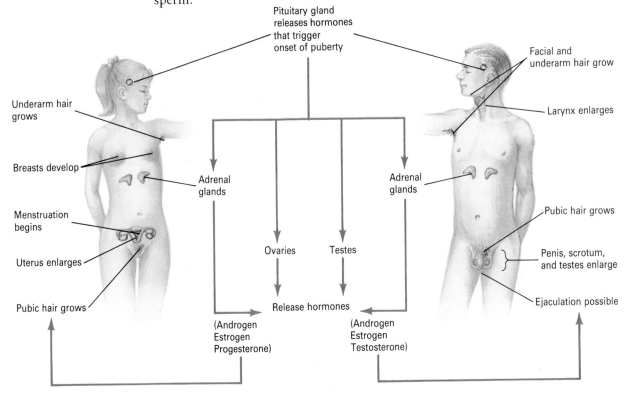

Figure 12.6
Physical Changes at Puberty

At puberty, dramatic physical changes occurring in both sexes trigger the onset of reproductive maturity.

The timing of the onset of puberty varies dramatically from person to person. Some children begin to mature physically at age eight; others at age sixteen or seventeen. Socioeconomic factors account for some of this variation. Children who are well fed and healthy tend to enter puberty earlier than those who are not. In fact, over the last century, as our understanding of health and nutrition has increased, the onset of menstruation has moved forward as much as two years (Bullough, 1981).

Cognitive Development

Primary sex characteristics The reproductive organs.

Secondary sex characteristics Characteristics of the two sexes that are not essential to reproduction.

Hand in hand with the physical changes in adolescence go changes in the adolescent's cognitive abilities. Adolescence marks Piaget's final stage, the *formal operational stage.* Adolescents are capable of abstract thought. Here's an example:

$$a + a = ?$$

If you asked an eight-year-old to solve this equation, he would probably say, "You can't add letters." But a thirteen- or fourteen-year-old understands not only that the correct answer is $2a$ but also that the completed equation is an abstract statement about addition: if you add something to itself, you end up with two of that something. Adolescents newfound skills at abstraction mean that in analyzing a problem—how to organize a dance or solve a mathematical equation, for example—they are able to come up with a list of possible solutions, consider them, and choose one.

Adolescents understand that reasoning is a process that can be right or wrong in and of itself, totally separate from what the reasoning is about. In Chapter 8 we talked about syllogisms, like this one:

All pigs are purple.

This animal is a pig.

Therefore, this animal is purple.

Children in the concrete operational stage don't see the reasoning at work here. They'll say the syllogism is wrong because pigs aren't purple. But people in the formal operational stage are able to ignore the content of the syllogism and evaluate its form. It doesn't matter that what the first sentence says is wrong; the syllogism is correct because the reasoning is correct.

A procedure that's widely used to demonstrate the transition from concrete operational to formal operational thinking is the pendulum test (Inhelder & Piaget, 1958; Martorano, 1977). The subject receives three weights that can be suspended from three lengths of string and is asked to decide which factors determine the speed of the pendulum swing: the size of the weight, the length of the string, or the distance at which the pendulum is pulled back before being released.

Concrete operational thinkers randomly try different combinations of weight, string length, and pendulum displacement, and usually announce—incorrectly—that some combination of these variables determines the rate at which the pendulum swings. They are apt to proceed in that way because they confuse their own actions with those of the pendulum and because they lack any abstract concept of a variable.

Formal operational thinkers are much more likely to systematically explore the effects of varying each variable. Using a single string length and displacement, they might try the different weights. Then they might leave the weights and string length the same and try different displacements. Finally, they might hold weight and displacement the same and try different string lengths. In this way, they quickly come to the correct conclusion that string length, and only string length, affects the speed at which a pendulum swings.

Their newfound ability to form abstractions means that adolescents are often very idealistic. In family discussions, they tend to take highly principled positions based on concepts like "love" and "fairness" and "freedom." One abstraction that's particularly important is the "self." Unlike children, who go through the day without worrying about how one activity relates to another, adolescents tend to wonder how their tennis, dancing, and chemistry are related to their concept of "self."

The capacity for abstract thought also contributes to **adolescent egocentrism:** adolescents tend to assume that everybody is thinking the way they do about the same things that they're thinking about. So, for example, when a teenager who's worried about how his hair looks walks into a room, he's likely to assume that everyone in the room is looking at his hair. Adolescent egocentrism may well be one reason why some teenagers are very shy (Elkind & Bowen, 1979).

Adolescent egocentrism The tendency of adolescents to assume that everybody is thinking the way they do about the same things that they are thinking about.

Carol Gilligan has identified two different types of moral judgment at the highest developmental levels. Men's moral judgments tend to be based on abstract moral principles; women's moral judgments are more strongly rooted in the context of human life.

The Development of Moral Reasoning

According to Kohlberg, most young people enter adolescence at the stage of conventional moral reasoning: they base their thinking about what is right or wrong on law and social rules. In adolescence, they begin to apply abstract principles to moral dilemmas—a process Kohlberg called *postconventional reasoning*. Sometimes these principles underlie social conventions; but on occasion they conflict with and supersede such conventions.

Let's go back to Heinz's dilemma. Should he steal the drug to save his wife's life? Conventional moral reasoners might say "no" because stealing is against the law, or "yes" because Heinz has a responsibility to take care of his wife. Postconventional moral reasoners go beyond the law or convention to the principle that underlies it. No, he shouldn't steal the medicine because our society depends on a system of laws we all agree on, and when we break the law, we put the structure of our society at risk. On the other side, the postconventional person might conclude that Heinze should steal it because husbands and wives have a duty to care for each other. In fact, in our society, we are all responsible for one another. Human life must have a greater value than property.

The change in moral reasoning from conventional to postconventional probably relates to the gradual extension of the adolescent's social frame of reference (Damon, 1983). As young people move from junior to senior high school and from senior high school to college and the workplace, they encounter an ever-widening range of people and standards. Moreover, their newfound skill at formal operations quickly teaches them that almost any action can be justified in terms of one or more moral principles.

By tying his stages of moral reasoning to Piaget's stages of cognitive development, Kohlberg implied that moral development follows automatically from the individual's growing cognitive ability. But does it? Researchers have had difficulty finding evidence of Kohlberg's stages across all cultures or even among certain groups within our culture. And some argue that Kohlberg's theory leaves out or minimizes moral concepts that are important in other cultures (Boyes & Walker, 1988). For example, in Chinese culture, many moral judgments are apparently rooted in feelings of love and respect for one's parents, in a way that is not captured by Kohlberg's system.

Other researchers point out that Kohlberg's stages don't apply particularly well to women. Remember that Kohlberg's original studies were done with boys and young men. When researcher Carol Gilligan (1982) tried to duplicate his findings with young women, she found some important differences in their responses to Kohlberg's dilemmas.

Does this mean that young women are less capable of abstract moral reasoning than young men? Gilligan didn't think so. She argued that Kohlberg's scoring procedures confuse the *way* we reason with the *values* we reason with. Because young women place a high value on personal relationships, they're concerned about the moral impact of moral decisions on others. As a result they seem to be at the conventional stage of moral reasoning when, in fact, they are at the postconventional stage. She insisted that men's responses to Kohlberg's dilemmas indicate not a higher level of moral reasoning but, rather, a bias in Kohlberg's scoring system toward the comparatively abstract and impersonal values that men hold in our society (Gilligan, 1982).

Finally, even if Kohlberg's descriptions of moral reasoning are accurate, they may not characterize moral action. A child who would say that Heinz should take the drug "because he wants it" still might give his teacher the dollar he found in the school corridor. In a review of the literature on moral cognition and moral action, Augusto Blasi (1980) did not find conclusive evidence that people's actual ethical choices and level of moral reasoning are linked.

Social Development

Adolescence is a time of comparative freedom. Parents exert less and less control, and the responsibility of taking care of children or aging parents lies far in the future for most young people in this age group. This freedom allows adolescents to be spontaneous, to experience all kinds of new things. It also has a downside. In part because they lack long-term commitments to other people, adolescents are prone to uncertainty, moodiness, depression, as well as to drug and alcohol abuse.

Social Groups and Sexuality   In adolescence, patterns of social interaction—*social organization*—gradually change (Dunphy, 1963). In early adolescence, youngsters tend to form small cliques—groups of two or three close friends, segregated by gender. But by late adolescence, we find several opposite-sex couples, loosely associated in a social circle (see Figure 12.7).

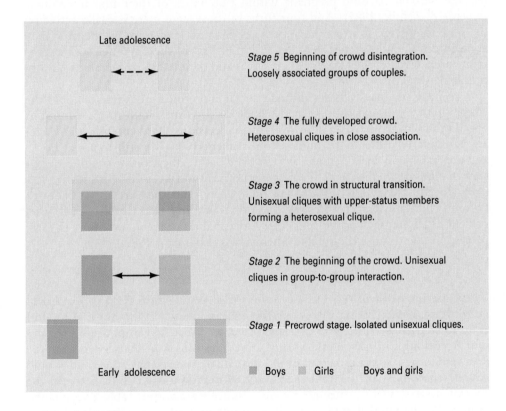

Late adolescence

Stage 5 Beginning of crowd disintegration. Loosely associated groups of couples.

Stage 4 The fully developed crowd. Heterosexual cliques in close association.

Stage 3 The crowd in structural transition. Unisexual cliques with upper-status members forming a heterosexual clique.

Stage 2 The beginning of the crowd. Unisexual cliques in group-to-group interaction.

Stage 1 Precrowd stage. Isolated unisexual cliques.

Early adolescence

■ Boys ■ Girls ■ Boys and girls

Figure 12.7
Changes in Association Patterns During Adolescence

During adolescence, social interactions change from exclusively same-sex groups toward confederations of couples.

Source: Dunphy, 1963.

With the formation of couples comes increased sexual intimacy and, ultimately, sexual intercourse. The age of first intercourse varies widely by sex and race, but more than 60 percent of all teenagers have had intercourse by age nineteen (Moore et al., 1987).

The increased incidence of sexual intercourse brings with it the risk of sexually transmitted disease and unwanted pregnancy. A surprisingly small proportion of adolescents understand how these diseases are transmitted or how methods of contraception work (Coles & Stokes, 1985; DiClemente, Boyer & Morales, 1988). And many of those who do understand the risks ignore them (Kegeles, Adler & Irwin, 1988), insisting that "it can't happen to me."

AIDS has made this confusion and carelessness potentially lethal. Because of the long delay—as much as eight to ten years—between exposure to the disease and the onset of symptoms, the risks of contracting AIDS while an adolescent are much greater than the present number of adolescents with AIDS would suggest (Flora & Thoresen, 1988). As of May 1988, only 1 percent (705 cases) of all reported cases of AIDS in the United States involved people between the ages of thirteen and twenty-one. But young adults in their twenties account for 20 percent of all reported AIDS cases. And in most of these cases AIDS was probably contracted when the victims were adolescents (Curran et al., 1988).

Though usually not life threatening, an unwanted pregnancy can have profound effects on a teenager. Yet less than half of all teenagers use contraception during their first sexual intercourse (Brooks-Gunn & Furstenberg, 1989). One study found that only two-thirds of sexually active urban adolescents use contraception of any kind, and a fourth of these adolescents use high-risk methods, such as withdrawal or rhythm (Zelnick & Kantner, 1980). Although pregnancy rates among teenagers have been declining since the 1970s (Furstenberg, Brooks-Gunn & Chase-Lansdale, 1989), more than a third of all sexually active teenage women become pregnant within two years of their first intercourse (Koenig & Zelnik, 1982). And four-fifths of those who were sexually active by the time they were fourteen have been pregnant at least once by the time they are eighteen (Coates, Petersen & Perry, 1982). Few of these women seek appropriate prenatal care, thus leaving themselves and their babies vulnerable to health problems (Makinson, 1985).

A teenage pregnancy raises difficult social and ethical questions. Should the couple marry? Should they keep the baby or give the child up for adoption? Should the woman have an abortion? These decisions, hard enough at any age, are particularly difficult for high school students who are still living at home and dependent on their parents, without the basic education or training necessary to support themselves. Teenagers who bear and keep their babies are less likely to complete high school than their peers, and they are more likely to become child abusers. Yet despite these discouraging facts, approximately 50 percent of all pregnant adolescents carry their babies to term, and more than 90 percent decide to raise their babies themselves (Edleman, 1987).

The Question of Identity   Puberty ushers in Erikson's fifth stage of psychosocial development. During this stage, the issue is identity: Who am I? Who do I want to be friends with? Who do I want to date? What do I want to do with my life? According to Erikson, answering these questions was relatively easy in the low-technology societies of centuries ago. In these societies, the child would have learned most of the skills necessary to function as an adult between the ages of six and twelve, during Erikson's industry stage (see Table 12.3). Then, at puberty, the child would be ready to move into adult society and adopt an adult identity. In our high-technology society, however, the knowledge needed to function as an adult requires many more years to learn. Erikson argued that, as a result, children could not acquire full-fledged adult identities until they were eighteen or twenty-one, or even older. The result was that adolescents were stuck in a *moratorium,* during which they were developmentally ready to work on their identities but unable to complete the process successfully.

That process, as Erikson described it, is not easy. He identified three responses to the adolescent identity crisis—responses that are fortunately temporary:

- *Identity foreclosure* The adolescent fixes prematurely on a particular identity, usually one closely related to the hopes and expectations of his or her parents. The problem with identity foreclosure is that the identity arrived at is not particularly enduring, for which reason the individual may find himself or herself reliving an adolescent identity crisis in middle age.

- *Negative identity formation* Here the adolescent responds to parental expectations by choosing a career or lifestyle of which his or her parents do not approve.
- *Identity diffusion* The adolescent casts off his or her childhood identity but doesn't search for a new identity. Instead he or she drifts aimlessly, planning one career one day, another the next.

For a majority of adolescents, however, the process of identity formation goes relatively smoothly, and they gradually acquire a stable identity. As Erikson has noted, the sign that someone has acquired an identity is that they no longer think about it: they can take themselves and who they are for granted.

Adolescent Vulnerability   For adolescents in the throes of a difficult identity crisis, adolescence can be a time of inner turmoil, leaving them vulnerable to substance abuse, criminal behavior, and the risk of suicide. (We talked about the hazards of hard drugs in Chapters 2 and 5.) Although drugs like cocaine and crack can be very harmful and have received justifiable public attention, the less notorious drugs—alcohol, tobacco, and marijuana—affect many more lives because their use is so widespread. According to a nationwide survey, only a minority of high school seniors have ever used hard drugs, but 92 percent have used alcohol and 24 percent, marijuana. Among those using alcohol, 5 percent reported that they drank *daily* (Newcomb & Bentler, 1989).

Although many adolescents are under enormous stress and do face serious conflict, for most teenagers the transition from childhood to adulthood is gradual and relatively calm (Savin-Williams & Demo, 1984). One research team repeatedly interviewed a group of adolescents from age eleven to age eighteen. Far from finding evidence of crisis, the researchers discovered that their subjects' views about themselves, their sexuality, and the world changed gradually (Dusek & Flaherty, 1981). Nor is there evidence that a dramatic separation from parents necessarily occurs during this period. Among a sample of seventeen-year-olds, 70 to 80 percent reported that they felt close to their parents. And when asked to list their heroes, college students often named their fathers and mothers (Starke, 1986). In short, adolescence may be not a period of crisis for all individuals so much as a period in which some individuals experience crises so dramatic that they capture our attention and concern.

Recap

- Adolescence is the developmental stage between childhood and adulthood.
- Hormones secreted by the pituitary gland trigger the onset of puberty, the period of physical change that prepares the body for reproduction.
- Testosterone and the estrogens control the development of the reproductive organs and the secondary sex characteristics.
- The timing of the onset of puberty varies dramatically from person to person, partly as a result of socioeconomic factors.
- Adolescence marks Piaget's final stage of cognitive development, the stage of formal operational thought.
- The capacity for abstract thought contributes to adolescent egocentrism, the tendency of adolescents to assume that everybody thinks the way they do about the same things they think about.

- Kohlberg linked the capacity for abstract thought with postconventional reasoning, the ability to apply abstract principles to moral dilemmas.

- Critics argue that Kohlberg's levels of moral reasoning, if they exist at all, are specific to males in this culture and are not necessarily tied to moral behavior.

- With the change in social organization in adolescence comes increased sexual intimacy.

- In Erikson's fifth stage of psychosocial development, the primary issue is identity.

- Erikson identified three different responses to the adolescent identity crisis: identity foreclosure, negative identity formation, and identity diffusion.

- For most teenagers, the transition from childhood to adulthood is gradual and relatively calm.

Figure 12.8
Stages in Family Development

Family systems psychologists see individual development within the context of the developing family, usually a complex association of three or more generations. Coincidences in the life events of the different generations that make up a family can have a tremendous influence on an individual's development. Consider, for example, what it is like for adults in middle age when the departure of their children from home happens to coincide with the death of one or more of their own parents.

Adulthood

At one time, adulthood was thought of as the culmination of all the developmental processes that go on in infancy, childhood, and adolescence—as the peak from which we descend into old age. But in recent years, psychologists have come to see adulthood as simply another stage of development, marked by physical, cognitive, and social change.

Seeing adulthood as just one stage of life is, in part, a way of viewing human development known as the *lifespan perspective.* In this approach to developmental psychology, the lives of individuals are studied from birth to death and understood in terms of the familial, societal, and historical contexts in which they are lived (Hareven, 1982; Smelser & Erikson, 1980). Moreover, the lifespan perspective is often combined with a *family systems approach,* which focuses on the fact that most of us grow up in families—complex associations with other

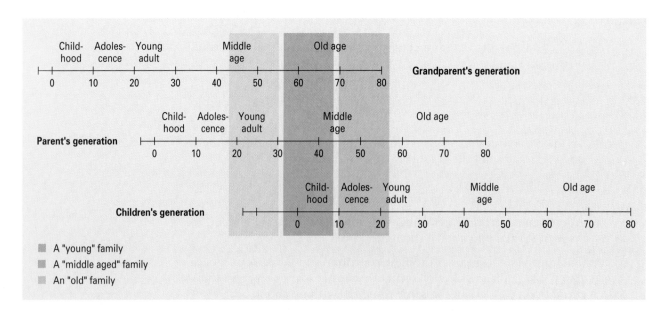

How Do We Know That?

Research on adulthood, to a greater extent than research on any other stage of development, is troubled by cohort effects. A *cohort* is a group of people raised during the same era. And *cohort effects* are historical influences—wars, economic crises, social upheavals—that affect people born at a particular time but do not affect people in general. The problem with cohort effects is that they leave researchers unable to decide whether the differences among subjects are caused by differences in age or by membership in different cohorts. For example, suppose we want to study the effects of age on sexual activity. The most obvious way is to carry out a *cross-sectional study,* for which we would recruit people of different ages and ask them about the frequency of their sexual behavior. If our older subjects reported less frequent sexual activity than did our younger subjects, we could conclude that sexual activity declines with advancing age.

But how confident can we be about that conclusion? To recruit subjects of different ages, we have to recruit subjects from different cohorts. Our sixty-year-olds would need to have been born in the 1930s; our forty-year-olds, in the 1950s; our twenty-year-olds, in the 1970s. Suppose our sixty-year-old subjects are less active sexually, not because of their age but because they were raised at a time when sexual activity was less accepted than it is now. Maybe our 1930s cohort has always been less active sexually. Here cohort effects might cause us to overestimate the decline of sexual activity in adulthood.

The only way to eliminate cohort effects is to perform a *longitudinal study,* a study that examines the same cohort repeatedly throughout its lifetime. Because all members of a given cohort are subject to the same historical events, any differences we find cannot be attributed to being born and raised at a particular time.

But longitudinal studies are vulnerable to sampling bias because of the long time it takes to complete them. Many longitudinal studies outlive the researchers who initiated them. And because longitudinal studies take such a long time to complete, many subjects drop out of them. The researchers can hope that the subjects who remain are representative of the original sample, but that's not always the case. In our hypothetical study, some subjects might drop out because they're embarrassed by our persistent questions about their sex lives. If these people are also less active sexually (which seems reasonable given their embarrassment), then our results might underestimate the decline of sexual activity in adulthood.

So how do we study the relationship between age and sexual activity? The solution is the one we have encountered before: use more than one method. In this case, we would combine cross-sectional and longitudinal studies. The former allow us to avoid sampling bias; the latter, cohort effects.

---

people who are developing as well (Minuchin & Baker, 1978). To fully understand adult development, then, we have to examine how the family develops.

Figure 12.8 shows the stages of family development. They begin with a young couple, alone, often recently separated from their parents; then the couple has children, with grandparents in the wings; as the children grow to adolescence, the grandparents age and die; and, finally, the children leave home, forming new families themselves (Aldous, 1978; Galinsky, 1981).

Puzzle It Out!

To a lifespan developmentalist, the historical and economic context of family life is an important focus of study. Dramatic economic changes can completely alter the structure of a family and affect the development of the children growing up in that family.

For example, consider the special historical and economic events that have affected your development if you were born around 1970:

- When you were an infant, the political disruptions of the Vietnam War were taking place.
- When you were a child, there was an extraordinary increase in the cost of living. Interest rates skyrocketed, and young families had a difficult time making ends meet. Many families had to forgo dreams of owning a home. Inflation drove mothers into the workforce in record numbers, contributing to such child-rearing phenomena as daycare centers and latchkey children.
- Your adolescence took place during a severe recession, in which many workers lost their jobs, many businesses went bankrupt, and many families lost their homes.
- Your early sexual development took place at the beginning of the AIDS crisis and the peak of the right-to-life movement. Both developments cast doubt on the sexual revolution that had characterized your parents' early adulthood.
- As you move into adulthood, some of the important factors that will affect your life are already evident. One is the increasing longevity of the elderly (Dietz, 1988). The proportion of elderly to the total population during the middle age of your cohort is going to be greater than ever before in American history and may place an extraordinary social and economic burden on your generation.

What do you suppose the impact of all these events has been and will be on the lifespan development of yourself and your friends?

Physical Development

Sometime during early adulthood (ages twenty to thirty-five), and usually in the early twenties, most individuals reach the peak of physical fitness. They are as healthy as they have ever been and more healthy than they will be for the rest of their lives.

Physiological Aging   From the early twenties on, the functioning of the body begins a steady decline that continues throughout adulthood. In middle adulthood (ages thirty-five to sixty-five), the decline is gradual. A middle adult who eats well and exercises can easily outperform a younger person who has failed to keep fit. But by late adulthood (age sixty-five and beyond), the effects of this decline become evident. Late adults are physically weaker. Their joints are less limber, their muscles are less powerful, and their heart and lungs have less capacity.

Also in late adulthood, sensory and perceptual processes are less sharp. Late adults find it increasingly difficult to distinguish among multiple stimuli and may become confused in complex perceptual situations. The acuteness of their hearing diminishes, particularly the hearing of high-pitched sounds. Moreover, the lenses of their eyes stiffen, reducing vision. And as late adults have weaker senses of taste and smell (Stevens & Cain, 1987), they like their food saltier and sweeter than younger people do (Murphy & Withee, 1986).

Reproductive Aging   Fertility also declines with age, but the pattern of decline differs by gender. In the male, the decline is gradual: over time, both the number and the viability of the man's sperm decrease. In the female, the decline is gradual at first. Then, at around age fifty, the ovaries sharply cut back their production of estrogens. Without estrogens the woman enters **menopause;** when both ovulation and menstruation stop.

Sexual activity in both genders seems to decline gradually throughout adulthood, falling from an average of two to three orgasms a week in the twenties to an average of less than one a week in the sixties. These figures probably underestimate sexual interest in late adulthood because some people become sexually inactive for reasons of illness or bereavement, not for lack of interest (Brecher, 1984). In addition, as discussed earlier, we cannot rule out the possibility of cohort effects.

As these cyclists would testify, the vast majority of people in late adulthood lead healthy and active lives.

The Quality of Life in Late Adulthood   Despite these many changes, most late adults adapt well to their physical difficulties and carry on productive lives. In fact, what we fear most about the quality of life in old age apparently isn't so much a problem for the elderly. Table 12.5 shows the results of a Harris poll that compared the responses of late adults with those of young and middle adults to several questions concerning the quality of life in old age (National Council on Aging, 1976). Although most early and middle adults expected that a large number of the elderly would characterize themselves as afraid, sick, poor, lonely, and lacking adequate medical care and housing, only a small percentage of the elderly actually did so. In fact, the vast majority of late adults are satisfied with their lives; they are healthy and able to live independently.

An important factor in maintaining the physical health of late adults is an active social life. Indeed, the number of family and friends an older person can call on is a significant statistical predictor of physical health (Cutrona, Russell & Rose, 1986).

Menopause The cessation of menstruation.

	Percentage of Those Describing Area as a "Very Serious Problem"	
	Personal Experience	**Public Expectation**
Fear of crime	23	50
Poor health	21	51
Not enough money to live on	15	62
Loneliness	12	60
Not enough medical care	10	44
Not feeling needed	7	54
Not enough to do	6	37
Not enough friends	5	28
Not enough job opportunities	5	45
Poor housing	4	35

Source: Adapted from the National Council on the Aging, 1975.

Cognitive Development

Recent studies of cognitive development in adulthood have focused on two issues: first, whether adult thinking represents a distinct stage or stages of cognitive development; and, second, whether, to what degree, and in what ways our ability to think changes in middle and late adulthood.

Is There Cognitive Development After Formal Operations?   At least two theorists, Klaus Riegel (1973) and Michael Basseches (1984), have suggested that the stage of formal operations characteristic of adolescence is succeeded by another stage of cognitive functioning, a stage they call **dialectical reasoning.** During this stage, adults learn to apply the principles of abstract reasoning acquired during adolescence to the practical issues of living. Thinking here is more open, more flexible, and more pragmatic than the formal operational thought characteristic of adolescents (Labouvie-Vief, 1980). In particular, dialectical reasoning takes conflicting principles and uses them to generate a solution that best meets the situation at hand.

How does it work? Let's take the issue of whether the federal government should fund daycare centers. There are good arguments on both sides. One person, starting from the principle that the federal budget should be balanced, might argue that the government cannot afford to pay for daycare centers. Another person, arguing from the principle that child welfare should be society's primary concern, might insist that the federal government is obligated to support daycare centers. Both of these arguments are well founded; both are the product of formal operational thought.

Dialectical reasoning allows us to recognize the value of both arguments. It also leads us to see that in the real world each generates its own contradiction. For example, the person arguing for a balanced budget should realize that if children are neglected in their early years, it's going to cost society a lot more to deal with their health and behavior problems later than with their daycare

Dialectical reasoning The application of the principles of abstract reasoning to everyday issues of living.

now. In a sense, the government can't afford *not* to care for children. Conversely, the person arguing for government support should recognize that high levels of government spending lead to inflation, which increases the economic stress on young families with children, which in turn reduces the quality and quantity of time that parents can spend with their children.

Of course, dialectical reasoning doesn't lead infallibly to a solution. But it does reveal that any real and enduring solution to a real-world problem usually requires integrating and perhaps compromising the abstract principles that formal operations thinkers find so compelling.

Although dialectical reasoning may be a distinct form of thought, there is only weak evidence to suggest that it represents a distinct stage in adult development. Adults engage in this sort of reasoning some of the time; but, as Basseches (1984) discovered, it is by no means a characteristic of all or even most adults in all or even many situations.

Does the Ability to Think Decline in Adulthood?

We know that the gradual physical decline that takes place during adulthood affects the nervous system, slowing reaction time (Birren, Woods & Williams, 1980) and complicating simple tasks such as copying and substituting digits (Salthouse, 1985a, 1985b). But what about cognitive abilities? How does aging affect our capacity to reason?

Not surprisingly, tests that demand rapid processing of sensory material often show the elderly at a disadvantage (Birren et al., 1980). Yet skills that demand reflection and complexity of understanding often show older people to be equal or at an advantage. For example, if a spoken text is read more rapidly, an older person will have more difficulty understanding it than a younger person will. But if the text is made longer or more complicated, the older person will do at least as well as the younger one (Stine, Wingfield & Poon, 1988).

Many psychologists believe that certain cognitive abilities actually continue to improve in adulthood. In 1956, K. Warner Schaie did a cross-sectional study on the effect of aging on reasoning, mathematical ability, spatial visualization, and verbal comprehension and fluency. He studied 490 people, ages twenty-five to sixty-seven, in groups of 70. And he did observe a decline from his youngest to his oldest subjects on many of his measures.

Schaie initially concluded that aging does decrease cognitive ability. Then, concerned about possible cohort effects, he began to retest his subjects at seven-year intervals. In these tests he discovered that the performance of many of his cohorts actually improved with age (see Figure 12.9). It seems that cohort effects (for instance, the younger subjects' greater experience with tests), not aging, were responsible for the decrease he found in his original study, and that cognitive ability actually holds steady or improves with aging until late adulthood (Schaie & Herzog, 1983).

Other psychologists insist, however, that certain cognitive skills do grow weaker as we age. John Horn (1985) makes a distinction between two kinds of intelligence: crystallized intelligence and fluid intelligence. **Crystallized intelligence** allows us to put to use information we've already learned. When we cook a meal we've cooked many times before, change a tire, add or subtract numbers, or solve familiar problems, we are usually using our crystallized intelligence. **Fluid intelligence** allows us to acquire new knowledge and skills. When we learn a new dance step, operate an unfamiliar piece of machinery, or learn a new language, we're using our fluid intelligence. (These concepts are discussed in greater detail in the section on assessment in Chapter 13).

Although most tests of intelligence attempt to measure fluid intelligence, they inevitably measure crystallized intelligence as well because it's very difficult to

Crystallized intelligence Knowledge and skills that have been memorized and can be put to use in familiar situations.

Fluid intelligence The ability to learn new information and skills.

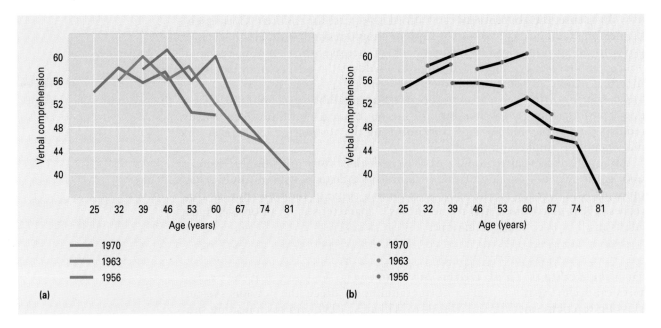

Figure 12.9
The Effects of Aging on Cognitive Development

Schaie measured the intellectual ability of a sample of subjects in 1956 and again in 1963 and 1970. Because he tested the same subjects on three different occasions, he was able to provide both (a) a cross-sectional and (b) a longitudinal analysis. Notice that the cross-sectional analysis shows that verbal comprehension begins to decline in the forties; the longitudinal analysis shows that only the cohorts in their sixties at the beginning of the study showed a decline. Schaie originally attributed the differences he found between his older and younger subjects to age. Later he concluded that those differences were the effects of educational differences among the cohorts.

Source: Adapted from Cole & Cole, 1989; data from Schaie, 1983.

design a test of fluid intelligence that does not make use of a person's factual knowledge and know-how. Horn (1982) argues that aging does affect fluid intelligence but that this effect is masked in studies like Schaie's by a simultaneous increase in crystallized intelligence.

Most problems in everyday life require the joint application of crystallized and fluid intelligence. So the outcome of this controversy is that both sides agree that, for most purposes, older people function as well as or better than they did when younger.

Social Development

Erikson identified three stages of social development in adulthood. In the first, early adulthood, the individual focuses on establishing a primary relationship with another person. Positive resolution at this stage leads to intimacy; negative resolution, to isolation.

In the second stage, middle adulthood, the issue is productivity or, as Erikson calls it, *generativity*. The individual's sense of achievement can be a product of raising children, a career, a hobby, a community activity, or a combination of them all. The objective here is a sense of accomplishment and involvement.

Finally, in late adulthood, the individual reflects on his or her life. If that life seems meaningful, the individual has a sense of fulfillment; if not, the individual is likely to fall victim to despair.

There are several other stage theories of adult social development, all of them based on Erikson's work. Like Erikson, Roger Gould (1978) believed that in each stage of development the individual has a psychological task to accomplish that eases the transition to the next stage. But Gould's task is the same throughout all stages: casting off a false assumption. Only the assumptions themselves change from stage to stage.

Gould identified seven transformations between the ages of sixteen and sixty. In the first, "leaving our parents' world," the false assumption is "I'll always belong to my parents and believe in their world." This "major" false assumption has several component assumptions—for example, "Only my parents can guarantee my safety" and "If I get any more independent, it will be a disaster." These are reasonable assumptions for a child, but less reasonable for the individual moving through adolescence. According to Gould, the individual must discard the major false assumption and its component parts before moving on to the next stage, when "I'm nobody's baby now."

Where Gould's theory focuses on beliefs, Daniel Levinson's focuses on changes in *life structure,* the "underlying pattern or design" of the individual's life (1977, p. 41). The elements that make up the life structure are our mate, our home, our job, and the roles we play at home, at work, and in the community. According to Levinson, development consists of alternating periods of building up and tearing down life structures. He called the building-up periods *stages* and the tearing-down periods *transitions.*

During Levinson's first stage, "entering the adult world," the individual must explore different possibilities and begin to put together a provisional life structure. Perhaps the young adult marries and starts a job. But in Levinson's system, each stage contains the germ of its own destruction. Inevitably there comes a transition—a time of soul searching and confusion—and then a new stage and new choices. Maybe there's a decision to start a family or a new job offer. With each new decision the individual's life structure changes, as do the relationships within that structure. Figure 12.10 compares the three theories.

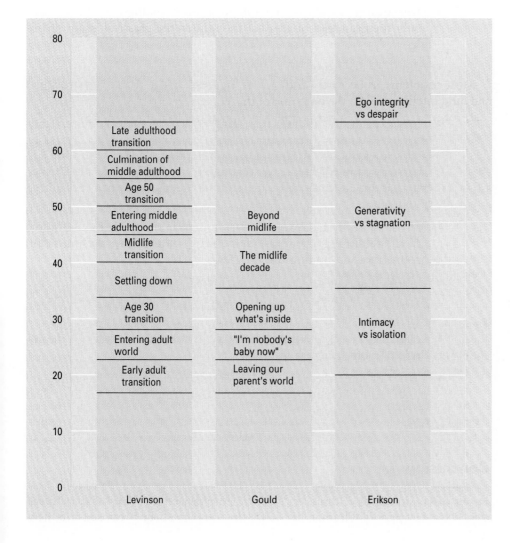

Figure 12.10
Comparison of Adult Transitional Stages

These three theories of adult development share some common themes—to build a family, to feel productive and effective, to be content with one's life—although the ages where these themes become dominant differ.

One point on which adult development theorists seem to agree is that there are times of crisis in adulthood, periods of uncertainty and conflict. And it is this point that most concerns the critics of adult stage theories. In interviews with many different subjects, they have found that few adults describe specific periods of crisis in their lives (Valliant, 1977; Haan, 1981; McCrae & Costa, 1982). Subjects are much more likely to report a gradual working out of issues and problems throughout their lives. Thus it seems that the idea of a universal midlife crisis, like the idea of a universal identity crisis in adolescence, is not supported by research.

Recap

- The lifespan perspective is an approach to developmental psychology in which the lives of individuals are studied from birth to death and understood in terms of the familial, societal, and historical contexts in which they are lived.

- From the early twenties on, the functioning of the body begins a steady decline that continues throughout adulthood.

- Despite their physical difficulties, most late adults lead productive and satisfying lives.

- Dialectical reasoning is a flexible form of reasoning that allows us to apply the principles of abstract thought to the practical issues of living.

- Although dialectical reasoning may be a distinct form of thought, there is only weak evidence to suggest that it represents a distinct stage in adult development.

- Horn explains the findings that aging does not weaken cognitive abilities by making a distinction between crystallized intelligence (skills and knowledge we already have) and fluid intelligence (the ability to learn new things). He insists that aging does affect fluid intelligence but that this effect is masked by a simultaneous increase in crystallized intelligence.

- According to Erikson, social development in the adult involves three tasks: establishing a primary relationship with another person, being productive, and finding meaning in one's life.

- Gould's stages of development are linked to false assumptions, to beliefs that have to be discarded in order for the individual to move on to the next stage.

- Levinson's stages of adult development focus on changes in the individual's life structure.

- Critics of stage theories of adult development argue that people are much more likely to gradually work out problems in their lives than to face a single period of crisis.

Conclusion

In our discussion of development, we have emphasized a variety of stage theories. For every period of human life, stage theories have been proposed and then, almost as often, have been opposed. Obviously, stage theories don't explain all of the many changes that we undergo in the process of development. Some theories fail to pinpoint the timing of different stages; others describe forms and levels of reasoning or patterns of resolution that simply don't exist generally. Yet despite these problems, many people find value in the concept of development in stages. Why?

The answer may lie in a principle we have encountered in earlier chapters. In Chapter 4, on perception, we discussed the Gestalt principle, which describes how many separate bits of information are automatically integrated into a larger whole. Similarly, in Chapter 7, we discussed the role of chunking: faced with a large array of information, people cope by grouping bits of information together.

A similar process may be at work in our perception of our own development. Faced with such an enormous array of knowledge about how we change over our lifetimes, we naturally collect that information into temporal groupings—what we call *stages*.

Ultimately, it doesn't matter whether all children develop concrete operational thought at the same age or whether moral reasoning is universal or whether adolescents and adults face crises at particular times. The stage concept will probably survive because it helps us grasp and remember the complex details of the changes that take place as we grow older.

Chapter 13   Psychological Assessment

Interval in Six Scales: Per II, Alfred Jensen, 1963

13

Gateways In previous chapters we have emphasized the processes and characteristics that most human beings have in common. We have approached behavior as if everyone learns in roughly the same way, has the same emotional reactions, falls prey to the same mistakes of perception and memory. Now we shift to a focus on *differences* among people. In this chatper we look at how psychologists seek to measure differences—and how they make sense of their measurements—as they assess intelligence and personality.

Differences in intelligence include differences in the kinds of thinking described in Chapter 8, as well as differences in the ability to learn (Chapter 6) and to remember (Chapter 7). The assessment of individual differences is especially relevant to Chapter 14 on personality, in which we consider other differences among people. Further, in Chapter 15, the adequate assessment of psychological disorders is a critically important issue.

My friend Susan was never much of a student. In high school, she had to work hard to get Cs and low Bs. My grades were only a little better, but school was always easy for me; I just didn't study very hard. The day that the white and blue envelopes came with my SAT scores, I called Susan to see how she had done. Her scores were barely high enough to get her into a local community college, but she was pleased. Mine were 300 points higher, and I could certainly go to a more "competitive" school.

After we went off to college, Susan and I saw each other occasionally during vacations, but we each had new friends and new experiences, and somehow weren't as close as we had been. Susan was doing all right at school, still working hard for Cs and an occasional B. She got married right after graduation. She invited me to the wedding, but I had a summer job doing research and couldn't go. Then we lost touch. Neither of us was much of a letter writer, and, anyway, we really weren't close any more.

I didn't speak to Susan again until our twenty-fifth high school reunion. Susan was living near Washington and had become a contractor, building houses. She'd started by renovating one house, and then went on from there. Well, as it turned out, she didn't actually hammer nails any more; she had crews who did the building. In fact, she had lots of crews. And she didn't actually spend that much time with the building projects because she had a couple of other businesses. Susan confessed that she had flown in—on her own airplane. Did she know how to fly? Well, no. She had a pilot!

How could it be? Good old Susan, a great friend, but not especially smart in school. How could she have made millions? Was it luck? Probably not. She'd done it at least three times, in different businesses. I was happy for Susan, more than a little envious, and really puzzled. What, I wondered, do the SATs really measure? And what, if anything, do test scores have to do with success?

There are three points to remember here. First, the SATs and tests like them are quite good at predicting performance in schools. They should be because that's what they're designed to do. You've probably noticed that better students usually get higher scores on the SATs, although there are always some exceptions. Second, despite their limitations, the tests have immense social power to shape the lives of every member of our society. Now that you're in college, you're probably beginning to see the impact of SAT scores on the direction of people's lives. Those scores really do make a difference as to where you go to college, and that makes a difference as to who your friends are, the kind of job you get after college, even who you marry and where you live.

Third, and most important, as Susan's success makes clear, the tests may predict success in school, but they don't measure many other important abilities. You haven't yet had the chance to see your friends becoming much less or much more successful than you would have expected from their performance in school. But that chance will come, too.

The SATs are an example of one of the largest practical applications of psychology, *psychological testing*. The SATs are a test of mental ability. Mental ability tests determine admission to schools, hiring decisions, and certification to practice a profession. Psychologists also use tests to measure people's motives and personality traits, and to diagnose psychological disorders. In this chapter we discuss the instruments psychologists use to learn about people and the way those instruments are designed.

The Properties of Effective Measures

As the science of psychology has developed, so have the methods used to improve the accuracy of psychological tests. To help you understand the problems inherent in psychological testing and the ways in which psychologists resolve those problems, we focus our initial discussion on one typical test, the Self-Monitoring Scale, developed by Mark Snyder (1974).

Snyder began with the idea that most people worry about what other people think of them. He believed that some people are especially sensitive to the expectations of others—about how they should behave, think, and feel—and that these people adjust their behavior to those expectations. At the other extreme are people who are oblivious to the expectations of others, who just do whatever seems reasonable to themselves. Snyder described these differences as variations in the degree of **self-monitoring.**

Ideas like this, ideas generated by theories, are called **theoretical constructs.** Any concept that is part of a theory is a theoretical construct, but in this chapter we will be concerned primarily with the constructs used to describe differences between people. We have already met a number of these individual-difference constructs in earlier chapters: the need for achievement, Type A personalities, and temperaments are all examples.

Theories generate and define the constructs we measure with psychological tests. They also guide every step of the process of developing and using an assessment method. For example, Snyder's first task was to devise a measure that would reflect the differences he believed exist among people. He began by writing a series of sentences, statements like "I guess I put on a show to impress or entertain others," or "In different situations and with different people, I often act like very different persons." (See Table 13.1.) Snyder assumed that these statements reflect some aspect of self-monitoring. Next, he asked people whether or not they agreed with the statements. To each response he assigned a numerical value; then he used the total value of each subject's responses to calculate a self-monitoring score for that individual.

Was Snyder's scale an adequate measure of self-monitoring? To answer that question, Snyder needed to deal with the two possible problems with any measure, which we discussed in Chapter 1. The first is the possibility that the measure doesn't reflect what it's supposed to reflect. This is a question of *validity*. If you want to know how heavy your brother is, measuring him with a yardstick isn't a very good way to find out. Granted, there might be some connection between your yardstick measurement and the ease with which you can pick up your brother, because taller people do tend to be heavier. But a yardstick isn't a valid measure of weight. It is, however, a valid measure of your brother's height. Notice that a measure is valid for a particular purpose, not in general.

Now imagine that your yardstick is made of rubber, so that every time you measure something, the yardstick stretches or contracts. If you measure your brother over and over, each time you're going to get a different measurement. Now and again you might get the right measurement, but most of the time the measurements are going to be wrong. Instruments that yield the wrong measurements are not reliable. *Reliability* is the second kind of problem psychologists have with tests.

Self-monitoring   The tendency to be especially aware of the expectations of others and to adjust one's behavior to fit those expectations.

Theoretical construct   A concept or idea that is part of a theory.

Correlation   A statistical technique used to measure the degree to which two variables are related.

1	I find it hard to imitate the behavior of other people.
2	At parties and social gatherings, I do not attempt to do or say things that others will like.
3	I can only argue for ideas which I already believe.
4	I can make impromptu speeches even on topics about which I have almost no information.
5	I guess I put on a show to impress or entertain others.
6	I would probably make a good actor.
7	In a group of people I am rarely the center of attention.
8	In different situations and with different people, I often act like very different persons.
9	I am not particulary good at making other people like me.
10	I'm not always the person I appear to be.
11	I would not change my opinions (or the way I do things) in order to please someone or win their favor.
12	I have considered being an entertainer.
13	I have never been good at games like charades or improvisational acting.
14	I have trouble changing my behavior to suit different people and different situations.
15	At a party I let others keep the jokes and stories going.
16	I feel a bit awkward in public and do not show up quite as well as I should.
17	I can look anyone in the eye and tell a lie with a straight face (if for a right end).
18	I may deceive people by being friendly when I really dislike them.

Source: Snyder & Gangestad, 1986.

Table 13.1
Snyder's Self-Monitoring Scale

The *Self-Monitoring Scale* measures the degree to which people care about how they appear to others. The higher the score, the greater the tendency toward self-monitoring. To find out how much of a self-monitor you are, read each item on the scale and decide whether it's true or false for you. The total score is the number of answers that match the following key: *false*—1, 2, 3, 7, 9, 11, 13, 14, 15, and 16; *true*—4, 5, 6, 8, 10, 12, 17, and 18.

Reliability

A psychological measurement is reliable to the extent that it is error-free (see Table 13.2). How do we gauge the reliability of an instrument like the Self-Monitoring Scale? One way is to administer the scale at two different times and see if people get the same or at least similar scores. If the scores are pretty much the same, then there probably isn't too much error.

Correlation is the statistical technique generally used to measure the degree to which two variables are related. (The two variables here are the scores on the first test administered and the scores on the second.) The *correlation coefficient* is a measure of relatedness between the two variables. The value of a correlation coefficient varies from +1.00 to −1.00. Strong relationships between variables are represented by numbers close to 1.00, and weak relationships by numbers

Reliable Measurements	Unreliable Measurements
A butcher's scale	A butcher's scale with a thumb pressing on it
Mile markers on highways	Odometers on most cars
Degrees on a thermometer	Judging that you have a fever
Counting calories	Feeling full
Police radar	Judging your own driving speed

Table 13.2
Reliable and Unreliable Measurements

The unreliable measurements are much more likely to be in error than the reliable measurements of the same quantity.

close to 0.00; positive numbers indicate that a high value of one score is associated with a high value of the other. Negative numbers mean that a high value of one score is associated with a low value of the other. (Figure 13.1 shows what the different values mean.)

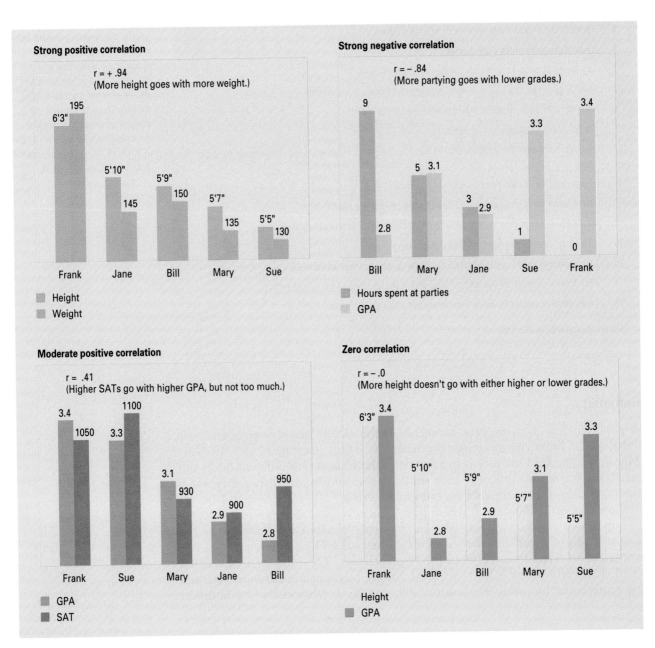

Figure 13.1
Examples of Correlations

These are examples of relationships that you already know about. The sample numbers depict the values of the correlation coefficients that correspond to strong positive and negative relationships, moderate relationships, and no relationships at all.

When we give the same test twice to the same group of people, we're assessing **test-retest reliability.** If scores on the two tests don't correlate highly, then the test is not reliable.

Even if the test-retest correlation is high, we can't be positive that the correlation represents high reliability. For example, if we administered the Self-Monitoring Scale a second time after only an hour, the subjects might remember their responses on the first go-round and try to reproduce them, thus making the scale seem more reliable than it is. To avoid this problem, we would wait a week or two before administering the test a second time.

Now a new issue emerges. Comparisons of scores obtained weeks apart test the **stability** of the measurements. If the thing being measured doesn't change from week to week, then any differences would be due to unreliability. But the scores could also vary because the thing being measured actually has changed. If we measured someone's mood on two successive weeks, we would expect to see some change, because moods do change from day to day and week to week. In fact, a measure of mood that didn't change would be a bad measure.

So, when we examine stability, what we hope to find depends on our theory about what we are measuring. Our theory determines whether we consider stability of measurements to be an estimate of the reliability of the test.

Because Snyder's theory included the assumption that self-monitoring would not change, he was able to use stability as an estimate of reliability. Indeed, he found that the test-retest reliability of his measure was .66, a value that is high enough.

If we had two measures of the same thing, we could get around the reliability-stability confusion. We could give one measure on the first occasion, and then give the second shortly afterward. This procedure establishes **alternate-forms reliability.** Unfortunately, we rarely have two measures to work with; but we can approximate the process by dividing a single scale into two halves. For example, we could divide the eighteen items on the Self-Monitoring Scale into two halves, each with nine items. In this case we would expect the scores on each half to be highly correlated, thus establishing **split-half reliability.**

We can carry this logic further. Many instruments, including the Self-Monitoring Scale, consist of items that reflect the same attribute. If all of the individual items measure the same thing, the scores on one item should be highly correlated with the scores on every other. Instead of dividing the items into two groups, then, we could look at the relationship between each item and all of the other items. A measure in which the individual items are all highly related to one another has high **internal consistency.**

In general, internal consistency is a good thing. In a specific case, however, it has to do with your theory about the measure. For example, test items are often deliberately selected to be somewhat different from one another. On the Wechsler intelligence tests, for example, there are subtests that consist of different kinds of items. One tests general knowledge; another tests vocabulary; a third tests the ability to remember lists of numbers. These different subtests were included because the test developer assumed that the abilities they measure are *not* perfectly correlated. So, when correlating items on these subtests with items on other subtests, we would neither expect nor want to find high internal consistency.

Of course, perfect internal consistency would be silly. If every item on a test correlated perfectly with every other item, all you'd need is a one-item test. If you knew someone's answer to that one item, you could predict the answers to any other item. So the ideal level of internal consistency is moderately high but not perfect. And how high it should be depends on your theory about the thing you're measuring.

This is an important point. How stable or internally consistent a measure "should" be depends on the attribute you're measuring and on your theory about the measure. We can't say that every test must be very stable or highly consistent. But there are some rules of thumb. Generally, we expect stability estimates above .60 for short time spans, and internal consistency estimates above .70. If the stability or internal consistency of a measure falls much short of these values, you should demand a well-developed theoretical explanation as to why. Otherwise, you may be working with a poorly developed measure—a rubber yardstick.

Test-retest reliability An estimate of reliability obtained by administering the same test twice, separated by a span of time.

Stability The degree to which a test produces the same or similar scores on two separate occasions; a measure of an instrument's reliability.

Alternate-forms reliability An estimate of reliability obtained by administering two different forms of the same measure at two different times.

Split-half reliability An estimate of reliability obtained by dividing a test in half and then relating the score on one half to the score on the other half.

Internal consistency An estimate of the reliability of a psychological measure obtained by relating each item of a multi-item measure to every other item.

Snyder's Self-Monitoring Scale does have acceptable values for both stability and internal consistency. The individual items on the scale are not intended to measure different aspects of self-monitoring. So we would expect to find a reasonably high level of internal consistency, and indeed we do. The correlation is about .70 (Snyder & Gangestad, 1986). Now we have reason to believe that the Self-Monitoring Scale is reliable. The next question is whether it's valid.

Validity

The basic question about validity is whether the instrument actually measures what it's supposed to measure (see Table 13.3). Sometimes the answer to this question is simple. Some tests are developed to predict a particular performance in the world. For example, the SATs are designed to predict how well a student is going to do in college. Other kinds of tests are designed to predict how well someone is going to perform on a job or even what kind of work the individual is going to find most satisfying. Here the validity of the test is measured by how well scores on the test correlate with performance in school or on the job, or with job satisfaction. This kind of validity is called **criterion validity.** There is a criterion—some observable standard—against which we can evaluate the test.

Table 13.3
Valid and Invalid Measurements

Both valid and invalid measurements may seem to reflect the same attribute, but the invalid measurements actually reflect some other factor.

Valid Measurements	Invalid Measurements
Of what you know Your grade on a well-designed exam	Your mother's judgment of your scholastic ability
Of the ability to drive safely A blood alcohol test	A person's judgment of their ability
Of baseball skill Batting average, win/lose record, home runs	A ballplayer's salary
Of political attitudes The way people vote	Bumper stickers; radio talk shows
Probability of your future success How hard you work	Your horoscope

Notice that for tests of this sort, the objective is an essentially practical one. We want to predict how well people are going to do in school because it's neither efficient nor kind to accept them at a school if they can't do the work. These tests are designed to do a particular job, and that's all. Scores on these tests have nothing to do with a specific theory (although the choice of measurement procedures is highly dependent on theory). The tests are simply tools that allow us to predict performance.

Tests that measure a theoretical construct such as self-monitoring have a different logic. These tests aren't trying to predict a single observable outcome. There is no one behavior that tells us whether an individual is especially sensitive to the opinions of others; many different behaviors are part of the overall pattern. So we don't have a criterion to validate the Self-Monitoring Scale against. What do we do?

To begin with, we can use our judgment about the items in the scale. The Self-Monitoring Scale *looks* like a good measure of self-monitoring; that is, the

Criterion validity   The degree to which a test that is designed to predict an observable outcome actually does predict that outcome.

statements all look like the kinds of statements that gauge the degree to which people worry about other people's opinions of what they do. On the surface, then, the measure seems valid. This kind of validity is called **face validity,** but it's virtually useless. A "handsome face" on a test—like a handsome face on a person—doesn't necessarily mean any real substance behind it. The scales published in popular magazines that supposedly measure whether you are a leader or how successful your romance is all have face validity. But we have no reason to think that any of them actually work (see Figure 13.2).

If we don't have a criterion, and if face validity isn't a real measure of validity, how do we validate a test like the Self-Monitoring Scale? The answer is **construct validity,** which once again involves the theory we're working with. A

Are you a giver or a taker?

1. A neighbor who's helped you out in the past is going away for two weeks and has asked you to look in on her aging mom. Alas, her mother happens to be rather quarrelsome and crotchety–a real pain. What do you do?

a. Oblige; you pay your debts.
b. Agree to check on her once or twice.
c. Invent some plausible excuse to get you off the hook.
d. Suggest a more agreeable way to pitch in–by doing the womans shopping, say.

2. A well-heeled, slightly impetuous pal decides you're in need of some R and R. She proposes to send you, all expenses paid, on a Caribbean cruise. Do you

a. Feel her out to see if she's sincere; if so, who are you to spoil her fun?
b. Give her a hug but remain noncommittal? By tomorrow, she'll probably regret her magnanimous impulse.
c. Gently decline? You'd be uncomfortable doing anything else.
d. Thank her profusely and pack before she changes her mind?

3. When the boss asks you to put in some (unpaid) overtime, your response is to

a. Get right to work.
b. Help out as long as it's convenient.
c. Plead a prior commitment.
d. Agree just this once, making it clear that you won't stay late again–not without fair compensation.

4. Your idea of the perfect birthday is

a. A lively party with good friends, good food, good music.
b. A cozy dinner for just you and a few close pals.
c. An intimate evening á deux.
d. Time to yourself for doing exactly what *you* want.

5. Imagine you overhear some catty acquaintances putting you down. Which epithet would hurt worst?

a. "Selfish"
b. "A control freak"
c. "A doormat"
d. "Insensitive"

6. As a child, you felt

a. Cherished.
b. Mistreated.
c. MIldly deprived.
d. Smothered with love.

7. If there's anything you hate, it's people who (choose just one)

a. Bottle up feelings. You believe in *airing* deepest thoughts.
b. Impinge on your privacy. *Space* is high on your list of priorities.
c. Try to manipulate you through guilt.
d. Refuse to pull their own weight.

8. When sharing digs, you solve the housework problem by

a. Doing most of the chores yourself–the easiest way to avoid hassles.
b. Hiring a cleaning person.
c. Splitting the tasks fifty-fifty.
d. Letting the dust bunnies lie where they may.

Scoring

Give yourself points as follows:

1. a-3	b-1	c-0	d-2
2. a-1	b-2	c-3	d-0
3. a-3	b-2	c-1	d-0
4. a-3	b-0	c-2	d-1
5. a-3	b-2	c-1	d-0
6. a-3	b-2	c-1	d-0
7. a-0	b-3	c-2	d-1
8. a-2	b-3	c-1	d-0

Source: Dritchell, 1990.

Figure 13.2
Face Validity

This scale claims to determine whether you are a "giver" or a "taker" in your relationships with others. The items seem plausible, and perhaps the scale scores actually do reflect how selfish or unselfish you are. But no research has been done to establish this fact. Instead, the scale relies solely on face validity. To get your score, add up the points in the scoring key that correspond to your answers. The higher your score, the more unselfish you are.

Face validity   The degree to which a test appears to measure what it's supposed to measure.

Construct validity   The confidence in a test of a theoretical construct (and its related theory), which is developed by repeated successful use of the test in confirming hypotheses.

measure has construct validity if it works in the way our theory predicts. If we can use our measure to predict other things people do, then we can begin to have confidence in its validity. The process of developing construct validity is complicated, so let's consider the example of self-monitoring.

According to Snyder, people who are high in self-monitoring should be especially effective at communicating emotions intentionally because they know how they appear to others. We can check this hypothesis by administering the Self-Monitoring Scale to a group of subjects and then seeing how well they communicate emotion. As it turns out, people who score high on the Self-Monitoring Scale *do* communicate emotions more effectively (Snyder, 1974). This is a reassuring finding because it confirms one of our theoretical ideas about self-monitoring: people identified by the scale as high in self-monitoring behave the way the theory predicts they should. It also suggests that the Self-Monitoring Scale does what it's supposed to do—measure the degree to which the individual monitors his or her behavior in response to the opinions of others.

Snyder also believed that people who are high in self-monitoring pay more attention to others. To assess this part of his theory, researchers tested a group of people who had taken the Self-Monitoring Scale on their ability to remember information about other people. They found that those who had scored high on the Self-Monitoring Scale *did* remember more about other people (Berscheid et al., 1976). This finding, like the one about communicating emotion, makes us feel more confident—both about the measure and about Snyder's self-monitoring theory.

In developing the Self-Monitoring Scale, Snyder and his associates repeated this kind of research over and over. In the process, they made several discoveries about people who are high in self-monitoring (Snyder & Gangestad, 1986):

- These people are more affected by situational definitions of "good" behavior.
- They are less consistent in their behavior across situations that seem to demand subtle differences in behavior.
- They are more affected by ads that talk about the prestige of using a product.
- They choose their friends and romantic partners on the basis of more "external" dimensions, such as attractiveness and prestige.
- They are less likely to behave in a way that is consistent with their attitudes and, instead, do what is expected in a given situation.

Each of these findings contributes a little bit of confidence to the theory. And each finding adds to our confidence in the scale. If the measure was not reflecting something like self-monitoring, then the predictions would not be confirmed so consistently. This confidence—the product of years of experimentation and repeated use of the scale—is construct validity.

Notice that research doesn't validate the measure alone. Construct validity is really a property of both the instrument and the theory in which the construct is embedded. If we had an excellent measure of self-monitoring and a weak theory, we'd be unable to use the instrument to predict behavior, and could never build up confidence in the measure. For example, if our theory predicted that people high in self-monitoring are better students, we'd be disappointed. There's no relationship between the degree of self-monitoring and school performance.

Notice, too, that construct validity is acquired gradually, each study adding an increment of confidence. In a sense, the process is never completed because every time the measure is used, some small amount of confidence is added or subtracted.

Throughout this section we've emphasized the role of the theory in defining both reliability and validity. Without a theory about the construct that's supposed to be measured, we'd have no way to decide what levels of stability and internal consistency to expect. Even more important, without a theory we'd be unable to generate the predictions that become the material for increasing construct validity. The theory plays a critical role in defining the observations that build confidence in a measure. At the same time, those observations—the knowledge we acquire from research—help refine the theory; the theory is constantly evolving in light of our findings. In short, theory and method are woven together, in a single fabric.

Recap

- As the science of psychology has developed, so have the methods used to improve the accuracy of psychological tests.

- Ideas generated by theories are called theoretical constructs.

- Reliability is the absence of error in measurement.

- Correlation is a statistical technique used to measure the degree to which two variables are related.

- Test-retest stability is an estimate of an instrument's reliability.

- An instrument in which the individual items are all highly related to one another has high internal consistency, a measure of reliability.

- The degree of stability or internal consistency that psychologists look for in a measure depends on both the theory on which the measure is based and the element being measured.

- An instrument is valid if it measures what it's supposed to measure.

- Criterion validity is the degree to which a test designed to predict an observable outcome actually does predict that outcome.

- Determining construct validity is an ongoing process; the confidence psychologists have in an instrument is a product of years of experimentation and repeated administrations of the test that confirm and refine the theory on which the test is based.

Assessment Techniques

Any opportunity to acquire information about another person can be an assessment technique. Some assessment techniques are informal. Interviews, for example, can be as casual as a conversation. The SATs, by contrast, are the product of very sophisticated measurement and statistical procedures. Each technique has a different combination of strengths and weaknesses.

Interviews

Certainly the oldest and still most common assessment technique is the **interview.** You've probably been on the receiving end of an assessment interview, for a job or college admission. Some interviews are highly structured: in such cases, the interviewer has a list of questions that must be asked, sometimes in a particular order. Other interviews are much less formal, just an unstructured way of getting to know someone.

Interview An assessment technique that uses verbal questions and answers to collect information about a subject.

The most commonly used assessment technique is the interview because of its flexibility. Although the interviewer has a list of questions she expects to ask, she can alter her inquiry to explore topics that her client raises.

The obvious advantage of an interview is its freedom. Interesting topics can be pursued and uncertainties cleared up. In addition, the interviewer is able to watch the interviewee's behavior, which can be a source of information in itself. And, in the course of conversation, the interviewee may feel free to talk about things he or she would not want to write down.

Clinical interviews—the type of interviews mental health professionals conduct with clients—are a complex mix of activities and goals. The clinician may be simultaneously getting to know more about a client, forming a relationship with the client, and trying to persuade the client to behave differently.

The principal weakness of the interview is the unknown quality of the information. Because the information collected in an interview does not come in quantitative form, it's reliability is difficult to assess. If one interviewer decides someone "has a very vivid imagination" and another interviewer decides that person is "very imaginative," do they agree or disagree? And to what extent?

Furthermore, when the reliability of interview results has been estimated, it tends to be poor. For example, diagnoses of psychological disorder based on interviews are notoriously unreliable. Two clinicians who use interviews to assign diagnoses to the same individuals agree only about 80 percent of the time on which of sixteen major diagnostic categories the client belongs in (Robins & Helzer, 1986). (Notice that this is a kind of alternate-forms reliability estimate. Each interview is, in effect, a different form of the assessment instrument.) The implication is that at least one in five people is misdiagnosed on the basis of clinical interviews.

Because interviews are flexible and encourage the exploration of new issues, they are especially appropriate in the early, exploratory stages of measurement—when the interviewer isn't exactly sure what information is needed. But because of their lack of reliability and their uncertain validity, interviews are not very effective for evaluating theories and specific hypotheses. They are also less reliable than tests for school or job selection. Probably the reason they continue to be used so often in selection situations is that they are easy and have a great deal of face validity.

Observation

Behavioral assessment An assessment technique that uses the direct observation of an individual's behavior as a predictor of future behavior.

Sometimes the best source of information about people is what they actually do. If you want to learn about Ms. Johnson's fear of driving, the best way is to go with her and make careful observations. Not surprisingly, **behavioral assessment** is the technique of choice among behaviorists, those who believe that the study of psychology should be focused on the study of observable activity.

Obviously psychologists can't always be there, watching what their clients do. So they must often rely on *self-observation*. For example, behavioral therapists might ask their clients to keep a diary, to note every time they behave in a certain way and to describe what's going on when it happens. These diaries can reveal unexpected relationships between behaviors and situations. In one case, a young woman reported that she often felt depressed for no reason. But her diary revealed that these bouts of depression always took place after a visit from her mother—a connection she'd never made.

Behavioral assessments are most useful when the focus of attention is a relatively concrete behavior—such as feeling depressed or anxious, or performing a task. They are often used in hiring situations because the best predictor of how people will do on a job is how they do during a trial run. In a sense, behavioral assessments have high criterion validity because the behavior itself is the criterion. Conversely, direct assessment is usually not appropriate for measuring abstract dispositions toward behavior, such as the need for achievement or self-monitoring.

In one case of indirect observation, a psychologist was able to identify which exhibits in a museum were most popular by studying the patterns of wear in the flooring in front of the exhibits (Webb et al., 1966).

Self-Prediction

Often the reason we want to assess someone is to be able to predict how that person will behave in the future. But no one is better placed to observe us than we are ourselves. It's not surprising, then, that **self-predictions** can be the best predictors of behavior. For example, college students' predictions about their own performance in college are as accurate as predictions based on SAT scores and high school grades (Schranger & Osberg, 1981). Likewise, the best predictors of the success of a smoking cessation program are the subjects' own predictions (Tiffany, Martin & Baker, 1986).

Although self-prediction can be and often is reasonably accurate, the method is seldom effective when subjects have a stake in the way the assessment is going to be used or when they're reluctant to reveal their thoughts and feelings. Students may be able to predict their college grades as accurately as their scores on the SATs and their high school grades. But admissions officers can't use self-predictions to choose the members of next year's freshman class. And although people can predict their own behavior, they are less successful when asked to describe their more abstract attributes, such as the dimensions of personality we've been talking about. We just don't think about ourselves in the abstract very well.

Self-prediction An assessment technique that uses the individual's predictions about his or her own behavior or performance in some future situation.

Objective Tests

In an **objective test,** the questions and the format of the responses are defined and the same for everyone taking the test. In one kind of objective test, the questions have right or wrong answers, and the purpose of the test is to measure aptitude or achievement. In another type of objective test—designed to assess motives, attitudes, or personality traits—the questions don't have right or wrong answers. Instead, each response is taken to reflect some aspect of the subject's nature. The Self-Monitoring Scale is an example of this second type.

Aptitude and Achievement Tests   **Aptitude tests** measure the subject's ability to do some task; **achievement tests** measure what the subject already has done. Both kinds of tests are often validated against a criterion of actual performance. For instance, a test of mechanical aptitude might consist of items that have been answered correctly by skilled mechanics and answered incorrectly by those who are all thumbs. Similarly, tests like the SATs are validated against actual performance in college. Such tests tend to be highly reliable and to have at least moderate criterion validity. But they often lack construct validity: people aren't quite sure what the tests measure, if anything, other than the probability of success at an activity.

Objective Personality Tests   These tests are often called *self-report measures* because they depend on the subjects' answering questions about themselves—about their behavior and their feelings. The difference between these measures and self-predictions or interviews is the way in which the respondents' answers are understood and used. In an interview, for example, the interviewer asks a question because he or she wants to know the answer. The respondent's answers may reveal more about the individual than was intended, but the answers themselves are of specific interest to the interviewer. On an objective personality test, however, the subject's answers are interesting only as a reflection of something else. For example, on the Bem Sex Role Inventory (Bem, 1985), subjects are asked to describe themselves using trait terms such as *ambitious, aggressive, kind,* and *caring.* The subjects are reporting what they're like, but the experimenter isn't really interested in how aggressive or kind they think they are. Instead, the experimenter is interested in whether the subjects tend to choose adjectives that are stereotypically masculine (like the first two), feminine (like the last two), or a mixture. The final scores of this test are for masculinity, femininity, or androgyny, not for aggression or kindness.

Indirect measurement is usually used for two reasons. First, the subjects may not be willing to reveal certain things about themselves. If a scale is intended to measure honesty, for example, simply asking a subject whether he's honest isn't going to work.

Second, most people just can't recognize their own levels of a particular quality. One reason is that we tend to see ourselves in a good light. For example, you couldn't ask a subject to tell you how vain he is because it's the essence of vanity to believe that one of his better features is humility (and with so much to be humble about, too!). Or the problem may be that the attribute being measured is so abstract that the subject has never thought of herself in that way. Self-monitoring is an example: most of us never think carefully about how much our behavior is affected by those around us.

Projective Techniques

We've made much of the role of the theory in shaping how we measure and what we measure. Nowhere is that role clearer than in the development of **projective tests.** These tests have been developed by people who believe, as Freud

---

Objective test An assessment technique in which the questions and the response format are defined and the same for everyone tested.

Aptitude test An instrument that is designed to predict the subject's potential ability to perform a task.

Achievement test An instrument that measures the subject's current actual ability.

Projective test An instrument that indirectly measures motives, desires, or emotions by asking the subject to respond to an ambiguous stimulus (such as an inkblot, a vague photograph, or an open-ended sentence).

Puzzle It Out!

As part of my training to be a clinical psychologist, I was required to practice administering the Rorschach inkblot test to friends and acquaintances. One of my friends produced a chilling set of responses: on almost every inkblot, he saw bizarre sexual and aggressive objects. Was he revealing some terrible underlying pathology? I was immensely relieved when, at the end of the session, he remarked that although he knew one was supposed to see sexual things in the ink blots, he had found it very difficult to do so, and he hoped he hadn't spoiled my practice testing.

What does this experience suggest about projective tests? And how might an experienced tester deal with this kind of problem?

did, that many of the causes of behavior are unconscious. Because people aren't aware of these motives, desires, or emotions, tests to detect them must be indirect. All projective tests ask subjects to respond to an ambiguous stimulus of some sort—to describe what they see in the shape of an inkblot, to create a story about what the people in a photograph are doing, to complete an open-ended sentence ("When I think of mother . . .").

People respond very differently to these projective stimuli. And because there's no structure that determines how subjects should respond to these kinds of stimuli, the assumption is that the individual's responses must reflect something about that individual. For example, if every inkblot looks like some kind of food to you, it's reasonable to assume that you're preoccupied with eating.

The advantage of projective tests is that most subjects don't recognize how they work, so their responses usually aren't affected by "trying to look good." Projective tests also have moderate stability, at least over shorter time periods (Groth-Marnat, 1984). At the same time, it's very hard to know what subjects' responses mean. Remember that the purpose of these tests is to assess a motive or an emotion that even the subject isn't aware of. Obviously, then, it's difficult to estimate the criterion validity of these tests.

When projective tests have been used to predict diagnoses of psychological disorders, the predictions are not very strong (Groth-Marnat, 1984). The kind of construct validity that has been built up around the Self-Monitoring Scale and other objective tests has not been developed for most of these tests. The problem here may be with the theory half of the construct validity equation because at least one projective test, the Thematic Apperception Test, has been used successfully in the extensive program of research on the need for achievement that we described in Chapter 9. If the test achieved adequate construct validity as a measure of need achievement, perhaps it could do the same for other motives as well.

Recap

- Any opportunity to acquire information about another person can be an assessment technique.

- Interviews can vary from highly structured to very informal. The interview form is very flexible, but the quality of the information gathered in an interview is difficult to assess.

- Behavioral assessment uses the direct observation of an individual's behavior as a predictor of future behavior. It is most effective when a specific behavior is of interest; it is much less effective when the focus of the assessment is an abstract disposition toward behavior.

- Self-prediction can be accurate, but its effectiveness is limited when subjects have a stake in they way the assessment is going to be used or are unwilling to reveal their thoughts and emotions.

- In an objective test, the questions and the format of the responses are defined and the same for everyone taking the test.

- Aptitude and achievement tests are an example of objective tests. In these tests, the questions have right or wrong answers.

- Objective personality tests are designed to assess motives, attitudes, or personality traits. Here the questions don't have right or wrong answers; instead, each response is taken to reflect some aspect of the subject's nature.

- Projective tests ask subjects to respond to an ambiguous stimulus of some sort. They are based on the assumption that people aren't aware of all their motives, desires, and emotions, so tests of these elements must be indirect.

Measures of Intelligence

Intelligence tests are probably the most highly developed psychological tests, and certainly the most influential. They affect decisions about hiring and schooling that can in turn affect every other part of people's lives. We're going to examine this last point in some detail around the question of whether different groups in our society—blacks and women, for example—"naturally" perform differently on these tests.

The Origins of Intelligence Testing

Tests of mental abilities are so pervasive in our society that it's startling to realize that they've been around for only about eighty-five years. In fact, until the end of the nineteenth century, teachers and school systems got along very nicely without tests. At this time, the French educational bureaucrats decided that poor students might do better if they could be grouped in special classes. In order to act on this idea, however, they needed a way to identify students who were not performing well in the regular classroom. In 1904 they sought the help of psychologist Alfred Binet. They asked him to develop a test to identify poor students, a test that was more objective than teacher judgments and suitable for use throughout the French school system.

A Test of General Knowledge   A test of learning ability might ask students to learn something and then see how they do. The problem is finding something that none of the students has learned already. Even if the material is only similar to things some children have learned, those children might have an advantage. For example, if you ask students to learn the meaning of several Latin words, children who've studied Latin would probably do better than those who haven't, even if the words themselves are new.

So Binet decided to go in the opposite direction. Instead of looking for material no one had learned already, he looked for material that *everyone* should have learned: he designed a test of general knowledge. That test included items such as these:

Alfred Binet, a French psychologist, devised the first test of school aptitude. Originally designed to predict school performance, it led to the development of intelligence tests.

- Point to your foot.
- Give me three pencils (from a bunch placed in front of the child).

For older children the questions were like these:

- Define the word *bland*.
- What does the proverb "A stitch in time saves nine" mean?

Binet and his associate, Theodore Simon, had teachers identify children in their classes who had difficulty learning. Then they asked these children—and a sample of their more successful classmates—a great many questions. Only those questions that were answered more often by the good students were included in the final version of the test. When Binet was finished, he had a wide variety of questions, all of which presumably could be answered using the information every child is exposed to, and which in fact were answered correctly more often by good students than by poor ones (Binet & Simon, 1916).

Binet had done just what he set out to do: he'd devised a way to predict performance in school. In other words, he had established criterion validity for the test. Binet explicitly denied that the test was a measure of any theoretical construct, such as intelligence, so he wasn't concerned about the issue that we now call construct validity.

The Question of Age   Older children know more than younger children. On a test of general knowledge, then, a thirteen-year-old poor learner should answer more questions correctly than a six-year-old good learner. Accordingly, Binet and Simon created a series of subtests, each of which consisted of items that were usually answered correctly by children at a particular age. The final score generated by the test was a **mental age.** A mental-age score of 12 meant that the child had performed like an average twelve-year-old.

In the final version of Binet and Simon's test, poor students were those whose mental age was significantly lower than their actual or chronological age. This shift to mental-age scores was very reasonable, but it changed the way of thinking about the results. Instead of talking about predicting how a child would do in school, people began talking about some "property" of the child. And that property was generalized from school performance to whatever is implied by the broad category of "mental abilities."

The Intelligence Quotient   Talking about mental ages was clumsy because each child's mental age had to be compared to his or her chronological age. Obviously a single number would simplify things. Another psychologist, William Stern, proposed that the best single number would be the ratio of mental age to chronological age multiplied by 100 (to clean up the decimals):

$$\frac{\text{Mental age}}{\text{Chronological age}} \times 100$$

Because mental age is divided by chronological age, the result is a quotient—an **intelligence quotient (IQ).** Table 13.4 shows how IQ is calculated.

Mental age The average age of the people who performed at the same level as the subject on a test that predicts performance in school.

Intelligence quotient (IQ) Originally, mental age divided by chronological age, multiplied by 100; more generally, a score on an intelligence test.

Table 13.4
Sample Calculations of IQ Scores

The original formula for calculating the intelligence quotient was mental age divided by chronological age, multiplied by 100. The result was that whenever someone's mental age was the same as their chronological age, their IQ was 100.

Mental Age	Chronological Age	Formula		IQ
8	10	8/10 × 100	=	80
10	10	10/10 × 100	=	100
12	10	12/10 × 100	=	120
14	14	14/14 × 100	=	100

Notice that with this formula, if a child's mental and chronological ages are identical, the child's IQ is 100. This is the number that has represented exactly average intelligence since Stern's IQ concept was adopted.

The transition to IQ scores made good sense, but it moved us closer toward generalizing and finally obscuring the meaning of the tests. The concept of "mental age" had retained the sense of a process of learning and growing, but IQ was a number that seemed to define—once and for all—some property of the child. Furthermore, as a permanent property of the person, IQ was no longer just something we needed to know just about schoolchildren. We could now ask about IQ differences among adults as well.

IQ Without Ages   The IQ formula relates mental age to chronological age. This makes sense when we're talking about schoolchildren, who are still learning. But beyond a certain age, we don't expect people to know more and more about geography and proverbs. In fact, the number of additional items answered correctly each year begins to drop sometime between ages sixteen and thirty. At this point the IQ formula begins to yield silly numbers. For example, a twenty-one-year-old whose mental age is 21 would have an IQ score of 100 (21/21 × 100). At age forty-two, if her mental age hasn't changed, her IQ score would be 50 (21/42 × 100), but she would actually know just as much as when she was younger. The numbers generated by the formula suggest that people become less intelligent as they get older. Although many college students believe this (especially about their parents!), most psychologists are old enough to be skeptical.

The solution to the problem was to change the way that IQ scores are calculated for both adults and children. Today we use **standard scores,** scores that tell us how each individual compares to the average of a large standardization sample of people who took the test earlier.

The way IQ scores originally were calculated, the average score was 100. For standard scores, that value was retained, but with a standard deviation of 15. This means that 68 percent of the people who take IQ tests score between 85 and 115, and that 95 percent score between 70 and 130. Only 3 percent of scores fall below 70 or above 130 (see Figure 13.3). Because these scores are expressed in terms of standard deviations, they're called *deviation IQ scores.*

Figure 13.3
The Distribution of Deviation IQ Scores

This curve is a theoretical distribution of deviation IQ scores. Actual test distributions vary slightly, however.

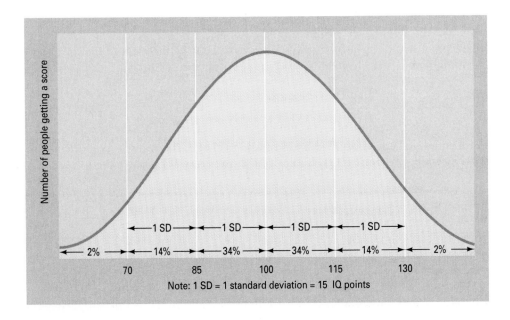

With the development of the deviation IQ score, the IQ test moved even further away from Binet's original task. IQs could now be calculated for adults, so the question of school performance was lost completely. And the calculation of scores had become so complex that only experts retained a sense of what the numbers really mean. Each of the transitions from mental-age scores to deviation IQ scores has made good sense, but their cumulative effect has been to obscure the purpose of tests of general knowledge. They were designed to predict performance in school, and that's all they should do. They may reflect more or less accurately an individual's abilities in other areas as well. But this would clearly be an extension of their application.

As soon as IQ tests began to be used as measures of "intelligence" rather than as predictors of school performance, a question about their validity arose. Intelligence is a theoretical construct, and a measure of a theoretical construct must meet construct validity standards. So the simple school-performance criterion validity that was good enough for Binet is not good enough at all.

Defining and Measuring Intelligence: The Problems

Binet never assumed that his test did anything but predict performance in school. But most psychologists—including Lewis Terman (1916), who developed an English version of Binet's test called the Stanford-Binet—believed that the test measured innate intelligence.

What do we mean by *intelligence*? Psychologists have struggled with this question since Binet's time, and all of the definitions they've come up with seem inadequate somehow. **Intelligence** has something to do with being able to solve problems and accomplish socially defined tasks, but its exact boundaries are unclear. The source of this problem may lie in the general difficulties of defining any concept, a difficulty that we talked about in Chapter 8. Just as we seem to understand the concept of "chair" by reference to protypical chairs, in order to define *intelligence* we should probably work with a prototype of someone everyone agrees was or is intelligent, not with a description of attributes (Neisser, 1979). For example, Einstein's intelligence is what distinguished him from the rest of us.

The problem of definition is compounded by the fact that psychologists strongly disagree about whether intelligence is one ability or many different kinds of abilities. And if there is more than one kind of intelligence, how are they related?

Binet's original test contained an assortment of tasks, thus suggesting that he believed several different kinds of mental abilities all contribute to school performance. However, the fact that the test generated just one score implies that all of the separate abilities were parts of one general capacity, a view held by Terman (1916).

The early champion of "one intelligence" was a British researcher, Charles Spearman (1927). He believed that there may be a few specific intellectual abilities, but that underlying them is a general ability that he called *g*.

A similar assumption guided David Wechsler, the designer of the IQ tests used most commonly today. He developed two tests, the Wechsler Adult Intelligence Scale, or WAIS, and the Wechsler Intelligence Scale for Children, or WISC. In the WAIS, Wechsler (1958) explicitly included eleven subtests of two broad types that generate two subscores in addition to an overall IQ score. Each subtest contributes to a score on **verbal IQ** or **performance IQ.** Items in the verbal subtests consist of such tasks as defining words, explaining proverbs, answering questions of general knowledge ("How far is it from New York to Chicago?"), and remembering lists of numbers. Items in the performance subtests

Standard score A score that compares each individual's score with the scores of a large standardization sample; the difference between a particular score and the mean of all scores, divided by the standard deviation.

Intelligence The capacity to solve problems and cope successfully with one's environment.

Verbal IQ A score on an IQ test that reflects the subject's ability to carry out tasks that involve language (for example, defining terms and answering questions that require general knowledge).

Performance IQ A score on an IQ test that reflects the subject's ability to carry out nonverbal tasks (for example, arranging blocks in a pattern and putting a series of pictures into a sequence that "tells" a story).

How Do We Know That?

The particular advantage of psychological tests, as opposed to other kinds of assessments, is that we can assign numbers to different performances. The problem is figuring out what those numbers mean. If a person scores 24 correct out of 35 on an IQ test, is that good or bad? Do 12 high-need-for-achievement themes in 20 stories indicate a strong motive? Does a score of 8 on an optimism scale mean that the individual is optimistic?

By themselves, these numbers mean very little. In order to interpret them, we need to know how other people did on the same test. If most people get 28 or 29 items correct, a score of 24 on an IQ test isn't very good. But if most people get 15 correct, a score of 24 is excellent.

The first step, then, is to describe the group's performance—that is, to determine the *group mean*, the average score of all of the people who've taken the test. If the group mean on an IQ test is 18 and a subject scores 24, obviously he's done well. His score is 6 points above the mean.

But how good is 6 points above the mean? Very good? Is this the highest score anyone ever got on the test? Or just pretty good? Did some people get all 35 items correct? The mean doesn't tell us everything we need to know about a test score. We also have to look at the way all the scores are *distributed*, the way they're spread out.

If you give any test to a random group of adults, you're going to find a wide range of performance. Most people's scores are going to fall pretty close to the average, but some are going to be much higher or lower. Figure 13.A shows a sample of test-score data. The horizontal axis represents numbers of correct answers; the vertical axis, the number of people who've received a score.

Figure 13.A
The Normal Curve

In this figure, the numbers of people receiving a particular score are represented by bars. More commonly, the tops of these bars are connected by a line, which is smoothed out to produce a figure like a bell.

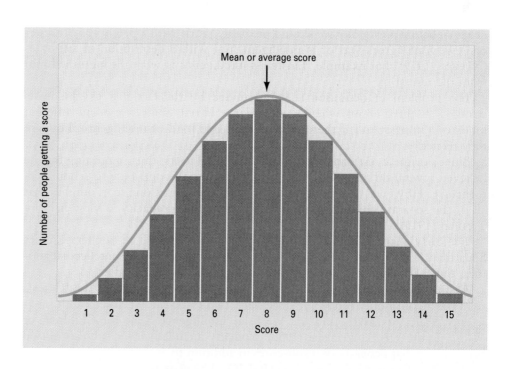

You may recognize the shape of the curve in Figure 13.A. It's called the *normal curve*. It's the curve people usually refer to when they talk about grad-

(Continued on next page)

ing "on the curve." And it's the curve we find again and again when we measure natural phenomena such as the heights of men and women or the amount of rain that falls each month in Chicago.

The mean of the measurements depicted in a normal curve falls in the middle of the curve. Notice that the curves for the heights of men and women are identical, except that the men's curve is shifted to the right because, on average, men are taller than women. This difference in the mean is one important difference among normal curves.

Another important difference among normal curves has to do with the distribution of the measurements, how widely they're spread out. We measure "spread" with a statistic called the *standard deviation,* which is roughly the average difference of all the individual scores from the mean. Curves with large standard deviations exhibit large differences between the scores and the mean. They look like the blue curve in Figure 13.B. And curves with small standard deviations are more tightly packed around the mean, like the orange curve.

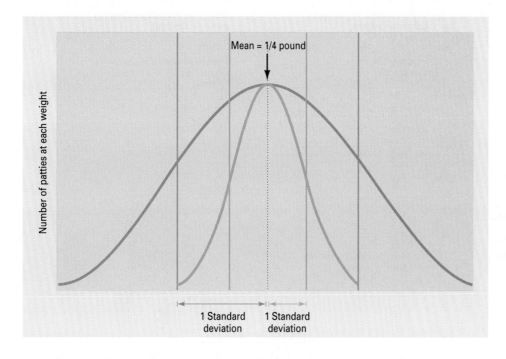

**Figure 13.B
Standard Deviation**

These are the sorts of curves that might result if you were trying to make hamburger patties that weighed exactly a quarter of a pound. If you picked up a handful of meat without weighing it, you might average a quarter of a pound, but if you did this continually you would end up with a number of patties that weighed more or less than a quarter of a pound. This would yield a standard deviation like the one shown by the blue curve. On the other hand, if you used a scoop to pick up the meat, you might still make some errors, but they would be much smaller, so the standard deviation of your patties would be smaller, as shown by the orange curve.

Now we can deal with the problem of interpreting a score of 24 out of 35 on an IQ test for which the group mean is 18. We can express the score of 24 as the difference from the mean, divided by the standard deviation. This is called a *standard score.*

Normal curves are very similar to one another; so if we know the mean and standard deviation of a group of measurements, we can infer a great deal more. For example, in all normally distributed measurements, 68 percent of the scores fall within 1 standard deviation below or above the mean; and 95 percent of the scores fall within 2 standard deviations below or above the mean. Let's go back to our example. If we assume the mean of our scores is 18 and the standard deviation is 6, a score of 24 is 1 standard deviation above the mean: it's higher than the scores of 84 percent of the people who've taken the test.

ask the subjects to construct patterns from blocks, put pictures in sequence so that they "tell" a story, and substitute "code" figures for letters (see Figure 13.4).

Wechsler assumed that some people find it easier to work with words and that others find it easier to visualize and manipulate objects. But he also believed that these two abilities were parts of a single general capacity.

In contrast, L. L. Thurstone (1938) argued that there exist at least 7 separate abilities that are not necessarily related to one another. Other psychologists have suggested anywhere from 3 to well over 100 separate abilities. The record holder seems to be J. P. Guilford (1982), who identified 150 different kinds of mental abilities!

Figure 13.4
The Wechsler Intelligence Scale for Children—Revised

The various subtests of the WISC-R are intended to measure components or aspects of intelligence. The two major groupings of the subtests generate separate scores for verbal and performance IQ, as well as a total score combining both.

Test	What Is Tested	Example
Verbal Scale		
Information	General information	Who wrote *Tom Sawyer*?
Comprehension	Understanding of cultural facts and customs	What is the advantage of keeping money in the bank?
Arithmetic	Simple arithmetic operations	If two buttons cost 15 cents, what will be the cost of a dozen buttons?
Similarities	The ability to perceive relationships among concepts	In what way are a circle and a triangle alike?
Vocabulary	The ability to define words	What does *govern* mean?
Performance Scale		
Picture completion	The ability to identify missing portions of a picture	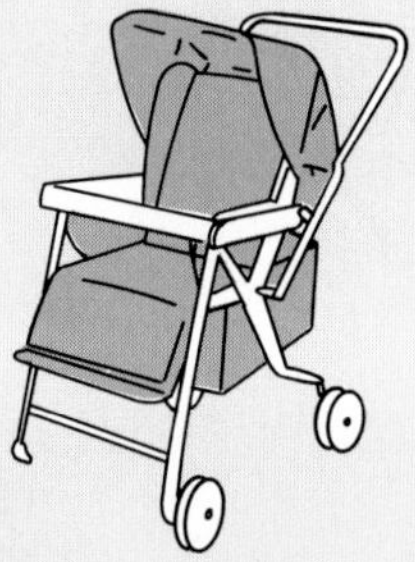
Picture arrangement	The ability to recognize a series of events	
Object assembly	The ability to put together the pieces of an object to make a whole	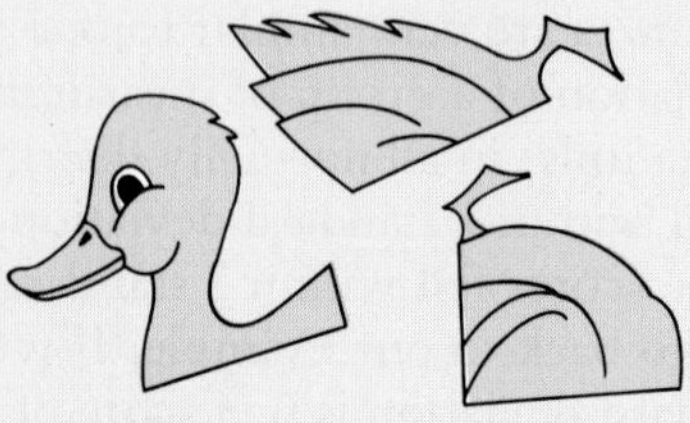

Source: The Psychological Corporation.

Howard Gardner identified seven different abilities. The three people pictured here represent three of them: Ceasar Chavez, a labor organizer, has an enormous ability to understand the needs of others; Tracy Chapman, a popular singer, excels musically; and Greg Louganis, an Olympic gold medalist, excels physically.

The controversy over the number of different mental abilities and the relationships among them stemmed in part from the difficulty of establishing the construct validity of intelligence tests. There was no theory that predicted different levels of performance on different tasks.

If one part of a test measures one ability and another part measures a different ability, then we would expect some people to do well on one part but not the other. That is, we couldn't predict how well someone would do on one part from his performance on the other. Earlier in this chapter we described how correlation is used to measure the relationship among the parts of a test. There we said that a high correlation is good because it indicates a high level of internal consistency. But if a test sets out to measure more than one kind of ability, the parts *should not* be too highly correlated.

The question of internal consistency was the focus of the early combatants in the "one" versus "many" battle. They spent most of their energies analyzing the pattern of relationships within IQ tests. Unfortunately, as long as they stayed within the tests themselves, their findings were circular and inconclusive (Gould, 1981).

More recently, psychologists have begun looking for evidence of different abilities in the real world. Howard Gardner (1983), for example, has studied people who are very talented in just one area and those who are noticeably lacking in some particular skill. From his work, he has identified seven different abilities: verbal and mathematical abilities; the musical and spatial abilities that make for great musicians and architects; the ability to understand oneself and the ability to understand others; and the ability to take intelligent physical action, as great dancers or athletes do.

Another psychologist, Robert Sternberg (1985), identified three kinds of mental skills: *Componential skills* are the analytical and critical skills that are needed to excel in school; these are measured by IQ tests. *Experiential skills* involve relating ideas to one another, creative thinking, and seeing new relationships among concepts. And *contextual skills* consist of knowing how to get things done in the real world, of achieving one's goals. This is practical intelligence.

So how many kinds of intelligence are there? At this point the best answer seems to be quite a few. What are they? That's a bit more difficult to say. We're not even sure whether different mental abilities are aspects of a general underlying ability. But it is clear that whatever aspects of mental ability are measured by conventional intelligence tests, the tests do not measure all mental abilities.

Francis Galton, a nineteenth century psychologist, was one of the first individuals to study intelligence and in particular the role inheritance plays in it.

The Question of Heredity

The question of whether intelligence is inherited may be the oldest question in the science of psychology. Francis Galton (1869), a distant cousin of Charles Darwin, began studying the inheritance of "eminence" in the middle of the nineteenth century. Upon discovering that eminent people are more likely than ordinary people to have eminent relatives, Galton concluded that eminence is biologically inherited. From our modern perspective, however, he seriously underestimated the potential impact of the family environment on eminence. Eminent parents tend not only to direct their children to fields such as science (where eminence is possible) but also to help them in many ways to become eminent in those fields.

The Evidence for Heritability In the years since Galton's work on eminence, the techniques of *behavioral genetics* (described in Chapter 11) have become far more sophisticated.

A good place to begin a study of intelligence and heredity is with the correlation between the IQ scores of parents and those of their children. Remember that an individual parent and child share 50 percent of their genes. And parent-child correlations of IQ scores usually fall between .40 and .60, thus indicating a substantial relationship between the intelligence of parents and that of their children. On the average, siblings also share 50 percent of their genes, and the correlations of IQ scores between siblings are similar to those between parents and children, ranging from .45 to .70 (Bouchard & McGue, 1981). Although the level of these correlations is consistent with the idea that intelligence is inherited, it's also consistent with the idea that intelligence is acquired through the family environment.

One way to separate the genetic similarity from the environmental similarity is to compare the IQ scores of adopted children with the scores of both their adoptive and their biological parents. The effects of environmental factors should be about the same whether a child is adopted or not. So any difference we find in the correlations between IQ scores should be a function of genetic differences. In fact, there are substantial differences. In one study of more than two hundred children who had been adopted at birth, the correlation with the IQs of their adoptive mothers was .15; the correlation with the IQs of their biological mothers was .32 (Munsinger, 1975).

If genes are important, identical twins should have higher correlations than siblings or even fraternal twins. The correlations for fraternal twins range between .65 and .75, slightly higher than the correlations between siblings. But for identical twins, IQ correlations are substantially higher, between .88 and .92 (Bouchard & McGue, 1981).

This array of correlations is shown in Figure 13.5. Notice that the genetic similarity of the pairs increases as you move from left to right in the chart, as does the size of the correlations. Within the 50 percent genetic relationship group, environmental similarity also increases as you move from left to right.

The Evidence for Environmental Determinants Figure 13.5 also contains clear evidence that environmental factors are important too. First, notice that the correlation for fraternal twins is higher than that for siblings, although both fraternal twins and siblings share the same 50 percent of their genes. The higher correlation for fraternal twins must be a function of environment. Because fraternal twins are the same age, their environments are more alike than the environments of other siblings. Notice, too, the difference in correlations between biological parents who are raising their children and biological parents who are not. When a child is raised by his or her biological parents, their IQ scores are more similar.

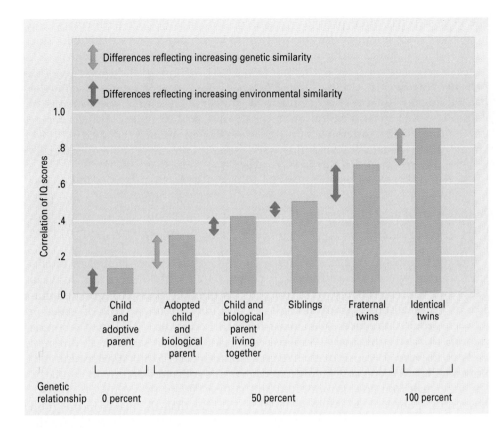

Figure 13.5
Heredity, Environment, and Intelligence

The height of the bars reflects the similarity in IQ scores. Notice that both genetic and environmental similarity increase from left to right. Increases in similarity of IQ related to increases in both heredity and environment can be seen.

The importance of environmental factors is demonstrated even more clearly in studies of extreme variations in environment. For example, the negative effects of unstimulating environments have been demonstrated over and over (see, for example, Hunt, 1982). Children who are raised in an environment where they have little experience with or encouragement to do intellectual tasks may score as many as 20 points lower on an IQ test than children who are raised in more stimulating environments.

If an unstimulating environment can reduce IQ scores, can an enriched environment increase them? Apparently not; at least not very much beyond some point. If children are raised in a reasonably normal, stimulating environment, then additional special treatments have little effect on their later intellectual ability (Scarr & Carter-Saltzman, 1982).

Can We Use IQ Scores to Compare Groups?

Intelligence testing has been the focus of one of the most passionate intellectual debates of this century. The acrimonious arguments about intelligence test scores and the races illustrates the confusion that can be sewn when social prejudices get mixed up with scientific debates. Similar debates have flared up occasionally around differences between other groups as well, especially men and women.

In all such cases, debate opens with the observation that some group consistently scores less well on intelligence tests than some other group. The slide into prejudice begins with the assumption that if blacks or women don't do as well on these tests, perhaps it's *because* they're black or female. The descent is accelerated by the obvious fact that people are black or female because of something in their biological makeup—specifically, the fact that they have different genes.

The next step has often proved irresistible—to conclude that performance on intelligence tests is caused by the same kind of genetic factors that make skin black or gender female. This just isn't so. Let's consider the evidence.

Race and Intelligence   In the United States blacks, on average, do score lower than whites on IQ tests. On standard IQ tests, most simple comparisons of black and white groups reveal a difference of about 15 points in the average score, although this difference has grown smaller in recent years (Jones, 1984; Angoff, 1988). Asians, on the other hand, score higher than whites, especially on tests of mathematical abilities (Stevenson, Lee & Stigler, 1986).

Early in this century, these differences were casually attributed to differences in genetic endowment. Later, as society's values became more democratic, psychologists attributed black-white IQ differences to environmental factors. Then, in the late 1960s, educational psychologist Arthur Jensen (1969) reopened the question of genetics.

One of Jensen's arguments was that since the differences we find in intelligence among whites are a product of genetic factors, the differences between blacks and whites probably were too. But his thinking was wrong. The influence of genes within a group doesn't say anything about the role of genes in between-group differences. Geneticist Richard Lewontin (1976) used a simple example to clarify this point. Suppose you plant a bag of seeds of all different kinds of flowers. Because of their genes, some species grow short, some tall. Now imagine that you sow half the seeds in fertile soil and water them regularly. The other half you sow in poor soil and ignore. When the plants are grown, those in the poor soil are going to be much shorter than the plants in the good soil. But within each group, the taller plants have the taller ancestors, and the shorter plants have the shorter ancestors. What Lewontin was saying is that genetics can predict within-group differences (like the difference in height) but still have nothing to do with between-group differences. In the same way, if one group of people is kept on its knees, the shorter reach of its members has nothing to do with genetics (see Figure 13.6).

Are there environmental factors that might account for the black-white differences in IQ scores? Definitely. Within the white population, parents who are better educated, have better jobs, and earn more money have children who score

Figure 13.6
Differences Within Groups

Within a group, differences in height are determined largely by heredity. But if everybody must kneel, the group's overall height will be shorter, even though the height differences within the group are still attributable to heredity.

better on IQ tests (Broman, Nichols & Kennedy, 1975). Blacks in our society generally have less access to education, lower status jobs, and less money. So the differences between black and white children may reflect socioeconomic factors, not genetic endowment (MacKenzie, 1984).

To test this possibility, numerous studies have attempted to equate groups of blacks and whites on these socioeconomic variables. The more successfully these matches are accomplished, the smaller the differences between the IQ scores. Perhaps the best match was achieved in a study of the children of U.S. servicemen in Germany. All of these children had white German mothers, and some had white and others African-American fathers. The two groups of children had essentially identical IQ scores.

Modern gene mapping technology has permitted a direct test of the role of genes in group differences. "Black" is a social category, not a biological reality. Many people who consider themselves black have ancestors from all over Europe, as do many whites. If black-white differences in IQ scores are caused by genetic factors, then the proportions of African and European ancestry should be related to IQ scores. A group of researchers used blood tests to determine the extent of white ancestry in a black population and found that the degree of white ancestry was not related to IQ scores (Scarr et al., 1977). These studies and countless others demonstrate that black-white differences in IQ scores are not due to genetic differences between the groups.

Cultural Differences and Test Bias   A second, equally important criticism of intelligence tests and how they are used leads to the same conclusion. The question is whether conventional IQ tests are valid for populations that do not share the culture of the original target population. Remember that many IQ tests assess general knowledge, the knowledge that people acquire in their everyday lives. But our everyday lives are very different. We live in a variety of geographical and social settings. For instance, one of the items on the Wechsler Adult Intelligence Scale is similiar to the question, "How far is it from New York to Chicago?" Someone who comes from New York or Chicago probably has an advantage on this question, compared to someone from Florida or Hawaii. And someone from Australia would have no more idea of the answer than you would know how far it is from Melbourne to Sidney.

These are minor differences in location; but differences between cultures can be more extreme. Whereas most people in the United States know the meaning of proverbs such as "A stitch in time saves nine," we would not expect people from New Guinea or France or India to have any idea.

Whether a person has learned something depends not only on how easily they learn but also on their opportunity to learn. Whenever a person's culture is different from the culture of the people for which a test was developed, the validity of the test *for that person* is suspect.

In response to this problem, psychologists have worked hard to develop *culture-fair tests* (see Figure 13.7). Because language differences among cultures are so obvious, most culture-fair tests attempt to avoid language items. However, critics point out that cultures differ in other kinds of experiences as well. For example, children play with blocks in some cultures, and don't in others. Can these kinds of differences make a difference in test scores? Definitely! Children who have just half an hour's experience playing with the blocks from the Wechsler block-design subtest do significantly better on that test. In fact, they do so much better that if they could increase their scores on all of the performance subtests by this amount, their overall performance IQ scores would go up 15 to 25 points (Dirks, 1982).

In sum, IQ tests vary in terms of how obviously their content is derived from a specific culture, but some cultural impact is always present. When the cultural content is less obvious, white-black differences in intelligence are smaller.

Figure 13.7
A Culture-Fair Test

Tests like the Raven Progressive Matrices Test were designed to avoid the use of language and to minimize the effects of differences among cultural experiences, which cannot be entirely removed.

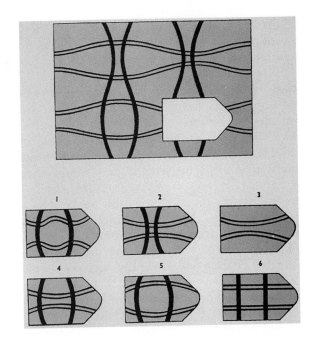

Source: Raven, 1948.

Gender and IQ Test Performance

We have focused on black-white differences, but the same issues arise in gender as well, though with an interesting twist. On most tests, overall IQ differences between men and women are not observed. But that is because the tests are scored differently for the two sexes, to make sure that no difference in IQ scores will occur. This was a theory-driven decision by the test developers who assumed men and women did not differ. Because differences in overall scores are not observed, the issue in regard to gender concerns differences in the *kinds* of intellectual abilities.

Commonly, boys do better than girls on tests of spatial relations and some kinds of mathematical reasoning, whereas girls are superior at verbal tasks (Halpern, 1986). Whether these differences are due to biological or cultural factors is still unclear. In any case, the differences, though commonly observed, are quite small (Hyde & Lynn, 1988) and don't justify any differences in what is expected of individual men and women.

Recap

- By searching out material that all children should learn, Alfred Binet designed a test of general knowledge, a test that could predict children's performance in school.

- Binet's test generated a mental-age score; later, William Stern used that score in a formula that calculates intelligence quotient.

- With the development of deviation IQ scores—scores that are expressed as standard deviations—the purpose of the tests to predict school performance was obscured.

- Binet never assumed that his test did anything but predict performance in school; however, many of the psychologists who followed him believed that his test measured intelligence.

- One of the difficulties in defining intelligence has to do with the nature of intelligence: Is it a single general ability, or many different kinds of abilities?

- There is strong evidence that intelligence is inherited; from the research on the correlation between IQ scores and genetic similarity comes evidence for environmental factors as well.

- Genetics may predict within-group differences without having anything at all to do with between-group differences.

- The differences we find in the IQ scores of black and whites are a product of socioeconomic and other environmental factors, not genetics.

- To the extent possible, culture-fair tests avoid language and other cultural influences that could lower the test scores of subjects who are not members of the original target population.

The Assessment of Personality

Tests of personality measure differences among people in terms of their motives, attitudes, styles, and characteristic ways of behaving and responding. These measures are used in research and in the processes of diagnosing psychological disorders, making hiring decisions, career counseling, and other life choices.

Although a measure that's been developed for one purpose is occasionally used for another, most personality tests have very specific objectives. For example, the instruments that researchers use to study personality—such as Snyder's Self-Monitoring Scale—tend to focus on one or two theoretically defined variables. In contrast, measures that are used for diagnosis or selection assess a wide variety of attributes.

In the next few pages we describe several measures of personality—their form, their function, and their limitations. These measures are characteristically divided into two groups: the objective personality tests and the projective tests.

Objective Tests of Personality

Personality tests generally consist of groups of questions that have specific answers. For example, many of them ask respondents just to decide whether an item does or does not describe themselves.

The Minnesota Multiphasic Personality Inventory (MMPI)   MMPI is the most widely used and studied measure of personality in recent times (Lanyon, 1984). The test consists of 556 items, each a statement about what the subject believes or feels or does. For example:

- "I sometimes wish I could be a better person."
- "I am afraid of losing my mind."
- "I have confidence in my abilities."
- "Sometimes I hear voices when no one is there."

Each item is answered true or false.

The items on the MMPI are divided into ten subscales (Hathaway & McKinley, 1940; Hathaway et al., 1989), each corresponding to a psychological disorder. From the scores on the different subscales, psychologists can prepare a profile of each client, like the ones in Figure 13.8.

**Figure 13.8
MMPI Profiles**

A score greater than 70 on any subscale indicates that the person is in the top 5 percent of people on that scale. The profile of the male indicates that he is hostile and impulsive, feels that others are persecuting him, and experiences delusions. The profile of the female indicates that she is tense, depressed, and has difficulty relating to other people.

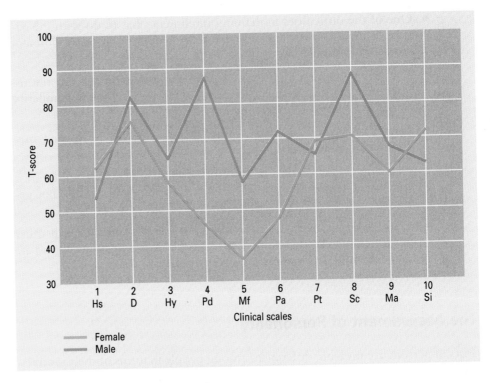

Source: Adapted from Duckworth & Anderson, 1986.

The clinical scales abbreviated in the figure are as follows: 1. Hypochondriasis (Hs) (concern with bodily functions and symptoms); 2. Depression (D) (pessimism, hopelessness, slowed thinking); 3. Hysteria (Hy) (use of physical or mental symptoms to avoid problems); 4. Psychopathic deviate (Pd) (disregard for social customs; emotional shallowness); 5. Masculinity/femininity (Mf) (interests associated with a particular sex); 6. Paranoia (Pa) (delusions, suspiciousness); 7. Psychasthenia (Pt) (worry, guilt, anxiety); 8. Schizophrenia (Sc) (bizarre thoughts and perceptions); 9. Hypomania (Ma) (overactivity, excitement, impulsiveness); 10. Social introversion (Si) (shy, insecure).

The developers of the MMPI wanted an objective diagnostic test. The procedure they followed was a straightforward application of criterion validity. First they asked groups of people already diagnosed with a psychological disorder to respond to a large pool of items. Then they compared the responses of these groups of patients to those of a control group of people considered to have no disorder. If an item was answered significantly differently by the criterion group (the group of patients), it was included in a subscale.

Does the MMPI work? The diagnostic scales do distinguish people who have psychological disorders from those who don't. Patterns of scores on the MMPI also predict diagnostic category moderately well (Dahlstrom, Welsh & Dahlstrom, 1975; Parker, Hanson & Hunsley, 1988).

Projective Tests of Personality

Projective techniques share the assumption that a person's imaginative creations will reflect his or her personality. They vary in terms of the way they stimulate the person's imagination.

Rorschach Inkblot Test   The inkblot test, which was named for its developer, Herman Rorschach, was the first (and is still the most famous) of the projective tests. The Rorschach test consists of ten inkblots, similar to the one in Figure 13.9. The subjects' task is to look at the inkblots and describe the kinds of things they see in them.

People see all sorts of different things in the inkblots. For example, an inkblot might look like a motorcyclist driving away to one person, like a pair of ele-

Clinical Versus Statistical Prediction: The Computer and the Clinician

The MMPI has been at the center of a controversy about how best to use psychological tests. Frequently, psychologists are asked to predict a person's behavior, such as how well that person will respond to psychotherapy, or whether he or she should be released from a psychiatric hospital. To answer such questions, psychologists have traditionally administered a group of tests and then made a judgment based on their overall impression of the client. This kind of judgment is called *clinical prediction*. Paul Meehl (1954, 1956) argued that such specific predictions could be made much more accurately by means of purely mathematical techniques. The *statistical prediction* he recommended is based simply on the specific scores of tests such as the MMPI. If a person scored above a certain level on a test, or received a certain combination of scores on different tests, that person was deemed more likely to be a success outside the hospital. But if the individual scored below that, an in-hospital stay was advised.

This controversy raged for some time, but the conclusion finally arrived at was that, for specific predictions about behavior, the statistical approach was superior (Sawyer, 1966). The research continues to demonstrate that if the measures are reliable and valid, and if they have been tested for each specific prediction, a mathematical equation does produce more accurate predictions than do global clinical judgments (Dawes, Faust & Meehl, 1989). The clinical interpretation is more appropriate, however, when neither the test nor the base of observations is available for the development of the statistical prediction (Holt, 1970).

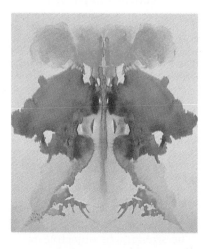

Figure 13.9
Rorschach Inkblots

Look at this inkblot for a moment, and then describe what it looks like to you. What you see is assumed to reflect your personality.

phants to another, and like an old woman's face to a third. But, of course, it really doesn't look much more like any one of these than any other. In this test, as in all projective tests, there is no structure that determines what the subject sees. The subject creates the structure. As the Rorschach is usually used, three aspects of a person's response are important. The first is content. The second is what determined the response—the shape, the shading, the color. The third is how well the response fits the shape. If a subject looking at the inkblot shown here sees the Los Angeles Dodgers on a bus tour, we could assume that she's extremely preoccupied with sports. The blot doesn't look anything like the Los Angeles Dodgers! (At least to us.)

The Rorschach test has been used for years, so a great deal of information about it has been collected. Testers can compare a person's responses against catalogues of responses for each whole or major part of the inkblots. This degree of standardization makes for relatively reliable scoring on the individual parts of the test. However, neither the reliability of the total scores (Reznikoff, Aronow & Rauchway, 1982) nor their validity (Korchin & Schuldberg, 1981) is very good.

Clinicians continue to use the Rorschach because they feel they can learn things from it. But it has essentially become the focus of a kind of structured interview rather than a diagnostic tool in itself (Anastasi, 1988).

The Thematic Apperception Test (TAT)   The TAT is another well-known projective test. It consists of twenty pictures, mostly of people alone or in small groups doing something ambiguous (see Figure 13.10 for a simulated example). The subjects' task is to make up a story about what's happening in the picture, what led up to it, what the people are feeling, and how it will all turn out.

The basic rationale of the TAT is exactly that of the Rorschach: both assume that the subjects' inner processes create structure from a vague stimulus. Because the pictures don't reveal much about the characters in them, the subjects themselves have to decide what kinds of stories to tell.

The TAT was developed by Henry Murray (1938), a trait theorist whose work we talked about in Chapter 9, in our discussion of the need for achievement. Murray believed that TAT stories reflect the kinds of needs that are most important to us.

David McClelland (1985) and his associates have used the TAT extensively to measure the need for achievement and other needs from Murray's list. This research grew out of an attempt to demonstrate the validity of the TAT as a measure of needs. McClelland began by developing a scoring system, based on the number of stories that contained themes of achievement or other motives. Then he related these scores to people's actual achievements, to child-rearing patterns, and eventually to patterns of economic development of whole countries. This extensive program of research provided strong support for the construct validity of the TAT measure of the need for achievement.

Although the TAT has been very useful in research, it doesn't work in quite the way it was originally conceived. Murray hoped the measure could be used to identify a person's needs and predict his or her behavior, in much the same way that a person's school performance could be measured by an IQ test. However, TAT measures of motives are not nearly as precise as IQ scores. They allow for broad distinctions among people who are relatively high or low in motives, distinctions that are useful in research on large groups. But they don't yield the kinds of specific predictions about an individual's behavior that Murray had hoped for.

Figure 13.10
The Thematic Apperception Test (a Simulation)

What do you think is happening in this picture? What led up to it, and how will it turn out? The stories people tell about the pictures in the TAT reflect their individual psychological processes, since the pictures themselves don't clearly define what is happening.

Measures of Personality: Pros and Cons

The strength of objective personality measures—scales such as the MMPI—is that we can usually be clear about both their reliability and their validity. But we never get something for nothing. These measures also have two important weaknesses.

The first weakness has to do with their application. We can use objective measures of personality to compare large groups of people, but they're not very accurate at predicting individual behavior. Even though objective tests statistically predict better than anything else, they still make many errors. Because this is a problem with both measurement and theory, we shall come back to it in Chapter 14, in our discussion of personality.

The second problem is a practical one. Because a great deal of work is required to establish reliability and validity, measures of many interesting variables do not exist. Take cool-headedness, for example. None of the tests of person-ality measure this attribute. And until someone tackles the work of developing a scale, there won't be a reliable and valid measure of cool-headedness. The result is that psychologists often study what they can measure, not what they're really interested in.

What about the projective tests? These tests were developed in an era when personality theorists believed that people are not conscious of the essential de-terminants of behavior. So the tests were designed to reveal these inner pro-cesses. But neither the theories nor the measures they inspired have fared too well in recent times. Psychologists have come to expect theories to predict things that actually happen and measures to demonstrate adequate reliability and validity. And projective tests simply don't meet these expectations.

Of course, some projective tests, especially the TAT, are being used effec-tively in nontraditional ways. And others continue to be used by psychologists primarily as the focus of interviews. The accuracy of the information gleaned from these interviews seems to owe much more to the insight of clinicians than to the testing procedure itself.

Recap

- Tests of personality measure differences among people in terms of their motives, attitudes, styles, and characteristic ways of behaving and responding.

- The Minnesota Multiphasic Personality Inventory is an objective measure of personality that was developed using criterion groups. The scale is used to diagnose psychological disorders.

- Test scores can be used to mathematically predict some kinds of be-havior. If the measures are reliable and valid, and if the predictions have been adequately tested, such statistical prediction is superior to the intuitive judgments of clinicians.

- The Rorschach inkblot test is a projective test that asks subjects to describe what they see in the shape, shading, and color of inkblots. The objective is to reveal the subjects' unconscious motives, emo-tions, and needs. Like most projective tests, the Rorschach is not highly reliable or valid; in fact, it's used primarily as the basis of struc-tured interviews.

- The Thematic Apperception Test asks subjects to create stories about the people in pictures; these stories, in turn, help psychologists define the subjects' motives. Unlike most other projective tests, the TAT has been validated through years of research.

- Objective measures of personality allow broad comparisons among groups of people but are not very accurate at predicting individual behavior; in addition, they are not available for every important at-tribute.

- Neither the theory behind projective measures nor the measures themselves meet today's standards of reliability and validity.

Psychological Assessment in Practice

In the real world, psychological tests are used for two major purposes. One is to choose people for admission to school or for a job. Related to this is the use of assessment techniques to counsel clients about career and other life choices. The other purpose is the clinical diagnosis of psychological disorders. Both purposes are associated with particular practices. Both also raise some important ethical questions.

Assessment and Selection

Unless you flip a coin, any decision about who to admit to a school or who to hire for a job reflects some kind of assessment. Most of the time these decisions are based on interviews and reports of past performance in other schools or jobs. As we've seen, interviews and behavioral assessments have advantages, especially that of convenience. But they have a serious disadvantage, too: they don't work very well. Interviews are neither very reliable nor valid, and predictions from past behavior are successful only if the past and present situations are similar. This is why almost all selective schools and many employers have turned to more formal psychological tests for help in making selection decisions.

The use of tests for selection has generated both controversy and changes in practice. At one time, employers used the MMPI and even the Rorschach to make hiring decisions. But they found that job applicants resented what they believed was an invasion of their privacy. Furthermore, these tests did not predict job performance any better than interviews.

A second body of concerns grew up around aptitude tests, including IQ tests. As they were used more widely, it became obvious that, although IQ tests do predict performance in some jobs, they do not predict success in many others (Schmidt & Hunter, 1981). And because certain minority groups do not score as well as other groups, the effect was to exclude their members from many jobs (Garcia, 1981). In response, the Equal Employment Opportunity Commission (1970) issued regulations that require every employer to demonstrate the criterion validity of any test used for selection. As a result, aptitude tests now tend to be highly specific to particular jobs and more closely connected to the actual nature of the work.

Tests are also used to help people make work choices. For instance, aptitude tests are intended to identify skills that, with practice, could develop into abilities. And general aptitude tests are somewhat similar to IQ tests in that they measure verbal and mathematical aptitude, and also include measures of reasoning, spatial relations, and the speed and accuracy of work. Notice that these skills are not unique to particular kinds of work. At their best, tests like these indicate broad categories of work that may be suitable for the individual.

Interest tests, such as the Strong-Campbell Interest Inventory (Campbell & Hansen, 1981), consist of items that ask a subject to choose between activities—say, baking bread or playing chess. The items have previously been answered by criterion groups, people who are happily working in some job. The more the subject's choices match those of a particular profession, the more his or her interests are deemed to fit that job. Of course, these tests don't guarantee that the subject will be satisfied in a particular profession, but they do suggest some directions to think about.

Clinical Assessment

Assessment has been central to the job description of clinical psychologists since the emergence of the profession. One of the goals of testing is to diagnose psychological disorders and determine methods of treatment. Traditionally, psychologists don't use single tests; instead, they tend to employ a battery of tests, the most popular of which are the MMPI, the WAIS, and the Rorschach (Lubin et al., 1985). Information from all of the tests is usually integrated in a summary report that describes the main features of the test-taker's personality, including strengths, weaknesses, and problems (Tallent, 1976).

The utility of these reports depends on the setting, the selection of tests, and the skills of the clinician. Ideally, the clinician is able to augment the information collected by the tests with interpretations of the client's behavior and any special circumstances of the test situation.

Recap

- In the real world, psychological tests are used to make selection decisions or clinical diagnoses.

- Recognizing the limited reliability and validity of interviews, many schools and employers have turned to more formal psychological tests to help them make selection decisions.

- Today most employers must demonstrate the criterion validity of any test used to make hiring decisions.

- At their best, tests of interests indicate broad categories of work that may be suitable for an individual.

- Most psychologists base their diagnoses of psychological disorders on a battery of tests and a summary of test results.

Conclusion

Psychological tests often have a major impact on people's lives. Beginning with the first school years, tests can determine the course of children's school careers. Later tests affect college admissions, and still others affect admission to graduate schools and to professions such as medicine and law. Psychological tests are also used to decide who to hire and promote and, in some cases, even who must be confined to an institution. Clearly, testing is an important business.

Equally clear is the fact that psychological testing is complex, difficult, and fallible. At least a few errors are inevitable. When such important decisions depend on instruments that can make mistakes, it is no wonder that people worry about the role of tests. Periodically, politicians and editorial writers cite examples of the most disturbing errors and call for the elimination of testing.

Could we do away with tests? If we did, what would the alternative be? After all, we cannot stop making the decisions guided by tests. Not everyone can attend this school or be hired at that job, so choices need to be made. And if we don't use tests to help us choose, what can we use? The only basis that remains is our intuitive impressions of the candidates involved. But these impressions are far more susceptible to prejudice and prone to error than tests. Without tests, we would be returning to the problem that Binet set out to solve: that some decisions are too important to be left to unaided human judgment. We human beings need all the help we can get, and tests are one kind of help. They may not make us perfect, but they do make us better. Uncritical rejection of tests is no better than uncritical acceptance.

Chapter 14

Personality

Head, Alexej Jawlensky, 1913

14

Gateways Why am I the way I am, with my particular collection of likes and dislikes, motives, habits, and quirks, and why aren't you like me? To many psychologists who study personality, this is perhaps the central question of psychology.

As this chapter explains various psychological perspectives on the differences among people, you will revisit a number of theorists whose ideas appeared in earlier chapters (as well as encountering some new theorists). For example, Freud and Erikson proposed stage theories of development (Chapters 11 and 12) to explain personality. We also considered Freud's ideas in Chapter 5 on consciousness and Chapter 9 on motivation. Other approaches to personality derive from the principles of learning and, to some extent, the principles of cognition, discussed respectively in Chapters 6 and 8. Theoretical conceptions of personality are particularly important to Chapter 15 on psychological disorders and Chapter 16 on treatment.

"Dick's so strong. He sits quietly and calmly, while everyone else is just kidding around. He's so wonderful."

Years ago, when my cousin pointed out her new friend at a family party, I knew that she had fallen hard. And she had. As the weeks went by, she found new qualities she admired. Dick was brave (his favorite sport was racing motorcycles). Dick was smart (he was a chemist). Dick was wise beyond his years (he didn't like "wasting" money in bars).

I finally talked to this perfect man—at their wedding. He told me how much he liked Louise's personality, how much he admired her sense of humor and the ease and enthusiasm with which she entered social situations. Well, I thought, opposites do attract.

Shortly after their wedding, Louise and Dick moved away. Ten years would pass before I saw Louise again. She was getting a divorce.

"We have nothing in common. He's so boring! All he wants to do is go off and race motorcycles. The rest of the time he sits around, saying nothing. And he doesn't like going out to restaurants or parties or anything!"

It sounded like Dick, all right. Maybe opposites don't attract after all.

You can imagine how surprised I was when Louise called some time later to announce that she and Dick were getting married again!

"I just didn't appreciate him. We had a big problem with our son, but Dick was so calm and never got rattled and just took care of it. And he's so reassuring to be with. He just quietly does whatever needs to be done."

Unfortunately, the marriage didn't work this time either. Two years later, Louise and Dick split up again.

"He drove me crazy. He never talks, and he doesn't have any sense of humor. He wanted to invest the little money we have in wild schemes. And now that he's getting too old for motorcycle racing, he wants to take up flying!"

Obviously Louise and Dick were very different from each other. And despite the years they lived together, neither of them changed very much. When things were good, Louise saw Dick's quiet but daring personality in a good light. When things were bad, she didn't see him differently—she just felt differently about the way he was. And Dick probably felt the same way about Louise.

Personality: The Definition of the Individual

Each of us is unique. We all have our own ways of thinking and feeling and behaving that distinguish us from everyone else. These long-standing patterns of thought, emotion, and behavior make up **personality.**

The essential task of the study of personality is to describe and understand what makes each individual unique. But to do this, we also need to study what is common to all people. The scientific study of personality began at the end of the nineteenth century with the development of several elaborate theories that attempted to explain "everything" about people's personalities. In the first part of this chapter we describe how these theories evolved through the middle of the twentieth century.

Personality The long-standing patterns of thought, emotion, and behavior that distinguish an individual from other people.

393

Each of these "grand" theories gave rise to competing theories. But, clearly, these contradictory theories cannot all be correct. So, after we've examined the theories, we discuss the question of choosing among them. Finally, we close by talking about some of the research generated by the theories and the direction this research is taking.

Freud and the Psychodynamic Theories

The **psychodynamic theories** explain behavior in terms of the motives—especially the unconscious motives—that underlie behavior. These theories were the work of Sigmund Freud, his supporters, and also some of his most important critics.

Origins

Freud's theory grew very naturally out of his work as a neurologist. In late-nineteenth-century Vienna, neurologists often came across patients, usually women, who suffered from what was then called *hysteria*. These patients seemed to have a problem with their nervous system. Some were paralyzed; others were unable to feel anything in their hands or legs. But when the physicians examined the patients more closely, they found that the symptoms had no neurological cause (see Figure 14.1).

Figure 14.1
An Impossible Neurological Symptom

In the late 19th century, patients diagnosed as "hysteric" often presented symptoms that were apparently caused by nerve damage, but which were in fact neurologically impossible to experience. One example was a "glove anesthesia," in which the patient reported no feeling in the hand, but normal feelings in the rest of the arm (part a). As you can see in part b, the nerves of the hand and arm are connected in such a way so that if one of the nerves in the hand is damaged, sensations can still be felt in other parts of the hand, though sensations from parts of the arm will be lost.

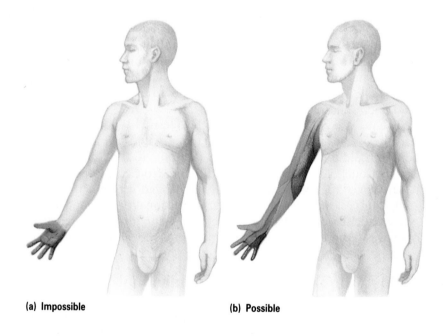

(a) Impossible   (b) Possible

Psychodynamic theories A group of theories of personality that assume the most important causes of behavior are motives, especially unconscious motives.

The most influential of these hysterical patients was Anna O., who was treated by Freud's early collaborator, Josef Breuer. Anna suffered from a series of problems that loosely mimicked injuries to the brain or nervous system. At one point, she was unable to swallow, although careful examination of her throat revealed no physical abnormalities.

A second symptom led to a "cure" for the first. Almost every afternoon Anna would fall into a kind of trance. One day, while Breuer watched, Anna fell into a trance and began to complain about "her English lady-companion whom she did not care for, and went on to describe, with every sign of disgust, how she had once gone into that lady's room and how her little dog—horrid creature!—had drunk out of a glass there." Still in the trance, she asked for and drank some water, and then woke "with the glass at her lips," her difficulty in swallowing gone (Breuer & Freud, 1896/1982, p. 34). Later, Anna reported that she had completely forgotten the episode of the dog drinking from the glass—until she was in the trance.

Breuer treated Anna's other symptoms in the same way. As soon as she spontaneously fell into a trance, he asked her to talk about her problem; each time, she remembered an unpleasant event and again, upon awakening, was cured.

Breuer and Freud had found what seemed to be a cure for hysteria: helping patients remember something unpleasant that they had forgotten. The problem was that most patients weren't as accommodating as Anna; they didn't conveniently fall into a trance every afternoon. The solution was to induce a trance through hypnosis. Once hypnotized and asked to talk about their symptoms, the patients readily reported unpleasant experiences that they, too, had forgotten. And when they woke, their symptoms, like Anna's, were gone.

Notice three things here. First, the patients—when hypnotized—reported memories of incidents they hadn't remembered before. Second, those memories were unpleasant. And, third, there was a relationship between the content of the memories (the feeling of disgust at the dog drinking from a water glass) and the patients' symptoms (the inability to swallow).

In these observations lay the germ of two ideas that are central to Freud's theory: that memories and feelings can exist in the mind but be inaccessible to the conscious, and that these unconscious memories can affect behavior.

Freud continued to study and treat hysteria—but without Breuer, who had returned to his conventional medical practice. Freud eventually stopped using hypnosis, replacing it with the technique of free association. In free association, Freud asked his patients to say anything that came to mind, without critical thought or censorship.

As he explored his patients' minds, Freud found that memories seemed to emerge in layers. In the first layer were incidents like Anna's memory of the dog; in the second layer—a layer uncovered only after repeated treatment—were memories of sexual experiences at very young ages, usually involving the parent of the opposite sex. At first, Freud believed that hysteria was caused by these experiences. Later, he realized that many of these events could not have happened; in one case, for example, a supposed seducer was absent for a year or more during the critical time. So Freud concluded that these memories must have been constructed after the fact.

At this point, Freud sharply modified his theory. He argued that hysteria and other psychological disorders are created by the difficulties of dealing with forbidden sexual desires. The memories of seductions that never happened were actually *expressions* of those desires.

Here we have the basis of two other concepts that are central to Freud's theory. Because his patients' memories so regularly pertained to sexual matters, Freud came to believe that sexual needs are the most important needs. And because the memories were so often of childhood events, he began to see that the adult's personality is shaped by the child's experiences.

Notice that Freud's experiences with his patients were the source for the central ideas of his theory—that memories and feelings can be unconscious, that these unconscious contents shape our everyday behavior, that these unconscious causes are often sexual, and that the origin of these unconscious memories and feelings is childhood. In the next few sections we will describe the specific details of the theory he built on these foundations.

Freudian Theory

Freud's theory consisted of three interrelated parts. One centers on the structure of the mind, or *psyche;* the second, on the nature and development of the sexual drive; the third, on psychological defense mechanisms.

The Structure of the Psyche   Based on his work with hysterical patients, Freud identified three levels of consciousness. He believed that the mind contains large reservoirs of memories, feelings, and biological motives, or drives, that the individual is not aware of. He called this part of the psyche the **unconscious mind.** In contrast, the part of the psyche currently being experienced by the individual is the **conscious mind.** The third part—the **preconscious mind**— contains the many memories that the individual isn't aware of right now but could become aware of if necessary. The preconscious mind is where you store phone numbers until you need them, for example.

Later, Freud developed an additional model of the mind based on the ways in which the different parts of the mind function. He called these functional parts of the psyche the *id,* the *ego,* and the *superego* (see Table 14.1). The way in which Freud saw these models fitting together appears in Figure 14.2.

Table 14.1
The Functional Parts of the Psyche

Structure	Development	Characteristic Activities
Id	Present at birth	The psychological aspect of the biological needs; wants all needs satisfied instantly; operates under the pleasure principle
Ego	Gradual, from birth to about age 5	Satisfies the demands of the id within the limitations of physical and social reality; perceives, thinks, remembers, and feels emotion; operates under the reality principle
Superego	About age 7 through identification with parents	Defines right and wrong; punishes wrong with guilt; sets standards of behavior

Unconscious mind The large reservoirs of memories, feelings, and drives that the individual is not aware of.

Conscious mind The memories, feelings, and drives that the individual is aware of right now.

Preconscious mind The memories, feelings, and drives that the individual is not aware of now but could become aware of if necessary.

Id In Freudian theory, the part of the psyche that consists of the psychological feelings of biological needs.

Pleasure principle In Freudian theory, the principle under which the id operates: satisfaction now, without regard for what is feasible.

Ego In Freudian theory, the part of the psyche that satisfies the id's demands within the limitations of physical and social reality.

Reality principle In Freudian theory, the principle under which the ego operates; satisfaction within the constraints of physical and social reality.

The id   A newborn is little more than a bundle of biological needs or drives; the **id** is the psychic representation of those needs. The id is concerned with wanting, but not with the ways in which wants are satisfied. Freud believed that the id operates on the **pleasure principle:** satisfaction now, at any cost. The id doesn't think about the consequences of its demands or even about whether those demands are feasible in the real world. And because it's impossible to satisfy all of the id's needs at the same time (for example, a person can't eat and sleep simultaneously), some of those needs are inevitably frustrated, at least temporarily.

The ego   Because the id isn't able to deal with reality, another part of the psyche must do so. That part is the ego. The **ego** consists of all the mental abilities that help the individual understand the world and get things done. Sensing and perceiving the external world, thinking about it, learning, remembering, feeling emotions—all are functions of the ego.

These abilities, and hence the ego itself, are not present at birth. They develop over time to help satisfy the id's needs: the id's inevitable frustrations focus psychic energy first on its frustrated needs and then on the possible means of satisfying them. The product is the ego.

The ego's job is to satisfy the id as much as possible within the limits of physical and social reality. Thus the ego operates under the **reality principle.**

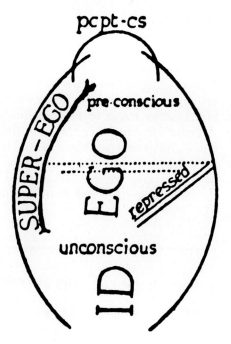

Source: Freud, 1933.

Figure 14.2
Freud's Psychic Structures

In this drawing by Freud, he depicts the relationships among the psychic structures and the levels of consciousness. The very small perceptual-conscious area at the very top is our conscious mind, which is primarily ego with a small part of the superego. The preconscious area is also ego. The ego extends into the unconscious area, as does the superego. The id is entirely unconscious, and parts of the id are "walled off" from consciousness by repression.

It finds acceptable ways to satisfy the id's impulses. Young children suck their thumbs; adults in our society don't. So if your id is crying out for something to suck (a need left over from infancy and early childhood), your ego finds a socially acceptable substitute—a piece of candy or a stick of gum.

The superego   The third psychic structure, the **superego,** is the home of moral functions. The superego defines right and wrong, punishes wrong with guilt, and sets standards of behavior. According to Freud, the superego develops at around age seven, as a result of the child's identification with his or her parents and adoption of their moral standards.

Your superego, like your ego, wouldn't approve of your sucking your thumb—but for different reasons. The ego is concerned with the results: "If you suck your thumb, people will make fun of you, and you will not be able to get as many other id satisfactions." But the superego just makes a moralistic judgment, without any necessary logical basis: "Thumb sucking is disgusting. You *shouldn't* suck your thumb."

The role of the psychic structures in behavior   Freud believed that behavior is a product of conflicts among the id, the ego, and the superego. The resolution of those conflicts is reflected in what the individual thinks or feels or does.

According to Freud, one of the ways in which people differ has to do with the relative strength of the three psychic structures. For example, people with weak egos are impulsive; they're inclined to satisfy their wants now at the expense of trouble later. And people with weak superegos have no compunctions about hurting and taking advantage of others, whereas people with excessively strong superegos tend to be rigid and guilt-ridden.

Instinctual Drives   Freud believed that underlying every behavior are the basic needs for survival, or drives. Some of these basic drives—for food, for shelter, for sleep—are satisfied relatively easily. But two drives in particular—for sexual satisfaction and for aggression—are often at odds with society and its conventions. It is for this reason, Freud argued, that these needs often generate conflicts and frequently must be satisfied indirectly.

Superego In Freudian theory, the part of the psyche that defines right and wrong, punishes wrong with guilt, and sets standards of behavior.

Freud focused most of his theoretical attention on the **libido**—the energy that moves the individual to seek pleasure. He believed that the libido is more than the sexual drive, although it encompasses that drive. He defined it as a "comprehensive bodily function, having pleasure as its goal" (S. Freud, 1905, p. 70).

According to Freud, libidinal needs take on different forms at different stages of life. Sexual activity is the primary source of sensual pleasure in adulthood, but at earlier stages sensual pleasure is obtained in other ways.

Freud identified five stages of libidinal development: oral, anal, phallic, latency, and genital (see Table 14.2). He further suggested that the first three stages are particularly important in shaping the adult's personality. If the needs in one of these stages are not satisfied, or if they are "oversatisfied," the individual *fixates* on that stage and continues to look for this kind of satisfaction later in life.

Table 14.2
Freud's Stages of Libidinal Development

Stage	Age	Form of Satisfaction	Effects of Fixation on Adult Personality and Behavior
Oral	0–2 ±	Sucking	Dependent personality; preoccupation with getting things; oral activities (smoking, chewing gum)
Anal	2–5 ±	Retaining and expelling feces	Obsessions with neatness, punctuality, and cleanliness, or with extreme slovenliness and disorder; collecting, saving, accumulating wealth
Phallic	5–7 ±	Obtaining exclusive attention of opposite-sex parent	Strength of conscience, sex-role identification, choice of mate
Latency	7–13 ±	Consolidating effects of phallic stage	None
Genital	13 +	Sexual activity	None; fixations of earlier stages integrated

Is it possible to get just the right amount of satisfaction at any stage? Freud didn't think so. He argued that almost all adults are fixated to some degree at each of the early stages of libidinal development, and that these fixations are reflected in behavior.

Oral stage   When a child is born, the libidinal drive centers on the mouth. In the **oral stage,** sucking gives the infant sensual pleasure. Fixation at this stage leaves the adult with oral needs that, according to Freud, often lead to such habits as smoking or nailbiting.

Children in the oral stage can't take care of themselves; all they can do is cry when they want something. And adults who are strongly fixated at this stage may be dependent, passively sitting back and waiting for others to take care of them.

Anal stage   Around age two, children are able to control their bowels. At this age toilet training becomes the major life issue, and the focus of libidinal urges shifts to the anus.

The **anal stage** centers on cleanliness, order, and, more generally, control. Children must learn to retain their feces until the appropriate time and place, and then expel them on demand. Freud argued that if toilet training is too lax, the individual may never learn any kind of self-control; and if that training is too harsh, the individual may become preoccupied with neatness and order.

Libido   In Freudian theory, the energy that moves the individual to seek pleasure.

Oral stage   In Freudian theory, the first stage of libidinal development; during this stage the focus of satisfaction is the mouth.

Anal stage   In Freudian theory, the second stage of libidinal development; during this stage the focus of satisfaction is the anus.

If your room looks like this, Freud would have said you were fixated at the anal stage. Messiness, lateness, problems managing money are all signs of anal fixation; so too are excessive neatness, punctuality, and stinginess.

Phallic stage   Around age five, the center of libidinal needs moves again—this time, to the genital area. Accordingly, this stage is called the **phallic stage.** The phallic stage begins when the child recognizes that his or her father is a serious rival for mother's affections. Freud believed that this recognition generates a powerful array of conflicting emotions, which he called the **Oedipus complex.** The impact of the Oedipus complex on boys is very different from that on girls.

When a boy recognizes the potential rivalry with his father, he begins to feel jealousy, even hatred, and an increasingly intense desire to possess his mother. Freud did not say that boys want to have sexual intercourse with their mothers; at the phallic stage, the libidinal impulse focuses on possession.

The boy's hatred of his father is mixed with **castration anxiety,** a fear rooted in his discovery of the anatomical differences between the sexes: perhaps girls have somehow lost their penises; and perhaps he too could lose his penis, castrated by his father.

The fear of castration resolves the Oedipus complex. The child forces his feelings for his mother into the unconscious mind. And to further placate his father, he attempts to be as much like him as possible, in both action and imagination—a process called **identification.**

One of the most important consequences of identification with the father is the creation of the superego. Boys learn to punish themselves for moral failings (based on what their fathers say rather than how they actually act). According to Freud, these internalized moral teachings constitute the superego.

For girls, the phallic stage begins in much the same way it does for boys. Girls are primarily attached to their mothers and become jealous of their fathers. Like boys, girls discover the anatomical differences between the sexes, but they feel no anxiety because, according to Freud, they have nothing left to lose. Instead, they envy their fathers and are disappointed with their mothers. This cluster of feelings, called **penis envy,** leads girls to shift their affections from their mothers to their fathers.

At this point, girls are in much the same situation as boys: primarily attracted to the parent of the opposite sex. But nothing analogous to castration anxiety causes girls to repress their attraction to their fathers or to identify with their mothers. As a result, Freud believed, girls' superegos are not as powerful as those of boys.

Phallic stage   In Freudian theory, the third stage of libidinal development; during this stage the focus of satisfaction is on the exclusive possession of the parent of the opposite sex.

Oedipus complex   In Freudian theory, a child's desire to possess the parent of the opposite sex; sometimes called the *Electra complex* in girls, although Freud did not use this term.

Castration anxiety   In Freudian theory, the boy's fear, during the phallic stage, of castration by his father in retaliation for the child's Oedipal feelings.

Identification   The process by which the individual tries to be as much like someone else as possible; in Freudian theory, a boy's response to castration anxiety.

Penis envy   In Freudian theory, the envy girls feel during the phallic stage because they don't have a penis.

Puzzle It Out!

Freud locates one major developmental transition at around age 6 to 7, with the resolution of the phallic stage. Piaget and many others have demonstrated a major change in cognitive operations at about this same age. What aspects of this change in cognitive functioning might have led Freud to perceive changes in personality functioning at the same time?

There's no question that Freud's thinking here was sexist. He explicitly held that women's development isn't just different from men's but inferior. Freud himself admitted that his theoretical understanding of women's libidinal development was not very adequate (S. Freud, 1905).

Latency stage   Once the commotion of the phallic stage has been resolved, the child moves into the *latency stage*. Freud believed that during this stage, which lasts from about age seven until age thirteen or so, libidinal urges are inactive.

Genital stage   With the onset of puberty, children move into the final stage of libidinal development, the *genital stage*. During this stage, satisfaction takes its final form—adult sexual activity. Because this stage marks the end of the development process, it has little impact on personality.

Psychological Defenses   One of the ego's most important tasks is to control the free expression of the id's desires. Usually it does so by finding acceptable substitutes for those things the id wants. Freud would have argued, for example, that someone with very aggressive urges might find an acceptable expression of those urges by becoming a surgeon. This strategy is called **sublimation**, and it is the strategy most of us use most of the time.

What happens if the ego can't find an acceptable substitute? When the ego is forced to work directly with the id's impulses, it uses **defense mechanisms.** These processes keep impulses in the unconscious mind or transform them so that they aren't threatening (A. Freud, 1946).

The most basic defense mechanism is **repression.** If you think of the id as energy pressing upward, toward consciousness, then repression is an equal force of energy holding the impulses down, into the unconscious mind (see Figure 14.3a).

Repression uses a lot of energy while combatting the upward force of the id. Other defense mechanisms are variations on repression that in one way or another make the job easier. For example, **denial** consists of bolstering repression with conscious energy, by asserting the opposite of the unconscious feeling (see Figure 14.3b). You have probably had the experience of someone telling you very firmly that she was *not* angry at you, leaving you wondering whether perhaps she really was. Denial is like that, except that the speaker would be unaware of the underlying feeling.

A similar defense, **reaction formation**, also "borrows" energy from the conscious mind. This defense converts the impulse into behavior that is diametrically opposed to the impulse. Consider the individual filled with aggression—with impulses that the ego cannot allow to "surface"—who claims to love animals. The clue that reaction formation is at work is the extent to which that individual is willing to go to assert that claim. Someone who's prepared to kill a human being in order to protect an animal is most likely motivated by aggression.

Sublimation   A defense mechanism in which an unacceptable impulse is satisfied by an acceptable behavior.

Defense mechanism   A process that keeps impulses in the unconscious mind or transforms them so that they are not threatening.

Repression   A defense mechanism that uses psychic energy to keep threatening impulses in the unconscious mind.

Denial   A defense mechanism in which the opposite of the unconscious feeling is asserted.

Reaction formation   A defense mechanism that converts an impulse into a behavior that is diametrically opposed to that impulse.

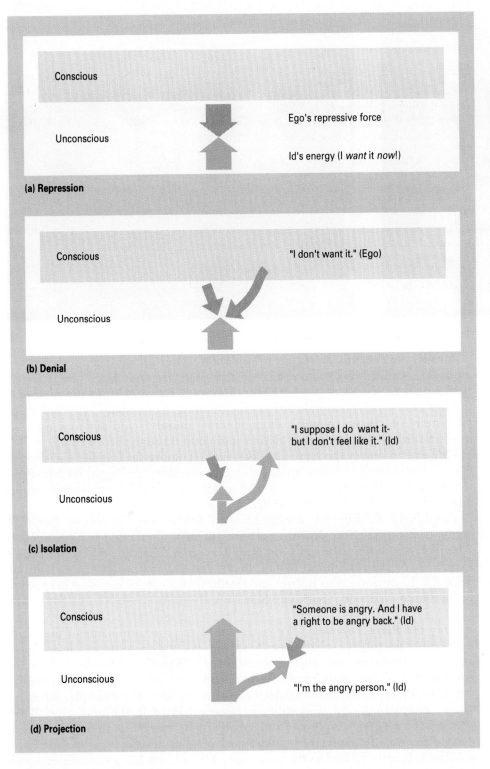

Figure 14.3
Defense Mechanisms

(a) In *repression*, the force of the id pressing toward consciousness is opposed by the equally repressive force of the ego. This occurs in the unconscious. (b) In *denial*, the ego uses some energy from its conscious activities to help keep the id material in the unconscious. (c) In *isolation*, feelings are repressed, but cognitions are permitted into consciousness as "cold" thoughts. (d) In *projection*, only the original source of the feeling (commonly anger) in the self is repressed, and the feeling is attributed to others. As a result, the feeling is often justified.

Another defense, termed **isolation,** involves a two-step process (see Figure 14.3c). First, unconscious feelings are separated from their associated unconscious thoughts and memories. Then, just the feelings are repressed; the thoughts and memories move into the conscious mind. This separation allows the individual to respond matter of factly to what are usually emotional stimuli. Isolation is at work when, for instance, a friend very casually remarks that he doesn't like one or both of his parents.

Isolation A defense mechanism that separates unconscious feelings from unconscious thoughts and memories, and then represses the feelings.

Marilyn Monroe usually played the stereotypical "dumb blond" who always seemed to have her head in the clouds. This character is a caricature of the hysterical personality, whose heavy reliance on repression and denial as defenses also lead the person to be unaware of much of what is going on around them. Mr. Spock was always depicted as extremely intellectual and unemotional—a caricature of the obsessive personality. The use of intellectualization as a defense leads the person to feel no emotions because they are repressed, with all the energy directed toward abstract thought.

Intellectualization elaborates on isolation. After unconscious feelings and ideas are separated and the feelings are repressed, the individual does a lot of thinking about the ideas. In that way, more of the energy from the repressed feelings can be expressed indirectly in the thinking. For instance, psychologists who study or choose to write about libidinal impulses and defenses may be intellectualizing, satisfying their desires indirectly through their writing.

One way to reduce the repressive load is to recognize the impulse and simply blame it on someone else—a process called **projection** (see Figure 14.3d). Projection occurs most often in conjunction with aggressive impulses: someone who's angry accuses those around her of being angry *at her.*

People rely on different combinations of defense mechanisms—a fact that accounts for some of the differences among people. On the one hand, someone who represses or denies the id's impulses may seem forgetful or unconcerned— like the stereotypical "dumb blond" in the movies and on television. On the other hand, someone who isolates and intellectualizes those impulses may seem unemotional—like Mr. Spock on "Star Trek."

Putting the Parts Together   We've described three determinants of the adult personality: the relative strength of the id, the ego, and the superego; how much a person is fixated at each stage of libidinal development; and the defense mechanisms used by the individual. Freud identified some common personality types, which represented combinations of these factors. For example, the individual with a hysterical personality is heavily fixated in the oral stage. This person has a relatively weak ego and superego, and tends to use repression and denial defenses. By contrast, the individual with an obsessive-compulsive personality is heavily fixated in the anal stage. This person has a stronger ego and often a very strong, punitive superego, and tends to use the defense mechanisms of isolation and intellectualization.

Intellectualization A defense mechanism that separates feelings from cognitive content, and then represses the former while closely examining the latter.

Projection A defense mechanism in which the unconscious impulse is attributed to other people rather than to the self.

The Response to Freud's Work

Many of the people who worked and studied with Freud eventually developed their own psychodynamic theories of personality. Carl Jung, at one time Freud's favorite disciple, quarreled with Freud over a theoretical disagreement about the nature of the major motive force. Freud believed that this force is libidinal; Jung (1933) believed that it's a striving for *self-actualization,* for the fullest development of all of one's capacities.

Although Jung rejected many of Freud's theoretical constructs, others found their way into his theory in different forms. For example, Jung rejected Freud's division of the psyche into the id, ego, and superego; but he preserved the idea that the mind is divided into a number of psychic structures—seven of them!

Jung also shared Freud's belief that behaviors are produced by unconscious forces. But he expanded those forces to include the **collective unconscious**— the "psychic residue" of our ancestral past, a kind of memory of our species' experiences. According to Jung, the collective unconscious contains *archetypes,* which are innate tendencies to understand the world in particular ways. One archetype, for example, is the "wise man," which leads us to assume that all bearded old men are wise. And the "earth mother" archetype tends to make us believe that all plump older women are nurturing.

Another of Freud's disciples, Alfred Adler, also developed his own psychodynamic theory. Like Freud and Jung, Adler argued that human diversity is the product of a single unconscious motive, but he believed that this motive is a striving for superiority (Adler, 1929).

According to Adler, we inevitably feel inferior in infancy and childhood because in fact we are inferior to the adults around us. The particular kinds of inferiority we experience shape our adult behavior, as we work to overcome them. These feelings of inferiority are unconscious and irrational; in addition,

Carl Jung, who began as Freud's disciple, developed a theory in which he assumed the basic motive behind human behavior was the full development of the self. He argued that many religious symbols expressed this motive for self-actualization. The mandala, with its perfect circular symmetry, was a particularly strong symbol of this development.

Collective unconscious   In Jungian theory, the part of the unconscious mind that holds memories of the ancestral past; those memories are the source of archetypes that lead us to understand the world in particular ways.

they are complicated by the collection of memories, thoughts, and fantasies that have developed around them over the years. Adler called this collection of unconscious memories, thoughts, and feelings the **inferiority complex.**

Erik Erikson (1963), whose theory of development we talked about in Chapters 11 and 12, was another of Freud's followers. His contribution was to redefine Freud's stages of libidinal development in social terms. In the process, he came to believe that events beyond age seven do make an important contribution to adult personality.

Karen Horney, like Freud, believed that a single, largely unconscious motive is at the center of most behavior. That force is the need to overcome feelings of insecurity, the basic anxiety that arises in childhood.

Horney's theory was in part a response to the weaknesses of Freud's theory of women's development. She argued that penis envy is actually an anatomical metaphor for the social condition of women, insisting that it is only natural for women to envy the opportunities and power that society allocates to men (Horney, 1939). Moreover, like Adler and Erikson, Horney believed that social interactions are the most powerful force in shaping personality.

All of the psychodynamic theories assume that some unconscious motive underlies behavior. And most assume that the psyche is divided into often conflicting parts. By definition, we can't observe unconscious motives or psychic structures; so it's not surprising that disputes among psychodynamic theorists were not easily resolved.

Recap

- Psychodynamic theories explain behavior in terms of the unconscious motives that underlie what people feel and think and do.

- As Freud worked with hysterical patients, his patients discovered forgotten memories of unpleasant incidents that were related in some way to their symptoms. He concluded that memories and feelings the individual is not aware of can exist in the mind and affect behavior.

- Because his patients' memories were so regularly of sexual matters and so often rooted in their childhood, Freud came to believe that the sexual drive is a primary force underlying behavior and that the adult's personality is shaped by the child's experiences.

- Freud's theory has three primary parts: the structure of the psyche, the nature and development of the sexual drive, and psychological defense mechanisms.

- Freud identified three levels of consciousness: the unconscious mind, the conscious mind, and the preconscious mind.

- According to Freud, the id is the psychic representation of the instinctual needs; the ego is the part of the psyche that satisfies the id's demands within the limitations of physical and social reality; and the superego is the home of moral functions.

- Behavior, according to Freud, is a product of conflict among the id, the ego, and the superego.

- The libido, the energy that moves the individual to seek pleasure, is satisfied in different ways at different stages of life. Freud believed that the first three stages of libidinal development—oral, anal, and phallic—are particularly important in shaping the adult's personality.

Inferiority complex In Adlerian theory, the collection of unconscious feelings of inferiority that develop in infancy and childhood and later shape adult behavior.

- When the ego can't find an acceptable substitute for what the id wants, it uses repression and other defense mechanisms to control the id's impulses.

- The three determinants of the adult personality—the relative strength of the psychic structures, libidinal development, and defense mechanisms—combine to produce personality.

- Several of Freud's followers eventually developed psychodynamic theories of their own. All of these theories assume that some unconscious motive underlies behavior, although they often disagree on what that motive is.

The Behaviorist Approach

In Chapter 1 we described how, at the beginning of this century, a group of psychologists began to study human behavior by focusing on what is observable. The behaviorists knew perfectly well that human beings think and feel and remember. But they argued that a science of psychology should focus only on what people actually did—their behavior. In their view, personality consists of the patterns of behavior, and the explanation of personality was to be found in how we learn to behave as we do.

The basic principles of behaviorist learning theory were described earlier, in Chapter 6. They consist of the principles of learning. The task for behaviorism as a personality theory, then, was to use these principles to explain the variety of ways in which people behave and hence, the differences between people.

These principles easily explain many aspects of behavior, such as why people go to work (for the reinforcer of money) or why they are frightened of dogs (they were classically conditioned by bad experiences with a dog). However, some of the more complex kinds of human behavior presented challenges to behaviorists. B. F. Skinner was especially creative in finding ways to answer these challenges.

Identifying the Reinforcer

Behaviorists such as Skinner argued that behavior was maintained by its reinforcers. Thus, to understand a behavior was to understand how it was being reinforced. The problem, however, was the frequent difficulty involved in identifying any reinforcer. If, for instance, someone does volunteer work without any recognition, what is the reinforcer?

One solution to this problem is to recognize that the behavior may be reinforced by a secondary reinforcer. Remember that if a previously neutral stimulus leads to a primary reinforcer, such as food or water, the neutral stimulus may become a *secondary reinforcer.* Any object or experience may become a secondary reinforcer through association with primary reinforcers. And each individual's unique learning history determines which, if any, kinds of events become secondary reinforcers. Thus, a behavior may be maintained by a secondary reinforcer that the observer can not recognize.

For example, you probably remember at least one child you went to school with who was constantly getting in trouble and being sent to the principal's office. On its surface, this behavior seems inconsistent with behaviorist principles, because the child did not receive any obvious reinforcer. Indeed, the consequence of the child's behavior was more likely to be punishment. The behav-

Some reinforcers, like food, are obviously related to biological needs, but the origins of others are more difficult to identify. Perhaps human beings have an innate need for physical affection, though hugs may have become reinforcing through their association with feeding in infancy. But some reinforcers, like money, are clearly derived from other more basic reinforcers.

iorists point out, however, that we may have misunderstood. In particular, the "punishment" of a trip to the principal's office and a scolding may instead have been experienced by the child as a reinforcer, as a form of "attention." So, instead of extinguishing disruptive behavior, this kind of attention reinforced it.

A second reason we may have difficulty identifying reinforcers has to do with their schedule. In real life, reinforcers are rarely administered after every behavior. (Your teacher doesn't compliment you each day you do your homework; for instance.) Rather, most reinforcers are administered only intermittently. And obviously, it can be difficult to identify a reinforcer that's not being administered during a particular behavior.

In sum, behaviorists argue that although some behaviors appear not to be reinforced, they actually are. In such cases, however, the reinforcers may be events we don't recognize as reinforcing, or they may occur so infrequently that we are able to detect them only after prolonged observation.

Shaping Complex Behavior

A second problem for behaviorist personality theory is the sheer complexity of human behavior. We can easily imagine how someone could be reinforced for stopping at traffic lights, or for saying "please" and "thank you." However, personality involves far more complex performances. For example, your performance as a student in college requires that you have a complicated set of motives and skills. How could a behaviorist explain such complicated actions as these?

Skinner's answer was *shaping*. Remember that shaping is the reinforcement of responses that gradually move closer to the desired response. Skinner believed that extremely complex patterns of behavior are created by a lifetime of shaping.

By extension, a behaviorist might explain your college-going behavior as the product of years of reinforcement: the hug your mother gave you each time you brought something home from kindergarten, the gold stars your teachers put on your papers in elementary school, the good grades you earned on a history project in junior high, the encouragement your guidance counselor gave you when you talked about career choices. All of these reinforcers gradually shaped your behavior: they all played a part in your desire to go to college and in the development of your skills.

Superstitious Behavior

Behaviorists assume that, at some very basic level, human beings behave rationally: everything we do, we do because "it pays" in terms of reinforcement. The problem for behaviorists, then, is to explain irrational behavior—behavior that doesn't seem to make sense.

In this connection, Skinner pointed to what he called **superstitious behavior,** which he believed was produced by random reinforcement. Skinner discovered the effects of random reinforcement by accident. In Chapter 6 we described his favorite apparatus, the Skinner box, an automated reinforcing machine in which animals could "earn" reinforcers continuously. One morning Skinner came into the laboratory and found some pigeons acting very peculiarly in their boxes. He discovered that the apparatus had malfunctioned and was giving the birds reinforcers at random intervals. Yet these random reinforcers had shaped behavior, just as systematic reinforcers do. The pigeons were hopping and twisting because these behaviors had been reinforced. According to Skinner, society, too, administers many reinforcers on a random basis and, consequently, produces equally peculiar behavior in humans.

You can get an idea of how random reinforcers might work, as well as why Skinner called the resulting behavior "superstitious," if you think about how minor superstitions develop. For example, suppose you won a tennis match that you expected to lose. What could have made you play better than usual? Maybe it was the new socks. Next time you play, you'd be sure to wear those socks, even if they're dirty. And if you win again—which "proves" that the socks are lucky!—you're going to wear those socks until they disintegrate. Each win, though in reality only randomly related to what socks you were wearing, nevertheless reinforces your belief in lucky socks. Research has demonstrated that superstitious behavior can be created in children through precisely this pattern of reinforcement (for example, see Wagner & Morris, 1987).

In sum, Skinner and other behaviorists were able to devise clever hypotheses to explain how many of the most complicated human behaviors might have arisen from schedules of reinforcement. Even when the reinforcers were not at all obvious, they could generally find a reinforcement explanation.

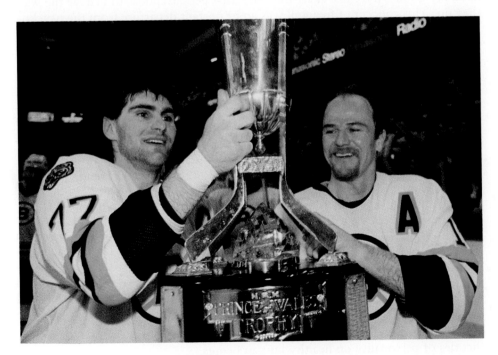

A conventional superstition in the National Hockey League is that during the playoffs, no one should shave. Each win reinforces nonshaving.

Superstitious behavior In behaviorism, the kind of behavior produced by random reinforcement.

Recap

- The behaviorists argued that learning—not thoughts or feelings or memories—shapes behavior.

- According to the behaviorists, people are different because they have different learning histories.

- Skinner believed that in order to understand a behavior, we have to identify what is reinforcing the behavior.

- According to the behaviorists, the reinforcers for much human behavior may be difficult to identify because they are either administered intermittently or are secondary reinforcers.

- Reinforcement explains how complex behaviors are maintained; the shaping process explains how they are created in the first place.

- According to Skinner, irrational behavior—what he called superstitious behavior—is produced by random reinforcement.

Humanistic/Phenomenological Theories

Although psychodynamic and behaviorist theories are very different, they are also similar in that they view human behavior as being caused by forces of which most people are completely unaware. Psychodynamic theories explain personality in terms of unconscious motives; behaviorist theory explains behavior in terms of reinforcement and shaping. But missing from both is *experience,* the conscious awareness of the individual's intentions, plans, thoughts, and feelings.

Phenomenology is the study of experience. Phenomenological psychologists believe that human behavior is a product of human experience—of the individual's thoughts and feelings, especially about the self.

The humanistic part of the name for these theories reflects their view of people as dignified and complex. Most of these theorists assume that people are naturally good. And most share the belief that people choose to behave the way they do. This concept of free will was an important departure from the psychodynamic and behaviorist theories. People cannot control impulses they aren't even aware of, nor can they control their learning histories.

The theories of two men—Abraham Maslow and Carl Rogers—typify the humanistic/phenomenological approach to personality.

Abraham Maslow and the Hierarchy of Needs

Abraham Maslow argued that the methods of both the psychodynamic theorists and the behaviorists were logically flawed. Remember that Freud's theories evolved from his work with patients, who were consulting him about their problems in living. How, Maslow wondered, could Freud be sure that his observations were relevant to all people? Perhaps healthier people followed different principles.

Maslow, who had been trained to study animal behavior, was equally skeptical about the behaviorists' procedures. In research on animals, he would never assume that rats would behave the same way as monkeys do. Why, then, should we expect principles developed through experimentation with rats and pigeons to apply to people? Instead of studying either animals or people with psychological disorders, Maslow (1970) insisted that psychologists should base their theories of personality on healthy human beings.

Phenomenology The study of experience.

Maslow (1968) himself began a study of great figures in history—among them Socrates, Abraham Lincoln, Albert Einstein, and Eleanor Roosevelt. He found that these people didn't seem to be motivated by the biological needs that Freud had talked about or that define the primary reinforcers. Instead, they focused on gathering knowledge, creating beauty, establishing justice—a collection of motives that Maslow called the *need for self-actualization* (see Table 14.3).

Remember that in Chapter 9 we described Maslow's theory about the hierarchy of needs, ranging from physiological needs such as hunger at the bottom to these self-actualizing needs at the top. He emphasized that social needs are as much a part of human nature as physiological needs. And he believed that the need for self-actualization is within each of us, but that we may be too preoccupied with lower-level needs ever to act on it.

**Table 14.3
Characteristics of
Self-Actualizing People**

1. Superior perception of reality

2. Increased acceptance of self, of others, and of nature

3. Increased spontaneity

4. Increase in problem centering

5. Increased detachment and desire for privacy

6. Increased autonomy and resistance to enculturation

7. Greater freshness of appreciation and richness of emotional reaction

8. Higher frequency of peak experiences

9. Increased identification with the human species

10. Changed interpersonal relations

11. More democratic character structure

12. Greatly increased creativeness

13. Certain changes in the value system

Source: Maslow, 1968.

Carl Rogers and the Self-Concept

Carl Rogers believed that human beings have an innate tendency to develop and exercise all of their capacities. Like Maslow, Rogers (1951) called this tendency *self-actualization* and believed it was the primary force in people's lives. Maslow and Rogers differed, however, in their explanation of why so many people fail to fully develop and use their abilities.

Maslow argued that most people are so busy meeting lower-level needs that they can't even begin to deal with their need for self-actualization. In contrast Rogers argued that **self-concepts**—the system of ideas and beliefs about the self—are usually the source of people's failure to self-actualize. Indeed, for Rogers a positive self-concept is an essential ingredient for a healthy life.

Rogers believed that people develop self-concepts by observing their own actions and feelings, and that the more accurate their observations, the healthier they are. But the accuracy of those observations is limited by the reactions of others. From infancy, parents and others impose what Rogers called **conditions of worth** on children. They tell children—through their words and actions—that they are more lovable when they act and feel in some ways than when they act and feel in others. The children, in turn, so badly want approval that they avoid recognizing their own actions and feelings for what they are. Instead, they try to adjust their self-concepts to reflect what their parents and others tell them their actions and feelings should be.

Self-concept The system of ideas and feelings one has about one's self.

Conditions of worth According to Rogers, the conditions placed on the individual by parents and others that limit the individual's ability to develop an accurate self-concept.

The problem is that many of the acts and feelings rejected by adults are in fact normal and inevitable. For example, a child who sees another child get something special may be told, "Don't be jealous." So the child tries not to be jealous. However, jealousy is a normal reaction, so the child is still going to feel jealous—but without being able to recognize that feeling or to cope with it. And according to Rogers (1959), the failure to fully understand one's feelings and actions prevents the individual from reaching his or her potential, from self-actualizing.

Our adult personalities reflect the compromises between our self-concepts and the realities of our true nature. When we cannot recognize our true selves, we develop superficial—and ultimately unsatisfying—ways of being.

Recap

- Phenomenological theories of personality assume that human behavior is a product of human experience—of the individual's thoughts and feelings, especially about the self.

- All of these theories share the basic assumption that people are naturally good; and most share the belief that people choose to behave the way they do.

- Maslow questioned the relevance of theories that developed from the study of people with psychological disorders or from experimentation with animals.

- From his studies of historical figures, Maslow identified a collection of motives that he called the need for self-actualization.

- Maslow believed that all people have a need for self-actualization, but that most are too preoccupied with lower-level needs ever to act on it.

- Like Maslow, Rogers believed that the need for self-actualization is the primary force in people's lives, but he argued that the failure to fully develop and use their abilities stems from their faulty self-concepts.

- According to Rogers, the conditions of worth imposed by parents and others limit the accuracy of the individual's self-concept and prevent the individual from reaching his or her potential.

Trait Theories

A **trait** is a consistent way of behaving, thinking, or feeling that distinguishes an individual from other people. "Generous," "grumpy," and "extraverted" are all trait names. You use traits to describe people and to make sense of their behavior. You know you can borrow money from your generous friends, should avoid your grumpy friends in the morning, and are going to have fun with your extraverted friends at the party Friday night. Trait theories of personality use traits in much the same way—to describe people and make sense of their behavior.

The English language contains more than 4,500 names for traits, even after obvious synonyms have been excluded (Allport & Odbert, 1936). Many trait theories focused on reducing that number to a manageable level. Often this meant creating broad categories, or *types,* of specific traits.

One interesting theory was proposed by William Sheldon (1942), a physician and psychologist. Sheldon identified three kinds of temperament: one associated

Trait In personality theory, a consistent way of behaving, thinking, or feeling that distinguishes the individual from other people.

with sociability, warmth, and even-temperedness; another, with aggression, enthusiasm, and competitiveness; and a third, with restraint and privateness. Sheldon's categories were not particularly novel; but his insistence that each type of temperament is associated with a specific body type was uncommon (see Figure 14.4). Sheldon believed that our temperaments arise from our body types.

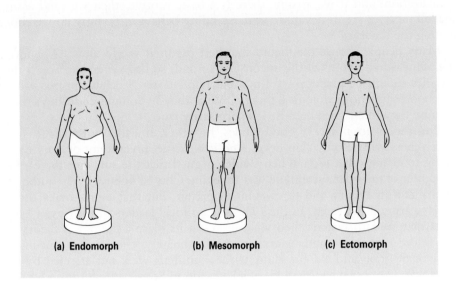

(a) Endomorph   (b) Mesomorph   (c) Ectomorph

Figure 14.4
Traits and Body Types

Sheldon's theory linked body types and temperaments. Endomorphs were supposed to be jolly and placid; mesomorphs, aggressive and confident; and ecotomorphs, timid and shy.

Sheldon's theory seemed little more than a collection of stereotypes—the jolly fat man, the aggressive jock, the timid bookworm. But in his research and in a number of subsequent studies, a relationship between temperament and body type was found. This relationship isn't very strong: there are lots of exceptions to the patterns Sheldon described. Furthermore, the distinction between cause and effect isn't always clear. Some people, for instance, may act according to the stereotype associated with their body type, rather than the reverse (Carver & Scheier, 1988). But Sheldon's body-type theory may have some merit.

Gordon Allport (1937), another early trait theorist, did not believe that just a few trait dimensions could be used to describe everyone. He argued that each individual is best described by some subset of the whole array of traits. Traits that affect many aspects of a person's behavior, in most situations, he called **cardinal traits.** For Einstein, curiosity might have been a cardinal trait; for Stalin, it may have been a rage for power. **Central traits**, such as altruism or ambition, describe large parts of the individual's behavior but do not have the broad effects that cardinal traits do. And, finally, **secondary traits**—such as preferences and likings—affect only small domains of behavior.

Recap

- A trait is a consistent way of behaving, thinking, or feeling that distinguishes the individual from other people.

- Trait theories of personality use traits to describe people and make sense of their behavior.

- Many of the original trait theories created broad categories of traits.

- William Sheldon's trait theory linked three different types of temperament to three distinctive body types.

- Gordon Allport argued that each individual is best described by a subset of all traits.

Cardinal trait A trait that describes most of the individual's behavior.

Central trait A trait that describes a large part of the individual's behavior but does not have the broad effects of a cardinal trait.

Secondary trait A trait that describes only a small part of the individual's behavior.

Choosing Among the Personality Theories

The personality theories we've been talking about make very different, often contradictory, assumptions. And, as noted earlier, they can't all be correct. The basic motive underlying behavior can't be libidinal satisfaction *and* self-actualization; and if we assume there is a basic motive, then we can't assume that all motives are irrelevant to understanding behavior. So how do we choose among the theories?

Many people choose the theory that best fits their world view: "I believe in the unmeasured depths of the unconscious mind, so I'm a Freudian" or "I think theories should be practical, so I'm a behaviorist" or "I believe in free will, so I'd choose a phenomenological theory." What they're doing is choosing a theory because they like it, not because it's necessarily true.

Preferences are not very good guides, however. If a theory isn't true, its attractiveness will be only skin-deep. And if it is true, no amount of denying it is going to change that fact. When Galileo argued that the sun, not the earth, is the center of the solar system, he was attacking Church doctrine. The authorities didn't like his theory and threw him in prison, but that didn't make the sun revolve around the earth. In the 1930s the political leaders of the Soviet Union discarded modern genetic theory, adopting in its place a biological theory that was more consistent with Marxism. Unfortunately, the laws governing the growth of grain and the breeding of farm animals were not affected by their ideology. The result was decades of stagnation in Soviet agriculture.

If not personal preference, what can we use to choose a theory? The answer lies in the theories themselves. Every theory is a claim about what's happening in the world. The test of a theory, then, is comparison of what is actually happening in the world with what the theory claims. This is so simple that you're probably wondering why we've spent so much time talking about these conflicting theories. Surely the theories have been around long enough for us to know which theory or theories meet the simple test of truth.

Indeed a lot of work has been done to test the theories we've talked about. But as studies of personality have become increasingly concrete and specific, the theories have slipped into the background. At one time a study might have grappled with the issue of whether Freud's ideas about repression are accurate. Then, as the research developed, the issue changed—and became the more general question of the nature of unconscious activity. But at that point the research no longer focused on the theory.

One reason research drifted away from the theories was that psychologists became interested in the phenomena they were studying and stopped thinking about the theories. More important, however, the research revealed that the theories were not specific enough to be tested directly. It wasn't that the theories seemed right or wrong, but that they were ambiguous. So new, more precise definitions and concepts were developed, and these new definitions and concepts were not closely connected to the theories.

The "grand" personality theories inspired much of the research we describe below. From that research we've learned many things about personality, but it hasn't helped us demonstrate the validity of the original theories. Which, if any, of the grand personality theories are true? We still don't know.

Research in Personality

In the next few sections, we will trace the evolution of some representative research programs, each of which was based on one of the grand personality theories.

The Psychodynamic Perspective

We've already discussed a lot of research that was inspired by Freud's thinking. For example, in Chapter 5 on consciousness we described Calvin Hall's elaborate studies of dreams, studies that were designed to explore Freud's theory that dreams are a way of working through the conflicts we experience in our daily lives (Hall et al., 1982). Similarly, the work on the impact of subliminal material had its roots in psychodynamic thinking. Then, in Chapter 7 on memory we described research that demonstrates a clear relationship between emotion and memory—albeit a relationship very different from Freud's description of repression. Apparently it's not the nature of an experience that makes the individual more or less likely to remember the experience but, rather, the individual's mood at the time he or she is remembering (Laird et al., 1982). We simply don't remember bad experiences when we're happy.

When we presented this research, we focused on the conclusions, not the process, and indeed did not mention Freud at length. To highlight the evolution that has taken place in research programs of this sort, we describe here one more example of how research that set out to test a psychodynamic theory evolved into something else.

One dimension of personality or trait theory has to do with sociability—the degree to which people seek out and enjoy their interactions with other people. At one end of the spectrum are **extraverts,** people who don't like being alone and who thrive on social occasions. At the other end are **introverts,** people who prefer to be alone, who find more pleasure in solitary activities than in being with people.

The extraversion-introversion dimension dates back to the ancient Greeks, whose theory of personality was based on the balance of four body fluids, or *humors:* blood, phlegm, black bile, and yellow bile. They would have said that the people we call extraverts have an excess of blood. Much later, Jung introduced this extraversion/introversion dimension to modern psychology.

Hans Eysenck's (1970) decision to study extroversion was based at least in part on his desire to test one of Jung's predictions. Jung had suggested that if extraverts developed a psychological disorder, they would become hysterics. Introverts, by contrast, would develop obsessive-compulsive disorders. (We talk more about these disorders in the next chapter.)

Extravert A person who enjoys social activity and does not like solitude.

Introvert A person who prefers being alone and does not enjoy social activity.

The public persona of Bette Midler is that of the classic extravert—gregarious, confident, loud, and impulsive. In contrast, Woody Allen's public image is that of the classic introvert—inhibited, shy, solitary, quiet, and introspective.

Eysenck began by collecting a variety of measurements on patients with psychological disorders. Using these measurements he identified two dimensions of personality: extraversion-introversion and emotional stability-instability (see Figure 14.5). And he found support for Jung's hypothesis: people who seemed to be extraverted according to his measures were more likely to be hysterical, whereas those who seemed introverted tended to be obsessive-compulsive or very anxious.

Figure 14.5
Eysenck's Personality Dimensions

The two strongest personality factors emerging from Eysenck's work were extraversion/introversion and emotionality. These dimensions correspond to a typology as old as the ancient Greeks: melancholic, choleric, phlegmatic, and sanguine. The traits that correspond to these personality types appear in the outer ring.

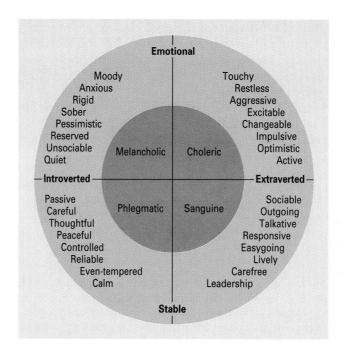

Source: Eysenck & Rachman, 1965.

Encouraged by this success, Eysenck developed an extraversion-introversion scale (Eysenck & Eysenck, 1975). Then he and others began to test the construct validity of the scale by exploring the differences among people who scored at one or the other end of the range of scores. They found that subjects who scored high on the extroversion scale do spend more time with others, enjoy parties more, are unhappy when alone, are more likely to conform to social pressures, and hold more lively conversations with one another (Eysenck, 1970; Thorne, 1987).

Eysenck next questioned *why* extraverts like to spend time with others. He was aware of some much earlier work by Pavlov (1927) that seemed to suggest an answer. Pavlov, you will remember from Chapter 6, on learning, had done much of his research on classical conditioning using dogs. Pavlov observed that his dogs reacted very differently to the conditioning experiments. Some dogs, who were outgoing, energetic, and friendly while running around loose, rapidly lost interest when confined in the boring experimental apparatus and even fell asleep. Other dogs, who were rather timid and withdrawn when loose, responded well to the experimental situation, once they became used to the experimenter and the apparatus. Pavlov concluded that these dogs differed in terms of the balance between two factors that affect the activity of the brain: excitation and inhibition.

Pavlov thought that the dogs who went to sleep in the apparatus exhibited a larger proportion of inhibitory activity in their brains and needed more stimulation than the apparatus provided. Yet these dogs could deal readily with high levels of external stimulation, such as the excitement of meeting new people. By contrast, the timid dogs who stayed awake in the apparatus had brains that were more heavily balanced toward excitatory processes.

Eysenck thought that Pavlov's inhibited and excited dogs sounded just like extraverts and introverts. He then proposed that extraverts' brains were dominated by inhibitory processes. Accordingly, extraverts needed lots of outside activity such as noise, parties, and other people just to stay awake; but they could tolerate, and even enjoy, very stimulating environments. In contrast, introverts were dominated by excitatory processes and tended to overreact to external stimulation. They needed to live quiet, unexciting lives, and to avoid being overpowered by their reactions.

Have you ever wondered why your sister or brother or roommate wants to study with the radio blaring and keeps jumping up to talk to people every little while? As Eysenck's theories about the balance of inhibition and excitation predict, extraverts seem to need this stimulation to keep alert enough to study. Conversely, introverts need more quiet when they study because they are more distractable (Campbell & Hawley, 1982).

Indeed, numerous studies have demonstrated that extraverts are much less distractable than introverts (Eysenck & Levey, 1972; Geen, 1984; Geen, McCown & Broyles, 1985). However, extraverts are not good at tasks that require continuous, careful attention, such as monitoring a long string of numbers for the occurrence of particular patterns (Claridge, 1967). In sum, there is considerable support for Eysenck's combination of ideas from Jung and Pavlov (Eysenck, 1985).

Notice what has happened in this research tradition. Eysenck began with an idea from Jung, a psychodynamic theorist. Later, he adopted another central idea from Pavlov, who was one of the earliest sources of behaviorist thought. And his basic approach is very much in the tradition of trait theories. Most striking of all, Eysenck no longer focuses on any of these theories in his work. Instead, he is concerned with the phenomenon of extraversion/introversion, and his explanations tend to be stated in terms of physiological and genetic factors. Finally, although we have focused on Eysenck, you may have noted that many of the experiments we mentioned were done by others. In every area of modern research, many people contributed to the development of research programs; and single individuals, like Eysenck, could at most be the most prominent of a large group. As we shall see, this kind of evolution occurred in all of the theoretical perspectives.

The Behaviorist Perspective

You may be wondering whether behaviorist theories are an exception to the shift away from the broad theories of personality. After all, behaviorism's defining characteristic is its emphasis on what is observable. Surely research would not require much change in behaviorist theories?

In principle, behaviorist theories are just such an exception. However, as behaviorism developed from a methodology to a theory of the origins of personality differences, it left some of its roots behind. This new, more general form of behaviorism was called **social learning theory** (Dollard & Miller, 1950) because it assumed that we learn from a society that reinforces various behaviors.

Yet the new principles or new applications required by social learning theory were often not directly observable. For example, the concept of shaping makes sense; we can imagine the process by which behavior is gradually shaped, in increments. But it has rarely been observed in actual childrearing. Although Skinner and other behaviorists have done vast amounts of research on the effects

Social learning theory The application of learning theory to the study of complex human behavior; assumes that social behavior is a product of reinforcement patterns.

of reinforcers on animals and on simple responses in humans, most of their explanations of complex human behavior are as speculative, and as difficult to test, as Freud's ideas about the unconscious and Rogers's ideas about conditions of worth. Moreover, as psychologists tried to test the behaviorists' theories, they found that the theories themselves were changing.

Observational Learning   Albert Bandura (1977) was responsible for a major shift in behaviorist thinking (see Chapter 6). He found that children can acquire very complicated new behaviors through observation, without any of the complex shaping that earlier behaviorists had described. The addition of observational learning to the behaviorists' repertoire of processes forced them to focus attention on the mechanisms by which complex information is acquired and stored; in particular, it forced the behaviorists to think about cognitive variables.

Expectancy and Locus of Control   Behaviorists began to add cognitive variables to their theories for a second reason: they observed that similar histories of reinforcements might produce quite different behavior in different people.

According to psychologist Julian Rotter (1954), a history of reinforcement allows us to expect that certain reinforcers are going to follow certain actions. So our behavior in any situation is determined by the reinforcement we expect to receive and the value of that reinforcement to us.

Rotter believed that we develop both specific and generalized expectancies about reinforcement. *Specific expectancies* concern the particular behaviors and reinforcers that may be present in a particular situation. For example, based on your experience, you probably assume that if you study, you're more likely to get a good grade in a course. The probability of your studying, then, is a product of your expectation that studying will produce a good grade and the value you place on a good grade. And whether you decide to study or not depends on the probable value of the grade to you in comparison to the probable value of the reinforcers of other behaviors—visiting a friend, going to the movies, reading a mystery. Although Rotter talks about expectancies, this part of his theory is fundamentally similar to traditional behaviorist theories.

But Rotter believed that we also develop a *generalized expectancy* about our ability to control our own reinforcement. He called this expectancy the **locus of control.** People with an *internal* locus of control usually believe that if they do the right things, they are going to be reinforced. These people tend to work harder to get what they want and to achieve more. By contrast, those with an *external* locus of control believe that their own actions—right or wrong—have nothing to do with reinforcement, that reinforcement is controlled by luck or other people. These people tend to be more passive.

Rotter (1966) developed a locus of control scale to measure general expectancies, as shown in Figure 14.6. Literally hundreds of studies have demonstrated the effects of locus of control. For example, people with an internal locus of control work harder and do better in school and at work, are more active in supporting causes they believe in, and are more independent (Phares, 1976). And, as we pointed out in Chapter 10 on stress and emotion, these people are also more resistant to stress and disease.

Rotter's work, like Bandura's, demonstrated the importance not only of a reinforcement history but also of the individual's beliefs about reinforcement. Here, too, we have the introduction of an abstract concept—what we think about reinforcement—into the behaviorist mainstream.

Learned Helplessness   The importance of cognitions has been demonstrated in research on a closely related concept, **learned helplessness.** Some people believe they have no control over their lives. Could this feeling of helplessness be learned? As a first step toward finding out, Martin Seligman (1975) administered

Locus of control   The generalized expectancy that one can control one's own reinforcements or, conversely, that they are controlled by luck or outside forces.

Learned helplessness   The expectation, stemming from the experience of failure, that one cannot succeed and so should not even try.

1.a. Many of the unhappy things in people's lives are partly due to bad luck.
  b. People's misfortunes result from the mistakes they make.

2.a. In the long run people get the respect they deserve in this world.
  b. Unfortunately, an individual's worth often passes unrecognized no matter how hard he tries.

3.a. Without the right breaks one cannot be an effective leader.
  b. Capable people who fail to become leaders have not taken advantage of their opportunities.

4.a. In the case of the well-prepared student there is rarely if ever such a thing as an unfair test.
  b. Many times exam questions tend to be so unrelated to course work that studying is really useless.

5.a. Becoming a success is a matter of hard work; luck has little or nothing to do with it.
  b. Getting a good job depends mainly on being in the right place at the right time.

6.a. The average citizen can have an influence in government decisions.
  b. This world is run by the few people in power, and there is not much the little guy can do about it.

Figure 14.6
Rotter's Locus of Control Scale

Here are some samples from Rotter's scale. For each item, the respondent chooses one alternative or the other as being more true. The number of choices like those that are underlined is the externality score.

Source: Abridged from Rotter, 1966.

electric shocks to animals who could not escape them. At first the animals struggled; but very shortly they settled down and passively accepted the shocks. Because they couldn't do much else, passive acceptance made sense. Later, Seligman made escape possible, but the animals didn't even try to escape, even though nothing was stopping them. They passively accepted shocks that they easily could have avoided.

Next, Seligman tried several less extreme experiments with humans. In one, for example, he gave his subjects a series of anagram puzzles to solve. In the experimental group, some of the puzzles had no solution; in the control group, all of the puzzles could be solved. Later, he asked both groups to work on a new set of problems that could be solved relatively easily. He found that those subjects who had struggled with the impossible problems not only didn't try very hard on the second batch but also solved far fewer puzzles than those in the control group. Seligman concluded that the insoluble problems had induced learned helplessness in the experimental subjects. These people felt there was no point in trying because they obviously were not very good at solving these kinds of problems.

What this experiment and others have shown is that people learn expectations and that those expectations affect their behavior (Peterson & Seligman, 1984; Brown & Siegel, 1988). Studies of learned helplessness were another step in behaviorism's transition from what can be observed to what can't be observed. Because conditioning alone has not adequately explained behavior, behaviorism has become increasingly cognitive (for example, see Abramson, Metalsky & Alloy, 1989).

A New Behaviorism: Cognitive Social Learning Theory   The research on observational learning, locus of control, learned helplessness, and other variables has expanded the social learning perspective to include cognition—that is, people's understanding of the world and themselves. To reflect the addition of the cognitive factor to their interests, behaviorists today speak about **cognitive social-learning theory,** or *social-cognitive theory* (Bandura, 1986).

Cognitive social-learning theory
The belief that behavior is a product of social learning, which includes people's understanding of the world and themselves; also called *social-cognitive theory*.

How Do We Know That?

A friend is describing someone she met at work. Suppose she tells you he's excitable, touchy, and moody. With each adjective you'd probably begin to feel that you're being told pretty much the same thing over and over: that the man is emotional. And if she says that he's outgoing, friendly, and gregarious, you'd probably say to yourself that this man is sociable. Your sense is that the six different trait terms really represent just two kinds of information—that is, two dimensions of variation among people. The same problem confronts psychologists who study traits. They need to pare down the bewildering variety of different traits, to find their common core of meanings.

How would you test your intuition that these six traits really represent two underlying personality dimensions? You would probably start by using a rating scale like those discussed in Chapter 13 to collect measurements on all six traits for a number of people. Then you could calculate a correlation coefficient that describes the relationship between the ratings on each trait and the ratings on all the other traits. This is what we've done with several traits in Table 14.4.

Table 14.4
Sample Correlations Among Trait Terms

The correlation between any two measures can be found at the intersection of the columns and rows. *Xs* indicate the correlation of a measure with itself.

Traits	Excitable	Touchy	Moody	Outgoing	Friendly	Gregarious
Excitable	X	.75	.72	.04	.09	.01
Touchy		X	.67	−.10	.12	.00
Moody			X	.03	.01	.11
Outgoing				X	.82	.76
Friendly					X	.87
Gregarious						X

If your sense that all of these trait terms define just two dimensions of personality is correct, then you'd expect to find a high correlation between some of the terms. For example, if "outgoing" and "friendly" measure pretty much the same thing, then people who are rated high on one will be rated high on the other. We would also expect that measures from different clusters, such as "touchy" and "friendly," would not correlate very highly. And that's exactly what you do find. Notice that the correlations among the first three traits and the correlations among the last three traits are very high. The traits in each group seem to "belong" together. Now look at the correlations between any trait in the first group and any trait in the second. Here they're very low, near zero. So you've identified two discrete dimensions of personality—emotionality and sociability.

You started with a list of six trait terms. But the process is a lot more complicated for trait theorists, who start with thousands of trait terms. Their job is to examine an array of correlations, find groups of measures that are highly related to one another, and identify the underlying dimensions reflected in those relationships. To do this, they use a statistical technique called *factor analysis*. Factor analysis accomplishes the same sort of result you achieved by looking at the table of correlations, but it does so mathematically.

(Continued on next page)

Factor analysis helps organize the measurements you have on hand; but it doesn't tell you anything about measurements that are missing. This is an important point: factor analysis describes the structure of the measurements, not the objects being measured. It will help you separate the six trait terms along two dimensions, but it won't tell you that these are the only two dimensions in personality. If, for instance, you added confidence and aggressiveness to the list, you'd find that these new traits aren't related to any of the others, that they constitute a third factor altogether.

Factor analysis does a good job of imposing a structure on a group of measurements without reference to a theory. But a theory is essential both to your choice of the measurements that are going to be analyzed in the first place and to your interpretation of the meaning of the factors.

Factor analysis is utilized in many areas of research. In addition to its use in the area of personality traits, it has been employed to identify dimensions underlying intelligence test results and to define basic dimensions of emotion.

This is more than an expanded definition of behaviorism. What we're seeing here is the introduction of elements that are ordinarily associated with other schools of thought. As with psychodynamic theory, behaviorism exhibits a new concern with emotions and motives. And the emphasis on people's perception of their world and themselves is similar to that of the phenomenological approach. Moreover, locus of control and learned helplessness are obviously trait dimensions. The behaviorists' narrow focus—their unwillingness to look at anything but behavior—has all but disappeared. What remains is a healthy preoccupation with keeping explanations closely tied to what can be observed, an objective shared today with almost everyone studying human personality.

The Phenomenological Perspective

The phenomenological perspective has had relatively little direct impact on research, although its influence is reflected in the very active research done on the self.

Maslow, Rogers, and many before them asserted that an accurate and positive self-concept is essential for a healthy and happy life. We need to know ourselves as we actually are—and to like what we see. Ironically, modern research suggests that the two usually aren't compatible. We seem to have to choose either a realistic recognition of our limitations or an inflated but reassuring belief in ourselves. Given this choice, most of us opt for the positive over the accurate.

For example, most people believe that they are above-average in abilities (Campbell, 1986). And when asked to compare themselves to other people, they tend to find more good qualities in themselves than in others (Brown, 1986). These tendencies are closely linked to the way individuals explain their successes and failures (Greenwald, 1980). Most of us take credit for our successes ("I really worked for that A in world history") but blame our failures on other things or other people ("That test didn't cover any of the material in the text").

In one study of this positive bias, subjects took what appeared to be an IQ test. Later, they were told at random that they had done very well or poorly; in other words, they were simply assigned scores. Then, the subjects were asked to evaluate the test. Those who thought they had done well, based on their assigned scores, claimed the test was valid and important; those who thought they had done poorly argued that the test was neither valid nor important (Greenberg, Pyszczynski & Solomon, 1982).

There is one group of people who seem to be able to assess their own abilities realistically—people who are depressed (Coyne & Gotlib, 1983). It's just not that these people have a low opinion of themselves; it's just that their opinions are a better reflection of reality. In fact seeing ourselves as we really are—with all our shortcomings—may be one cause of anxiety or depression (Higgins, 1989). For some, it can even lead to suicide (Baumeister, 1990).

In the overall scheme of things, then, it's better to be positive about oneself than to be accurate. A sense of control—even the illusion of control—moves the individual to act decisively and effectively (Taylor & Brown, 1988). Like the Little Engine, we need to think "we can."

The Trait Perspective

Modern trait research has focused on two issues: one is identifying the basic dimensions of personality differences. The second is the importance of traits in determining behavior.

Basic Personality Factors   More than 4,500 traits have been identified, and some psychologists are busy inventing more. But the priority of trait theories today is less a matter of adding to the list of terms we use to describe personality than one of finding the basic dimensions that underlie specific groups of traits.

Factor analysis has played an important role in the process of identifying the basic dimensions of traits. For example, psychologist Raymond Cattell (1965, 1985) used the technique to distinguish between **surface traits,** the trait terms we use in our everyday language to describe people, and **source traits,** the basic dimensions that underlie all of the surface traits.

Cattell started by rejecting the approximate synonyms of ordinary language, leaving 171 trait terms. Next, he asked a group of student judges to rate large samples of people on these traits. Finally, by using factor analysis, he reduced the whole array to just 16 source traits (see Figure 14.7).

A different, smaller list of basic trait dimensions was generated by Eysenck (1970). Also using factor analysis, he identified three basic dimensions of personality. In addition to the extraversion-introversion and emotional stability-instability scales noted earlier is Eysenck's third factor, called *psychoticism,* which has to do with the individual's hostility and cruelty, versus the willingness to cooperate.

Cattell points to sixteen factors; Eysenck, to three. Other people have found other numbers. In fact, about every factor analysis that's been conducted has produced a different number of factors or factors with slightly different names. Instead of simplifying matters, the process has seemingly added to the confusion.

A major source of the differences between results is the diversity of measures used. Factor analysis identifies relationships between variables; but it can't identify a relationship if a variable isn't among those being analyzed. So, to some extent, both the type of factors and the number found depend on which measures are being used. One solution, then, is to analyze as many variables as possible, so that all the major ones are included.

Use of this approach has led to the consistent emergence of five basic dimensions of personality (McCrae & Costa, 1987). Two of these dimensions are familiar from Eysenck's system: emotional stability and extraversion. The other three factors are openness to experience, agreeableness, and conscientiousness. The five factors together seem to account for most of the variation in scores on a great many personality inventories (Digman & Inouye, 1986).

Surface trait According to Cattell, the trait terms commonly used to describe personality.

Source trait According to Cattell, one of the sixteen basic dimensions underlying the surface traits.

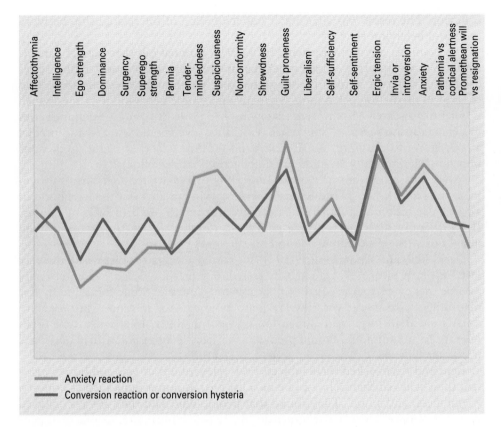

Figure 14.7
Cattell's Sixteen Personality Factors

Cattell identified sixteen personality factors that he argued lay "beneath" the surface traits of such tests as the MMPI. His *source traits* are characteristically depicted in profiles like these, which are characteristic of people suffering anxiety disorders or conversion disorders.

Anxiety reaction
Conversion reaction or conversion hysteria

Source: Cattell, 1965.

So, is the matter settled? Are there five basic dimensions of personality? Perhaps. The results of many factor analyses support this conclusion, but factor analysis isn't the only statistical technique available. Other procedures tend to produce somewhat different numbers and types of factors (for example, see A. Buss & Finn, 1987). It may well be the case that both the number and kind of factors depend on how those factors are being used.

Traits Versus Situations Some years ago, Walter Mischel (1968) launched an assault on personality research in general and trait theories in particular—an assault from which they are only now recovering. He argued that people's personalities really don't have much effect on their behavior, that far and away the most important cause of behavior is the situation people are in.

To get a sense of his argument, think about how you behave in class: You and your classmates file into the room, sit in your usual chairs, listen, and take notes. If you speak at all, you speak quietly. Now think about your behavior at a party. You and your friends move around, dance, talk often and sometimes loudly. There's a very big difference between your behavior in a classroom and your behavior at a party; and there are few differences among people's behaviors within either situation.

To support his argument, Mischel pointed out that the usual personality measures, such as the extraversion scale, did not predict very accurately. A large group of people who scored at the extraverted end of the scale might attend more parties, but the difference between their frequency of partying and that of introverts would be rather small.

Mischel's argument was greeted with the professional version of howls of outrage, followed by a serious examination of whether and how traits predict behavior. The result was a far better understanding of the relationship between traits and behavior.

For example, Seymour Epstein (1979, 1983) pointed out that tests of personality are prone to error. (Remember that it's for this reason most rating scales use lots of different items.) He suggested that we should expect the same kind of error in predicting behavior if we focus on a single behavior at a time, which is what the research Mischel was reviewing had done. Instead of using measures of personality to predict a single behavior, then, we should use them to predict a collection of behaviors. As Epstein expected, the accuracy of his predictions improved dramatically when he used collections of behavior.

David Buss and Kenneth Craik (1983, 1985) have argued that this improvement is exactly what should happen, because traits predict not the likelihood of a particular action but, rather, the general tendency to perform *kinds* of actions. Being friendly may mean saying hello to a stranger at one time and listening quietly to a friend's troubles at another.

Daryl Bem and Andrea Allen (1974) suggested another problem with the way in which trait measures were usually tested: in everyday usage, we don't really assume that every trait is equally applicable to all people. Some traits "fit" better than others. We might describe Jay Leno as jovial, for instance—but joviality doesn't seem an important dimension of George Bush. In short, a trait that's relevant to an individual should predict his or her behavior better than one that's irrelevant (Cheek, 1982).

Bem and Allen asked their subjects how relevant a trait was and how consistent they believed themselves to be on a list of trait dimensions such as honesty, friendliness, and so on. They found that people who said they always behaved the same way on a particular dimension were much more predictable than people who said they sometimes behaved one way, sometimes another. So in those cases when people (or their friends) say that a trait describes them, and that they always behave the way the trait describes, the accuracy of prediction is still higher (Zuckerman et al., 1988).

In the end, Mischel's criticisms led to the discovery of numerous practical ways to improve the accuracy of the predictions that psychologists can make on the basis of personality traits. In the process, psychologists have learned that both situations and traits shape behavior in powerful ways (Kenrick & Funder, 1988).

Recap

- Much of the research that was designed to test psychodynamic theories of personality eventually led to new areas of inquiry that were unconnected to psychodynamic theories.

- The research on observational learning, locus of control, and learned helplessness has expanded the social learning perspective to include cognitive factors—people's understanding of the world and themselves. Today the behaviorists' narrow focus on what can be directly observed has all but disappeared.

- Contemporary research suggests that self-concepts can be accurate or positive, but seldom both; and that most people choose positive self-concepts over accurate ones.

- Factor analysis identifies relationships between variables; but it can't identify a relationship if a variable isn't among those being analyzed.

- The factor analysis of a large number of trait terms has identified five basic dimensions of personality.

- Apparently, both situation and traits shape behavior in powerful ways.

Conclusion

The era of grand personality theories is past. Today the study of personality is much like the study of other topics we've talked about in other chapters: many psychologists working on various problem areas, testing each new theoretical premise carefully, building their theories slowly and cautiously from their observations. Some argue that much of the work in personality has a flavor of behaviorism. And, indeed, it is true that current research is closely tied to observation and to the experimental context in which psychologists make observations. But the interest of even the behaviorists themselves has expanded into the cognitive arena. Today, thoughts and feelings are at the center of personality research.

If the grand old personality theories are no longer relevant, why have we talked so much about them in this chapter? One reason is that these theories have had a major impact on our culture and science. Another is that many people still use these theories today, when they need help understanding human behavior. Sometimes we can't wait for academic psychology to develop a new theoretical direction; we need a perspective that can help us now to make decisions and get on with our work.

The most common context in which this need arises is psychotherapy. Therapists have developed a number of specific techniques from the scientific findings described in this book. But therapists have to choose and adapt these techniques, and sometimes devise new ones, for individual clients. To guide their decisions, they often apply one or more of the grand theories of personality.

These theories are also used by scholars in other disciplines who need a framework for understanding human behavior in order to do their work. Historians, sociologists, economists, literary critics, and philosophers often cite Freudian theory. Some refer to Jung or Rogers. Maslow's hierarchy of needs is very popular among management theorists. And educators frequently turn to Skinner's work. In all of these contexts, the theories provide at least some confidence and a coherent place from which to start.

Chapter 15   Psychological Disorders

Woman in a Window, Richard Diebenkorn, 1957

15

Gateways Sometimes the differences among human beings become intensified. For some people, an ordinary situation such as shopping in a supermarket becomes terrifying. Other people, instead of merely having "down days," experience long spells of profound hopelessness and alienation. Most of us will not experience the worst of these disorders, but almost everyone encounters them in others, even in people who are close to us. A range of psychologists study abnormal behavior not only to help the afflicted, but to understand better the mechanisms that guide normal behavior and to recognize the pressure points at which those mechanisms are vulnerable.

As you read this chapter—especially as you read about anxiety and depression—you may recall Chapter 10 on emotion and stress. One theory of depression implicates mood and memory, as discussed in Chapter 7. Distortions of perception and thinking are illuminated by principles presented in Chapters 4 and 8. Finally, many disorders seem to involve learned behavior or problems in neurotransmitter systems—or both; these topics were covered, respectively, in Chapters 6 and 2.

The year 1971 saw a peculiar epidemic of hospital admissions. On a particular day, people appeared at eight different mental hospitals all over the country complaining of exactly the same symptoms. They heard voices when no one was speaking. When asked, they replied that they weren't sure what the voices were saying, but the words sounded like "empty," "hollow," and "thud." Sadly, every day people are admitted to mental hospitals because they hear voices, but eight people hearing exactly the same thing is certainly unusual.

The eight people who complained of hearing voices were in fact part of a study by David Rosenhan (1973). Among them were three psychologists (including Rosenhan), a psychiatrist, a graduate student in psychology, a pediatrician, a painter, and a housewife—all presumably well adjusted, with no history of psychiatric problems. The eight pseudo-patients disguised their identities, and those who were mental health professionals disguised their occupations as well. Otherwise, they answered questions honestly. All eight behaved as they ordinarily would during their admission interviews and throughout the time they spent in the hospital, except for saying during the admissions interview that they heard voices.

Despite the fact that Rosenhan and the rest of his subjects were not actually suffering from any psychiatric problem, they all were admitted to hospitals, most with a diagnosis of schizophrenia (considered to be the most serious psychological disorder). And despite the fact that they never reported any further symptoms, their stays in the hospital ranged from seven to fifty-two days, with an average of nineteen days.

Moreover, when the subjects were discharged from the hospital, their diagnosis was usually "schizophrenia in remission"—suggesting that, although no symptoms were currently observable, the disorder was not considered cured. In other words, the diagnosis implied that the symptoms could return at any time.

Rosenhan's experiment has important implications regarding the extent to which diagnoses are reliable, an issue that we shall discuss later. But the most important implication is that the people inside mental institutions and the people outside institutions are not very different. Even people who are seriously disturbed act pretty much like the rest of us most of the time, and even professionals can have difficulty distinguishing seriously disturbed people.

We are not trying to minimize the impact of these problems. People with psychological disorders do behave very strangely at times, and that behavior can have devastating effects on their lives and on the lives of those around them. But it's equally important to realize that most of the people who are suffering from these disorders are like you in more ways than they are different. They may be people suffering from a disorder, but they are people first and foremost.

This may explain why the hospital staff didn't question the seeming normality of the Rosenhan "patients." Because staff members see patients only occasionally, they wouldn't have been surprised not to observe any unusual behavior. Interestingly, although the professional staff in the hospitals never realized that Rosenhan's volunteers were not schizophrenic, a substantial number of their fellow patients—35 out of 118—did. Because they all lived together, twenty-four hours a day, the patients realized that Rosenhan's people *never* behaved abnormally.

Defining Abnormal Behavior and Psychological Disorder

Often abnormal behavior is unmistakable. You have probably seen a strangely dressed, disheveled person standing on a street corner, talking animatedly with no one at all. You may not have known what was wrong, but you knew instantly that this person was acting abnormally. Although sometimes we can identify abnormal behavior quite easily, defining it is more difficult. The problem is that no single criterion or group of criteria distinguishes normal from abnormal: some varieties of abnormal behavior meet one set of criteria, while others meet a different set. Consider a few potential criteria.

The word *abnormal* itself means uncommon, and most psychological disorders are uncommon. However, there must be more to the meaning of *abnormal* than just uncommon, because many uncommon behaviors are highly desirable. Einstein's scientific ability and Bach's musical genius were uncommon, but they were not abnormal in the sense that we mean it here. To avoid this confusion, we shall use the term *psychological disorder* hereafter.

At the least, disordered behavior is uncommon and undesirable. Who decides what is undesirable? That is clearly a social judgment, a matter of what the society values and rejects. Thus, to some extent what is considered psychologically disordered is defined by society. For example, in some societies, hearing voices in certain religious contexts is acceptable or even desirable. (Presumably the voices have more to say than "thud.")

However, most societies seem to share a perception of the basic kinds of disorder (Murphy, 1976). For example, in a study of ten countries, including those as diverse as India, Colombia, Nigeria, and a variety of European and North American countries, extremely similar patterns of symptoms of schizophrenia were observed (Sartorius et al., 1986). Certainly, then, there is more to psychological disorder than just a social role.

Another characteristic of some disordered behavior is that it is irrational, or self-defeating. Some kinds of disordered behavior, such as hearing voices, seem to have no rational basis; but unfortunately for our definition, others do seem rational. For example, people who are called sociopaths exploit others shamelessly (and guiltlessly) for their own ends. This behavior, though surely "rational," is considered disordered.

Another possibility is to define disorder as causing the individual distress. Certainly many psychological disorders do cause great suffering. Indeed, the essence of depression and anxiety disorders is that people feel miserable. Like the other criteria we have examined, however, suffering per se cannot form the core of our definition of disorder. Sometimes people martyr themselves for some cause and suffer greatly as a result of their own behavior, but are not disordered. Further, some kinds of disordered behavior, such as the frenzied activity of individuals in a manic state, do not cause the person any distress. (Rather, it is often the people around such individuals who are distressed.) In sum, suffering is commonly a part of psychological disorder, but not invariably so.

The problem with defining disordered behavior is very much like the problem we discussed in Chapter 8, on thought and language, when we tried to define the concept of "chair." The research suggests that concepts do not have unique definitions. Their meaning is drawn from prototypes, or complex conjunctions of criterial attributes. Just as "chair" takes its meaning from our prototype of a chair, so too our concept of **psychological disorder** may be rooted in a prototype (Cantor & Genero, 1986). Clear examples of disorder are those that possess more of these attributes: behavior that violates social norms; distresses the individual or other people around him or her; is inefficient, maladaptive, or irrational.

Psychological disorder A pattern of behavior, thought, or feeling that is abnormal, socially unacceptable, irrational, or painful to the individual or those around the individual.

There are a great many psychological disorders. In this chapter we describe one diagnostic system that categorizes disorders. And we talk about the factors that individually or in combination produce these disorders. In the next chapter, we describe how the disorders are treated.

DSM-III-R: A Classification System

A first step in diagnosing and treating psychological disorders is to distinguish among them. Following the general medical tradition, psychiatrists in the nineteenth century proposed a number of different systems for classifying psychological disorders. And as early as 1917, the American Psychiatric Association published a manual of its official diagnostic system. Since then, this system has been refined, elaborated, and revised continually. The current system is described in *The Diagnostic and Statistical Manual of Mental Disorders* (3rd Edition, Revised) (DSM-III-R).

The DSM-III-R system was developed by the American Psychiatric Association. Though not universally accepted by members of other mental health professions, such as psychologists and social workers, nor even by some psychiatrists (McReynolds, 1989), it is by far the most commonly used diagnostic system.

The Five Axes of Diagnosis

DSM-III-R asks the clinician to collect information about the client along five dimensions, or "axes":

Axis I: Psychological disorders—the type of disordered behavior displayed by the person

Axis II: Personality disorders—the more or less permanent characteristics of the individual as distinct from the particular problem from which he or she is suffering at the moment

Axis III: Physical problems that are relevant to the individual's disorder (for example, signs of malnourishment in an individual with anorexia or evidence of brain damage in an alcoholic)

Axis IV: Environmental stresses that may have precipitated the individual's problem

Axis V: How the individual is functioning—in family and other relationships, and on the job—now and over the last year

This system compels the clinician to focus attention on the "whole" person, to consider more than just the acute problems described along Axis I. The individual's ordinary personality functioning, his or her physical condition, level of stress, and ability to function are all important components of a treatment plan.

An Overview of the Diagnostic Categories

Table 15.1 shows the sixteen major categories described along Axis I and the developmental and personality disorders described along Axis II. In total, the system identifies more than two hundred specific disorders. Many of them are quite rare. In fact, more than 80 percent of all the disorders fall into just three main categories (Robins et al., 1984).

Table 15.1
DSM-III-R Diagnostic Categories

Axis I (Major Mental Disorders)

1. *Disorders usually first evident in infancy, childhood, or adolescence* Includes mental retardation, hyperactivity, conduct disorders, anxiety disorders, eating disorders, and gender-identity disorders. The common feature of these disorders is that they first appear in infancy, childhood, or adolescence.

2. *Organic mental syndromes and disorders* Includes delirium, dementia (senile and presenile), and disorders caused by the physical deterioration of the brain, such as Alzheimer's disease. Also includes disorders caused by brain damage from alcohol and drug abuse.

3. *Psychoactive substance use disorders* Includes disorders involving abuse of and dependence on psychoactive drugs (cocaine, PCP, marijuana, LSD, etc.), alcohol, and nicotine.

4. *Schizophrenia* Includes disorders involving bizarre behavior and thinking. Hallucinations and motor disturbances are also symptomatic. Five types: catatonic, disorganized, paranoid, undifferentiated, and residual.

5. *Delusional disorders* Includes false beliefs about being loved, inflated views of one's abilities (delusions of grandeur), and feelings of persecution (paranoid delusions). Essential feature is that the delusions cannot be attributed to another disorder, such as schizophrenia.

6. *Other psychotic disorders* Includes mental problems that are similar to but less intense than schizophrenic and delusional disorders.

7. *Mood disorders* Includes disorders characterized by disturbances in mood, such as depression, mania, manic-depression (bipolar disorder), and the milder forms of cyclothymia and dysthymia.

8. *Anxiety disorders* Includes panic disorder, phobias, generalized anxiety disorder, obsessive-compulsive disorder, and post-traumatic stress disorder. The chief features of all these disorders are anxiety and avoidance behavior.

9. *Somatoform disorders* Includes conversion disorder, hypochondriasis, and somatization disorder. These disorders are characterized by physical symptoms that cannot be attributed to organic causes.

10. *Dissociative disorders* Includes multiple-personality disorder, psychogenic fugue, and psychogenic amnesia. These disorders are characterized by disturbances in consciousness, memory, and identity.

11. *Sexual disorders* Includes (1) paraphilias, disorders characterized by sexual arousal through unusual objects or situations such as red shoes or watching others engage in sexual activity; and (2) sexual dysfunctions, disorders characterized by disturbed patterns in the sexual response cycle.

12. *Sleep disorders* Involves problems in the sleep cycle, including insomnia and sleepwalking.

13. *Factitious disorders* Involves psychological or physical conditions that are intentionally faked to satisfy some need.

14. *Impulse-control disorders* Includes gambling, fire setting, and kleptomania. These disorders are characterized by an inability to control impulses.

15. *Adjustment disorders* Involves the inability to adjust to both difficult and ordinary life events.

16. *Psychological factors affecting physical condition* Includes physical problems, such as headaches and ulcers, that are caused or made worse by psychological factors, such as anxiety.

Axis II (Developmental and Personality Disorders)

1. *Specific developmental disorders* These disorders impair cognitive, social, language, and motor development. They include mental retardation, autism, and developmental disorders related to reading, math, and language.

2. *Personality disorders* These disorders are characterized by behavior patterns that interfere with normal functioning. They include borderline personality disorder, conduct disorder, narcissistic personality disorder, and antisocial and avoidant personality disorders.

Look at Table 15.2. The data show the incidence of psychological disorders in a careful survey of three cities: New Haven, Connecticut; Baltimore, Maryland; and St. Louis, Missouri (Robins et al., 1984). Notice that alcohol and drug abuse accounts for almost half of all mental disorders. Anxiety disorders are the

Disorders	New Haven	Baltimore	St. Louis
Any disorder	28.8	38.0	31.0
Substance use	15.0	17.0	18.1
Alcohol	11.5	13.7	15.7
Drugs	5.8	5.6	5.5
Schizophrenic	2.0	1.9	1.1
Affective (mood)	9.5	6.1	8.0
Major depression	6.7	3.7	5.5
Manic	1.1	.6	1.1
Anxiety	10.4	25.1	11.1
Phobia	7.8	23.3	9.4
Panic	1.4	1.4	1.5
Obsessive-compulsive	2.6	3.0	1.9
Antisocial personality disorder	2.1	2.6	3.3

Table 15.2
Prevalence of Mental Disorders

Source: Robins et al. 1984.
Note: Figures are in percentages. Some individuals reported multiple disorders.

next most prevalent, followed by mood disorders. Schizophrenic disorders are not very common, afflicting only one or two people in a hundred. However, because schizophrenic disorders are often very resistant to treatment, schizophrenia is one of the most serious problems for society.

In our discussion of these disorders, we begin with the most prevalent and work down. We don't discuss some of the rare disorders.

Intern's Syndrome

The first disorder you need to know about is not in DSM-III-R. It's *intern's syndrome*—a common phenomenon among medical students and interns. As they learn about the symptoms of each new disease, interns often think that they themselves are suffering from it.

Keep intern's syndrome in mind as you read this chapter. The behavior that defines psychological disorders is continuous with normal behavior. Don't be surprised, then, if you find that you share certain behaviors with the people we describe. To make the nature of the disorders clear, we are going to draw many parallels with your experience. We believe that this procedure will further your understanding, but it may also heighten your feeling that you might be suffering from one (or all) of the disorders we talk about.

The odds are very much against your actually suffering from any of these disorders. But if you're uncertain or unhappy after you've finished this chapter, you might want to speak to a psychologist or psychiatrist. Your school undoubtedly offers some sort of psychological counseling through its health service or a separate counseling center. Most people who use counseling services are not suffering from any serious disorder, and the therapists there will be happy to talk with you about your feelings.

Recap

- Classification systems are used to distinguish among psychological disorders, so as to facilitate their diagnosis and treatment.

- The third edition, revised, of *The Diagnostic and Statistical Manual of Mental Disorders* (DSM-III-R) is currently the most widely used diagnostic system.

- DSM-III-R asks the diagnostician to judge five axes, or aspects, of the individual's life: the psychological disorder, personality, physical condition, stressors in the environment, and how the individual functions in the world.

- DSM-III-R identifies sixteen major categories of psychological disorders along Axis I and twelve personality disorders along Axis II.

- More than 80 percent of all disorders fall into three main categories: alcohol and drug abuse, anxiety disorders, and mood disorders.

- Intern's syndrome is the tendency among people who are learning about a disease to believe, incorrectly, that they are suffering from the disease themselves.

Axis I Disorders

The Axis I disorders are relatively acute, specific patterns of behavior and feeling that the sufferer often feels are not part of his or her normal personality. These are the kinds of problems most people think of as mental illness.

Psychoactive Substance Use Disorders

The most common psychological disorders are psychoactive substance use disorders, and the most common substance that is used, and abused, is alcohol. Because alcohol use is so accepted in our society, we don't readily recognize its effects. But, in fact, the social effects of alcohol abuse are appalling. More than 50 percent of traffic accidents and nearly half of all domestic crimes involve alcohol. And more than half of the people who commit violent crimes and rapes are drunk at the time (National Institute of Justice, 1985). In one study of 204 people who successfully committed suicide, 101 had serious alcohol or other substance abuse problems (Rich et al., 1988). In addition, alcohol abuse can produce some very serious physical effects on the drinker, including heart disease, fatal damage to the liver, and permanent brain damage, as in Korsakoff's syndrome.

With alcohol, as with other drugs, we need to distinguish between abuse and dependence. *Alcohol abuse* refers to those people who use too much of the substance and, on some occasions, are unable to stop using it. Such use also produces problems in their lives, such as arguments with family or friends, missed work, automobile accidents, or encounters with the law. A person who abuses alcohol, or any other substance, may not be dependent on it, and may go long periods of time between incidents of abuse.

Alcohol dependence involves a separate set of problems. When someone is physically dependent on alcohol, he or she shows increased tolerance, so that larger and larger amounts are required to produce the same behavioral effects. More important, these changes seem to represent the adaptation of the body to the presence of alcohol. If the alcohol-dependent person doesn't get his or her usual ration, the individual will experience *withdrawal* symptoms. Withdrawal from alcohol dependence may produce delirium tremens, or "DTs." Its symptoms are terrifying, and include sweating, trembling, disorientation, and sometimes hallucinations.

Many people whose use of alcohol is causing serious problems in their lives reassure themselves that they are not "alcoholics" because they are not physically dependent on alcohol. Others who are dependent feel they have no problem because their drinking doesn't cause interpersonal or social problems. The two cases can be quite distinct from one another. Many people who are physically dependent do not get in trouble and, so long as they can get a drink at regular intervals, have no problems except damaged health. Others, who can go for weeks without drinking, get in serious trouble with their families or society when they do drink. Obviously, either pattern has serious effects on one's life. Perhaps because of stereotypes about alcoholism, many people assume it's a problem that usually occurs later in life. Actually, alcohol use disorders are most prevalent among young adults (see Figure 15.1).

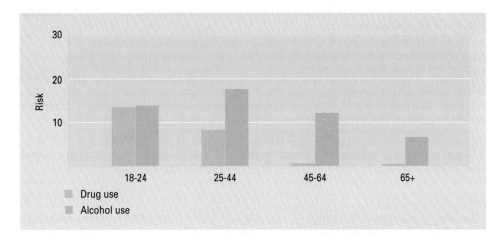

Figure 15.1
Age and Substance Abuse

People between the ages of twenty-one and thirty-four are most prone to problem drinking and many of the other substance abuse disorders.

Source: Data from Helzer, 1987.

The same problems, of abuse or dependence, are associated with the other psychoactive drugs discussed in Chapter 5. Practically any substance producing pleasurable effects has the potential to be abused and to disrupt a person's life.

Anxiety Disorders

Your heart pounds, sweat breaks out on your forehead and palms, your body tenses and stiffens, and you want to run away. As we discussed in Chapter 10, this pattern of behaviors and feelings—the fight-or-flight response—probably evolved as a mechanism to help you confront or escape danger (Cannon, 1927).

When the danger is obvious, we call this pattern of responses *fear.* But when there is no real danger, or when the responses seem out of proportion to the actual danger, we call these behaviors and feelings **anxiety.** If you're terrified of a bear, that's fear. If you're terrified of a small bird, that's anxiety.

Anxiety, by definition, is irrational. But knowing that anxiety is irrational doesn't make it go away. The essence of the experience of anxiety is the knowledge that the terror is unreasonable. For example, many people feel anxious when they have to speak before a large group. They know that the situation isn't really dangerous, and they tell themselves it's silly to be scared, but these reassurances don't really help. *Anxiety disorders* are simply more pervasive or intense versions of this kind of experience.

Simple Phobias   *Phobias* are unreasonable fears of ordinary objects or situations that limit the individual's participation in everyday activities. In years gone by, therapists enjoyed concocting complex Greek names for each phobia as it was

Anxiety Physical and emotional responses of fear or dread that are unwarranted by their object.

discovered; two examples are *arachnophobia* (a fear of spiders) and *herpetophobia* (fear of snakes). Table 15.3 lists some examples of phobia names.

Many phobias are common, among them the fear of flying, the fear of high places, and the fear of dogs or snakes. The degree to which specific phobias are debilitating depends on the object of the phobia and the conditions of the person's life. A fear of flying isn't a problem for the majority of people in the United States, who don't have to travel by plane. And snake phobias don't bother most city-dwellers. However, if your job demands that you travel long distances, a flying phobia is a serious problem. One Manhattanite we know couldn't visit friends in New Jersey because she was afraid of both high bridges and tunnels, the only convenient means of reaching her friends.

In general, the extent to which a simple phobia is disruptive depends on how often the individual has to come in contact with the object of the phobia. Many people manage to tolerate simple phobias by structuring their lives to avoid the things or situations they fear.

Social Phobias   Unreasonable fears of social situations and activities are called **social phobias.** You can avoid snakes, airplanes, perhaps even high bridges without disrupting your life, but you cannot avoid other people. Unfortunately, many people suffer from irrational fears of social situations. They are afraid of making fools of themselves, of being unable to perform adequately, and, especially, of speaking to groups. In themselves, these fears aren't all that unusual. They become a psychological disorder only when people begin to avoid social situations.

Generalized Anxiety   A feeling of anxiety that is more or less constant but not attached to a particular object or situation is known as **generalized anxiety.** It's an uneasiness that has no focus. People who suffer from generalized anxiety are jumpy and nervous, and often have difficulty sleeping and eating. Although they feel anxious, they are unable to identify the source of their anxiety. As a result, they are constantly on guard—a condition that colors every experience.

One woman reported that, initially, she felt vaguely anxious at work, a feeling she attributed to the competitive pressures she believed were prevalent there. Subsequently, however, she found that her anxious feelings began to occur at home and when she was out with other people. She felt so strongly that something was threatening her that she constantly analyzed every interaction and worried about every act.

Generalized anxiety can be triggered by a traumatic event, although the connection is usually neither direct nor obvious (Blazer, Hughes & George, 1987). The woman described above fits this pattern inasmuch as her father had died a few months before her anxiety symptoms appeared.

Panic Disorder and Agoraphobia   The primary symptom of panic disorder is a **panic attack,** the sudden unexpected onset of the physical symptoms of anxiety. Without warning—and for no apparent reason—your heart starts pounding, you begin to sweat, you feel faint, and you have difficulty breathing.

One sufferer described a panic attack that started in a supermarket:

> The first sign is a feeling of being slightly nervous without apparent reason. Then, bang! Your pulse elevates and you think "I must return to the car. What if I can't find it? What if the panic is so bad that I can't move?" Then complete and utter panic. You can't move. You look around, panting, to find that all is faintly unreal. The familiar shelves and trolleys are strangely daunting; the people like puppets. You somehow find the exit and yes, relief, the car is there. Soon the panic has passed. Usually an attack lasts about two minutes. One hundred and twenty seconds of hell—a two-minute eternity. (Clarke & Wardman, 1985, p. 37)

Social phobia An unreasonable fear of social situations or activities that limits the individual's participation in those situations or activities.

Generalized anxiety A feeling of anxiety that is more or less constant but not attached to a particular object or situation.

Panic attack The sudden unexpected onset of the physical symptoms and feelings of anxiety.

Agoraphobia Literally, the fear of public places, but actually a fear of panic attacks that occur in public places.

Table 15.3
Some Phobias

This method of classification once implied that the object of the phobia was an important part of the diagnosis. But as most mental health professionals no longer believe that the object of a phobia is particularly important, these names are really just historical curios.

Acrophobia—fear of heights	*Microphobia*—fear of germs
Agoraphobia—fear of open spaces	*Monophobia*—fear of being alone
Ailurophobia—fear of cats	*Mysophobia*—fear of contamination or germs
Algophobia—fear of pain	*Nyctophobia*—fear of the dark
Arachnophobia—fear of spiders	*Ochlophobia*—fear of crowds
Astrapophobia—fear of storms, thunder and lightning	*Pathophobia*—fear of disease
Aviophobia—fear of airplanes	*Phobophobia*—fear of phobias
Brontophobia—fear of thunder	*Pyrophobia*—fear of fire
Claustrophobia—fear of closed spaces	*Syphilophobia*—fear of syphilis
Dementophobia—fear of insanity	*Topophobia*—fear of performing
Genitophobia—fear of genitals	*Xenophobia*—fear of strangers
Hematophobia—fear of blood	*Zoophobia*—fear of animals or some particular animal

Source: Sue, Sue & Sue, 1990.

For some people the panic attacks remain their only problem. But when people believe that a place or situation in some way triggers a panic attack, they often learn to avoid that place or situation. This leads to a more complicated set of behaviors and feelings called **agoraphobia** (from the Greek for marketplace, or *agora*), which literally means a fear of public places.

Agoraphobia is very different from the specific phobias because the fear isn't really of public places. That is, although people who suffer from agoraphobia are unable to go out into public places, it's not because they are afraid of the places themselves. What they really fear is a panic attack and, as a consequence, any place or situation in which they've had a panic attack or think that they're likely to have one. The result for some people is that they come to fear more and more situations, until they are unable to leave home.

Obsessive-Compulsive Disorders   You're getting ready for a big trip. Your travel arrangements have been made for weeks. You know what time you have to leave for the airport; you know how long the ride to the airport takes, allowing for traffic; and you know what time you have to board the plane. Still, you go over the plans in your mind again and again. Nothing's changed; there's no reason to keep going over the arrangements. But for some reason you find the mental checking and rechecking reassuring.

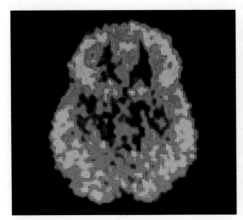 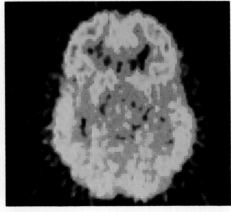

In these Pet scans, red and yellow indicate higher levels of activity. As you can see, the brain of the person with obsessive-compulsive disorder (right-hand photo) is much more active than the normal brain. Whether this higher activity level is a cause or a result of the disorder is unclear, though evidence suggests a biological contribution to the disorder.

When you packed last night, you put your travelers' checks, passport, and plane tickets in the pocket of your carry-on bag. You know they're there, but you find yourself reaching into the bag repeatedly, just to be sure.

Going over your travel plans again and again is a kind of **obsession**—a thought or a pattern of thoughts that is repeated simply for reassurance. Checking your carry-on bag for the eleventh time is a kind of **compulsion**—an action that is repeated to reduce your anxiety. Most of us have minor obsessions and compulsions from time to time. But when obsessive thoughts or compulsive actions are irrational and dominate someone's life, such that every day is filled with activities designed to ward off anxiety, the individual is suffering from an *obsessive-compulsive disorder.* In the absence of those activities, the individual feels intense anxiety.

In his later years, Howard Hughes, one of the richest men in the world, developed an obsession with dirt. He lived an extremely isolated, reclusive life, devoted to rituals designed to protect him from contamination. His fear of dirt and his rituals were typical symptoms of obsessive-compulsive disorder. But perhaps his wealth made his disorder worse, by permitting him to live such an abnormal life.

Obsession A thought or pattern of thoughts that the individual repeats again and again to ward off anxiety.

Compulsion An action that the individual repeats again and again to ward off anxiety.

Major depression A psychological disorder in which the primary symptoms are long term, and/or profound feelings of sadness and hopelessness.

Bipolar disorder A psychological disorder in which the individual goes back and forth between episodes of depression and mania; at one time called *manic-depressive disorder.*

Mania A state in which the individual is extravagantly (and often unrealistically) happy, optimistic, and energetic.

People can carry these patterns of thought and behavior to remarkable degrees. Toward the end of his life, multimillionaire Howard Hughes developed an obsessive fear of germs and contamination that led him to avoid most human contact. He devised elaborate rituals for cleaning his food and opening cans of food. He insisted that everything handed to him be wrapped in sheets of tissue. Hughes had the money to hire an army of people to carry out these rituals, but the disorder left him almost entirely shut off from the world and normal human contact (Brownstein & Solyom, 1986).

In contrast with the other anxiety disorders, in obsessive-compulsive disorder the anxiety itself is not obvious. It is the behaviors that are intended to control the anxiety that are the immediate problem. The anxiety underlying them becomes apparent only when the person cannot perform the ritualistic thoughts or actions.

Mood Disorders

There are two main kinds of mood, or affective, disorders; **major depression** and **bipolar disorder.** In both, the individual experiences profound sadness and hopelessness. But the individual suffering from bipolar disorder also experiences intervals of **mania,** during which he or she is extravagantly (and often unrealistically) happy, optimistic, and energetic.

Major Depression   Most of us know all too well the sadness, the hopelessness, the apathy that are at the core of depression. But for most of us, these feelings are brought on by a disappointment or a problem in our lives, and last only for hours or days. The difference between being sad and being depressed is the duration and the intensity of the symptoms. If the feelings last for more than two weeks, and either have no apparent cause or seem out of proportion to the cause, then they may be symptomatic of a full-fledged depression.

Depression is a common psychological disorder: it is estimated that as many as 20 percent of the population will have at least one episode during their lifetime (American Psychiatric Association, 1987). Even by the very stringent criteria of the study we discussed earlier (Robins et al., 1984), more than 5 percent of the population have suffered a depressive episode. Episodes generally last for a few months at most, and people tend to recover their normal mood levels spontaneously, whether or not they're in therapy. But some episodes are more serious and enduring, and often they recur.

People who are depressed characteristically feel sad, discouraged, and worthless. They take no interest in activities that previously gave them pleasure. Often they eat too much or too little. They complain of no energy, and their movements and thinking processes are slower than normal. In addition, their sleep patterns change: some individuals sleep all the time; others are unable to sleep at all. Finally, people who are depressed often think about death and suicide. For many, suicide seems the only escape from a life that is filled with hopelessness and sorrow.

One writer described his experience with depression as follows:

> My life had turned inside out so that everything I saw was a photographic negative. Where there should have been joy, I could feel only an unending sadness. Where I should have felt hope, there was only despair. Where life with its continuing promise should have sustained me, only the oblivion of death attracted me now, for living had become a hell on earth. . . . I ached for sleep. Would I ever know restful sleep again? Even pills gave me only restless snatches in which I tossed and trembled. . . . And always I awoke in the darkest hours, just before dawn. . . . When I tried to find strength and comfort in things I had done, I found myself walking down ruined avenues between shattered houses on whose walls bits and pieces of remembered experience flashed briefly into focus, and out again.
>
> . . . Some part of my mind that was still rational was aware that this was nonsense. But awareness made no difference: it was too late. I had passed the point of no return: death was my only escape. (Knauth, 1975)

There is always a danger of suicide among people who are seriously depressed, although not all people who commit suicide are depressed (Shneidman, 1987). As many as 15 percent of seriously depressed people commit suicide, and as many as 80 percent have at least considered it (Fawcett et al., 1987).

A number of misconceptions surround suicide. One is that people who talk about it rarely do it. The facts are exactly the opposite: the majority (70 percent) of people who have attempted suicide have tried to talk about it (Cohen, Motto & Seiden, 1966). This means that if someone you know admits to thinking about suicide, take it seriously and help the individual find therapeutic assistance. Another myth is that you shouldn't talk about suicide with someone who is considering it. Actually, if someone who is depressed wants to talk about suicide, it *is* helpful, especially if the talking leads to therapy.

Finally, you've probably heard that attempted suicide isn't "really serious." It's true that the majority of suicide attempts fail. According to Norman Farberow and Edwin Litman (1970), only 5 percent of people who attempt suicide choose a method that is certain to succeed. The same researchers estimate that

65 percent of people who attempt suicide aren't sure, and deliberately choose methods that are going to fail.

But these "cries for help" *are* serious. Any suicide attempt is dangerous. Even those who choose less than certain methods may take one too many pills or misgauge the speed with which a friend can reach them and get help. We should not minimize the meaning of the act simply because someone is uncertain about it. Even thinking about suicide is a sign of enormous strain.

Bipolar Disorder For some people, depressive episodes are mixed with mood swings beyond the normal to mania, a state of increased excitement and energy. In the manic state, people sleep little, have tremendous energy, and make grandiose plans. In fact, they are often very productive. Many famous people, including Isaac Newton, Abraham Lincoln, Friedrich Nietzsche, and Ernest Hemingway reported the pronounced mood swings typical of bipolar disorder. Moreover, the intense energy of the manic phase may have contributed to their achievements (Andreason & Glick, 1988).

Unfortunately, for most people with bipolar disorder, mania progresses rapidly from productivity to increasingly unreasonable plans and activities. In extreme manic states, such people often believe they can accomplish great deeds such as wiping out disease in the world or making vast sums of money. As their schemes become more and more irrational, they may spend enormous amounts of money and disrupt family relationships.

Manic states ordinarily do not last more than a few weeks. In addition, they are often followed by intense depressions, as the person's mood swings back again. In some people, the mood swings are less intense, leading to a diagnosis of *cyclothymia,* a milder form of bipolar disorder.

A concert in Washington D.C. held a few years ago showed the possible role of mania in creativity by including only the music of composers who suffered from bipolar disorder. These composers included Berlioz (right-hand photo), Handel (left-hand photo), Mahler, and Schumann (De-Angelis, 1989).

Schizophrenic Disorders

Schizophrenia A serious psychological disorder characterized by thought disturbances, emotional disturbances, motor disturbances, and social isolation.

All of the disorders we have discussed so far exhibit symptoms that are exaggerations of familiar behaviors and experiences. But the symptoms of **schizophrenia**—the most serious psychological disorder—fall outside of ordinary experience. The closest parallel can be found in our dreams. In many dreams, events follow one another in no obvious order and bizarre connections between things and people occur. Another common feature of dreams is that your emo-

These images were painted by people with schizophrenia. One can only imagine the thought processes that were at work during the creation of these wonderful, but bizarre pictures.

tional reactions to events seem inappropriate: you should be sad but you are not, or perhaps you are frightened of something innocuous. These are two of the most distinctive features of schizophrenia: bizarre thinking and inappropriate emotional reactions. The similarity between dreams and schizophrenia suggests that schizophrenia might not be too unpleasant. But quite the opposite is true: schizophrenia is more like a nightmare than a dream.

Schizophrenia is not only the most debilitating behavioral disorder, it is also one of the most difficult to treat. Though much less common than substance abuse, anxiety disorders, and mood disorders, schizophrenia is probably the major mental health problem in our society today. More than half of all patients in mental hospitals suffer from schizophrenia, as do large numbers of people "on the streets."

The symptoms of schizophrenia are diverse, and not all people suffering from schizophrenia show all of them. One of the saddest diagnostic signs of schizophrenia is the age of onset, which is ordinarily in the teens or early twenties. Most commonly, the person may have seemed a bit strange or socially isolated in earlier years and then, sometime between the ages of fifteen and twenty-five, the individual begins to suffer from some of the following symptoms.

Thought Disturbances   The word *schizophrenia,* which comes from the Greek, literally means a "splitting of the mind." But schizophrenia is not a form of multiple personality. Rather, it involves a separation of the individual from reality. While suffering from schizophrenia, an individual is not able to think rationally about the world. This problem takes a number of forms.

Delusions, false beliefs about the world, are one form of thought disturbance. The most common delusion among those with schizophrenia is the belief that people or forces are conspiring against them. They may insist that aliens control their thoughts or that radio waves are affecting their behavior. Moreover, some patients believe they are famous historical figures, such as Jesus Christ, George Washington, or Napoleon.

Delusion A false belief about what is happening or true in the world.

Another kind of thought disorder involves perception—seeing or, more commonly, hearing things that are not there. Perceptions of sights and sounds that are not really there are called *hallucinations*. The voices that Rosenhan (1973) and his subjects reported hearing were examples of hallucinations. Although the Rosenhan group claimed to have heard single words ("empty," "hollow," "thud"), people suffering from schizophrenia usually report that the voices tell them what to do or say nasty things about them.

Both delusions and hallucinations appear in this woman's description of a schizophrenic experience as she watched television in a hospital:

> There was a commercial for Ore-Ida tater tots (similar to oven chips). There was a shot of the tater tots falling out of the package and then they fell right out of the TV screen onto the dayroom floor. At first they just sat on the floor and then they disappeared. . . .
>
> As I stared at the spot where the tater tots had been they suddenly reappeared, glowing red-hot.
>
> They are radioactive! We are all getting a lethal dose of radiation! This is a Sign from The Other Side that something is about to happen. Should I say something to the other patients about the radiation that they apparently are not aware of? Should I tell them The Other Side might be trying to gain control of our minds with the rays from the tater tots? (Farr, 1982, pp. 5–6)

Another, more pervasive kind of thought disorder—*formal thought disturbance*—is the simple inability to think coherently. Thoughts follow each other, not in logical progression, but in a sequence determined by the way words rhyme or by the memories they spark. Here's an example:

> It occurs to me to point out to you that not all people enjoy or improve [sic] of double blind experiments. Also, there are some husbands who do not appreciate the succulence of ambiguous statements when they are getting it from all sides. Also, there are some experimental variables which respond better to positive reinforcement, say incoming calls or even invitations as opposed to systems of ration which drive them to other things. And when one or more go so far as to lower themselves to invasioning [sic] tactics, in truly egalitarian systems this would imply ultimate reversal. (Goldstein, Baker & Jamison, 1986, pp. 116–117)

The individual sentences seem to make sense, but in fact they don't.

Affective Disturbances   *Schizophrenia* also refers to a split within personality, between feelings and thoughts. In the case of one such affective disturbance, *flattened affect,* the victims do not react emotionally to events; no matter what happens, they remain relatively impassive and unresponsive. In a second form, their emotional reactions are inappropriate such that, for example, they laugh at funerals and weep when someone tells a joke.

Motor Disturbances   People who suffer from schizophrenia may also display bizarre body movements and actions. For example, some rock back and forth endlessly. Others don't move, holding the same position for hours. In this **catatonic stupor,** they ignore other people and do not speak.

Social Isolation   All of the symptoms we've been talking about—delusions, hallucinations, bizarre emotional reactions and physical movements—obviously interfere with social interaction. However, beyond these effects, many people suffering from schizophrenia seem to withdraw from human contact, spending most of their time alone.

Catatonic stupor A motor disturbance in schizophrenia, in which the individual does not move or speak for long periods of time.

Subtypes of Schizophrenia   DSM-III-R identifies three major forms of schizophrenia, each representing a different combination of symptoms.

1. People with **disorganized schizophrenia** exhibit the most profound thought disorders. They are unable to think coherently, and have both delusions and hallucinations. Their emotional responses are usually very flat or extremely inappropriate, and they neglect their appearance and hygiene.
2. The most striking symptom of **catatonic schizophrenia** is some sort of movement disorder. People may remain motionless or refuse to speak for long periods of time. Or they may show elaborate disruptive movements.
3. In **paranoid schizophrenia,** the most obvious symptoms are delusions and hallucinations, with strong themes of persecution. The woman who described the radioactive tater tots would have been diagnosed with paranoid schizophrenia. People with this disorder are characteristically less impaired than those with disorganized or catatonic schizophrenia—perhaps partly because of the age of onset. Since the symptoms of paranoid schizophrenia normally appear when people are in their twenties rather than in their teens, they have more opportunity to develop strengths.

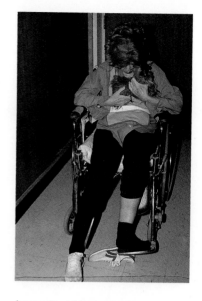

Among the striking symptoms of schizophrenia are movement disorders. Some people repeat strange movements over and over, while others like this woman may sit or stand motionless as statues for long periods of time.

Delusional Disorders

Delusional disorders are characterized by a single well-organized delusion. The core of the delusion is usually the idea that other people are paying unusual attention to you. It's something like being acutely aware of the pimple on your chin and imagining that everyone you meet is looking at it. Of course, with a moment's thought you'd realize that you don't spend your time looking at your friends' complexions, so they probably don't spend their time looking at yours. But you can't help feeling an irrational self-consciousness. If you can imagine this feeling greatly exaggerated, you'd have some idea of one of the central experiences of delusional disorders—the belief that the people around you are watching you (when in fact they're not thinking about you at all). These kinds of delusions are called *ideas of reference.*

Another example: You see two of your friends talking together. As you notice them, they both look at you and then turn away and begin to talk animatedly. For a minute you wonder if they are talking about you; then you forget the whole thing. Someone suffering from a delusional disorder, however, might create an elaborate, irrational explanation for the experience. The friends aren't really friends; they're agents working for the CIA. And they're not simply talking about the individual; they're planning his or her assassination.

ROTHCO

"You know what I wish? I wish I were paranoid - then at least I would THINK people were noticing me."

Kenlyne

Disorganized schizophrenia The most profoundly disturbed type of schizophrenia characterized by hallucinations, delusions, and disturbed emotional responses.

Catatonic schizophrenia A type of schizophrenia in which the most striking symptom is some sort of movement disturbance.

Paranoid schizophrenia A type of schizophrenia characterized by hallucinations and delusions of persecution and/or grandiosity.

Delusional disorders Psychological disorders in which the individual experiences a single well-organized delusion.

The emotional contents of delusions are suspicion and hostility, leading to the label of *paranoid delusion*. Like those with paranoid schizophrenia, people who have paranoid delusions believe that their "enemies" are trying to persecute them. But here the delusion is well organized and, except for some unlikely central assumption (the friends are working for the CIA), may even be logical.

Most people who are diagnosed with a delusional disorder are able to function very well in the spheres of their life that are not related to the delusion. A husband who believes irrationally that his wife is unfaithful, vigorously rejecting even the most compelling evidence that his suspicions are wrong, may not be able to function within the family but would probably have little trouble functioning at work.

Delusional disorders tend to develop later in life than paranoid schizophrenia, thus leaving more of the individual's functioning intact; in addition, people are much more likely to recover from delusional disorders.

Somatoform Disorders

The central symptoms of **somatoform disorders** are physical complaints with a psychological basis.

Conversion Disorders   The most famous, and once the most common, somatoform disorders are **conversion disorders.** This is the modern name for the hysteria that we described in Chapter 14. Like Anna O., people with conversion disorders report impossible symptoms—physical problems that seem to be the product of nerve damage but can't be.

Although conversion disorders were very common in Freud's time, they are much less so today. It may be that people now know more about the way their bodies work and about the effects of modern medicine and thus experience their bodies and their infirmities differently.

Somatization Disorders   Less specific physical complaints that also have a psychological basis are usually diagnosed as **somatization disorders.** Victims report fatigue; aches and pains in the head, body, or back; and vague problems with their digestion and bowels.

Dissociative Disorders

Dissociative disorders involve a disturbance of memory. Imagine that exams and papers have piled up, and you're sitting at your desk in despair. You're never going to get all of the work done in time. And it's all so boring anyway. Wouldn't it be nice just to give it all up, head for the Caribbean, and get a job on a boat? Everyone has feelings like this at some time or another, but most of us don't act on them. Why not? Because we don't want to disappoint our families, and because life on a boat doesn't really fit our sense of who we are and what we want to do.

People who suffer from dissociative disorders disassociate themselves from their history and sense of self. *Amnesia* is the simplest kind of dissociation: people with amnesia simply can't remember some portion of their life. Closely related is *fugue*. Here the individual not only forgets his or her past life but leaves familiar surroundings and people, and sometimes even builds a new life in a different place, as a different person. The most complex dissociative state is *multiple personality*. People with multiple personalities behave as though more than one person is inhabiting their bodies.

Somatoform disorders Psychological disorders in which the major symptoms are physical complaints of illness, fatigue, discomfort, or paralysis.

Conversion disorders Disorders in which the sufferer reports a loss of movement or sensation in some part of the body, for which there is no neurological basis.

Somatization disorders Disorders in which the individual complains of vague physical symptoms—such as fatigue, dizziness, and headaches—that have no physical basis.

Dissociative disorders A group of psychological disorders in which the individual is unable to remember recent events, his or her identity, or parts of his or her personality.

Psychogenic amnesia Loss of memory due to psychological rather than physical causes.

Fugue A dissociative disorder in which the individual forgets his or her own identity and may leave familiar surroundings to live at least briefly in a new place, with a new identity.

Multiple personality disorder A dissociative disorder in which the individual seems to have more than one personality controlling behavior at different times.

Psychogenic Amnesia   Loss of memory due to psychological rather than physical factors is known as **psychogenic amnesia.** By far the most common causes of amnesia are physical injuries, which disrupt the brain's activities. But some cases of amnesia stem from psychological factors. People with psychogenic amnesia forget their own identity and those of the people around them. This kind of amnesia seems to function as an escape from the problems or responsibilities of life. Psychogenic amnesia is very uncommon, and episodes are usually relatively brief.

Fugue   "Flight" is what **fugue** means, and that's just what this disorder is about. People who are in fugue states are amnesic, but they also leave familiar surroundings. Sometimes they leave one life and establish an entirely new life and identity in some other place, without any memory of their first life. (Usually, however, their new life is in some place like Akron or Wichita, not the Caribbean.) More commonly, the fugue lasts at most a few days, at the end of which the individual "wakes up" in a strange place, with no idea how he or she got there. Fugues, like episodes of psychogenic amnesia, seem to occur when the individual is under a great deal of stress.

Multiple Personality   One of the rarest forms of mental disorder is **multiple personality disorder.** Victims, who usually have an ordinary, everyday personality, may report blackouts or periods of time about which they can't remember anything. During these blackouts, a different personality takes over. In psychotherapy, people have reported from three or four different personalities up to as many as twenty-one personalities. It is not unusual in these cases for the everyday personality to be quiet and repressed, and for at least one of the alternate personalities to be uninhibited and unrestrained. These alternate personalities seem to exist in order to do and feel things the first personality is incapable of doing and feeling. Usually the second (or third or fourth) personality knows about the first, but the first is not aware of the others.

Probably the most famous case of multiple personality was described in the movie *The Three Faces of Eve* (Thigpen & Cleckley, 1954). The dominant personality was Eve White, a quiet timid woman. She was unaware of a second personality, Eve Black, who was much more exciting, impulsive, and seductive. During therapy, a third personality emerged, called Jane, who was more interesting and confident than Eve White, and more mature and controlled than Eve Black. Eventually, with therapy, the three personalities merged into one that was most like Jane.

In 1926, Agatha Christie, already the most famous mystery writer in the world, disappeared. She was discovered a few days later in a distant city. She never explained what happened, and the mystery of her disappearance has never been solved. But it was known that she was under great stress at the time, and perhaps her flight was a case of fugue.

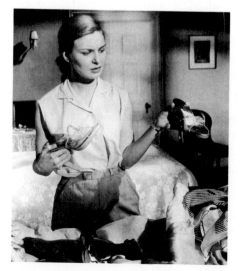

In the movie the *Three Faces of Eve,* Joanne Woodward played a woman with three personalities. Depicted here are two of them— the uninhibited, sensual Eve Black and the constricted, timid Eve White, who was unaware of Eve Black and often puzzled by the evidences of Eve Black's personality.

As we noted earlier, this kind of "split personality" is very different from schizophrenia. The sufferer may have separate personalities, but none of the personalities exhibit the severe thought or emotional disturbances that are characteristic of schizophrenia.

In all of the dissociative disorders, the effect is to help the individual deny responsibility for his or her actions—by forgetting them, running away from them, or attributing them to some other personality (Spanos, Weekes & Bertrand, 1985). For this reason, considerable skepticism has surrounded some cases of multiple personality. The question in each case is whether the person is demonstrating a kind of unconscious escape from intolerable conflict or simply faking. The fact that the emergence of different personalities produces different patterns of EEG activity in the brain (Braun, 1983) indicates that at least some cases are genuine.

Although dissociative disorders make good drama, they are in fact very rare. Even with the increased number of such cases in recent decades, only an average of about five cases a year are reported in the United States (Boor, 1982). Most therapists never see a single case of multiple personality in their whole career.

Recap

- One sign of psychoactive substance abuse is the inability to function normally at work or within personal relationships.

- Anxiety is the physical and emotional responses of fear or dread of an object or situation that is either not dangerous at all or not dangerous enough to warrant the responses.

- Simple phobias, social phobias, generalized anxiety, panic disorder, agoraphobia, and obsessive-compulsive disorders are all forms of anxiety disorders.

- In both depression and bipolar disorder, the individual experiences profound sadness and hopelessness. But the individual suffering from bipolar disorder also experiences intervals of mania.

- The danger of suicide is serious in people who are depressed: as many as 15 percent of seriously depressed people commit suicide, and as many as 80 percent at least consider it.

- Schizophrenia is a serious psychological disorder characterized by thought disturbances, emotional disturbances, motor disturbances, and social isolation.

- DSM-III-R identifies three major forms of schizophrenia: disorganized schizophrenia, catatonic schizophrenia, and paranoid schizophrenia.

- Somatoform disorders are psychological disorders in which the major symptoms are physical complaints of illness, fatigue, discomfort, or paralysis.

- Delusional disorders are characterized by a single well-organized delusion, often of persecution.

- Dissociative disorders—psychogenic amnesia, fugue, and multiple personality—all involve a disturbance of memory that helps the individual deny responsibility for his or her actions.

Axis II Disorders

Unlike the Axis I disorders, Axis II disorders are enduring, even lifelong patterns of behavior.

Personality Disorders

Many of the personality disorders bear names similar to the psychological disorders that make up Axis I because they refer to similar behaviors (see Table 15.4). But personality disorders are different from psychological disorders. Characteristically, the person doesn't experience them as problems. To the person, they're "just the way I am."

Cluster A   People with these disorders often exhibit odd or eccentric behavior.

- Paranoid personality disorder
- Schizoid personality disorder
- Schizotypal personality disorder

Cluster B   People with these disorders often exhibit dramatic, emotional, or erratic behavior.

- Antisocial personality disorder
- Borderline personality disorder
- Histrionic personality disorder
- Narcissistic personality disorder

Cluster C   People with these disorders often exhibit anxiousness or fearfulness.

- Avoidant personality disorder
- Dependent personality disorder
- Obsessive-compulsive personality disorder
- Passive-aggressive personality disorder
- Other

Note: "Other" refers to conditions that affect functioning but do not meet enough criteria to be classified as specific disorders.

Table 15.4
Personality Disorders

Consider obsessive-compulsive personality disorder. People with this disorder are preoccupied with neatness, order, punctuality, and planning. Their preoccupation with organizing is like the obsessional thinking characteristic of the psychological disorder, but it's less extreme. Often individuals with an obsessive-compulsive personality disorder will not perceive their preoccupations as problems but, instead, are likely to complain about the slovenliness of everyone around them.

Although personality disorders are usually not experienced as a problem by those who exhibit them, they can create problems for others. Thus people are rarely diagnosed with or treated for a personality disorder unless someone else has urged them to get help. A good example is the antisocial personality.

People with an **antisocial personality** pose a major problem for society. These people seem to have a moral deficiency. They don't care about other people or their feelings, and they never seem to experience guilt or remorse. As a result, they lie, cheat, steal, and or even kill. These people also seem to be much less affected by fear and anxiety than most people, so that they often take wild risks quite calmly. Typically average or above average in intelligence, and charming, they make expert liars and con artists.

Antisocial personality   A personality disorder in which the individual feels no sympathy for other people and no guilt or remorse for his or her actions.

Fortunately for the rest of us, most people with antisocial personalities are impulsive, not much given to elaborate planning. So their crimes tend to be minor and unsystematic. But some of the most notorious mass murderers in recent times—including Kenneth Bianchi (the Hillside Strangler) and Ted Bundy—clearly had antisocial personalities.

Developmental Disorders

A second group of disorders included in Axis II are the disorders that emerge in childhood and adolescence. These disorders include mental retardation and autistic disorder. One picture of autism was presented in the movie *Rain Man,* modeled on the story of a real man. Autistic children and adults characteristically have very disrupted social interactions. Autistic children seem to ignore other people and often do not speak. Many such children are originally diagnosed as retarded. However, they are usually less sociable than retarded children and often exhibit a few intellectual abilities that are normal, or even unusually high.

Recap

- Characteristically, personality disorders are milder and more enduring than psychological disorders, and are less likely to be considered a problem by the disordered individual.

- Although personality disorders are rarely experienced as a problem by those who exhibit them, they can create problems for others.

- People with an antisocial personality don't care about other people and never seem to experience guilt or remorse.

A Question of Reliability

Although each group of disorders we've discussed seems to have unique symptoms, we seldom find a "textbook" case in real life. First, people are complex, and any individual is likely to present a complex mixture of symptoms. Second, despite careful probing, clinicians sometimes do not uncover all of the individual's symptoms. Third, the very process of acknowledging a disorder and coming for treatment can generate feelings of anxiety or depression, feelings that can mask the symptoms of the real disorder. The result is that diagnoses of psychological disorders are not always reliable or consistent.

In Chapter 13 we noted that any system for measuring or classifying people is prone to some degree of error or unreliability. A good assessment system minimizes such error. What about the reliability of DSM-III-R? When two clinicians use the system to assign diagnoses to the same individuals, they usually agree about 80 percent of the time on which of the sixteen major categories of Axis I the person belongs in (Robins & Helzer, 1986). Eighty percent agreement is certainly better than chance, but it's a long way from perfect. (Not surprisingly, there is less agreement on the specific subcategories—a diagnosis of disorganized schizophrenia versus paranoid schizophrenia, for example.)

Probably the largest source of errors in the system is the variability of people. But part of the problem lies in the system itself. DSM-III-R, like its predecessors, underwent lengthy discussion among many groups of mental health professionals before it was adopted by the board of trustees of the American Psychiatric Association. Of course, these discussions involved a great deal of scientific debate, but they also reflected political and social concerns. Inevitably, then, the system was shaped by more than just patients' behaviors.

Consider the sheer number of diagnostic categories, for example. To some extent, that number seems determined by economics, not psychology. In this country, the majority of all psychotherapeutic services are paid for by health insurance. Naturally, the health insurance industry is reluctant to pay claims unless an individual definitely needs treatment. The means by which the industry ensures that someone needs treatment is to require a diagnosis in one of the categories defined in DSM-III-R. So if mental health professionals want to be paid for their work, they have to find labels for all of their patients (McReynolds, 1989). And as they find new problem areas, the number of diagnostic categories grows larger (Schacht, 1985).

The diagnostic system also reflects social attitudes. For example, until recently homosexuality was a diagnostic category; then, society became increasingly tolerant, and the category was dropped. The diagnosis had been included in response to social attitudes, and it was dropped when those attitudes changed. At no time did the decision hinge on science.

In the discussions surrounding the latest revision of the *Diagnostic and Statistical Manual,* several new categories were proposed. One—paraphilic coercive disorder—described men who derive sexual pleasure from the coercive aspects of rape. Critics argued that the diagnosis might provide a psychiatric defense for rapists that would help them escape punishment (Holden, 1986). The diagnosis was dropped. Here, too, the issue wasn't science but, rather, the practical consequences of using this kind of diagnostic category.

In sum, the official diagnostic system reflects not only current knowledge about abnormal behavior but also more practical, social, and professional concerns. Some of the difficulty involved in applying diagnostic categories accurately may arise from the multidimensional basis of the system.

Recap

- The variability of people, the clinician's failure to uncover all symptoms, and the feelings evoked by the process of acknowledging and accepting treatment for psychological disorders combine to complicate the diagnosis of those disorders.

- When two clinicians use the DSM-III-R system to assign diagnoses to the same individuals, they agree about 80 percent of the time when the diagnoses fall within the sixteen major categories along Axis I.

- Although the largest source of errors in the DSM-III-R system is probably the variability of people, part of the problem lies in the system itself—a system shaped by social and political forces as well as by science.

Origins of Psychological Disorders

The first thing we need to realize about the origins of psychological disorders is that we really don't know what they are. Despite decades of intense research, at most we have only inklings of what the causes of some disorders might be. So what follows is a kind of progress report on our current state of knowledge.

The Traditional Theories

Psychologists working from four different perspectives have tried to explain abnormal behavior. Although research supports each of these groups of theories, the consensus today is that the theories are not so much rivals as different pieces to the same puzzle. Along with that consensus, efforts to demonstrate individual theories have given way to models that integrate the different perspectives and to research that supports this integration.

Biological Theories The biological (or medical) theories assume that the source of abnormal behavior is some malfunction of the nervous system. At one time this was just a very plausible hypothesis, without much evidence to support it. But more recently, as part of the mushrooming research on brain function (see Chapter 2), a great deal of evidence has accumulated revealing the role of biological factors in some psychological disorders.

Psychodynamic Theories Remember that Freud developed his theories on the basis of his work with patients (see Chapter 14). He believed that abnormal behavior arises out of conflict within the individual, a conflict whose roots lie in the individual's development. Moreover, because people aren't aware of many of the motives that drive their behavior, they aren't able to control it.

Many opponents of Freud, notably the humanistic theorists, shared with him the belief that disorders emerge from maladaptive ways of thinking and feeling about the world and one's self.

Behaviorist Theories The behaviorists, too, assumed that people don't understand the origins of their own behavior. But they also believed that all patterns of behavior—both normal and abnormal—are learned. If people behave abnormally, it's because they've learned to do so through conditioning. And if psychologists want to change their behavior, they have to teach these people new ways to behave and think.

Social Systems Theories These theories share the assumption that psychological disorders stem from a disruption in the individual's social systems. The most elaborate kind of social systems theory focuses on the family system. It argues that all people are embedded in social systems, and that the family is the most important of those systems. If the family system is disrupted in some way, the behavior of all the people in the family is inevitably affected. One effect could be abnormal behavior by one or more family members. And the way to change that behavior is by changing relationships within the family.

Another type of social systems theory argues that psychological disorders are caused by the stress that society places on some of its members. Disorders emerge in individuals because they are members of certain socioeconomic classes or live in certain neighborhoods or belong to certain social groups.

A third approach links psychological disorders with crime and other kinds of deviant behavior. It argues that societies create deviant behavior by creating rules. For example, a society with no rules protecting private property has no thieves. Some theorists argue that people with psychological disorders are considered unusual because of the implicit "rules" in our society about how people should think and feel. When someone violates these rules, that person is treated as deviant. Because most of the ways we treat deviant people are unpleasant, this accounts for much of the distress that accompanies psychological disorder.

An Integrative Approach: The Diathesis-Stress Model

Integrative approaches to explaining psychological disorders recognize the differences among the traditional theories—but they also recognize that those theoretical differences developed because the theorists were looking at different aspects of the disordered person's life.

One integrative model is called the **diathesis-stress model**, which is illustrated in Figure 15.2. It holds that all kinds of disorders—physical and mental—stem from both a predisposition to a disorder, a *diathesis,* and a triggering factor, a *stressor.* Neither the diathesis without the stressor nor the stressor without the diathesis is sufficient to produce a disorder.

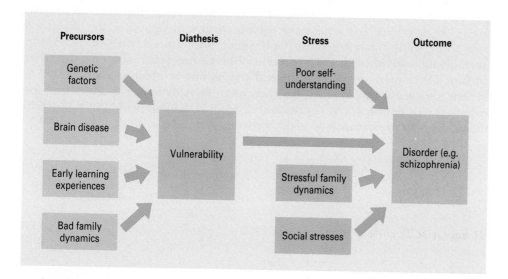

Figure 15.2
The Diathesis-Stress Model

Environmental stresses coupled with a predisposition to a disorder may increase a person's vulnerability to that disorder.

A diathesis-stress model can integrate the traditional theories. Perhaps biological factors create a diathesis. Or the diathesis may be created or aggravated by events during maturation, as both the psychodynamic and the behavioral approaches suggest. However, stressors in later life are necessary to produce the final psychological disorder. These stressors might include those produced by poor self-understanding, bad family dynamics, unfortunate social circumstances, or any combination of these factors.

Evidence for the Different Hypotheses

Until recently, most of the evidence concerning the origins of disorder has focused on separate factors. Consequently, in the next few sections, we will follow that separation. Bear in mind, though, that all the factors may contribute in some integrated way.

Biological Factors   Although neuroscientists are busy looking for specific evidence of brain malfunctions that cause psychological disorders, most of the evidence about biological factors is indirect. It consists of three general kinds of observations:

1. *Many psychological disorders are predictable from heredity.* If people "inherit" a predisposition to a disorder, it must be through some biological mechanism.
2. *The brain structures and functions of people with disorders appear different.* If there are differences in the chemistry or anatomy of these people's brains, those differences may be the source of the differences in their behavior.

Diathesis-stress model The belief that physical and mental disorders arise from both a predisposition (the diathesis) and some triggering factor (the stressor).

How Do We Know That?

We have already talked about the genetics of behavior in our discussions of temperament and intelligence. The same principles apply to the research on psychological disorders. In all behavior-genetic investigations, the researcher obtains information about the incidence of a disorder among the relatives of people who do and do not have the disorder. In general, if we find that people who are more alike genetically are also more likely to share a disorder, we begin to have confidence in our assumption that the disorder has a genetic basis.

The research on schizophrenia shows how the process works. We begin with the basic rate—the frequency of schizophrenia in the general population—which is between 1 and 2 percent. That is, one person in one hundred in the general population is diagnosed with schizophrenia at some time (Robins et al., 1984). But if an individual has a parent or sibling with schizophrenia, the likelihood rises to between 7 and 9 percent (Gottesman, McGuffin & Farmer, 1987). On average, the individual shares 50 percent of his or her genes with each parent or sibling. Obviously, then, the increased risk is not as great as the increase in genetic similarity. But the fact that there is an increase suggests a genetic contribution (see Figure 15.A). Furthermore, if both parents have schizophrenia, the risk rises to greater than 37 percent (Gottesman, McGuffin & Farmer, 1987).

Figure 15.A
Genetics and the Risk of Schizophrenia

Note that the more similar people are in their genetic endowment, the more likely it is that if one person is diagnosed as schizophrenic, the other one will be too.

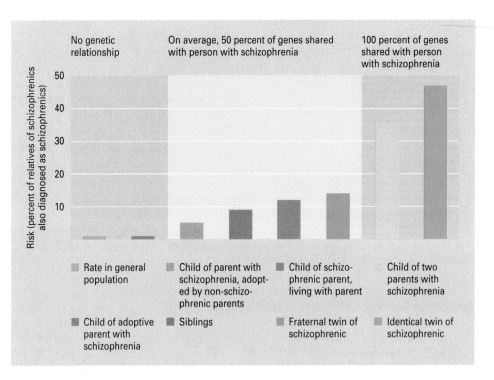

Source: Data from Gottesman, McGuffin & Farmer, 1987.

The problem is that the increased risk we find in these cases could be due to other factors. For example, imagine what it would be like to be raised by parents who sometimes hallucinate or suffer delusions. This kind of environment, by itself, could very well produce disordered behavior.

To estimate the influence of the environment, we can study identical and fraternal twins. Remember that identical twins have the same genes; whereas

(Continued on next page)

fraternal twins, like other siblings, share just half of their genetic makeup. But because both kinds of twins are the same age, they tend to share more similar environments than siblings. If we find that the risk of a disorder is much greater between identical twins than between fraternal twins, we have evidence of a genetic contribution. In fact, the risk *is* greater. If one identical twin is diagnosed as having schizophrenia, the risk to the other twin is about 46 percent. By contrast, if one fraternal twin is schizophrenic, the risk to the other is 14 percent, a great deal lower (Gottesman et al., 1987). Note, however, that this risk is higher than that for siblings, thus suggesting a role for experiential factors as well.

In ordinary families, the impact of genetic factors and environment are very difficult to separate. Perhaps, for example, identical twins are treated more similarly than other siblings, precisely because they look more similar. To solve this problem, psychologists have found that the best evidence of the role of genetics comes from studies of children who've been adopted very early in life. In such instances, one family supplies the genes and a completely different family provides the childrearing experiences.

If the biological mother has been diagnosed with schizophrenia, an adopted child is at greater risk of developing the disorder (Gottesman & Shields, 1982). And if the biological parents are not schizophrenic but one of the adoptive parents is, there is no increased risk (Wender et al., 1974).

All of this evidence makes it clear that genetic factors contribute to schizophrenia. However, these results do not mean that there is one or more genes that directly "cause" schizophrenia. Rather, the genetic factors may produce a condition that is only indirectly related to the disorder.

A parallel example that may clarify this point is the "genetics" of basketball playing. You can certainly predict the likelihood that someone will be a good basketball player from knowing whether his or her parents and siblings, especially identical twins, are basketball players. The reason is not, however, that there is a gene for basketball playing. Instead, height is largely controlled by genetic factors, and tall people tend to be good basketball players whereas very short people do not. So, the "genetics" of basketball skill are indirect, depending completely on the presence of both genes for height and a culture in which basketball is played. Note that in a culture without basketball, the genes would have no expression at all. The genetics of psychological disorder may be similarly indirect.

A related question concerns the relative contribution of genetic and environmental factors. Proposed answers are sometimes presented as a *heritability ratio*, the ratio of genetic to nongenetic factors. If one collects data about, say, schizophrenia from a group of identical twins raised in different environments, this ratio can easily be calculated. However, all heritability ratios should be pondered with care. They represent the relative contribution of genes and environment *only in this particular sample*. If there are more extreme environments or different genetic factors at work, then the ratio will change. Accordingly, a heritability ratio for schizophrenia is difficult to establish and is, at best, an estimate based on a particular sample.

---

3. *Biological treatments improve many psychological disorders.* If a biological treatment works, the disorder may arise out of a biological condition.

The genetics of psychological disorders   The genetic contribution to many disorders has been studied. The most extensive research has been directed at schizophrenia, which we'll refer to in our discussion of behavior genetics.

Pictured here are Nora, Iris, Myra, and Hester Genain, monozygotic quadruplets. Because they are monozygotic, they all share the same genes. In addition, they were all diagnosed with schizophrenia. Evidence like this and related research results suggest a genetic contribution to the genesis of schizophrenia.

Schizophrenia is not the only disorder with a substantial genetic component. The evidence is equally clear that genetic factors contribute to the development of bipolar disorder. For example, if one identical twin has bipolar disorder, the other twin has a 72 percent chance of developing the disorder (Allen, 1976). And the children of one parent with bipolar disorder have a greater than 30 percent chance of developing the disorder (see Figure 15.3).

Figure 15.3
Genetics and the Risk of Mood Disorders

The probability that a person will suffer a major depression increases if an identical twin already has the disorder. But the probability is greater for bipolar disorder.

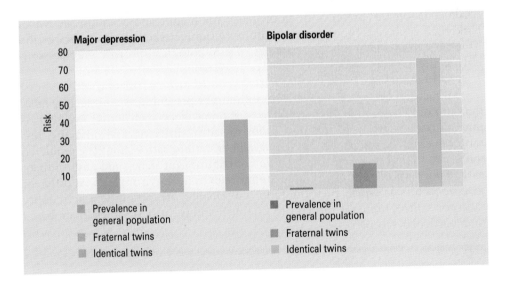

Source: Data from Allen, 1976.

Particularly striking evidence of a genetic factor in bipolar disorder comes from the Amish, a group of about 13,000 people of German descent living in Pennsylvania. Bound by strong religious and cultural ties, the Amish tend to marry within their own community. They also keep very good records of births and deaths and marriages—records that go back several generations, making it easy to trace family histories. Those records tell us that all of the cases of bipolar disorder in the Amish community, and all of the cases of suicide, have occurred in just a few families (Kolata, 1986). In fact, the pattern is so clear that we can tell that, in this group, the diathesis for bipolar disorder is produced by a single gene that leads to the actual disorder in about 62 percent of the members of the affected families (Egeland et al., 1987). Bipolar disorder itself is not necessarily produced by this single gene, however. Studies of other groups also show strong genetic influences but implicate entirely different genes (Biron et al., 1987).

The evidence of genetic factors in other disorders is less systematic than in schizophrenia and bipolar disorder. But genetic factors do seem to contribute to the occurrence of obsessive-compulsive disorders (Turner, Beidel & Nathan, 1985), generalized anxiety disorder (Noyes et al., 1987), alcoholism (Guze et al., 1986), and antisocial personality as well as anorexia nervosa (Loehlin, Willerman & Horn, 1988). In these instances, too, fewer than half of the people with a genetic predisposition to a psychological disorder actually develop that disorder.

In short, there is considerable evidence that a number of psychological disorders are significantly more likely to occur in individuals who have a genetic predisposition. In addition, since genes work most directly through their influence on biological processes, some nervous system abnormalities seem likely to be involved.

Differences in brain function and anatomy   Much of the work on the relationship between brain function and anatomy, and psychological disorders has focused on schizophrenia. The computer-imaging techniques that we talked about in Chapter 2 reveal anatomical abnormalities in the brains of many, though not all, people with schizophrenia. The most common abnormality—found in about 50 percent of those diagnosed with schizophrenia—is enlargement of the ventricles. (Recall from Chapter 1 that the ventricles are the spaces in the brain through which the cerebrospinal fluid circulates.) In the normal brain, the ventricles are small because the space is packed with brain cells. In the brains of about half the patients with schizophrenia, however, the ventricles are larger (see Figure 15.4). This suggests that the brains of schizophrenics either have not developed adequately or have shrunk through some degenerative process (Shelton & Weinberger, 1986).

These differences, and those in glucose metabolism and brain activity (Mirsky & Duncan, 1986), support the idea that schizophrenia is associated with abnormalities of the brain. But, again, the association is not perfect. Some individuals with schizophrenia show no brain abnormalities, and some individuals who are not schizophrenic do show brain abnormalities. It may well be that any abnormality we find is only one of a number of physical diatheses that increase the likelihood of schizophrenia if combined with the right stressor.

The effects of biological treatments   Another powerful piece of evidence in support of the biological origin of mental illness is the fact that many disorders are helped by drugs. For example, the most common treatment for schizophrenia is a family of drugs known as the phenothiazines. These drugs reduce the amount of the neurotransmitter dopamine in the brain. Generally, the more extensively a drug acts against dopamine, the more effective it is at relieving the symptoms of schizophrenia (Creese, Burt & Snyder, 1976). This finding suggests that the patient with schizophrenia is producing too much dopamine, is highly sensitive to dopamine, or has too many dopamine receptors (Wong et al., 1986).

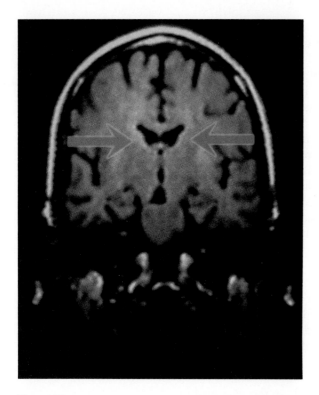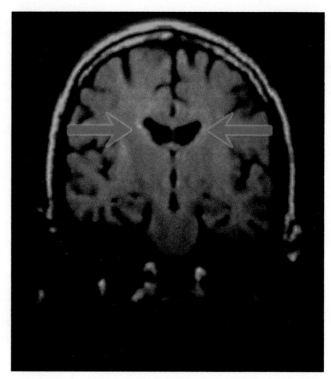

Source: Suddath et al., 1990.

Figure 15.4
Brain Structure in People with and Without Schizophrenia

The red arrows in these MRI images point to the ventricles, the spaces in the interior of the brain. The person on the right has schizophrenia and the much larger ventricles that are typical of many people with schizophrenia. The comparison between the two brains is even more dramatic because they belong to identical twins.

The dopamine theory is strengthened by what happens when a patient is given too much phenothiazine; bad side effects, such as shaking and stiff movements, result. This pattern of symptoms is called *Parkinsonism,* because it mimics the symptoms of Parkinson's disease.

Parkinson's disease seems to be due to too little dopamine in a particular group of motor neurons. People with Parkinson's disease can be helped by a drug called L-dopa, that increases dopamine. If they receive too much L-dopa, however, they may suffer hallucinations and delusions. Apparently, the human brain requires a certain level of dopamine activity. Too much may bring about the symptoms of schizophrenia; too little may result in Parkinsonism.

Unfortunately, the dopamine hypotheses suffer from a number of problems. For example, the phenothiazines take effect in hours, but the symptoms of schizophrenia do not abate for days. Still, the evidence suggests that some abnormality in the production, level, or use of dopamine in the brain is responsible for those symptoms.

Other psychological disorders seem to involve other neurotransmitter systems. For example, depression is ordinarily treated with drugs that increase the effectiveness of norepinephrine and serotonin. Although the mechanisms are not yet clear, the problem seems to be with the sensitivity of receptor sites (McNeal & Cimbolic, 1986).

A completely different kind of drug therapy is used for bipolar disorder. Here the drug of choice is lithium carbonate. We don't understand exactly how the drug works, but the fact that it does work supports the distinction between depression and bipolar disorder, thus further suggesting that the two disorders involve neurological processes different from each other and from those involved in schizophrenia.

Puzzle It Out!

When treatment with a drug helps relieve a disorder, we are tempted to believe that the disorder was caused by a shortage of the drug or some related chemical. One disorder common among college students is procrastination, especially in regard to studying. Sometimes the solution is massive doses of caffeine, taken through the night. Does this mean that procrastination is caused by caffeine deficiency? More important, what does this suggest about the meaning of the drug treatments for our explanations of disorder?

In sum, a great deal of evidence has accumulated supporting the importance of biological factors in many disorders. The success of biological treatments, the findings linking behavior and genetic makeup, and the observations of brain abnormalities all indicate that biological factors are important. However, they don't tell the whole story. Many people who probably possess a genetic predisposition do not develop a disorder. Brain abnormalities occur in individuals whose behavior is completely normal. And the biochemical differences that presumably underlie the drug treatments are not observed in all sufferers of a disorder. For these reasons, most psychologists assume that biological factors must be combined with other, experiential causes to produce these disorders. Furthermore, some disorders do *not* seem to be associated with biological factors.

Psychodynamic Approaches   Freud believed that psychological disorders, like normal personality traits, are rooted in the early stages of libidinal development. The potential expression of these primitive libidinal urges may cause anxiety, which might be experienced as a symptom itself. And the defense mechanisms that relieve the anxiety could produce disordered behavior. So, for example, a phobia pertaining to bridges might be an expression of a fear of separation from the people we love, which in itself could be an expression of even more deeply repressed feelings of aggression toward those same people.

The psychologists who developed other psychodynamic theories would have attributed the conflict to different factors, but they would have shared with Freud the belief that psychological disorders are a residue of past experience and that the basic causes of those disorders are unconscious.

Most of the psychodynamic theorists actually treated patients. And most took the success of their therapies to be the ultimate test of their theories. It wasn't necessary to study the effects of childhood development or low self-esteem on the individual, they believed, so long as treatments directed toward the unconscious or toward increasing self-esteem worked. More recently, psychologists have recognized that successful psychotherapy doesn't "prove" that the theory guiding the therapy is correct. A therapy may be working for very different reasons than the theorist supposes.

Behavioral Approaches   The early behaviorists assumed that disordered behavior, like all behavior, is learned. They pointed to phobias as an example. In this connection, recall from Chapter 6 how John Watson used classical conditioning to teach a young child to fear a tame white rat (Watson & Rayner, 1920).

Like the psychodynamic theorists, the early behaviorists did not try to discover whether people with disorders had actually been conditioned through experience. They, too, were content to devise therapies based on their theories, and to take the success of those therapies as support for their theories.

In Chapter 14, we described an evolution in behaviorist theory that accommodated the influence of cognition in the realm of behavior. From this willingness to acknowledge feelings and thoughts have come two bodies of research on psychological disorders.

Formal thought disturbance—the inability to think coherently and systematically—is one of the symptoms of schizophrenia. According to one popular theory, the effect of a genetic or biological predisposition toward schizophrenia may be interference with normal cognitive processes, especially attention. This theory has stimulated much research on the relationship between schizophrenia and attention. Even when they are not actively suffering from the symptoms of schizophrenia, people with the disorder have difficulty focusing their attention (Mirsky & Duncan, 1986). Attention difficulties have also been observed in people whose genetic history suggests that they are at risk for schizophrenia, even though they show no symptoms of the disorder (Neuchterlein & Dawson, 1984). These studies show that attention deficits are associated with schizophrenia; but their role in the development of the disorder is still unclear.

Depression also seems to go hand in hand with a distinctive pattern of cognitive abnormality. Three processes have been identified, each beginning with an event that triggers a depressive reaction, which in turn produces an event that triggers another depressive reaction, and so on.

- *Loss of positive reinforcement*   Depressive episodes often begin with an event—the loss of a loved one, the loss of a job, a failure of some kind—that leaves the individual sad and apathetic (Lewinsohn et al., 1985). As a result of the apathy, the individual does not do things that give him or her pleasure, and so has further reason to be unhappy. And because no one enjoys being around someone who's sad and apathetic (Strack & Coyne, 1983), people begin to avoid the individual. The consequence is a downward spiral in which each step leaves the individual more isolated and less able to find pleasure.
- *Emotion-driven remembering*   In Chapter 7 we discussed a similar spiral involving mood and memory. When people are depressed, it's extremely difficult for them to remember good things or happy experiences. Instead, they remember things and experiences whose emotional tone matches their mood—failures and losses. And what they think about only reinforces and may even intensify their depression (Beck, 1982).
- *Learned helplessness*   We discussed the third factor—learned helplessness—in Chapter 14. Remember that when people experience a series of failures, they tend to work less hard on subsequent tasks, thus increasing the likelihood of further failure and the potential for another downward spiral.

  Subsequent research has demonstrated that the experience of failure alone is not enough to produce learned helplessness. The subjects must also blame themselves for that failure (Abramson, Seligman & Teasdale, 1978). And, of course, people who are depressed do tend to take the blame for failure. The relationship here is so strong that the tendency to accept blame is a reliable predictor of depression (O'Hara, Behm & Campbell, 1982).

All three of these processes may well contribute to the downward spiral of depression. Perhaps the tendency to act in one or more of these ways is the stressor that, in combination with a genetic diathesis, brings depression into full flower.

Social Approaches   Many of the stressors that could activate the diathesis appear to stem from family and social environments. There is considerable evidence that family and social stressors are associated with an increased risk of psychological disorders. But, again, environmental stress at best is only part of the answer. Many people face enormous stress in their everyday lives without developing a disorder.

The family system   The most famous theory of the impact of the family on a psychological disorder focused on the effects of family communication patterns on schizophrenia (Bateson et al., 1956; Watzlawick, Beavin, & Jackson, 1967). In families in which one member has been diagnosed as schizophrenic, a pattern of communication, called the *double bind,* has been observed: the speaker communicates one message verbally and a contradictory message in some other way. For example, a mother might say to her schizophrenic child, "Come sit in my lap" as she stands up, making her lap "disappear."

The early proponents of the double-bind theory believed that this kind of contradictory communication teaches the child to think in contradictory and illogical ways, a basis for the formal thought disturbance that is symptomatic of schizophrenia. Today the idea that parents "cause" schizophrenia seems unlikely, in part because of evidence supporting the role of heredity. However, there is some evidence suggesting that difficulties in communication can contribute to stress that may combine with a diathesis to produce schizophrenia. Two factors have been identified: *communication deviance* and *expressed emotion.* Communication deviance refers to confused and contradictory kinds of communications. Expressed emotion involves negative emotions primarily, as well as intrusive comments made to others such as "You have a bad attitude."

Expressed emotion in their families is a very powerful predictor of relapse among people who have previously been hospitalized for schizophrenia (Miklowitz et al., 1986). Some research indicates that it may be involved in the development of schizophrenia as well.

For example, one study identified a group of children who were seriously at risk for developing schizophrenia, and then followed their development for fifteen years. In families in which the parents communicated effectively, only 8 percent of the children developed schizophrenia or related disorders. However, in families in which the parents' communication deviance and expressed emotion had reached high levels, 50 percent of the children developed schizophrenia or related disorders (Goldstein, 1988). Of course, many other sources of stress may have existed in these families. But the findings tell us that genetic risk leads to schizophrenia only when stress is also present.

A similar point emerges from the research on children of schizophrenic mothers who were adopted by nonschizophrenic families. As a group, these children are as likely to develop schizophrenia or related disorders as children who remain with their biological mothers. But the outcome for adopted children depends on the nature of the family into which they are adopted. In one study, families were divided into "healthy" and "unhealthy" groups. Among the children who were adopted into healthy families, only 7 percent developed any kind of disorder; among the unhealthy families, 52 percent of the children developed psychological disorders (Mirsky & Duncan, 1986).

Socioeconomic status   A number of observations suggest that a person's position in the social fabric is a source of stress that can activate his or her vulnerability to psychological disorder. For example, in the United States, people at lower socioeconomic levels are exposed to more severe stresses (Thoits, 1983). This finding may account for the fact that poor people (Hollingshead & Redlich, 1958) and those who are less educated (Robins et al., 1984) are more likely to be diagnosed with schizophrenia or some other serious disorder.

But we find this pattern only in Western cultures. In many Third World countries, schizophrenia is more common among the middle and upper classes, at least in the cities. This finding has been attributed to the fact that in these countries, levels of stress are much higher for city-dwellers, who, though better off economically, are cut off from the fabric of the societies in which they grew up. By contrast, life in cohesive rural societies is economically harder, but the people there have much greater social support (Warner, 1985).

Other studies point to the role of additional socioeconomic factors in the development of schizophrenia. For example, in Western societies, people from lower socioeconomic classes seem to use less effective coping skills (Kessler, Price & Wortman, 1985). They have fewer and less effective ways of solving the problems in their lives. And they tend to have less social support as well (Liem & Liem, 1978). It may be that the disruptions caused by their economic problems tend to separate them from their families and friends, leaving them "nowhere to turn" when troubles strike.

At this point, we seem to have a wide array of promising leads but very little certainty about how psychological disorders develop. Certainly the evidence for biological and genetic contributions to some disorders is persuasive. However, the specific mechanisms of these factors are as yet quite unclear. Furthermore, they cannot be the whole story, given that people with identical genetics or (as far as we can tell) brain functions may differ dramatically in terms of how seriously they are affected—if they are affected at all.

Similarly, numerous strands of evidence indicate that people prone to schizophrenia, depression, and certain other disorders tend to exhibit unusual cognitive processes that may foster the development of disorders. And, clearly, people who are at greatest risk of developing disorders are also those whose lives are most filled with stress. The problem once again is that atypical cognitions or environmental stressors are at best only part of the answer. Many people exhibit similar patterns of thinking or face even greater stressors without developing a disorder.

Recap

- Despite decades of research, psychologists have only a basic understanding of the origins of psychological disorders.

- Biological theories, psychodynamic theories, behaviorist theories, and social systems theories have approached the question of the origin of psychological disorders from different perspectives; more recent theories are attempting to integrate these different perspectives.

- According to the diathesis-stress model, both physical and mental disorders stem from a predisposition (the diathesis) and a triggering factor (the stressor). Neither the diathesis nor the stressor is sufficient by itself to produce a disorder.

- The role of genetic factors in psychological disorders, comparisons of the brain physiology of people with and without disorders, and the effects of biological treatments on psychological disorders all support the idea of a biological vulnerability to psychological disorders.

- The individual's early development, learning, and cognitive functions are all individual factors that seem to increase the vulnerability to psychological disorders.

- Social factors—including family dynamics and socioeconomic level—seem to be a primary source of the stress that activates the diathesis.

Conclusion

In truth, every chapter in this book is only a progress report: we will know more next year, and every year after that. But this chapter seems particularly tentative. The diagnostic system is admittedly not very precise, and it is certain to be revised soon. Our understanding of the origins of the various psychological disorders is equally incomplete.

Nevertheless, we are making rapid progress toward understanding these processes. And you will see in the next chapter, we are also making progress at developing successful treatments, even though we are not yet sure how the disorders arise.

Chapter 16

Treatment of Psychological Disorders

Dust Motes Dancing in Sunlight, Vilhelm Hammershøi, 1900

16

Gateways The treatment of psychological disorders can provide wonderful opportunities. Psychologists who do therapy have the chance to help people by applying the theories and research findings of psychology. Their clients have the chance not only to heal inner wounds but, in most cases, to become better educated about their own motives and needs.

Every approach to therapy examined in this chapter harkens back to principles discussed earlier. The psychodynamic approach should bring to mind discussions of Freud in several chapters. Behaviorist approaches derive to a great extent from principles of learning discussed in Chapter 6. Cognitive therapies are rooted in principles presented in Chapter 8 on thought and language, Chapter 10 on emotion and stress, and Chapter 14 on personality. The systems approach, with its emphasis on communication within families, evokes themes we talked about in Chapters 11 and 12 on human development, as well as ideas we explore in forthcoming chapters on social psychology. Biological approaches draw on information about the nervous system, especially neurotransmitters, presented in Chapter 2.

I was talking to an elderly woman recently at a family wedding. When she learned that I was a psychologist, she asked if she could tell me a story. This is the story she told: "Once when I was a child my mother went to the city to do some shopping and left me with an unfamiliar baby sitter, a starched sort of woman who brought along a large boring-looking book and didn't seem to take much interest in me. Before departing, my mother made a very special point of telling me to be good "for Mrs. Adelson." And she particularly reminded me not to go near the gas jets on the new heater that had recently been installed.

"I had sized up Mrs. Adelson correctly. She found her novel a great deal more interesting than she found me, and I was left pretty much to my own devices. Although I tried hard to find other things to do, I did eventually get around to fooling with the gas jets. As luck would have it, Mrs. Adelson chose that precise moment to come see what I was up to. She announced sternly that I had been a very bad girl and that 'my mother would have to be told!'

"In due course my mother appeared, her arms filled with parcels. Mrs. Adelson delivered her report with an icy satisfaction and my mother, after giving me a preliminary scolding, sent me to my room to await a punishment equal to my crime. When she finally came to my room, she had a large box, sealed with tape, which seemed to contain something just purchased at a department store. She also carried brown wrapping paper, a pen, and string.

"She said to me: 'This box contains a doll that I bought you while I was shopping. Since you haven't been a good girl, I want you to help me wrap up the box, address it, and carry it to the post office, and we'll mail it to the orphanage where it will make some *good* little girl happy.' All of this we did.

"That was sixty years ago. Since that time, I must have relived wrapping that box a thousand times: the sound of the crisp wrapping paper being folded, the feel of the twine as I held my finger to the knot, the weight of the box as I carried it down the street, the sound as it slid down the brass chute at the post office. How strange to still be thinking about a doll I lost more than fifty years ago!

"But about two years ago my mother died, and six months later I woke up one night with a stunning realization. *The box had been empty.* It was too light to contain a doll. There never had been a doll. The box had been empty the whole time!

"I felt like an enormous burden had been lifted from my shoulders. At that moment, I understood why I kept thinking about that doll all my life. You see, although the thought of the lost doll was terrible, it was less terrible than the truth: that even if I had been good, my mother wouldn't have given me anything because she hadn't brought me anything. Once I let myself realize how selfish and manipulative my mother had been that afternoon, I finally could let it go.

"Now, what I want to know is—my realizing the box was empty—was that an example of *insight*?"

In Chapter 8 we talked about one kind of insight, the sudden recognition of the solution to a problem. And some of what the woman was describing—her recognition that there had never been a doll—was this kind of insight. But there's another kind of insight, too: what we call *therapeutic insight*. This kind of insight is the recognition and understanding of the unconscious thoughts and feelings that drive behavior. The woman did experience a therapeutic insight, but it wasn't about the doll. It was her recognition of her need to feel that her mother loved her and how the intensity of that need made her ignore the evidence of her own senses, that the box was too light to hold a doll.

The woman's story shows that people can achieve insights into their thoughts and feelings on their own. But it also shows that these kinds of insights don't come easily: the woman had mulled over the incident for sixty years before she recognized her feelings. The goal of many kinds of psychological treatment is to help people achieve these kinds of insights more easily.

Therapeutic Approaches

Therapists may use any of four broad approaches in treating the people who come to them for help. These approaches correspond to the groups of theories we talked about in Chapter 15. Those theories have been used to explain the origins of psychological disorders; it makes sense, then, that they also form the basis for treating psychological disorders.

- One group of treatments is called *insight-oriented therapies* because treatment consists of talking with clients to help them gain insight into their problems. The insight-oriented therapies divide naturally into two subgroups: those that were inspired by psychodynamic theories and those that were inspired by humanistic theories.
- The second group, *behavioral therapies,* follow the principles of behaviorism. Their objective is to help people learn new ways of behaving and even thinking and feeling. Just as the behaviorist theories have become more cognitive in recent years, the behavioral therapies, too, have come to focus more on clients' thoughts and feelings, as well as on their behaviors. Both insight-oriented and behavioral therapies focus on the individual. And they both are forms of **psychotherapy,** treatments that are primarily verbal and directed at the individual.
- A third group of treatments, *systems approaches,* focus on the group to which the individual belongs. For example, family therapies start with the assumption that the disorder occurs in the family system, not in the individual.
- The fourth group, the *biological therapies,* again focus on the individual. These therapies assume that the source of psychological disorders is a physiological abnormality, and they attempt to treat that abnormality with medication or other forms of direct physical intervention.

We begin this chapter by describing these different therapies. Then we examine their effectiveness. Finally, we take a brief look at the ethical issues raised by their use.

It's natural to think that one treatment method is better than another. This tendency is reinforced by the fact that some mental health professionals act as though the different therapies are in some sort of competition with one another. But remember what we said in Chapter 15. Many different factors can contribute to the development of a psychological disorder; perhaps for that reason, many different therapies can contribute to its treatment. For example, suppose a person is experiencing intense anxiety. We can treat the physical symptoms and feelings with drugs. With psychotherapies we can help the individual uncover the unconscious source of the anxiety or learn new behaviors to overcome the anxiety. Finally, by understanding the dynamics of family interaction, we can change them and so reduce the individual's anxiety. In sum, any or all of the therapies can help.

Psychotherapy Any primarily verbal set of techniques for treating psychological disorders that focuses on the individual's behaviors, thoughts, and feelings.

Psychodynamic therapy A therapy based on the fundamental idea that the symptoms of psychological disorders can be alleviated by the resolution of intrapsychic conflict.

We don't mean to say that all therapies are equally effective for every condition. But as you read about the different treatments, you should think of them as potential collaborators, not rivals. In actual practice, different kinds of therapies are often combined.

Insight-Oriented Therapies

A number of different approaches assume that psychological disorders arise from people's failure to understand themselves and, therefore, focus on improving that understanding. Although there are some differences in technique, the biggest difference among the insight-oriented therapies concerns the kind of self-understanding they focus on. These therapies are based on the long-standing personality theories we talked about in Chapter 14. As noted, many of these personality theories were developed by practitioners, in the course of their work as therapists. The first of these theorist-practitioners was Sigmund Freud.

Psychoanalysis and Other Psychodynamic Therapies

The therapies based on the idea of intrapsychic conflict are called **psychodynamic therapies.** All of them arise, in one way or another, from *psychoanalysis,* the system of understanding and treatment developed by Sigmund Freud and systematized and expanded by others after his death.

Classical Psychoanalysis   Remember that Freud believed adult behavior is rooted in libidinal impulses that often are preserved more or less unchanged from infancy and childhood. Because these impulses are repressed in the unconscious mind, they are expressed only indirectly. Some psychological disorders were assumed to consist of these indirect expressions. For example, a series of unsatisfactory romantic relationships might all have been attempts at symbolic satisfaction of Oedipal desires for the opposite-sex parent. Other kinds of disorders, such as somatoform paralysis, may actually be part of the mechanism that keeps forbidden impulses, memories, and thoughts repressed—a paralyzed person cannot act on unacceptable sexual desires.

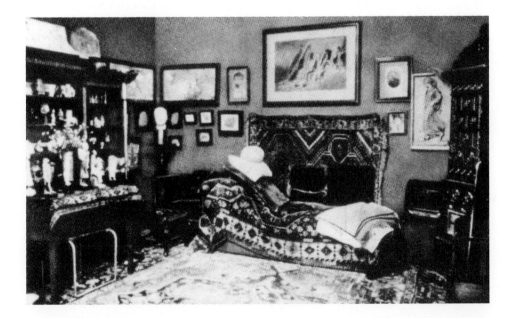

One reason Freud claimed he sat behind his patients was that he couldn't "put up with being stared at by other people for eight hours a day (or more)" (Freud, 1913/1961).

The basic goal of psychoanalytic therapy is **therapeutic insight,** the recognition of the unconscious drives that underlie behavior. The process of helping clients achieve insight into both their intrapsychic conflicts and the effects of these conflicts on behavior is what Freud called **psychoanalysis.** Psychoanalysis has developed into an intense, prolonged exploration of the individual's psyche. In classical psychoanalysis, the client is seen five or six times a week, often for several years.

Psychoanalysis involves two steps: helping the client gain insight into the unconscious motives that drive behavior, and then working through the conflicts that insight reveals.

Gaining insight   The first step in psychoanalysis is to help the client gain insight—to bring the client's unconscious thoughts and feelings into consciousness. The basic technique Freud used is called **free association.** He would ask his patients to say everything that they thought during a session, without censoring anything—no matter how unimportant or silly it might have seemed. "Say whatever goes through your mind. Act as though you were a traveller sitting next to the window of a railway carriage and describing to someone the changing views which you see outside" (Freud, 1913/1961a, p. 135). Throughout the session the patient would be lying on a couch, while Freud sat out of view.

According to Freud, the psychoanalyst should not focus on any particular aspect of what the patient is saying. Instead, he or she should listen with "evenly hovering attention" so that the individual's free associations come together in a whole, their meaning integrated through the action of the analyst's own unconscious.

Through this combination of the patient's free association and the analyst's evenly hovering attention, the therapist gradually comes to understand the conflicts that lie behind the patient's symptoms. Once these unconscious conflicts are understood, the analyst can use his or her understanding to provide an **interpretation.** The analyst's interpretation is only an aid to the client's understanding, since the essential result is that the client truly understand his or her behavior, rather than merely receive an expert opinion from the analyst.

The analyst can use a variety of phenomena to understand, and help the patient understand, the unconscious. Freud believed that dreams, for example, are a source of rich material for discovering repressed conflicts, because in dreams those conflicts appear in symbolic form. (It was partially through an analysis of his own dreams that Freud developed his psychoanalytic theories.)

Resistance is another source of clues to unconscious impulses. Often when clients come close to gaining insight into their motives, they try to change the subject, devalue its importance, or reject their analyst's interpretations. By watching for signs of resistance, analysts can infer an underlying motivation.

Freud believed that **transference** was another crucial source of information. He argued that when people have unresolved conflicts from their past—conflicts with their parents for example—they tend to repeat those conflicts in their daily interactions with others. In therapy, clients begin to play out unresolved conflicts with their analyst, projecting people from their past onto the analyst and acting toward the analyst as they used to act toward those people. Providing the maximum opportunity for projection is the major reason Freud gave for the analyst's sitting out of view of the client.

Working through the conflicts   Once clients understand the conflicts that underlie their behavior, they have to integrate that understanding into their lives. This *working through the conflicts* is what Freud called "the part of the work that effects the greatest changes in the patient" (1914/1961b, p. 155).

A colleague described a case that exemplifies many of these elements. A successful professional woman consulted a woman psychoanalyst because she was

Therapeutic insight   The recognition of the unconscious thoughts and feelings that underlie behavior.

Psychoanalysis   The process developed by Freud of helping a client achieve insight into and work through intrapsychic conflict.

Free association   In psychoanalysis, the process of saying whatever comes to mind, no matter how unimportant it seems.

Interpretation   In psychoanalysis, a psychological explanation that the analyst provides in everyday language to patients in order to help them understand their own feelings and behavior.

Resistance   A defense mechanism through which a client evades insight when it is close at hand; for the psychoanalyst, a source of information about the client's underlying motivation.

Transference   The client's projection of unresolved conflicts onto his or her relationship with the psychoanalyst.

having difficulty establishing an enduring relationship with a man. In the course of the therapy, the analyst realized that her client always sought out lovers who were older than she and then became increasingly dependent on them. The relationships seemed to founder because the men were unwilling or unable to "father" her. The analyst attempted a series of interpretations, based on this understanding, but the client didn't seem able to understand or accept them. Eventually the therapist found that her client was becoming increasingly dependent on her, and was able to point out the parallel between this transference relationship and the way the client had tried to relate to her father in her childhood. (Notice that the client had begun treating her female therapist like a father. Transference is not logical, after all.) For the first time, the client recognized the pattern of her behavior; she had a genuine insight. But it was several months of working through before she came to fully understand the implications of that insight and began to change her behavior with men.

Variations on Classical Psychoanalysis   Variations on classical psychoanalysis have emerged for both theoretical and practical reasons. In Chapter 14 we noted that several of Freud's disciples disagreed with his theories and eventually separated from him to begin their own schools of psychoanalysis. However, their therapeutic techniques often varied less than their theories. Both Jung and Adler, for instance, continued to use techniques that focused on understanding unconscious forces. But for Jung those forces involved archetypes; for Adler they were unconscious strivings to overcome inferiority complexes.

In psychoanalysis, the therapist strives to understand and interpret the unconscious sources of the client's problems. Most commonly, clients lie on a couch facing away from the therapist, but many psychoanalytic sessions are conducted face to face, as well.

Practical considerations have also influenced the development of psychoanalysis. Classical psychoanalysis, because of the time and cost involved, is not well suited to the delivery of care to large numbers of troubled people. Accordingly, many therapists, instead of seeing clients five or six times a week, now see their clients less often, sometimes just once a week and sometimes just for a few sessions. These briefer treatments seem to be effective (Goldfried, Greenberg & Marmar, 1990). In addition, psychoanalysis has been adapted to treat groups of clients.

Object relations theory is a recent development in psychoanalysis. Starting with Melanie Klein (1981), some psychoanalysts began focusing on the early relationships children had with their parents, particularly their mothers. Freud had emphasized these relationships, of course, but his focus was on the way in which they affect libidinal development. By contrast, object relations theorists emphasize the way in which these early relationships affect, and are often replayed in, adult relationships with others (Kernberg, 1975).

Humanistic Approaches

In Chapter 14 we noted that humanistic theories were a reaction to the influence of the psychodynamic and behavioral theories, and to the limited role they assigned the individual in controlling his or her behavior. Psychodynamic theories seemed to reduce the individual to a battleground for warring mental factions; behaviorist theories, to a pawn of the environment.

Humanistic psychologists wanted to develop a therapy that emphasized the individual as an integrated human being, a therapy consistent with their belief that people are responsible, that they are capable of seeking help, making decisions, and taking action. In the humanists' view, the therapist's job is not to interpret the client's motivations or to teach the client new behaviors; it is simply to provide a setting in which the client ultimately can solve his or her own problems.

Just as there are schools of psychodynamic therapy, there are schools of humanistic therapy. The most influential has been Carl Rogers's person-centered therapy. Other important approaches include Viktor Frankel's existential analysis and Fritz Perls's Gestalt therapy.

Carl Rogers was one of the most influential humanistic psychologists. He developed a theory of personality, a distinctive type of psychotherapy, and was a pioneer in conducting research on the process and effectiveness of psychotherapy. Later in life, he was one of the leaders of the human potential movement.

Rogers's Person-Centered Therapy   Carl Rogers (1951) believed the most important aspect of humanity is the inherent tendency to *actualize*, to mature and to enrich our lives. He argued that psychological disorders develop when this need to grow is obstructed. Those obstructions arise because, from early childhood on, other people approve or don't approve of the things that we do. Because we all want to be liked and loved, we may take that approval or disapproval of our *actions* to be one of us as *people*. Then we may try to deny natural feelings in ourselves (such as anger and jealousy) simply because we think others won't like us if we have those feelings. The result of this process is that our experience and our self-image become *incongruent,* such that we see ourselves as different than we really are.

Here's an example. A woman is angry with her father. She doesn't show her anger for fear of being rejected, so she denies the feeling and tries to see herself as a person who does not get angry at her parents. Rogers believed that this kind of incongruence is central to most psychological disorders.

The goal of therapy is to help the individual eliminate the obstructions that stand in the way of *congruence*—a self-concept that is in line with the self. Rogers believed that we all have within us the resources to develop and improve ourselves. So the therapist should not try to change the client but, rather, should attempt to create the kind of environment in which the client can realize his or her potential.

According to Rogers, three major elements of the therapist-client relationship make it possible for the client to change:

- First, the therapist must have what Rogers called *unconditional positive regard* for the client, an acceptance that is not contingent on the client's actions, thoughts, or feelings. In other words, the therapist must be nonjudgmental; he or she can disapprove of the client's actions but not of the person.

- Second, the therapist must be genuine, open, and honest about his or her feelings while interacting with the client.
- Third, the therapist must display an accurate empathic understanding. That is, he or she must be able to understand the experience and feelings of the client at each moment in therapy. The objective here is to reflect back to the client, not the content, but the emotion that underlies each statement the client makes (Rogers et al., 1967).

According to Rogers, the moment of change in therapy comes when the client experiences the feelings—the anger or sadness or jealousy—that he or she has been denying in an effort to gain the approval of others.

Person-centered therapy sessions are very different from psychoanalytic sessions. The Rogerian therapist always seems to be tentatively stating the obvious. But this is no accident: it's what is obvious about the client's thoughts and feelings that the client needs to hear affirmed. Here's an exchange between a Rogerian therapist and a female client:

> CLIENT: *It seems to be really apparent to me that I can't depend on someone else to give me an education. [very softly] I'll really have to get it myself.*
>
> THERAPIST: *It really begins to come home—there's only one person that can educate you—a realization that perhaps nobody else can give you an education.*
>
> CLIENT: *Um-hum. [long pause—while she sits thinking] I have all the symptoms of fright. [laughs softly]*
>
> THERAPIST: *Fright: That this is a scary thing, is that what you mean?*
>
> CLIENT: *Um-hum. [very long pause—obviously struggling with feelings in herself]*
>
> THERAPIST: *Do you want to say any more about what you mean by that? That it really does give you the symptoms of fright?*
>
> CLIENT: *[laughs] I, uh . . . I don't know whether I quite know. I mean . . . well, it really seems like I'm cut loose [pause], and it seems that I'm very—I don't know—in a vulnerable position, but I, uh, I brought this up and it, uh, somehow it almost came out without saying it. It seems to be . . . it's something I let out. (Gendlin, 1970, pp. 129–173)*

Notice the humanistic themes in this fragment of therapy. First, the exchange focuses on the client's taking charge of her own life. Second, there's the distinctive Rogerian technique whereby the therapist reflects back to the client the emotional content of each of her statements. Hearing her own feelings and thoughts expressed in a positive way, the client begins to recognize and deal with them.

Carl Rogers made an important contribution to the study and practice of psychotherapy by being the first major theoretician of therapy to tape-record his sessions. Those recordings made it possible for others to hear what he actually did during therapy, rather than just what he said he did. He was also one of the first therapists to conduct extensive research on the effectiveness of psychotherapy (Rogers, 1985).

Existential Therapies   Existentialism is a group of philosophies that flowered in the twentieth century. It acknowledges that people are responsible for making their own decisions, but recognizes that they do so without certain knowledge of what is right or wrong. Its emphasis, then, is on the meaning of life and finding coherence in life.

After the Second World War, with the growing popularity of existential philosophies and writings, many psychotherapists began to combine theories based on existentialism with their therapies. For example, Victor Frankl (1962), like other existentialists, believed that much of modern life is alienating, leaving people feeling deeply alone and adrift. From these feelings stem psychological disorders. Thus, for Frankl, the essential task of psychotherapy is to help people find meaning in their lives.

Another therapist in this group was Fritz Perls (1973), who called his method of treatment *Gestalt therapy*. We talked about Gestalt psychology in Chapter 4, in our discussion of perception. The Gestalt psychologists believed that perceptions are organized into "wholes" (remember that *Gestalt* is the German word for "whole"). Perls extended this thinking to people. He believed that every individual is a potential "whole," an organized network of all of his or her thoughts and feelings and behaviors. By denying certain thoughts or feelings, the individual disrupts the whole. The role of therapy, then, is to help clients become aware of all of their parts and processes. Perls believed, like Rogers, that people have an innate tendency to integrate and actualize themselves; and that, with awareness, this tendency takes over. Perls also believed that the best way to integrate oneself was to focus on what was happening at the present moment. Thus Gestalt therapy deals with how clients are feeling and thinking during the therapy session, not with their past history.

Group Therapy

Many of the psychodynamic and humanistic therapeutic techniques have been adapted for use with groups of people. In these groups, a therapist leads and monitors the group's activities, and may help interpret an individual's behavior. At the same time, the members of the group express their thoughts about one another's problems.

Group therapy is not a systems approach. First of all, the group members do not ordinarily constitute a group except for therapy, and they come together only to work on their individual problems. Furthermore, the theoretical assumption underlying group therapy is that the members are suffering from problems that are individual to each of them.

Its advocates say that group therapy has two advantages. First, it expands the therapist's effectiveness by allowing the therapist to treat more people in the same period of time. Second, many therapists believe that the structure is more effective for some clients because the group gives them a new perspective. Members not only learn that other people have similar problems; they also get a consensus from the group about their own behavior.

Viktor Frankl developed his theory while in a Nazi concentration camp. He observed that he and a few other victims survived when many who seemed stronger died. He attributed the difference to his role as a physician, which gave meaning to his life. He concluded that human beings needed a sense of the meaningfulness of life, even more than adequate food or shelter. He began doing his therapy by helping people find meaning in the camps. After the war, he found that people in everyday life needed meaning in their lives just as much.

Recap

- Insight-oriented therapies assume that psychological disorders arise from the failure to understand oneself, and thus focus on improving that understanding.

- Psychodynamic therapies are based on the idea of intrapsychic conflict.

- The basic goal of psychoanalytic therapy is therapeutic insight, recognizing the unconscious drives that affect behavior. The process of helping a client achieve insight into and work through intrapsychic conflicts is called psychoanalysis.

- In an effort to help his patients gain insight, Freud asked them to free-associate. The role of the therapist at this stage is to make order out of the patient's free associations, to help the patient understand the conflicts that lie behind the patient's symptoms.

- Freud believed that dreams, resistance, and transference are all important sources of information about the individual's psyche.

- Once clients understand the conflicts that underlie their behavior, they have to integrate that understanding into their lives.

- Variations on classical psychoanalysis continue to focus on understanding unconscious forces, but they define those forces differently.

- Humanistic therapies broaden the role of the client. The therapist's job here is simply to provide a setting in which the client ultimately can solve his or her own problems.

- Carl Rogers believed that psychological disorders develop when the individual's need to actualize is obstructed. The goal of his person-centered therapy is congruence, a self-concept that is in line with the true self. To this end, the therapist creates an accepting, emotionally open setting in which the client can realize his or her potential.

- The essential task of existential therapy is to help people discover ways to make their lives meaningful.

- According to Gestalt therapy, a form of existential therapy, the role of therapy is to help clients become aware of all of their parts and processes so that they can organize them into an integrated "whole."

- Group therapy is an adaptation of individual approaches in which the therapist treats a number of individuals simultaneously.

Behavioral Therapies

In practice, the insight-oriented therapies tend to be complex and even a little mysterious because they assume that much of their effectiveness depends on the therapist's sensitivity and ability to discern the truth about the client. In contrast, the basic concepts of behavioral therapies are much simpler and more straightforward.

Behavioral therapies are based on the learning theories of theorists such as Pavlov, Thorndike, Skinner, and especially the cognitive-behaviorists we talked about in Chapters 6 and 14. Behavioral therapists agree with the psychodynamic therapists that psychological disorders stem from the individual's experience. But they disagree with the idea that the best way to treat those disorders is by searching for and understanding unconscious motivations.

Behavioral therapists believe that the symptoms of psychological disorders are simply a special form of learned behavior or feeling or thought. Their goal is to change the unwanted behavior or feeling or thought by using principles of learning. Depending on the nature of the client's problem, these therapists use a variety of techniques—ranging from classical conditioning to directly teaching people new habits of thought.

Techniques from Classical Conditioning

Classical conditioning is the learning that takes place when a response ordinarily elicited by one stimulus comes to be elicited by another stimulus because the two stimuli have been paired (see Chapter 6). Both systematic desensitization and flooding draw on the principles of classical conditioning to treat anxiety disorders.

Puzzle It Out!

How is a phobic person like an animal in an avoidance learning experiment?

Systematic Desensitization   One pioneer of behavioral therapies, Joseph Wolpe (1958), based his therapy on the assumption that anxiety disorders, especially phobias, are caused by classical conditioning. Wolpe reasoned that phobias are the product of the pairing of what was a neutral situation with a frightening situation or stimulus. He believed that people become afraid of social situations, spiders, supermarkets, or elevators because these relatively innocent stimuli have come to elicit anxiety responses through being paired with a terrifying experience.

Remember that classically conditioned responses usually disappear once the pairing of conditioned and unconditioned stimuli stops. When the response is fear, however, the individual avoids the situation and so never learns that it's harmless. A special technique, then, is needed to extinguish fear.

In his behavioral therapy for phobias, Wolpe used a two-part procedure he called **systematic desensitization.** First, the client and therapist work together to construct a hierarchy of feared situations, starting with the most feared and going down to the least feared. Figure 16.1 shows a hierarchy that was constructed by a student being treated for a crippling fear of examinations. The hierarchy proceeds from the most intense stimulus, 1, to the least intense, 14. (Notice that for this student, driving to the examination produces more anxiety than actually sitting down to take the test.)

Figure 16.1
A Hierarchy of Fears

This is a list of fears worked out by Wolpe and a client who was afraid of taking exams. The least feared item is at the end of the list; the most feared at the top. To help the client become less fearful and anxious, Wolpe had the person relax while imagining each item beginning with the last and gradually working up the list to the most terrifying.

1. On the way to the university on the day of an examination.
2. In the process of answering an examination paper.
3. Before the unopened doors of the examination room.
4. Awaiting the distribution of examination papers.
5. While the examination paper lies face down before her.
6. The night before an examination.
7. On the day before an examination.
8. Two days before an examination.
9. Three days before an examination.
10. Four days before an examination.
11. Five days before an examination.
12. A week before an examination.
13. Two weeks before an examination.
14. A month before an examination.

Source: Wolpe & Lazarus, 1966.

The next step is to teach the client a relaxation response. By learning to relax each muscle group in turn, the client is able to induce a deep state of physical and mental relaxation.

Once the hierarchy has been agreed on and the relaxation response learned, the therapist asks the client to relax and then to imagine as vividly as possible the least threatening item on the list. If the client is able to stay relaxed while thinking of that item, the therapist moves on to the next item on the list. If the client begins to feel anxious about one of the more frightening items, the therapist tells the client to stop thinking about that item, to relax, and to move back to a less frightening one. Gradually working up the hierarchy, the client learns to associate relaxation with what used to be frightening situations or objects.

Systematic desensitization   A behavioral therapy, developed by Joseph Wolpe to treat phobias, in which a relaxation response is used to prevent the previous fear response.

The desensitization process can work in the real world, too. For example, programs designed to help people lose their fear of flying gradually move the individual through a hierarchy of flying fears, from packing a suitcase to driving to the airport to eventually taking a short flight.

Flooding   Another technique used by behavioral therapists to treat phobias is **flooding**—a process in which clients are asked to imagine being in the situation that terrifies them most (Boudewyns & Shipley, 1983). For example, the client who constructed the hierarchy in Figure 16.1 might be asked to imagine as vividly as possible that she's driving to school to take an exam. An even more intense version brings the client into the feared situation in real life. In treating a man who fears heights, for instance, the therapist might take him to a high building and spend several hours with him there.

On the surface, flooding seems cruel; and in untrained hands it would be. But when carefully monitored by a skilled therapist, flooding can reduce phobic fears. The prolonged exposure to the feared situation allows the individual to see that it's actually harmless. And, in time, the fear diminishes.

Operant Techniques

Operant conditioning is learning through reinforcement. Several therapeutic techniques use reinforcement to guide and change behavior, especially where more verbal approaches have failed.

Time Out   Operant learning theory argues that all behavior is maintained by reinforcement. Accordingly, to remove an undesired behavior, one must avoid reinforcing it. **Time out** is a way to prevent reinforcement, even when we don't know what the nature of the reinforcement is. This is accomplished by isolating the individual every time the unwanted behavior is exhibited.

One of the striking characteristics of much disordered behavior is that the behavior seems irrational and self-defeating, and so apparently is not rewarded. But behaviorists believe that if the behavior continues, it *is* being reinforced—even though the nature of the reinforcement may not be understood.

Consider the problem behaviors of an eight-year-old named Mike:

> Mike . . . had episodes of severe tantrumming and negativistic behavior both at home and in various other settings including school. . . . Mike's mother . . . reported a long history of difficulty in controlling Mike, more so in public places. A typical episode involved his being allowed to push the shopping cart in a grocery store, whereupon he promptly banged into displays and people. When his mother tried to control his cart, he emitted high-pitched screams. If he became hungry while shopping, he would again scream, cry, roll on the floor, and throw objects off the shelves if not *immediately* fed. . . . At the time of the behavioral assessment, his mother stated that life with Mike was "intolerable, hell on earth." (Ayllon & Skuban, 1973/1977, pp. 377–389)

Both Mike and his mother seemed to be suffering throughout these episodes. So why did they continue? Behaviorists argue that the people in the situation surrounding an unwanted behavior are somehow rewarding the behavior without meaning to do so. Mike, for example, may have been reinforced by his mother's attention to his tantrums.

Although it would be nice to identify the reinforcers in every instance, it's not necessary. Time out can work whether we know what the reinforcer is or not. An unwanted response can be weakened by removing the individual from the social situation whenever the response is made. In Mike's case, time out consisted of putting him in a quiet room by himself every time he threw a

Flooding A behavioral therapy for phobias that asks clients to imagine being in the situation that terrifies them most, or that actually places them in that situation, until the fear subsides.

Time out In behavioral therapy, a program of treatment in which the individual is prevented from receiving reinforcement for an unwanted response by removing the individual from the social situation whenever the response is made.

tantrum. In this way, whatever was reinforcing the tantrum behavior was not being administered. And in time, Mike's tantrums did diminish.

Token Economies   We talked about *token economies,* programs of treatment that reward behavior with tokens that can be exchanged for privileges or treats, in Chapter 6. Token economies are sometimes used to manage residents of chronic-care wards in mental hospitals, most of whom have been diagnosed as schizophrenic.

Some of these people do not feed, clean, or dress themselves; others cannot even go to the toilet by themselves. Staff efforts are devoted to merely keeping the clients alive, and little time can be devoted to rehabilitation. Under these circumstances, any treatment program that improves clients' willingness and ability to care for themselves would greatly improve their lives. One successful program encouraged patients to help care for themselves. The first step was for staff members to stop feeding patients in their rooms. In short order, the patients began coming to the dining room for meals.

> For the therapists, however, this was only the beginning. Their plan was to use meal taking as a privilege—a reward for doing other things. . . . A turnstile was installed at the door of the dining room. Tokens were required to pass through the turnstile. At first the nurses guided the patients through. . . . A little later they handed the patients tokens at the turnstile which the patients themselves deposited. Still later the patients were required to come to the nurses for their tokens. These new demands on the patients were made slowly, but successfully.
>
> The patients were then required to earn their tokens. Each patient was set a few tasks by the nurses and the therapists which, if successfully completed, would produce a token. They centered exclusively on self-maintenance—washing, combing their hair, dressing, going to the bathroom, and the like. The patients performed their tasks readily, and before long the nurses were almost completely freed from the caretaking functions which had occupied most of their time. The patients looked more alert, clean, and active than anyone could remember. (Schwartz, 1984, pp. 252–253)

Reinforcement principles worked with these patients where other therapies had failed. And although the treatment did not "cure" the patients' schizophrenia, it did dramatically improve their behavior.

Punishment   Punishment is another behavioral technique. Remember that punishment weakens a response by taking away something the individual likes or by giving the individual something he or she dislikes (see Chapter 6). The idea is that people stop doing whatever causes them discomfort. Actually, punishment is used very rarely in therapy, and only in certain circumstances and with the client's agreement. One reason punishment is used so rarely is that many learning theorists, especially Skinner, have argued that it is an ineffective means of controlling behavior. As noted in Chapter 6, punishment can rarely be administered quickly, consistently, and severely enough to produce the desired effects.

Cognitive-Behavioral Techniques

The behavioral techniques we've talked about so far do not depend on people's abilities to think and solve problems. In the last few decades, as behaviorist theories have incorporated social and cognitive factors, a number of cognitive-behavioral techniques have been developed; today they play a major role in behavioral therapies. These techniques are behavioral in the sense that they make use of such behaviorist concepts as learning and reinforcement; but they are cognitive in the sense that the things that are learned or reinforced are patterns of thinking, not actual responses.

Modeling   The process of **modeling** is based on the idea that the individual can learn by simply observing a behavior and the consequences of that behavior (Bandura, 1986). You may recall from our discussions of observational learning and development that modeling is a primary source of complex new behaviors.

Sometimes even the therapist serves as a model. For example, in the treatment of some phobias, the therapist moves toward and interacts with the feared object, while the client follows each step (Ladouceur, 1983). In this case, the therapist/model is demonstrating that there is nothing to fear, that there are no bad consequences.

Modeling is also an important part of *social skills training*. Many people who suffer from disorders, especially social anxiety, lack basic social skills. Therapists often teach these skills by modeling appropriate social behaviors themselves and then encouraging their clients to imitate them (Curran, 1981).

Cognitive Restructuring   As the behaviorists began to incorporate cognitive factors into their understanding of learning, a number of them recognized that many disorders center on how people think about themselves and the world. One way to change how people think about themselves is to change how they talk *to* themselves *about* themselves. People who are busy telling themselves that they can't do something obviously aren't going to be able to do it (Meichenbaum, 1977).

Suppose every time you begin to read this textbook, you say to yourself, "I can't understand this. Psychology is too hard for me. I'm going to flunk." You certainly would have a hard time paying attention to the book. The solution is to change the way you think, to say something like, "It seems difficult, but if I work at it, I can master it." A number of therapies focus on changing cognition in this general way.

One, developed by Albert Ellis (1962), is called **rational-emotive therapy.** Ellis insists that many psychological disorders are caused by common but irrational beliefs. An example: thinking that everyone you know has to love you or approve of you. Obviously, this is impossible. But the more strongly you believe it, the more likely you are to feel unhappy, and the greater the risk of your choosing self-defeating behavior in what can only be an unsuccessful attempt to be loved. Ellis's therapy is very direct and combative. He often argues with clients, pointing out contradictions in their thinking and the foolishness of these kinds of beliefs.

Aaron Beck (1976) also believes that psychological disorders arise from faulty thinking. Beck is best known for his therapy for depression, which focuses on the spiraling effects of depression on the way people think about themselves. As we noted in our discussions of memory and the origin of psychological disorders, he argues that being depressed makes it difficult to remember happy experiences or to think positively about oneself, thus increasing the depression. One of the most important of Beck's therapeutic techniques focuses on teaching clients to say positive things to themselves, rather than the negative, self-defeating kinds of self-talk that is their custom.

An Overview of Behavioral Therapies

At one time, behavioral therapies were clearly distinct from the insight-oriented therapies because they were so firmly rooted in classical learning theory. More recently, as thoughts and feelings have been incorporated into the behavioral

Modeling In behavioral therapy, a program of treatment in which a wanted response is strengthened or an unwanted response is weakened by using a model to demonstrate the behavior and the consequences of the behavior.

Rational-emotive therapy Treatment method in which client's irrational beliefs are challenged and alternatives to them are provided; developed by Albert Ellis.

therapies, the differences have begun to blur. But they still exist. Cognitive behavioral approaches tend to focus more narrowly on the individual's particular problem and the context in which that problem occurs. Cognitive therapists also tend to be more concerned with the experimental underpinnings of their therapies. Although they often use the success of a therapy as evidence of the accuracy of the theory it rests on, they also have invested heavily in studying the techniques of their therapies.

Recap

- Behavioral therapies assume that psychological disorders are a special form of learned behavior or feeling or thought, and their goal is to change the unwanted behavior or feeling or thought by using principles of learning.

- Both systematic desensitization and flooding draw on the principles of classical conditioning to treat anxiety disorders.

- Time out and token economies are operant techniques that use reinforcement to guide and change behavior.

- Cognitive-behavioral therapies use modeling and cognitive restructuring to change behavior.

Systems Approaches

Systems approaches to psychological disorders are based on the idea that the individual's problems are expressions of disturbances in the group—the system—to which the individual belongs. According to these approaches, it's the family or some other group, or even the community, that's functioning poorly, not necessarily the individual.

Family Systems Therapies

Family systems therapies focus on the structure of the individual's family. Consider the following case (modeled on Minuchin, 1974).

> Bobby R., a six-year-old, is referred to a clinic because he is experiencing severe anxiety, accompanied by attacks of asthma, every morning when he goes to school.

How should Bobby be treated? Insight-oriented therapists might explore Bobby's fears of separation from his parents. Behavioral therapists might explore the events that take place each morning to see how Bobby is being reinforced for exhibiting anxious behavior. And therapists using a biological approach would probably prescribe medication for the child's asthma and perhaps a drug to relieve his anxiety.

But suppose the case report goes on to say:

> Bobby is brought into the clinic by his mother and father, and an interview is held with all three present. After the therapist obtains a history of Bobby's symptoms and how and when they appear, he asks about the family's home life. It turns out that with Bobby in school all day, Mrs. R. feels that "it's time" for her to go back to work. Mr. R., whose father always said, "It's the man's job to earn the money," is uneasy about his wife leaving the house. As the therapist continues to probe, it becomes evident that Bobby's parents have a substantial continuing disagreement over this and related issues. They begin to argue, and as they do, Bobby's breathing grows labored and he begins to wheeze. The parents turn to him to see what's the matter and ask if he is all right. As the focus shifts to the child, the parents' arguing gradually stops.

What's going on here? A family systems therapist would argue that even though it's Bobby who has the symptoms (anxiety and asthma), the problem is not primarily with Bobby as an individual but with the **family system** of which he is a part. Even though Bobby may have been born with an organic predisposition to asthma, his symptoms now come and go with the family situation around him. To help Bobby, the therapist would have to find out what function Bobby's symptoms play in the family system. Only then could the reasons for Bobby's behavior be understood.

The interview tells us that the R. family exhibits a particular pattern of interaction: when the parents start to argue, Bobby's symptoms get worse; and when Bobby's symptoms get worse, the parents forget their own conflict and focus on him. In short, Bobby's symptoms serve a purpose in the family: they help maintain the family's equilibrium. By focusing on Bobby, the parents are distracted from their disagreements and stop fighting.

Family systems therapists would say that as long as the family's pattern of interaction doesn't change, Bobby's symptoms are unlikely to change, no matter how much individual treatment (whether psychodynamic, humanistic, behavioral, or biological)—he receives. Furthermore, they would say that if someone *did* manage to cure Bobby's symptoms, the family would find another way to protect its structure.

Notice that a family systems perspective takes a very different view of the actual disorder. It's not just that there's a marital conflict in the family. And it's not just that Bobby is reinforced for certain behaviors. It's that the family system *as a whole* reacts badly to stress—the stress in this instance being Bobby's going to school, Mrs. R.'s desire to return to work, and Mr. R's attitudes about her working.

There are several different kinds of family systems therapies, but all share five basic assumptions (Gurman & Kniskern, 1981):

Family system The aggregate of people, property, relationships, rights, responsibilities, expectations, and traditions that constitute a family.

1. The parts of the family are interrelated.
2. One part of the family cannot be understood in isolation from the rest of the system.
3. Family functioning cannot be fully understood simply by understanding each of its parts.
4. The family's structure and organization play an important role in determining the behavior of family members.
5. Patterns of interaction within the family system shape the behavior of family members.

A good example of this approach was developed by Salvador Minuchin (1974) in what he calls *structural family therapy*. The object of the therapy is to change the experiences of family members by changing the structure of the family and the ways in which family members interact.

Part of Minuchin's work has involved families in which a child suffers from a psychophysiological disorder (such as asthma or diabetes) or an eating disorder (such as anorexia nervosa). Physical disorders that are aggravated by psychological factors were previously called "psychosomatic," and for that reason Minuchin calls these families *psychosomatic families*. Notice that he talks about the *family*, not the child or the disorder. What he's saying is that the disorder is not just the child's; rather, it's the family structure that produces the disorder, and everybody, including the child, plays a part (Minuchin, Rosman & Baker, 1978).

Minuchin sees the boundaries within a family as one of the critical elements of any family system, disordered or not. Those boundaries establish the responsibilities and prerogatives of each family member within the spouse subsystem or sibling subsystem. In healthy families, boundaries are clearly defined: each person knows his or her "place," but all are related to each other. In some disordered families, however, the boundaries aren't clear, making it hard to tell the adults and children apart. In these *enmeshed* families, the children (particularly the child with the problem) tend to be involved in their parents' conflicts. And the parents—like Bobby's mother and father—use the child's problem to avoid confronting their own marital problems, a behavior Minuchin called *detouring*. At the other extreme are families in which the members are *disengaged*, so that they have too little involvement in each others' lives.

Because family systems therapists believe it's important to understand how the family system functions as a whole, some insist on having the whole family present during therapy sessions so that the therapist can observe the members of the group interacting. For example, when meeting a family with a child who has an eating disorder, Minuchin typically schedules the interview at lunch so that he can see how the family interacts at mealtimes.

Other family systems therapists feel that it's the systems approach, not the number and identities of the people attending, that defines a family systems therapy session. The systems approach can be used with just one family member if the focus of the therapy is on "the way in which the one person contributes to maintaining the family's repetitive interactions" (Szapocznik et al., 1986, p. 396).

The Community Mental Health Movement

Family systems therapy expanded the focus of treatment from the individual to a small social organization. The community mental health movement works with larger structures: institutions and communities.

During the 1960s and 1970s, groups of mental health professionals became disillusioned with conventional treatment approaches especially with hospitalization, which was routine for serious disorders. In the 1960s especially, the care

and treatment of patients in psychiatric hospitals received a great deal of criticism. Stories of inadequate budgets, poor care, minimal treatment, and a general feeling of hopelessness among patients were common. In addition, many patients seemed to have adjusted too successfully to being in a hospital; they were simply unable to leave.

The solution seemed obvious: **deinstitutionalization.** Instead of confining people to hospitals and sanitoriums, let them live in the community, among healthy people, and provide treatment there. Near family, friends, and opportunities for employment, deinstitutionalized patients could be reintegrated into the community.

With the help of federal aid, new community mental health centers began to blossom all over the country. The basic goal of these centers was to provide for all the mental health needs of a particular community. The services would extend beyond traditional hospital treatment, to include outpatient services, alcohol and drug abuse programs, and much more. More important, these centers would establish programs to prevent psychological disorders by identifying and improving unhealthy conditions in the community (Cowen, 1983).

Has it worked? Certainly there was a major reduction in the number of patients hospitalized in institutions that were designed for long-term care (see Figure 16.2). Between 1969 and 1981, the average number of psychiatric inpatients in the United States fell from approximately 469,000 to 211,000. In roughly the same period, the median length of stay in county and state mental hospitals dropped from forty-one days to twenty-three days. And there were 53 percent fewer psychiatric beds available in 1982 than in 1970 (Taube & Barrett, 1985).

But these effects were only partly a product of the community mental health movement. Much more important factors have been the increasing use of drug therapies and changes in the law that have made involuntary commitment more difficult.

In large measure, the promise of care in the context of the community has actually not been met. The literature suggests that half of deinstitutionalized patients receive little or no psychiatric care (Iscoe & Harris, 1984). And those who do are more often than not treated by family practice doctors or other primary-care physicians in the general health sector (Jones & Knopke, 1987).

Prior to the 1960s, most people with serious psychological disorders were treated in mental hospitals. Most of these institutions were far from the patients' homes and provided little treatment. Moreover, conditions were often depressing. Community mental health centers were intended to provide better and more efficient services in the person's own community; people were much less likely to be confined to hospitals for long periods of time. But treatment in the community was rarely available, and many people with serious disorders became, instead, homeless "street people." This situation prevails today.

Deinstitutionalization The practice of releasing chronic mental patients from large mental hospitals to transitional institutions, in the process of reintegrating them into the larger community.

Figure 16.2
Declining Population of Mental Hospitals

The number of people confined to mental hospitals has plummeted drastically since the peak in the mid-1950s. The decline began with the introduction of drugs that dramatically reduced the symptoms of schizophrenia. Continued development of drug therapies for the most serious disorders and changes in legal procedures for involuntary hospitalization have contributed to the trend.

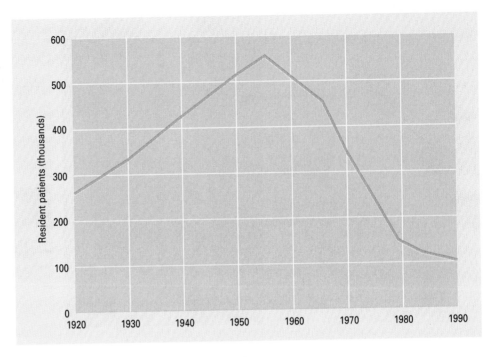

Source: Data from the National Institute of Mental Health.

One consequence of the lack of specialized outpatient care is that outpatient admissions to psychiatric hospitals and wards more than doubled between 1969 and 1979. Also, more than 70 percent of all admissions to psychiatric wards and hospitals are now patients who have previously been hospitalized (Taube & Barrett, 1985). Figure 16.3 shows the shift from mental hospitals to general hospitals for patient care.

Where are all the deinstitutionalized patients living? Many have simply been transferred to other forms of institutions—to private hospitals or nursing homes, for example. Others live more or less permanently in halfway houses,

Figure 16.3
Changing Locations for Psychiatric Hospitalization

Part of the decline in the mental hospital population is an illusion, produced by a shift in the location of treatment. As the number of people in mental hospitals has declined, the number treated in general medical hospitals has increased.

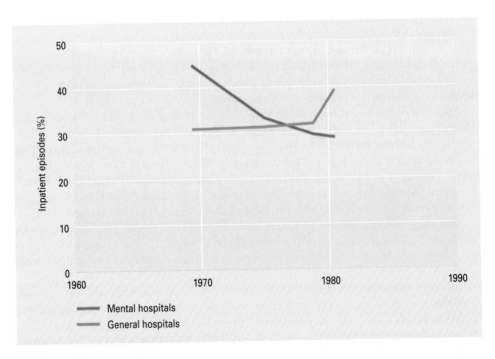

Source: Data from the National Institute of Mental Health.

residences that were intended to be temporary and to facilitate rapid reintegration into the community. Still others have joined the increasing number of people living on the streets. In fact, the problems associated with homelessness are one reason we're seeing a reaction against deinstitutionalization. For instance, New York City has hired a team of mental health professionals to evaluate people who've been deinstitutionalized to determine who should be put back into hospitals (Stengel, 1987; Hornblower, 1987). It seems we are moving back into an era of institutional care for psychiatric patients.

Why did the community mental health movement fail? One reason was that just as it was beginning, the Vietnam War began to make increasing demands on the federal budget. Fewer than half of the projected community mental health centers were ever built, and sufficient resources have never been committed to the care of the seriously psychologically disordered.

Although the community mental health movement did not yield the expected outcome, it did focus public attention on legitimate problems associated with the care of people who are mentally ill. Overcrowding in mental hospitals, lack of individualized treatment, the isolation of patients, and care that is not responsive to the needs of certain groups are problems that still must be addressed.

Recap

- Systems approaches to psychological disorders are based on the idea that the individual's problems are expressions of disturbances in the groups—the systems—to which the individual belongs.

- Family systems therapy focuses on the structure of the individual's family.

- According to family systems therapists, the individual's behavior cannot change as long as the family's pattern of interaction does not change.

- According to Salvador Minuchin, the boundaries in healthy families are clearly defined; they are not well defined in disordered families.

- The community mental health movement was a response to the routine hospitalization of mental patients and to the conditions in institutions providing long-term care.

- The goal of the community mental health movement was deinstitutionalization, the reintegration of patients into the community through programs of psychiatric and social services.

- Throughout the 1970s, the number of psychiatric patients in institutions and hospitals in the United States dramatically diminished, as did the average stay in mental hospitals. But only a small part of this shift can be attributed to the community mental health movement.

- The failure of the community mental health movement was in large part a product of new priorities in the government.

Biological Approaches

In Chapter 15 we talked about the evidence that biological factors contribute to psychological disorders. Many of the treatments we describe here are directed at those biological factors.

Prior to the introduction of psychoactive drugs, mental hospitals were often very chaotic places. Severely disturbed people often behaved in bizarre ways, and the staff of those institutions were unable to do more than keep some order and provide minimal care. This woodcut of a women's day room in a nineteenth century insane asylum provides a sense of the ineffectiveness of those early institutions and treatment methods.

As we discuss the three broad types of biological therapies—drugs, electroconvulsive therapy, and surgery—you'll notice that we keep saying that the mechanisms by which the treatments work are unclear. This is generally true. For the most part, these therapies have been discovered more or less by accident, not through the systematic examination of the role of brain chemistry and physiology in psychological disorders.

Furthermore, most of the biological treatments are not "cures." Although they relieve some of the worst symptoms of certain disorders, they bypass others. This is not to say that biological treatments are not useful. They certainly are. At the very least, they make life easier. And with their help, some patients eventually make full recoveries, even from the worst disorders.

Pharmacological Treatments

Since the early 1960s, drug therapies have come into widespread use and are now an integral part of the treatment of psychological disorders. In fact, drugs are the most common form of treatment for all psychological disorders, and they have revolutionized the treatment of the most severe mental disorders.

Most drugs are used to treat a specific disorder. Table 16.1 lists the major drug treatments and the disorders for which they're prescribed.

Antianxiety Drugs   A family of drugs called **tranquilizers** alleviate the symptoms of anxiety. The most common tranquilizers are the benzodiazepines, which include Librium and Valium. These drugs seem to work by increasing the release of the neurotransmitter GABA, which generally has an inhibitory effect on nerve cells. Accordingly, the drugs tend to lower the level of activity in the relevant systems (Insell, 1986).

Although tranquilizers are relatively mild in comparison to some other drugs, their use does carry serious risk. In particular, they are often overprescribed and abused. In 1979, an estimated 3 million Americans were addicted to tranquilizers (Hughs & Brewin, 1979). Yet despite their addictive properties, these drugs have been prescribed for "a huge range of ills with a casualness unequaled by any other group of prescription drugs" (Melville & Johnson, 1982).

Tranquilizers A family of drugs that reduce the symptoms of anxiety.

Category	Generic Name	Brand Name
Antianxiety drugs	Meprobamate	Miltown, Equanil
	Chlordiazepoxide	Librium
	Diazepam	Valium
	Clomipramine	Anafranil
	Alprozolam	Xanac
Antipsychotic drugs	Chlorpromazine	Thorazine
	Trifluoperazine	Stelazine
	Thioxanthene	Haldol
		Prolixin
	Clozapine	Clozaril
Antidepressants	Phenelzine	Nardil
	Isocarboxazid	Marplan
	Tranylcypromine	Parnate
	Imipramine	Tofranil
	Doxepin	Sinequan
	Amitriptyline	Elavil
	Fluoxetine	Prozac
Antimanic drugs	Lithium	Eskalith

Source: Adapted from Sue, Sue & Sue, 1990.

Table 16.1
The Major Drug Treatments for Psychological Disorders

Antidepressants   Two separate families of drug treatments are used for major depression and for bipolar disorder. The **antidepressants**, such as the MAO (monamine oxydase) inhibitors and the tricyclics, are used to treat the profound sadness and withdrawal that are symptoms of chronic major depression. Currently, the most popular antidepressant drug is Prozac, a member of a third family of drugs, the tetracyclics. These drugs appear to increase the production of noradrenalin, and may also act on dopamine and serotonin (Georgotas, 1985). In short, they seem to excite circuits that energize the brain and quiet circuits that slow it down.

All of the antidepressants have side effects, ranging from fatigue, dry mouth, and blurred vision to impotence and tremors. People who are taking MAO inhibitors must follow dietary restrictions: they cannot eat cheese or other foods that are aged; nor can they drink wine or eat chocolate. Patients who don't follow these diet restrictions run the risk of a catastrophic rise in blood pressure, which in turn can cause intracranial bleeding, severe headaches, sweating, nausea, and vomiting.

A different treatment is used for bipolar disorder. One of the most striking successes attained with drugs has been the treatment of bipolar disorder with **lithium.** Remember that people who suffer from bipolar disorder experience wild mood swings between depression and mania. In 1949, researchers accidentally discovered that the chemical element lithium greatly reduces the severity and frequency of mood swings in both directions (Cade, 1949) and completely prevents the symptoms in two-thirds of patients (Janicak & Bushes, 1987). We don't know how the drug works, but it does have potential for serious side effects if the patient is not carefully monitored.

Antipsychotic Drugs   Yet another group of drugs—the **antipsychotic drugs**—are used to treat the symptoms of schizophrenia. The primary effect of these drugs is to ease delusions and hallucinations; however, they have very little effect on the "negative" symptoms of schizophrenia—the failure to respond emotionally or the social isolation that is symptomatic of the disorder. The antipsy-

Antidepressants A group of drugs used to treat the symptoms of chronic depression.

Lithium A mineral that has been highly successful in the treatment of patients with bipolar disorder.

Antipsychotic drugs A group of drugs that reduce or stop the delusions and hallucinations that are symptomatic of schizophrenia.

chotic drugs seem to work by affecting the sensitivity of the dopamine system, but the exact mechanisms are still unclear.

The first widely used antipsychotic drug was chlorpromazine (marketed under the name Thorazine), which was developed in 1952. Chlorpromazine is one of the phenothiazines. Although these drugs are helpful, they can cause some very serious side effects. The worst of these is *tardive dyskinesia,* a condition that afflicts about 20 percent of the people who have taken phenothiazines for many years (Kane et al., 1986). The patients develop irreversible neurological problems, including uncontrolled movements of their faces and difficulty walking. For this reason, other drugs—among them Haldol and Clozapine—are replacing chlorpromazine in the treatment of schizophrenia.

Although drugs are not a "cure" for schizophrenia, they have played a part in reducing the number of long-term patients in mental hospitals. By reducing the number of schizophrenic episodes and minimizing hallucinations and delusions, antipsychotic drugs have enabled many patients to move back into the community. The discovery that patients thought to be incurable could be helped with drugs changed mental hospitals from institutions with an essentially custodial function to institutions concerned with therapy and rehabilitation.

Drugs to Combat Hyperactivity   *Attention-deficit hyperactivity disorder* (Whalen & Henker, 1980) is a disorder of childhood in which the child (most often a boy) is extremely active physically and has great difficulty maintaining attention, particularly in school. Paradoxically, this hyperactivity is often treated with a stimulant, Ritalin, which has the effect of calming children who are hyperactive and increasing their ability to focus attention.

Like other psychoactive drugs, Ritalin can have side effects, including nausea, insomnia, weight loss, and reduction in growth (Salholz, 1987). In recent years, moreover, controversy has surrounded its use. According to some physicians, psychologists, and parents, Ritalin is being given to children without attention problems just to keep them manageable.

Electroconvulsive Therapy

Electroconvulsive therapy (ECT)—what you probably think of as shock treatment—is not a punishment; it's a treatment for serious psychological disorders. A current of electricity is passed through the patient's cortex for just a second. The current triggers a convulsion similar to an epileptic seizure, which continues for several seconds after the current is turned off. During the seizure, electrical activity in the patient's brain is disrupted and he or she loses consciousness. Upon awakening, the patient does not remember the treatment or the events immediately surrounding the treatment.

In the 1930s and 1940s, before the discovery of the antipsychotic drugs, there were no treatments for serious disorders such as schizophrenia and severe depression. During this period, ECT was used extensively to treat many disorders. But with the development of psychoactive drugs, ECT came to be used much less frequently. Its use today is restricted almost exclusively to people who are severely depressed and who have not responded to antidepression drug treatments (Weiner, 1985).

The reason ECT is still used is that it does seem to improve depression. In a recent study of patients with depression, over a twelve-year period, 70 percent of those given ECT exhibited "marked improvement" (Black, Winokur & Nasrallah, 1987). ECT apparently improves not only mood but also the disturbances of sleep, eating, and sexual behavior that often go hand in hand with chronic depression (Fink, 1979). We still don't understand why ECT works, but the evidence is clear that it does so in cases of severe depression.

Electroconvulsive therapy (ECT) The use of electric current to generate a kind of seizure that alleviates some of the symptoms of severe chronic depression.

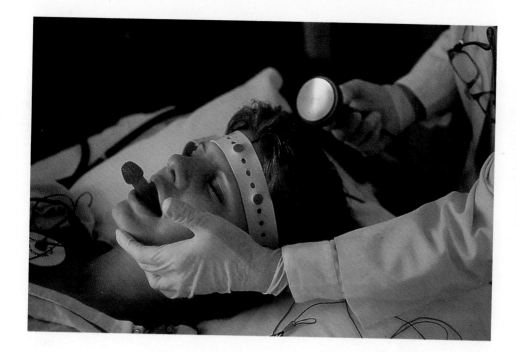

Before a patient undergoes ECT, anaesthesia and muscle relaxants are administered to reduce both the patient's discomfort and the risk of harm from the seizure. One or two electrodes are placed on the skull and a current of about 140 volts is administered for a period of 0.6 to 1.25 seconds. This produces something like an epileptic seizure, which lasts for 25 to 30 seconds (Weiner, 1985).

ECT does have potential side effects. In the early days, the patient ran all the risks of a seizure, including heart failure, bone breakage, and choking. But by carefully screening patients for heart conditions and through the use of muscle relaxants, anesthesia, and other refinements, psychiatrists have minimized these hazards.

Yet other side effects remain. Temporary or even permanent loss of memory for events around the time of treatment seems to be an unavoidable consequence of ECT. And even more frightening for the patient is the fact that a treatment can impair the ability to form new memories for several weeks. Finally, personality changes can develop after several treatments. Confusion, disorientation, and passivity may become more evident as the treatments are repeated (Taylor & Carroll, 1987).

Because of these potential side effects, ECT remains a treatment of last resort. Nevertheless, as many as 100,000 patients undergo the treatment in an average year (Bower, 1985). Most of these patients are severely depressed people for whom ECT is their last hope.

Psychosurgery

The most drastic biological treatment of mental illness is **psychosurgery**, surgery on the brain. *Prefrontal lobotomy,* the only kind of psychosurgery to have been widely practiced, is no longer performed. In this operation, the connections between the prefrontal lobes and subcortical areas of the brain, especially the thalamus, are severed. The procedure was usually performed on people who were diagnosed as schizophrenic and considered incurable. It was supposed to eliminate violent behaviors.

Although the theoretical rationale for the prefrontal lobotomy was weak, the procedure was performed during the 1940s with astonishing frequency, perhaps as many as a thousand each year. It was used for illnesses as diverse as schizophrenia, depression, and obsessive-compulsive disorders. In the era before antipsychotic drugs, many disorders, especially schizophrenia, were so awful that this kind of extreme treatment seemed justified. And because the surgical procedure was fairly simple, the operation could be performed quickly. But despite

Psychosurgery An operation performed on the brain to control a patient's behavior or experience.

Egaz Moniz, a Portuguese neurologist, won a Nobel Prize for his work on the frontal lobotomy. He was later shot by one of his lobotomized patients. His fate seemed an appropriate, if ironic, commentary on the wisdom of the treatment he invented.

the early wave of enthusiasm for lobotomies, it soon became clear that they were not a reliable form of treatment. Although some symptoms were alleviated in many patients, other symptoms, such as hallucinations, were not. In addition, the side effects—including apathy and a total loss of initiative—were both unpredictable and very much unwanted. Eventually, as antipsychotic drugs came into use, lobotomies were no longer performed.

Prefrontal lobotomies may be a thing of the past, but there is ongoing discussion as to whether other forms of psychosurgery might someday be used to help treat intractable personality disorders. Studies of animals suggest that parts of the limbic system play a major role in mediating emotion, aggression, and hostility. Based on these findings, some experts have experimented with the use of psychosurgery on hospitalized patients with long-term records of unpredictable violence or sexual delinquency (Donnelly, 1985). But these experimental procedures have been vigorously opposed on ethical grounds (Rodin, 1987; Lowinger, 1987), and it seems unlikely that they will come into widespread use.

Recap

- Although at present, most biological therapies don't really cure psychological disorders, they can play an important role in the patient's recovery.

- In the last thirty years, drug therapies have come into widespread use and are now an integral part of the treatment of psychological disorders.

- Most drugs are used to treat a specific disorder.

- All drugs—including those used to treat psychological disorders—involve the risk of serious side effects.

- By triggering a seizure, electroconvulsive therapy alleviates some of the symptoms of severe chronic depression.

- Prefrontal lobotomy, the only kind of psychosurgery that has ever been widely practiced, is no longer performed.

Matching Treatments and Disorders

At the beginning of this chapter, we said that the different therapies are not rivals; indeed, most treatment regimens use two or more of them at a given time. But certain therapies are commonly employed with certain disorders. For example, the insight-oriented therapies are used most often in the treatment of anxiety disorders, somatoform disorders, and dissociative disorders; they are used less often to treat schizophrenia. The behavioral therapies are used for many of the same disorders and are particularly effective in treating phobias and other anxiety disorders. And some of the cognitive-behavioral therapies were designed especially to treat chronic depression.

Family systems therapies are often used to treat eating disorders, somatoform disorders, and adjustment problems within the family. And drug therapies work remarkably well with certain symptoms of schizophrenia, whereas psychotherapy and systems approaches don't have the same effect.

These associations between treatments and disorders reflect general inclinations, not firm rules or even guidelines. Indeed, they raise the question we now turn to: How well do the various therapies work?

The Process of Evaluation

We've talked about a wide variety of treatment approaches. And we've said that these different approaches are not simply different practices but, in fact, completely different ways of looking at people and their problems. It's not surprising, then, that psychologists have tried to find ways to compare and evaluate the different therapies—sometimes to show that therapy is better than nothing, and sometimes to show that some therapies are more effective than others. This kind of research is beset with serious methodological problems.

Despite these methodological difficulties, many attempts have been made to judge the effectiveness of therapies. Early reviews of this research suggested that psychotherapies aren't particularly effective. Hans Eysenck (1952) created a furor when he compared the results of two studies of untreated clients with twenty-four studies of clients treated by psychoanalysis or psychotherapy, and concluded that the clients who were *not* treated improved more than the clients who were! As you might imagine, these findings generated numerous rebuttals and counterarguments among psychotherapists (for example, see Luborsky, 1954). Some subsequent studies, however, supported Eysenck's findings (Bergin 1971; Rachman, 1971).

The result of this controversy was a storm of research that was better designed. The results of this research, though complex, generally seemed to show that psychotherapy does help people after all (Luborsky, Singer & Luborsky, 1975).

Meta-Analysis

Eventually the volume of research grew so large that interpreting it became very difficult. This difficulty was solved in part with **meta–analysis,** a sophisticated technique in which statistical methods are used to combine the results of many studies into one set of conclusions.

Meta-analysis A statistical technique that combines the results of many studies into one set of conclusions.

How Do We Know That?

Psychologists face several problems in trying to evaluate therapies. The most obvious is defining the criteria of success. Who is going to judge whether a client is better or worse? The therapist? Surely the therapist has a vested interest in thinking his or her treatment was a success. Independent judges? Any outside person is going to be a poor judge of the pain that the client was feeling when the therapy started. The client? Certainly the customer's satisfaction is a useful criterion in evaluating a washing machine, but is it appropriate with a psychological therapy? For instance, would we call a therapy for alcoholism successful because the client is now able to drink without guilt? Probably not. What about the client's friends and relatives? Like the therapist, they may have personal reasons for believing the client is sick or healthy. Ultimately, we have to use many different measures and check carefully to see what different kinds of effects the therapy has had.

An additional problem emerges when we try to compare different treatments because they often have different definitions of success. A behaviorist might be satisfied that a phobia of public speaking has been cured once the client has made a speech in front of a large group of people. But what about insight-oriented therapists, who see the fear as an expression of intrapsychic conflict or the inability to accept one's real self? To these latter therapists, the simple removal of the fear doesn't mean that the basic problem has been solved.

To some extent, the solution to the criteria problem is also a solution to this one. If we use many different measures, then some can fit each perspective. We might expect to find that clients treated by one set of techniques would be improved by the standards of that theory, but not by the standards of a different theory. That is, each kind of therapy might have different effects. So we might have to conclude that the therapeutic techniques differed in terms of which effects they produced, not in terms of how large the effects were.

Meta-analysis has dramatically changed the process of interpreting therapeutic research. In one meta-analysis of the outcomes of psychotherapy, the researchers were able to examine 475 separate controlled studies of psychotherapy outcome and 90 studies of drug therapy outcome (Smith, Glass & Miller, 1980). From their analyses, they reached four general conclusions:

1. When all of the different kinds of psychotherapy are considered as a group, psychotherapy is "unequivocally" effective.
2. Different types of psychotherapy (for example, client-centered therapies, psychoanalysis, or behavioral therapies) do not produce different types or degrees of benefit.
3. When psychotherapy is compared to drug therapy for all major mental disorders, psychotherapy is about equally effective.
4. Differences in the way therapy is conducted (individually or in a group, long term or short term) make no difference in the outcome of the therapy.

The first two conclusions have attracted the most attention. First of all, it's reassuring to find that psychotherapy is effective. But for most therapists, the finding that different kinds of therapy are equally effective was more disturbing. Nevertheless, this conclusion has been confirmed by a number of related studies, conducted to investigate it.

Puzzle It Out!

One explanation for the fact that all treatments are about equally successful is that some do one thing, some another. Even therapists themselves sometimes argue that they have different goals. What effects do you think different treatments have? Consider a psychodynamic therapy, a humanistic therapy, a cognitive-behavioral therapy, and a drug treatment. If you were feeling stressed out, what sorts of effects would you expect from these different kinds of treatment? Should this expectation have any bearing on the kinds of treatment you choose?

For example, other meta-analyses of other groups of studies have found similar results. In addition, psychotherapy has been found to be effective with children; but here, too, few differences among the types were found (Casey & Berman, 1985; Kazdin, 1990; Weisz et al., 1987). The same is true of therapies for alcoholism (Nathan & Skinstad, 1987) and, with perhaps a less substantial research base, for family systems therapies for a variety of problems (Hazelrigg, Cooper & Borduin, 1987). In all of these different reviews of different kinds of therapies and for different groups, the same conclusions emerge: therapy works, and no therapy seems clearly better than any other.

The third conclusion of the study by Smith, Glass & Miller (1980)—that psychological therapies are comparable to drug treatments—is also important. In fact, for at least one disorder, psychotherapy has been shown to be superior. A meta-analysis of fifty-six outcome studies of drug therapy and psychotherapy found psychotherapy to be preferable in the treatment of unipolar depression in adults (Steinbruek, Maxwell & Howard, 1983).

The same conclusions were drawn recently in one of the most elaborate and careful studies of psychotherapy outcome ever performed (Elkin et al., 1990). In this study of treatment for depression, a psychodynamic therapy, a cognitive-behavioral therapy, and a standard drug treatment for depression were compared to one another and to a no-treatment control. The result was that all three treatments were equally effective, and all subjects showed significant improvement compared to untreated control subjects.

What does this result mean? If all treatments are equally successful, what produces the change? One possibility, common to all treatments (or at least to all the psychotherapies), is that most therapists provide support and reassurance. In most cases, therapist and client agree to work together in a "therapeutic alliance," which in itself may make the client feel more in control (Goldfried, Greenberg & Marmar, 1990). Another possibility takes into account the origins of psychological disorders. If disorders stem from multiple factors, then it makes sense that different kinds of treatment work equally well, each by its own methods.

Recap

- Although different therapies tend to be used more or less often to treat different disorders, the associations between therapies and disorders are not rules or even guidelines.

- The process of evaluating therapies has focused on the effectiveness of treatment versus no treatment, and on the effectiveness of one treatment versus others.

- There are serious methodological problems involved in designing a study to gauge the effectiveness of a therapy.

- Although early reviews of research on psychotherapies suggested that they aren't particularly effective, later, better-designed studies indicated that psychotherapies do work.

- Meta-analysis allows researchers to compare the findings of a large number of research studies.

- Psychologists explain the comparable effects of different therapies by pointing to a factor most share—the therapist's support—and to the multidimensional sources of psychological disorders.

Finding a Therapist

Nearly 20 percent of Americans have a diagnosable psychological disorder and might seek a therapist. Many people who do not have a disorder also consult therapists. So the odds are very high that you or someone you know well is going to want to consult a mental health professional for treatment at some time. Table 16.2 lists several different kinds of therapists. How do you choose among them?

The research on therapy outcomes suggests a simple rule to follow when choosing a therapist: look for a therapist with whom you feel comfortable. Of course, talking about your troubles to a stranger is never going to be easy. But it's important that you and your therapist be compatible (Bateman, 1988; Orlinsky & Howard, 1986). Study after study has shown that the client's involvement in the therapy process is crucial to the success of the process (Gomes-Schwartz, 1978). Study after study has shown that successful therapy rests on the client's perception that the therapist is empathic, understanding, and accepting (Rogers, 1961; Truax & Carkhuff, 1967). And study after study has shown that compatibility between therapist and client is helpful to the therapy process (Garfield & Bergin, 1986).

People sometimes wonder if it's a good idea to choose a therapist of the same sex, race, or ethnic identity as oneself. It is if you think it is. If these factors are going to promote a good working relationship between you and your therapist, then by all means consider them. But if you're comfortable working with a person of the opposite sex, or of another race or ethnic identity, then ignore these factors in your choice of a therapist. The evidence does not suggest that ethnic or racial similarity between therapist and client promotes a good therapy outcome (Sue, 1988).

In summary, the best advice in choosing a therapist is to visit one and see if you can form a good working relationship with that person. If you can, all is well and good. If you can't, explain the problem to the therapist; he or she may be able to get the therapy back on the right track or help you find a therapist who better suits your particular needs. Or, if you really feel out of touch with your therapist, you can quit and find another yourself. Don't be too concerned about the therapist's feelings. Therapists are well aware that the "fit" between therapist and client is crucial to the success of treatment, and they are accustomed to having clients come and go in their search for a satisfying therapeutic relationship.

How do you get started? Most colleges and universities maintain a mental health clinic or counseling center. If the people at these facilities cannot help, they can refer you to somebody who can. Or you might accept the recommendation of a friend who has had a good experience with a therapist, or ask your family doctor or clergyman to recommend someone.

Table 16.2
Mental Health Providers

Many different professionals provide the various treatments we've described. Each tends to specialize in slightly different kinds of treatments and to have slightly different kinds of skills.

Providers	Training	General Focus/Form of Therapy
Psychiatrists	Four years of medical school, leading to M.D. degree; three years of residency in psychiatry	Psychiatrists may use all the talking therapies. They are the only mental health professionals authorized to prescribe drugs or perform ECT. They work in hospitals, clinics, and in private practice.
Clinical psychologists	Four or five years of graduate training, leading to a Ph.D. or Psy.D. degree; internship of at least one year	Clinical psychologists use all of the talking therapies but cannot prescribe drugs. They are specially trained in testing and diagnosis, and in research methodology. They work in hospitals, clinics, and in private practice.
Social workers	Two years of graduate work and a one-year internship to earn a master of social work degree (M.S.W.)	Social workers specialize in counseling people who are having difficulty integrating into society. Their clients may be on probation or welfare, or may suffer from a psychological disorder. Social workers serve in hospitals and clinics.
Professional counselors	A degree in counseling from a school of psychology, social work, divinity, or education	Counselors tend to focus on helping people with short-term, practical problems of adjustment. They practice in clinics and educational institutions.
Psychiatric nurses	An R.N. degree in nursing; an advanced degree such as M.A. or Ph.D. is also possible	Psychiatric nurses provide many therapeutic services; in hospitals they are often in charge of patients' day-to-day activities.

The Ethics of Therapy

Treatment is one of the relatively few activities in which psychologists and other mental health professionals deliberately try to change another person's behavior. And as we've seen, these attempts are generally successful. But the power to change people carries with it serious ethical responsibilities.

Perhaps these responsibilities are clearest, and most difficult to resolve, in the area of biological treatments. For example, it's not uncommon for patients who've been taking lithium for bipolar disorder to stop taking their medication, perhaps because they miss the "highs" of the manic stage (Jamison et al., 1980). Similarly, people suffering from schizophrenia often stop taking antipsychotic drugs because the side effects are unpleasant (Van Putten et al., 1981). The result in both cases is usually relapse. The ethical question here is whether family and society have the right to *require* people to take their medications. Obviously the same kind of question arises with respect to the use of ECT and confinement to a hospital.

The first reaction of most people is to say, yes, family and society do have the right to see that patients take their medications. After all, it's for their own good. But to understand the complexity of the problem, step back a moment and consider the treatments used by "the father of American psychiatry," Benjamin Rush.

Rush, a signer of the Declaration of Independence, was a well-meaning man who argued that disordered people should be treated more humanely, with respect and dignity (Sue, Sue, & Sue, 1990). But in keeping with contemporary theories about the balance of mental and physical forces in the individual, he implemented procedures in his hospital that appall us today. For example, he immobilized patients for long periods of time, immersing them in hot and cold water until they nearly drowned, or strapped them to a centrifuge and whirled them around until they were unconscious (see Figure 16.4).

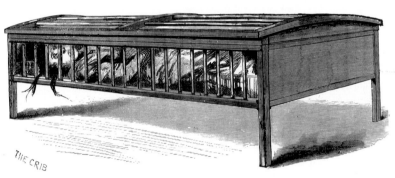

THE CRIB

Figure 16.4
Early Treatments for Psychological Disorders

Benjamin Rush (1746–1813) was famous for arguing for more humane treatment of people with psychological disorders. These are some of his treatments—a crib for restraining violent patients and a centrifugal machine in which a patient would be spun until he or she lost consciousness. Although these treatments seem horrible from our modern perspective, the fact that treatment was at least attempted was a step forward.

From our modern perspective, we can only assume that if these kinds of extreme measures sometimes worked, they did so because patients suppressed their symptoms rather than face more treatment. Rush performed these actions for the patients' own good; he really believed that they worked. But we cannot use good intentions as our sole criterion of the morality of imposing treatment on an individual.

In modern times, the debate over biological treatments focuses on two issues: costs and benefits on the one hand, and the client's consent on the other. Clinicians agree that a client has a right to a treatment whose probable benefits outweigh its possible costs. And most authorities agree that the benefits of well-established drug therapies far outweigh the risks of side effects and addiction. But clearly some clients don't agree.

Although many mental health professionals have profound misgivings about ECT because of its associated costs, most would agree that for clients whose depression cannot be reached by any other treatment, the benefits of ECT outweigh its costs.

The issues are less clear for insight-oriented, behavioral, and family systems therapies, primarily because the costs are less obvious. However, the expense in terms of both time and money can be substantial for these therapies. That's part of the reason so much attention has been focused on measuring the effectiveness of psychotherapies. If they don't work, the benefits can't outweigh the costs.

Probably the most difficult issue here concerns the client's consent to be treated. In the case of insight-oriented, behavioral, and family systems therapies (therapies that depend on the client's active cooperation), we can assume that the client is able to make a rational decision to participate. And in the case of a drug therapy for depression or anxiety, we also can assume that the client, after being fully informed of the costs and benefits of the therapy, is capable of choosing to participate.

But when we turn to treatments for people with more serious disorders, such as the victims of schizophrenia, we have a problem. Often these people behave in irrational ways, and one of their irrational behaviors may be to refuse treatment. Do we treat these people without their consent?

In times past, it was relatively easy to treat patients without their consent by confining them to a mental hospital. If family members and mental health professionals agreed that an individual was likely to be a danger to himself or herself, or to others, commitment was a simple procedure. Of course, forcing someone into even the nicest institution wasn't pleasant, and family members and professionals had to weigh their choices carefully. But in the last fifteen to twenty years, this kind of decision making has largely moved from the mental health arena to the courts. Civil commitment is a legal procedure, and the courts have ruled that an individual has the right to a court hearing. The result is that far fewer people are being confined and treated involuntarily today (Kiesler & Sibulkin, 1989).

The reduction in the rate of involuntary treatment is a mixed blessing. In making their decisions, the courts have to rely on expert testimony from mental health professionals about the "danger" the individual poses to self and society. Unfortunately this judgment is extremely difficult to make because opposing sides can readily find professionals to testify either way. The result is that the decision often rests on the individual's behavior in the courtroom (see, for example, Davison & Neale, 1990). The problem here is that many seriously disordered people act just like everyone else for long periods of time. So there are people who are seriously in need of treatment who aren't getting it. These people make up a disproportionate share of the homeless, and their lives are anything but easy. But society has made the tacit decision that they have the right to choose to live the way they want to.

Conclusion

Deciding how to help people in psychological distress is a complex and difficult undertaking. We have few definitive answers, and more remains to be done before we can know exactly what works when, with whom, under what circumstances, and, of course, why. Given the vast differences among the ways in which the different therapeutic approaches define disordered behavior, it's not surprising that we have so few answers. But what we do know is that the different therapeutic approaches are really different approaches to life. And it makes intuitive good sense to conclude that the best therapeutic outcomes are likely to result when client and therapist share similar approaches toward therapy and other basic life issues.

Chapter 17   Relations Between Individuals

A Conversation, Vanessa Bell, 1913–1916

17

Gateways In preceding chapters we have focused mainly on the individual person. But we are very social animals, almost constantly interacting with other people. In these final two chapters we look at how people think about and act toward one another. Liking and loving, manipulating, attacking, and helping—these are all kinds of relationships we have with others. We cannot have them alone.

Every social relationship begins with our perception of another person—our sense of what the person is like and of the reasons for his or her actions. We develop social knowledge in much the same way that we learn about other things, and many principles discussed in Chapter 8 on thought and language appear again in this chapter. Also reappearing here is a question that pervaded Chapter 14 on

personality: how do we distinguish between the individual's characteristics and situational factors in understanding the motives behind others' behavior? Finally, our discussion of aggression and altruism should remind you of research on learning through imitation (Chapter 6) and the effects of mass media on children (Chapter 12).

Reflecting on his first year of college, a young friend, Rick, recently wrote: "My first semester in college, I made some unusual friends. I met the first one in the first hour I was there, as I was lugging boxes up the stairs to my dorm room. My father was taking stuff out of the car and piling it on the curb, my mother was threatening to unpack my suitcases and put my clothes away, like I was ten years old, 'Just so you can start neatly.' And then this guy walked into the room and introduced himself, while I tried to stand in front of my mother so he wouldn't see her putting socks in the bureau drawer. He said he lived next door, asked where my roommate was and did I like it here. Then he asked me where I went to school before, like we were going to have a big conversation, while my father hollered from down below to come get another load, and my mother folded underwear. I couldn't believe him.

"But after my folks left, I was kind of glad when Harold came back. Neither of us knew exactly where to go for dinner, so we went off together to find the place. The next day, both Harold's roommate, Frank, and my roommate, Mark, had shown up, and we all went to the orientation meetings together. We all ate together just about every meal. In fact, a couple of times I was really hungry but didn't want to eat alone, so I waited for them. We didn't have many of the same classes, but we usually got together afterward.

"At Christmas that year, I spent a couple of days at Mark's house, which wasn't very far from our town, and Harold and Frank stopped over at our house on their way back to school. We talked about getting summer jobs at some resort area that would be fun, but we never quite got it organized. And by spring, when we had to plan who we were going to room with next year, I was relieved when Mark told me he was going to room with one of his friends from home, and Harold and Frank also had other roommates. By then I had gotten real friendly with some guys I met on the campus newspaper and some other guys from the soccer team, so I roomed with some of them. And after that, I never did see that much of Harold, Frank, or Mark. Our group that first year just drifted apart.

"To tell the truth, I really didn't have much in common with any of them, and Harold was actually a total jerk. So why did I spend so much time with him? And how come I didn't realize what he was like? Or that I really didn't have anything in common with the others?"

Social Psychology

In this chapter, we look for answers to these questions in the research that psychologists have conducted on how people get to know and understand other people. We examine perceptions of other people, the way first impressions are formed, liking and disliking, the relationship between attitudes and behaviors, and the way persuasion influences both attitudes and behavior. Finally, we turn to extreme forms of liking and disliking—altruism and aggression.

The moment we lay eyes on a new person we begin to form an impression of them, based on their appearance, their smallest actions, and of course what they say. We form impressions so effortlessly that even in a large group of strangers, we can come away with a wide variety of impressions.

All of these topics move us into **social psychology,** the scientific study of how people think, feel, and act in relation to other people. In this chapter we concentrate primarily on the smallest social interactions: one person's interactions with one other person. In the next chapter, we look at the relationships between individuals and social groups, and how groups affect behavior.

Interpersonal Perception

In any social encounter you begin to form an impression of the other person almost immediately. In fact, the response is so quick, so automatic, that you really can't help yourself. As fast as you receive information about the other person, you transform that information into an impression of what the person is like (Uleman, 1989).

Our impressions of other people consist largely of individual traits. If the professor you just met warmly shakes your hand, you immediately think "He's a *friendly* person," and you remember the trait—friendly—more than the professor's actual behavior.

In Chapter 14 we described a controversy in trait theory: the debate over the relative contributions of traits and situation to the individual's behavior. The same issue confronts all of us as everyday trait theorists. If your boss maintains her distance at work, is it because she's unfriendly? Or is the situation dictating her behavior?

Social psychology The scientific study of how people think, feel, and act in relation to other people.

Attribution theory A theory of how people understand the behaviors of others, by ascribing those behaviors to properties of the individual, to the situation, or to chance.

Attributions: Explanations for What You Observe

Attribution theory is one way of describing how people explain behavior. Harold Kelley (1967, 1972) proposed that people make sense of a particular action by looking for consistent patterns among the target action and other actions. Does the person always act this way? In many situations? Or does everyone act this way in this situation? To see how this process works, consider the following example.

Suppose your friend Millicent just got an A on an exam in Governing Under Tyranny. Did she get the A because she's a real scholar? Or is G.U.T. an easy course? Or was she lucky: Did the exam cover the one thing she'd studied? Three equally reasonable explanations. How do you decide among them?

According to Kelley, you need more information. You have to examine the behavior (Millicent's getting an A in G.U.T.) along three dimensions:

- *Consistency: Has the person done the same thing before in the same situation?* How has Millicent done on other exams in this course? If she's done well, you can say that her behavior is consistent and probably has to do with her own abilities. But if this is the only good grade she's gotten in G.U.T., then her behavior is not consistent and the A grade probably has to do with luck.
- *Consensus: How did other people behave in the same situation?* Was consensus high? Did lots of people in the class get As on the exam? If they did, Millicent's A really doesn't tell you very much about her as an individual. It probably means that the exam—the situation—was easy. The more people act alike in a situation, the more likely it is that the behavior is caused by the situation, not by something in the people.
- *Distinctiveness: How does the individual behave in other situations?* How is Millicent doing in her other courses? If she's getting good grades in other courses, then her behavior in this course is not distinctive. And if this behavior is not distinctive, it probably has something to do with Millicent herself—let's say she's a good student—rather than with the situation. But if Millicent is not doing well in her other courses, chances are it's this course—this situation— that's responsible for her behavior.

To attribute a behavior to a trait—some characteristic of the individual—a particular pattern of information along these three dimensions has to exist. First, consistency must be high because a trait is an enduring property. Consensus must be low because a trait points out differences among people. And distinctiveness must be low because a trait applies to behaviors in a wide variety of situations (see Figure 17.1).

Pattern of information	Example
High consistency + Low consensus + *Low distinctiveness* = Person attribution	Millie always gets A's in this course. No one else got an A on this exam. *Millie gets A's on all her exams.* Millie is an excellent student.
High consistency + High consensus + *High distinctiveness* = Situation attribution	Millie always gets A's in this course. Everyone got an A on this exam. *Millie doesn't get A's on all her exams.* GUT is an easy course.
Low consistency + Low consensus + *High distinctiveness* = Chance attribution	Millie usually doesn't get A's in this course. No one else got an A on this exam. *Millie doesn't get A's on all her exams.* Millie was lucky this time.

Figure 17.1
The Patterns of Information That Lead to the Attribution of Behavior

The way we make sense of an event is determined by the patterns of information that surround it. Here we present some of the more common patterns and show how they lead us to understand the event of Millie getting an A on an exam.

Do people actually think this way? The research says yes. When information is varied along these dimensions, peoples' attributions generally vary the way the theory predicts (McArthur, 1972; Hilton & Slugoski, 1986). And although the analysis looks difficult, in fact it's almost automatic.

Self-Attributions

Attribution theory also explains in part how people come to understand their own behavior. Suppose you're the one who just got an A on the exam in G.U.T. How do you decide whether you're a good student, G.U.T. is an easy course, or you were just lucky?

You would have to collect information. You'd think about your other grades in this course (consistency); you'd ask other people in the class how they did on the test (consensus); and you'd think about your grades in other courses (distinctiveness). If you find that you always get good grades in this class (high consistency), that no one else got an A on this test (low consensus), and that you tend to get good grades in your other courses (low distinctiveness), you can feel pretty confident that the A was a product of your ability, not of the situation or chance.

Now you may not realize that when you think about your grades in this class or your other classes, or ask a classmate how he did on the exam, that you're evaluating your own performance—but you are. Research on the ways in which college students explain their success and failure in their courses demonstrates that they do use the attribution process (Vallerand & Richer, 1988).

In Chapter 9 we described Bernard Weiner's findings that differences in need achievement involve differences in attribution. People with a high level of need achievement tend to attribute their successes to their own traits (intelligence, ability, study skills) and their failures to the situation (a difficult test, an unreasonable professor) or chance (Weiner, 1986).

Attribution Biases

To identify the causes of behavior, you need a tremendous base of observations about many behaviors in many situations. When the behavior is your own or your sister's or a close friend's, you may have this kind of information. But most of the time you don't have nearly enough information to make a full attribution analysis. You meet a new person, watch him move, listen to him talk, notice his reactions to your own behavior, and in seconds form an impression of him. The problem is that when you work with incomplete information—the kinds of observations you make at a first meeting—you tend to make mistakes.

The Fundamental Attribution Error

The most common error people make is underestimating the contribution of the *situation* to behavior. This tendency is so strong that it's called the **fundamental attribution error** (Ross, 1977).

When someone—particularly someone in authority—asks you to do something, usually you do it. So a direct request very clearly can shape behavior. To demonstrate the effects of the fundamental attribution error, several studies have examined situations in which the subjects knew that behavior was a product of a direct request, yet failed to attribute the behavior to the situation. In the first (Jones & Harris, 1967), students were asked to judge a speaker's opinion after reading a speech for or against Fidel Castro, supposedly given by a student. One group of subjects was told that the writer chose which side to argue; when members of this group were asked the writer's opinion, they assumed it matched the speech. Another group was told that the writer was assigned a pro or anti position. Although the differences were smaller, these subjects still assumed that the writer's opinion at least to some extent matched the speech (see Figure 17.2).

Fundamental attribution error
The tendency to underestimate the role of the situation in determining behavior.

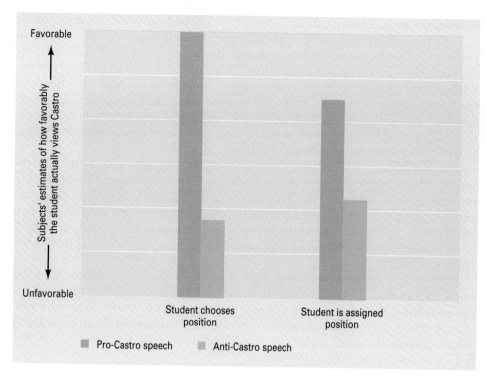

Source: Brehm & Kassin, 1990; data from Jones & Harris, 1967.

Figure 17.2
The Fundamental Attribution Error

When students thought the position taken in a speech had been freely chosen by a speaker, they assumed it reflected the person's own attitudes. They still tended to assume the speaker believed the speech even after they found out the viewpoint presented had been assigned to the speaker and didn't necessarily reflect that person's opinion.

In a similar study conducted years later, student subjects actually assigned the pro and anti speeches to another student, but they still tended to assume that the student's own opinions matched their assigned speech (Gilbert & Jones, 1986).

Why do people tend to underestimate the impact of situational demands on behavior? A major cause seems to be the kind of information we attend to. Our attention is usually focused on the person. When the person's actions are particularly dramatic (perhaps he or she is making a strong speech on a controversial subject), the actions attract our attention especially strongly. Then, since we are paying attention to the person, we look for the causes of the action in the person (see Figure 17.3).

Figure 17.3
Why Is This Man Running Away?

When our focus is on the man, we attribute his behavior to something about him—his fear. But when we see the tiger chasing him, we pay more attention to the role of the situation in his behavior.

Just being different is enough to affect attributions. People who stand out because they are a different age or sex than the rest of the group are perceived as playing a larger role in the group's activities, even when their actual contribution is the same as everyone else's.

Even the way questions about behavior are phrased can affect what we attend to, and promote or reduce the fundamental attribution error. Most questions focus attention on the actor. For instance, the usual question pertaining to the speech maker would be something like "Why did that student make a pro-environmental speech?" But notice the shift in emphasis if we asked, "Why did the experimenter's request lead the student to make a pro-environmental speech?" The grammatical form of the second question is sufficient to shift the focus of attention from the person to the situation, and it changes the attribution as well (Higgins & Bargh, 1987).

Another factor contributing to the fundamental attribution error may be the way in which people go about using the information they have. The attribution process seems to work in two stages. In the first stage, you look at the other person's behavior and attribute it to an individual trait—some property of that other person. This is the stage that is almost automatic. In the second, you check to see if there are any situational factors that could change your initial attribution (Gilbert, 1989).

Studies that support the two-stage theory usually ask subjects to form impressions of other people while the subjects are busy doing something else at the same time (for example, see Gilbert, Pelham & Krull, 1988). When the subjects are busy, they're more likely to commit the fundamental attribution error. Why? Because they still make the automatic attribution, but they're too distracted to correct their first impression.

Actor-Observer Differences   People are very quick to commit the fundamental attribution error when they're observing other people's behavior; they are much less likely to commit the error when their own behavior is at issue. In fact, there's a strong tendency to go in the other direction—to believe that their own behavior is a "natural" reaction to the situation in which they find themselves. As a result, people tend not to recognize the consistent patterns of their own behavior (Nisbett & Ross, 1980).

To the observer, this boy looks industrious. As observers, we instantly make the person attribution. But the boy may well be thinking about his situation and how unfair it is that his parents have demanded that he mow the lawn.

First Impressions

In his letter, Rick asked why at first he didn't recognize what Harold and the others were really like. You can probably begin to answer that question now. Certainly there were situational forces affecting Rick's own behavior. He was alone, his parents were gone, and he was a little nervous about starting at a new school. If you had asked him, he might even have described the situational forces that made him want to have dinner with Harold.

However, because of the fundamental attribution error, he probably failed to appreciate how much those same forces were operating on Harold. Instead, he may well have felt that Harold was genuinely warm and friendly.

In one study, while student subjects were being asked to volunteer to help a charity, they were watched through a one-way mirror by observer subjects. When the volunteers (the actors) and the observers were asked to explain why the students had volunteered their time, the two groups gave very different answers. The actors said that they volunteered because the cause was a good one, because the person asking was persuasive, or for some other reason that located the reason for their action in the situation. By contrast, each of the observers attributed the behavior to individual traits, describing all of the volunteers as kind, generous people (Jones & Nisbett, 1971).

Why do actors and observers have such different explanations? It seems to be a matter of perspective. When observers are watching an actor, the actor is the center of attention; so they tend to explain the actor's behavior in terms of traits. But the actors don't pay much attention to themselves. Because they're trying to deal with the situation, they immediately look for answers in the situation.

One effective demonstration of the importance of perspective used television cameras and monitors to reverse the perspectives of actors and observers (Storms, 1973). When the actors watched a picture of themselves in action, they attributed their behavior to their own properties. At the same time, observers who watched a picture of the situation as seen by the actors attributed the actors' behavior to the situation.

Actor-observer differences can be a powerful source of misunderstanding between people. An example: asking a professor for more time to complete an assignment. We professors—momentarily forgetting the fundamental attribution error—are usually sure that the delay reflects something about the student (maybe laziness, maybe a lack of organization, maybe a lack of responsibility). From the student's perspective, however, it's the situation (maybe an illness, maybe an unreasonable assignment in another class, maybe even a social event too good to pass up) that's causing the problem.

Self-Serving Bias   People don't always attribute their own actions to the situation. When they're happy with the outcome of a behavior, they are much more likely to attribute that behavior to themselves. And when they're not happy with the outcome of a behavior, they are much more likely to attribute that behavior to the pressures of the situation. This is called the **self-serving bias** (Nisbett & Ross, 1980). As we discussed in Chapter 14, people use a variety of strategies to select—and even distort—information about their lives so that they maintain a positive view of themselves. Deciding when to take credit for an action and when to blame the situation is one of our best techniques.

Self-serving bias The tendency to attribute successful behaviors to oneself and unsuccessful behaviors to situational pressures.

Puzzle It Out!

Psychotherapists have long believed that their clients are particularly incapable of self-understanding—that they often overlook the most obvious patterns in their behavior. How might the fundamental attribution error and actor-observer differences in attributions explain some of these problems?

The Organization of Impressions

Through the attribution process, you collect bits of information, which immediately begin to be organized. The first piece of information you collect stands by itself; but every subsequent bit of information is interpreted in light of what you already know. Suppose a friend describes a man she knows as "kind." Your impression of that man—someone you've never met—has already begun to form. Now, when your friend says that the man is also "calm," you have a sense that he's "even-tempered." This is very different from the impression you'd have if your friend had told you that the man was "cruel" and then "calm." "Cruel" and "calm" conjure up "calculating," not "even-tempered."

You don't assign a list of isolated attributes to other people. Instead, you develop an organized system of ideas, a **person schema** (Taylor & Crocker, 1981). We talked about schemas in Chapter 7. There we said that schemas are organizing structures, frameworks you impose on your knowledge to help you understand and remember your experiences. Person schemas are exactly the same, except that they apply to your knowledge of people and their attributes.

Making Information Consistent   The impressions you form of other people tend to be coherent and consistent. You may know that people's behaviors are often contradictory, but your impressions don't reflect that knowledge. Instead, you tend to make everything fit together. For example, if we tell you that someone is brilliant and foolish, that sounds like a contradiction. How can anyone be both? But you probably already have a mental image of the typical absentminded professor (Asch & Zukier, 1984). Notice that not only have you made sense of what seemed to be a contradiction but also that you've done so by adding a new trait dimension—absentmindedness.

The **balance principle** describes one of the ways in which people resolve inconsistencies (Heider, 1958). According to that principle, good things belong with other good things, and bad things belong with bad.

Suppose we tell you that a woman you've never met is "generous and warm, and unreliable and dishonest." The contradiction here is different from the brilliant-foolish contradiction because it doesn't lie in the meaning of the words. We didn't say that the woman is generous and stingy. Rather, the contradiction is between positive and negative qualities.

Many experiments have given subjects descriptions that mix positive and negative characteristics. When asked to describe again the person initially described, the subjects characteristically change the information in some way to make it more consistent (Crockett, 1968). Sometimes the subjects find a third quality that allows them to incorporate both positive and negative qualities (just as absentminded incorporates both brilliant and foolish). Often, particularly when people aren't attentive, they remember just the individual's good or bad qualities, not both. The balance principle leads them to forget half of the information, as Figure 17.4 illustrates.

Person schema An organized system of ideas about a person's attributes.

Balance principle One principle that organizes impressions of people and events, in which good things are assumed to belong with other good things, and bad things belong with bad.

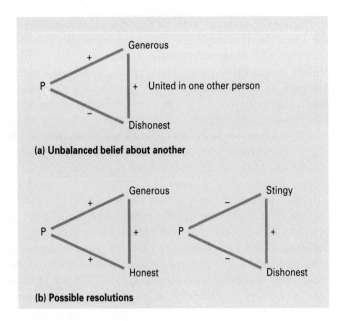

Figure 17.4
Balance and Impression Formation

The balance triangle is a way of depicting consistent and inconsistent relationships among ideas. In part a, P (the subject) is told that another person is generous, a trait P feels positively about, and dishonest, a trait P feels negatively about. Since these two traits are united in one person, P's feelings are unbalanced.

The balance principle reappears in a number of other psychological phenomena, as we will note from time to time below. At least two other general kinds of organizing principles have important effects on the impressions we form of others.

Stereotypes   Preconceived generalizations about the attributes or traits of people in different social groups are called **stereotypes.** For example, at most colleges you can hear people talk about the extroverted, "party" type of person. Other common stereotypes include the "jock," who is assumed to have muscles instead of brains; the "preppie," who cares most about wearing the right sort of clothing; the "grind," who studies night and day; and so on.

Most stereotypes are negative, and we all know that they are silly oversimplifications. Accordingly, most people try not to use them. The research suggests that when people are paying attention and thinking carefully about an individual, they usually don't use stereotypes (Higgins & Bargh, 1987). But even the most careful people are affected by stereotypes when they are distracted or when they don't have any other basis for judgment (Bodenhausen & Wyer, 1985). When we don't know anything else about a person except that he or she has a few of the attributes of a stereotyped group, most of us are likely to assign the person to that group, and then to assume the individual has all the other attributes of the stereotype as well.

People also tend to remember information that conforms to a stereotype better than information that doesn't (O'Sullivan & Durso, 1984). It's much easier to remember that Susan plays basketball if you have stereotyped her as a jock than if you think of her as a grind. This is the same effect we talked about in Chapter 7, where we said that creating a complex whole or "chunk" helps people remember details, but also leads to errors of memory.

Physical Attractiveness   One set of stereotypes is based on physical appearance. The moment you lay eyes on someone, his or her appearance begins to influence your impression of that person.

The most powerful aspect of appearance is attractiveness: just knowing that someone is physically attractive (according to the prevailing cultural standards) is enough to shape your impression of many of the individual's other attributes.

Stereotype A generalization about the attributes or traits of people in a social group.

For example, research tells us that the more attractive a woman is judged to be, the more likely people are to assume that she is better adjusted personally and socially, and more competent at various tasks (Dion, Berscheid & Walster, 1972). In another study, physical attractiveness played a role in the subjects' evaluations of writing samples. Even mediocre essays were judged acceptable when the writers were attractive (Landy & Sigall, 1974). Moreover, the impact of attractiveness extends beyond the individual to the individual's companions: people assume not only that a beautiful woman is smart and witty and kind, but also that the man with her is a better person (Sigall & Landy, 1973).

One explanation of these effects is the "what is beautiful is good" stereotype (Dion, Berscheid & Walster, 1972), which is a special case of the "what is good is good" balance principle (see Figure 17.5). As the balance principle predicts, the effect seems to work the other way, too. That is, people's judgments of physical attractiveness are affected by everything else they know about the individual. If Ann has been described as good and generous and kind, you would probably find her more attractive than if she'd been described as mean and stingy and cruel (Gross & Crofton, 1977). Even if someone merely agrees with you on a subject, you tend to see that person as more attractive (Klentz et al., 1987).

Clearly, physical attractiveness is one of numerous attributes involved in balance processes. If we initially perceive someone as attractive, that perception will sway us to see the person as positive in other ways. But if we initially know other good things about that person we will find him or her more attractive.

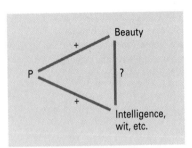

Figure 17.5
Balance and Physical Attractiveness

If your first impression of someone is that he or she is attractive, you tend to see the individual in all kinds of positive ways. And if your first impression is of good things, you tend to find the individual more attractive.

First Impressions: The Effects

Once an impression is organized, it affects the way you process everything else you learn about another person. First impressions not only resist change; they even affect how well you can remember information about a person. Your first impression of someone may even affect how the other person behaves.

Resisting Change   One effect of person schemas is the notorious *first-impression effect.* We've talked about the perils of the attribution process, so it's clear that first impressions can be wrong. They also can be very hard to change.

Consider the following information about two people, George and Clarence. After you read it, stop and think about the kind of person each man is; then continue reading.

George is intelligent, industrious, and impulsive.

Clarence is critical, stubborn, and envious.

Now here's some more information about George and Clarence:

George is envious, stubborn, and critical.

Clarence is impulsive, industrious, and intelligent.

Who do you think you'd like better, George or Clarence?

Obviously we've given you exactly the same information about the two men, but your tendency is to like George more because the first things you read about him were positive.

This example is taken from a classic experiment by Solomon Asch (1946), in which one group of subjects was given the positive information first and the other was given the negative first. The group who received the positive information first formed more positive impressions. The reason, of course, is that whatever information comes first—positive or negative—biases the interpretation of later information.

Once you form a first impression, you tend to see new behavior through the filter of that impression. In one demonstration of this effect, a group of college students watched a videotape of a young girl who seemed to be from a poor family. Another group saw a videotape of the same girl, but this time she seemed to come from an upper-middle-class family. Then half the subjects in each group were asked what kind of student they thought the girl was. Not unexpectedly, the girl's socioeconomic status had an effect (a small one) on the subjects' thinking, thus indicating the slight influence of stereotypes.

To counteract that influence, all of the subjects watched the same videotape in which the girl answered questions on school tests. This videotape showed the girl to be about average, answering some questions right and others wrong. Remarkably, information that was intended to counteract the influence of the socioeconomic stereotypes actually increased their effect, as Figure 17.6 makes clear (Darley & Gross, 1983). Apparently the subjects who expected the girl to be a poor student paid more attention to her errors, whereas those who expected her to be a better student paid more attention to her successes. The result was that each group believed their stereotyped impressions had been confirmed by the girl's performance, so the effects of their stereotypes were exaggerated.

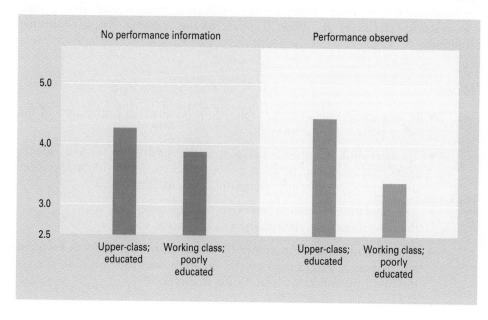

Figure 17.6
The Effects of Stereotypes on Information Selection

When subjects were given information just about a child's background, the information had only a small effect on the subjects' judgment of the girl's school performance. But after watching a tape showing both successes and failures, the subjects stereotyped more.

Source: Data from Darley & Gross, 1983.

The Effect of First Impressions on a Person's Behavior   First impressions not only bias the way you interpret later information about another person; they also can affect that person's behavior, leading the individual to act in ways that confirm your first impression.

In a classic study of this effect, the researchers asked men and women—strangers—to get to know each other on the telephone (Snyder, Tanke & Berscheid, 1977). Each of the men received a photograph of the woman he was supposedly going to be talking to. Half saw a photograph of a very beautiful woman; the other half, of a woman who was not attractive. Neither photograph was actually of the women the men were going to speak with on the phone.

After their conversation, the men who had seen the photograph of the attractive woman thought that their phone partner was much friendlier, more interesting, and wittier than did the men who had seen the photograph of the unattractive woman. This is the effect we described above, of attributing lots of good qualities to people who are attractive.

The really dramatic findings came from tape recordings of the phone conversations. The men's half of the conversations was edited out, so that only the women's half remained. Then judges listened to these half-conversations and evaluated them in terms of friendliness, interest, wittiness, and so on. According to these judges, the women whose partners had believed they were physically attractive actually acted friendlier than the women whose partners had believed they were unattractive. Their telephone partners' impressions had affected the women's behavior. When their partners believed they were attractive, the women acted more attractive.

The same effect, of expectations on reality, has been observed in connection with other attributes. People's expectations have made students act more or less extroverted (Snyder & Swann, 1978), and teachers' expectations have had an impact on school performance and even intelligence test scores (Rosenthal & Jacobson, 1968).

In general, then, it seems that stereotypes can function as self-fulfilling prophecies. Expecting people to act in a stereotyped way can lead people to act in ways that confirm those stereotypes. We should note, however, that like many of the less desirable and less rational behaviors that psychologists have discovered, this effect of expectations is much reduced if either the individual holding the impression (Neuberg, 1989) or the individual with whom that person is interacting (Darley et al., 1988) is aware of the potential for self-fulfilling prophesy.

Recap

- In any social encounter, people begin to form an impression of the other person almost immediately.

- To determine whether a behavior is the product of the individual's traits, the situation, or luck, people collect information along three dimensions: consistency, consensus, and distinctiveness.

- The fundamental attribution error is made when one underestimates the contribution of the situation to behavior.

- The fundamental attribution error arises from the tendency to focus on the person rather than on the situation, and the failure to correct the first impression with later information.

- When the behavior in question is their own, people are much more likely to attribute it to the situation—particularly when the behavior is not successful or desirable.

- The first piece of information collected about an individual stands by itself; every subsequent bit of information is interpreted in light of what's already known.

- A person schema is an organized system of ideas about a person's attributes.

- The balance principle describes one of the ways in which people resolve inconsistencies in the information they have about other people.

- When people are distracted or when they don't have better information, stereotypes affect their judgments of other people.

- Perceiving someone as physically attractive is enough to bias people's impressions of many of the individual's other attributes, to the good. Similarly, knowing that someone has positive qualities tends to bias people's opinions of their physical attractiveness, again to the good.

- First impressions are difficult to change, in part because they often bias the interpretation of new information.

- An individual's behavior can be affected by other people's expectations.

Interpersonal Attraction

Human beings are social animals. We spend most of our lives in groups and families, drawn together by liking and loving. Understanding how we are attracted to one another is central to understanding much of our behavior.

Liking

Coming to know other people is a pretty complicated process; liking them, on the other hand, is relatively simple. The research indicates that you like other people who live near or spend time with you, who are similar to you, and who like you back.

Propinquity   One of the strongest predictors of friendship is *propinquity*, or nearness. You are much more likely to be friends with someone who lives or works near you than with someone who lives or works far away. If you're shaking your head no because your best friend lives a thousand miles away, think again. Where did the two of you live when you first met? It's not that you can't become close to people who live far away; it's just that you usually don't (Festinger, Schachter & Back, 1950).

Robert Zajonc has suggested that we like familiar things just because they are familiar. In Chapter 10 we described a study in which Zajonc showed his subjects a long list of Chinese characters. Later they were shown pairs of characters—in each case, one they'd seen previously and one that was new. The subjects couldn't remember the characters they had already seen with anything better than chance accuracy. But when asked to choose the character they liked better in each pair, the subjects consistently chose the character they had seen before (Zajonc, 1968).

Zajonc and his colleagues have demonstrated this effect over and over again—with Turkish words and with pictures of strangers, for example (Moreland & Zajonc, 1982). And they've found that "mere exposure" to something is enough to induce a preference for that object. Certainly if mere exposure is enough to make people like Chinese characters, being around a person a lot should make them feel positive about that person.

Yet there are limits to the potential impact of propinquity. If your neighbor turns out to be a combination of Pig Pen and Genghis Khan, no amount of nearness is going to create closeness. Of course, if you yourself are a little like Pig Pen and Genghis Khan, you may have found a friend after all—which brings us to the role of similarity in attraction.

Similarity   You may have noticed that people who are alike seem to hang around together, and the evidence is clear that friends are more similar in their attitudes and values than are nonfriends. But the reason for that similarity isn't so clear. It could be that people choose to be friendly with people like themselves, but it's equally possible that friends come to share attitudes and values because of common experiences and lots of talk.

A classic study at the University of Michigan found both effects. Entering freshmen were given the opportunity to live free in a dormitory in return for answering lots of questions during the year about their lives and friendships. Early in the year, they were asked to describe how they and their new friends in the dormitory felt about a number of issues. The students reported that their friends shared many of their attitudes and values; and they described their friends as much more similar to themselves than were nonfriends. But this was actually a misperception. Pairs of friends weren't really more similar than non-friends; they just thought they were.

As the year went on, the students seemed better able to identify one another's attributes, and their friendships began to change. By the end of the year, the students had made friends who actually did have similar values (Newcomb, 1961). In fact, the researcher found that his predictions of friendship patterns at the beginning of the school year (based on similarity on a measure of values) were closer to the final friendship patterns than were the students' first choice of friends. Many other studies have confirmed that people who share the same attitudes like each other more than people whose attitudes are different (Byrne, 1971).

The effect of similar attitudes on attraction is another example that fits the balance principle (see Figure 17.7). If you like chess a lot and meet another person who likes chess a lot, that is a strong positive feature of the new person. Since the balance principle holds that good goes with good, you will tend to like the person as well as his or her hobby. And if you find that your new acquaintance shares your opinions on politics and art and sports, there are going to be more and more links reinforcing your feelings toward that other person.

What about the idea that opposites attract, that people come together because each partner brings different strengths to the relationship? The evidence just doesn't support it. Friends and spouses are much more likely to be similar than to be complementary to each other (Buss, 1984). And among married couples, the more similar they are, the more stable the marriage (Byrne, 1971). Perhaps the reason so many people believe that opposites attract is that they tend to take their similarities with friends and spouses for granted, noticing only the few areas in which they disagree with or complement each other.

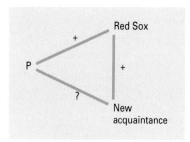

Figure 17.7
Balance and Similarity

If you (P) are a Red Sox fan, and you meet a person who is also a fan, the balance principle indicates that you will begin to like your new acquaintance.

Reciprocity   Although propinquity and similarity are factors in attraction, the strongest determinant of all seems to be **reciprocity**—liking people who like you.

Of all the things you like in the world, you probably like yourself best (at least most people do). The balance principle would predict, then, that the most important determinant of your feeling toward another person is that person's feeling toward you (see Figure 17.8) (Heider, 1958). And that seems to be the case. More than anything, you like the people who like you (Kenny & Nasby, 1980).

Just hearing that someone likes you is enough to make you like that person (Berscheid & Walster, 1978). (Remember the messages that went back and forth in the hallways of your high school, about who liked whom?) Furthermore, people who believe that someone likes them act in ways that induce the other person to actually like them—another example of self-fulfilling prophecy (Curtis & Miller, 1986).

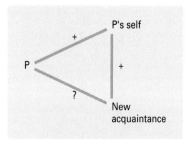

Figure 17.8
Balance and Reciprocity

If we like ourselves (and most of us do) then a new acquaintance who seems to like us will be liked in return. After all, this new person is demonstrating excellent judgement.

Romantic Love

Many psychologists suggest that when we talk about love—romantic love—we're talking about two different kinds of feelings and phenomena. Ellen Berscheid and Elaine Walster (1974) called them *passionate love* and *companionate love.*

Putting the Attraction Principles Together

As noted, we tend to be friendly with people we see often, people who are similar to us, and people who like us. Let's go back to Rick's experience to see how all of these observations fit together.

Propinquity is probably the least powerful of the determinants of attraction; but it is the most effective one early in a relationship. Through repeated exposure, you may begin to like your neighbors a little. That feeling is probably enough just to ensure some additional interaction, within which you can explore your similarities. In the long run, however, real similarities and reciprocity determine whom you like.

All of these principles were at work in Rick's friendships during his first year of school. The first, propinquity, is the most obvious. His friends consisted of his roommate and two people who lived next door. In this case, reciprocity may have been a kind of illusion for Rick and his friends. All of the group members acted as though they liked the others, although in fact they probably wanted company in general, rather than the company of these particular people. But because they all thought that the others liked them, reciprocity probably strengthened their relationship. Missing in all of this, of course, were any real similarities. And as that lack became increasingly apparent, the friendships dissolved.

Passionate love is the intense emotional condition in which the sight or even the thought of the person you love sets your heart pounding. This is the kind of love Shakespeare was describing in *Romeo and Juliet*.

Passionate love is an emotional experience marked by high levels of autonomic arousal and characteristic patterns of behavior—gazing into each other's eyes, touching, sharing secrets, and doing and feeling all the other things that poets write about. Passionate love is consuming, the lovers spending as much time together as possible. And, perhaps because of its intensity, it almost always begins to fade within a year or two (Hill, Rubin & Peplau, 1976).

Is romantic love a more intense form of liking, determined by the same principles, similarity being one of them? Dating services operate on that assumption. They use computers to match people on as many dimensions as possible in order to maximize similarity.

Reciprocity People's tendency to like people who like them.

Passionate love The intense form of romantic love in which the presence or even the thought of the loved one produces excitement and physiological arousal.

As the intensity of passionate love fades, the relationship either dissolves or evolves into a less exciting but perhaps deeper kind of love (see Figure 17.9). **Companionate love** is based on intimacy, trust, and respect, and seems to be a lot like friendship in the sense that greater similarity between the partners is associated with greater stability in the relationship (Berscheid & Walster, 1978, Hatfield, 1988).

Figure 17.9
The Course of Love

Generally, passionate love declines within a year or so, and in many cases, it is replaced by companionate love, a deeper, more enduring kind of love.

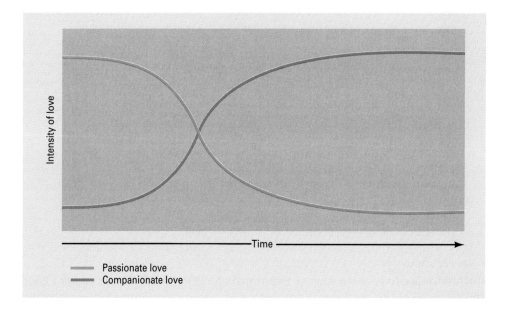

By sharing interests and values, lovers, like friends, give each other positive experiences. They reinforce each other's ideas and behaviors, and they take pleasure from sharing activities.

The role of passionate love may be to see to it that two people spend time together, discovering each other, sharing their thoughts and feelings (Holmes & Rempel, 1989). Passionate love helps the lovers explore their similarities.

And for most couples, passionate love does fade, perhaps evolving into companionate love. Yet most people in our culture believe that passion can and should last forever, and that if it disappears from a relationship, the relationship should end (Berscheid, 1983). So most people begin romantic relationships with an expectation that seems certain to cause problems in the future. It's no wonder, then, that the rate of divorce is so high (Simpson, Campbell & Berscheid, 1986).

Recap

- People like people who live near or spend time with them, who are similar to them, and who like them.

- Romantic love actually may be two different kinds of feelings and phenomena: passionate love and companionate love.

- Perhaps because of its intensity, passionate love almost always begins to fade within a year or two, ending the relationship or changing it.

- Companionate love is a kind of intense liking that's based on the lovers' similarities.

Companionate love The form of romantic love that is based on the lovers' similarities; an intense liking.

Prejudice

We turn in the opposite direction now, from liking and loving to prejudice. **Prejudice** is a strong negative feeling or belief about another person based only on that individual's membership in a social group.

Prejudice is different from stereotyping in that it usually includes a strong feeling of dislike or hatred for the other group. However, many prejudiced people hold very negative stereotyped beliefs about the individuals in a group while genuinely liking them. The best example is the attitude of many conventionally sexist men who like women but persist in believing that women are inferior to men in various ways. Accordingly, the definition of prejudice should include negative stereotyped beliefs about a group, whatever the associated feelings.

A number of explanations for prejudice have been proposed. Some focus on the motives and needs of the dominant group; others focus on their modes of thinking.

The Social-Motivational Origins of Prejudice

In many societies, prejudice arises and is maintained by social tradition. The attitudes of whites toward blacks in South Africa, for example, have been taught to succeeding generations for centuries. Within these societies, prejudice may act as an outlet for the frustrations of the dominant culture. The target group functions as a *scapegoat*, something to blame for the troubles of the dominant culture. Some support for this view comes from a study of the number of lynchings of blacks in the American South between 1880 and 1930. Lynchings were most common in years when the price of cotton, the region's principal crop, was lowest (Hepworth & West, 1988).

A related source of prejudice may be the need to maintain and reassert one's status. The groups who are most prejudiced in a society tend to be those who have the least status within the dominant group. These people at the bottom of the hierarchy of the dominant group strive to feel superior at least to the objects of their prejudice. In one test of this mechanism, when individual college students were made to feel foolish, they expressed more prejudiced attitudes (Meindl & Lerner, 1984). Apparently they used prejudice to overcome their own feelings of inferiority.

The Cognitive Sources of Prejudice

The motivational sources of prejudice are augmented by a series of cognitive mechanisms that tend to create and maintain negative stereotypes. Many of the normal mechanisms of attribution and impression formation have the potential to foster prejudice.

Ingroup-Outgroup Differences   People have a strong tendency to attach themselves to their **ingroups,** groups or categories of people to which they "belong." At the same time, they have a tendency to separate themselves from **outgroups,** groups or categories of people to which they either don't belong or think they don't belong. A number of studies have demonstrated the impact of the most trivial distinctions between "we" and "they." For example, ingroups and outgroups have been formed on the basis of eye color, the color of people's pencils and notepads, even the tendency to over- or underestimate the number of dots on a screen (Tajfel, 1982).

Prejudice A strong negative feeling or belief about another person based only on that individual's membership in a social group.

Ingroup Any group to which the individual belongs.

Outgroup Any group of which the individual is not a member or is not aware of membership.

These delegates at the 1988 Democratic National Convention probably recognized that they were a diverse group, with individual interests and needs; but to them, Republicans are all the same—just conservatives. Republicans, of course, recognize their own diversity, but to them, "Democrat" is just another word for "liberal."

The first effect of this kind of separation is that people begin to exaggerate their similarities to members of the ingroup and their differences from members of the outgroup (Wilder, 1981). Remember that similarity is an important determinant of liking. One effect, then, of believing that the members of the ingroup are more like you and that the members of the outgroup are less like you is that you like the ingroup more and the outgroup less.

A second effect of the ingroup-outgroup distinction has to do with behavior. People treat the members of their ingroups better than they do the members of their outgroups. This effect is almost immediate. In one study, for example, the subjects were asked to distribute money among members of randomly created ingroups and outgroups. They gave much less to their outgroups (Tajfel, 1982).

This kind of behavior reinforces feelings about "we" and "they." Naturally, if members of the ingroup treat you preferentially, you like them more; in addition, that liking is reflected in your own behavior. And if members of the outgroup discriminate against you, you like them less—and that dislike, too, is reflected in your interactions with them.

People also tend to see the structure of their ingroups differently from the structure of their outgroups, in ways that parallel actor-observer differences in attributions. For example, if the groups are something people can choose to join, such as teams or organizations, members think that the other ingroup members joined for situational reasons ("It's a good group," "We get to travel all over") but that members of other outgroups joined for personality reasons ("He's that kind of person"). In other words, "we" are individuals and "they" are all alike.

In these effects—exaggerating the differences from members of the outgroup, treating the members of the outgroup differently from the members of the ingroup, and failing to recognize that the members of the outgroup are individuals—lie the embryo of prejudice.

The Just-World Phenomenon   Another subtle process that contributes to prejudice is the **just-world phenomenon**—another special case of the balance principle, that good goes with good. Many people behave as if they believed in a just world, in which bad things don't happen to good people. Of course, the world isn't just; and earthquakes, hurricanes, famine, and disease all strike at random. However, to the extent that people follow the just-world principle, they tend to think that the victims of tragedy somehow deserve their fate (Ler-

Just-world phenomenon The belief that the world is just and, therefore, that bad things happen only to bad people.

ner, 1980). Certainly we all know better; but as with other cases in which balance processes occur, if we are not paying attention we may tend to exhibit the just-world phenomenon.

In a classic series of studies of this effect, Melvin Lerner (1980) asked college students to watch another student receive a number of electric shocks. The subjects then rated the personalities of the two students. Despite the fact that the subjects knew that the student who received the shocks was chosen by chance, they described her more negatively. Apparently they believed that if a bad thing happened to this woman, she must have been a bad person.

The same effect has been observed in the real world, among people who blame the victims of crime (Ryan, 1971). Not long ago, a woman was savagely attacked while jogging in Central Park, by a gang of boys who raped and beat her and left her for dead. One of the common reactions reported in the newspapers was that "she had no business jogging there." This tendency to blame the victim is so strong that victims sometimes blame themselves (Comer & Laird, 1976; Baumeister & Scher, 1988).

Many of the groups who are victims of prejudice are victims of other misfortunes as well. In varying degrees, they may be poor, powerless, and demoralized. If we believe in a just world, we are likely to believe they deserve their problems. And so we assume that they're bad people, thus reinforcing the prejudice that may well have contributed to these other conditions in the first place. At the same time, of course, we've constructed a convenient rationalization for our prejudice.

Ingroup favoritism, in- versus outgroup attribution, and belief in the just world are all normal processes that probably occur in everyone. In short, prejudice seems to grow naturally from our habitual patterns of thought. It can be avoided, however, if we pay diligent attention to the logic of our thinking about others (see Table 17.1).

Combating Prejudice

Can people avoid or lose their prejudice? The evidence from social psychology indicates that they can. The process begins with information and experiences that are inconsistent with the prejudice. Although stereotypes exert pressure to-

Table 17.1
The Cognitive Sources of Prejudice

Ingroup-outgroup differences and the just-world phenomenon reflect habitual patterns of thought, common to all people. So we are all at risk of developing prejudices.

The Source	The Pattern of Thought
Ingroup-outgroup differences	The people in my group are more like me than the people in your group.
	I like the people in my group better than I like the people in your group.
	I treat the people in my group better than I treat the people in your group.
	The people in my group treat me better than the people in your group.
	The people in my group are individuals; the people in your group are all alike.
Just-world phenomenon	If bad things are happening to your group, you must deserve them.

ward redefining or ignoring discrepant information, that information cannot be ignored if it is compelling enough.

In order to change the negative stereotypes that underlie many prejudices, people have to see one another in action; they have to see that the stereotypes don't apply. A classic demonstration of the growth and cure of prejudice was conducted by Muzafer Sherif and a group of other social psychologists (Sherif et al., 1961/1988). At a summer camp, they divided boys randomly into two groups and then created a series of competitions between the groups. In short order, ingroup-outgroup differences appeared and the two groups came to hate each other. A number of fights had to be broken up. Obviously competitive contact created and strengthened prejudice.

Now the researchers set about weakening the prejudice. They set up a number of situations in which the two groups had to cooperate to solve a mutual problem. For example, both groups had to work together to repair the camp's water system. After a series of tasks that forced them to cooperate, the hostility between the groups disappeared, and the two groups in effect became one cohesive group.

A similar solution has been used to promote interracial harmony in the classroom by giving students equal status and setting up an opportunity for cooperative contact. Eliot Aronson developed a technique called the *jigsaw classroom,* in which each student learns a different part of the material and then teaches it to the other students. In this way, every child is dependent on every other child and learns to appreciate each child's contribution. The effect is an improvement in a variety of academic skills and attitudes, as well as a dramatic drop in prejudice (Aronson et al., 1978).

In sum, contact alone is not enough. But if the situation brings people together with equal status and, most important, compels them to work together toward a common goal, then contact does reduce prejudice.

Recap

- Prejudice is a strong negative feeling about another person based only on that individual's membership in a social group.

- Motivational theories argue that prejudice functions as an outlet for people's frustrations and as means of overcoming their own feelings of inferiority.

- Ingroups are the groups or categories that people belong to; outgroups are the groups or categories that they don't belong to or think they don't belong to.

- The just-world phenomenon reinforces prejudice while at the same time providing a convenient rationalization for prejudice.

- An effective technique to combat prejudice is to bring people together with equal status in a situation that compels them to cooperate with one another.

Attitudes and Persuasion

In our discussions of attraction and prejudice, we've been talking about the individual's likes and dislikes of other people. Social psychologists call these feelings **attitudes.** Attitudes are the feelings of liking and disliking for people or for objects (Tesser & Shaffer, 1990). Attitudes also involve the way people think about and behave toward the objects of their feelings.

Obviously people aren't the only thing people like or dislike. I like spinach and skiing; I dislike committee meetings and polka music. You may like polkas and hate spinach. People like or dislike just about every object we can identify; so we can say that people have an attitude toward just about everything.

Do Attitudes Affect Behavior?

Most people assume that there's a close cause-and-effect relationship between attitudes and behaviors: you attend polka dances *because* you like polkas, and you never choose a seafood restaurant *because* you dislike fish. But for a time, research seemed to demonstrate that attitudes were actually very poor predictors of behavior. In the characteristic study of this sort, subjects would be asked to use a rating scale to describe their attitude toward something—say, dancing. Then the ratings would be used to predict whether or not the subjects would show up at a dance. Surprisingly, the accuracy of the predictions was very poor (Wicker, 1969).

The problem here was a lot like the trait-versus-situation controversy we described in Chapter 14. In fact, both controversies were going on at the same time, involved some of the same people, and were resolved in much the same way. The product in this case was a much better understanding of the relationship between attitudes and behavior, and as a result a more accurate prediction.

One factor that improves our ability to predict behavior from attitudes is knowing whether the subject believes that the action is socially appropriate (Ajzen & Fishbein, 1980). Even if a person really likes eating spaghetti with his fingers, he probably won't do it. Another important factor is the variety of alternatives. Even if you love to dance, you may not go to a dance because you'd rather go to a basketball game the same night or because you have no money or because you have to study for an exam. One way to allow for these factors is to use measures of attitudes to predict many behaviors over a span of time (Kahle & Berman, 1979). Another important factor is whether you happen to think of your attitude at the time you choose to act. You don't remember every attitude at exactly the time it's relevant; and, obviously, if you don't remember an attitude, your behavior isn't likely to be related to the attitude (Fazio, 1986).

In short, behavior is determined by a whole constellation of factors, only one of which is your attitude. Your actions fit your attitudes only when

Attitude A feeling of liking or disliking that also involves the way people think about and behave toward the object of their feeling.

- the action is clearly linked to an attitude.
- other social or practical factors don't interfere.
- you remember an attitude at the time you're acting.

For example, if you want to predict how someone is going to vote in an election, it's not enough to ask which candidate the individual likes best. You also have to ask how the individual thinks other people feel about the candidates; determine the other activities that are scheduled for election day; and decide how likely the individual is even to remember to vote.

Does Behavior Affect Attitudes?

The result of all the research on the role of attitudes in behavior has been to confirm and refine the common-sense belief that attitudes do affect behaviors. But does the relationship work in reverse? Do behaviors also affect attitudes?

Your first response, like most people's, is probably no. But think for a minute. Have you ever watched a conversation turn into a heated debate, each participant becoming more and more committed to his or her "side"? Or have you ever noticed that people who are required by their jobs to act in certain ways start to act that way off the job? There's the waiter, who's always helpful; or the professor, with a long-winded explanation for everything.

In point of fact, people do change their attitudes to conform to their behaviors. In the next few pages we discuss why.

Cognitive Dissonance   Leon Festinger proposed that whenever people acted in a way that was inconsistent with their attitudes, they would experience **cognitive dissonance**. According to Festinger cognitive dissonance is uncomfortable, a *negative motivational state*. One way of reducing or eliminating cognitive dissonance is to change your attitudes to match your behavior.

Festinger and Merrill Carlsmith (1959) carried out a classic experiment on cognitive dissonance. Imagine that you've volunteered for what you think is a study of manual performance. Your task is to pack wooden spools onto a tray, one by one, over and over again. You are bored to tears and heartily sick of packing spools by the time the experiment is over.

As you're getting ready to leave, the researcher explains that you actually were a member of the control group in an experiment on the effect of expectations on performance. His coworker—who is supposed to give the subjects in the experimental group their instructions and tell them that the work is really fun—is sick. Would you be willing, for a dollar, to administer the instructions to the subject who's scheduled to arrive in a few minutes? You agree. And when the new subject comes, you describe how much you enjoyed the experiment.

As you leave, another student comes up to you and says that he's doing a survey for the psychology department on people who have been subjects in research. One of the questions he asks is "How much did you enjoy the experiment?" What do you think you would answer?

Because the experimental task was so boring, you probably think that you and any other subjects in their right minds would say that it was boring. But you're wrong. Most of the subjects who had been asked to tell a new subject that the experiment was fun went on to tell the student taking the survey that the experiment was relatively enjoyable. These subjects rated the task as much more enjoyable than the real control subjects, who hadn't been asked to tell someone the task was fun (see Figure 17.10). In short, the subjects had changed their attitudes to conform to their behavior (telling the subject that the task was fun).

Cognitive dissonance The discomfort produced by acting in a way that is inconsistent with one's attitudes; a negative motivational state.

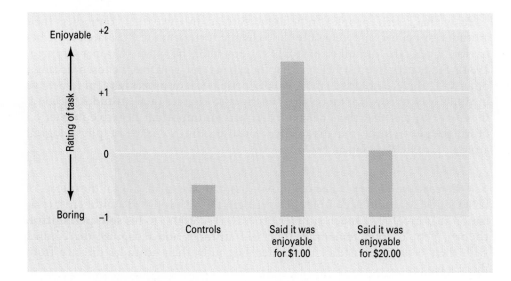

Figure 17.10
Cognitive Dissonance

When people said the task was enjoyable and did not have a strong ($20) reason for saying it, they reported that they really did enjoy the task.

Source: Data from Festinger & Carlsmith, 1959.

Festinger and Carlsmith believed that the subjects were experiencing cognitive dissonance, the product of the conflict between their feelings (the task was boring) and their behavior (telling another person that the task was fun). The only way to eliminate the dissonance was to resolve the conflict. Because the behavior had already happened, their attitude toward the task had to change.

This interpretation was reinforced by another variable in the study. Some of the subjects who were asked to tell a new subject that the task was fun were offered $20. Most people, and most psychologists at the time, assumed that the attitudes of the $20 group would change more than those of the $1 group, that the members of the $20 group would have more positive feelings about the whole experience. But the findings were exactly the opposite: the $20 group didn't change at all, whereas the $1 group changed a lot.

According to Festinger and Carlsmith, the reason was simple. The people in the $20 group didn't feel any dissonance when they said they enjoyed the task: they'd been paid to do it so they had a good reason. Conversely, a dollar isn't enough to justify lying to someone, so the members of the $1 group were faced with cognitive dissonance and had to change their attitudes to reduce it.

These findings and those of subsequent studies by Festinger and his students were startling, controversial, and exciting. They generated a tremendous volume of research, totaling nearly a thousand published studies that confirmed the basic effect (Cooper & Fazio, 1984). Table 17.2 describes what some of these studies found.

Table 17.2
Behavior and the Effects of Cognitive Dissonance

Behavior	Effect
Eat spinach	Like spinach more
Eat a caterpillar	Dislike eating caterpillars less
Suffer to join a group	Like the group better
Choose not to play with a toy	Like the toy less
Choose one appliance over another	Like the chosen appliance better
Pay more money for a product	Value the product more
Insult someone	Like the person less
Make a speech on an issue	Change beliefs to match the speech

As we have seen, people can be induced to act in a way that contradicts their attitudes or beliefs; and generally they change their attitudes to match their behavior. There are a number of qualifications here, however (Cooper & Fazio, 1984). First, people must believe that their behavior was freely chosen because, otherwise, there is no dissonance. Paying people $20 or ordering them to behave in some way makes it unnecessary for them to change their attitudes. Second, they have to feel that their behavior has had an important negative impact on other people. Third, the dissonance must produce a state of physiological arousal (Croyle & Cooper, 1983).

Self-Perception Theory   The cognitive-dissonance explanation of the effects of behavior on attitudes is complex. Daryl Bem (1972) proposed a different explanation that involves a much simpler process. According to his **self-perception theory,** people don't remember their old attitudes and recognize the conflict with their behavior; instead, they often just infer their attitudes directly from their behavior.

Dissonance theory proposes a process that runs something like this:

1. You act as though you believe A. (You make an antitax speech.)
2. You interpret that action as meaning you believe A. ("I must oppose higher taxes.")
3. You remember your previous attitude, not-A. ("I've always favored higher taxes when necessary.")
4. You recognize the inconsistency between the implication of your action, A, and your previous attitude, not-A. ("It's inconsistent for me to make a speech opposing higher taxes when I favor higher taxes.")
5. To remove the inconsistency, you change your attitude to A. ("I must oppose higher taxes.")

Notice that the last step in the process is the same as Step 2. In both cases your conclusion is "I must oppose higher taxes."

Bem argued that the process sometimes goes only as far as Step 2. If you don't remember an inconsistent attitude, you might just adopt the attitude implied by your behavior. Notice that Bem's self-perception theory would make exactly the same predictions as dissonance theory in all of the classic dissonance experiments. Because the usual dissonance resolution in Step 5 is to adopt the position in Step 2 after going through Steps 3 and 4, the outcome is the same.

Bem argued that what the dissonance experiments may have been demonstrating is that people infer their own attitudes from observing their own behavior, in just the same way an outside observer would infer their attitudes. If an outside observer heard you say that you loved an experiment, he or she would assume you did like it. But if the outside observer knew you'd been paid $20 to say that you liked the experiment, he or she would not assume you believed what you were saying.

The critical difference between self-perception theory and dissonance theory involves Steps 3 and 4: Do people remember their initial attitude, and do they experience dissonance? Because the dissonance process seems to be largely unconscious, this isn't an easily resolved dispute. As cognitive dissonance theory would predict, people sometimes do experience the dissonance of Step 4 (Zanna & Cooper, 1974). Furthermore, actions that are inconsistent with attitudes cause detectable physiological arousal, which indicates the presence of some negative motivational state like dissonance (Croyle & Cooper, 1983).

On the opposite side of the controversy, as self-perception theory would predict, people often seem to be unaware of their previous attitudes (Bem, 1972). Self-perception theory also has found support in a number of places where dissonance theory is irrelevant. For example, the James-Lange theory of emotion

Self-perception theory The theory that people come to know their own attitudes the same way they come to know the attributes of others, by unconsciously observing and interpreting behavior and the situation in which it occurs.

(discussed in Chapter 10) shares the assumption that feelings are the result, not the cause, of emotional behaviors. Self-perception theory is also central to the understanding of intrinsic motivation (discussed in Chapter 9).

Both the cognitive-dissonance and self-perception explanations are supported by solid evidence. It's no surprise, then, that researchers have concluded that both processes probably occur under different circumstances (Fazio, 1987). When a behavior is not too discrepant with a person's attitudes, the self-perception processes go to work. When the discrepancy is larger, however, the conflict generates dissonance and triggers the usual dissonance-reduction processes.

Both dissonance theory and self-perception theory tell us that the relationship between attitudes and behaviors is more complex than most people believe. In at least some situations, attitudes are a product of behaviors. The basic fit between what people believe and how they act is (at least sometimes) constructed after the actions have been completed.

Persuasion and Attitude Change

One way to change people's attitudes is to change their behavior. Another is to use more symbolic, verbal means—a *message*. **Persuasion** is the attempt by one person, the communicator, to change the attitudes of another, the audience, through a message. Acting together, these three components—communicator, audience, and message—determine the success of persuasion.

Determining the most effective combination of communicator and message properties for a particular audience is complicated by the fact that there seem to be two very different kinds of persuasive processes. In one, called the *central route* (Petty & Cacioppo, 1986) or *systematic processing* (Chaiken, Liberman & Eagly, 1989), people pay close attention, consciously processing the information in the message and about the communicator. In the other, the *peripheral route* or *heuristic processing,* people don't pay close attention and the information is not processed systematically.

The Audience   Audiences who are more involved with an issue and who know more about it are more likely to process arguments centrally. That is, they tend to examine the arguments relatively carefully and to be affected by the quality of the arguments rather than by the "peripheral" factors that we describe below (Tesser & Shaffer, 1990).

In addition, John Cacioppo and Richard Petty (1982) argue that people differ in their *need for cognition,* the degree to which they like to think about things or solve problems. People high in the need for cognition are more likely to process persuasive information centrally and, hence, are more responsive to the quality of an argument.

The Message   One of the questions you must answer in any attempt to persuade someone is whether to present just your side of the argument, or to present opposing arguments as well and then try to refute them. The one-sided strategy works best when your audience is not very well informed or not very thoughtful, conditions that minimize the likelihood of central processing (McGuire, 1985). For instance, if you're trying to persuade people to eat less meat for their health and you think they know very little about health issues, a simple one-sided argument works best.

However, if the audience knows about the issue and is intelligent, and especially if they initially disagree with you (as beef farmers might), you can assume that they're going to know the opposing arguments. In this case, it's more effective to present the opposing arguments and then to explain why they're wrong (Petty & Cacioppo, 1981).

Persuasion The attempt to change someone's attitudes or beliefs through a verbal message.

During his presidency, Ronald Reagan earned the title of the "Great Communicator" because he was especially successful at winning support for his policies from the general populace. His effectiveness as a communicator seemed to be unrelated to central factors, such as the actual content of his message. Instead, his effectiveness derived from peripheral factors—his audience perceived him as attractive and sincere.

If you're going to present both sides, which should come first? Should you talk about the antimeat arguments or the pro-meat arguments first? In the research on first impressions, we suggested that the first information people get affects how they process later information. The same principle applies here. So, in general, you want to present your side first. The only exception is a situation in which your audience is going to have to act immediately after hearing the two arguments, without much time to think about them. Here, it may be best to put your arguments last, so that they'll be fresh in the audience's mind as they make a decision (McGuire, 1985).

A good strategy for the communicator is to explicitly state the conclusions that should be drawn from the argument. Another technique is to ask for a big commitment immediately. In general, the more you ask for, the more you'll get—but only to a point. At that point, you lose credibility and the audience stops responding (McGuire, 1985). In your anti-meat campaign, for instance, you should tell the members of the audience that they should quit eating meat immediately, if you think they will not reject your arguments completely.

How emotional do you make your appeals? Should you talk graphically about the horrors of strokes and heart disease brought on by cholesterol, or should you keep the argument less emotional? Generally, the more fear a message provokes, the more effective it is (Robberson & Rogers, 1988), but only if it also supplies a clear course of action for avoiding the feared outcome (Leventhal, 1970).

The Communicator   What makes a good communicator? The main characteristics of successful persuaders are expert status, attractiveness, and credibility. However, as expert status and attractiveness are not necessarily tied to the quality of the arguments, these factors affect only peripheral attitude change processes (see Table 17.3). Consequently, both factors affect an audience only if the audience is not paying close attention. Even credibility has to be reflected in the quality of the message; otherwise, it's effective only during peripheral processing (Maddux & Rogers, 1980). In sum, the effects of persuader variables occur only when conditions favor peripheral routes to persuasion (DeBono & Harnish, 1988).

Table 17.3
Central and Peripheral Factors in Persuasion

Central Factors
- The quality of the argument
- The credibility of the communicator (in support of an argument only)

Peripheral Factors
- The attractiveness of the communicator
- The expertise of the communicator (independent of the quality of the argument)
- The similarity of the communicator to the audience
- The length of the message
- The style of the presentation
- The emphasis of the message
- Agreement among multiple sources
- The audience's mood
- The likability of the communicator

Persuasion in the Real World   The findings we've been describing are particularly applicable to the needs of advertisers and politicians. Most of the commercials you see on television or the ads you see in magazines aren't trying to make rational arguments; they've been designed to follow the peripheral route. They try to persuade you by linking the object for sale to other objects you like or by

Manipulation

Social psychologists have identified two particularly manipulative ways to change attitudes—techniques that the practical psychologists who sell encyclopedias door to door or used cars have long used intuitively.

The foot-in-the-door technique   The idea here is to ask first for a small favor and then for a large one. In one study, housewives in California were asked to sign a petition for safe driving. This was such a small request that they all agreed. But a week later the researchers were back, this time asking for permission to erect a large ugly sign on the front lawn. People who had signed the petition—compared to those who hadn't been asked—were much more likely to agree to the sign (Freedman & Fraser, 1966).

This strategy is at work when you get a mail offer that promises more information (usually something that's going to cost you money) if you return a postcard or call an 800 number. Most people don't stop to think that the organizations could have sent the information to begin with. The intent is to get you to make a small first step toward them (Cialdini, 1985).

How does it work? Your first behavior—signing the petition or calling the 800 number—is a behavior that implies you agree with the cause or are interested in the object that's being sold. Your self-perception processes may lead to a more favorable attitude as a result. And when the second request comes, you are likely to respond in line with your new attitude (DeJong, 1979).

The door-in-the-face technique   This technique works the other way around. Here the persuader starts off with a large request that he or she expects to be refused, then follows with a smaller request that you're more likely to agree to. The first refusal seems to create a sense of obligation that you meet by agreeing to the second request (Cialdini, 1985).

In one study, college students were asked to volunteer large amounts of time to a counseling program for delinquents. After they had refused, they were asked to spend two hours one day taking a group of delinquents to the zoo. Fewer than a fifth of those who received only the second request agreed to the zoo trip, but half of those who had refused the larger request agreed to go (Cialdini et al., 1975).

We have described these techniques so that you can be alert. Knowing that they are being used is the best way to avoid falling prey to them. A natural response is also to wonder if you could use these techniques to good advantage. We strongly recommend against any such effort. Obviously there are moral problems with these manipulative acts. And from a practical standpoint, the costs of discovery are likely to outweigh any gains, since people are often offended by such highly manipulative techniques.

separating the object from other objects you dislike. Why don't advertisers use techniques aimed at more rational, intelligent, informed audiences? The answer is that they can't. An ad is not a credible source: it's been bought and paid for by a manufacturer or a politician. Time and space are factors, too. There usually isn't enough time in a thirty-second commercial or enough space on a full-page ad to present a solid argument.

Recap

- An attitude is a feeling of liking or disliking that also involves the way people think about and behave toward the object of that feeling.

- Behavior is determined by a large number of factors, only one of which is the individual's attitude toward a person or object.

- People change their attitudes to conform to their behaviors—because they want to eliminate cognitive dissonance or because they infer their attitudes directly from their behaviors.

- Persuasion is the attempt by one person, the communicator, to change the attitudes of another, the audience, through a message.

- When an audience is knowledgeable and paying close attention, persuasion should take the central route, relying on the quality of the message. But when an audience is not particularly knowledgeable or attentive, peripheral factors, like the attractiveness of the communicator, become more important in generating a change in attitudes.

Aggression and Altruism

We close this chapter with a discussion of two topics in which schemas and balance and other more or less cognitive principles do not play a central role. This isn't surprising because aggression and altruism are the two areas in which the social behavior of humans most closely parallels that of animals.

Aggression

One man punches another in a bar. A woman is knocked down on the street, her purse stolen. One country invades another, occupying its territory. These are all instances of **aggression,** behavior that's intended to injure another person. Where does aggression come from? And what can we do to control it?

Where Does Aggression Come From? Some psychologists argue that human beings have an innate, and hence inevitable, tendency to behave aggressively. Others insist that aggression is learned and can be radically altered by learning.

Is aggression innate? As we described in Chapter 14, Sigmund Freud (1920/1959) believed that people have an innate aggressive drive. Accordingly, he believed that people need suitably symbolic and indirect outlets for their aggressive impulses, in order to avoid the impulses being expressed more directly. This notion of relieving built-up instinctual energy Freud called **catharsis.**

Konrad Lorenz (1966) shared Freud's belief that aggression is innate. We talked about Lorenz's work with animals in Chapter 11. He and other ethologists (people who study animals' behavior in their natural environment) pointed out that behavior seemingly analogous to human aggression can be observed in a great many animals: dogs fight until one runs off whimpering; robins threaten each other to defend their patches of lawn; even fish charge rivals that are trying to invade their breeding grounds. Lorenz believed that aggression is a natural way of settling disputes over scarce resources.

Direct evidence of a biological foundation for aggression is quite scarce, but there is considerable indirect evidence that links aggression to both genetics and biochemistry:

Aggression Behavior that is intended to hurt another person.

Catharsis The process of relieving an impulse by expressing it directly or indirectly.

Aggressive behaviors occur in a wide variety of animal species, although each species has its own way of carrying out aggression.

- *Genetics* Think for a minute about the temperaments of pitbulls and golden retrievers. Obviously animals can be bred to act more or less aggressively. In our discussion of development, we noted that human temperament, including the tendency toward aggression, also seems to be shaped by genetic factors (Tellegen et al., 1988).

- *Biochemistry* The male is physically more aggressive than the female—a difference that is common to most mammals (Eagly & Steffen, 1986). This gender difference suggests that aggression might be linked to testosterone, the sex hormone that males produce in much greater quantity than do females (Moyer, 1983).

Do such findings mean that aggression is an innate drive, as Freud and Lorenz hypothesized? Not at all. At most, they demonstrate that people, like most mammals, are built such that one of the many kinds of responses they are capable of making is aggression. People are also built such that they can respond in other ways to the same situations. Which kind of response occurs may depend on learning.

Is aggression learned?   On the other side of the issue, many researchers point to evidence that adults and children are more or less aggressive depending on their exposure to aggressive models and on their experience—their success or failure—using aggression. For example, children whose parents use physical punishment tend to be more physically aggressive, perhaps because they've learned by watching their parents (Bandura, Ross & Ross, 1961). And, as we discussed in Chapter 6, there is strong evidence that watching violence on television increases the likelihood of acting aggressively (Eron & Huesmann, 1984; Rule & Ferguson, 1986).

Closely related to the TV/violence question is the question of whether pornography fosters rape or violence toward women. As you might imagine, collecting persuasive evidence on this question is difficult, and most psychologists are uncertain in their conclusions. Nevertheless, numerous studies have demonstrated distressing results of exposure to pornography that features violent treatment of women and/or rape. After viewing violent pornography, men react less negatively to violence toward women and view rape less negatively as well (Linz, Donnerstein & Penrod, 1988). A frequent fictional theme is the "rape myth," which depicts women as becoming aroused during a physical assault and ultimately becoming attracted to the assailant. Viewing even nonpornographic depictions of the rape myth can increase men's acceptance of it (Malamuth & Check, 1981).

In sum, there is little evidence that pornography leads to rape or violence. But numerous negative effects of pornography (especially violent pornography) on violence-related attitudes and beliefs have been demonstrated. Concern is certainly justified.

The Role of the Environment   Whatever their genetic makeup or learning history, people do not act aggressively all of the time. They act aggressively only in response to certain environmental factors. One of those factors is temperature. As the temperature rises above 90 degrees, the number of violent crimes increases dramatically (Anderson & Anderson, 1984).

Overcrowding and economic hard times are also associated with higher crime rates (Fleming, Baum & Weiss, 1987). These factors probably work by increasing tension and discomfort. In Chapter 10 we talked about how physiological changes can be misattributed to other sources. In this case, the arousal and discomfort of heat and hard times may be transformed into anger and aggression (Zillman, 1983).

One early theory held that all aggression is a product of frustration: if people can't get what they want, they respond with aggression (Dollard et al., 1939). But, depending on how it's understood, frustration apparently leads to a variety of responses, including apathy, withdrawal, and even renewed effort. Frustration seems to be only one of the causes of aggression (Buss, 1961).

Altruism and Helping

As natural as our capacity to hurt one another is our capacity to help one another. Every year people all over the world donate millions of dollars to charities. Newspapers and magazines carry stories about the firefighter who risked life and limb saving an infant, the doctor who traveled to Iraq to save the lives of wounded citizens, the missionary who has spent a lifetime helping the poor in the slums of Calcutta. In this section we explore the sources of helping behaviors and the sometimes surprising conditions that increase and inhibit those behaviors.

Where Does Altruism Come From?   The phenomenon of **altruism**—helping another without any obvious prospect of reward—poses a puzzle for psychologists. Psychologists find it easier to believe that people are motivated by what are essentially selfish concerns. So when they try to explain altruism, they often look for selfish motives underlying what are apparently unselfish behaviors.

According to one approach, for example, most societies have more or less explicit expectations that their members are going to help one another. When those expectations aren't met, members of the society express their disapproval in a variety of ways, ranging from saying something nasty to imprisoning the offender (Berkowitz, 1972). Societies make not helping "cost" more than helping.

Another kind of cost is bad feelings. If not helping someone makes you feel badly, then you may help just to avoid those feelings. A "selfish" theory based on this observation argues that people always act to maximize their benefits. This means that if the "costs" of helping are too high, people are going to try to find some other way of dealing with their bad feelings (Piliavin et al., 1981). A less selfish version argues that people have a tendency to empathize with those in distress, to share their suffering (Batson, 1987). This empathy moves people to help—especially when they feel close to the victim—despite the costs of helping (Batson et al., 1988).

Ethologists, trying to explain altruistic behavior in animals, have pointed to a deeper level of selfishness that's captured in the title of one of the early books on the subject, *The Selfish Gene* (Dawkins, 1976). The theory of evolution assumes that organisms that exist now do so because they have been able to reproduce more successfully than those that couldn't. As a group, they survived. Because organisms are defined by their genetic structure, what's really at stake is the survival of the gene. Thus, the selfishness—the tendency to try to thrive at all costs—may exist only in the gene. The survival of individual animals makes sense only as long as their survival is best for the survival of the gene.

Altruism Helping another without any expectation of a reward.

Helping is widespread in the animal kingdom. For example, this otter, which was covered in oil from the 1989 Exxon Valdez spill, is helping another otter (left). And, in 1987, the entire town of Midland, Texas was involved in the rescue of two-year-old Jessica McClure from a 22-foot well (right). Helping and altruism are so common in animals that some inherited mechanism seems likely to exist.

So, for example, it makes good evolutionary sense for an aging adult animal to lay down its life for its children, who carry the adult's genes.

An extension of this idea appeared in Chapter 9, where we discussed the theory that animals might sacrifice themselves for others to the extent that they share genes. The implication is that animals would be most willing to help their close relatives. But because the vast majority of the genes of every member of a species are the same, altruism should extend to any member of the species (Wilson, 1978).

The selfish-gene concept is still being debated. Certainly it might explain why people feel badly when someone else is hurt and why they're inclined to help. But some psychologists insist that the theory trivializes altruism. Alternatively, we might marvel at evolutionary processes that may make human beings innately helpful to each other.

The Role of the Situation   Whether altruism is an innate response or not, it's clear that people don't always help other people. The factors that increase or reduce helping behaviors seem to be rooted in the situation.

Everyday situations   Generally, people are more likely to help someone if the costs of helping aren't too high or if they empathize with the victim. Seeing someone else help is also a strong spur to helping. In one clever demonstration of this principle, researchers created the appearance that a motorist had stopped on a throughway to help a woman change a tire. A mile down the road, they stationed another woman with a flat tire. They found that people were much more likely to help if they had seen the helping model (Bryan & Test, 1967). People who ask for money on the street know the truth of this principle. That's why they always put some money into their cup or basket or hat before they start to pass it.

Another determinant of everyday helping is mood. Many studies have shown that anything that makes people happier is likely to make them help more—even something as trivial as being given a cookie or finding change in a phone booth (Isen, 1987).

Helping in Emergencies   In New York City, one night in 1964, a woman named Kitty Genovese was attacked on the street in a middle-class neighborhood. She screamed for help, struggled with her attacker, and escaped, still screaming. Her cries attracted the attention of the people living nearby. At least thirty-eight men and women watched from their apartment windows as the man caught her, stabbed her, was frightened away by her struggles and screams, and then came back and finally killed her—thirty minutes after the attack began. During that time, not a single person helped her. No one even called the police.

The newspaper accounts of this incident attributed the onlookers' unwillingness to help to the stony indifference bred by life in the big city. Psychologists

John Darley and Bib Latané disagreed, and they set about studying the conditions under which people help in an emergency.

They identified a number of factors that might have interfered with her neighbors' decision to help Genovese. One is *diffusion of responsibility,* which reduces the individual's responsibility to act. They believed that a single individual probably would have taken action, but that in a group, each person assumed others would help. To test this idea, Darley and Latané (1968) set up an apparent emergency. They told their subjects that they were studying the ways people talk about personal things. To protect their anonymity, the subjects would sit in individual cubicles and talk over an intercom. Even the researcher wouldn't listen in; he was seated at a desk down the hall.

Shortly after the discussions began, one of the subjects seemed to have a seizure and could be heard calling for help. In fact, there was only one real subject each time the experiment was conducted; all of the others, including the one who had the "seizure," were the tape-recorded voices of actors. Because the real subjects had not seen the person who apparently was having a seizure, and did not know where he was, the only way they could help was to get up and tell the researcher. The question was, would they?

Some subjects believed the group consisted of just two people, themselves and the person having the seizure. So these subjects believed they were the only ones who knew about the seizure and the only ones who could help. In this condition, 86 percent of the subjects helped within two minutes (see Figure 17.11). Another group of subjects believed that there were three people in the group, that another person could help. Only 62 percent of this group went to get help. In a third group of subjects, who believed that four other people were taking part in the discussion, only 30 percent helped. The people who didn't help certainly did believe there was a real emergency because they asked anxiously about the seizure victim as soon as the experimenter appeared. But they did not help.

Figure 17.11
Helping in Groups

When subjects believed that other people knew about an emergency and could offer assistance, they were less likely to help. The number of potential helpers was also a factor—the more people available to help meant the less likely any of them would.

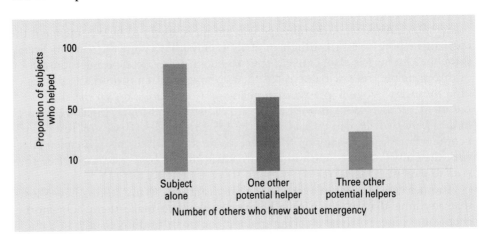

Source: Data from Darley & Latané, 1968.

What Darley and Latané had found was that as the number of potential helpers increased, the likelihood that any one of them actually would help decreased. This is called the **bystander effect,** and it's been demonstrated in many experiments involving thousands of subjects (Latané & Nida, 1981).

The people who failed Kitty Genovese were not unusual. The problem lay in the situation. The more people who were watching, the less likely any individual was to help. Because all of the onlookers could see at least some of the others at their windows, they assumed that someone else had taken responsibility and had phoned the police. Even in crowds, if everyone can see that no one else is helping, people do act (Piliavin, Rodin & Piliavin, 1969).

Bystander effect As the number of potential helpers increases, the likelihood that any one of them actually will help decreases.

How Do We Know That?

John Darley and Bib Latané believed that the Kitty Genovese case had been misunderstood. The reason no one helped her was not because city dwellers are callous, but because there were so many people involved. Yet their explanation could not be tested by even the closest analysis of newspaper accounts of real life events. To identify the actual causes of helping, they needed to perform experiments.

As they designed their experiments, they were facing a problem that is common among social psychologists especially, but one that all psychologists must handle. The problem was to make an inevitably artificial experiment match a real-life situation. That is, they needed to "model" the essential elements of a real-life emergency situation. However, they also had to avoid any real dangers, and to arrange the procedures so that they could observe subjects' behaviors systematically.

We have seen some other examples of modeling of complex social situations in this chapter. In his studies of the just-world phenomenon, Lerner needed to reproduce the essentially random misfortunes that befall people. Festinger's studies of cognitive dissonance were actually inspired by his observations of the effects of the members' actions on their devotion to a cult. And, indeed, most studies of aggression must somehow mimic real aggression.

In all of these cases, the results of the studies contradicted common sense to some degree. Small wonder, then, that one criticism of all these experiments has been that the model did not accurately capture the true nature of the real-life situation. Perhaps in real life the presence of other people does not inhibit helping?

The essential task of the experimenter in such studies is to persuade the audience that the essential features of the real-life situation have been reproduced. Of course, no one can prove that the reproduction has been successful; this conclusion can only be argued plausibly. However, once new principles have been discovered or confirmed in the laboratory model, the experimenters must return to the real world. If the experiments have been successful, they will have yielded new insights that can be used in the real world. Once again, we see that real confidence lies in the results of programs of research employing many different methods.

There's another problem with helping in an emergency situation: recognizing that there is an emergency. One day on Wall Street, at noon, when the most densely populated area in the world poured thousands of people onto the street for lunch, a man had a heart attack. As he lay on the sidewalk, conscious but unable to move, people passed right by him. No one helped. The problem may have been that people didn't realize he needed help. After all, although he was dressed like every other Wall Street denizen, he could have been drunk.

In their analysis of the effects of crowds on helping, Latané and Darley (1970) identified a number of different steps that must be followed to help in an emergency. These steps are shown in Figure 17.12. Note that Step 2 is recognizing that an emergency exists. Latané and Darley suspected that the presence of others can interfere with this step, too, and constructed another experimental model to explore their hypothesis.

In this study, subjects were brought into a room on a high floor of a New York building and then were asked to fill out some papers. While they were doing this, harmless but very realistic smoke was pumped into the room

Figure 17.12
The Steps in Helping in an Emergency

A person will help another only if all the steps identified by Latané and Darley are passed. At many of these steps, the presence of others actually interferes.

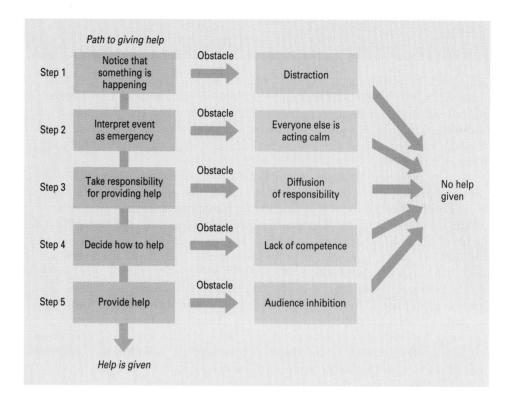

Source: Adapted from Brehm & Kassin, 1990; data from Latané & Darley, 1970.

through an air conditioning duct, while the experimenters observed the subjects' behavior through a one-way window. The subjects were either alone or with three other subjects. To respond to this "emergency," the subjects again had to leave the room and inform a researcher waiting outside.

When individual subjects were alone in the smoke-filled room, most informed the researcher. However, when four subjects (none of whom were confederates of the experimenter) were together in the room, fewer than a quarter told anyone. In fact, the groups of subjects were slower to notice the smoke at all, apparently because each subject in a group was focused on his or her own part of the room. Later, when asked to explain their reactions, the subjects said they had looked around and noticed that no one else seemed to be worried about the smoke, so they concluded that the situation must be all right. Not wanting to seem foolish, they went back to their work.

Notice that when a subject went back to work, he or she was providing a cue to the other subjects that everything was all right. When the next person looked up, he or she would find the reassuring sight of the others working. So each person reassured the others, creating a kind of joint myth of safety. In the same way, each passerby on Wall Street must have been reassured by the apparent indifference of those around, and so concluded that there was no emergency.

What all of this research tells us is that, by their very presence, other people can seriously inhibit help in an emergency. If other people are around, you are less likely to recognize that an emergency exists. Even if you do recognize it, you are likely to let someone else help unless it's obvious that no one's going to do so. There is a moral to this story. Someday you are going to be faced with a situation that might be an emergency. When that happens, don't hesitate to help: probably no one else will. Moreover, if you're unsure about the situation, don't judge what's going on by the apparent reactions of those around you. They probably don't know either. And, remember, even if you aren't sure of your competence to deal with the situation, you can at least summon people who are.

Recap

- Aggression and altruism are the two areas in which the social behavior of humans most closely parallels that of animals.

- Aggression is behavior that's intended to injure another person.

- There is considerable indirect evidence that links aggression to genetics and biochemistry.

- Although the capacity to make aggressive responses may be innate, evidence suggests that people are more or less aggressive depending on their exposure to aggressive models and on their experience using aggression.

- Among the environmental factors that increase aggression are high temperatures, overcrowding, and economic hardship.

- Altruism is the act of helping another without any obvious prospect of reward.

- Among the explanations that psychologists have proposed for altruism are societal pressures, empathy, and the selfish gene.

- The factors that increase or reduce helping behaviors seem to be rooted in the situation.

- Among the determinants of helping in everyday situations is seeing someone else help.

- Studies of helping in emergency situations demonstrate the bystander effect: as the number of potential helpers increases, the likelihood that any one of them actually will help decreases.

- Another obstacle to helping in an emergency is the failure to recognize that an emergency exists.

Conclusion

Many of the processes we have described in this chapter occur without our intent or conscious recognition as we go about responding to and trying to understand our social world and ourselves. The research presented here often portrays human behavior—our behavior—as simple-mindedly primitive. For example, to blame victims for their misfortunes or to blindly assume that beautiful people are good and good people beautiful are the kinds of thinking we all would like to avoid. No better are the cognitive processes that support the development of prejudices against anyone who is different from us.

The research also implies some surprising weaknesses. We can be induced to change our attitudes and beliefs by just acting as if we believed the new attitudes. The foot-in-the-door and the door-in-the-face techniques trick us into agreeing to unreasonable requests. And the conditions under which we will, or more depressingly, will *not* help someone in distress cannot make us feel proud.

This bleak picture of human behavior is true, but only partly true. We act and think in these ways when we are not paying close attention, when we are responding automatically. Only when we are caught up in social situations that sweep us along inattentively do these undesirable kinds of behavior emerge. One moral of this chapter is clear, then. If we are to be strong, moral, and rational, we must be thoughtful, attentive, and informed.

Chapter 18

The Individual and the Social Group

Les Constructeurs, Fernand Léger, 1950

18

Gateways "Most people would never hurt another human being if they could help it." "If only everyone acted rationally, environmental problems could be solved." "People make better decisions and are more productive when they work together rather than alone." Although most people would agree with these propositions, research strongly suggests they are wrong. In this chapter, as we examine the effects of groups on individuals, we encounter some of the most startling research findings in psychology. These findings demonstrate that most people do not appreciate how powerfully groups can shape the individual's behavior. That is a key reason why social psychologists find it so important to study social groups.

We hope this chapter calls to mind our discussion of counterintuitive research results in Chapter 1. Because much of the behavior described here derives from learning of which we are unaware, this chapter also echoes earlier discussions of attention (Chapters 4 and 5) and of learning (Chapter 6). Finally, in documenting the individual's vulnerability to social forces, this chapter casts additional light on the relative importance of personal and situational factors, discussed in Chapter 17.

A student was waiting outside the door to my office, pacing back and forth.

"Professor, I think I need some help."

He certainly looked like he did—harried and tense. As we walked into the office, I asked what the problem was, all the time thinking that I would urge him to contact the counseling center.

"Well, I hurt someone, a bunch of people, for no reason. I just don't know why I did it. I've always tried to treat people right, but this time I just, I don't know, I just got too involved or something, lost control or something."

Puzzled by his vagueness, I asked him to back up and start again from the beginning.

"Well, you see, I guess it started when I joined the fraternity. I had gotten to know a bunch of guys who I liked a lot and who were all in one of the fraternities, so it was natural for me to join. You know the school has a big rule against any hazing during initiation, but the members kind of ignored that. In fact, one of the things we had to do was to sign a big oath that we would never tell anyone about our initiation. And some of that stuff was awful. But whenever I felt like it just wasn't worth it, I'd look at the other pledges, and they weren't complaining, so I told myself if they could do it, so could I. And the members said they'd done the same kind of things when they joined. So anyhow, I stuck it out, and afterward I was really glad because I enjoyed being a member.

"Now that I'm a member, my older sister, who graduated last year, says I sound just like everyone else in the fraternity. She says I even dress like all of them. I always hate it when she says that, but I guess she's right. In fact, when we were talking last week in class about how similarity led to friendship, I thought that sounded just like us.

"Last weekend, it was time to initiate the new members, and that was the problem. It was O.K. in the beginning, but then it got worse and worse. I mean we didn't do anything really bad, like you read about in the papers—no one would have gotten hurt real bad. In fact, it was pretty much the same stuff that was done to us last year. But it was pretty tough on them. At first I didn't think anything of it. After all, last year it would have been me. But there was this one kid who was really scared, and he began to shake, and I wanted to stop, but the others said we had to finish, so I went ahead.

"Anyhow, it was afterward that I really began to feel bad. I had no business treating another person like that. I just can't believe that I spent a night making a bunch of other people, people I really like, feel miserable, and for no reason. I just feel real lousy because I never thought I was that kind of a person. So what do you think I should do?"

"Well," I said, "I think you would have felt differently about yourself if you'd waited to hear what we're going to be talking about in class this week. It won't excuse your behavior; you're going to have to make up for that by trying to change how your fraternity behaves in the future. But at least you'd understand why you acted the way you did. And you'd realize that what you did probably had very little to do with your personality and more to do with the situation."

527

I went on to describe some of the research we talk about in this chapter, about the ways—sometimes very surprising ways—in which social situations and the forces they generate shape the individual's behavior.

We begin with a discussion of conformity, the tendency of individuals to adjust their behavior to the expectations of others, and obedience, the response individuals make to the explicit demands of others. Then we talk about social roles, the organized sets of expectations that groups hold for their members. Next we discuss the effects of groups on performance and decision making. Finally, we look at the sources of conflict and the effect of cooperation on resolving conflict. Throughout, you may be very surprised at what the research reveals about the group's influence on the individual.

Conformity

Why do college students wear bell-bottoms in one decade and torn jeans in the next? Why do professors wear tweeds and stockbrokers, gray pin-stripes? Why do hemlines rise and fall in unison? And why did my student act and even dress so much like the other members of his fraternity? These are all examples of **conformity**—instances in which individuals change their behavior, feelings, or beliefs to match the expectations of those around them.

All groups have expectations about how their members will act, think, and even look.

Norms

The standards of behavior that the members of a group share are called **norms.** Some norms are explicit; they may even be written down. For example, most campus organizations have very clear rules: "You should come to meetings," "You should wait to be recognized before speaking," "You should get your committee reports in on time."

Most organizations also have less explicit norms. For example: "You shouldn't sneer when others make suggestions," "During the business session, you shouldn't talk about how you spent the weekend," "You shouldn't come to meetings drunk." These kinds of norms probably aren't written down. In fact, they probably aren't even discussed until someone sneers at someone else's suggestion or holds a private conversation during the business session or comes to a meeting drunk. But there's no question that the group expects its members to behave in certain ways and that these behaviors aren't appropriate.

Even less explicit are the norms that govern the way people dress or cut their hair. Norms like these are usually characteristic of less formal groups, such as groups of friends.

Finally, one kind of norm is so difficult to recognize that even when someone fails to meet it, we may not know what's happening. We just feel uncomfortable, and know that the violator is acting peculiarly. These most-hidden norms govern the details of how people interact with one another—where they look during a conversation, how loudly they speak, even how they hold their bodies (Goffman, 1967).

An example of these covert norms are those that govern conversational distance. When two people speak, they ordinarily position themselves at a distance from each other—a distance that reflects the nature of their conversation and the nature of their relationship. In our society, for example, friends ordinarily stand or sit about two to four feet apart. Acquaintances, or people doing business, stand four to six feet apart (Hall, 1966). In other cultures, the norms that govern conversational distance are different. In many Arab cultures, for example, friends interact at a much closer distance: they aren't comfortable unless each can feel the other's breath. In Western cultures, however, that distance is reserved for only the most intimate relationships. A friend or acquaintance who stands too close makes us uncomfortable (Sommer, 1969).

Because we are all unaware of these norms, you have probably experienced them without knowing it. You didn't say to yourself that this person is standing too close or too far away; instead you had a sense that the individual was pushy or cold.

Every culture has norms regarding the relationship between people and how close or far apart they stand when conversing. You might suppose these two men are good friends because they are standing so close to each other. But this may not be the case. Conversational distances in Middle Eastern countries are generally much closer than in Western countries, so even though these two men could be friends they could just as easily be business acquaintances.

How Norms Work

The norms of conversational distance reveal how powerful the norms of our groups can be. Norms influence us in two ways—by defining what is "true" and by defining what is "proper" behavior (Deutsch & Gerard, 1955).

Informational Social Influence   One of the ways in which norms influence people is by defining their reality. Often it's impossible for individuals to collect information about the world themselves, so they must rely on group norms to tell them what's "true." For example, unless you're an astronomer, you have to rely on your culture's explanation of the heavens. The people in some cultures believe the stars are departed spirits; in our culture, we believe they are distant suns. But in all cultures, including our own, most people have to accept the culture's opinion.

In other cases, what's being defined isn't "truth"; it's what's "correct" or "proper." Whether you hold your fork in your left hand or your right doesn't affect how the food tastes or how nutritious it is. But it does reflect your culture. In this country, people hold their forks in their right hand; in England, they hold their forks in the left. There's no intrinsic right or wrong here; the culture defines what's "correct" and what isn't. So the group influences its members by supplying them with information—about what is true and what is proper. This is called **informational social influence.**

In one of the earliest studies of social psychology, Muzafer Sherif (1936) came up with a way to study the development and influence of norms about truth. He began by seating his subjects—individual college students—in a dark room. Nothing was visible in the room but a tiny point of light. Although the light was actually fixed, in the dark it seemed to move. Sherif asked each subject to estimate how far the light had moved. Because the movement was entirely an illusion, there was no "real" answer, and the estimates varied widely from person to person.

Conformity Changing one's behavior, feelings, or beliefs to match the expectations of the group.

Norm A pattern of behavior shared and required by members of a group.

Informational social influence The capacity of a group to influence behaviors and attitudes by defining what is true or correct.

The next day the subjects returned and repeated the procedure, but with one difference: this time Sherif placed three subjects together in the dark room. The subjects each made a number of estimates that the others could hear. Naturally the members of the group began with different estimates of how far the light had moved, based on their experience the day before. But very quickly, the estimates moved up or down as the group converged on a distance that was usually somewhere in the middle. Each group returned two more days; by the last day, the members of each group agreed almost perfectly (see Figure 18.1).

Figure 18.1
The Creation of Norms

The three subjects were sitting in the dark, observing a light that actually didn't move. Initially, each subject estimated the amount of movement differently, but by the third session their opinions had converged.

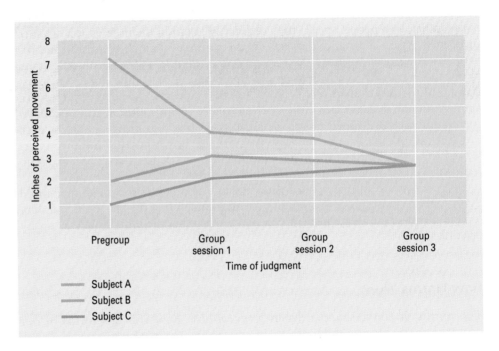

Source: Brehm & Kassin, 1990; data from Sherif, 1936.

Notice that at no time during this procedure did anyone attempt to directly influence anyone else. The subjects just announced their individual judgments and gradually came to agree. And when interviewed later, the subjects were confident that their individual judgment was accurate, although it had changed to match the rest of the group. Without any discussion at all—without realizing what was happening—the group had developed a norm about what was "really" happening, and this norm determined what the members of the group believed they saw.

Another classic study of group influence showed the same effect in real life (Newcomb, 1943). In the 1930s, most of the students at Bennington College came from wealthy conservative families. When they arrived on campus, they held the same conservative political attitudes as their families. However, with each year they spent at Bennington, their attitudes became more liberal: by the time they graduated, most were Democrats. Theodore Newcomb pointed out that there was virtually no direct pressure on new students to adopt more liberal attitudes. Instead, they were exposed to groups of older students and faculty who held these attitudes, and they just gradually accepted them as truth.

Normative Social Influence Another way groups influence behavior is by "punishing" those who don't conform. If you don't act the way others in your group think you should, they may give you funny looks or make a joke about your behavior. If you persist in deviating, they may tell you that you're behav-

ing badly. If you still persist, they may stop letting you share in the group's activities or even expel you from the group. In the end, then, one reason group members act alike is that if they don't, they won't continue to be members of the group. When group members change their behavior to avoid the group's disapproval, they are responding to **normative social influence.**

Solomon Asch (1956) devised a fiendishly simple way to study normative social influence. A college student arriving to take part in what was supposedly a study of perception would be seated near the end of a row of other subjects, who were apparently being run at the same time. Then all of the subjects were shown a standard line and three comparison lines, like the ones in Figure 18.2. Their task was to indicate which of the three comparison lines was most like the standard line.

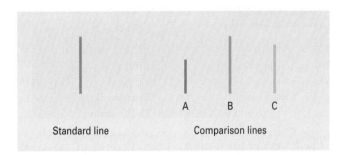

Standard line   Comparison lines

Figure 18.2
Asch's Conformity Experiment

Clearly, line B is most like the standard line. Yet one after the other, the members of the group chose line C.

On the first trial, everyone would choose the correct line, like B in the figure. After a few trials, however, the subject would be first surprised and then confused to hear one after another of the other subjects choose an obviously incorrect line, like C. As you've probably realized, all the "subjects" except one were working with Asch, whose real goal was to find out how the real subject would react to this unanimous agreement on what was clearly the wrong answer.

What Asch found was that a surprising proportion of the people went along with the group. More than 70 percent of the subjects agreed with the group at least once, and about 50 percent conformed more than half the time. Notice that in this situation, the subjects knew there was a conflict between what the members of the group said and what they themselves saw. In contrast to Sherif's subjects, Asch's subjects were aware that when they agreed with the group, they were denying the evidence of their own eyes. In fact, many said afterward that they agreed with the group only to avoid looking foolish or different.

Normative social influence The capacity of a group to influence its members by the threat of its disapproval.

This is an important difference. What Sherif found was *true conformity,* in which the influence of the group changed both what the subjects said and what they genuinely believed. What Asch found was **compliance:** most of his subjects changed their behavior, but their beliefs did not change (Kelman, 1961). Although Asch's subjects went along with the group, they knew full well that the group was wrong.

Norms and Conformity

Conformity for either informational or normative reasons depends on a balance between the individual and the group. The individual's tendency to submit to informational influence is a function of confidence in his or her own judgment versus confidence in the group's judgment. Normative influence depends on the balance between the individual's fear of the group's disapproval and the individual's commitment to his or her own opinion.

The Individual's Confidence   In the balance between the individual and the group, one side of the equation is the confidence individuals have in their own judgment. To test the role of confidence, Asch made the comparison lines more similar in length (see Figure 18.3), making the subjects' task more difficult. As the task became more difficult, the subjects conformed more (Asch, 1956). In another variation, the subjects were given a pretest and told they were either very good or very bad at the task. They conformed less or more depending on what they'd been told. More general feelings of confidence have similar affects, since people who have low self-esteem, or a high need for social approval, also are more likely to conform (M. Snyder & Ickes, 1985).

Figure 18.3
Increasing Conformity

As the lines become more similar in length, the judgment gets more difficult, and the subjects are more likely to conform.

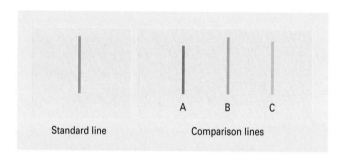

Standard line   Comparison lines

The Power of the Group   The other half of the influence equation is the group's power. There are numerous ways in which the group can have a bigger impact. For example, more attractive and more expert groups tend to produce more conformity (Lott & Lott, 1961).

Bigger groups also increase conformity, although Asch initially found that increasing the size of the group made little difference once the group had three or four members (Asch, 1956). Apparently his conclusion was correct in this specific situation, in which the subject was aware that each group member knew the responses of all the other members. However, a later study showed that when a subject believed the other subjects were unaware of each other's judgments, each additional independent judgment continued to exercise some additional influence. In this study, subjects heard various-sized groups of people give their (incorrect) opinions. When a group of six knew each other's judgments, they did not generate much more conformity than a group of three had generated (see Figure 18.4). However, when the subjects believed the six people were two completely independent groups of three, the effect was greater. And when

Compliance Changing one's external behavior without changing one's beliefs.

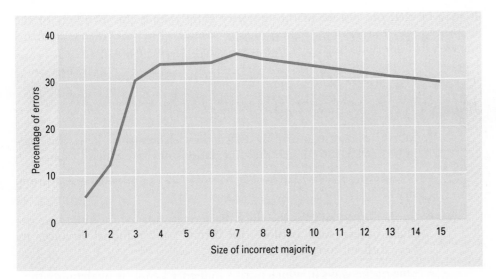

Figure 18.4
Conformity and Group Size

In Asch's original studies, increasing the number of people who chose the incorrect line did not increase conformity beyond three.

they believed the six were three groups of two, the effect was greater still (Wilder, 1977).

Ironically, these findings suggest that subjects in conformity experiments understand conformity, too. They seem to realize that if more than three people agree on the wrong answer, any others who agree may just be conforming to the group. The larger the group, then, the more likely subjects are to discount the opinions of its members when those opinions are obviously wrong and have been voiced in the presence of all the group's members.

The group's power depends on unanimity. If just one person in the group dissents, the group loses almost all of its influence (Asch, 1956). It may be that others see the dissenter as an ally, or that the dissenter serves as a model of "bravery" in the face of social pressure. In one study, the members of a group were asked to make judgments in two separate tasks. In the first, someone posing as a subject disagreed with the group—and with the real subject—by making a judgment that was clearly an error. But this model of independence was enough to make the real subjects resist conforming on the second task, in which all of the group members chose the wrong alternative (Nemeth & Chiles, 1988).

The Influence of the Minority

Most of what we've been describing sounds very much like a tyranny of the majority. Yet we know that a minority can sway the majority. Many changes in our society—among them the extension of civil rights to blacks and women—initially were supported only by small minorities.

To explore the impact of the minority, Serge Moscovici (1976) designed an experiment similar to Asch's but with four real subjects and two confederates. The group's task was to describe the color of a series of blue stimuli of varying shades. The real subjects announced that the stimuli were blue. But when the two confederates disagreed with the majority, insisting that the stimuli were green, more than 8 percent of the real subjects agreed with them. This is not a very big effect, but it is important when you consider that it was achieved in the face of unequal numbers and meant agreeing with an obvious error (Moscovici, Mugny & Van Avermaet, 1985).

Numerous other studies have confirmed that a minority can influence a majority (Nemeth, 1986). The exact mechanisms of influence aren't clear, however.

It may be that the dissent of the minority simply leads the members of the majority group to reexamine their positions carefully. But the evidence confirms the idea that a serious consistent minority can move the majority.

Recap

- Individuals are conforming when they change their behavior, feelings, or beliefs to match the expectations of those around them.

- Norms are the standards of behavior that the members of a group share.

- Some norms, such as the rules that govern formal meetings, are explicit; others, such as those that dictate conversational distance, are very difficult to recognize.

- One of the ways in which norms influence people is by defining their reality—what's "true" or what's "correct."

- Another way groups influence behavior is by "punishing" those who don't conform.

- In his moving-light experiment, Sherif found true conformity: the influence of the group changed the individual's behaviors and beliefs. By contrast what Asch found in his conformity experiments was compliance: the subjects' behavior changed, but their beliefs did not.

- The more confident individuals are in their own judgment, the less likely they are to conform to the group's judgment.

- The attractiveness of a group, its size, the seeming independence of group members' judgments, and unanimity are key factors in the influence of the group.

- Experimental evidence confirms the idea that a serious consistent minority can move the majority.

Obedience

At the time of his capture and trial in the early 1960s, Adolf Eichmann was the most notorious Nazi war criminal alive. The Israeli prosecutors presented overwhelming evidence of the appalling atrocities for which he was responsible, but his defense seemed almost as monstrous as his actions. Eichmann claimed over and over again that he was not guilty because he had just been following orders. Like other Nazis who had been tried before him, he seemed to sincerely believe that it was his duty to carry out immoral orders. The Israeli court, and world opinion, rejected Eichmann's defense. He was hanged in 1962.

Milgram's Experiment

Obedience Complying with the direct request or order of another person.

Eichmann's defense and a general concern with the role and effects of authority inspired one social psychologist, Stanley Milgram (1963), to explore the factors that affect **obedience**. In contrast to conformity, which is a relatively subtle influence on the individual, obedience is the response to—the compliance with—a direct demand for action.

Milgram's research raised several difficult issues, both practical and, especially, ethical. We shall talk about these issues later in the section. But, first, we look at the research itself, probably the most famous single program of research in psychology.

We want you to imagine that you're a subject in Milgram's initial experiment. You're living in New Haven, Connecticut, and answer an ad in a newspaper asking interested people to participate in a study on learning. When you arrive at the laboratory, at Yale, you meet a distinguished-looking professor and another volunteer who also is going to take part in the study. The other volunteer, a man of about fifty, seems nice.

The professor explains that the research concerns the role of punishment in learning, and that this particular study will consider the effects of an escalating schedule of punishments—a series of electric shocks. He goes on:

> We're going to choose one of you, at random, to be the teacher and one to be the learner. The learner is going to go into the next room, where we're going to sit you down in front of a problem box and attach electrodes to you. The teacher is going to stay in this room, to administer the problems and, if necessary, any punishments for errors. Now, let's decide who's going to do what.

At this point, you select one of two cards that designate your role. When you turn it over, your card reads TEACHER. Because you agreed to be in the experiment, you would have taken your shocks bravely if you had to. But you're relieved: this is definitely a case where it's better to give than to receive.

You watch the other volunteer as he's strapped into his chair and the electrodes are attached, and then you return to the next room. The experimenter gives you a sample shock of 45 volts, which is unpleasant but not really painful. Then you sit down in front of the shock generator. It has a series of buttons on it labeled 15 VOLTS at one end and going up by 15-volt increments to 450 VOLTS on the other. Groups of buttons also have labels, from SLIGHT SHOCK at the very lowest voltages to VERY STRONG SHOCK at around 200 volts, DANGER: SEVERE SHOCK at around 400 volts, and XXX at 450 volts. Each time the learner makes a mistake, you're told to increase the shock by 15 volts.

As the experiment begins, the learner gets the first few answers right but then begins to make more and more mistakes. You give him 15 volts, then 30, 45, 60 and 75. At this point, you can hear the learner grunt in the next room, and he continues to grunt and moan with each succeeding shock. Unfortunately, although he gets some of the questions right, he keeps making mistakes, and you have to give him more shocks. At 150 volts you can hear the man asking to be released, saying he wants to quit the experiment.

What about you? What do you think you'd be doing at this point? You probably think that you would refuse to continue. But if you say something, the experimenter sternly says, "Please go on." If you don't do as he says, he insists, saying, "You have no choice. You must go on."

If you proceed, the learner continues to protest and to ask to be released from the experiment. He screams in agony at each successive shock, and at 300 volts he announces that he is not going to answer any more questions. You look at the researcher, who tells you that the lack of a response must be treated as an error and has to be punished. At 315 volts the man stops answering the questions but "shrieks in agony whenever a shock is administered" (Milgram, 1977, p. 123). If you continue to obey the experimenter's demands, you keep on increasing the voltage and administering shocks until you reach the 450 volt maximum—the one labeled XXX.

How far do you think you would go? Do you think you'd go all the way to 450 volts? Perhaps not. But the odds are that you would, because just about two

Figure 18.5
Administration of Shocks in Milgram's Experiment

Over 60 percent of the subjects continued to administer shocks to the 450 volt maximum. Forty psychiatrists failed to predict this behavior.

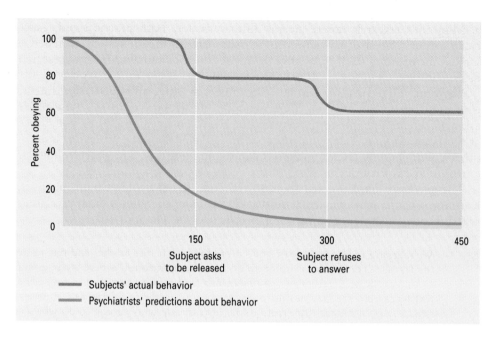

Source: Adapted from Milgram, 1974.

out of every three people in Milgram's experiment did. The findings are shown in Figure 18.5. As you can see, a few subjects stopped at around 150 volts, and a few more at around 300 volts; but 62 percent went all the way to 450 volts.

Explaining Away the Findings

Everyone is stunned by Milgram's findings. Could it be true that subjects are so careless of one another's well-being? Whenever I describe these experiments to students in my classes, they insist that no one would go all the way to 450 volts. This opinion was shared by a group of forty psychiatrists questioned by Milgram (1974). The psychiatrists predicted unanimously that no more than one person in a thousand would go all the way. Milgram himself didn't anticipate anything like these results. Why, then, did a group of people like you and me hurt a total stranger? A great many explanations have been proposed, some of which attempt to explain the effect away.

It may have been that the subjects didn't believe they were actually hurting the learner. And, in fact, they weren't. The learner was never actually shocked. He was a confederate of Milgram's, and the drawing was rigged so that the real subjects were always the teachers. Perhaps the subjects saw through the deception and somehow knew that the other volunteer wasn't really being hurt seriously (Orne & Holland, 1968).

However, Milgram filmed some of the subjects during the experiment. One look at that film tells us that these subjects had no doubt they were hurting someone seriously. Milgram's subjects were extremely upset, pleading with the researcher to be allowed to stop, moaning themselves, and saying things like "Oh God, let's stop it" and "He can't stand it. I'm not going to kill that man in there. You hear him hollering? He's hollering. He can't stand it. What if something happens to him?" (Milgram, 1977, p. 112). (The man who said these things went all the way to 450 volts.) Milgram's subjects certainly believed they were hurting someone, perhaps seriously.

Another explanation is that the subjects were an unusually compliant group. Perhaps Milgram's findings were a fluke; maybe the same thing wouldn't happen with a different group of people. Unfortunately, this isn't true either. The same sort of experiment has been replicated many times, with many different kinds of subjects, in a number of countries, even Germany. Milgram himself ran experiments involving "almost a thousand adults" (Milgram, 1977, p. 120). Furthermore, Milgram's subjects were recruited by newspaper ads, and included people of all ages and from all walks of life. The results were always the same: the majority of people delivered the shocks. Incidentally, the German subjects behaved no worse or no better than people from other countries. Apparently this kind of blind obedience knows no geographic boundaries.

Milgram's results cannot be explained away as experimental error. Nor can we say that his findings pertain to some special group of people. What Milgram discovered was a quality that is common to most of us. But what is that quality?

Are People Inherently Cruel?

Did Milgram tap a sadistic streak that's inside all of us? Probably not. In variations on Milgram's experiment, subjects actually punished themselves. In one study, subjects assumed the role of both learners and teachers, and were told to punish themselves whenever they made a mistake. The subjects wore earphones, and the punishment was a loud, high-pitched noise. The subjects had been told that the noise could severely damage their hearing (actually, it wasn't dangerous); yet, in response to the experimenter's urging, they continued to administer the punishment to themselves (Martin et al., 1976).

In another study, the subjects' punishment was to eat crackers that had been soaked in an extremely bitter solution (Kurdika, 1965, cited in Milgram, 1977, p. 133). Again, the majority of subjects responded to the experimenter's demands by eating the crackers.

Clearly, Milgram did not find a potential for violence toward others. What he found was a willingness to obey. The horror of the Jonestown suicides show the degree to which people are willing to obey. In 1978, almost a thousand people killed themselves—parents helping their children drink poisoned Kool-Aid—in response to the order of their leader, Jim Jones.

In Jonestown in 1978, almost a thousand men, women, and children drank poison because their leader, Jim Jones, ordered them to do so. Although they knew they and their families were going to die, their willingness to obey Jones was stronger than their desire to stay alive.

The Force of the Experimental Situation

Since so many people obeyed in Milgrim's experiment, the explanation for their remarkable behavior must lie in the situation, not the people. Several dimensions of the experimental situation seem to be important: the distance between teacher and learner, the gradual evolution of the situation into a moral dilemma, and the authority of the individual issuing the orders.

The Distance Between Teacher and Learner   Milgram observed that his subjects tried to avoid looking in the direction of their victim. He suspected that the high rates of compliance he had found might be due, at least in part, to the fact that teacher and learner were separated physically. To test the role of distance, he ran four versions of the experiment:

1. In the most distant, the teacher could not hear the learner at all.
2. In the next most distant, the teacher could hear but not see the learner.
3. In the third condition, the learner sat next to the teacher.
4. In the closest condition, the teacher was required to hold the learner's hand on the metal plate that supposedly delivered the shocks.

As Milgram expected, the closer the teachers were to their victim, the lower was the number of teachers who complied as the voltage rose (see Figure 18.6). But even in the closest condition, the rate of full compliance was still 30 percent. When ordered to do so, 30 percent of the subjects held a stranger's hand on a shock plate to administer the maximum shock!

Figure 18.6
Obedience as a Function of the Closeness to the Victim

As the subjects were required to be nearer to their victims, the number of those willing to administer maximum shock declined, but 30 percent were induced to hold the victim's hand on a shock plate, to the maximum voltage.

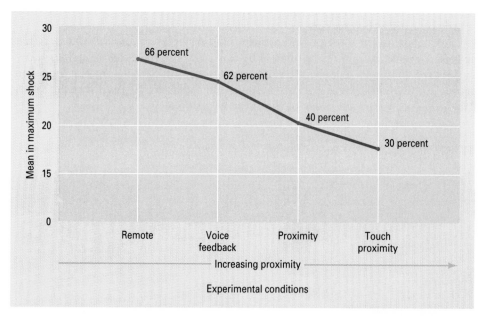

Source: Milgram, 1977.

Although the distance between teacher and learner affects the rate of obedience, distance does not explain the basic effect itself because a substantial percentage of subjects continue to comply even at the closest distance. In fact, two other elements of the situation were also at work. First, the moral status of the situation changed very gradually. Second, there was no question about the legitimacy of the authority figure—the person issuing the orders.

Gradual Evolution into a Moral Dilemma   Look again at Figure 18.5. Notice that no one dropped out until 150 volts. Then the line is level for a bit. At 300 volts, we begin to see a steady drop in compliance. What happened at 150 and 300 volts? These were the points at which the learner started to act very differently: at 150 volts he said he wanted to stop the experiment, and at 300 volts he stopped responding. Something about his behavior produced defiance in the teacher.

When we described the experiment to you, we tried to give you a feel for the very gradual way in which the situation changed. In the beginning, there is no moral issue: you're asked to administer a shock much milder than the one you just received yourself, to someone who freely chose to participate, and you have no reason to believe that you're going to have to administer more than a few shocks.

Once the experiment begins, you increase the voltage very gradually, in 15-volt increments. This gradual evolution probably contributed to the subjects' behavior. By changing the situation gradually, from one that was morally proper to one that became morally repulsive, Milgram made it difficult for his subjects to notice the change (Gilbert, 1981). Figure 18.7 shows a visual representation of a gradually changing situation. Notice how difficult it is to determine exactly when the light part of the illustration changes to dark.

A third factor causing compliance was the social force created both by the experimenter's urging and by his institutional role. We all respond to norms that ask us to respect legitimate authority and to obey reasonable requests from people in charge. Without these kinds of norms, society would be unable to function. The problem in Milgram's experimental situation was that these norms were too powerful; the subjects weren't able to resist when they should have.

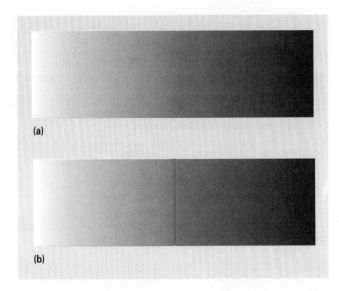

Figure 18.7
The Milgram Experiments: A Physical Analogue

As we move from the left side of the figure to the right side, there is no point at which we notice any change between light and dark. But when we add a line separating the two sides, they look very different.

What would happen, Milgram wondered, if he weakened the force of the norms by weakening his own authority? What if he removed from the equation the fact that he was a professor at a famous university? Would the rate of compliance fall? To find out, Milgram ran the basic obedience experiment in a rented office in Bridgeport, a neighboring industrial town, and never mentioned Yale. And the rate of compliance did fall—but only from 62 percent to 48 percent. Milgram concluded that people are willing to obey authority figures, even if they are not clearly reputable (Milgram, 1974).

Milgram also explored another way to change the balance between the experimenter-authority and the subject, by giving the subject allies. He ran several new versions of the experiment in which three "subjects" worked together to administer the shocks. In fact, two of these subjects were Milgram's confederates, one of whom was told to quit at 150 volts and the other, at 210 volts. Figure 18.8 shows the percentage of subjects still administering shocks at each level. Notice that as soon as one other person objected, a significant portion of the subjects quit. In fact, after both confederate-subjects quit, only 12 percent of the real subjects continued to the end.

Finding an ally was by far the most effective way to reduce compliance. When another subject objected strongly enough, the real subjects were freed from the social constraints that had kept them in front of the shock generator.

Figure 18.8
Obedience When Other Subjects Refuse

Milgram reported that "of the score of experimental variations . . . none was so effective in undermining the experimenter's authority as the manipulation reported here" (Milgram, 1974, p. 194).

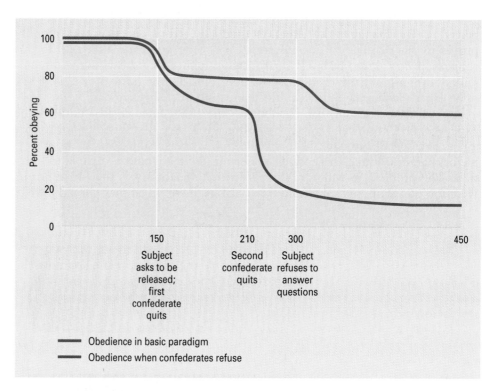

Source: Adapted from Milgram, 1974

Some Final Thoughts on Obedience

We've spent a lot of time on Milgram's research for two reasons. One is its powerful moral about obedience: all of us have the potential to be led astray by the authorities we ordinarily trust unthinkingly. Obedience is undoubtedly a good thing; but like all good things, it can be excessive. And it can lead us a terrifying distance from our moral principles. We must be vigilant, then, in watching out for the gradual evolution of perfectly acceptable situations and expectations into those we would not and should not accept.

The other important lesson of Milgram's experiments is about dissent. What is shown by the ally study, and by several of the conformity studies, is the power of the individual who dissents. When you begin to feel uncomfortable in a group situation, you can't rely on the apparent acceptance of others. *You* have to act; *you* have to speak out. Your objection may be all that's needed to turn what seems to be compliance into dissent.

How Do We Know That?

Many of Milgram's subjects suffered intensely in the course of the experiment, because they felt they were doing something horrible. Once his findings were published, a group of psychologists argued that he had no right to put his subjects through that kind of psychological pain (for example, see Baumrind, 1964; Miller, 1986). Milgram defended himself vigorously, pointing out that he carefully explained the research to the subjects when they'd finished, assuring them that they hadn't actually hurt anyone, and that they had behaved the way most people did. He argued that none of his subjects left the experiment with any lasting emotional scars, and he noted that the majority (84 percent) of his subjects said on a later questionnaire that they were somewhat or very glad they had participated. Only a few more than 1 percent of his subjects were sorry to have been in the experiment (Milgram, 1964).

Milgram also argued that many of the ethical objections to his research were actually directed at his findings, not at his procedures. He pointed out that if all of his subjects had stopped at 150 or 200 volts, no one would have objected at all (Milgram, 1977). On this point he was apparently correct. In one study, researchers described Milgram's procedures but said that only 10 percent of the original subjects complied. Most of the people who heard the 10 percent figure had little trouble accepting the experiment on ethical grounds (Schlenker & Forsyth, 1977).

Stanley Milgram demonstrated the incredible force of social pressure to induce people to act in ways they truly felt were immoral.

The controversy over Milgram's work highlights one of the central problems of psychological research: How do we balance the costs and benefits of a research program? All research imposes some "costs" on the subjects—at the very least, on their time and energy. And sometimes they're asked to endure embarrassment, anxiety, anger, even mild physical pain. Subjects pay these psychological costs to the research effort in the belief that they are helping the progress of science. Scientific progress, then, is the ultimate justification for asking people to participate. Any particular experiment is justified only if the potential benefits to society and, directly or indirectly, to the subjects exceed the potential costs to the subjects.

Yet, unfortunately, neither subjects nor researchers are in a position to weigh the costs and benefits fairly. The subjects characteristically do not know enough about the field, much less about the whys and wherefores of the experiment. And researchers, despite their good intentions, are moved by the same self-interested motives that shape the behavior of all people. They are more likely to be impressed by the benefits of their work than by the costs.

To provide informed but objective judgments about the ethics of proposed experiments, all research institutions now maintain independent-review committees. These committees are required at any institution that receives research funding from the federal government. Even unfunded research is routinely reviewed to ensure that it does not pose risks to subjects.

How would a research committee evaluate Milgram's work? Did the benefits balance the costs? We believe that Milgram's initial study certainly was justified. First of all, he was as surprised as everyone else with the results, so he could not have predicted the costs. And when they appeared, he did everything he could to minimize them.

Furthermore, given the potential importance of his findings, it seems to us that many of the follow-up studies had acceptable cost-benefit ratios. At some point, however, the ratio definitely tipped the other way. We believe, and think most review committees would agree, that any new information collected now could not justify any more replications of the basic effect.

Puzzle It Out!

We reported above that after the ethical controversy arose, Milgrim questioned many of the subjects in his obedience studies. The vast majority said they were glad they had participated, and felt the studies were important. How would Festinger's cognitive dissonance theory or self-perception theory explain the subjects' judgments?

Milgram's research gives us a rationale for open discussion of the moral dimensions of public policy. It also explains why this kind of discussion is often so effective. As demonstrated by events in the United States over the last few decades, when a relatively small number of dissenters speak out against discrimination, against prejudice, against irrational war, society often begins to see how discrimination and prejudice and war conflict with its values.

Recap

- Obedience is compliance with a direct demand for action.

- About 62 percent of Milgram's subjects fully complied with the task, administering what they thought was a dangerous electric shock to someone who had done nothing at all to them.

- Several factors in the experimental situation—the distance between teacher and learner, the gradual steps toward compliance, and the authority of the researcher—contributed to the effects that Milgram found.

- Finding an ally is by far the most effective way to reduce compliance.

- There are two important lessons to be learned from Milgram's research. First, all people have the potential to be led astray by authority. And, second, a lone dissenter has the power to reduce the rate of compliance, to remind others of the moral issues at stake.

Social Roles

In our discussion of conformity and obedience, we dealt with more or less isolated norms, created in the laboratory or invoked by the experimenter. In the real world, however, the structure of norms and the ways in which they affect our actions are more complex.

Norms don't apply equally to every member of a group. Instead, there are different norms for different people. Furthermore, these norms tend to be organized into groups, each group an integrated set of expectations about how different people should behave. These "packages" of norms are called **social roles;** they describe the way the individual should act. And all the people who hold the same social role are expected to act the same way.

One social role you're called on to play regularly is "student." That role defines your behavior in school. When you go to a lecture class, you're expected to sit quietly, to pay attention to the professor, and to take notes. You're not expected to talk or dance or sleep. Conversely, the person in the professor role

Social role An organized system of norms assigned to one or more individuals in a group.

is expected to talk, but only about the subject of the course. (Obviously, it's also true that we all occasionally slip out of our roles.) Notice that it would be just as inappropriate for the professor to come into class and not say a word as it would be for a student to walk in and never stop talking. Notice, too, that these roles are closely coordinated: a student can't take notes if a professor doesn't talk; and a professor can't talk if students are singing and dancing. Most roles cannot be enacted by the player alone.

The Power of Social Roles

People move from social role to social role so easily that we're usually not aware of the extent to which social roles shape our behavior. Although you may talk animatedly with your friends before class, then sit silently for an hour, then pick up your conversation again after class, you probably don't recognize the dramatic changes in your behavior because you take them for granted.

Psychologist Philip Zimbardo wanted to see what would happen to a normal group of college students playing social roles full time for a couple of weeks. He hired a group of Stanford University students to play the roles of prisoners and guards in a pretend prison. The students who signed up for the study were tested carefully in advance, so as to ensure that they were mentally and physically healthy. Then they were assigned by the toss of a coin to be either prisoners or guards.

Zimbardo went to exceptional lengths to create a realistic prison. The cells were real, and the prisoners and guards wore realistic uniforms. The "prisoners" were "arrested" and "booked" by real policemen. And from that point on, they were referred to only by number. At the jail, the guards, in their uniforms, wore dark sunglasses that obscured their faces; they, too, were not identified by name. The guards were told that their only duty was to preserve law and order.

Both prisoners and guards fell naturally into their routines, the guards enforcing the rules and the prisoners trying to get around them. On the second day, the prisoners rebelled, and the guards overcame them by threatening them with billy clubs and spraying them with fire extinguishers. From then on, the guards became increasingly abusive and strict. Any breach of the rules was punished with the loss of "privileges," including eating and sleeping. To further humiliate and punish errant prisoners, the guards invented demeaning tasks, such as forcing the prisoners to clean the toilets with their bare hands.

As the guards became more abusive, the prisoners became increasingly demoralized. Some were so upset that they had to be removed from the prison and released from the experiment. Others grew apathetic or sullen. The experiment was supposed to have lasted two weeks, but Zimbardo became so concerned about the changes in the students' behavior that he ended it after just six days (Zimbardo et al., 1973).

When it was over, the students reported that at the time they felt they were behaving in the only way that made sense, but they were shocked at their own behavior. The guards could not understand how they could have treated the prisoners the way they did. And the prisoners were appalled at their own lack of stability, at how easily they had become demoralized.

What happened here? Zimbardo argues that the students were immersed in their social roles. They knew how prisoners and guards supposedly acted, and they began, like method actors, to live their roles. And those roles inevitably generated hostility.

Think what it must have been like for the guards. Their task was simple: keeping order. The prisoners' revolt must have seemed like a deliberate attempt to make them look bad. So the guards responded vigorously, with anger and violence. Once order was reestablished, it must have seemed to the guards that

Many institutions, such as the military or the prison system, use deindividuation to increase control of their members. Here, prison inmates are dressed alike, given identical haircuts, and are often called by their last names only. This treatment tends to undermine their sense of identity and makes them more responsive to institutional definitions of correct behavior.

the way to maintain discipline was to constantly remind the prisoners that the guards were all-powerful. How did they accomplish this? By dominating and demeaning the prisoners at every turn. Meanwhile, the prisoners' response to the guards' treatment of them either reinforced the dominating behavior (when the prisoners acted demoralized and passive) or escalated the antagonism between the two groups (when the prisoners rebelled).

Notice that a policy of intimidation almost inevitably leads to increasing brutality. Yesterday's unreasonable demand becomes today's standard policy, so there's a constant need to keep increasing the unreasonableness of demands. Furthermore, being overbearing, arbitrary, and cruel works reasonably well in the short term, but in the long run breeds resistance. So escalation is built into the policy along with a rationale for that escalation (each step being a "reasonable" response to some action of the prisoners). What Zimbardo's study suggests is that the very structure of the guard and prisoner roles has built into it a mechanism that produces repression and cruelty—the kinds of behaviors we usually attribute to people who aren't nice.

Zimbardo's findings weren't that different from Milgram's, although the behaviors that the "teachers" and "guards" exhibited did stem from different sources. In Milgram's experiments, those behaviors were the product of obedience, the norm that says you should respond the way someone in authority says you should respond. But in Zimbardo's study, those behaviors were the product of a system of norms that defined the roles the students were playing.

There was another similarity between the obedience and social role experiments. In Zimbardo's experiment, as in Milgram's, the situation gradually evolved from a benign bit of play-acting to outright cruelty. The guards' brutality increased over time, much like the gradual increase in voltage observed in Milgram's studies. What we see in both cases isn't an immediate plunge into the depths of immorality but a kind of moral drift.

Deindividuation: The Release from Normative Control

In our discussion of norms and social roles, we've focused on the negative aspects of compliance—in part because those aspects so dramatically reveal the power of norms and social roles. Here we see that compliance isn't always bad; sometimes noncompliance is much more dangerous.

People often do things in groups that they would never think of doing alone. The revelers at Mardi Gras are an example. Once a year they party and dance and sing and drink on the streets of New Orleans, doing all kinds of things they would ordinarily never do. The most extreme examples of this phenomenon are the times when mobs become violent. In Holland not too long ago, a mob of English fans rioted at a soccer match and killed thirty-two people—over a mere game. And in New York City, a gang of young boys, most of whom had no history of violence, raged through Central Park, attacking, raping, and almost killing a woman jogger.

What is it that leads people to act so differently in large groups? To answer this question, we have to think about the factors that are different in the group context. Perhaps the most striking difference is that in the middle of a mass of people, the individual is no longer recognized as an individual. In a very real sense, it's almost impossible to single any one person out of a mob and to hold that person responsible for his or her actions. In fact, it may well be that the individual loses a sense of being responsible for those actions. This effect—the loss of one's sense of individual identity—is called **deindividuation.**

A number of studies have tested the effects of deindividuation by reducing the subjects' sense of their own identity and then examining their behavior. One

Deindividuation The loss of a sense of personal identity, with a consequent increase in the impact of situational factors on behavior.

Mardi Gras has the reputation of being a festival in which people act with far less inhibition than they normally do. The tradition of wearing costumes that disguise and deindividuate the revelers may be partially responsible for their behavior.

of Zimbardo's studies is an excellent example (Zimbardo, 1970). His subjects were all women who didn't know one another. They arrived in groups of four. Zimbardo created two conditions, one that emphasized each woman's identity (which he called the *individuation condition*) and one that minimized it (the *deindividuation condition*). In the individuation groups, the women were asked to wear their best clothes (on the assumption that these would also be their most distinctive clothes); then they were placed in a brightly lit room and addressed by name. The women in the deindividuation groups were asked to wear old clothes. When they arrived, they were placed in a dimly lit room and immediately given oversized white lab coats and hoods to put on. These women were identified only by numbers.

All of the women had been told that the focus of the study was their empathy with someone under stress. But of real interest to Zimbardo was their willingness to create that stress by administering electric shocks to two "subjects," one who seemed as obnoxious as the other seemed nice. By now you certainly know enough about this kind of research to have guessed that the supposed victims were confederates, and that no shocks were actually administered. And you probably wouldn't be surprised to learn that the women in the individuated condition were less willing to comply than were the women in the deindividuated condition. The women whose identities were emphasized not only administered fewer shocks but also discriminated between the two victims: they administered even fewer shocks to the "nice" victim than they did to the "obnoxious" one. In the deindividuated condition, by contrast, the victim's personality made no difference: the subjects administered shocks to both victims indiscriminately (Zimbardo, 1970).

Zimbardo's findings indicate that deindividuation leads to increased and indiscriminate aggression against others in the laboratory. But a number of observations indicate that the deindividuation effect is present in the real world, too. For example, among primitive cultures, warfare is much more savage when the warriors paint their faces, wear masks, or in some other way disguise themselves before battle (Watson, 1973). The phenomenon is no less evident in more "civilized" societies. You've seen news reports of people standing on the ledge of a building, threatening suicide. Apparently when a small crowd gathers, and when it's daylight, the crowd simply watches. But when the crowd is large, and when it's dark out, the crowd is likely to urge the person on, chanting "Jump, jump" (Mann, 1981).

Puzzle It Out!

Now that you have seen some of the ways in which social situations can shape and compel behavior, can you explain the experience and behavior of the student we described at the beginning of this chapter? What might the student have done to change the way his fraternity members behaved?

Deindividuation can have serious effects. The costumes of the Ku Klux Klan may permit their members to act outside the bounds of civilized behavior. Members of mobs are able to be more violent because they are deindividuated.

Does deindividuation always lead to violence? Definitely not. The effect of deindividuation is simply to reduce the individual's awareness of himself or herself as an individual. With the loss of identity comes the release of inhibitions that are rooted in the individual's sense of responsibility or fear of punishment, either of which makes the individual more responsive to situational influences (Prentice-Dunn & Rogers, 1989). Those situational influences can work to the good or the bad. In one replication of Zimbardo's experiment, groups of women were dressed in nurses' uniforms instead of the vaguely Ku Klux Klan–like hoods Zimbardo used. The benevolent situational cue of the nurses' uniforms was such that these women administered fewer shocks than did the individuated women (Johnson & Downing, 1979).

Deindividuation seems to reduce people's connection to the usual norms and rules that govern their conduct. It allows them to step out of "character"; it frees them from their inhibitions, to act according to the situation, whatever that might be.

A Comment on Group Norms, Social Roles, and Individual Values

All of the research we've been talking about depicts a conflict between group and individual forces in the control of behavior. On one side are the group norms and social roles that demand compliance from the individual; on the other are the individual's judgment and values. In Milgram's obedience experiments and Zimbardo's prison study, those judgments and values were submerged by group norms and social roles. In these studies morality was clearly on the side of individual judgment and values. But the deindividuation experiments tell us that morality is just as likely to be on the side of social forces. Here the immoral behavior emerged when the social forces were removed.

Although our examples focus on the conflict between social forces and individual values, you should recognize that the two aren't necessarily or even usu-

Cults

Many of the processes we've described in this chapter and the last one show up in the ways cults induct new members. The characteristic beginning is a warm, friendly invitation to spend a few days with the group, "just to find out more about us." This first agreement is a "foot in the door" toward a later change in attitude. During the visit, prospects find themselves in an entirely new environment, surrounded by strangers who in a very nice way take complete control of their experience.

All day long, recruits are kept busy doing things with the group, surrounded by people who unanimously sing the praises of the group (sometimes literally) and encourage the recruits to do the same. The combination of little opportunity for critical thought and immersion in the group's enthusiasm creates tremendous pressure to conform.

Finally, the norms require that the recruit join in the group's activities, which often consist of singing and talking about how wonderful the group is. Since the recruit is induced to do these pro-group activities by means of relatively unnoticeable social pressure, no coercion is apparent. Thus (as we discussed in the previous chapter), through the workings of cognitive dissonance, or self-perception, the recruits are likely to adopt the pro-group attitudes that these activities imply.

Once recruits have joined, the cult's control over their experience grows stronger. Recruits are deindividuated, cut off completely from their previous identities—from their friends and families, from their usual activities, from familiar places. In some cults, recruits are even given new names.

Group members continually define and reinforce their vision of reality for one another. This vision frequently includes the idea that the larger society is hostile to the group (which is often the case), thus reinforcing the individual's dependence on the group.

Often members are expected to make sacrifices for the group, including giving up most contacts with their loved ones, working hard, long hours, and turning over any proceeds of their work to the group. Again, as we know from the principles discussed in the previous chapter, making sacrifices for a group increases its attractiveness. Since these people are making really major sacrifices, dissonance reduction or self-perception requires that they believe the group is worth it.

Cult leaders seem to be very clever practical psychologists. They seem to have an intuitive understanding of cognitive dissonance, self-perception, deindividuation, and the impact of the group on the individual's behavior and attitudes.

ally in conflict. People usually choose to act in just the ways that society's norms and social roles lead them to act. Even people with severe psychological disorders usually deviate in only a few ways. The conflict between social and individual forces makes for dramatic research precisely because it's relatively rare.

Another thing to remember. Many of the dramatic findings we've described seem to depend on the gradual evolution of the situation from one in which social and individual inclinations are identical toward one in which they conflict. Without this kind of gradual evolution, and hence without the difficulty it creates for the individual in terms of monitoring his or her behavior, many of these effects probably would not occur.

Based on what you know about deindividuation, why do you suppose these people are all dressed alike and wear their hair the same way?

Recap

- Social roles describe the way individuals within the group are expected to act.

- People move between social roles so easily that they're usually not aware of the extent to which these roles shape their behavior.

- The behavior of the subjects in Zimbardo's prison experiment was the product of a system of norms that defined the roles the subjects were playing.

- One effect of the group is deindividuation, the individual's loss of his or her sense of identity.

- Deindividuation often leads people to do things in groups that they would never think of doing alone.

- Zimbardo's findings indicate that deindividuation can lead to increased and indiscriminate aggression against others.

- Deindividuation does not always lead to violence; it simply makes the individual more responsive to situational influences.

- People usually choose to act in just the ways that society's norms and social roles lead them to act.

The Effects of Others on Performance

The presence of others can affect people's level of performance as well as their morality. Both work and thought can be improved or disrupted by the presence of others.

Social Facilitation and Interference

Social facilitation The positive effect on the individual's performance produced by the presence of other people.

In some circumstances, just having other people around can improve performance. This effect is called **social facilitation,** and it was first demonstrated in one of the very earliest social psychological studies.

Norman Triplett (1898) began with the not-too-surprising observation that bicycle racers go much faster when a competitor is nearby. To examine this effect, he arranged his own "race" and timed different racers riding alone, competing against the clock, and competing with another racer. As a comparison condition, he also had the racers ride alongside another rider with whom they were not competing. Of course, he found that bicycle racers go faster when they're competing. But he also found that they go faster when riding with a noncompeting rider.

Why should the simple presence of another rider increase performance? One possibility is that people can't avoid a little informal competition. But many later studies suggested that this was not the case, most obviously because performance also improves when others are only observing, not participating. Furthermore, we find the same effect in other species. For example, cockroaches run faster when another cockroach is present (Zajonc, Heingartner & Herman, 1969).

The theoretical situation grew more confusing inasmuch as it soon became apparent that an audience sometimes doesn't improve performance but, in fact, worsens it (Bond & Titus, 1983). This effect is called **social interference.** How do we explain what seem to be contradictory findings?

Physiological Arousal   Robert Zajonc (1965) suggested that both facilitation and interference are the products of increased physiological arousal. Lots of earlier research had established the fact that arousal improves performance on simple or routine tasks, but disrupts performance when a task is more complex. (Some of this research was discussed in Chapter 9.) The physiological arousal produced by the presence of an audience, then, could improve performance on simple tasks but inhibit performance on more complex tasks.

The evidence is generally consistent with this hypothesis, even where cockroaches are concerned. Cockroaches run faster with a companion when the runway is simple. But if we complicate things by adding a turn to the runway (one turn is about all the complexity a cockroach can handle), their performance drops (Zajonc, Heingartner & Herman, 1969).

The problem with arousal theory is that arousal measures, such as measures of heart rate and galvanic skin responses, fail to show that audiences consistently increase arousal (Moore & Baron, 1983). However, researchers have proposed several alternative theories that share Zajonc's basic insight: that the presence of other people improves performance on well-learned or simple tasks, and that it interferes with performance on more complex tasks. Two of the most likely theories target evaluation apprehension and self-consciousness.

Evaluation Apprehension   One possibility is that even when people are only being observed, they may feel that they are being evaluated and become apprehensive. And this apprehension could very well increase their effort, leading to an improvement of their performance on simple tasks but to a disruption of their performance on difficult tasks. Consistent with this hypothesis is the finding that an audience that is blindfolded does not affect performance (Cottrell et al., 1968).

Self-Consciousness   Roy Baumeister has proposed a related idea, that an audience affects performance by making the individual pay closer attention to what he or she is doing. If the task is simple, focusing on how you're accomplishing the task may help. But paying too much attention to how you're doing may actually impede your performance (Baumeister & Scher, 1988). If you want to hit a golf or tennis ball well, thinking about how you're moving your arms is more confusing than helpful.

Social interference   The negative effect on the individual's performance produced by the presence of other people.

One of Baumeister's tests of his hypothesis was to look at the effects of audiences on professional sports teams. He points out that, although there is a home field or home court advantage in sports, it doesn't extend to really critical games. He argues that being in front of your home audience increases performance when things aren't too tense, which is why the home team wins most of the games in the beginning of the World Series or the NBA playoffs. However, when the games become really crucial, the home audience makes the players so self-conscious—so concerned with how they're doing—that it interferes with their ability to play. This is the reason the home team loses most of the games toward the end of the World Series or the playoffs (Baumeister & Steinhilber, 1984).

In short, there is reasonably consistent evidence to suggest that an audience enhances performance if the task is not too complex. Which of the many proposed mechanisms is responsible remains less clear. Perhaps all contribute.

Social Loafing

The social facilitation/interference research demonstrates the complex effects of having other people watch you work. But what if you're all working together? We might hope that, at least on simple tasks, the presence of coworkers would improve everyone's performance. Unfortunately, the usual result is the opposite. The presence of coworkers seems to lead to **social loafing.** When people work together on a task, each individual is likely to work less hard.

In one study, for example, subjects were asked to pull as hard as they could on a rope, in a simulated tug-of-war. When the subjects believed that three other subjects were pulling on the rope behind them, they pulled about 80 percent as hard as they did when they were alone (Ingham et al., 1974). Furthermore, as the group gets bigger, the individual expends less effort. Figure 18.9 shows the relationship between group size and effort among a group of people who were asked to clap and cheer as loudly as they could (Latané, Williams & Harkins, 1979).

Figure 18.9
The Relationship Between Group Size and Effort

The subjects in this experiment were asked to make as much noise as they could by cheering and clapping. They believed they were either working alone or with one, three, or five others. Notice that the amount of effort each subject expended declined in relation to the number of other participants each subject thought was involved.

Social loafing The tendency to work less hard when a number of other people are sharing the work.

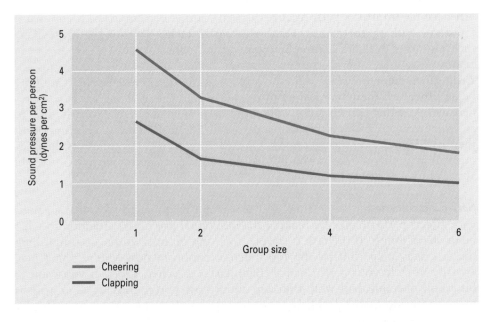

Source: Lantané, Williams & Harkins, 1979.

Social loafing is not a matter of deliberately choosing to slack off. When people in the studies were asked how much effort they felt they were making under each condition, they reported no difference.

Obviously social loafing could be a serious problem for society. Most people assume that "many hands make light work." But, in fact, it may well be that many hands make the people work lightly.

How do psychologists explain social loafing? We have to start by examining the circumstances in which it occurs. Social loafing occurs when people are working together to produce something that is identifiable only as the group's output. In a tug-of-war, for example, we know only how much force the whole group is exerting; we have no idea how much each individual is contributing. Notice that this is the exact opposite of the situation in which social facilitation occurs, wherein the individual's performance is apparent to the audience.

It could be that the presence of coworkers produces either social facilitation or social loafing, depending on whether observers can tell how each individual is doing. To test this possibility, Stephen Harkins (1987) varied both the number of people working (alone or in a group) and the nature of the output (whether the group could tell how well each individual was doing). He found two distinct effects: people working with others did better than those working alone, and both groups did better when their individual work could be evaluated.

It appears, then, that social facilitation and social loafing are aspects of the same basic phenomenon. People work harder when other people can see how they're doing, and they also work harder in groups, perhaps because the group they work with becomes an important source of normative pressure. However, if no one, including group members, can tell how hard the individual is working, the individual expends less effort.

A second, related factor may be the individual's own lack of information about his or her effort. In many of the social-loafing experiments, the individual subject is as much in the dark as the coworkers are. For example, in a tug-of-war, each person feels he or she is pulling as hard as possible, but no one has any real sense of how much he or she is contributing to the total effort. To test this possibility, the experimental task was rearranged so that workers knew how they were doing. When they know, they work just as hard as when they work alone, and it doesn't matter whether anyone else is watching or not (Szymanski & Harkins, 1987). In a sense, this result is consistent with the effects of biofeedback (see Chapter 10). When people don't have information about the effects of their own behavior, they can't control it. And in many cases where people seem to lack ability, what they really lack is information.

Where do we stand, then, regarding the effects of other people on performance? The particular applications may be complex, but the principles are straightforward:

- People always work better if they themselves know how they are doing.
- The fact that other people know how they're doing can also improve performance if the task is not too complex or challenging.
- All things being equal, just the presence of others can improve performance.

Although these children probably believe they are exerting as much force as they can in this game of tug-of-war, research demonstrates that in fact each child would pull significantly harder if they were pulling alone.

Recap

- Apparently the presence of others improves performance when the task is simple or routine, but disrupts performance when the task is complex.

- The effects of social facilitation and interference can be explained in terms of physiological arousal, evaluation apprehension, and self-consciousness.

- Social loafing is the tendency to work less hard when a number of other people are sharing the work.

- Apparently the most important factor in performance is the individual's ability to gauge how he or she is doing.

Group Decisions

"Many hands make light work" is often not true, as we now know. But what about this proverb: "Many heads are better than one"? Most people would say that when decisions are important, groups make better decisions than individuals do. But that isn't always the case either. Group decision making is prone to its own set of problems.

Groupthink

Groupthink is a term coined by Irving Janis (1983) to describe a pattern of decision making that limits not only the alternatives considered by a group but also the critical evaluation of those alternatives.

The following example is adapted from one that Janis analyzed extensively.

> The president of the United States and his advisers are meeting to make a critical decision. The revolutionary government of a Latin American country has become increasingly hostile to the United States, and an increasing annoyance to the president and his government. A large group of dissidents from the country have organized a resistance movement; they've been training in a neighboring country for an invasion of their homeland. An invasion would involve the United States in the conflict, and carries the risk of other superpowers being drawn into an escalating war. The advisers, and ultimately the president, must decide whether to authorize the invasion.

Would you be more comfortable if the president makes the decision alone or with the group? Most people feel that the group decision would be better because it's more likely to be moderate and to consider all of the pros and cons carefully.

You may have thought this example referred to relatively recent events in Panama or Nicaragua or Grenada, and to decisions by Presidents Reagan or Bush. But, in fact, the president was John Kennedy and the question was whether to authorize an invasion of Cuba in 1961. Kennedy and his cabinet approved the invasion, and it was a fiasco. A small band of Cuban exiles landed on the beach at the Bay of Pigs, hoping to oust communist leader Fidel Castro. They believed the people of Cuba would rise to support them—but they didn't. Most of the exiles were killed or captured almost immediately. And the United States, which had armed and trained the exiles, took the brunt of world blame.

Later, all of those involved in the decision to go ahead with the invasion felt they should have recognized that it would fail. But no one did. They had all been victims of groupthink.

According to Janis, Kennedy and his advisers made a bad decision because of certain characteristics of the group. First, the group was a very cohesive one: the members valued one another and wanted to stay together as a group. Accordingly, each member was reluctant to challenge the prevailing opinion of the group. Second, all of the members of the group had tremendous respect for the president—their leader—and for one another. So they all were swayed by

Groupthink A pattern of decision making that limits the alternatives the group considers and the critical evaluation of those alternatives.

the president's opinion and the apparent unanimity with which these bright, knowledgeable people agreed. Each, in effect, looked at the others and thought, "If these exceptional people are in favor of the invasion, then it must be a good idea." Third, the group was isolated from outside opinions and had no procedures in place for raising objections or coming up with new alternatives. In the end, this group of very intelligent people failed to consider all of the possible consequences, performed a highly selective analysis of the facts, and made a lousy decision.

Janis believes that groups—particularly cohesive groups with a strong leader—have to protect themselves from groupthink by encouraging their members to express their doubts, by creating an atmosphere in which dissent is acceptable. He suggests, for example, that one person be designated to play the role of devil's advocate; that the group divide into subgroups for discussion, so that different points of view will emerge; and that outside experts be consulted.

Group Polarization

If we can protect groups from the dangers of groupthink, do they make better decisions than individuals do? If by "better" we mean more moderate, the answer is still no. Groups tend to take more extreme positions than at least the average position of their members. This tendency is called **group polarization.**

For example, in one classic set of studies (Stoner, 1961), the subjects were asked to make a series of decisions. One involved an engineer who had reached his limit in his current job and was deciding whether to quit and form his own company. The subjects were told that if he stayed in his present job, he would have security and a comfortable paycheck; but that if he formed his own company, he could lose everything or make a tremendous amount of money. Then the subjects were asked what odds the engineer should require before he decided to quit. Should he quit his job even if the odds were only 1 in 10 that his new company would succeed? Should he stay with the old company even if the odds were 9 in 10 that his new company would succeed?

After each subject had made his or her judgment individually, they all discussed the problem, eventually reaching a decision they all agreed on. You'd expect that the group decision would be pretty near the average of the individual decisions—that if the individual members of the group thought on average that 5 chances in 10 of success were enough to justify the engineer's quitting his job, the group decision would be near 5 in 10. But it wasn't. The group decision was more like 2 or 3 in 10. That is, the group decision was noticeably "riskier" than the average of the individual decisions.

It's not that group decisions are always riskier than individual decisions. Sometimes they're more conservative. For example, in a decision as to whether a child should have an operation that would improve the quality of her life but carries some risk of death, the group's decision is likely to be more conservative than the average of the decisions of its members.

The point is that group decisions are *polarized*, more extreme than the average of the decisions of its members. On some issues that means more risky; on others, more conservative.

One by-product of group polarization is the effect on the group's members. By the time the group has made its decision, the thinking of individual members has moved in the direction of the group's thinking: their own opinions have become more polarized (see Figure 18.10). In Sherif's conformity experiment, remember how the individual judgments of distance converged over time? Group decision making apparently causes a similar unnoticed drift—in this case, toward more extreme positions.

Group polarization The tendency for a group's decisions to be more extreme than the average decision of individual group members.

Figure 18.10
Group Polarization

Everyone in the group believes a moderately risky position is best and thinks they are willing to be slightly more risky than most people. When members of the group discover that others are equally or more willing to take a riskier position, they all move toward that position.

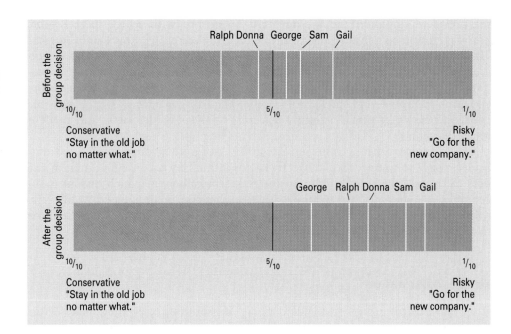

Why are group decisions more extreme? A couple of factors in combination seem to produce this effect. First, potential arguments usually tend to polarize the discussion. Second, once the members know more about the group, they compare themselves to the others and adjust their position to fit (Isenberg, 1986).

The Arguments   The group begins the discussion moderately favoring the position it will adopt more extremely later. So at the beginning of a discussion, few arguments are heard opposing the group's position; instead, the members hear new reasons to strengthen their position. Consistent with this view is that the more arguments a group hears, the more polarized the members' attitudes become (Hinsz & Davis, 1984).

In addition, it's much easier to make an argument for an extreme. If you think that the engineer should take a 7 in 10 risk, you don't say, "I think the engineer should be moderately brave and accept an intermediate level of risk." Instead, you say something like, "He's got to have some guts; he should go for it!"

Social Comparison   The conformity research tells us that people don't want to be too different from others. But they also don't want to be exactly the same (C. Snyder & Fromkin, 1980). They're faced with a careful balancing act—wanting to be different, but not too different, from those around them. This tendency seems to contribute to the polarization of the group.

The polarizing effect begins with each individual thinking that he or she is slightly more extreme, in the "right" direction, than the average other person (Lamm & Myers, 1978). If the issue is one in which risk is valued (as in the engineer example), each group member may feel that he or she is more daring than average. But the group discussion produces the disappointing news that other people are just as daring, maybe more so. To maintain his or her distance from the group, the individual has to become more extreme. And if everyone in the group does the same thing, the outcome is group polarization.

To test this effect, researchers gave a group of subjects information about one another's positions, without any opportunity for discussion. Just hearing what the other subjects had decided was sufficient to produce change toward more polarized positions on the part of many group members (Goethals & Zanna, 1979).

The group polarization effect may have been at work among Kennedy and his advisers. It may well have led the group to its initial position, which groupthink then prevented the members of the group from evaluating fully. Kennedy was a politician, an aggressive, ambitious man. And the members of his Cabinet were no less ambitious. Certainly the daring of the invasion—the "big act"—would have appealed to them. Then they took turns persuading one another, each trying to be more daring than the last.

Recap

- Groupthink is a pattern of decision making that limits not only the alternatives considered by the group but also the critical evaluation of those alternatives.

- Three conditions seem to increase the vulnerability of the group to the groupthink effect: the cohesiveness of the group, the respect group members have for their leader and one another, and the group's isolation from outside opinions.

- According to Janis, groups can protect themselves from the dangers of groupthink by creating an atmosphere that encourages dissent.

- Groups tend to take more extreme positions than the average of the individual positions of their members—a tendency called group polarization.

- One by-product of group polarization is the effect on the group's members: by the time the group has made its decision, the thinking of individual members has moved in the direction of the group's thinking.

- Two factors—the nature of the arguments for or against an alternative and people's desire to be different, but not too different, from those around them—seem to produce the group polarization effect.

Cooperation and Conflict

In this section we discuss some of the origins of conflict and the ways in which conflict can be resolved. People tend to think that conflict arises only through misunderstanding; but in many situations conflict is actually the inevitable result of different interests. All the more important, then, to understand how to deal with conflict when it develops.

Social Dilemmas: A Source of Conflict

Social dilemmas are situations in which the perfectly rational behavior of individuals produces irrational and often conflictual outcomes for themselves and others. Sometimes there is an intrinsic conflict between the group and the individual. This kind of conflict gives rise to social dilemmas. Here are some familiar examples:

- Time and again, newspapers report tragic fires in theaters and other public places. The crowd panics, people jam the exits, and many die either because they cannot escape or because they are trampled. Inevitably some authority observes that if only people had kept their heads about them, if only they had filed out in an orderly way, no one would have been hurt.

Social dilemma A situation in which the rational behavior of different individuals has negative cumulative effects on both the individuals and the people around them.

- In our large cities, the air is being poisoned by automobile exhaust, and traffic makes the shortest trip a stop-and-go nightmare. People bring their cars into the city but then don't use them because they're afraid they'll never find another parking space. Mass transit systems could help solve these problems, but relatively few people use them. Instead they keep driving into the city each day.
- It used to be that the college green was green—an expanse of grass perfect for lying out in the sun or tossing a ball. Today, at many schools, the green areas are crisscrossed by worn dirt paths that, depending on the weather, are either muddy or dusty and hard. By using the grass, people have made the grass unusable.

In all of these cases, people were doing what made sense for themselves—moving as fast as possible to an exit, choosing the comfort of their own cars, playing ball on the grass. But the outcomes made no sense: what should have turned out well for each individual turned out badly instead.

The Tragedy of the Commons   Our college-green example depicts a social dilemma that is much like a problem described by Garrett Hardin (1968). At one time the commons—the grassy area in the center of the village—played an important role in farming. This large pasture was owned by all the people in the village, and everyone had equal rights to keep cows there.

Now, suppose that in one village there was enough grass on the common to maintain twenty cows. If there were ten villagers and each put two cows on the commons, all would thrive. And if just one of the villagers put a third cow on the commons, the effect on everyone would have been extremely small. Each cow might have given a little less milk, but the difference would hardly have been noticeable. And for the one villager, the payoff would have been really big: the milk from three cows instead of two. So, for the individual villager it made good sense to add a cow.

The problem is that what one villager found reasonable, other villagers did too. Soon each villager had three, then four cows on the commons. They added more and more cows until the commons was no longer a pasture, until there was too little grass to support even one cow. Hardin called this the "tragedy of the commons." The cumulative effect of individually rational behavior was the destruction of the commons.

To make matters worse, many people, upon realizing that something is growing scarce, very rationally try to get as much of it as possible, as quickly as possible, before "the others" destroy the "commons." In the process they accelerate that destruction (Rutte, Wilke & Messick, 1987).

Notice the parallel with the college-green example. Each person who cuts across the grass doesn't have a noticeable impact on the lawn, and each gains a significant advantage in time saved. From the individual's perspective, the cost-benefit ratio makes sense. And if only one person ever walked across the green, it really would be the right thing to do. The lawn would never be damaged, and that person would save time. But the effect of hundreds of students making the same rational decision is an irrational result: the lawn is destroyed.

The same analysis obviously applies to our example of automobiles in the city. And though less obvious, it also applies to the case of theater panic. If only one person pushes ahead of the others to the exit, circumstances don't change appreciably for the other people and that one person is definitely going to escape. But if everyone makes the same "rational" decision and tries to push ahead, the exits will be jammed and no one is going to escape (Brown, 1965).

All of the problems of the environment are "commons" dilemmas. Any single coal-burning factory or smoky automobile saves its owners lots of money and contributes little to pollution, but together they poison the atmosphere. Each whale killed makes little difference to the population and produces a major profit for the whaler, but together the whalers are killing off the whales.

How do we stop the tragedies of the commons? We might begin by asking why common pastures worked well for hundreds of years and then failed. The answer is that they worked in small, tightly knit communities, communities in which no one would have felt that the decision to add a cow was a decision that could be made alone. People in smaller groups (Dawes, 1980), or those who feel more connected to the group (Orbell, van de Kragt & Dawes, 1988), are much more likely to behave cooperatively in a commons situation. The problem with the commons started when communities were no longer small enough or cohesive enough to induce true sharing.

So one solution would be to return to smaller communities. But many problems, like those of the environment, won't be solved by making communities smaller. The reason is that sometimes even small communities make "rational" decisions, such as discharging raw sewage into a river, that have disastrous consequences only if many communities make the same decision.

To solve the dilemma of the environment, we have to invent formal procedures for conserving scarce resources. The most direct approach is simply to regulate behavior. The Environmental Protection Agency was established, in effect, to change the balance of costs and benefits by invoking fines or other penalties that make what was once a rational choice to pollute no longer rational.

One kind of regulation that is successful in laboratory examples is to impose a rule that the largest user must pay all of the costs of restoring a common resource if it's overused. At least in experiments, this is a very effective way to ensure that actual use remains within the capacity of the system (Sato, 1987). Each user exerts self-control because the potential cost of excess is so high. If this rule were in force, and Japan had to pay all of the costs of restoring the whale population, whaling would probably stop very quickly.

Before going on, we should point out one policy implication of social dilemmas. Americans have always been skeptical of Big Government, and the failure of the "command economies" of the Soviet bloc has reinforced that skepticism. In response, recent U.S. administrations have tried to reduce government regulation, in the belief that the natural forces of the marketplace would produce the common good in the long term. But the commons dilemma tells us that this faith is misplaced. Yes, in some circumstances, common good does follow from each individual's rational pursuit of what's best for himself or herself. But in other circumstances (the savings and loan scandal being a case in point), what's rational for the individual is disastrous for society or the nation as a whole. It's important to determine when regulation is necessary and when it's not, and to avoid the simple-minded assumption that regulation is either good or bad in and of itself.

If only one person leaves trash behind in a common area, it has little impact on the area's attractiveness. But if everyone did it, the park would soon become a dump that no one could enjoy.

The Prisoner's Dilemma

In the commons dilemma, rational behavior on the part of the individual ultimately hurts the individual and those around. In a related situation, two individuals or two groups or two countries are led into conflict solely by making what seem to be perfectly rational decisions.

A classic example of this effect is the **prisoner's dilemma.** Imagine that you're one of two prisoners suspected of committing a crime together. You and your partner are separated, and the police tell each of you that if your partner confesses and turns state's evidence, and you don't, you're going to get fifteen

Prisoner's dilemma A model of the real-world situation in which two competing rational decisions produce a worse outcome than two cooperative decisions that seem much less rational.

years. If both of you confess, you'll get only ten years. And if both of you hold out and don't confess, they're going to charge each of you with a lesser crime and you'll each get four years. Finally, if your partner doesn't confess and you do, you'll go free while your partner gets fifteen years.

Complicated, isn't it? Each of you has just two choices, confess or not. But whatever you do, your partner can either confess or not. In effect, each of you has to choose the decision that is best for you individually. Figure 18.11 shows each of the outcomes you would get depending on how each of you acts.

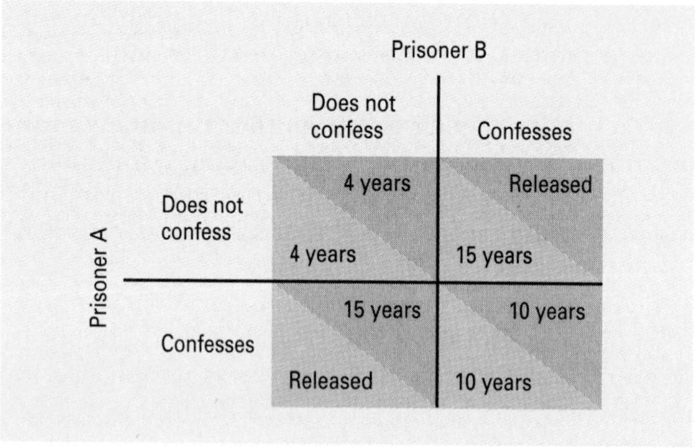

Figure 18.11
The Prisoner's Dilemma

Imagine that you are Prisoner A and consider your choices based on what Prisoner B does. You will see that it is always to your advantage to confess. The same is true for Prisoner B. So, if you both act rationally, you will both confess and spend 10 years in jail. But if neither of you confesses, you each will serve only four years.

What should you do? Let's examine what your partner might do and what you should do in each case. First, your partner might not confess. If you don't confess either, you'll spend four years in jail. But if you do confess, you'll go free. It makes sense, then, for you to confess.

Now assume that your partner does confess. If you don't, you're going to spend fifteen years in jail. If you do, you serve only ten years. So, once again, the rational choice is for you to confess. It doesn't matter whether your partner confesses or not: in either case, you're better off if you confess.

Your partner faces exactly the same set of choices, and it's equally rational for him or her to confess, whatever you do. So if you both act rationally, choosing the choice that is best for each of you, both of you are going to confess and both of you are going to wind up serving ten years. But suppose you cooperate with each other; suppose that neither of you confesses. Now you both serve just four years. You can see why this is called a *dilemma;* the rational choice by each individual leads to an irrational outcome for both.

How can rational decisions produce an irrational result? The answer lies in the difference between what is rational for the individual and what is rational for the group (which in this case is the smallest possible group, two people). As long as you and your partner think only in terms of yourselves, you can't make the best choice.

Variations on the prisoner's dilemma called the *prisoner's dilemma game,* have been used in psychological laboratories for years, and the results are almost invariably the same. People are far more likely to make the competitive, and ultimately self-defeating choice, than the cooperative choice. In part, this competitiveness may reflect an aspect of Western culture. Certainly the way in which people react to these games is related to the degree of their competitiveness or cooperativeness in everyday life (Bem & Lord, 1979).

But the personality of the players has relatively little impact on the outcome of a social dilemma. Far more important are the payoffs. The better the competitive choice for the individual, the greater the competition—even if the ultimate result is worse for both players. Why? Again, because the basic problem in a social dilemma is that the competitive choice is the more rational choice from the perspective of each individual.

Social Dilemmas in International Relations

Although the prisoner's dilemma is just a game, the principles embodied in it are very real. Indeed, they underlie some of the most serious problems in the world today.

Perhaps the clearest example is the arms race that raged between the United States and the Soviet Union for forty-five years. The expense of the weapons seems to have been a major factor in the final economic collapse of the Soviet Union, and it caused many social problems to go unsolved in the United States; yet both sides were unable to stop for years.

Figure 18.12 depicts a vastly simplified version of the payoffs for both countries of arming or disarming. For both sides, the choice is to spend on weapons or on domestic problems. And, clearly, the best solution for both would be domestic spending. However, as in all social dilemmas, the actual choice is not what's best for both sides. If we assume the Soviets will build arms, and if we don't build arms, we might be conquered. This is a terrible outcome, so we must build arms ourselves. Similarly, if we assume the Soviets have not built arms, then we would be able to influence world events more successfully if we did build arms. So in this case, too, we build arms, even though we have no intention of making war on the Soviets.

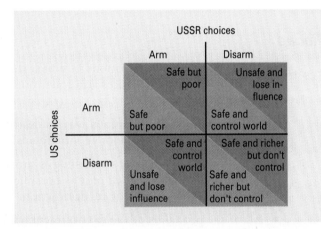

Figure 18.12
Payoffs in the Arms Race

The arms race between the U.S. and the Soviet Union was a perfect example of the prisoner's dilemma. The best solution for both countries would have been to disarm. Each country would have been safer and richer. But instead, both countries armed and were much poorer. Now with improved relations, each country is moving toward the best position.

Probably the same is true of the Soviets. Today, in the era of *glasnost,* we've learned that the arms race has been terribly costly for the Russians. If they could have been sure that we would disarm, they would rather not have armed; and they certainly didn't want to conquer us and have another hostile territory to try to govern. Unfortunately, both the Soviet Union and the United States have been caught in a payoff matrix that produced the cold war treadmill, each country building more and more arms.

Is there a way out of this dilemma? Both laboratory studies and recent history suggest that there is. We've implied that people or countries make these decisions just once. However, the cold war is an ongoing prisoner's dilemma game. Laboratory studies have found that playing the prisoner's dilemma game over and over gives the players an opportunity to change their strategy. For example, if one player repeatedly chooses the competitive alternative, the other invariably chooses the competitive alternative, too. Unfortunately, however, if one player always chooses the cooperative strategy, the other player is very likely to take advantage of this "weakness."

In the laboratory, one strategy leads toward mutual cooperation. This is the "tit-for-tat" strategy, one player following the other's moves. If your opponent competes, you compete as well. But if your opponent cooperates, so do you (Axelrod & Dion, 1988).

The Soviet bloc and Western countries were for decades locked in a social dilemma, in which each side spent more on arms than was wise or desirable. Everyone knew that mutal disarmament was a better policy, but it was only recently that both sides felt they had to take the first steps in that process.

Charles Osgood (1962) developed a real-world variation of the tit-for-tat strategy. He called the technique *graduated reciprocated initiatives in tension-reduction,* or GRIT for short. The first step in GRIT is to announce your intention to cooperate with your opponent. The announcement makes the meaning of your subsequent moves clear. The next step is to make a move, or better yet a number of small moves, in your opponent's favor. Then you wait for your opponent to respond in kind. If your opponent does so, you make a new move of the same sort. The eventual outcome—assuming that you continue to cooperate—is peace.

Notice that your moves are graduated: you don't give up too much too soon. GRIT is not a strategy of appeasement. Notice also that your moves must be reciprocated by your opponent. You retain the capacity to retaliate if your opponent tries to take advantage of you. In laboratory studies, the various parts of the strategy have been found to work as predicted (Lindskold & Han, 1988).

The late 1980s saw an abrupt change in the relationship between the United States and the Soviet Union. Obviously much of that change was rooted in the internal politics and economy of the Soviet Union. But many of the early moves toward *glasnost* were reciprocated by the United States such that, intentionally or not, the progress of the relations between the two nations began to follow the path that Osgood described.

Recap

- Social dilemmas are situations in which the perfectly rational behavior of individuals produces irrational outcomes for themselves and others.

- The tragedy of the commons was its destruction, the cumulative effect of the rational behavior of individuals.

- When people realize that something is growing scarce, they very rationally try to get as much of it as possible, as quickly as possible. In the process they accelerate its destruction.

- All of the problems of the environment are commons dilemmas.

- The problem with the commons started when communities were no longer small enough or cohesive enough to induce true sharing.

- The prisoner's dilemma is a model of the real-world situation in which two competing rational decisions produce a worse outcome than two cooperative decisions that seem much less rational.

- The better the competitive choice for the individual, the greater the competition, even if the ultimate result is worse for both players.

- The GRIT strategy outlines a step-by-step process for achieving world peace.

- GRIT is not a strategy of appeasement: the moves must be graduated and reciprocated in turn by each player.

Conclusion

This chapter continues a theme begun in the last—that much of our social behavior is determined by processes and forces we usually overlook. In this chapter we have seen how powerfully norms and the social situation can shape our behavior. We can be led to commit horrible acts simply by the demands of an authority or the requirements of our social roles. Less dramatically, but more commonly, we conform to those around us, to avoid looking unusual; and we may even adopt the group's opinion as our own. The mere presence of other people affects how hard we work, and how well we think. Even when the group does not affect our individual behavior directly, even when everyone in a group behaves rationally, we sometimes produce cumulative effects that none of us wanted or intended.

These effects are dramatic, but even more striking is our ignorance of them. We continue to believe in our rationality and independence, perhaps at the very moment that we are conforming slavishly. One reason for this ignorance is undoubtedly the fundamental attribution error: when we see people acting in bizarre, unexpected ways, we assume that they are strange people, not people much like ourselves who have been caught in a bizarre situation.

Are we really mere pawns of social forces? Absolutely not. These effects depend on the inattention and ignorance of the people involved. Note that, in the context of each topic in this chapter, the effects of the social situation would diminish or disappear if the participants were alert and aware. If we are vigilant, and if we understand these social forces, we can shape or resist them, to achieve the ends that our conscious reason has chosen. These phenomena are good examples of a point we made in Chapter 1: that by increasing our psychological knowledge we increase our freedom. People have succumbed to authority, conformed, been carried away by their social roles, and been thwarted by social dilemmas for centuries. Now that we are beginning to understand these issues, we may free ourselves from them.

Appendix

Statistics in Psychological Research

Whether psychologists conduct experiments, field studies, case studies, naturalistic observations, or surveys, their investigations usually generate a large amount of data: numbers that represent their findings and provide the basis for their conclusions. In Chapter 1, we described how psychologists obtain their findings, and we discussed several factors vital to research design if that research is to yield meaningful data. No matter how well a study is designed, however, understanding and interpreting the results also depend on the adequacy of the researcher's **statistical analyses;** that is, on the methods used for summarizing and analyzing the data. In this appendix, we consider various **descriptive statistics** that psychologists use to describe and present their data. Then we discuss **inferential statistics,** the mathematical procedures used to draw conclusions from data and make inferences about what they mean.

Describing Data

To illustrate our discussion, consider a hypothetical experiment on the effects of incentives on performance. The experimenter presents a simple list of mathematics problems to two groups of subjects. Each group must solve the problems within a fixed time, but for each correct answer, the low-incentive group is paid ten cents, while the high-incentive group gets one dollar. The experimenter of course expects that the high-incentive group will work harder.

Assume that the experimenter has obtained a random sample of subjects, assigned them randomly to the two groups, and done everything possible to avoid the research problems discussed in Chapter 1. The experiment has been run, and the psychologist now has the data: a list of the number of correct answers reported by each subject in each group. Now comes the first task of statistical analysis: describing the data in a way that makes them easy to understand.

The Frequency Histogram

The simplest way to describe the data is to draw up something like Table A.1, in which all the numbers are simply listed. After examining the table, you might discern that the high-incentive group seems to have done better than the low-incentive group, but the difference is not immediately obvious. It might be even harder to see if there were more subjects and if the scores included three-digit numbers. A picture is worth a thousand words, so a more satisfactory way of presenting the same data is in a picturelike graphic known as a **frequency histogram** (see Figure A.1).

Source: This appendix is adapted from "Statistics in Psychological Research," in Bernstein, D.A., Roy, E.J., Srull, T.K. & Wickens, C.D. (1991), *Psychology,* 2d ed. Boston, MA: Houghton Mifflin Co. Used with permission.

Statistical analyses The mathematical methods used to summarize and analyze research data.

Descriptive statistics Numbers that summarize a pool of research data.

Inferential statistics A set of procedures that provides a measure of how likely it is that research results came about by chance.

Frequency histogram A graphic presentation of data that consists of a set of bars, each of which represents how frequently different values occur in a data set.

Table A.1
A Simple Data Set

Here are the test scores obtained by thirteen subjects performing under low-incentive conditions and thirteen subjects performing under high-incentive conditions.

Low Incentive	High Incentive
4	6
6	4
2	10
7	10
6	7
8	10
3	6
5	7
2	5
3	9
5	9
9	3
5	8

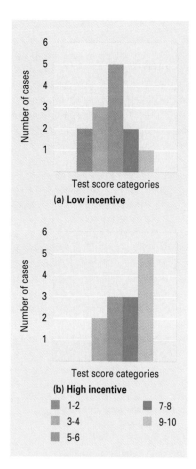

Figure A.1
Frequency Histogram

The height of each bar of a histogram represents the number of scores falling within each range of score values. The pattern formed by these bars gives a visual image of how research results are distributed.

Construction of a histogram is simple. First, divide the scale for measuring the dependent variable (in this case, the number of correct solutions) into a number of categories, or "bins." The bins in our example are 1–2, 3–4, 5–6, 7–8, and 9–10. Next, sort the raw data into the appropriate bin. (For example, the score of a subject who had 5 correct answers would go into the 5–6 bin, a score of 8 would go into the 7–8 bin, and so on.) Finally, for each bin, count the number of scores in that bin and draw a bar up to the height of that number on the vertical axis of a graph. The set of bars makes up the frequency histogram.

Because we are interested in comparing the scores of two groups, there are separate histograms in Figure A.1: one for the high-incentive group and one for the low-incentive group. Now the difference between groups that was difficult to see in Table A.1 becomes clearly visible: more people in the high-incentive group obtained high scores than in the low-incentive group.

Histograms and other pictures of data are useful for visualizing and better understanding the "shape" of research data, but in order to analyze data statistically, the data making up these graphic presentations must be handled in other ways. For example, before we can tell whether two histograms are different statistically or just visually, the data they represent must be described in more precise mathematical terms.

Descriptive Statistics

The numbers that summarize a pool of data are called *descriptive statistics*. The four basic categories of descriptive statistics (1) measure the number of observations made; (2) summarize the typical value of a set of data; (3) summarize the spread, or variability, in a set of data; and (4) express the correlation between two sets of data.

N The easiest statistic to compute, abbreviated as N, simply describes the number of observations that make up the data set. In Table A.1, for example, $N = 13$ for each group, or 26 for the entire data set. Simple as it is, N plays a very important role in more sophisticated statistical analyses.

Measures of Central Tendency   It is apparent in the histograms in Figure A.1 that there is a difference in the pattern of scores between the two groups. In order to compare the two groups without graphs, however, a single number to represent each group's performance would be convenient. Numbers that represent the group are called *measures of central tendency*. There are three measures that are used in this way, the mode, the median, and the mean. Each is most useful for some purposes or with some kinds of data.

The **mode** is the value or score that occurs most frequently in the data. It is computed most easily by ordering the scores from lowest to highest, as has been done in Table A.2. The mode is 5 in the low-incentive group and 10 in the high-incentive group. Notice that these modes do indicate that the two groups are very different and that the mode of 5 does capture the flavor of the low-incentive group (it falls about in the middle). But, in the case of the high-incentive group, the mode (10) is actually an extreme score; it does not provide a value representative of the group as a whole. Thus, the mode can act like a microphone for a small but vocal minority, which, though speaking most frequently, does not represent the views of the majority.

Low Incentive	High Incentive
2	3
2	4
3	5
3	6
4	6
5	7
Mode → ⑤ ← Median →	⑦
5	8
6	9
6	9
7	10 ⎤ ← Mode
8	10
9	10 ⎦
Total = 65	Total = 94
Mean = 65/13 = 5	Mean = 94/13 = 7.23

Table A.2
Measures of Central Tendency

Reordering the data in Table A.1 makes it easy to calculate the mean, median, and mode of the scores of subjects in the high- and low-incentive groups.

Unlike the mode, the **median** takes all of the scores into account. The median is the halfway point in a set of data: half the scores fall above the median, half fall below it. To compute the median, arrange the scores from lowest to highest (as in Table A.2) and count the scores from lowest to highest until the halfway point is reached; that point is the median. If there is an even number of observations, so that the middle lies between two numbers, the median is the value halfway between those two numbers. Thus, if the midpoint is between 17 and 18, the median is 17.5. There are 13 scores in Table A.2; so the median is the seventh score, which is 5 for the low-incentive group and 7 for the high-incentive group.

Mode The value or score that occurs most frequently in a data set; a measure of central tendency.

Median The halfway point in a set of data (half the scores fall above and below it); a measure of central tendency.

The third measure of central tendency is the **mean,** which is the *arithmetic average*. When people talk about the "average" in everyday conversation, they are usually referring to the mean. To compute the mean, add the values of all the scores and divide by N (the total number of scores). For the scores in Table A.2, the mean for the low-incentive group is $65/13 = 5$, and for the high-incentive group, the mean is $94/13 = 7.23$.

Like the median (and unlike the mode), the mean reflects all the data to some degree, not just the most frequent data. Because the mean is more representative than the median of the value of all the data, it is often preferred as a measure of central tendency. Notice, however, that the mean reflects the *actual value* of all the scores, whereas the median gives each score equal weight, whatever its size. This difference can have a huge effect on how well the two statistics reflect the values of a particular set of data. Suppose, for example, that you collected data on the incomes of all fifty families in one small town and that the mean and the median incomes were the same: $20,000. A week later, a person moves to town with an annual income of $1 million. When you reanalyze the income data, the median will hardly change at all, because the millionaire just counts as one score added at the top of the list. However, when you compute the new mean, the actual *amount* of the millionaire's income is added to everyone else's income and divided by the original 50 plus just one more; as a result, the mean might double in value to $40,000. Although the mean is usually the favored measure of central tendency, sometimes, as in this example, the median may be better because it is less sensitive to a few extreme scores.

Measures of Variability The variability, or spread, or dispersion of a set of data is often just as important as its central tendency. In the histograms in Figure A.1, for example, you can see that there is considerable variability in the low-incentive group; all five bins have at least one score in them. There is less variability in the high-incentive group; only four bins are represented, so the numbers are more "tightly packed." This variability can be quantified by measures known as the range and the standard deviation.

The **range** is simply the difference between the highest and the lowest value in the data set. For the data in Table A.2, the range for the low-incentive group is $9 - 2 = 7$; for the high-incentive group, the range is $10 - 3 = 7$. Like the median, the range does not reflect the values of all scores.

In contrast, the **standard deviation,** or **SD,** measures the average difference between each score and the mean of the data set. To see how the standard deviation is calculated, consider the data in Table A.3. The first step is to compute the mean of the set, in this case $20/5 = 4$. Second, calculate the difference, or *deviation* (D), of each score from the mean by subtracting the mean from each score, as in column 2 of Table A.3. Third, find the average of these deviations. However, if you calculated the average by finding the arithmetic mean, you would sum the deviations and find that the negative deviations exactly balance the positive ones, resulting in a mean difference of 0. Obviously there is more than zero variation around the mean in the data set. So, instead of employing the arithmetic mean, we compute the standard deviation by first squaring the deviations (which removes any negative values), summing these squared deviations, dividing by N, and then taking the square root of the result. These simple steps are outlined in more detail in Table A.3.

The standard deviation is a particularly important characteristic of any data set. For example, suppose you are a substitute teacher who comes to a new school hoping for an easy day's work. You are offered the choice of teaching one of two classes. In each, the students' mean IQ is 100. At first glance, there would appear to be no major difference between the classes' IQ scores. But it

Mean The arithmetic average of the scores in a set of data; a measure of central tendency.

Range The difference between the highest and lowest value in a data set; a measure of variability.

Standard deviation (SD) The average difference between each score and the mean of the data set; a measure of variability.

Raw Data	Difference from Mean = D		D^2
2	2 − 4	= −2	4
2	2 − 4	= −2	4
3	3 − 4	= −1	1
4	4 − 4	= 0	0
9	9 − 4	= 5	25
Mean = 20/5 = 4			ΣD^2 = 34

$$\text{Standard deviation} = \sqrt{\frac{\Sigma D^2}{N}} = \sqrt{\frac{34}{5}} = \sqrt{6.8} = 2.6$$

Note: Σ means "the sum of."

Table A.3
Calculating the Standard Deviation

The standard deviation of a set of scores reflects the average degree to which those scores differ from the mean of the set.

turns out that one class has an SD of 16; the SD of the other is 32. Since a higher standard deviation means more variability, the class with the SD of 32 is likely to be more difficult to teach because its students vary more in ability.

The Normal Distribution Now that we have described histograms and some descriptive statistics, we will reexamine how these methods of representing research data relate to some of the concepts discussed elsewhere in the book.

In most subareas in psychology, when researchers collect many measurements and plot their data in histograms, the pattern that results often resembles that shown for the low-incentive group in Figure A.1. That is, the majority of scores tend to fall in the middle of the distribution, with fewer and fewer occurring as one moves toward the extremes. As more and more data are collected, and as smaller and smaller bins are used (perhaps containing only one value each), the histograms tend to smooth out, until they resemble the bell-shaped curve known as the **normal distribution,** or *normal curve,* which is shown in Figure A.2a. When a distribution of scores follows a truly normal curve, its mean, median, and mode all have the same value. Furthermore, if the curve is normal, we can use its standard deviation to describe how any particular score stands in relation to the rest of the distribution.

Remember that in Chapter 13 we discussed the normal curve and how it applies to IQ scores. They are distributed in a normal curve, with a mean, median, and mode of 100 and an SD of 15 (see Figure A.2b). In such a distribution, half of the population will have an IQ above 100 and half will be below 100. The shape of the true normal curve is such that 68 percent of the area under it lies within one standard deviation above and below the mean. In terms of IQ this means that 68 percent of the population has an IQ somewhere between 85 (100 minus 15) and 115 (100 plus 15). Of the remaining 32 percent of the population, half falls more than 1 SD above the mean, and half falls more than 1 SD below the mean. Thus, 16 percent of the population has an IQ above 115, and 16 percent of the scores below 85.

Another way of describing these relationships is with percentiles. A **percentile score** indicates the percentage of people or observations that fall below a given score in a normal distribution. In Figure A.2b, for example, the mean score (which is also the median) lies at a point below which 50 percent of the scores fall. Thus, the mean of a normal distribution is at the 50th percentile. What does this mean for IQ? If you score 1 SD above the mean, your score is at a point above which only 16 percent of the population falls. This means that

Normal distribution The "bell curve" distribution of scores such that the mean, median, and mode all have the same value.

Percentile score The percentage of people or observations that fall below a given score.

Figure A.2
The Normal Distribution

Many kinds of research data approximate the symmetrical shape of the normal curve, in which most scores fall toward the center of the range.

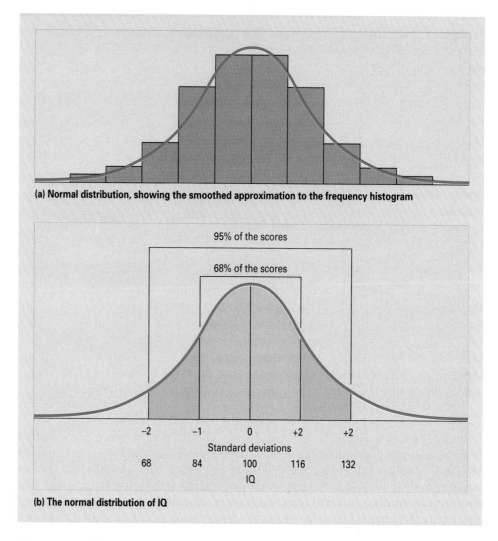

(a) Normal distribution, showing the smoothed approximation to the frequency histogram

(b) The normal distribution of IQ

84 percent of the population (100 percent minus 16 percent) must be below that score; so this IQ score is at the 84th percentile. A score at 2 SDs above the mean is at the 97.5 percentile, because only 2.5 percent of the scores are above it in a normal distribution.

Scores may also be expressed in terms of their distance in standard deviations from the mean, producing what are called **standard scores.** A standard score of 1.5, for example, is 1.5 standard deviations from the mean.

Correlation   Histograms and measures of central tendency and variability describe certain characteristics of one dependent variable at a time. However, psychologists are often concerned with describing the *relationship* between two variables. Measures of correlation are often used for this purpose. We discussed the interpretation of the **correlation coefficient** in Chapters 1 and 13; here we describe how to calculate it.

Recall that correlations are based on the relationship between two numbers associated with each subject or observation. The numbers may represent, say, a person's height and weight or the IQ of a parent and child. Table A.4 contains this kind of data for four subjects from our incentives study who took the test twice. (As you may recall from Chapter 13, the correlation between their scores would be a measure of *test-retest reliability* or stability.) The formula for computing the Pearson product-moment correlation, or *r*, is as follows:

Standard score A value that indicates the distance, in standard deviations, between a given score and the mean of all the scores in a data set.

Correlation coefficient A measure of the degree to which two variables are related.

$$r = \frac{\Sigma(x - M_x)(y - M_y)}{\sqrt{\Sigma(x - M_x)^2 \Sigma(y - M_y)^2}}$$

where

x = each score on variable 1 (in this case, test 1)
y = each score on variable 2 (in this case, test 2)
M_x = the mean of the scores on variable 1
M_y = the mean of the scores on variable 2

Table A.4
Calculating the Correlation Coefficient

Though it appears complex, calculation of the correlation coefficient is quite simple. The resulting r reflects the degree to which two sets of scores tend to be related, or to covary.

Subject	Test 1	Test 2	$(x - M_x)(y - M_y)$[b]
A	1	3	$(1 - 3)(3 - 4) = (-2)(-1) = +2$
B	1	3	$(1 - 3)(3 - 4) = (-2)(-1) = +2$
C	4	5	$(4 - 3)(5 - 4) = (1)(1) \quad = +1$
D	6	5	$(6 - 3)(5 - 4) = (3)(1) \quad = +3$
	[a]$M_x = 3$	$M_y = 4$	$\Sigma(x - M_x)(y - M_y) \quad = +8$

[c]$\Sigma(x - M_x)^2 = 4 + 4 + 1 + 9 = 18$
[d]$\Sigma(y - M_y)^2 = 1 + 1 + 1 + 1 = 4$
[e]$r = \dfrac{\Sigma(x - M_x)(y - M_y)}{\sqrt{\Sigma(x - M_x)^2 \Sigma(y - M_y)^2}} = \dfrac{8}{\sqrt{18 \times 4}} = \dfrac{8}{\sqrt{72}} = \dfrac{8}{8.48} = +.94$

The main function of the denominator in this formula is to ensure that the coefficient ranges from $+1.00$ to -1.00, no matter how large or small the values of the variables being correlated. The "action element" of this formula is the numerator. It is the result of multiplying the amounts by which each of two observations (x and y) differ from the means of their respective distributions (M_x and M_y). Notice that, if the two variables "go together" (so that, if one is large, the other is also large, and if one is small, the other is also small), then either both will tend to be above the mean of their distribution or both will tend to be below the mean of their distribution. When this is the case, $x - M_x$ and $y - M_y$ will both be positive, or they will both be negative. In either case, their product will always be positive, and the correlation coefficient will also be positive. If, on the other hand, the two variables go opposite to one another, such that, when one is large, the other is small, one of them is likely to be smaller than the mean of its distribution, so that either $x - M_x$ or $y - M_y$ will have a negative sign, and the other will have a positive sign. Multiplying these differences together will always result in a product with a negative sign, and r will be negative as well.

Now we can compute the correlation coefficient for the data presented in Table A.4. The first step (step a in the table) is to compute the mean (M) for each variable. M_x turns out to be 3 and M_y is 4. Next, calculate the numerator by finding the differences between each x and y value and its respective mean and by multiplying them (as in step b of Table A.4). Notice that, in this example, the differences in each pair have like signs, so the correlation coefficient will be positive. The next step is to calculate the terms in the denominator; in this case, as shown in steps c and d in Table A.4, they have values of 18 and 4. Finally, place all the terms in the formula and carry out the arithmetic (step e). The result in this case is an r of $+.94$, a high and positive correlation suggesting that performances on repeated tests are very closely related. A subject doing well the first time is very likely to do well again; a person doing poorly at first will probably do no better the second time.

Recap

- Statistics are methods for describing and drawing conclusions from data.

- Visual representations, such as *frequency histograms,* provide visual descriptions of data, making the data easier to understand.

- Descriptive statistics summarize a body of data.

- Measures of central tendency include the mean, median, and mode; variability is typically measured by the range and by the standard deviation.

- Sets of data often follow a normal distribution, which means that most scores fall in the middle of the range, with fewer and fewer scores occurring as one moves toward the extremes.

- The correlation coefficient measures the relationship between two sets of scores.

Inferential Statistics

The descriptive statistics from the incentives experiment tell the experimenter that the performances of the high- and low-incentive groups differ. But some uncertainty remains. Is the difference large enough to be important? Does it represent a stable effect or a fluke? The researcher would like to have some *measure of confidence* that the difference between groups is genuine and reflects the effect of incentive on mental tasks in the real world, rather than the effect of the particular subjects used, the phase of the moon, or other random or uncontrolled factors. One way of determining confidence would be to run the experiment again with a new group of subjects. Confidence that incentives produced differences in performance would grow stronger if the same or a larger between-group difference occurs again. In reality, psychologists rarely have the opportunity to repeat, or *replicate,* their experiments in exactly the same way three or four times. But inferential statistics provide a measure of how likely it was that results came about by chance. They put a precise mathematical value on the confidence or probability that rerunning the same experiment would yield similar (or even stronger) results.

The hypothesis that is actually tested is the **null hypothesis,** the assertion that the independent variable manipulated by the experimenter will have no effect on the dependent variable measured by the experimenter. In this case, the null hypothesis holds that the size of the incentive (the independent variable) will not affect performance on the mathematics task (the dependent variable). Inferential statistics tell us how likely it is that we would have observed the results we did if there was actually no difference between the groups. It is similar to figuring out how likely it is that a coin flipped ten times would come out heads every time. If the probability of this result is low, we reject the null hypothesis—that the coin is equally likely to come out heads or tails, or that the incentive groups are identical. If we reject the null hypothesis, then our orginal experimental hypothesis is probably true.

Null hypothesis The assertion that the independent variable manipulated by the experimenter will have no effect on the dependent variable measured by the experimenter.

How low does the probability of the null hypothesis have to be in order to reject it? There is no fixed answer, but in psychology the convention is one time in twenty. If a result happens less than one in twenty times, or 5 percent of the time by chance, then we reject the chance explanation—the null hypothesis—and decide that our results are not due to chance. In this case, we conclude that the incentive treatments did have an effect on performance.

Differences Between Means: The t Test   One of the most important tools of inferential statistics is the *t* **test.** It allows the researcher to ask how likely it is that the difference between two means occurred by chance rather than as a function of the effect of the independent variable. When the *t* test or other inferential statistic says that the probability of chance effects is small enough (usually less than 5 percent), the results are said to be *statistically significant*. Conducting a *t* test of statistical significance requires the use of three descriptive statistics.

The first component of the *t* test is the size of the observed effect, the difference between the means. In the example shown in Table A.2, the difference between the means is $7.23 - 5 = 2.23$.

Second, the standard deviation of scores in each group must be known. If the scores in a group are quite variable, the standard deviation will be large, indicating that chance may have played a large role in producing the results. The next replication of the study might generate a very different set of group scores. If the scores in a group are all very similar, however, the standard deviation will be small, which suggests that the same result would probably occur for that group if the study were repeated. Thus, the *difference* between groups is more likely to be significant when each group's standard deviation is small.

Third, we need to take the sample size, *N,* into account. The larger the number of subjects or observations, the more likely it is that a given difference between means is significant. This is because, with larger samples, random factors within a group—the unusual performance of a few people who were sleepy or anxious or hostile, for example—are more likely to be canceled out by the majority, who better represent people in general. The same effect of sample size can be seen in coin tossing. If you toss a quarter five times, you might not be too surprised if heads comes up 80 percent of the time. If you get 80 percent heads after one hundred tosses, however, you might begin to suspect that this is probably not due to chance alone and that some other effect, perhaps some bias in the coin, is significant in producing the results.

To summarize, as the differences between the means get larger, as *N* increases, and as standard deviations get smaller, *t* increases. This increase in *t* raises the researcher's confidence in the significance of the difference between means.

Now we will calculate the *t* statistic and show how it is interpreted. The formula for *t* is:

$$t = \frac{M_1 - M_2}{\sqrt{\frac{(N_1 - 1)S_1^2 + (N_2 - 1)S_2^2}{N_1 + N_2 - 2}\left(\frac{N_1 + N_2}{N_1 N_2}\right)}}$$

where:

M_1 = mean of group 1
M_2 = mean of group 2
N_1 = number of scores or observations for group 1
N_2 = number of scores or observations for group 2
S_1 = standard deviation of group 1 scores
S_2 = standard deviation of group 2 scores

t-test An inferential statistic that allows a researcher to ask how likely it is that the difference between two means occurred by chance rather than as a function of the effect of the independent variable.

Despite appearances, this formula is quite simple. In the numerator is the difference between the two group means; t will get larger as this difference gets larger. The denominator contains an estimate of the standard deviation of the *differences* between group means; in other words, it suggests how much the difference between group means would vary if the experiment were repeated many times. Since this estimate is in the denominator, the value of t will get smaller as the standard deviation of group differences gets larger. For the data in Table A.2,

$$t = \frac{M_1 - M_2}{\sqrt{\frac{(N_1 - 1)S_1^2 + (N_2 - 1)S_2^2}{N_1 + N_2 - 2}\left(\frac{N_1 + N_2}{N_1 N_2}\right)}} = \frac{7.23 - 5}{\sqrt{\frac{(12)(5.09) + (12)(4.46)}{24}\left(\frac{26}{169}\right)}}$$

$$= \frac{2.23}{\sqrt{.735}} = 2.60 \text{ with 24 df}$$

To determine what a particular t means, we must use the value of N and a special statistical table called, appropriately enough, the t *table*. We have reproduced part of the t table in Table A.5.

Table A.5
The t Table

This table allows the researcher to determine whether an obtained t value is statistically significant. If the t value is larger than the one in the appropriate row in the .05 column, the difference between means that generated that t score is usually considered statistically significant.

df	P-Value		
	.10 (10%)	.05 (5%)	.01 (1%)
4	1.53	2.13	3.75
9	1.38	1.83	2.82
14	1.34	1.76	2.62
19	1.33	1.73	2.54
22	1.32	1.71	2.50
24	1.32	1.71	2.49

First, find the computed value of t in the row corresponding to the degrees of freedom, or df, associated with the experiment. In this case, degrees of freedom are simply $N_1 + N_2 - 2$ (or two less than the total sample size or number of scores). Since our experiment had 13 subjects per group, df $= 13 + 13 - 2 = 24$. In the row for 24 df in Table A.5, you will find increasing values of t in each column. These columns correspond to decreasing p values, the probabilities that the difference between means occurred by chance. If an obtained t value is equal to or larger than one of the values in the t table (on the correct df line), then the difference between means that generated that t is said to be significant at the .10, .05, or .01 level of probability. Suppose, for example, that an obtained t (with 19 df) was 2.00. Looking along the 19 df row, you find that 2.00 is larger than the value in the .05 column. This allows you to say that the probability that the difference between means occurred by chance was no greater than .05, or 5 in 100. If the t had been less than the value in the .05 column, the probability of a chance result would have been greater than .05. As noted earlier, when an obtained t is not large enough to exceed t table values at the .05 level or better, it is not usually considered statistically significant.

The t value from our experiment was 2.60 with 24 df. Because 2.60 is greater than all the values in the 24 df row, the difference between the high- and low-incentive groups could have occurred by chance less than 1 time in 100.

Beyond the* t *Test Many experiments in psychology are considerably more complex than simple comparisons between two groups. They often involve three or more experimental and control groups. Some experiments also include more than one independent variable. For example, suppose we had been interested not only in the effect of incentive size on performance, but also in the effect of problem difficulty. We might then create six groups whose subjects would perform easy or difficult problems with low, high, or very high incentives.

In an experiment like this, the results might be due to the incentive, the problem difficulty, or the combined effects (known as the *interaction*) of the two. Analyzing the size and source of these effects is typically accomplished through procedures known as *analysis of variance*. The details of analysis of variance are beyond the scope of this book, but the statistical significance of each effect is influenced by differences between means, standard deviation, and sample size in much the same way as described for the *t* test.

For more detailed information about how analysis of variance and other inferential statistics are used to understand and interpret the results of psychological research, consider taking courses in research methods and statistical or quantitative methods.

Recap

- Inferential statistics estimate the probablity that the observed results could have been due to chance.

- The null hypothesis asserts that any relationships between variables are due only to chance. Inferential statistics test the null hypothesis. When an inferential statistic indicates that the experimental results had a low probability of occurring by chance, the results are said to be statistically significant.

- The *t* test assesses the likelihood that differences between two means occurred by chance.

- When more than two groups must be compared, researchers typically rely on analysis of variance.

Glossary

Absolute threshold   The smallest amount of stimulation that can be noticed. (*p. 84*)

Accommodation   (1) The process of adapting behavior and thinking to meet the demands of a new situation. (*p. 314*) (2) In vision, the process of changing the shape of the lens to bring objects into focus on the retina. (*p. 69*)

Achievement test   An instrument that measures the subject's current actual ability. (*p. 370*)

Acquisition   The process by which experience changes behavioral tendencies. (*p. 152*)

Action potential   The electrochemical impulse that travels down a neuron. (*p. 32*)

Acuity   The ability to see the visual field in fine detail. (*p. 70*)

Adaptation   The process of adjusting to a stimulus; in the case of the eye, to the brightness of light. (*p. 72*)

Addiction   Reliance on a substance to carry on everyday activities. (*p. 145*)

Adolescence   The developmental stage between childhood and adulthood. (*p. 341*)

Adolescent egocentrism   The tendency of adolescents to assume that everybody is thinking the way they do about the same things that they are thinking about. (*p. 343*)

Adrenal glands   A pair of endocrine glands that secrete hormones involved in long- and short-term reactions to stress. (*p. 44*)

Aggression   Behavior that is intended to hurt another person. (*p. 518*)

Agoraphobia   Literally, the fear of public places, but actually a fear of panic attacks that occur in public places. (*p. 433*)

Alcohol   A term applied to a variety of beverages containing ethyl alcohol; the most widely abused legal psychoactive drug. (*p. 147*)

Algorithm   A systematic procedure that produces the solution to a problem. (*p. 218*)

Alpha waves   The pattern of brain waves at a frequency of 8 to 13 cycles per second that is characteristic of a state of resting wakefulness. (*p. 126*)

Alternate-forms reliability   An estimate of reliability obtained by administering two different forms of the same measure at two different times. (*p. 363*)

Altruism   Helping another without any expectation of a reward. (*p. 520*)

Ambient flow   A pattern of motion in relation to objects in the environment that gives the individual information about the size, distance, and shape of those objects. (*p. 112*)

Amphetamines   Powerful manufactured stimulants whose effects last for several hours. (*p. 146*)

Amplitude   The energy of a sound wave, usually measured in decibels. (*p. 61*)

Anal stage   In Freudian theory, the second stage of libidinal development; during this stage the focus of satisfaction is the anus. (*p. 398*)

Anorexia nervosa   An eating disorder in which the individual starves himself or herself. (*p. 254*)

Antidepressants   A group of drugs used to treat the symptoms of chronic depression. (*p. 479*)

Antipsychotic drugs   A group of drugs that reduce or stop the delusions and hallucinations that are symptomatic of schizophrenia. (*p. 479*)

Antisocial personality   A personality disorder in which the individual feels no sympathy for other people and no guilt or remorse for his or her actions. (*p. 443*)

Anxiety   Physical and emotional responses of fear or dread that are unwarranted by their object. (*p. 431*)

Aptitude test   An instrument that is designed to predict the subject's potential ability to perform a task. (*p. 370*)

Assimilation   The process of adapting a new experience to an existing schema. (*p. 314*)

Attachment   The process by which a bond is formed between infant and primary caregiver; the bond itself. (*p. 320*)

Attention   The mental function that makes the individual fully conscious of an element in the environment. (*p. 120*)

Attitude   A feeling of liking or disliking that also involves the way people think about and behave toward the object of their feeling. (*p. 511*)

Attribute   A property or characteristic of an object. (*p. 208*)

Attribution theory   A theory of how people understand the behaviors of others, by ascribing those behaviors to properties of the individual, to the situation, or to chance. (*p. 492*)

Auditory hair cells   The receptor cells for sound; they run along the surface of the basilar membrane. (*p. 64*)

Auditory localization   The process of determining the source of a sound using cues provided by the sound itself. (*p. 94*)

Autonomic nervous system   The part of the peripheral nervous system that controls the smooth muscles in the body's organs and glands. (*p. 40*)

Availability heuristic   The tendency to estimate the frequency of an event by the ease with which it's remembered. (*p. 226*)

Aversive stimulus   A stimulus that a subject tries to avoid. (*p. 158*)

Avoidance conditioning   A form of instrumental aversive conditioning in which the subject responds to a neutral stimulus that signals the onset of the aversive stimulus, thereby avoiding the aversive stimulus. (*p. 171*)

Axon   In a neuron, a fiber that carries information away from the cell body. (*p. 30*)

Axon terminal   A fine fiber at the end of an axon that connects the neuron to a muscle, gland, or other neuron. (*p. 30*)

Balance principle   One principle that organizes impressions of people and events, in which good things are assumed to belong with other good things, and bad things belong with bad. (*p. 498*)

Barbiturate   A powerful depressant drug that is especially dangerous because of its effect on the respiratory system. (*p. 147*)

Behavior   Any activity that can be observed. (*p. 3*)

Behavioral assessment   An assessment technique that uses the direct observation of an individual's behavior as a predictor of future behavior. (*p. 368*)

Behaviorism   A school of psychology that believes the study of psychology must be limited to the study of observable activity; associated with the work of John Watson, E. L. Thorndike, and B. F. Skinner. (*p. 10*)

Beta waves   The pattern of brain waves at a frequency of 14 to 30 cycles per second that is characteristic of a high level of activity in the cerebral cortex. (*p. 126*)

Binocular disparity   A perceptual cue for distance; the difference in the images projected on the retinas of the eyes. (*p. 105*)

Biofeedback   A procedure that allows control of one's own autonomic responses by providing information about them. (*p. 293*)

Biological clock   The internal mechanism that helps maintain the body's circadian rhythms. (*p. 124*)

Bipolar disorder   A psychological disorder in which the individual goes back and forth between episodes of depression and mania; at one time called *manic-depressive disorder*. (*p. 434*)

Brain stem   The part of the brain just above the spinal cord; includes the medulla oblongata, the pons, and the midbrain. (*p. 38*)

Brightness   The intensity of light; related to the amplitude of lightwaves. (*p. 74*)

Broca's area   A small area in the left frontal lobe of the brain that is necessary for the production of speech. (*p. 54*)

Bulimia nervosa   An eating disorder in which the individual regulates his or her weight by alternately binging and purging. (*p. 254*)

Bystander effect   As the number of potential helpers increases, the likelihood that any one of them actually will help decreases. (*p. 522*)

Cardinal trait   A trait that describes most of the individual's behavior. (*p. 411*)

Cartesian dualism   René Descartes's belief that mind and body operate under different principles and should be studied by different specialists. (*p. 7*)

Case study   The detailed examination of a single person or instance of a psychological phenomenon. (*p. 14*)

Castration anxiety   In Freudian theory, the boy's fear, during the phallic stage, of castration by his father in retaliation for the child's Oedipal feelings. (*p. 399*)

Catatonic schizophrenia   A type of schizophrenia in which the most striking symptom is some sort of movement disturbance. (*p. 439*)

Catatonic stupor   A motor disturbance in schizophrenia, in which the individual does not move or speak for long periods of time. (*p. 438*)

Catharsis   The process of relieving an impulse by expressing it directly or indirectly. (*p. 518*)

Central nervous system   The spinal cord and brain. (*p. 25*)

Central trait   A trait that describes a large part of the individual's behavior but does not have the broad effects of a cardinal trait. (*p. 411*)

Cerebellum   The finely wrinkled structure at the back of the brain that coordinates movement and helps maintain balance. (*p. 38*)

Cerebral cortex   The large, wrinkled balloon of gray matter that covers the rest of the brain structure in which the most complex processing occurs. (*p. 37*)

Characteristic attribute   An attribute shared by many but not all members of a concept category. (*p. 210*)

Chromosome   A strand of genetic material found in the nucleus of every cell. (*p. 301*)

Chunking   Organizing random elements into a meaningful whole. (*p. 185*)

Circadian rhythm   A cycle of activity that repeats every twenty-four hours or so. (*p. 124*)

Classical conditioning   The process of learning by which a neutral stimulus occurs with a stimulus that evokes a response, so that the neutral stimulus comes to evoke a similar response. (*p. 152*)

Closure   A Gestalt cue; the tendency to see solids where there are gaps or intruding elements. (*p. 103*)

Cochlea   The structure in the inner ear that houses the receptor cells for sound. (*p. 64*)

Coding   The process of translating sensory information into patterns of nerve activity that allow the brain to distinguish among the properties of a stimulus. (*p. 60*)

Cognition   All of the activities involved in gathering and using information. (*p. 208*)

Cognitive dissonance   The discomfort produced by acting in a way that is inconsistent with one's attitudes; a negative motivational state. (*p. 512*)

Cognitive map   A mental image of space. (*p. 169*)

Cognitive psychology   A school of psychology that emphasizes the mental processes by which people and animals come to understand the world. (*p. 10*)

Cognitive social-learning theory   The belief that behavior is a product of social learning, which includes people's understanding of the world and themselves; also called *social-cognitive theory*. (*p. 417*)

Collective unconscious   In Jungian theory, the part of the unconscious mind that holds memories of the ancestral past; those memories are the source of archetypes that lead us to understand the world in particular ways. (*p. 403*)

Common fate   A Gestalt cue; the tendency to group together visually objects that are parallel or that move together. (*p. 103*)

Companionate love   The form of romantic love that is based on the lovers' similarities; an intense liking. (*p. 506*)

Compliance   Changing one's external behavior without changing one's beliefs. (*p. 532*)

Compulsion   An action that the individual repeats again and again to ward off anxiety. (*p. 434*)

Computerized axial tomography (CAT)   A process that uses a computer-driven X-ray machine to map the structure of internal organs. (*p. 29*)

Concept   A way of thinking about objects, events, or people that makes them seem to go together. (*p. 208*)

Conditioned response (CR)   A response that has been learned. (*p. 153*)

Conditioned stimulus (CS)   A stimulus that elicits a response by being paired with an unconditioned stimulus. (*p. 153*)

Conditions of worth   According to Rogers, the conditions placed on the individual by parents and others that limit the individual's ability to develop an accurate self-concept. (*p. 409*)

Cones   The photoreceptor cells that are responsible for color vision. (*p. 70*)

Confirmation bias   The tendency to pay more attention to information that may confirm a hypothesis than to information that might disprove it. (*p. 223*)

Conformity   Changing one's behavior, feelings, or beliefs to match the expectations of the group. (*p. 528*)

Conscious mind   The memories, feelings, and drives that the individual is aware of right now. (*p. 396*)

Consciousness   An awareness of one's thoughts, feelings, and surroundings. (*p. 119*)

Conservation   The ability to understand that certain properties of an object stay the same despite a change in the shape or position of the object. (*p. 334*)

Consolidation   A hypothetical process in which short-term memories are transformed into long-term memories. (*p. 193*)

Constancy   The perception that an object is not changing when its image on the retina is changing. (*p. 98*)

Constructionist theory   The theory that the nervous system assembles fragments of sensory information into human experience. (*p. 90*)

Construct validity   The confidence in a test of a theoretical construct (and its related theory), which is developed by repeated successful use of the test in confirming hypotheses. (*p. 365*)

Continuity   A Gestalt cue; the tendency to see continuous lines where lines are broken. (*p. 102*)

Continuous reinforcement   A pattern of rewarding the subject whenever it responds correctly. (*p. 165*)

Control group   In an experiment, a comparison group that is not exposed to the variable being manipulated. (*p. 18*)

Convergence   The inward rotation of the eyes that keeps both eyes pointed at an image. (*p. 105*)

Conversion disorders   Disorders in which the sufferer reports a loss of movement or sensation in some part of the body, for which there is no neurological basis. (*p. 440*)

Cornea   Part of the eye; a transparent membrane that covers and protects the iris. (*p. 68*)

Corpus callosum   The nerve fibers that transmit impulses from one cerebral hemisphere to the other. (*p. 37*)

Correlation   A statistical technique used to measure the degree to which two variables are related. (*p. 361*)

Correlation coefficient   A measure of the degree to which two variables are related. (*p. A–6*)

Courtship   The exchange of stimuli and responses between two individuals that leads to sexual intercourse. (*p. 258*)

Creativity   The ability to come up with new and useful ideas or to combine information in new and useful ways. (*p. 228*)

Criterion validity   The degree to which a test that is designed to predict an observable outcome actually does predict that outcome. (*p. 364*)

Crystallized intelligence   Knowledge and skills that have been memorized and can be put to use in familiar situations. (*p. 353*)

Decision   The choice of a course of action. (*p. 224*)

Declarative memory   Memory for things that can be expressed in words; includes semantic and episodic memory. (*p. 192*)

Deductive inference   A conclusion about a specific case drawn from a general principle. (*p. 212*)

Defense mechanism   A process that keeps impulses in the unconscious mind or transforms them so that they are not threatening. (*p. 400*)

Deficit   A specific loss of ability. (*p. 27*)

Defining attribute   An attribute shared by all members of a concept category. (*p. 210*)

Deindividuation   The loss of a sense of personal identity, with a consequent increase in the impact of situational factors on behavior. (*p. 544*)

Deinstitutionalization   The practice of releasing chronic mental patients from large mental hospitals to transitional institutions, in the process of reintegrating them into the larger community. (*p. 475*)

Delta waves   The pattern of brain waves at a rate of 1 to 5 cycles per second that first appears in Stage 3 sleep and is characteristic of Stage 4 sleep. (*p. 127*)

Delusion   A false belief about what is happening or true in the world. (*p. 437*)

Delusional disorders   Psychological disorders in which the individual experiences a single well-organized delusion. (*p. 439*)

Dendrite   In a neuron, a fiber that carries information toward the cell body. (*p. 30*)

Denial   A defense mechanism in which the opposite of the unconscious feeling is asserted. (*p. 400*)

Deoxyribonucleic acid (DNA)   The large complex molecules that form the chromosomes. (*p. 301*)

Dependent variable   A variable that is expected to change as a function of an independent variable. (*p. 18*)

Depressants   A class of drugs that tend to relax the user. (*p. 147*)

Descriptive statistics   Numbers that summarize a pool of research data. (*p. A–1*)

Development   The regular sequence of physical and psychological changes that we pass through as we age. (*p. 297*)

Developmental norm   The average age at which an important behavior is first performed. (*p. 328*)

Diagnosticity   The capacity of a task to give information about the skills of the person who performs it. (*p. 264*)

Dialectical reasoning   The application of the principles of abstract reasoning to everyday issues of living. (*p. 352*)

Diathesis-stress model   The belief that physical and mental disorders arise from both a predisposition (the diathesis) and some triggering factor (the stressor). (*p. 447*)

Difference threshold   The smallest noticeable difference between two stimuli; also called *just noticeable difference threshold*. (*p. 85*)

Discriminated operant   A behavior that the subject performs only in the presence of a particular stimulus. (*p. 168*)

Discrimination   The ability to distinguish among similar stimuli by responding to them in different ways. (*p. 157*)

Disorganized schizophrenia   The most profoundly disturbed type of schizophrenia characterized by hallucinations, delusions, and disturbed emotional responses. (*p. 439*)

Display rules   Cultural norms that govern the expression of different emotions. (*p. 272*)

Dissociation   A state of consciousness in which attention is divided. (*p. 138*)

Dissociative disorders   A group of psychological disorders in which the individual is unable to remember recent events, his or her identity, or parts of his or her personality. (*p. 440*)

Drive   An internal stimulus that pushes the organism to behave in certain ways. (*p. 241*)

Drive reduction theory   The belief that the circumstances surrounding the relief of a biological drive become incentives themselves. (*p. 246*)

Drive stimulus   The discomfort caused by a biological need that increases the biological drive. (*p. 246*)

Echoic memory   The sensory register that briefly stores auditory information. (*p. 182*)

Ecological theory   James Gibson's theory that we perceive the world directly through our senses. (*p. 112*)

Ego   In Freudian theory, the part of the psyche that satisfies the id's demands within the limitations of physical and social reality. (*p. 396*)

Egocentrism   The inability to see the world from another's perspective. (*p. 334*)

Elaborative rehearsal   Encoding material into meaningful units by connecting it to what is already known. (*p. 187*)

Electroconvulsive therapy (ECT)   The use of electric current to generate a kind of seizure that alleviates some of the symptoms of severe chronic depression. (*p. 480*)

Electroencephalograph   A device that monitors and records electrical activity in the brain on a moving paper chart or computer screen. (*p. 28*)

Embryo   The developing human at two to eight weeks following conception. (*p. 305*)

Embryonic phase   The period following implantation, in which the placenta forms and the basic body organs develop. (*p. 305*)

Emotion   A complex automatic response to a situation, composed of emotional action, autonomic responses, expressive behavior and feeling. (*p. 268*)

Empiricists   Those who believe that perceptual principles are learned through experience with the environment. (*p. 92*)

Endocrine gland   A gland that delivers its secretions directly to the bloodstream. (*p. 43*)

Environmental invariants   Complex properties of the world that are apparent to active observers. (*p. 112*)

Episodic memory   Memory for personal experiences. (*p. 192*)

Erogenous zone   A sensitive part of the body, stimulation of which increases sexual motivation. (*p. 258*)

Escape conditioning   A form of instrumental aversive conditioning in which the subject's response terminates the aversive stimulation. (*p. 171*)

Expectancy   An assumption that is based on experience. (*p. 91*)

Experience   Feelings, thoughts, and perceptions. (*p. 3*)

Experiment   An observational context in which the psychologist manipulates the amount or presence of one or more variables and then observes the effects on other variables. (*p. 18*)

Experimental group   In an experiment, subjects who are exposed to the variable being manipulated. (*p. 18*)

Experimenter influence   The unintentional influence that a researcher exerts on a subject's responses. (*p. 141*)

Expressive behavior   A behavior that conveys information about an emotional state. (*p. 271*)

Extinction   The gradual disappearance of a conditioned response once the conditioned stimulus is no longer followed by the unconditioned stimulus or by reinforcement. (*p. 156*)

Extravert   A person who enjoys social activity and does not like solitude. (*p. 413*)

Extrinsic motivation   Motivation that is derived from the consequence of behavior. (*p. 241*)

Face validity   The degree to which a test appears to measure what it's supposed to measure. (*p. 365*)

Family system   The aggregate of people, property, relationships, rights, responsibilities, expectations, and traditions that constitute a family. (*p. 473*)

Feature detectors   Cells in the visual cortex that respond to specific elements in the sensory impulses transmitted from the eyes. (*p. 77*)

Feelings   The conscious experience of emotion. (*p. 273*)

Fetal phase   The last period of prenatal development—from about eight weeks after conception to birth. (*p. 306*)

Fetus   The developing human from about eight weeks after conception to birth. (*p. 306*)

Fight-or-flight response   The pattern of responses produced by the autonomic nervous system that prepares the organism for intense action. (*p. 269*)

Figure   The part of the visual field that interests the viewer. (*p. 102*)

Fixed-interval schedule   A pattern of reinforcement in which the subject is reinforced for responses made a certain number of seconds or minutes after its last reinforced response. (*p. 166*)

Fixed-ratio schedule   A pattern of reinforcement in which the subject must make a specified number of unreinforced responses for each reinforced response. (*p. 166*)

Flooding   A behavioral therapy for phobias that asks clients to imagine being in the situation that terrifies them most, or that actually places them in that situation, until the fear subsides. (*p. 469*)

Fluid intelligence   The ability to learn new information and skills. (*p. 353*)

Fovea   A small dip in the center of the retina where few receptors gather light for each ganglion cell; receptors are mostly cones. (*p. 70*)

Fraternal twins   Two individuals conceived and born at the same time who do not share the same genotype. (*p. 302*)

Free association   In psychoanalysis, the process of saying whatever comes to mind, no matter how unimportant it seems. (*p. 462*)

Frequency   The number of wave crests in a unit of time, it determines pitch. (*p. 61*)

Frequency histogram   A graphic presentation of data that consists of a set of bars, each of which represents how frequently different values occur in a data set. (*p. A–1*)

Frequency theory   The theory that the hair cells in the cochlea reproduce the frequency of sound waves in the nerve impulses they generate. (*p. 64*)

Fugue   A dissociative disorder in which the individual forgets his or her own identity and may leave familiar surroundings to live at least briefly in a new place, with a new identity. (*p. 441*)

Functional fixedness   The inability to think of a new use for a familiar object. (*p. 221*)

Functionalism   A school of psychology that believed behavior is governed by instincts that help the individual adapt to the environment; associated with the work of William James. (*p. 9*)

Fundamental attribution error   The tendency to underestimate the role of the situation in determining behavior. (*p. 494*)

Gate theory   The theory that neurons in the spinal cord can block the transmission of pain to the brain. (*p. 82*)

Gene   The basic unit of heredity that guides the physical processes of development of the organism. (*p. 301*)

General adaptation syndrome (GAS)   A pattern of responses to stressful circumstances that consists of the alarm, resistance, and exhaustion stages. (*p. 286*)

Generalization   The tendency to respond to different stimuli in the same way. (*p. 157*)

Generalized anxiety   A feeling of anxiety that is more or less constant but not attached to a particular object or situation. (*p. 432*)

Generalizing   Drawing conclusions about a whole population from the study of a representative sample. (*p. 14*)

Genotype   The individual's genetic makeup. (*p. 301*)

Germinal phase   The period of development from conception to the egg's implantation in the uterus. (*p. 305*)

Gestalt cues   Perceptual cues that help the individual see the different parts of an image as a whole. (*p. 102*)

Gestalt psychology   A school of psychology that believed the whole, not its parts, is the fundamental experience. (*p. 9*)

Glial cell   A nerve cell that supports and protects neurons. (*p. 30*)

Gonads   The male and female sex glands (testes and ovaries, respectively). (*p. 44*)

Ground   Everything in the visual field except the figure. (*p. 102*)

Group polarization   The tendency for a group's decisions to be more extreme than the average decision of individual group members. (*p. 553*)

Groupthink   A pattern of decision making that limits the alternatives the group considers and the critical evaluation of those alternatives. (*p. 552*)

Hallucination   A sensory experience that occurs in the absence of a sensory stimulus. (*p. 147*)

Hallucinogens   A class of drugs that distort perception. (*p. 147*)

Hardy personality   A type of personality consisting of several traits that seem to protect the individual from stress-related illness. (*p. 291*)

Heuristic   A problem-solving strategy that is neither systematic nor certain, but that is often efficient. (*p. 219*)

Hidden observer   The dissociated consciousness in a hypnotized subject. (*p. 140*)

Hierarchy of needs   Maslow's classification of motives. (*p. 249*)

Higher-order conditioning   Training a subject to respond to a conditioned stimulus by pairing it with the conditioned stimulus from a previous conditioning procedure. (*p. 156*)

Homeostasis   The relative stability of the body's internal environment. (*p. 42*)

Homeostatic mechanism   A mechanism that regulates the level of a physiological variable. (*p. 242*)

Hormone   A substance secreted into the bloodstream by an endocrine gland that has broad effects on physiology. (*p. 43*)

Hue   The psychological experience of color; related to the wavelength of light. (*p. 74*)

Humanistic psychology   A school of psychology that believes that people control their own actions and thoughts; associated with the work of Carl Rogers and Abraham Maslow. (*p. 10*)

Hypnotism   The process of inducing a state of relaxation in a subject who then can be made to perform suggested behaviors. (*p. 136*)

Hypothalamus   A tiny structure in the brain that monitors the body's internal environment, receives information about the body's external environment, and controls hunger and thirst. (*p. 38*)

Hypothesis   An expectation, based on a theory, of how something will behave under specific circumstances. (*p. 4*)

Iconic memory   The sensory register that briefly stores visual images. (*p. 182*)

Id   In Freudian theory, the part of the psyche that consists of the psychological feelings of biological needs. (*p. 396*)

Identical twins   Two individuals with exactly the same genotype. (*p. 302*)

Identification   The process by which the individual tries to be as much like someone else as possible; in Freudian theory, a boy's response to castration anxiety. (*p. 399*)

Illusion   A distorted perception of reality. (*p. 92*)

Image   A mental representation of visual information. (*p. 213*)

Imagery   The representation in thought of visual scenes. (*p. 203*)

Imprinting   Learning during a sensitive period. (*p. 320*)

Incentive   A circumstance or environmental stimulus that pulls the organism to behave in certain ways. (*p. 241*)

Incubation   Breaking away from a problem for a while before coming back to try to solve it again. (*p. 221*)

Independent variable   A variable that the experimenter manipulates. (*p. 18*)

Inductive inference   A generalization based on specific observations. (*p. 212*)

Inferential statistics   A set of procedures that provides a measure of how likely it is that research results came about by chance. (*p. A–1*)

Inferiority complex   In Adlerian theory, the collection of unconscious feelings of inferiority that develop in infancy and childhood and later shape adult behavior. (*p. 404*)

Informational social influence   The capacity of a group to influence behaviors and attitudes by defining what is true or correct. (*p. 529*)

Ingroup   Any group to which the individual belongs. (*p. 507*)

Inner ear   The cochlea; the part of the ear that transduces physical energy into nerve impulses. (*p. 64*)

Insight   The sudden recognition that a solution is the right solution to a problem. (*p. 222*)

Insomnia   A chronic problem with falling asleep or with the pattern of sleep. (*p. 134*)

Instinct   An innate tendency to respond to certain stimuli in certain ways. (*p. 244*)

Instrumental conditioning   Learning through reinforcement. (*p. 161*)

Intellectualization   A defense mechanism that separates feelings from cognitive content, and then represses the former while closely examining the latter. (*p. 402*)

Intelligence   The capacity to solve problems and cope successfully with one's environment. (*p. 375*)

Intelligence quotient (IQ)   Originally, mental age divided by chronological age, multiplied by 100; more generally, a score on an intelligence test. (*p. 373*)

Intensity   The level or loudness of sound; related to the energy of sound. (*p. 61*)

Interference   The disruption of memory by other memories. (*p. 202*)

Internal consistency   An estimate of the reliability of a psychological measure obtained by relating each item of a multi-item measure to every other item. (*p. 363*)

Interpretation   In psychoanalysis, a psychological explanation that the analyst provides in everyday language to patients in order to help them understand their own feelings and behavior. (*p. 462*)

Interview   An assessment technique that uses verbal questions and answers to collect information about a subject. (*p. 367*)

Intrinsic motivation   Motivation that is derived from the pleasure of behaving in a certain way. (*p. 241*)

Introspection   The procedure of confronting subjects with a stimulus and then asking them to describe their experience of it in detail; a method used by the structuralists. (*p. 9*)

Introvert   A person who prefers being alone and does not enjoy social activity. (*p. 413*)

Iris   The band of muscle that controls the amount of light that enters the eye. (*p. 68*)

Isolation   A defense mechanism that separates unconscious feelings from unconscious thoughts and memories, and then represses the feelings. (*p. 401*)

James-Lange theory   The theory that feelings are the result, not the cause, of emotional behaviors. (*p. 273*)

Just-world phenomenon   The belief that the world is just and, therefore, that bad things happen only to bad people. (*p. 508*)

K-complexes   Periods of long, high-amplitude EEG waves that along with sleep spindles are characteristic of Stage 2 sleep. (*p. 127*)

Kinesthetic sense   The sense of motion; it tells you where parts of your body are in relation to each other. (*p. 83*)

Language   The medium through which knowledge is acquired, organized, and communicated. (*p. 208*)

Latent content   The underlying meaning of a dream. (*p. 132*)

Latent learning   Learning that is not demonstrated immediately. (*p. 169*)

Lateralized function   An activity that is performed by just one side of the brain. (*p. 54*)

Law of effect   Responses that are reinforced are more likely to be repeated (learned) than those that are not reinforced. (*p. 161*)

Learned helplessness   The expectation, stemming from the experience of failure, that one cannot succeed and so should not even try. (*p. 416*)

Learning   An enduring change in behavior that is a product of experience. (*p. 151*)

Lens   The round clear fibrous material that adjusts the focus of light on the retina. (*p. 68*)

Lesion   An area of tissue that has been damaged. (*p. 27*)

Libido   In Freudian theory, the energy that moves the individual to seek pleasure. (*p. 398*)

Limbic system   A group of structures in the brain that play a role in emotional behavior and memory. (*p. 39*)

Lithium   A mineral that has been highly successful in the treatment of patients with bipolar disorder. (*p. 479*)

Locus of control   The generalized expectancy that one can control one's own reinforcements or, conversely, that they are controlled by luck or outside forces. (*p. 416*)

Logic   The rules for manipulating propositions to generate valid inferences. (*p. 212*)

Long-term memory   The memory system that preserves information for long periods of time. (*p. 180*)

Magnetic resonance imaging (MRI)   A process that uses the brain's magnetic fields to trace the cellular activity and chemical makeup of brain tissue. (*p. 29*)

Maintenance rehearsal   Repeating information over and over to retain it in working memory. (*p. 185*)

Major depression   A psychological disorder in which the primary symptoms are long term, and/or profound feelings of sadness and hopelessness. (*p. 434*)

Mania   A state in which the individual is extravagantly (and often unrealistically) happy, optimistic, and energetic. (*p. 434*)

Manifest content   The parts of a dream—the story, the characters—that the individual recognizes immediately. (*p. 132*)

Marijuana   The most widely used illegal psychoactive drug. (*p. 148*)

Maturation   The developmental processes that are determined by the individual's biological inheritance. (*p. 298*)

Mean   The arithmetic average of the scores in a set of data; a measure of central tendency. (*p. A–4*)

Means-end analysis   A heuristic for determining the way to arrive at a solution and the form of that solution. (*p. 219*)

Median   The halfway point in a set of data (half the scores fall above and below it); a measure of central tendency. (*p. A–3*)

Meditation   (1) A means of focusing attention to produce an altered state of consciousness. (*p. 143*) (2) Any of a wide variety of techniques for focusing attention that produces a calming effect on feelings and the body's activities. (*p. 294*)

Medulla oblongata   The lower part of the brain stem; relays information to and from the brain and controls heart rate, the rate of respiration, and the diameter of blood vessels. (*p. 38*)

Menopause   The cessation of menstruation. (*p. 351*)

Mental age   The average age of the people who performed at the same level as the subject on a test that predicts performance in school. (*p. 373*)

Meta-analysis   A statistical technique that combines the results of many studies into one set of conclusions. (*p. 483*)

Method of loci ('lo-si)   A memory aid involving the association of a list of unrelated items with images and the mental placement of those images in a familiar location. (*p. 203*)

Middle ear   The ossicles; the part of the ear that conducts sound from the outer ear to the inner ear. (*p. 63*)

Misattribution   The process by which bodily states produced by one cause lead to feelings as if they were produced by a different cause. (*p. 277*)

Mnemonic   A technique used to improve memory. (*p. 203*)

Mode   The value or score that occurs most frequently in a data set; a measure of central tendency. (*p. A–3*)

Modeling   In behavioral therapy, a program of treatment in which a wanted response is strengthened or an unwanted response is weakened by using a model to demonstrate the behavior and the consequences of the behavior. (*p. 471*)

Mood-congruent memory   A memory whose emotional tone is consistent with the individual's mood at the time of retrieval. (*p. 198*)

Morpheme   The smallest meaningful unit of language. (*p. 231*)

Motivation   The psychological factors that energize behavior and determine its direction. (*p. 241*)

Multiple personality disorder   A dissociative disorder in which the individual seems to have more than one personality controlling behavior at different times. (*p. 441*)

Myelin   A shiny white fatty substance, often coating the outside of axons, that speeds conduction. (*p. 30*)

Naming fallacy   A form of disordered logic in which a person tries to explain an event by merely giving it a name. (*p. 245*)

Narcolepsy   A disorder in which the individual falls asleep abruptly, in the middle of everyday activities. (*p. 135*)

Nativists   Those who believe that perceptual principles are present at birth. (*p. 92*)

Naturalistic observation   Watching subjects in a real-life situation to see how they behave. (*p. 13*)

Need for achievement (nAch) The need to meet challenges and to accomplish one's goals. (*p. 261*)

Negative afterimage The reverse visual image seen after examining a bright stimulus. (*p. 71*)

Negative reinforcement A procedure that strengthens learning by taking away from the subject something it dislikes. (*p. 170*)

Neonatal reflexes Patterns of autonomic behavior that are present at birth. (*p. 308*)

Neonate An infant through the first month of life. (*p. 307*)

Nerves Bundles of nerve fibers that carry information throughout the nervous system. (*p. 26*)

Nervous system The spinal cord, the brain, and the nerves that connect these structures to the muscles, glands, and sense organs. (*p. 25*)

Neuron A nerve cell that carries information in the form of electrochemical impulses. (*p. 30*)

Neuroscience The study of the components and processes of the nervous system. (*p. 27*)

Neurotransmitter A chemical produced by the presynaptic neuron that moves across the synaptic cleft and binds to receptor sites on the postsynaptic neuron. (*p. 33*)

Norm A pattern of behavior shared and required by members of a group. (*p. 528*)

Normal distribution The "bell curve" distribution of scores such that the mean, median, and mode all have the same value. (*p. A–5*)

Normative social influence The capacity of a group to influence its members by the threat of its disapproval. (*p. 531*)

Null hypothesis The assertion that the independent variable manipulated by the experimenter will have no effect on the dependent variable measured by the experimenter. (*p. A–8*)

Obedience Complying with the direct request or order of another person. (*p. 534*)

Obesity The maintenance of body weight at 25 percent or more above the average body weight for the individual's height and build. (*p. 255*)

Objective test An assessment technique in which the questions and the response format are defined and the same for everyone tested. (*p. 370*)

Object permanence The infant's recognition that an object exists outside his or her experience with it. (*p. 314*)

Observational learning Learning from watching the behavior of others and the consequences of that behavior. (*p. 175*)

Obsession A thought or pattern of thoughts that the individual repeats again and again to ward off anxiety. (*p. 434*)

Oedipus complex In Freudian theory, a child's desire to possess the parent of the opposite sex; sometimes called the *Electra complex* in girls, although Freud did not use this term. (*p. 399*)

One-word stage The stage of language development at which children use single words. (*p. 233*)

Operant A response that acts on the environment. (*p. 162*)

Operant conditioning A form of instrumental conditioning developed by Skinner that allows the subject to set the pace of learning. (*p. 162*)

Operation An action that a child can carry out and reverse entirely in his or her imagination. (*p. 333*)

Operational definition A description of particular procedures and measurements used in an experiment, which define the concepts being studied. (*p. 4*)

Opiate A depressant drug derived from or modeled on opium. (*p. 147*)

Opponent-process theory Ewald Hering's theory that all color experience derives from the activity of three pairs of color systems. (*p. 77*)

Optic chiasm Point at the midline of the brain where the optic nerves cross over to the opposite side of the brain. (*p. 45*)

Optimal arousal theory The theory that certain behaviors are motivated by the need to maintain a moderate level of excitement in the nervous system. (*p. 247*)

Oral stage In Freudian theory, the first stage of libidinal development; during this stage the focus of satisfaction is the mouth. (*p. 398*)

Orgasm The strong rush of sexual pleasure that occurs at the climax of sexual interaction. (*p. 258*)

Orienting reflex A response to an unanticipated or new stimulus. (*p. 153*)

Outer ear The pinna, auditory canal, and eardrum; the part of the ear that collects and focuses sound. (*p. 63*)

Outgroup Any group of which the individual is not a member or is not aware of membership. (*p. 507*)

Overjustification effect The weakening of an intrinsic motive for a behavior by introducing an extrinsic motive for the behavior. (*p. 248*)

Pancreas The gland that produces insulin and glucagon. (*p. 44*)

Panic attack The sudden unexpected onset of the physical symptoms and feelings of anxiety. (*p. 432*)

Paranoid schizophrenia A type of schizophrenia characterized by hallucinations and delusions of persecution and/or grandiosity. (*p. 439*)

Parasympathetic division The part of the autonomic nervous system that generally conserves energy. (*p. 42*)

Partial reinforcement A schedule of reinforcement that does not reinforce every response. (*p. 165*)

Passionate love The intense form of romantic love in which the presence or even the thought of the loved one produces excitement and physiological arousal. (*p. 505*)

Pegword method A memory aid in which a list of unrelated words is associated with words that have already been memorized. (*p. 203*)

Penis envy In Freudian theory, the envy girls feel during the phallic stage because they don't have a penis. (*p. 399*)

Percentile score The percentage of people or observations that fall below a given score. (*p. A-5*)

Percept   The product of perception—the thing we see, feel, or hear. (*p. 92*)

Perception   The process of organizing, interpreting, and integrating sensory information. (*p. 89*)

Perceptual cue   An element of sensory information from which perceptions are constructed. (*p. 91*)

Performance   The demonstration of learning in behavior. (*p. 152*)

Performance IQ   A score on an IQ test that reflects the subject's ability to carry out nonverbal tasks (for example, arranging blocks in a pattern and putting a series of pictures into a sequence that "tells" a story). (*p. 375*)

Peripheral nervous system   The portion of the nervous system that connects the spinal cord and brain to the rest of the body. (*p. 25*)

Periphery   Area in the retina surrounding the fovea where a great many receptors gather light for a single ganglion cell; the receptors are mostly rods. (*p. 70*)

Personality   The long-standing patterns of thought, emotion, and behavior that distinguish an individual from other people. (*p. 393*)

Person schema   An organized system of ideas about a person's attributes. (*p. 498*)

Persuasion   The attempt to change someone's attitudes or beliefs through a verbal message. (*p. 515*)

Phallic stage   In Freudian theory, the third stage of libidinal development; during this stage the focus of satisfaction is on the exclusive possession of the parent of the opposite sex. (*p. 399*)

Phenomenology   The study of experience. (*p. 408*)

Phenotype   The actual traits displayed by an individual; how a genotype is expressed in a particular environment. (*p. 301*)

Pheromone   An odor that communicates a social message. (*p. 79*)

Phobia   An unreasonable fear that limits the individual's participation in day-to-day activities. (*p. 159*)

Phoneme   A sound used to form spoken words that gives the words meaning in a particular language. (*p. 231*)

Physical dependence   The body's inability to function normally in the absence of a drug. (*p. 144*)

Pitch   The placement of sound on the musical scale; related to the frequency of sound. (*p. 61*)

Pituitary gland   The pealike structure in the brain that, with the hypothalamus, governs most of the body's automatic functions; called the *master gland*. (*p. 38*)

Placenta   The structure through which nutrients and oxygen are delivered to the embryo and wastes are removed. (*p. 305*)

Place theory   The theory that different frequencies target specific areas on the basilar membrane. (*p. 65*)

Pleasure principle   In Freudian theory, the principle under which the id operates: satisfaction now, without regard for what is feasible. (*p. 396*)

Population   All of the people or animals to which a theory applies. (*p. 14*)

Positive reinforcement   A procedure that strengthens learning by giving the subject something it likes. (*p. 170*)

Positron emission tomography (PET)   A process that uses a computer-driven X-ray machine and radioactive tracers to study the activity of internal organs. (*p. 29*)

Posthypnotic suggestion   A suggestion made during hypnotism that describes an action to be taken when the subject is no longer hypnotized. (*p. 137*)

Posttraumatic stress disorder   Recurring bouts of anxiety, depression, and other physiological and social disorders resulting from severe trauma. (*p. 292*)

Pragmatic inferential rules   Principles for making inferences that are similar to the rules of formal logic but are expressed in more concrete language. (*p. 213*)

Preconscious mind   The memories, feelings, and drives that the individual is not aware of now but could become aware of if necessary. (*p. 396*)

Prejudice   A strong negative feeling or belief about another person based only on that individual's membership in a social group. (*p. 507*)

Prenatal period   The period of development between conception and birth. (*p. 305*)

Preparedness theory   The idea that people are predisposed to acquire and maintain conditioned responses to biological hazards. (*p. 159*)

Primary sex characteristics   The reproductive organs. (*p. 342*)

Priming   Using cues to improve memory. (*p. 197*)

Principles of inference   Guidelines that tell the perceptual system how to interpret sensory information. (*p. 92*)

Prisoner's dilemma   A model of the real-world situation in which two competing rational decisions produce a worse outcome than two cooperative decisions that seem much less rational. (*p. 557*)

Proactive interference   The disruption of a later memory by an earlier one. (*p. 202*)

Problem   A question that appears to have an answer. (*p. 217*)

Procedural memory   Memory for action and skills. (*p. 192*)

Projection   A defense mechanism in which the unconscious impulse is attributed to other people rather than to the self. (*p. 402*)

Projective test   An instrument that indirectly measures motives, desires, or emotions by asking the subject to respond to an ambiguous stimulus (such as an inkblot, a vague photograph, or an open-ended sentence). (*p. 370*)

Proposition   An idea that links two or more concepts together by describing a relationship among them. (*p. 212*)

Prototype   The standard used to define a concept. (*p. 209*)

Proximity   A Gestalt cue; the tendency to see items that are clustered in a group as a single element. (*p. 102*)

Psychoactive drug   A substance that affects behavior or experience through its influence on synaptic activity. (*p. 144*)

Psychoanalysis   The process developed by Freud of helping a client achieve insight into and work through intrapsychic conflict. (*p. 462*)

Psychodynamic theories   A group of theories of personality that assume the most important causes of behavior are motives, especially unconscious motives. (*p. 394*)

Psychodynamic therapy   A therapy based on the fundamental idea that the symptoms of psychological disorders can be alleviated by the resolution of intrapsychic conflict. (*p. 461*)

Psychogenic amnesia   Loss of memory due to psychological rather than physical causes. (*p. 441*)

Psychological dependence   An emotional dependence on a drug. (*p. 144*)

Psychological disorder   A pattern of behavior, thought, or feeling that is abnormal, socially unacceptable, irrational, or painful to the individual or those around the individual. (*p. 426*)

Psychology   The science of behavior and experience. (*p. 3*)

Psychosocial theory   Erikson's theory that at each of various stages of life the individual must resolve a critical issue in his or her relationships to others. (*p. 330*)

Psychosurgery   An operation performed on the brain to control a patient's behavior or experience. (*p. 481*)

Psychotherapy   Any primarily verbal set of techniques for treating psychological disorders that focuses on the individual's behaviors, thoughts, and feelings. (*p. 460*)

Puberty   The period of physical change that prepares the body for reproduction. (*p. 341*)

Punishment   A procedure that weakens a response by taking away something the subject likes or by giving the subject something it dislikes. (*p. 170*)

Pupil   The transparent opening through which light enters the eye. (*p. 68*)

Random sample   A sample whose members are selected purely by chance, so that every member of the population has an equal chance of being included. (*p. 14*)

Range   The difference between the highest and lowest value in a data set; a measure of variability. (*p. A-4*)

Rating scale   An instrument used to measure a psychological variable, usually through the assignment of numerical values. (*p. 16*)

Rational-emotive therapy   Treatment method in which client's irrational beliefs are challenged and alternatives to them are provided; developed by Albert Ellis. (*p. 471*)

Reaction formation   A defense mechanism that converts an impulse into a behavior that is diametrically opposed to that impulse. (*p. 400*)

Reality principle   In Freudian theory, the principle under which the ego operates; satisfaction within the constraints of physical and social reality. (*p. 396*)

Reasoning   Generating new information by manipulating old information. (*p. 212*)

Reciprocity   People's tendency to like people who like them. (*p. 504*)

Reflex   An automatic response, originating within the spinal cord. (*p. 37*)

Reinforcement   The process of systematically following a response with a reward in order to increase the frequency of that response. (*p. 162*)

Reinforcement schedule   The pattern in which reinforcement is provided. (*p. 165*)

Reliability   The degree to which a measurement is error free, estimated by the degree to which measurements are repeatable. (*p. 16*)

REM sleep   Sleep characterized by rapid eye movement and high levels of activity in the brain and sympathetic nervous system, but very low levels of activity in the muscles; also called *paradoxical sleep*. (*p. 128*)

Representational thought   The ability to talk about events or people not taking place or present at the moment. (*p. 332*)

Representativeness heuristic   The tendency to assume that a person or object must be a member of a category if it represents that category especially well. (*p. 226*)

Representative sample   A sample whose characteristics are similar to those of the population from which it is drawn. (*p. 14*)

Repression   A defense mechanism that uses psychic energy to keep threatening impulses in the unconsciou mind. (*pp. 198 & 400*)

Resistance   A defense mechanism through which client evades insight when it is close at hand; for th psychoanalyst, a source of information about t client's underlying motivation. (*p. 462*)

Retina   The thin layers of light-sensitive tissue at back of the eye. (*p. 69*)

Retrieval   The process of finding information that been encoded and stored in memory, and transformi it back into usable form when it's needed. (*p. 196*)

Retroactive interference   The disruption of an earlie memory by a later one. (*p. 202*)

Rigidity   The unwillingness to give up a problem-solving strategy that no longer works or is not as effective as a new strategy. (*p. 220*)

Rods   The photoreceptor cells that are responsible for vision in dim light. (*p. 70*)

Sample   The small part of a population that is studied in order to collect information about the whole population. (*p. 14*)

Saturation   The purity of color; related to the number of wavelengths that combine to create a specific color. (*p. 74*)

Schema   An organizing structure for knowledge. (*p. 191*)

Schizophrenia   A serious psychological disorder characterized by thought disturbances, emotional disturbances, motor disturbances, and social isolation. (*p. 436*)

Science   A discipline that uses systematic observation and experimentation to describe, explain, and predict events in the world. (*p. 3*)

Scientific method   The procedures that help make observations more objective, precise, and reliable. (*p. 4*)

Secondary sex characteristics   Characteristics of the two sexes that are not essential to reproduction. (*p. 342*)

Secondary trait   A trait that describes only a small part of the individual's behavior. (*p. 411*)

Self-actualization   Development of the capacity to think, feel, and understand the world. (*p. 249*)

Self-concept   The system of ideas and feelings one has about one's self. (*p. 409*)

Self-efficacy   Belief in one's ability to achieve goals and exert control in life. (*p. 291*)

Self-monitoring   The tendency to be especially aware of the expectations of others and to adjust one's behavior to fit those expectations. (*p. 360*)

Self-perception theory   The theory that people come to know their own attitudes the same way they come to know the attributes of others, by unconsciously observing and interpreting behavior and the situation in which it occurs. (*p. 514*)

Self-prediction   An assessment technique that uses the individual's predictions about his or her own behavior or performance in some future situation. (*p. 369*)

Self-serving bias   The tendency to attribute successful behaviors to oneself and unsuccessful behaviors to situational pressures. (*p. 497*)

Semantic memory   Memory for general facts. (*p. 192*)

Semantic network   A network of ideas relating to a particular subject. (*p. 189*)

Semicircular canals   The vestibular organ, consisting of three curved tubes located just above the cochlea in the inner ear. (*pp. 64 & 83*)

Sensation   An awareness of conditions inside and outside the body. (*p. 59*)

Sense   A type of awareness produced by a sensory system, such as vision, hearing, and touch. (*p. 59*)

Sensitive period   A time of special sensitivity in the development of any organism in which certain events must occur or others must be avoided in order for the individual to develop normally. (*p. 298*)

Sensory memory   The memory system that briefly preserves perceptual information. (*p. 180*)

Sensory register   A memory system that briefly holds sensory information. (*p. 181*)

Sexual dysfunction   A problem that limits the sexual satisfaction for either or both partners in a relationship. (*p. 260*)

Shaping   The reinforcement of successive approximations to a desired response. (*p. 163*)

Similarity   A Gestalt cue; the tendency to cluster similar objects visually. (*p. 102*)

Sleep apnea   A breathing disorder that can deprive the individual of sleep. (*p. 136*)

Sleep spindles   Short bursts of high-frequency EEG waves that are one of two components characteristic of Stage 2 sleep. (*p. 127*)

Social dilemma   A situation in which the rational behavior of different individuals has negative cumulative effects on both the individuals and the people around them. (*p. 555*)

Social facilitation   The positive effect on the individual's performance produced by the presence of other people. (*p. 548*)

Social interference   The negative effect on the individual's performance produced by the presence of other people. (*p. 549*)

Socialization   The process by which children learn the customs and attitudes of their community. (*p. 336*)

Social learning theory   The application of learning theory to the study of complex human behavior; assumes that social behavior is a product of reinforcement patterns. (*p. 415*)

Social loafing   The tendency to work less hard when a number of other people are sharing the work. (*p. 550*)

Social phobia   An unreasonable fear of social situations or activities that limits the individual's participation in those situations or activities. (*p. 432*)

Social psychology   The scientific study of how people think, feel, and act in relation to other people. (*p. 492*)

Social role   An organized system of norms assigned to one or more individuals in a group. (*p. 542*)

Social–role theory   A theory that stresses social expectations and interpersonal relations in explaining a phenomenon. (*p. 138*)

Sociobiological theory   A theory of social behavior that claims that a genetic selfishness underlies all human behaviors, even altruistic behaviors. (*p. 245*)

Somatization disorders   Disorders in which the individual complains of vague physical symptoms—such as fatigue, dizziness, and headaches—that have no physical basis. (*p. 440*)

Somatoform disorders   Psychological disorders in which the major symptoms are physical complaints of illness, fatigue, discomfort, or paralysis. (*p. 440*)

Source amnesia   A phenomenon in which subjects perform posthypnotic suggestions but cannot report why. (*p. 142*)

Source trait   According to Cattell, one of the sixteen basic dimensions underlying the surface traits. (*p. 420*)

Spatial frequency perception   The ability to recognize spatial waves. (*p. 115*)

Split-half reliability   An estimate of reliability obtained by dividing a test in half and then relating the score on one half to the score on the other half. (*p. 363*)

Spontaneous recovery   The reappearance, with no additional training, of a conditioned response that has been extinguished. (*p. 156*)

Stability   The degree to which a test produces the same or similar scores on two separate occasions; a measure of an instrument's reliability. (*p. 363*)

Stage   A period in which behavior and experience change very little. (*p. 298*)

Standard deviation (SD)   The average difference between each score and the mean of the data set; a measure of variability. (*p. A–4*)

Standard score   A score that compares each individual's score with the scores of a large standardization sample; the difference between a particular score and the mean of all scores, divided by the standard deviation. (*pp. 374 & A–6*)

Statistical analyses   The mathematical methods used to summarize and analyze research data. (*p. A–1*)

Stereotype   A generalization about the attributes or traits of people in a social group. (*p. 499*)

Stimulants   A class of drugs that increase energy, endurance, and confidence. (*p. 146*)

Stress   The emotional reaction to elements that disrupt our equilibrium. (*p. 268*)

Stress responses   Patterns of responses made by the organism that help to mobilize its resources to deal with an environmental challenge. (*p. 286*)

Structuralism   A school of psychology that analyzed experience by breaking it down into basic elements; associated with the work of E. B. Tichner. (*p. 9*)

Sublimation   A defense mechanism in which an unacceptable impulse is satisfied by an acceptable behavior. (*pp. 246 & 400*)

Subliminal perception   The response to a stimulus below the absolute threshold. (*p. 123*)

Superego   In Freudian theory, the part of the psyche that defines right and wrong, punishes wrong with guilt, and sets standards of behavior. (*p. 397*)

Superstitious behavior   In behaviorism, the kind of behavior produced by random reinforcement. (*p. 407*)

Surface trait   According to Cattell, the trait terms commonly used to describe personality. (*p. 420*)

Syllogism   A series of premises and the conclusion that follows from them; in philosophy, the form of a deductive inference. (*p. 212*)

Sympathetic division   The part of the autonomic nervous system that generally mobilizes the body for vigorous action. (*p. 42*)

Synapse   The junction between two neurons. (*p. 33*)

Synaptic cleft   The submicroscopic space that separates the axon terminals of a presynaptic neuron from the dendrites of a postsynaptic neuron. (*p. 33*)

Syntax   The rules that govern the order in which words are used in a language. (*p. 232*)

Systematic desensitization   A behavioral therapy, developed by Joseph Wolpe to treat phobias, in which a relaxation response is used to prevent the previous fear response. (*p. 468*)

Telegraphic speech   The simple speech — without articles — that is characteristic of the two-word stage. (*p. 233*)

Temperament   The individual's fundamental disposition. (*p. 319*)

Teratogen   A substance that produces physical defects in the embryo. (*p. 305*)

Test-retest reliability   An estimate of reliability obtained by administering the same test twice, separated by a span of time. (*p. 362*)

Thalamus   Two masses of gray matter in the brain that relay most sensory impulses and interpret pain, temperature, and pressure. (*p. 39*)

Theoretical construct   A concept or idea that is part of a theory. (*p. 360*)

Theory   A general explanation of how things work based on a number of systematic observations. (*p. 4*)

Therapeutic insight   The recognition of the unconscious thoughts and feelings that underlie behavior. (*p. 462*)

Thinking   Using and manipulating knowledge to solve problems, make decisions, and create new understanding. (*p. 208*)

Thyroid gland   A gland that secretes hormones that regulate the body's metabolism, growth and development, and the activity of the nervous system. (*p. 44*)

Timbre   The tone and depth of sound; related to the complexity of sound frequencies. (*p. 62*)

Time out   In behavioral therapy, a program of treatment in which the individual is prevented from receiving reinforcement for an unwanted response by removing the individual from the social situation whenever the response is made. (*p. 469*)

Tip-of-the-tongue phenomenon   A situation in which people know they will be able to remember a fact that at the moment they cannot recall. (*p. 196*)

Token economy   A system of secondary reinforcement that rewards behavior with tokens that later can be exchanged for something the individual wants. (*p. 168*)

Tolerance   The body's increasing adaptation to a drug, such that larger doses are required to produce a constant effect. (*p. 144*)

Trait   (1) Any observable physical or behavioral characteristic of an individual. (*p. 301*) (2) In personality theory, a consistent way of behaving, thinking, or feeling that distinguishes the individual from other people. (*p. 410*)

Tranquilizers   A family of drugs that reduce the symptoms of anxiety. (*p. 478*)

Transduction   The process of converting a physical or chemical stimulus into a nerve impulse. (*p. 60*)

Transference   The client's projection of unresolved conflicts onto his or her relationship with the psychoanalyst. (*p. 462*)

Transformational grammar   According to Chomsky, the syntactic rules that allow the individual to express the core meaning of a sentence (the deep structure) in a variety of forms (the surface structures). (*p. 233*)

Transition   A period in which behavior and experience change abruptly. (*p. 298*)

Tricolor theory   Hermann von Helmholtz's theory that all color experience is the product of activity in red, yellow, and blue color systems. (*p. 76*)

***t*-test**   An inferential statistic that allows a researcher to ask how likely it is that the difference between two means occurred by chance rather than as a function of the effect of the independent variable. (*p. A–9*)

Two-word stage   The stage of language development at which children make two-word utterances. (*p. 233*)

Type A personality   A type of personality characterized by a chronic state of arousal. (*p. 289*)

Unconditioned response (UCR)   A behavior that is automatic. (*p. 153*)

Unconditioned stimulus (UCS)   A stimulus that automatically elicits a certain response. (*p. 153*)

Unconscious mind   The large reservoirs of memories,

feelings, and drives that the individual is not aware of. (*p. 396*)

Validity   The degree to which a measure relates to the factor it is supposed to be measuring. (*p. 16*)

Variable   In an experiment, a characteristic that can change. (*p. 13*)

Variable-interval schedule   An irregular pattern of reinforcement that rewards the subject after a certain period of time has elapsed on the average. (*p. 167*)

Variable-ratio schedule   An irregular pattern of reinforcement that rewards the subject after a number of unreinforced responses have been made on the average. (*p. 167*)

Verbal IQ   A score on an IQ test that reflects the subject's ability to carry out tasks that involve language (for example, defining terms and answering questions that require general knowledge). (*p. 375*)

Vestibular sense   The sense of balance; it provides information about the body's general movements. (*p. 83*)

Visual cliff   An apparatus used to test depth perception in infants and animals. (*p. 109*)

Voluntary nervous system   The part of the peripheral nervous system that controls striated muscles. (*p. 40*)

Weber's law   The ratio between the difference threshold and the intensity of a stimulus is a constant. Different senses have different values for the constant. (*p. 85*)

Wernicke's area   A small area in the left temporal lobe that is necessary for understanding speech. (*p. 54*)

Withdrawal   The physical and psychological effects of stopping drug use. (*p. 145*)

Working memory   A memory system, limited in both duration and capacity, that preserves information for processing; also called *short-term memory*. (*p. 180*)

References

Abrams, D. B., & Wilson, G. T. (1983). Alcohol, sexual arousal, and self-control. *Journal of Personality and Social Psychology, 45,* 188–198.

Abramson, L. Y., Metalsky, G. I., & Alloy, L. B. (1989). Hopelessness depression: A theory-based subtype. *Psychological Review, 96,* 358–372.

Abramson, L. Y., Seligman, M. E. P., & Teasdale, J. D. (1978). Learned helplessness in humans: Critique and reformulation. *Journal of Abnormal Psychology, 87,* 49–74.

Adams, P. R., & Adams, G. R. (1984). Mount Saint Helens' ashfall. *American Psychologist, 39,* 252–260.

Adelman, P. K., & Zajonc, R. B. (1989). Facial efference and the experience of emotion. *Annual Review of Psychology, 40,* 249–280.

Adler, A. (1929). *The practice and theory of individual psychology.* New York: Harcourt, Brace & World.

Ainsworth, M. D. S. (1979). Attachment as related to mother-infant interaction. In J. S. Rosenblatt, R. A. Hinde, C. Beer, & M. Busnel (Eds.), *Advances in the study of behavior* (Vol. 9). New York: Academic Press.

Ainsworth, M. D. S., & Bell, S. M. (1970). Attachment, exploration, and separation illustrated by the behavior of one-year-olds in a strange situation. *Child Development, 41,* 49–67.

Ajzen, I., & Fishbein, M. (1980). *Understanding attitudes and predicting social behavior.* Englewood Cliffs, NJ: Prentice-Hall.

Aldous, J. (1978). *Family careers: Developmental change in families.* New York: Wiley.

Alexander, C. N., Langer, E. J., Newman, R. I., Chandler, H. M., & Davies, J. L. (1989). Transcendental meditation, mindfulness and longevity: An experimental study with the elderly. *Journal of Personality and Social Psychology, 57,* 950–964.

Allderidge, P. (1979). Hospitals, mad houses, and asylums: Cycles in the care of the insane. *British Journal of Psychiatry, 134,* 321–324.

Allen, M. G. (1976). Twin studies of affective illness. *Archives of General Psychiatry, 33,* 1476–1478.

Allport, G. W. (1937). *Personality: A psychological interpretation.* New York: Holt.

Allport, G. W., & Odbert, H. S. (1936). Trait-names: A psycholexical study. *Psychological Monographs, 47* (Whole No. 211).

Amabile, T. M. (1983). *The social psychology of creativity.* New York: Springer.

Amabile, T. M. (1985). Motivation and creativity: Effects of motivational orientation on creative writers. *Journal of Personality and Social Psychology, 48,* 393–399.

American Psychiatric Association. (1980). *Diagnostic and statistical manual of mental disorders* (3rd ed.). Washington, DC.

American Psychiatric Association. (1987). *Diagnostic and statistical manual of mental disorders* (3rd ed., rev.). Washington, DC.

Amsel, A. (1962). Frustrative non-reward in partial reinforcement and discrimination learning. *Psychological Review, 69,* 306–328.

Anand, B. K., & Brobeck, J. R. (1951). Hypothalamic control of food intake in rats and cats. *Yale Journal of Biology and Medicine, 24,* 123–140.

Anastasi, A. (1988). *Psychological testing.* New York: Macmillan.

Anderson, C. A., & Anderson, D. C. (1984). Ambient temperature and violent crime: Tests of the linear and curvilinear hypotheses. *Journal of Personality and Social Psychology, 46,* 91–97.

Anderson, J. R. (1983). A spreading activation theory of memory. *Journal of Verbal Learning and Verbal Behavior, 22,* 261–295.

Anderson, J. R., & Bower, G. H. (1973). *Human associative memory.* New York: Wiley.

Andreason, N. C., & Glick, I. D. (1988). Bipolar affective disorder and creativity: Implications and clinical management. *Comprehensive Psychiatry, 29,* 207–217.

Andrews, F. M. (1975). Social and psychological factors which influence the creative process. In I. A. Taylor & J. W. Getzels (Eds.), *Perspectives in creativity* (pp. 117–145). Chicago: Aldine.

Angoff, W. H. (1988). The nature-nurture debate, aptitudes, and group differences. *American Psychologist, 43,* 713–720.

Anrep, G. V. (1920). Pitch discrimination in the dog. *Journal of Psychology, 53,* 380.

Antelman, S. M., & Rowland, N. (1981). Endogenous opiates and stress-induced eating. *Science, 214,* 329–331.

Antrobus, J. (1991). Dreaming: Cognitive processes during cortical activation and high afferent thresholds. *Psychological Review, 98,* 96–121.

Arnold, M. B. (1960). *Emotion and personality.* New York: Columbia University Press.

Aronson, E., Blaney, N., Stephan, C., Sikes, J., & Snapp, M. (1978). *The jigsaw classroom.* Beverly Hills, CA: Sage.

Asch, S. E. (1946). Forming impressions of personality. *Journal of Abnormal and Social Psychology, 41,* 258–290.

Asch, S. E. (1956). Studies of independence and conformity: A minority of one against a unanimous majority. *Psychological Monographs, 70* (Whole No. 416).

Asch, S. E., & Zukier, H. (1984). Thinking about persons. *Journal of Personality and Social Psychology, 46,* 1230–1240.

Aschoff, J. (1969). Desynchronization and resynchronization of human circadian rhythms. *Aerospace Medicine, 40,* 844–849.

Aschoff, J., & Weaver, R. (1981). The circadian system of man. In J. Aschoff (Ed.), *Handbook of behavioral neurobiology: 4. Biological rhythms* (pp. 311–331). New York: Plenum Press.

Asendorpf, J. B., & Scherer, K. R. (1983). The discrepant repressor: Differentiation between low anxiety, high anxiety, and the repression of anxiety by autonomic-facial-verbal patterns of behavior. *Journal of Personality and Social Psychology, 45,* 1334–1346.

Aserinsky, E., & Kleitman, N. (1953). Regularly occurring periods of eye motility and concomitant phenomena during sleep. *Science, 118,* 273–274.

Aslin, R. N. (1987). Motor aspects of visual development in

infancy. In P. Salapatek & L. Cohen (Eds.), *Handbook of infant perception, 1: From sensation to perception.* Palo Alto, CA: Annual Reviews Inc.

Aslin, R. N., & Smith, L. B. (1988). Perceptual development. *Annual Review of Psychology, 39,* 435–473.

Atkinson, J. W. (1957). Motivational determinants of risk-taking behavior. *Psychological Review, 64,* 359–372.

Atkinson, R. C., & Shiffrin, R. M. (1968). Human memory: A proposed system and its control processes. In K. W. Spence & J. T. Spence (Eds.), *The psychology of learning and motivation* (Vol. 2, pp. 89–195). New York: Academic Press.

Averill, J. R. (1982). *Anger and aggression: An essay on emotion.* New York: Springer-Verlag.

Averill, J. R. (1980). On the paucity of positive emotions. In K. R. Blankenstein, P. Pliner, & J. Polivy (Eds.), *Assessment and modification of emotional behavior* (pp. 7–45). New York: Plenum.

Averill, J. R. (1983). Studies on anger and aggression. *American Psychologist, 38,* 1145–1160.

Axelrod, R., & Dion, D. (1988). The further evolution of co-operation. *Science, 242,* 1385–1390.

Ayllon, T., & Skuban, W. (1977). In S. J. Morse & R. I. Watson (Eds.), *Psychotherapies: A comparative casebook* (pp. 377–389). New York: Holt, Rinehart and Winston. (Original work published 1973)

Baddeley, A. D. (1983). Working memory. *Philosophical Transactions Royal Society of London, 302,* 311–324.

Bahrick, H. P. (1984). Semantic memory content in permastore: 50 years of memory for Spanish learned in school. *Journal of Experimental Psychology: General, 113,* 1–29.

Bahrick, H. P., Bahrick, P. O., & Witlinger, R. P. (1975). Fifty years of memories for names and faces: A cross-sectional approach. *Journal of Experimental Psychology: General, 104,* 54–75.

Baillargeon, R., & Graber, M. (1987). Where's the rabbit? 5.5-month-old infants' representation of the height of a hidden object. *Cognitive Development, 2,* 375–392.

Bandura, A. (1973). *Aggression: A social learning analysis.* Englewood Cliffs, NJ: Prentice-Hall.

Bandura, A. (1977). *Social learning theory.* Englewood Cliffs, NJ: Prentice-Hall.

Bandura, A. (1986). *Social foundations of thought and action: A social cognitive theory.* Englewood Cliffs, NJ: Prentice-Hall.

Bandura, A. (1988). Self-efficacy mechanism in physiological activation and health-promoting behavior. In J. Madden, S. Matthysse, & J. Barchas (Eds.), *Adaptation, learning and affect.* New York: Raven.

Bandura, A., Ross, D., & Ross, S. A. (1961). Transmission of aggression through imitation of aggressive models. *Journal of Abnormal and Social Psychology, 63,* 575–582.

Banks, M. S. (1987). Infant refraction and accommodation. *International Ophthalmology Clinics, 20,* 205–232.

Banks, M. S., & Dannemiller, J. L. (1987). Infant visual psychophysics. In P. Salapatek & L. Cohen (Eds.), *Handbook of infant perception, 1: From sensation to perception.* New York: Academic Press.

Barber, T. X., Spanos, N. P., & Chaves, J. F. (1974). *Hypnosis, imagination and human potentialities.* New York: Pergamon.

Barclay, C. R., & Decooke, P. A. (1988). Ordinary everyday memories: Some of the things of which selves are made. In U. Neisser & E. Winograd (Eds.), *Remembering reconsidered: Ecological and traditional approaches to the study of memory* (pp. 99–125). New York: Cambridge University Press.

Barron, F., & Harrington, D. M. (1981). Creativity, intelligence and personality. *Annual Review of Psychology, 52,* 439–476.

Bar-Tal, D., & Saxe, L. (1976). Perceptions of similarly and dissimilarly attractive couples and individuals. *Journal of Personality and Social Psychology, 33,* 772–781.

Bartlett, F. C. (1932). *Remembering.* Cambridge, Eng.: Cambridge University Press.

Basseches, M. (1984). *Dialectical thinking and adult development.* Norwood, NJ: Ablex.

Bateman, J. (1988). *Client dropout as a function of client-therapist interaction in the initial intake session at a CMHC.* Unpublished doctoral dissertation. Clark University, Worcester, MA.

Bateson, G., Jackson, D. D., Haley, J., & Weakland, J. H. (1956). Toward a theory of schizophrenia. *Behavioral Science, 1,* 251–264.

Batson, C. D. (1987). Prosocial motivation: Is it ever truly altruistic? In L. Berkowitz (Ed.), *Advances in experimental social psychology* (Vol. 20, pp. 65–122). New York: Academic Press.

Batson, C. D., Dyck, J. L., Brandt, J. R., Batson, J. G., Powell, A. L., McMaster, M. R., & Griffitt, C. (1988). Five studies testing two new egoistic alternatives to the empathy-altruism hypothesis. *Journal of Personality and Social Psychology, 55,* 19–39.

Baumeister, R. F. (1990). Suicide as escape from self. *Psychological Review, 97,* 90–113.

Baumeister, R. F., & Scher, S. J. (1988). Self-defeating behavior patterns among normal individuals: Review and analysis of common self-destructive tendencies. *Psychological Bulletin, 104,* 3–22.

Baumeister, R. F., & Steinhilber, A. (1984). Paradoxical effects of supportive audiences on performance under pressure: The home field disadvantage in sports championships. *Journal of Personality and Social Psychology, 47,* 85–93.

Baumrind, D. (1964). Some thoughts on the ethics of research: After reading Milgram's "Behavioral Study of Obedience." *American Psychologist, 19,* 421–423.

Bayley, N. (1969). *Manual for the Bayley scales of infant development.* New York: Psychological Corporation.

Beach, L. R., Campbell, F. L., & Townes, B. D. (1979). Subjective expected utility and the prediction of birth-planning decisions. *Organizational Behavior and Human Performance, 24,* 18–28.

Beck, A. (1976). *Cognitive therapy and the emotional disorders.* New York: International Universities Press.

Beck, A. T. (1982). *Depression: Clinical, experimental and theoretical aspects.* New York: Harper & Row.

Beck, A. T., Rush, A. J., Shaw, B. F., & Emery, G. (1979). *Cognitive therapy of depression.* New York: Guilford Press.

Beck, S., Ward-Hull, C., & McLear, P. (1976). Variables related to women's somatic preferences of the male and female body. *Journal of Personality and Social Psychology, 34,* 1200–1210.

Bednar, R. L., Burlingame, G. M., & Masters, K. S. (1988). Systems of family treatment: Substance or semantics? *Annual Review of Psychology, 39,* 401–434.

Bell, A. P., Weinberg, M. S., & Hammersmith, S. K. (1983). *Sexual preference: Its development in men and women.* Bloomington, IN: Indiana University Press.

Belsky, J., & Rovine, M. J. (1988). Nonmaternal care in the first year of life and the security of infant-parent attachment. *Child Development, 59,* 157–167.

Bem, D. J. (1972). Self-perception theory. In L. Berkowitz

(Ed.), *Advances in experimental social psychology* (Vol. 6). New York: Academic Press.

Bem, D. J. (1983). Constructing a theory of the triple typology: Some (second) thoughts on nomothetic and idiographic approaches to personality. *Journal of Personality, 47*, 566–577.

Bem, D. J., & Allen, A. (1974). On predicting some of the people some of the time: The search for cross-situational consistencies in behavior. *Psychological Review, 81*, 506–520.

Bem, D. J., & Lord, C. G. (1979). Template matching: A proposal for probing the ecological validity of experimental settings in social psychology. *Journal of Personality and Social Psychology, 37*, 833–846.

Bem, S. J. (1985). Androgyny and gender schema theory: A conceptual and empirical integration. *Nebraska symposium on motivation, 32*, 179–226.

Benedict, H. (1979). Early lexical development: Comprehension and production. *Journal of Child Language, 6*, 183–200.

Benson, H., & Proctor, W. (1984). *Beyond the relaxation response.* New York: Times Books.

Berger, P. A., & Dunn, M. J. (1986). The biology and treatment of drug abuse. In P. A. Berger & H. K. H. Brodie (Eds.), *American handbook of psychiatry: Biological psychiatry* (Vol. 8, 2nd ed., pp. 810–867). New York: Basic Books.

Bergin, A. E. (1971). The evaluation of therapeutic outcomes. In A. E. Bergin & S. L. Garfield (Eds.), *Handbook of psychotherapy and behavior change: An empirical analysis.* New York: Wiley.

Berkowitz, L. (1972). Social norms, feelings, and other factors affecting helping and altruism. In L. Berkowitz (Ed.), *Advances in experimental social psychology* (Vol. 6, pp. 63–108). New York: Academic Press.

Berlyne, D. E. (1960). *Conflict, arousal and curiosity.* New York: McGraw-Hill.

Bernard, L. L. (1926). *Introduction to social psychology.* New York: Holt.

Bernstein, D. A., Roy, E. J., Srull, T. K., & Wickens, C. D. (1991). *Psychology* (2nd ed.). Boston: Houghton Mifflin.

Bernstein, I. L. (1978). Learned taste aversions in children receiving chemotherapy. *Science, 200*, 1302–1303.

Berry, D. S., & McArthur, L. Z. (1986). Perceiving character in faces: The impact of age-related craniofacial changes on social perception. *Psychological Bulletin, 100*, 3–18.

Berscheid, E. (1983). Emotion. In H. H. Kelley, E. Berscheid, A. Christenson, J. H. Harvey, T. L. Huston, E. L. Levinger, E. McClintock, L. A. Peplau, & D. R. Peterson (Eds.), *Close relationships* (pp. 110–168). New York: Freeman.

Berscheid, E., & Walster, E. (1978). *Interpersonal attraction.* Reading, MA: Addison-Wesley.

Berscheid, E., & Walster, E. (1974). A little bit about love. In T. Huston (Ed.), *Foundations of interpersonal attraction.* New York: Academic Press.

Berscheid, E., Graziano, E., Monson, T., & Dermer, M. (1976). Outcome dependency: Attention, attribution and attraction. *Journal of Personality and Social Psychology, 34*, 978–989.

Biederman, I., Mezzanote, R. J., Rabinowitz, J. C., Franeolin, C. M., & Plude, D. (1981). Detecting the unexpected in photo-interpretation. *Human Factors, 23*, 153–163.

Bigelow. (1977). Infant vision. In P. Salapatek & L. Cohen (Eds.), *Handbook of infant perception, 1: From sensation to perception.* New York: Academic Press.

Binet, A., & Simon, T. (1916). *The development of intelligence in children.* Baltimore: Williams & Wilkins.

Biron, M., Risch, N., Hamburger, R., Mandel, B., Kushner, S., Newman, M., Drumer, D., & Belmaker, R. H. (1987). Genetic linkage between X-chromosome markers and bipolar affective illness. *Nature, 326*, 289–292.

Birren, J. E., Woods, A. M., & Williams, M. V. (1980). Behavioral slowing with age: Causes, organization, and consequences. In L. W. Poon (Ed.), *Aging in the 80's: Psychological issues.* Washington, DC: American Psychological Association.

Black, D. W., Winokur, G., & Nasrallah, A. (1987). The treatment of depression: Electroconvulsive therapy versus antidepressants: A naturalistic evaluation of 1,495 patients. *Comprehensive Psychiatry, 28*, 169–182.

Blanchard, E. B. (1979). Biofeedback and the modification of cardiovascular dysfunctions. In R. J. Gatchel & K. P. Price (Eds.), *Clinical applications of biofeedback: Appraisal and status.* Elmsford, NY: Pergamon.

Blanchard, E. B., Andrasik, F., Ahles, T. A., Teders, S. J., & O'Keefe, D. (1980). Migraine and tension headache: A meta-analytic review. *Behavior Therapy, 11*, 613–631.

Blaney, P. H. (1986). Affect and memory: A review. *Psychological Bulletin, 99*, 229–246.

Blasi, A. (1980). Bridging moral cognition and moral action: A critical review of the literature. *Psychological Bulletin, 88*, 1–45.

Blazer, D., Hughes, D., & George, L. D. (1987). Stressful life events and the onset of a generalized anxiety syndrome. *American Journal of Psychiatry, 144*, 1178–1183.

Block, J. (1981). Some enduring and consequential structures of personality. In A. I. Rabin (Ed.), *Further explorations in personality.* New York: Wiley.

Block, J. H. (1983). Differential premises arising from differential socialization of the sexes: Some conjectures. *Child Development, 54*, 1335–1354.

Block, V., Hennevin, E., & LeConte, P. (1977). Interaction between post-trial reticular stimulation and subsequent paradoxical sleep in memory consolidation processes. In R. R. Drucker-Colin & J. L. McGaugh (Eds.), *Neurobiology of sleep and memory.* New York: Academic Press.

Bock, P. K. (1980). *Continuities in psychological anthropology.* San Francisco: Freeman.

Bodenhausen, G. V., & Wyer, R. S., Jr. (1985). Effects of stereotypes on decision making and information-processing strategies. *Journal of Personality and Social Psychology, 48*, 267–282.

Bond, C. F., Jr., & Titus, L. T. (1983). Social facilitation: A meta-analysis of 241 studies. *Psychological Bulletin, 94*, 265–292.

Boor, M. (1982). The multiple-personality epidemic. *Journal of Nervous and Mental Disease, 170*, 302–304.

Boring, E. G. (1942). *Sensation and perception in the history of experimental psychology.* New York: Appleton-Century-Crofts.

Bouchard, T. J., Jr. (1984). Twins reared together and apart: What they tell us about human diversity. In S. W. Fox (Ed.), *Individuality and determinism.* New York: Plenum Press.

Bouchard, T. J., Jr., & McGue, M. (1981). Familial studies of intelligence: A review. *Science, 212*, 1055–1059.

Boudewyns, P. A., & Shipley, R. H. (1983). *Flooding and implosive therapy: Direct therapeutic exposure in clinical practice.* New York: Plenum.

Bower, B. (1985). Panel okays ECT, calls for U.S. survey. *Science News, 127*, 389.

Bower, G. H. (1981). Mood and memory. *American Psychologist, 36*, 129–149.

Bower, G. H., & Clark, M. C. (1969). Narrative stories as

mediators for serial learning. *Psychonomic Science, 14,* 181–182.

Bower, G. H., & Mayer, J. D. (1989). In search of mood-dependent retrieval. *Journal of Social Behavior and Personality, 4,* 121–156.

Bowerman, M. (1989). Learning a semantic system: What role do cognitive predispositions play? In M. Rice & R. L. Schiefelbusch (Eds.), *The teachability of language* (pp. 133–169). Baltimore: Paul H. Brookes.

Bowlby, J. (1951). *Maternal care and mental health.* Geneva: World Health Organization.

Bowlby, J. (1969). *Attachment and loss.* New York: Basic Books.

Boyes, M. C., & Walker, L. J. (1988). Implications of cultural diversity for the universality claim of Kohlberg's theory of moral reasoning. *Human Development, 31,* 44–59.

Bozarth, A., & Wise, R. A. (1985). Toxicity associated with long-term intravenous heroin and cocaine self-administration in the rat. *Journal of the American Medical Association, 254*(1), 81–83.

Brackbill, Y., McManus, K., & Woodward, L. (1985). *Medication in maternity: Infant exposure and maternal information.* Ann Arbor: University of Michigan Press.

Brand, R. (1978). Coronary-prone behavior as an independent risk factor for coronary heart disease. In T. M. Dembrowski, S. M. Weiss, J. L. Shields, S. G. Haynes, & M. Feinleib (Eds.), *Coronary-prone behavior* (pp. 11–24). New York: Springer-Verlag.

Bransford, J. D., & Franks, J. J. (1971). The abstraction of linguistic ideas. *Cognitive Psychology, 2,* 331–350.

Bransford, J. D., & Johnson, M. K. (1972). Contextual prerequisites for understanding: Some investigations of comprehension and recall. *Journal of Verbal Learning and Verbal Behavior, 11,* 717–720.

Braun, B. G. (1983). Neurophysic changes in multiple personality due to integration: A preliminary report. *American Journal of Clinical Hypnosis, 26,* 84–92.

Brecher, E. M. (1984). *Love, sex, and aging.* Boston: Little, Brown.

Brehm, S. S., & Kassir, S. M. (1990). *Social psychology.* Boston: Houghton Mifflin.

Brende, J. E., & Parson, E. R. (1985). *Viet Nam veterans: The road to recovery.* New York: Plenum

Breuer, J., & Freud, S. (1982). *Studies in hysteria* (J. Strachey, Trans. and Ed., with A. Freud). New York: Basic Books. (Original work published 1895)

Brizzolara, D., Chilosi, A. M., de Nobili, G. L., & Ferretti, G. (1984). Neuropsychological assessment of a case of early right hemiplegia: Qualitative and quantitative analysis. *Perceptual and Motor Skills, 59,* 1007–1010.

Broadbent, D. E. (1958). *Perception and communication.* New York: Pergamon.

Brobeck, J. R., Tepperman, T., & Long, C. N. (1943). Experimental hypothalamic hyperphagia in the albino rat. *Yale Journal of Biology and Medicine, 15,* 831–853.

Broca, P. (1865). Sur la siège de la faculté du language articulé. *Bulletin of Social Anthropology, 6,* 377–393.

Brodal, A. (1981). *Neurological anatomy in relation to clinical medicine* (3rd ed.). New York: Oxford University Press.

Broman, S. H., Nichols, P. I., & Kennedy, W. A. (1975). *Preschool IQ: Prenatal and early developmental correlates.* Hillsdale, NJ: Erlbaum.

Brooks-Gunn, J., & Furstenberg, F. F. (1989). Adolescent sexual behavior. *American Psychologist, 44,* 249–257.

Brown, J. D. (1986). Evaluations of self and others: Self-enhancement biases in social judgments. *Social Cognition, 4,* 353–376.

Brown, J. D., & Siegel, J. M. (1988). Attributions for negative life events and depression: The role of perceived control. *Journal of Personality and Social Psychology, 54,* 316–322.

Brown, R. (1965). *Social psychology.* New York: Free Press.

Brown, R., & McNeill, D. (1966). The "tip-of-the-tongue" phenomenon. *Journal of Verbal Learning and Verbal Behavior, 5,* 325–377.

Brownstein, M., & Solyom, M. (1986). The dilemma of Howard Hughes: Paradoxical behavior in compulsive disorders. *Canadian Journal of Psychiatry, 31,* 238–240.

Bruch, H. (1973). *Eating disorders.* New York: Basic Books.

Bruner, J. S. (1973). *Beyond the information given.* New York: Norton.

Bruzzlfon, T. B. (1984). *Neonatal behavioral assessment scale.* (2nd ed.). Philadelphia: J. B. Lippincott.

Bryan, J. H., & Test, M. A. (1967). Models and helping: Naturalistic studies in aiding behavior. *Journal of Personality and Social Psychology, 6,* 400–407.

Buck, R. (1985). Prime theory: An integrated view of motivation and emotion. *Psychological Review, 92,* 389–413.

Bullough, V. L. (1981). Age at menarche: A misunderstanding. *Science, 213,* 365–366.

Buss, A. H. (1961). *The psychology of aggression.* New York: Wiley.

Buss, A. H., & Finn, S. E. (1987). Classification of personality traits. *Journal of Personality and Social Psychology, 52,* 432–444.

Buss, A. H., Plomin, R., & Willerman, L. (1973). The inheritance of temperaments. *Journal of Personality, 41,* 513–524.

Buss, D. M. (1984). Toward a psychology of persons-environment (PE) correlation: The role of spouse selection. *Journal of Personality and Social Psychology, 47,* 361–377.

Buss, D. M., & Craik, K. H. (1983). The act-frequency approach to personality. *Psychological Review, 70,* 105–126.

Buss, D. M., & Craik, K. H. (1985). Why *not* measure that trait? Alternative criteria for identifying important dispositions. *Journal of Personality and Social Psychology, 48,* 934–946.

Byrne, D. (1971). *The attraction paradigm.* New York: Academic Press.

Cabanac, M. (1971). The physiological role of pleasure. *Science, 173,* 1103–1107.

Cacioppo, J. T., & Petty, R. E. (1982). The need for cognition. *Journal of Personality and Social Psychology, 42,* 116–131.

Cade, J. F. J. (1949). Lithium salts in the treatment of psychotic excitement. *Medical Journal of Australia, 36,* 349–352.

Cajal, S. R. (1967). The structure and connections of neurons. In *Nobel lectures: Physiology and medicine, 1901–1921.* Amsterdam: Elsevier. (Original work published 1906)

Campbell, D. P., & Hansen, J. C. (1981). *Manual for the SVIB-SCII Strong-Campbell Interest Inventory.* Stanford, CA: Stanford University Press.

Campbell, J. B., & Hawley, C. W. (1982). Study habits and Eysenck's theory of extraversion-introversion. *Journal of Research in Personality, 16,* 139–148.

Campbell, J. D. (1986). Similarity and uniqueness: The effects of attribute type, relevance, and individual differences in self-esteem and depression. *Journal of Personality and Social Psychology, 50,* 281–294.

Campbell, S. S., & Tobler, I. (1984). Animal sleep: A review of sleep duration across phylogeny. *Neuroscience and Biobehavioral Reviews, 8,* 269–300.

Cannon, W. B. (1927). The James-Lange theory of emotion:

A critical examination and an alternative theory. *American Journal of Psychology, 39,* 106–124.

Cannon, W. B. (1929). *Bodily changes in pain, hunger, fear and rage.* New York: Appleton.

Cannon, W. B. (1939). *The wisdom of the body* (2nd ed.). New York: Norton.

Cannon, W. B., & Washburn, A. L. (1912). An explanation of hunger. *American Journal of Physiology, 29,* 444–454.

Cantor, N., & Genero, N. (1986). Psychiatric diagnosis and natural categorization: A close analogy. In T. Millon & G. L. Klerman (Eds.), *Contemporary directions in psychopathology: Toward the DSM IV* (pp. 233–256). New York: Guilford.

Carlson, N. R. (1991). *The physiology of behavior.* Boston: Allyn and Bacon.

Carver, C. S., & Scheier, M. F. (1988). *Perspectives on personality.* Boston: Allyn and Bacon.

Casey, K. L. (1982). Neural mechanisms in pain and analgesia: An overview. In A. L. Beckman (Ed.), *The neural basis of behavior.* Jamaica, NY: Spectrum.

Casey, R. J., & Berman, J. S. (1985). The outcome of psychotherapy with children. *Psychological Bulletin, 98,* 388–400.

Castellucci, V. F. (1985). The chemical senses: Taste and smell. In E. R. Kandel & J. H. Schwartz, *Principles of neural science* (pp. 409–428). New York: Elsevier.

Castillo, M., & Butterworth, G. (1981). Neonatal localization of a sound in visual space. *Perception, 10,* 331–338.

Cattell, R. B. (1965). *The scientific analysis of personality.* Chicago, IL: Aldine.

Cattell, R. B. (1985). *Human motivation and the dynamic calculus.* New York: Praeger.

Centers for Disease Control. (1989). Contributions of birth defects to infant mortality—United States, 1986. *Journal of the American Medical Association, 262,* 1923–1924.

Chaiken, S., Liberman, A., & Eagly, A. H. (1989). Heuristic and systematic information processing within and beyond the persuasion context. In J. S. Uleman & J. A. Bargh (Eds.), *Unintended thought: Limits of awareness, intention and control.* New York: Guilford.

Charney, E., Goodman, H. C., McBride, M., Lyon, B., & Pratt, R. (1976). Childhood antecedents of adult obesity: Do chubby infants become obese adults? *New England Journal of Medicine, 295*(1), 6–9.

Chase, W. G., & Simon, H. A. (1973). Perception in chess. *Cognitive Psychology, 4,* 55–81.

Cheek, J. (1982). Aggregation, moderator variables and the validity of personality tests: A peer-rating study. *Journal of Personality and Social Psychology, 43,* 1254–1269.

Cheng, P. W., & Holyoak, K. J. (1985). Pragmatic reasoning schemas. *Cognitive Psychology, 17,* 391–416.

Cherry, E. C. (1953). Some experiments on the recognition of speech, with one and two ears. *Journal of the Acoustical Society of America, 25,* 975–979.

Chesney, M. A., & Rosenman, R. H. (Eds.). (1985). *Anger and hostility in cardiovascular and behavioral disorders.* Washington, DC: Hemisphere.

Chomsky, N. (1972). *Language and mind.* New York: Pantheon.

Chomsky, N. (1957). *Syntactic structures.* The Hague: Mouton.

Chugani, H. T., & Phelps, M. E. (1986). Maturational changes in cerebral function in infants determined by 18FDG positron emission tomography. *Science, 231,* 840–843.

Church, R. M., & Raymond, G. A. (1969). Influence of the schedule of positive reinforcement on punished behavior.

Journal of Comparative and Physiological Psychology, 63, 329–332.

Cialdini, R. B. (1985). *Influence: Science and practice.* Glenview, IL: Scott, Foresman.

Cialdini, R. B., Vincent, J. E., Lewis, S. K., Catalan, J., Wheeler, D., & Darby, B. L. (1975). Reciprocal concessions procedure for inducing compliance: The door-in-the-face technique. *Journal of Personality and Social Psychology, 31,* 206–215.

Claridge, G.S. (1967). *Personality and arousal.* New York: Pergamon.

Clark, D. M., & Teasdale, J. D. (1982). Diurnal variation in clinical depression and accessibility of memories of positive and negative experiences. *Journal of Abnormal Psychology, 91,* 87–95.

Clarke, J. C., & Wardman, W. (1985). *Agoraphobia: A clinical and personal account.* Sidney: Pergamon Press.

Clarke-Stewart, K. A. (1989). Infant day care: Maligned or malignant? *American Psychologist, 44,* 266–272.

Clement, C. A., & Falmagne, R. J. (1986). Logical reasoning, world knowledge, and mental imagery: Interconnections in cognitive processes. *Memory and Cognition, 14,* 299–307.

Coates, T. J., Petersen, A. C., & Perry, C. (1982). *Promoting adolescent health: A dialogue on research and practice.* New York: Academic Press.

Cohen, D. (1983). *Piaget: Critique and reassessment.* Bechenham, Kent, Eng.: Crown Helm.

Cohen, E., Motto, J. A., & Seiden, R. H. (1966). An instrument for evaluating suicide potential: A preliminary study. *American Journal of Psychiatry, 122,* 886–891.

Cohen, M. W., & Friedman, S. B. (1975). Nonsexual motivations of adolescent sexual behavior. *Medical Aspects of Human Sexuality, 9,* 9–31.

Cohen, N. J., & Squire, L. R. (1980). Preserved learning and retention of pattern-analyzing skill in amnesia: Dissociation of knowing how and knowing what. *Science, 210,* 207–210.

Coile, D. C., & Miller, N. E. (1984). How radical animal activists try to mislead humane people. *American Psychologist, 39,* 700–701.

Cole, M., & Cole, S. (1989). *The development of children.* New York: Freeman.

Cole, W. G., & Loftus, E. F. (1979). Incorporating new information into memory. *American Journal of Psychology, 92,* 413–425.

Coles, R., & Stokes, G. (1985). *Sex and the American teenager.* New York: Harper & Row, Collophon Books.

Collins, A. M., & Quillian, M. R. (1969). Retrieval time from semantic memory. *Journal of Verbal Learning and Verbal Behavior, 8,* 240–247.

Collins, G. B. (1985). Clues to cocaine dependency. *Diagnosis,* 57–65.

Collins, W. A., & Gunnar, M. R. (1990). Social and personality development. *Annual Review of Psychology, 41,* 387–416.

Colombo, M., D'Amato, M. R., Rodman, H. R., & Gross, C. G. (1990). Auditory association cortex lesions impair auditory short-term memory in monkeys. *Science, 247,* 336–338.

Comer, R., & Laird, J. D. (1976). Choosing to suffer as a consequence of expecting to suffer. *Journal of Personality and Social Psychology, 32,* 1, 92–101.

Condry, J. (1977). Enemies of exploration: Self-initiated versus other-initiated learning. *Journal of Personality and Social Psychology, 35,* 459–477.

Cooper, J., & Fazio, R. H. (1984). A new look at dissonance

theory. In L. Berkowitz (Ed.), *Advances in experimental social psychology* (Vol. 17, pp. 229–266). New York: Academic Press.

Cooper, J. R., Bloom, F. E., & Roth, R. H. (1986). *The biochemical basis of neuropharmacology* (5th ed.). New York: Oxford University Press.

Coren, S., Porac, C., & Ward, L. M. (1984). *Sensation and perception*. Orlando: Academic Press.

Cottrell, N. B., Wack, D. L., Sekerak, G. J., & Rittle, R. M. (1968). Social facilitation of dominant responses by the presence of an audience and the mere presence of others. *Journal of Personality and Social Psychology, 9,* 245–250.

Cousins, N. (1979). *The anatomy of an illness*. New York: Norton.

Cowen, E. L. (1983). Primary prevention in mental health: Past, present and future. In R. D. Felner, L. A. Jason, J. N. Moritsugu, & S. S. Farber (Eds.), *Preventive psychology: Theory, research and practice*. New York: Pergamon.

Coyne, J. C., & Gotlib, I. H. (1983). The role of cognition in depression: A critical appraisal. *Psychological Bulletin, 94,* 472–505.

Craik, F. I. M., & Lockhart, R. S. (1972). Levels of processing: A framework for memory research. *Journal of Verbal Learning and Verbal Behavior, 11,* 671–684.

Craik, F. I. M., & Tulving, E. (1975). Depth of processing and the retention of words in episodic memory. *Journal of Experimental Psychology: General, 104,* 268–294.

Creese, I., Burt, D. R., & Snyder, S. H. (1976). Dopamine receptor binding predicts clinical and pharmacological potencies of antischizophrenic drugs. *Science, 192,* 481–483.

Cregler, L. L., & Kaplan, H. (1986). Medical complications of cocaine abuse. *New England Journal of Medicine, 315*(23), 1495–1500.

Crick, F., & Mitchison, G. (1983). The function of dream sleep. *Nature, 304,* 111–114.

Crockenberg, S. (1986). Are temperamental differences in babies associated with predictable differences in care giving? In J. V. Lerner & R. M. Lerner (Eds.), *New directions for child development: Temperamental and social interaction during infancy and childhood*. San Francisco: Jossey-Bass.

Crockett, W. H. (1968). In L. Berkowitz (Ed.), *Advances in experimental social psychology*. New York: Academic Press.

Crowder, R. G. (1989). Modularity and dissociations in memory systems. In H. L. Roediger & F. I. M. Craik (Eds.), *Varieties of memory and consciousness: Essays in honor of Endel Tulving*. Hillsdale, NJ: Erlbaum.

Crowder, R. G., & Morton, J. (1969). Precategorical acoustic storage (PAS). *Perception and Psychophysics, 5,* 365–373.

Croyle, R., & Cooper, J. (1983). Dissonance arousal: Physiological evidence. *Journal of Personality and Social Psychology, 45,* 782–791.

Cummings, M. R. (1988). *Human heredity*. St. Paul, MN: West.

Curran, J. P. (1981). Social skills and assertion training. In W. E. Craighead, A. E. Kazdin, & M. J. Mahoney (Eds.), *Behavior modification: Principles, issues and applications* (2nd ed.) Boston: Houghton Mifflin.

Curran, J. W., Jaffe, H. W., Hardy, A. M., Morgan, W. M., Selik, R. M., & Dondero, T. J. (1988). Epidemiology of HIV infection and AIDS in the United States. *Science, 239,* 610–616.

Curtis, R. C., & Miller, K. (1986). Believing another likes or dislikes you: Behaviors making the beliefs come true. *Journal of Personality and Social Psychology, 51,* 284–290.

Cutrona, C., Russell, D., & Rose, J. (1986). Social support

and adaptation to stress by the elderly. *Psychology and Aging, 1,* 47–54.

Czeisler, C. A., Allan, J. S., Strogatz, S. H., Ronda, J. M., Sanchez, R., Rios, C. D., Freitag, W. O., Richardson, G. S., & Kronauer, R. E. (1986). Bright light resets the human circadian pacemaker independent of the timing of the sleep-wake cycle. *Science, 233,* 667–671.

Dahlstrom, W. A., Welsh, G. S., & Dahlstrom, L. E. (1975). *An MMPI handbook. Vol. 2: Research applications* (rev. ed.). Minneapolis: University of Minnesota Press.

Damasio, A. R. (1985). Prosopagnosia. *Trends in Neurosciences, 8*(3), 132–135.

Damasio, A. R., & Geschwind, N. (1984). The neural basis of language. *Annual Review of Neuroscience, 7,* 127–147.

Damon, W. (1983). *Social and personality development*. New York: Norton.

Damon, W., & Hart, D. (1980). The development of self-understanding from infancy through adolescence. *Child Development, 53,* 831–857.

Darley, J. M., & Gross, P. H. (1983). A hypothesis-confirming bias in labeling effects. *Journal of Personality and Social Psychology, 44,* 20–33.

Darley, J. M., & Latané, B. (1968). Bystander intervention in emergencies: Diffusion of responsibility. *Journal of Personality and Social Psychology, 8,* 377–383.

Darley, J. M., Fleming, J. H., Hilton, J. L., & Swann, W. B., Jr. (1988). Dispelling negative expectancies: The impact of interaction goals and target characteristics on the expectancy confirmation process. *Journal of Experimental Social Psychology, 24,* 19–36.

Darwin, C. (1859). *The origin of species*. London: Murray.

Darwin, C. (1872). *The expression of emotion in man and animals*. London: Murray. (Reprinted by the University of Chicago Press, 1965)

Davidson, R. J. (1987). Cerebral asymmetry and the nature of emotion: Implications for the study of individual differences and psychopathology. In R. Takahashi, P. Flor-Henry, J. Gruzelier, & S. Niwa (Eds.), *Cerebral dynamics: Laterality and psychopathology*. New York: Elsevier.

Davis, P. J. (1987). Repression and the inaccessibility of affective memories. *Journal of Personality and Social Psychology, 53,* 585–593.

Davis, P. J., & Schwartz, G. E. (1987). Repression and the inaccessibility of affective memories. *Journal of Personality and Social Psychology, 52,* 155–162.

Davison, G. C., & Neale, J. M. (1990). *Abnormal psychology*. New York: Wiley.

Dawes, R. M. (1980). Social dilemmas. *Annual Review of Psychology, 31,* 169–193.

Dawes, R. M., Faust, D., & Meehl, P. E. (1989). Clinical versus actuarial judgment. *Science, 243,* 1668–1674.

Dawkins, R. (1976). *The selfish gene*. New York: Oxford University Press.

DeAngelis, T. (1989). Mania, depression and genius. *The APA Monitor, 20,* 1.

DeBono, K. G., & Harnish, R. J. (1988). Source expertise, source attractiveness, and the processing of persuasive information: A functional approach. *Journal of Personality and Social Psychology, 55,* 541–546.

DeCasper, A. J., & Fifer, W. (1980). Of human bonding: Newborns prefer their mothers' voices. *Science, 208,* 1174–1176.

DeCasper, A. J., & Spence, M. J. (1986). Prenatal maternal speech influences newborns' perception of speech sounds. *Infant Behavior and Development, 9,* 133–150.

deCharms, R., & Carpenter, V. (1968). Measuring motivation in culturally disadvantaged school children. In H. J. Klausmeirer & G. T. O'Hearn (Eds.), *Research and development toward the improvement of education*. Madison, WI: Educational Research Services.

Deci, E. L., & Ryan, R. M. (1987). The support of autonomy and the control of behavior. *Journal of Personality and Social Psychology, 53,* 1024–1037.

De Groot, A. D. (1965). *Thought and chance in chess*. The Hague: Moulton.

DeJong, W. (1979). An examination of self-perception mediation of the foot-in-the-door effect. *Journal of Personality and Social Psychology, 37,* 2221–2239.

Dembrowski, T. M., & Costa, P. T., Jr. (1987). Coronary-prone behavior: Components of the Type A pattern and hostility. *Journal of Personality, 55,* 212–235.

Dement, W. C. (1960). The effect of dream deprivation. *Science, 131,* 1705–1707.

Dement, W., & Kleitman, N. (1957). The relation of eye movements during sleep to dream activity: An objective method for the study of dreaming. *Journal of Experimental Psychology, 53,* 339–346.

de Molina, A. F., & Hunsperger, R. (1959). Central representation of affective reactions in forebrain and brainstem: Electrical stimulation of amygdala, stria terminalis, and adjacent structures. *Journal of Physiology, 145,* 251–265.

Descartes, R. (1960). *Meditations on first philosophy* (J. Cottingham, Trans.) Indianapolis: Bobbs-Merrill. (Original work published 1641)

Desir, D., van Cauter, E., Fang, V. S., Martino, E., Jadot, C., Spire, J. P., Noel, P., Refetoff, S., Copinschi, G., & Goldstein, J. (1981). Effects of "jet lag" on hormonal patterns: I. Procedure variations in total plasma proteins and disruption of adrenocorticotropin-cortisol periodicity. *Journal of Clinical Endocrinology and Metabolism, 52,* 628–641.

Desmond, N. L., & Levy, W. B. (1986). Changes in the postsynaptic density with long-term potentiation in the dentate gyrus. *Journal of Comparative Neurology, 253,* 476–482.

Deutch, R. (1974). Conditioned hypoglycemia: A mechanism for saccharin-induced sensitivity to insulin in the rat. *Journal of Comparative and Physiological Psychology, 86,* 350–358.

Deutsch, M., & Gerard, H. B. (1955). Normative and informational social influence upon individual judgment. *Journal of Abnormal and Social Psychology, 51,* 629–636.

DiClemente, R. J., Boyer, C. B., & Morales, E. S. (1988). Minorities and AIDS: Knowledge, attitudes, and misconceptions among black and Latino adolescents. *American Journal of Public Health, 78,* 55–57.

Dienstbier, R. A., LaGuardia, R. L., Barnes, M., Tharp, G., & Schmidt, R. (1987). Catecholamine training effects from exercise programs: A bridge to exercise-temperament relationships. *Motivation and Emotion, 11,* 297–318.

Dietz, J. (1988, April 29). Aging boom dictating new focus in research. *Boston Globe,* p. 6.

Digman, J. M., & Inouye, J. (1986). Further specification of the five robust factors of personality. *Journal of Personality and Social Psychology, 50,* 116–123.

Dion, K., Berscheid, E., & Walster, E. (1972). What is beautiful is good. *Journal of Personality and Social Psychology, 24,* 285–290.

Dirks, J. (1982). The effect of a commercial game on children's block design scores on the WISC-R test. *Intelligence, 6,* 109–123.

Dixon, N. F. (1981). *Preconscious processing*. London: Wiley.

Dodwell, P. C., Humphrey, G. K., & Muir, D. W. (1987). Shape and pattern perception. In P. Salapatek and L. Cohen (Eds.), *Handbook of infant perception, 1: From sensation to perception*. New York: Academic Press.

Dollard, J., & Miller, N. E. (1950). *Personality and psychotherapy: An analysis in terms of learning, thinking and culture*. New York: McGraw-Hill.

Dollard, J., Doob, L., Miller, N., Mowrer, O. H., & Sears, R. R. (1939). *Frustration and aggression*. New Haven: Yale University Press.

Domjan, M., & Burkhard, B. (1986). *The principles of learning and behavior*. Monterey, CA: Brooks/Cole.

Donnelly, J. D. (1985). Psychosurgery. In H. I. Kaplan & B. J. Saddock (Eds.), *Comprehensive textbook of psychiatry* (4th ed., pp. 1563–1568). Baltimore: Williams & Wilkins.

Doty, R. L., Green, P. A., Ram, C., & Yankell, S. L. (1982). Communication of gender from human breath odors: Relationship to perceived intensity and pleasantness. *Hormones and Behavior, 16,* 13–22.

Duffy, E. (1957). The psychological significance of the concept of "arousal" or "activation." *Psychological Review, 64,* 265–275.

Duncker, K. (1945). On problem solving. *Psychological Monographs, 58*(270).

Dunn, J. (1983). *Parents labeling their newborn*. Colloquium talk delivered at the sub-Department of Animal Behavior, Cambridge University.

Dunphy, D. (1963). The social structure of urban adolescent peer groups. *Sociometry, 26,* 230–246.

Durlach, N. I., & Colburn, H. S. (1978). Binaural phenomena. In E. C. Carterette and M. P. Freidman (Eds.), *Handbook of perception* (Vol. 4.) New York: Academic Press.

Dusek, J. B., & Flaherty, J. F. (1981). The development of the self-concept during the adolescent years. *Monographs of the Society for Research in Child Development, 46* (4, Serial No. 191).

Dywan, J., & Bowers, K. S. (1983). The use of hypnosis to enhance recall. *Science, 222,* 184–185.

Eagly, A. H., & Steffen, V. J. (1986). Gender and aggressive behavior: A meta-analytic review of the social psychology literature. *Psychological Bulletin, 100,* 309–330.

Ebbinghaus, H. (1913). *Memory: A contribution to experimental psychology* (H. A. Ruger & C. E. Bussenius, Trans.). New York: Columbia University Press. (Original work published 1885)

Edleman, M. W. (1987). *Families in peril: An agenda for social change*. New York: Alan Guttmacher Institute.

Egeland, J. A., Gerhard, D. S., Pauls, D. L., Sussex, J. N., Kidd, K. K., Allen, C. R., Hostetter, A. M., & Housman, D. E. (1987). Bipolar affective disorders linked to DNA markers on Chromosome 11, *Nature, 325,* 783–787.

Eibl-Eibesfeldt, I. (1973). The expressive behavior of the deaf-and-blind-born. In M. von Cranach & I. Vine (Eds.), *Social communication and movement*. New York: Academic Press.

Eich, E. (1989). Theoretical issues in state-dependent memory. In H. L. Roediger & F. I. M. Craik (Eds.), *Varieties of memory and consciousness: Essays in honor of Endel Tulving* (pp. 331–354). Hillsdale, NJ: Erlbaum.

Eich, E., & Birnbaum, I. M. (1982). Repetition, cuing and state-dependent memory. *Memory and Cognition, 10,* 103–114.

Eimas, P. D., Siqueland, E. R., Jusczyk, P., & Vigorito, J. (1971). Speech perception in infants. *Science, 171* 303–306.

Ekman, P. (1982). *Emotion in the human face* (2nd ed). New York: Cambridge University Press.

Ekman, P., & Friesen, W. V. (1971). Constants across cultures in the face and emotion. *Journal of Personality and Social Psychology, 17,* 124–129.

Ekman, P., & Friesen, W. V. (1986). A new pan-cultural facial expression of emotion. *Motivation and Emotion, 10,* 159–168.

Ekman, P., Friesen, W. V., & Ellsworth, P. E. (1972). *Emotion in the human face: Guidelines for research and an integration of findings.* New York: Pergamon Press.

Ekman, P., Friesen, W. V., O'Sullivan, M., Chan, A., Dia-coyanni-Tarlatzis, I., Heider, K., Krause, R., LeCompte, W. A., Pitcairn, T., Ricci-Bitti, P. E., Scherer, K., Tomita, M., & Tzavaras, A. (1987). Universals and cultural differences in the judgments of facial expressions of emotion. *Journal of Personality and Social Psychology, 53,* 712–717.

Ekman, P., Levenson, R., & Friesen, W. V. (1983). Autonomic nervous system activity distinguishes between emotions. *Science, 221,* 1208–1210.

Elkin, I., Shea, T., Watkins, J. T., Imber, S. D., Sotsky, S. M., Collins, J. F., Glass, D. R., Pilkonis, P. A., Leber, W. R., Docherty, J. P. Fiester, S. J., & Parloff, M. B. (1989, November). NIMH treatment of depression collaborative research program: I. General effectiveness of treatments. *Archives of General Psychiatry, 46,* 971–982.

Elkind, D., & Bowen, R. (1979). Imaginary audience behavior in children and adolescents. *Developmental Psychology, 15,* 38–44.

Ellis, A. (1962). *Reason and emotion in psychotherapy.* Secaucus, NJ: Citadel Press.

Ellis, H. C., & Ashbrook, P. W. (1989). The "state" of mood and memory research: A selective review. *Journal of Social Behavior and Personality, 4,* 1–22.

Ellsworth, P. C., & Smith, C. A. (1988). Shades of joy: Patterns of appraisal differentiating pleasant emotions. *Cognition and Emotion, 2,* 301–331.

Empson, J. A. C., & Clarke, P. R. F. (1970). Rapid eye-movements and remembering. *Nature, 227,* 287–288.

Engen, T. (1982). *The perception of odors.* New York: Academic Press.

Epstein, S. (1979). The stability of behavior: I. On predicting most of the people much of the time. *Journal of Personality and Social Psychology, 37,* 1097–1126.

Epstein, S. (1983). Aggregation and beyond: Some basic issues on the prediction of behavior. *Journal of Personality, 51,* 360–392.

Equal Employment Opportunity Commission. (1970). Guidelines on employee selection procedures. *Federal Register, 35,* 12333–12336.

Erdelyi, M. H., & Goldberg, B. (1979). Let's not sweep repression under the rug: Toward a cognitive psychology of repression. In J. Kihlstrom & F. Evans (Eds.), *Functional disorders of memory* (pp. 355–402). Hillsdale, NJ: Erlbaum.

Erikson, E. H. (1963). *Childhood and society* (2nd ed.). New York: Norton.

Erikson, E. H. (1963). *Childhood and society.* New York: Norton.

Eron, L. D., & Huesmann, L. R. (1984). The control of aggressive behavior by changes in attitudes, values and the conditions of learning. In R. J. Blanchard & C. Blanchard (Eds.), *Advances in the study of aggression* (Vol. 1, pp. 139–171). New York: Academic Press.

Estes, W. K. (1944). An experimental study of punishment. *Psychological Monographs, 57.*

Estes, W. K., & Skinner, B. F. (1941). Some quantitative properties of anxiety. *Journal of Experimental Psychology, 29,* 390–400.

Eysenck, H. J. (1952). The effects of psychotherapy: An evaluation. *Journal of Consulting Psychology, 16,* 319–324.

Eysenck, H. J. (1970). *The structure of human personality* (3rd ed.). London: Methuen.

Eysenck, H. J. (1985). *Personality and individual differences: A natural science approach.* New York: Plenum.

Eysenck, H. J., & Eysenck, S. B. G. (1975). *The Eysenck Personality Questionnaire.* San Diego, CA: Educational and Industrial Testing Service.

Eysenck, H. J., & Levey, A. (1972). Conditioning, introversion-extraversion and the strength of the nervous system. In V. D. Nebylitsyn & J. A. Gray (Eds.), *Biological Bases of Individual Behavior.* New York: Academic Press.

Fallon, A. E., & Rozin, P. (1985). Sex differences in perceptions of desirable body shape. *Journal of Abnormal Psychology, 94,* 102–105.

Fantz, R. (1961). The origin of form perception. *Scientific American, 204,* 66–72.

Farley, J., & Alkon, D. C. (1985). Cellular mechanisms of learning, memory and information storage. *Annual Review of Psychology, 36,* 419–494.

Farr, E. L. (1982). Introduction: A personal account of schizophrenia. In M. T. Tsuang (Ed.), *Schizophrenia: The facts* (pp. 1–10). Oxford: Oxford University Press.

Faurion, A. (1988). Physiology of the sweet taste. *Progress in Sensory Physiology, 8,* 129–201.

Fawcett, J., Scheftner, W., Clark, D., Hedeker, D., Gibbons, R., & Coryell, W. (1987). Clinical predictors of suicide in patients with major affective disorders: A controlled prospective study. *American Journal of Psychiatry, 144,* 35–46.

Fazio, R. H. (1986). How do attitudes guide behavior? In R. M. Sorrentino & E. T. Higgins (Eds.), *The handbook of motivation and cognition: Foundations of social behavior* (pp. 204–243). New York: Guilford.

Fazio, R. H. (1987). Self-perception theory: A current perspective. In M. P. Zanna, J. M. Olson, & C. P. Herman (Eds.), *Social influence: The Ontario symposium* (Vol. 5, pp. 129–150). Hillsdale, NJ: Erlbaum.

Fernald, A. (1985). Four-month-olds prefer to listen to "motherese." *Infant Behavior and Development, 8,* 181–195.

Fernald, A., & Kuhl, P. (1987). Acoustic determinants of infant preference for motherese speech. *Infant Behavior and Development, 10,* 279–293.

Festinger, L. (1957). *A theory of cognitive dissonance.* Stanford, CA: Stanford University Press.

Festinger, L., & Carlsmith, J. M. (1959). Cognitive consequence of forced compliance. *Journal of Abnormal and Social Psychology, 58,* 203–210.

Festinger, L., Schachter, S., & Back, K. W. (1950). *Social pressures in informal groups: A study of human factors in housing.* New York: Harper.

Field, J., Muir, D., Pilon, R., Sinclair, M., & Dodwell, P. (1980). Infants' orientation to lateral sounds from birth to three months. *Child Development, 51,* 195–298.

Finger, S., & Stein, D. G. (1982). *Brain damage and recovery: Research and clinical perspectives.* New York: Academic Press.

Fink, M. (1979). *Convulsive therapy: Theory and practice.* New York: Raven Press.

Fleming, I., Baum, A., & Weiss, L. (1987). Social density and perceived control as mediators of crowding stress in high-density residential neighborhoods. *Journal of Personality and Social Psychology, 52,* 899–906.

Flora, J. A., & Thoresen, C. E. (1988). *American Psychologist, 43,* 965–970.

Folkard, S., Hume, K. I., Minors, D. S., Waterhouse, J. M., & Watson, F. L. (1985). Independence of the circadian rhythm in alertness from the sleep/wake cycle. *Nature, 313,* 678–679.

Folkins, C. E., & Sime, W. E. (1981). Physical fitness training and mental health. *American Psychologist, 36,* 373–389.

Forgays, D. G., & Belinson, M. J. (1986). Is flotation isolation a relaxing environment? *Journal of Environmental Psychology, 6,* 19–34.

Foulkes, D. (1985). *Dreaming: A cognitive-psychological analysis.* Hillsdale, NJ: Erlbaum.

Foulkes, D. (1966). *The psychology of sleep.* New York: Scribner's.

Fouts, R. S., Fouts, D. H., & Schoenfeld, D. J. (1984). Sign language conversational interaction between chimpanzees. *Sign Language Studies, 42,* 1–12.

Fouts, R. S., Fouts, D. H., & Van Cantfort, T. E. (1989). The infant Loulis learns signs from cross-fostered chimpanzees. In R. A. Gardner, B. T. Gardner, & T. E. Van Cantfort (Eds.), *Teaching sign language to chimpanzees* (pp. 280–292). New York: State University of New York Press.

Frankl, V. E. (1959). *Man's search for meaning: An introduction to logotherapy.* Boston: Beacon Press.

Frankl, V. E. (1962). *Man's search for meaning* (rev. ed.). New York: Washington Square Press.

Franklin, D. (1987). The politics of masochism. *Psychology Today, 21,* 52–57.

Freedman, J. L. (1984). Effect of television violence on aggressiveness. *Psychological Bulletin, 96,* 227–246.

Freedman, J. L. (1986). Television violence and aggression: A rejoinder. *Psychological Bulletin, 100,* 372–378.

Freedman, J. L., & Fraser, S. C. (1966). Compliance without pressure: The foot-in-the-door technique. *Journal of Personality and Social Psychology, 4,* 195–202.

Frese, M., & Harwich, C. (1984). Shift work and the length and quality of sleep. *Journal of Occupational Medicine, 26,* 561–566.

Freud, A. (1946). *The ego and the mechanisms of defense.* New York: International Universities Press.

Freud, S. (1905). *Sexuality and the psychology of love.*

Freud, S. (1933). New introductory lecture on psych-analysis. New York: Carlton House.

Freud, S. (1938/1900–1914). *The basic writings of Sigmund Freud* (A. A. Brill, Trans.). New York: Modern Library.

Freud, S. (1959). *Beyond the pleasure principle: A study of the death instinct in human aggression.* (J. Strachey, Trans.) New York: Bantam Books. (Original work published 1920)

Freud, S. (1961a). On beginning the treatment. (Further recommendations on the technique of psycho-analysis.) In J. Strachey (Ed. and Trans.), *The standard edition of the complete works of Sigmund Freud* (Vol. 12, pp. 123–144). London: Hogarth Press. (Original work published 1913)

Freud, S. (1961b). Remembering, repeating and working-through. (Further recommendations on the technique of psycho-analysis.) In J. Strachey (Ed. and Trans.), *The standard edition of the complete works of Sigmund Freud* (Vol. 12, pp. 147–156). London: Hogarth Press. (Original work published 1914)

Freud, S. (1962). *The ego and the id* (J. Riviere, Trans.). New York: Norton. (Original work published 1923)

Friedman, H. S., & Booth-Kewley, S. (1987). The "disease-prone personality": A meta-analytic view of the construct. *American Psychologist, 42,* 539–555.

Friedman, M., & Rosenman, R. H. (1959). Association of a specific overt behavior pattern with increases in blood cholesterol, blood clotting time, incidence of arcus senilis and clinical coronary artery disease. *Journal of the American Medical Association, 2169,* 1286–1296.

Friedrich-Cofer, L., & Huston, A. C. (1986). Television violence and aggression: The debate continues. *Psychological Bulletin, 100,* 364–371.

Fristrom, J. W., & Clegg, M. T. (1988). *Principles of genetics.* New York: W. H. Freeman.

Furstenberg, F. F. Jr., Brooks-Gunn, J., & Chase-Lansdale, L. (1989). Teenaged pregnancy and childbearing. *American Psychologist, 44,* 313–320.

Furuno, S. F., O'Reilly, K. A., Hosaka, C. M., Inatsuka, T. T., Allman, T. L., & Zeisloft, B. (1984). *Hawaii early learning profile (HELP).* Palo Alto, CA: VORT.

Galanter, I. (1962). Contemporary psychophysics. In R. Brown (Ed.), *New Directions in Psychology.* New York: Holt, Rinehart and Winston.

Galinsky, E. (1981). *Between generations: The six stages of parenthood.* New York: Berkeley.

Galton, F. (1869). *Hereditary genius: An inquiry into its laws and consequences.* London: Macmillan.

Garcia, J. (1981). The logic and limits of mental aptitude testing. *American Psychologist, 36,* 1172–1180.

Garcia, J., Ervin, F. R., & Koelling, R. A. (1966). Learning with prolonged delay of reinforcement. *Psychonomic Science, 5,* 121–122.

Garcia, J., Hankins, W. G., & Rusniak, K. W. (1974). Behavioral regulation of the *milieu interne* in man and rat. *Science, 185,* 824–831.

Garcia, J., Kimeldorf, D. J., Hunt, E. L., & Davis, B. P. (1956). Food and water consumption of rats during exposure to gamma radiation. *Radiation Research, 4,* 33–41.

Gardner, B. T., & Gardner, R. A. (1971). Two-way communication with an infant chimpanzee. In A. Schrier & F. Stollnitz (Eds.), *Behavior of nonhuman primates.* New York: Academic Press.

Gardner, H. (1983). *Frames of mind: The theory of multiple intelligences.* New York: Basic Books.

Gardner, R. A., & Gardner, B. T. (1969). Teaching sign language to a chimpanzee. *Science, 165,* 664–672.

Garfield, S. L., & Bergin, A. E. (Eds.). (1986). *Handbook of psychotherapy and behavior change* (3rd ed.). New York: Wiley.

Garner, D. M., & Davis, R. (1982). The clinical assessment of anorexia nervosa and bulimia nervosa. In P. A. Keller and L. G. Ritt (Eds.), *Innovations in clinical practice: A source book.* Sarasota, FL: Professional Resource Exchange.

Garner, D. M., & Isaacs, P. (1986). The fundamentals of psychotherapy for anorexia nervosa and bulimia nervosa. In P. A. Keller & L. G. Ritt (Eds.), *Innovations in clinical practice: A source book.* Sarasota, FL: Professional Resource Exchange.

Gazzaniga, M. S., & Sperry, R. W. (1967). Language after section of the cerebral hemispheres. *Brain, 96,* 131–148.

Geen, R. G. (1984). Preferred stimulation levels in introverts and extraverts: Effects on arousal and performance. *Journal of Personality and Social Psychology, 46,* 1303–1312.

Geen, R. G., McCown, E. J., & Broyles, J. W. (1985). Effects of noise on sensitivity of introverts and extraverts to signals in a vigilance task. *Personality and Individual Differences, 6,* 237–241.

Gehringer, W. L., & Engel, E. (1986). Effect of ecological viewing conditions on the Ames' distorted room illusion. *Journal of Experimental Psychology: Human Perception and Performance, 12,* 181–185.

Gelb, A. (1929). Die "farbenkonstanz" der Sehdinge. *Handbuch der Normalen und Pathologische Physiologie, 12,* 549–678.

Gendlin, E. T. (1970). A theory of personality change. In J. T. Hart & T. M. Tomlinson (Eds.), *New Directions in client-centered therapy* (pp. 129–173). Boston: Houghton Mifflin.

Excerpted in Patterson, C. H. (1986). *Theories of counseling and psychotherapy*. New York: Harper & Row.

Georgotas, A. (1985). Affective disorders: Pharmacotherapy. In H. I. Kaplan & B. J. Saddock (Eds.), *Comprehensive textbook of psychiatry* (4th ed., pp. 821–833). Baltimore: Williams & Wilkins.

Geschwind, N., & Levitsky, W. (1968). Human brain: Left-right asymmetries in temporal speech region. *Science, 161,* 186–187.

Gesell, A. (1928). *The mental growth of the pre-school child: A psychological outline of normal development from birth to the sixth year including a system of developmental diagnosis*. New York: Macmillan.

Getchell, T. V. (1986). Functional properties of vertebrate olfactory receptor neurons. *Physiological Review, 66,* 772–818.

Gibson, E. J., & Bergman, R. (1954). The effect of training on absolute estimation of distance over the ground. *Journal of Experimental Psychology, 48,* 473–482.

Gibson, E. J., & Walk, R. D. (1960). The "visual cliff." *Scientific American, 202,* 64–71.

Gibson, J. J. (1950). *The perception of the visual world*. Boston: Houghton Mifflin.

Gibson, J. J. (1966). *The senses considered as perceptual systems*. Boston: Houghton Mifflin.

Gibson, J. J. (1979). The ecological approach to visual perception. Boston: Houghton Mifflin.

Gibson, J. J. (1985). Conclusions from a century of research on sense perception. In S. Koch & D. E. Leary (Eds.), *A century of psychology as science*. New York: McGraw-Hill.

Gibson, J. J., & Gibson, E. J. (1957). Continuous perspective transformations and the perception of rigid motion. *Journal of Experimental Psychology, 54,* 129–138.

Gilbert, D. T. (1989). Thinking lightly about others: Automatic components of the social inference process. In J. S. Uleman & J. A. Bargh (Eds.), *Unintended thought: The limits of awareness, intention and control* (pp. 189–211). New York: Guilford.

Gilbert, D. T., & Jones, E. E. (1986). Perceiver-induced constraint: Interpretations of self-generated reality. *Journal of Personality and Social Psychology, 50,* 269–280.

Gilbert, D. T., Pelham, B. W., & Krull, D. S. (1988). On cognitive busyness: When person perceivers meet persons perceived. *Journal of Personality and Social Psychology, 54,* 733–740.

Gilbert, S. J. (1981). Another look at the Milgram obedience studies: The role of the graduated series of shocks. *Personality and Social Psychology Bulletin, 7,* 690–695.

Gilligan, C. (1982). *In a different voice: Psychological theory and women's development*. Cambridge, MA: Harvard University Press.

Ginsberg, H., & Opper, S. (1988). *Piaget's theory of intellectual development*. Englewood Cliffs, NJ: Prentice-Hall.

Giray, E. F. (1985). A life span approach to the study of eidetic imagery. *Journal of Mental Imagery, 9,* 21–32.

Glisky, E. L., Schacter, D. L., & Tulving, E. (1986). Computer learning by memory-impaired patients: Acquisition and retention of complex knowledge. *Neuropsychologia, 25,* 313–328.

Godden, D. R., & Baddeley, A. D. (1975). Context-dependent memory in two natural environments: On land and underwater. *British Journal of Psychology, 66,* 325–331.

Goethals, G. R., & Zanna, M. P. (1979). The roles of social comparison in choice shifts. *Journal of Personality and Social Psychology, 37,* 1469–1476.

Goffman, E. (1967). *Interaction ritual*. Garden City, NY: Doubleday.

Goldberg, J. (1990). *Journal of the American Medical Association.*

Goldfried, M. R., Greenberg, L. S., & Marmar, C. (1990). Individual psychotherapy: Process and outcome. *Annual Review of Psychology, 41,* 659–688.

Goldsmith, H. H., & Alansky, J. A. (1987). Maternal and infant temperamental predictors of attachment: A meta-analytic review. *Journal of Consulting and Clinical Psychology, 55,* 805–816.

Goldstein, M. J. (1988). The family and psychopathology. *Annual Review of Psychology, 39,* 283–299.

Goldstein, M. J., Baker, B. L., & Jamison, K. (1986). *Abnormal psychology: Experiences, origins, and interventions*. Boston: Little, Brown.

Golgi, C. (1967). The neuron doctrine—theory and facts. In *Nobel lectures: Physiology and medicine, 1901–1921.* Amsterdam: Elsevier. (Original work published 1906)

Gomes-Schwartz, B. (1978). Effective ingredients in psychotherapy: Prediction of outcome from process variables. *Journal of Consulting and Clinical Psychology, 46,* 1023–1035.

Goodstein, L. D. (1988). Report of the executive vice president: 1987: The growth of the American Psychological Association. *American Psychologist, 43,* 491–498.

Gottesman, I. I., & Shields, J. (1982). *Schizophrenia: The epigenetic puzzle*. Cambridge, Eng.: Cambridge University Press.

Gottesman, I. I., McGuffin, P., & Farmer, A. E. (1987). Clinical genetics as clues to the "real" genetics of schizophrenia. *Schizophrenia Bulletin, 13,* 23–47.

Gottlieb, G. (1976). The roles of experience in the development of behavior and the nervous system. In G. Gottlieb (Ed.), *Studies on the development of behavior and the nervous system: Vol 3. Neural and behavioral specificity*. New York: Academic Press.

Gough, H. G. (1957). *California Personality Inventory Manual*. Palo Alto, CA: Consulting Psychology Press.

Gould, K. B., Lee, A. F. S., & Morelock, S. (1988). The relationship between sleep and sudden infant death. *Annals of the New York Academy of Sciences, 533,* 62–77.

Gould, R. (1978). *Transformations: Growth and change in adult life*. New York: Simon & Schuster.

Gould, S. J. (1981). *The mismeasure of man*. New York: Norton.

Graziano, W., Brothen, T., & Berscheid, E. (1978). Height and attraction: Do men and women see eye-to-eye? *Journal of Personality, 46,* 128–145.

Greenberg, J., Pyszczynski, T., & Solomon, S. (1982). The self-serving attributional bias: Beyond self-presentation. *Journal of Experimental Social Psychology, 18,* 56–67.

Greene, E., Flynn, M. S., & Loftus, E. F. (1982). Inducing resistance to misleading information. *Journal of Verbal Learning and Verbal Behavior, 21,* 207–219.

Greenwald, A. G. (1980). The authoritarian ego: Fabrication and revision of personal history. *American Psychologist, 35,* 603–618.

Gregory, R. L. (1988). *Odd perceptions*. Routledge.

Griggs, R. A., & Cox, U. R. (1982). The elusive thematic-materials effect in Wason's selection task. *British Journal of Psychology, 73,* 407–420.

Grimsley, R. (1967). Jean-Jacques Rousseau. In Paul Edwards (Ed.), *The encyclopaedia of philosophy*. New York: Macmillan.

Gross, A. E., & Crofton, C. (1977). What is good is beautiful. *Sociometry, 40,* 85–90.

Groth-Marnat, G. (1984). *Handbook of psychological assessment*. New York: Van Nostrand.

Guilford, J. P. (1967). Crystallized intelligences: The nature of human intelligence. New York: McGraw-Hill.

Guilford, J. P. (1982). Cognitive psychology's ambiguities: Some suggested remedies. *Psychological Review, 89,* 48–59.

Gurman, A. S., & Kniskern, D. P. (Eds.) (1981). *Handbook of family therapy.* New York: Bruner Mazel.

Guttman, N., & Kalish, H. I. (1956). Discriminability and stimulus generalization. *Journal of Experimental Psychology, 51,* 79–88.

Guze, S. B., Cloninger, C. R., Martin, R., & Clayton, P. J. (1986). Alcoholism as a medical disorder. *Comprehensive Psychiatry, 27,* 501–509.

Haaf, R., & Brown, C. J. (1976). Infants' responses to facelike patterns: Developmental changes between 10 and 15 weeks of age. *Journal of Experimental Child Psychology, 22,* 155–160.

Haan, N. (1981). Common dimensions of personality development: Early adolescence to middle life. In D. H. Eichorn, J. A. Clausen, N. Haan, M. P. Honzik, & P. Mussen (Eds.), *Present and past in middle life* (pp. 299–319). New York: Academic Press.

Hagbarth, K. E. (1983). Microelectrode exploration of human nerves: Physiological and clinical implications. *Journal of the Royal Society of Medicine, 76,* 7–15.

Hall, C. S., Dornhoff, W., Blick, K. A., & Weesner, K. E. (1982). The dreams of college men and women in 1950 and 1980: A comparison of dream contents and sex differences. *Sleep, 5,* 188–194.

Hall, E. T. (1966). *The hidden dimension.* Garden City, NY: Doubleday.

Hall, G. S. (1904). *Adolescence* (Vols. 1 and 2). New York: Appleton-Century-Crofts.

Halpern, D. F. (1986). *Sex differences in cognitive abilities.* Hillsdale, NJ: Erlbaum.

Hamilton, W. D. (1964). The evolution of social behavior. *Journal of Theoretical Biology, 7,* 1–52.

Hardin, G. (1968). The tragedy of the commons. *Science, 162,* 1243–1248.

Hareven, T. K. (1982). *Aging and life course transitions: An interdisciplinary perspective.* New York: Guilford.

Harkins, S. G. (1987). Social loafing and social facilitation. *Journal of Experimental Social Psychology, 23,* 1–18.

Harlow, H. (1950). Learning and satiation of response in intrinsically motivated complex puzzle performance in monkeys. *Journal of Comparative and Physiological Psychology, 43,* 289–294.

Harlow, H. F., & Harlow, M. K. (1965). The affectional systems, A. M. Shrier, H. F. Harlow, & F. Stollnitz (Eds.), *Behavior of non-human primates.* (pp. 287–334). New York: Academic Press.

Harlow, H. F., & Zimmerman, R. R. (1959). Affectional responses in the infant monkey. *Science, 130,* 421–432.

Harris, T., Cook, E. F., Garrison, R., Higgins, M., Kannel, W., & Goldman, L. (1988). Body mass index and mortality among nonsmoking older persons: The Framingham heart study. *Journal of the American Medical Association, 259,* 1520–1524.

Harth, E. (1982). *Windows on the mind: Reflections on the physical basis of consciousness.* New York: William Morrow.

Hartup, W. W. (1974). Aggression in childhood: Developmental perspectives. *American Psychologist, 29,* 336–341.

Hartup, W. W. (1983). Peer relations. In P. H. Mussen (Ed.), *Handbook of child psychology: Vol. 4. Socialization, personality and social development.* New York: Wiley.

Hatfield, E. (1988). Passionate and companionate love. In R. J. Sternberg & M. L. Barnes (Eds.), *The psychology of love* (pp. 191–217). New Haven, Yale University Press.

Hathaway, S. R., & McKinley, J. C. (1940). A multiphasic personality schedule (Minnesota): I. Construction of the schedule. *Journal of Psychology, 10,* 249–254.

Hathaway, S. R., & McKinley, J. C., with Butcher, J. N., Dahlstrom, W. G., Graham, J. R., Telegen, A., & Kaemmer, B. (1989). *Minnesota multiphasic personality inventory-II: Manual for administration and scoring.* Minneapolis: University of Minnesota Press.

Hayes, C. (1951). *The ape in our house.* New York: Harper & Row.

Haynes, H., White, B. L., & Held, R. (1965). Visual accommodation in human infants. *Science, 148,* 528–530.

Hazelrigg, M. D., Cooper, H. M., & Borduin, C. M. (1987). Evaluating the effectiveness of family therapies: An integrative review and analysis. *Psychological Bulletin, 101,* 428–442.

Hearst, E. (1988). Fundamentals of learning and conditioning. In R. C. Atkinson, R. J. Herrnstein, G. Lindzey, & R. D. Luce (Eds.), *Stevens' handbook of experimental psychology: 2. Learning and cognition* (pp. 3–109). New York: Wiley.

Hebb, D. O. (1949). *The organization of behavior.* New York: Wiley.

Hebb, D. O. (1955). Drives and the CNS. *Psychological Review, 62,* 243–253.

Hecht, S., Shlaer, S., & Pirenne, M. (1942). Energy, quanta, and vision. *Journal of General Physiology, 25,* 819–840.

Heider, F. (1958). *The psychology of interpersonal relations.* New York: Wiley.

Heilman, K. M., Scholes, R., & Watson, R. T. (1975). Auditory affective agnosia: Disturbed comprehension of affective speech. *Journal of Neurology, Neurosurgery and Psychiatry, 38,* 69–72.

Helmholtz, H. (1968). Concerning the perceptions in general. In R. M. Warren and R. P. Warren (Ed. and Trans.), *Helmholtz on perception: Its physiology and development.* (pp. 171–203). New York: Wiley. (Original work published 1866)

Helson, H., Judd, D. B., & Wilson, M. (1956). Color rendition with fluorescent sources of illumination. *Illuminating Engineering, 51,* 329–346.

Helzer, J. E. (1987). Epidemiology of alcoholism. *Journal of Consulting and Clinical Psychology, 55,* 284–292.

Hepworth, J. T., & West, S. G. (1988). Lynchings and the economy: A time-series reanalysis of Hovland and Sears (1940). *Journal of Personality and Social Psychology, 55,* 239–247.

Herbert, W. (1983, June 25). Schizophrenia clues in angel dust. *Science News,* p. 407.

Herman, C., Polivy, J., Lank, C. N., & Heatherton, T. F. (1987). Anxiety, hunger and eating behavior. *Journal of Abnormal Psychology, 96,* 264–269.

Herrnstein, R. J. (1958). Some factors influencing behavior in a two-response situation. *Transactions of the New York Academy of Sciences, 21,* 35–45.

Herrnstein, R. J. (1961). Relative and absolute strength of response as a function of frequency of reinforcement. *Journal of the Experimental Analysis of Behavior, 4,* 267–272.

Higgins, E. T. (1989). Self-discrepancy theory: What patterns of self-beliefs cause people to suffer? In L. Berkowitz (Ed.), *Advances in experimental social psychology* (Vol. 22, pp. 93–136). New York: Academic Press.

Higgins, E. T., & Bargh, J. A. (1987). Social cognition and social perception. *Annual Review of Psychology, 38,* 369–425.

Hilgard, E. R. (1986). *Divided consciousness: Multiple controls in human thought and action.* New York: Wiley.

Hilgard, E. R. (1987). *Psychology in America*. New York: Harcourt Brace Jovanovich.

Hilgard, J. R. (1979). *Personality and hypnosis: A study of imaginative involvement* (2nd ed.). Chicago: University of Chicago Press.

Hill, C. T., Rubin, Z., & Peplau, L. A. (1976). Breakups before marriage: The end of 103 affairs. *Journal of Social Issues, 32,* 147–168.

Hilton, D. F., & Slugoski, B. R. (1986). Knowledge-based causal attribution: The abnormal conditions focus model. *Psychological Review, 93,* 75–88.

Hinsz, V. B., & Davis, J. H. (1984). Persuasive arguments theory, group polarization, and choice shifts. *Personality and Social Psychology Bulletin, 10,* 260–268.

Hirsch, J., & Leibel, R. (1988). New light on obesity. *New England Journal of Medicine, 318,* 509–510.

Hoffman, L. W. (1985). The changing genetics/socialization balance. *Journal of Social Issues, 41,* 127–148.

Holbreich, M. (1982). Asthma and other allergic disorders in pregnancy. *American Family Physician, 25,* 187–192.

Holden, C. (1980a). Identical twins reared apart. *Science, 207,* 1323–1325.

Holden, C. (1980b). Twins reunited. *Science, 80,* 55–59.

Holden, C. (1986). Proposed new psychiatric diagnoses raise charges of gender bias. *Science, 231,* 327–328.

Holland, J. H., Holyoak, D. J., Nisbett, R. E., & Thagard, P. T. (1986). *Induction: Processes of inference, learning and discovery.* Cambridge, MA: Bradford Books/MIT Press.

Hollingshead, A. B., & Redlich, F. C. (1958). *Social class and mental illness: A community study.* New York: Wiley.

Holmes, D. S. (1988). The influence of meditation vs rest on physiological considerations. In M. West (Ed.), *The psychology of meditation* (pp. 81–103). New York: Oxford University Press.

Holmes, D. S., Solomon, S., Cappo, B. M., & Greenberg, J. L. (1983). Effects of transcendental meditation versus resting on physiological and subjective arousal. *Journal of Personality and Social Psychology, 44,* 1244–1252.

Holmes, J. G., & Rempel, J. K. (1989). Trust in close relationships. In C. Hendrick (Ed.), *Close relationships* (pp. 187–220). Newbury Park, CA: Sage.

Holmes, T. H., & Rahe, R. H. (1967). The Social Readjustment Rating Scale. *Journal of Psychosomatic Research, 11,* 213–218.

Holroyd, K. A., & Lazarus, R. S. (1982). Stress, coping and somatic adaptation. In L. Goldberger & S. Breznitz (Eds.), *Handbook of stress: Theoretical and clinical aspects.* New York: Free Press.

Holt, R. R. (1970). Yet another look at clinical and statistical prediction: Or is clinical psychology worthwhile? *American Psychologist, 25,* 337–349.

Horn, J. L. (1982). The aging of human abilities. In H. J. Wolman (Ed.), *Handbook of developmental psychology.* Englewood Cliffs, NJ: Prentice-Hall.

Horn, J. L. (1985). Remodeling old models of intelligence. In B. B. Wolman (Ed.), *Handbook of intelligence: Theories, measurements, and applications.* New York: Wiley.

Hornblower, M. (1987, March 21). Down and out—but determined: Does a mentally disturbed woman have the right to be homeless? *Time, 130,* 29.

Horne, J. A. (1985). Sleep function, with particular reference to sleep deprivation. *Annals of Clinical Research, 17,* 199–208.

Horner, M. S. (1973). A psychological barrier to achievement in women: The motive to avoid success. In D. C. McClelland & R. S. Steele (Eds.), *Human motivation: A book of readings.* Morristown, NJ: General Learning Press.

Horney, K. (1939). *New ways in psychoanalysis.* New York: Norton.

Hoyenga, K. B., & Hoyenga, K. T. (1984). *Motivational explanations of behavior.* Monterey, CA: Brooks/Cole.

Hsu, L. K. G. (1980). Outcome of anorexia nervosa: A review of the literature (1954 to 1978). *Archive of General Psychiatry, 37,* 1041–1046.

Hubel, D. H., & Wiesel, T. N. (1979). Brain mechanisms of vision. *Scientific American, 241*(9), 150–168.

Huesmann, L. R., Eron, L. D., Lefkowitz, M. M., & Walder, L. O. (1984). Stability of aggression over time and generations. *Developmental Psychology, 20,* 1120–1134.

Huesmann, L. R., Laperspetz, K., & Eron, L. D. (1984). Intervening variables in the TV violence-aggression relation: Evidence from two countries. *Developmental Psychology, 20,* 746–775.

Hughes, M. J., & Donaldson, M. (1979). The use of hiding games for studying coordination of viewpoints. *Educational Review, 31,* 133–140.

Hughes, R., & Brewin, R. (1979). *The tranquilizing of America.* New York: Harcourt Brace Jovanovich.

Hull, C. F. (1943). *Principles of behavior.* New York: Appleton-Century-Crofts.

Hull, J. G., Van Treuren, R. R., & Virnelli, S. (1987). Hardiness and health: A critique and alternative approach. *Journal of Personality and Social Psychology, 53,* 518–530.

Hulse, S. H., Fowler, H., & Honig, W. K. (1978). *Cognitive processes in animal behavior.* Hillsdale, NJ: Erlbaum.

Hunt, J. McV. (1982). Toward equalizing the developmental opportunities of infants and preschool children. *Journal of Social Issues, 38,* 163–191.

Hurlburt, A., & Poggio, T. (1988). Synthesizing a color algorithm. *Science, 239,* 482.

Huston, A. C. (1985). The development of sex-typing: Themes from recent research. *Developmental Review, 5,* 1–17.

Huttenlocher, P. R. (1979). Synaptic density in human frontal cortex: Developmental changes and effects of aging. *Brain Research, 163,* 195–205.

Hyde, J. S., & Lynn, M. C. (1988). Gender differences in verbal ability: A meta-analysis. *Psychological Bulletin, 104,* 53–69.

Hyman, B. T., Van Hoesen, G. W., Damasio, A. R., & Barnes, C. L. (1984). Alzheimer's disease: Cell-specific pathology isolates the hippocampal formation. *Science, 225,* 1168–1170.

Ingham, A. G., Levinger, G., Graves, J., & Peckham, V. (1974). The Ringelman effect: Studies of group size and group performance. *Journal of Experimental Social Psychology, 10,* 371–384.

Inhelder, B., & Piaget, J. (1958). *The growth of logical thinking from childhood to adolescence.* New York: Basic Books.

Insell, T. R. (1986). The neurobiology of anxiety. In B. F. Shaw, Z. V. Segal, T. M. Wallis, & F. E. Cashman (Eds.), *Anxiety disorders* (pp. 35–49). New York: Plenum.

Iscoe, I., & Harris, L. C. (1984). Social and community interventions. *Annual Review of Psychology, 35,* 333–360.

Isen, A. M. (1987). Positive affect, cognitive processes and social behavior. In L. Berkowitz (Ed.), *Advances in experimental social psychology* (Vol. 20, pp. 203–253). New York: Academic Press.

Isen, A. M., Daubman, K. A., & Nowicki, G. P. (1987). Positive affect facilitates creative problem solving. *Journal of Personality and Social Psychology, 52,* 1122–1131.

Isen, A. M., Johnson, M. M. S., Mertz, E., & Robinson, G. F. (1985). The influence of positive affect on the unusualness of word associations. *Journal of Personality and Social Psychology, 38,* 1–14.

Isenberg, D. J. (1986). Group polarization: A critical review and meta-analysis. *Journal of Personality and Social Psychology, 50*, 1141–1151.

Ittleson, W. H. (1952). *The Ames demonstrations in perception.* Princeton, NJ: Princeton University Press.

Izard, C. E. (1971). *The face of emotion.* New York: Appleton-Century-Crofts.

Izard, C. E. (1990). Facial expressions and the regulation of emotions. *Journal of Personality and Social Psychology, 58*, 487–498.

Izard, C. E. (1977). *Human emotions.* New York and London: Plenum Press.

Jacobs, B. L. (1987). How hallucinogenic drugs work. *American Scientist, 75(4)*, 386–392.

Jacobs, B., & Trulson, M. (1979). Mechanisms of action of LSD. *American Scientist, 67*, 396–404.

Jacobson, E. (1938). *Progressive relaxation.* Chicago: University of Chicago Press.

James, W. (1890). *Principles of psychology.* New York: Henry Holt.

Jamison, K. R., Gerner, R. H., Hammen, C., & Padesky, C. (1980). Clouds and silver linings: Positive experiences associated with primary affective disorders. *American Journal of Psychiatry, 137*, 198–202.

Janicak, P. B., & Bushes, R. A. (1987). Advances in the treatment of mania and other acute psychotic disorders. *Psychiatric Annals, 17*, 145–149.

Janis, I. L. (1983). *Groupthink: Psychological studies of policy decisions and fiascoes* (2nd ed.). Boston: Houghton Mifflin.

Janis, I. L., & Mann, L. (1977). *Decision making: A psychological analysis of conflict, choice and commitment.* New York: Free Press.

Janis, I. L., & Wheeler, D. (1978). Thinking clearly about career choices. *Psychology Today, 11*, 67–77.

Janowitz, H. D. (1976). Role of gastrointestinal tract in the regulation of food intake. In C. F. Code (Ed.), *Handbook of physiology: Alimentary canal, 1*, 219–224.

Jemmot, J. B., & Locke, S. E. (1984). Psychosocial factors, immunologic mediation, and human susceptibility to infectious diseases: How much do we know? *Psychological Bulletin, 95*, 78–108.

Jensen, A. R. (1969). How much can we boost IQ and scholastic achievement? *Harvard Educational Review, 39*, 1–123.

Johnson, R. D., & Downing, L. J. (1979). Deindividuation and valence of cues: Effects of prosocial and antisocial behavior. *Journal of Personality and Social Psychology, 37*, 1532–1538.

Johnston, L. D., O'Malley, P. M., & Bachman, J. G. (1988). *Illicit drug use, smoking, and drinking by America's high school students, college students, and young adults, 1975–1987.* Rockville, MD: National Institute on Drug Abuse.

Johnston, W. A., & Dark, V. J. (1986). Selective attention. *Annual Review of Psychology, 37*, 43–75.

Jones, E. E., & Harris, V. A. (1967). The attribution of attitudes. *Journal of Experimental Social Psychology, 3*, 2–24.

Jones, E. E., & Nisbett, R. E. (1971). *The actor and the observer: Divergent perceptions of the causes of behavior.* Morristown, NJ: General Learning Press.

Jones, L. R., & Knopke, H. J. (1987). Educating family physicians to care for the chronically mentally ill. *Journal of Family Practice, 24*, 177–183.

Jones, L. V. (1984). White-black achievement differences: The narrowing gap. *American Psychologist, 39*, 1207–1213.

Josephson, W. L. (1987). Television violence and children's aggression: Testing the priming, social script, and disinhibition predictions. *Journal of Personality and Social Psychology, 53*, 882–890.

Jouvet, M. (1967). The stages of sleep. *Scientific American, 216*, 62–72.

Jung, C. (1933). *Modern man in search of a soul.* New York: Harcourt Brace Jovanovich.

Jusczyk, P. W. (1985). The high-amplitude sucking technique as a methodological tool in infant speech perception research. In G. Gottlieb & N. A. Krasnegor (Eds.), *Measurement of audition and vision in the first year of postnatal life: A methodological overview.* Norwood, NJ: Ablex.

Kaas, J. H. (1987). The organization of the neocortex in mammals: Implications for theories of brain function. *Annual Review of Psychology, 38*, 129–151.

Kagan, J. (1978, January). The baby's elastic mind. *Human Nature*, 66–73.

Kagan, J. (1989). Temperamental contributions to social behavior. *American Psychologist, 44*, 668–674.

Kahle, L. R., & Berman, J. (1979). Attitudes cause behaviors: A cross-legged panel analysis. *Journal of Personality and Social Psychology, 37*, 315–321.

Kahneman, D. (1973). *Attention and effort.* Englewood Cliffs, NJ: Prentice-Hall.

Kales, A., & Kales, J. D. (1984). *Evaluation and treatment of insomnia.* New York: Oxford University Press.

Kamin, L. (1959). The delay of punishment gradient. *Journal of Comparative and Physiological Psychology, 52*, 434–437.

Kandel, E. R. (1985). Brain and behavior. In E. R. Kandel & J. H. Schwartz (Eds.), *Principles of neural science* (pp. 3–12). New York: Elsevier.

Kane, J. M., Woerner, M., Weinhold, P., Wegner, J., Kinon, B., & Bornstein, M. (1986). Incidence of tardive dyskinesia: Five-year data from a prospective study. *Psychopharmacology Bulletin, 20*, 387–389.

Kanizsa, G. (1976). Subjective contours. *Scientific American, 234*, 48–52.

Kanner, A. D., Coyne, J. C., Schaefer, C., & Lazarus, R. S. (1981). Comparisons of two modes of stress measurement: Daily hassles and uplifts versus major life events. *Journal of Behavioral Medicine, 4*, 1–39.

Katz, S. (1987). Why there is no error in the direct theory of perception. *Perception, 16*, 537–542.

Kazdin, A. (1990). Psychotherapy for children and adolescents. *Annual Review of Psychology, 41*, 21–54.

Keesey, R. E., & Powley, T. L. (1986). The regulation of body weight. *Annual Review of Psychology, 37*, 109–133.

Kegeles, S. M., Adler, N. E., & Irwin, C. E. (1988). Sexually active adolescents and condoms: Changes over one year in knowledge, attitudes and use. *American Journal of Public Health, 78*, 460–461.

Kellerman, H. (1981). *Sleep disorders: Insomnia and narcolepsy.* New York: Brunnel Mazel.

Kellerman, J., Lewis, J., & Laird, J. D. (1989). Looking and loving: The effects of mutual gaze on feelings of romantic love. *Journal of Research in Personality, 23*, 145–161.

Kelley, D. K. (1985). Disorders of sleep and consciousness. In E. R. Kandel & J. H. Schwartz (Eds.), *Principles of neural science* (pp. 659–670). New York: Elsevier.

Kelley, H. H. (1967). Attribution theory in social psychology. In D. Levine (Ed.), *Nebraska symposium on motivation* (Vol. 15, pp. 192–241). Lincoln, NB: University of Nebraska Press.

Kelley, H. H. (1972). Attribution in social interaction. In E. E. Jones, D. E. Kanouse, H. H. Kelley, R. E. Nisbett, S. Valins, & B. Weiner (Eds.), *Attribution: Perceiving the causes of behavior.* Morristown, NJ: General Learning Press.

Kellogg, W. N., & Kellogg, L. A. (1933). *The ape and the child.* New York: McGraw-Hill.

Kelly, G. (1955). *The psychology of personal constructs*. New York: Norton.

Kelman, H. C. (1961). Processes of opinion change. *Public Opinion Quarterly, 25*, 57–78.

Kenny, D. A., & Nasby, W. (1980). Splitting the reciprocity correlation. *Journal of Personality and Social Psychology, 38*, 249–256.

Kenrick, D. T., & Funder, D. C. (1988). Profiting from controversy: Lessons from the person-situation debate. *American Psychologist, 43*, 23–34.

Kernberg, O. (1975). *Borderline conditions and pathological narcissism*. New York: Aronson.

Kerr, N. H. (1983). The role of vision in visual imagery experiments: Evidence from the congenitally blind. *Journal of Experimental Psychology: General, 112*, 265–277.

Kessler, R. C., Price, R. H., & Wortman, C. B. (1985). Social factors in psychopathology: Stress, social support and the coping process. *Annual Review of Psychology, 36*, 531–572.

Kiecolt-Glaser, J. K., & Glaser, R. (1988). Behavioral influences on immune function: Evidence for the interplay between stress and health. In T. Field, P. M. McCabe, & N. Schneiderman (Eds.), *Stress and coping across development*. Hillsdale, NJ: Erlbaum.

Kiesler, C. A., & Sibulkin, A. E. (1989). *Mental hospitalization: Myths and facts about a national crisis*. Newbury Park, CA: Sage.

Kihlstrom, J. F. (1985). Hypnosis. *Annual Review of Psychology, 36*, 385–418.

Kimble, G. A. (1961). *Hilgard and Marquis' conditioning and learning*. New York: Appleton-Century-Crofts.

Kimelberg, H. K. (1988). *Glial cell receptors*. New York: Raven Press.

Kinsey, A. C., Pomeroy, W. B., & Martin, C. E. (1948). *Sexual behavior in the human male*. Philadelphia: W. B. Saunders.

Kinsey, A. C., Pomeroy, W. B., Martin, C. E., & Gebhard, P. (1953). *Sexual behavior in the human female*. Philadelphia: W. B. Saunders.

Klaus, M., & Kennell, J. (1976). *Maternal-infant bonding*. St. Louis: Mosby.

Klein, M. (1981). *The writings of Melanie Klein* (Vol. 1, R. E. Money-Kyrle, Ed.). London: Hogarth Press.

Kleinginna, P. R., & Kleinginna, A. M. (1981). A categorized list of motivational definitions, with a suggestion for a consensual definition. *Motivation and Emotion, 5*, 263–291.

Kleinke, C. L., & Staneski, R. A. (1980). First impression of female bust size. *Journal of Social Psychology, 110*, 123–134.

Kleinmuntz, B., & Szucko, J. J. (1984). Lie detection in ancient and modern times: A call for contemporary scientific study. *American Psychologist, 39*, 766–776.

Kleitman, N. (1982). Basic rest-activity cycle—22 years later. *Sleep, 4*, 311–317.

Kleitman, N. (1963). *Sleep and wakefulness* (rev. ed.). Chicago: University of Chicago Press.

Klentz, B., Beaman, A. L., Mapelli, S. D., & Ulrich, J. R. (1987). Perceived physical attractiveness of supporters and nonsupporters of the women's movement: An attitude-similarity-mediated error (AS-ME). *Personality and Social Psychology Bulletin, 13*, 513–523.

Klopfer, P. H., & Klopfer, M. S. (1968). Maternal imprinting in goats. *Proceedings of the National Academy of Sciences, U.S.A., 52*, 911–914.

Kluver, H., & Bucy, P. C. (1939). Preliminary analysis of the functions of the temporal lobes in monkeys. *Archives of Neurology and Psychiatry, 42*, 979–1000.

Klymenko, V., & Weisstein, N. (1986). Spatial frequency difference can determine figure-ground organization. *Journal of Experimental Psychology: Human Perception and Performance, 12*, 324–330.

Knauth, P. (1975). *A season in hell*. New York: Harper & Row.

Knox, V., Morgan, A. H., & Hilgard, E. R. (1974). Pain and suffering in ischemia: The paradox of hypnotically suggested anaesthesias contradicted by reports from the "hidden observer." *Archives of General Psychiatry, 30*, 840–847.

Knudsen, E. I. (1984). The role of auditory experience in the development and maintenance of sound localization. *Trends in Neurosciences*, 326–330.

Kobasa, S. (1982). The hardy personality: Toward a social psychology of stress and health. In G. S. Sanders and J. Suls (Eds.), *Social psychology of health and illness* (pp. 3–32). Hillsdale, NJ: Erlbaum.

Koch, S. (1985). Foreword. In S. Koch & D. E. Leary (Eds.), *A century of psychology as science* (pp. 7–35). New York: McGraw-Hill.

Koenig, M. A., & Zelnik, M. (1982). The risk of premarital first pregnancy among metropolitan-area teenagers, 1976 and 1979. *Family Planning Perspectives, 14*, 239–247.

Kohlberg, L. (1963). The development of children's orientations towards a moral order. 1. Sequence in the development of moral thought. *Vita Humana, 6*, 11–33.

Kohlberg, L. (1976). Moral stages and moralization: The cognitive-developmental approach. In T. Lickona (Ed.), *Moral development and behavior*. New York: Holt, Rinehart & Winston.

Kohlberg, L., & Gilligan, C. (1971). The adolescent as a philosopher: The discovery of the self in a postconventional world. *Daedalus, 100*, 1051–1086.

Kohler, W. (1927). *The mentality of apes*. London: Routledge & Kegan Paul.

Kolata, G. (1986). Manic depression: Is it inherited? *Science, 232*, 575–576.

Korchin, S. J., & Schuldberg, D. (1981). The future of clinical assessment. *American Psychologist, 36*, 1147–1158.

Kosslyn, S. F. (1980). *Image and mind*. Cambridge, MA: Harvard University Press.

Kozulin, A. (1984). *Psychology in Utopia: Towards a social history of Soviet psychology*. Cambridge, MA: MIT Press.

Krantz, D. S., Baum, A., & Singer, J. E. (Eds.). (1983). *Handbook of psychology and health: Vol. 3. Cardiovascular disorders and behavior*. Hillsdale, NJ: Erlbaum.

Krantz, D. S., Grunberg, N. E., & Baum, A. (1985). Health psychology. *Annual Review of Psychology, 36*, 349–383.

Kubler-Ross, E. (1969). *On death and dying*. New York: Macmillan.

Kuczaj, S. A., II. (1978). Children's judgments of grammatical and ungrammatical irregular past-tense verbs. *Child Development, 49*, 319–326.

Kuhl, P. K. (1985). Methods in the study of infant speech perception. In G. Gottlieb & N. A. Krasnegor (Eds.), *Measurement of audition and vision in the first year of postnatal life: A methodological overview*. Norwood, NJ: Ablex.

Kuhl, P. K. (1987). Perception of speech and sound in early infancy. In P. Salapatek & L. Cohen (Eds.), *Handbook of infant perception, 2: From perception to cognition*. New York: Academic Press.

Kupferman, I. (1985a). Genetic determinants of behavior. In E. R. Kandel & J. H. Schwartz (Eds.), *Principles of neural science* (pp. 795–804). New York: Elsevier.

Kupferman, I. (1985b). Hemispheric asymmetries and the cortical localization of cognitive and affective functions. In E. R. Kandel & J. H. Schwartz (Eds.), *Principles of neural science* (pp. 673–687). New York: Elsevier.

Labouvie-Vief, G. (1980). Beyond formal operations: Uses

and limits of pure logic in life-span development. *Human Development, 23,* 141–161.

Lackner, J. R., & Garrett, M. F. (1972). Resolving ambiguity: Effects of biasing context in the unattended ear. *Cognition, 1,* 359–372.

Ladouceur, R. (1983). Participant modeling with or without cognitive treatment of phobias. *Journal of Consulting and Clinical Psychology, 51,* 942–944.

Laird, J. D., & Bresler, C. (1990). William James and the mechanisms of emotional experience. *Personality and Social Psychology Bulletin, 16,* 636–651.

Laird, J. D., Wagener, J. J., Halal, M., & Szegda, M. (1982). Remembering what you feel: Effects of emotion on memory. *Journal of Personality and Social Psychology, 42,* 646–657.

Laird, J. D., Cuniff, M., Sheehan, K., Shulman, D., & Strum, G. (1989). Emotion-specific effects of facial expressions on memory for life events. *Journal of Social Behavior and Personality, 4,* 87–98.

Lamm, H., & Myers, D. G. (1978). Group-induced polarization of attitudes and behavior. In L. Berkowitz (Ed.), *Advances in experimental social psychology* (Vol. 11, pp. 145–195). New York: Academic Press.

Landau, B., Spelke, E., & Gleitman, H. (1984). Spatial knowledge in a young blind child. *Cognition, 16,* 225–260.

Landy, D., & Sigall, H. (1974). Beauty is talent: Task evaluation as a function of the performer's physical attractiveness. *Journal of Personality and Social Psychology, 29,* 299–304.

Lanyon, R. I. (1984). Personality assessment. *Annual Review of Psychology, 35,* 667–701.

Lanzetta, J. T., Cartwright-Smith, J., & Kleck, R. E. (1976). Effects of nonverbal dissimulation on emotional experience and autonomic arousal. *Journal of Personality and Social Psychology, 33,* 354–370.

Latané, B., & Darley, J. M. (1970). *The unresponsive bystander: Why doesn't he help?* New York: Appleton-Century-Crofts.

Latané, B., & Nida, S. (1981). Ten years of research on group size and helping. *Psychological Bulletin, 89,* 308–324.

Latané, B., Williams, K., & Harkins, S. (1979). Many hands make light the work: The causes and consequences of social loafing. *Journal of Personality and Social Psychology, 37,* 822–832.

Laurence, J. R., & Perry, C. (1983). Hypnotically created memory among highly hypnotizable subjects. *Science, 222,* 523–524.

Lazarus, R. S. (1982). Thoughts on the relations between emotion and cognition. *American Psychologist, 37,* 1019–1024.

Lazarus, R. S. (1984a). Puzzles in the study of daily hassles. *Journal of Behavioral Medicine, 7,* 375–389.

Lazarus, R. S. (1984b). On the primacy of cognition. *American Psychologist, 39,* 124–129.

Lazarus, R. S., & Folkman, S. (1984). *Stress, appraisal and coping.* New York: Springer.

Leahy, T. H. (1987). *A history of psychology: Main currents in psychological thought.* Englewood Cliffs, NJ: Prentice-Hall.

Leakey, R. E., & Lewin, R. (1977). *Origins.* New York: Dutton.

Lehman, D. R., Lempert, R. O., & Nisbett, R. E. (1988). The effects of graduate training on reasoning: Formal discipline and thinking about everyday life events. *American Psychologist, 43,* 431–442.

Lenneberg, E. H. (1967). *Biological foundations of language.* New York: Wiley.

Lepper, M. R., Greene, D., & Nisbett, R. E. (1973). Undermining children's intrinsic interest with extrinsic reward: A test of the "overjustification" hypothesis. *Journal of Personality and Social Psychology, 28,* 129–137.

Lerner, M. J., & Simmons, C. H. (1966). Observers' reaction to the "innocent victim": Compassion or rejection? *Journal of Personality and Social Psychology, 4,* 203–210.

Lerner, M. L. (1980). *The belief in a just world: A fundamental delusion.* New York: Plenum.

Leuba, C. (1962). Relation of stimulus intensities to learning and development. *Psychological Reports, 1,* 429–455.

Leventhal, H. (1970). Findings and theory in the study of fear communications. In L. Berkowitz (Ed.), *Advances in experimental social psychology* (Vol. 5). New York: Academic Press.

Leventhal, H., & Scherer, K. (1987). The relationship of emotion to cognition: A functional approach to a semantic controversy. *Cognition and Emotion, 1,* 3–28.

Levine, F. M., & Sandeen, E. (1985). *Conceptualization in psychotherapy: The models approach.* Hillsdale, NJ: Erlbaum.

Levinson, D. J. (1977). *The seasons of a man's life.* Knopf: New York.

Lewinsohn, P. M., Hoberman, H., Teri, L., & Hautzinger, M. (1985). An integrative theory of depression. In S. Reiss & R. Bootzin (Eds.), *Theoretical issues in behavior therapy.* Orlando: Academic Press.

Lewontin, R. C. (1976). Race and intelligence. In N. J. Block & G. Dworkin (Eds.), *The IQ controversy* (pp. 78–92). New York: Pantheon Books.

Liem, R., & Liem, J. V. (1978). Social class and mental illness reconsidered: The role of economic stress and social support. *Journal of Health and Social Behavior, 19,* 139–156.

Light, L. L., & Carter-Sobell, L. (1970). Effects of changed semantic context on recognition memory. *Journal of Verbal Learning and Verbal Behavior, 9,* 1–11.

Light, P., Buckingham, N., & Robbins, A. H. (1979). The conservation task as an interactional setting. *British Journal of Educational Psychology, 49,* 304–310.

Lindskold, S., & Han, G. (1988). GRIT as a foundation for integrative bargaining. *Personality and Social Psychology Bulletin, 14,* 335–345.

Linton, M. (1978). Real world memory after six years: An in vivo study of very long-term memory. In M. M. Gruneberg, P. E. Morris, & R. N. Sykes (Eds.), *Practical aspects of memory.* Orlando, FL: Academic Press.

Linz, D. G., Donnerstein, E., & Penrod, S. (1988). Effects of long-term exposure to violent and sexually degrading depictions of women. *Journal of Personality and Social Psychology, 55,* 758–768.

Litwin, G. H. (1958). *Motives and expectancy as determinants of preference for degrees of risk.* Unpublished bachelor of arts thesis. University of Michigan, Ann Arbor.

Livingstone, M. S., & Hubel, D. J. (1987). Psychophysical evidence for separate channels for the perception of form, color, movement and depth. *Journal of Neuroscience, 7,* 3416–3468.

Loehlin, J. C., Willerman, L., & Horn, J. M. (1988). Human behavior genetics. *Annual Review of Psychology, 39,* 101–133.

Loftus, E. F. (1979). *Eyewitness testimony.* Cambridge, MA: Harvard University Press.

Loftus, E. F., & Palmer, J. C. (1974). Reconstruction of an automobile destruction: An example of the interaction between language and memory. *Journal of Verbal Learning and Verbal Behavior, 13,* 585–589.

Loftus, E. F., Miller, D. G., & Burns, H. J. (1978). Semantic integration of verbal information into a visual memory. *Journal of Experimental Psychology, 4,* 19–31.

Loftus, G. R. (1983). The continuing persistence of the icon. *The Behavioral and Brain Sciences, 1,* 43.

Loftus, G. R. (1985). Picture perception: Effects of luminance on available information and information-extraction rate. *Journal of Experimental Psychology: General, 114,* 342–356.

Lorenz, K. (1937). The companion in the bird's world. *Auk, 54,* 245–273.

Lorenz, K. (1966). *On aggression.* New York: Harcourt, Brace, World.

Lott, A. J., & Lott, B. E. (1961). Group cohesiveness, communication level, and conformity. *Journal of Abnormal and Social Psychology, 62,* 408–412.

Lowenstein, W. R., & Skalak, R. (1966). Mechanical transmission in a Pacinian corpuscle: An analysis and a theory. *Journal of Physiology, 182,* 346–378.

Lowinger, P. (1987). Two comments on psychosurgery. *New England Journal of Medicine, 316*(2), 114.

Lowrey, G. H. (1978). *Growth and development of children.* (7th ed.). Chicago: Year Book Medical Publishers.

Lubin, B., Larsen, R. M., Matarazzo, J. D., & Seever, M. (1985). Psychological test usage patterns in five professional settings. *American Psychologist, 40,* 857–861.

Luborsky, L. (1954). A note on Eysenck's article, "The effects of psychotherapy: An evaluation." *British Journal of Psychology, 45,* 129–131.

Luborsky, L., Singer, B., & Luborsky, L. (1975). Comparative studies of psychotherapies: Is it true that everyone has won and all must have prizes? *Archives of General Psychiatry, 32,* 995–1008.

Luchins, A. S. (1942). Mechanization of problem solving. *Psychological Monographs, 54*(248).

Luisada, P. V., & Brown, B. I. (1976). Clinical management of the phencyclidine psychosis. *Clinical Toxicology, 9,* 539–545.

Luria, A. R. (1979). *The making of mind.* Cambridge, MA: Harvard University Press.

Lykken, D. T. (1985). The probity of the polygraph. In S. M. Kassin and L. S. Wrightsman (Eds.), *The psychology of evidence and trial procedure.* Beverly Hills, CA: Sage.

Lykken, D. T. (1981). *A tremor in the blood: Uses and abuses of the lie detector.* New York: McGraw-Hill.

Lynn, S. J., & Rhue, J. W. (1987). Hypnosis, imagination, and fantasy. *Journal of Mental Imagery, 11,* 101–112.

Maccoby, E. E. (1990). Gender and relationships: A developmental account. *American Psychologist, 45,* 512–520.

Maccoby, E. E., & Jacklin, C. N. (1987). Gender segregation in childhood. In H. W. Reese (Ed.), *Advances in child development and behavior* (Vol. 20, pp. 239–288). New York: Cambridge University Press.

Maccoby, E. E., Snow, M. E., & Jacklin, C. N. (1984). Continuities and discontinuities in early mother-child interaction: A longitudinal study at 12 and 18 months. In M. E. Lamb & A. L. Brown (Eds.), *Advances in developmental psychology.* (Vol. 20, pp. 459–472). Hillsdale, NJ: Erlbaum.

Macfarlane, J. W. (1964). Perspectives on personality constancy and change from the guidance perspective. *Vita Humana, 7,* 115–126.

MacGregor, D. (1960). *The human side of enterprise.* New York: McGraw-Hill.

MacKenzie, B. (1984). Explaining race differences in IQ: The logic, the methodology, and the evidence. *American Psychologist, 39,* 1214–1223.

Madden, J., with D. Anderson. (1988). *One size doesn't fit all.* New York: Villard Books.

Maddux, J. E., & Rogers, R. W. (1980). Effects of source expertness, physical attractiveness and supporting arguments on persuasion: A case of brains over beauty. *Journal of Personality and Social Psychology, 39,* 235–244.

Maier, N. R. F. (1930). Reasoning in humans: II. The solution of a problem and its appearance in consciousness. *Journal of Comparative Psychology, 12,* 181–194.

Makinson, C. (1985). The health consequences of teenage fertility. *Family Planning Perspectives, 17,* 132–139.

Malamuth, N. M., & Check, J. V. P. (1981). The effects of mass media exposure on acceptance of violence against women: A field experiment. *Journal of Research in Personality, 15,* 436–446.

Mandler, G., & Nakamura, Y. (1987). Aspects of consciousness. *Personality and Social Psychology Bulletin, 13,* 299–313.

Mann, L. (1981). The baiting crowd in episodes of threatened suicide. *Journal of Personality and Social Psychology, 55,* 28–36.

Maranon, G. (1924). Contribution a l'étude de l'action emotive de l'adrenaline. *Revue française d'endocrinologie, 2,* 301–325.

Maratsos, M. (1983). Some current issues in the study of the acquisition of grammar. In P. H. Mussen (Ed.), *Handbook of child development: Vol. 3. Cognitive development* (Ed. J. H. Flavell & E. M. Markman, pp. 707–786). New York: Wiley.

Martin, G. B., & Clark, III, R. D. (1982). Distress crying in neonates: Species and peer specificity. *Developmental Psychology, 18,* 3–9.

Martin, J., Lobb, B., Chapman, G. C., & Spillane, R. (1976). Obedience under conditions demanding self-immolation. *Human Relations, 29,* 345–356.

Martorano, S. C. (1977). A developmental analysis of performance on Piaget's formal operations tasks. *Developmental Psychology, 13,* 666–672.

Marx, F. (Ed.). (1894). *Ad herennium (libri IV).* Leipzig: Teubner.

Maslow, A. H. (1962). *Toward a psychology of being.* New York: Van Nostrand.

Maslow, A. H. (1970). *Motivation and personality.* New York: Harper & Row.

Maslow, A. H. (1970). *Motivation and personality* (rev. ed.). New York: Harper & Row.

Masters, W. H., & Johnson, V. E. (1966). *Human sexual response.* Boston: Little, Brown.

Matas, L., Arend, R. A., & Sroufe, L. A. (1978). Continuity of adaptation in the second year: The relationship between quality of attachment and later competence. *Child Development, 49,* 547–556.

Matsumoto, D., & Ekman, P. (1989). American-Japanese cultural differences in intensity ratings of facial expressions of emotion. *Motivation & Emotion, 13,* 143–157.

Matthews, G. B. (1980). *Philosophy and the young child.* Cambridge, MA: Harvard University Press.

Maurer, D., & Barrera, M. (1981). Infants' perception of natural and distorted arrangements of a schematic face. *Child Development, 52,* 196–202.

Mayer, D. J., & Liebeskind, J. C. (1974). Pain reduction by focal electrical stimulation of the brain: An anatomical and behavioral analysis. *Brain Research, 68,* 73–93.

Mayes, A. R., Meudell, P. R., & Pickering, A. (1985). Is organic amnesia caused by a selective deficit in remembering contextual information? *Cortex, 21,* 167–202.

Mayeux, R., & Kandel, E. R. (1985). Natural language, disorders of language, and other localizable disorders of cognitive functioning. In E. R. Kandel & J. H. Schwartz (Eds.), *Principles of neural science* (pp. 688–703). New York: Elsevier.

McArthur, L. A. (1972). The how and what of why: Some

determinants and consequences of causal attribution. *Journal of Personality and Social Psychology, 22,* 171–193.

McBurney, D. H., & Collings, V. B. (1984). *Introduction to sensation perception* (2nd ed.). Englewood Cliffs, NJ: Prentice-Hall.

McCann, I. L., & Holmes, D. S. (1984). Influence of aerobic exercise on depression. *Journal of Personality and Social Psychology, 46,* 1142–1147.

McClelland, D. C. (1985). *Human motivation.* Glenview, IL: Scott, Foresman.

McClelland, D. C., & Pilon, D. A. (1983). Sources of adult motives in patterns of parent behavior in early childhood. *Journal of Personality and Social Psychology, 44,* 564–574.

McClelland, D. C., Atkinson, J. W., Clark, R. A., & Lowell, E. L. (1958). *The achievement motive.* New York: Appleton-Century-Crofts.

McCormick, D. A., & Thompson, R. F. (1984). Cerebellum: Essential involvement in the classically conditioned eyelid response. *Science, 223,* 296–299.

McCrae, R. R. (1984). Situational determinants of coping responses: Loss, threat, and challenge. *Journal of Personality and Social Psychology, 46,* 919–928.

McCrae, R. R., & Costa, P. T., Jr. (1982). Aging, the life course, and models of personality. In T. M. Field, A. Huston, H. C. Quay, L. Troll, & G. E. Finley (Eds.), *Review of human development* (pp. 602–613). New York: Wiley-Interscience.

McCrae, R. R., & Costa, P. T., Jr. (1987). Validation of the five-factor model of personality across instruments and observers. *Journal of Personality and Social Psychology, 52,* 81–90.

McDaniel, M. A., & Einstein, G. O. (1986). Bizarre imagery as an effective memory aid: The importance of distinctiveness. *Journal of Experimental Psychology: Learning, Memory and Cognition, 12,* 54–65.

McDougall, W. (1908). *An introduction to social psychology.* Boston: J. W. Luce.

McFarland, C., Ross, M., & DeCourville, N. (1989). Women's theories of menstruation and biases in recall of menstrual symptoms. *Journal of Personality and Social Psychology, 57,* 522–531.

McGarrigle, J., & Donaldson, M. (1975). Conservation accidents. *Cognition, 3,* 341–350.

McGaugh, J. L. (1983). Hormonal influences on memory. *Annual Review of Psychology, 34,* 297–323.

McGaugh, J. L., & Herz, M. J. (1972). *Memory consolidation.* San Francisco: Albion.

McGuire, W. J. (1985). Attitudes and attitude change. In G. Lindzey & E. Aronson (Eds.), *Handbook of social psychology* (pp. 233–346). New York: Random House.

McNally, R. J. (1987). Preparedness and phobias: A review. *Psychological Bulletin, 101,* 283–303.

McNeal, E. T., & Cimbolic, P. (1986). Antidepressants and biochemical theories of depression. *Psychological Bulletin, 99,* 361–374.

McReynolds, P. (1989). Diagnosis and clinical assessment: Current status and major issues. *Annual Review of Psychology, 40,* 83–108.

Mebert, C. J., & Kalinowski, M. F. (1986). Parents' expectations and perceptions of infant temperament: "Pregnancy status" differences. *Infant Behavior and Development, 9,* 321–334.

Meddis, R. (1979). The evolution and function of sleep. In D. A. Oakley & H. C. Plotkin (Eds.), *Brain, behavior and evolution* (pp. 99–125). London: Methuen.

Meddis, R., Pearson, A. J. D., & Langford, G. (1973). An extreme case of healthy insomnia. *EEG and Clinical Neurophysiology, 35,* 213–214.

Medin, D. L., & Smith, E. E. (1984). Concepts and concept formation. *Annual Review of Psychology, 35,* 113–138.

Mednick, S. A., & Mednick, M. T. (1967). *Remote Associates Test.* Boston: Houghton Mifflin.

Meehl, P. E. (1954). *Clinical vs. statistical prediction: A theoretical analysis and review of the evidence.* Minneapolis: University of Minnesota Press.

Meehl, P. E. (1956). Wanted: A good cookbook. *American Psychologist, 11,* 263–272.

Meichenbaum, D. (1977). *Cognitive-behavior modification: An integrative approach.* New York: Plenum.

Meijer, J. H., & Rietveld, W. J. (1989). Neurophysiology of the suprachiasmatic circadian pacemaker in rodents. *Physiology Reviews, 69,* 671–707.

Meindl, J. R., & Lerner, M. J. (1984). Exacerbation of extreme responses to an out-group. *Journal of Personality and Social Psychology, 47,* 71–84.

Meltzoff, A. N., & Moore, M. K. (1977). Imitation of facial and manual gestures by human neonates. *Science, 198,* 75–78.

Meltzoff, A. N., & Moore, M. K. (1983). Newborn infants imitate adult facial gestures. *Child Development, 54,* 702–709.

Melville, A., & Johnson, C. (1982). *Cured to death: The effects of prescription drugs.* Briarcliff Manor, NY: Scarborough House.

Melzack, R., & Wall, P. D. (1982). *The challenge of pain.* Harmondsworth, NY: Penguin.

Michaels, C. F. (1986). An ecological analysis of binocular vision. *Psychological Research, 48,* 1–22.

Miklowitz, D. J., Strachan, A. M., Goldstein, M. J., Doane, J. A., Snyder, K. S., Hogarty, G. E., & Falloon, I. R. H. (1986). Expressed emotion and communication deviance in families of schizophrenics. *Journal of abnormal psychology, 95,* 60–66.

Milgram, S. (1963). Behavioral study of obedience. *Journal of Abnormal and Social Psychology, 67,* 371–378.

Milgram, S. (1964). Issues in the study of obedience: A reply to Baumrind. *American Psychologist, 19,* 848–852.

Milgram, S. (1974). *Obedience to authority.* New York: Harper & Row.

Milgram, S. (1977). *The individual in a social world.* Reading, MA: Addison-Wesley.

Miller, A. G. (1986). *The obedience experiments: A case study of controversy in social science.* New York: Praeger.

Miller, G. A. (1956). The magical number seven, plus or minus two: Some limits on our capacity for processing information. *Psychological Review, 63,* 81–97.

Miller, N. (1960). Learning resistance to pain and fear: Effects of overlearning, exposure and rewarded exposure in context. *Journal of Experimental Psychology, 60,* 137–145.

Minuchin, S. (1974). *Families and family therapy.* Cambridge, MA: Harvard University Press.

Minuchin, S., Rosman, B. L., & Baker, L. (1978). *Psychosomatic families: Anorexia nervosa in context.* Cambridge, MA: Harvard University Press.

Mirsky, A. F., & Duncan, C. C. (1986). Etiology and expression of schizophrenia. *Annual Review of Psychology, 37,* 291–319.

Mischel, W. (1968). *Personality and assessment.* New York: Wiley.

Mogenson, G. J. (1987). Limbic-motor integration. *Progress in Psychobiology and Physiological Psychology, 12,* 117–170.

Monahan, L., Kuhn, D., & Shaver, P. (1974). Intrapsychic

versus cultural explanations of the "fear of success" motive. *Journal of Personality and Social Psychology, 29,* 60–64.

Mook, D. G., Brane, J., & Whitt, J. A. (1983). "De-satiation" in the rat: Reinstatement of feeding in the glucose-satiated rat. *Appetite, 4,* 15–34.

Moore, D. L., & Baron, R. S. (1983). Social facilitation: A physiological analysis. In J. T. Cacioppo & R. Petty (Eds.), *Social psychophysiology* (pp. 434–466). New York: Guilford.

Moore, K. A., Wenk, D., Hofferth, S. L., & Hayes, C. D. (1987). Trends in adolescent sexual and fertility behavior. In S. L. Hofferth & C. D. Hayes (Eds.), *Risking the future: Adolescent sexuality, pregnancy and childbearing* (p. 368). Washington, DC: National Academy Press.

Moore-Ede, M. C., Czeisler, C. A., & Richardson, G. S. (1983). Circadian timekeeping in health and disease. *New England Journal of Medicine, 309,* 530–536.

Morden, B., Mitchell, G., & Dement, W. C. (1967). Selective REM sleep deprivation and compensation phenomena in the rat. *Brain Research, 5,* 339–349.

Moreland, R. L., & Zajonc, R. B. (1982). Exposure effects in person perception: Familiarity, similarity and attraction. *Journal of Experimental Social Psychology, 18,* 395–415.

Morgan, A. H., Johnson, D. L., & Hilgard, E. R. (1974). The stability of hypnotic susceptibility: A longitudinal study. *International Journal of Clinical Experimental Hypnosis, 22,* 249–257.

Morse, S. J., & Watson, R. I. (1977). *Psychotherapies: A comparative casebook.* New York: Holt, Rinehart & Winston.

Moscovici, S. (1976). *Social influence and social change.* London: Academic Press.

Moscovici, S., Mugny, G., & Van Avermaet, E. (1985). *Perspectives on minority influence.* Cambridge and New York: Cambridge University Press.

Moskowitz, B. A. (1978). The acquisition of language. *Scientific American.*

Mountcastle, V. B. (1978). An organizing principle for cerebral function: The unit module and the distributed system. In G. M. Edleman and V. B. Mountcastle (Eds.), *The mindful brain* (pp. 21–42). Cambridge, MA: MIT Press.

Moyer, K. E. (1983). The physiology of motivation: Aggression as a model. In C. J. Scheier & A. M. Rogers (Eds.), *G. Stanley Hall lecture series* (Vol. 3). Washington, DC: American Psychological Association.

Munsinger, H. (1975). The adopted child's IQ: A critical review. *Psychological Bulletin, 82,* 623–659.

Murphy, C., & Withee, J. (1986). Age-related differences in the pleasantness of chemosensory stimuli. *Psychology and Aging, 3,* 303–311.

Murphy, J. (1976). Psychiatric labeling in cross-cultural perspective. *Science, 191,* 1019–1028.

Murray, H. A. (1938). *Explorations in personality.* New York: Oxford University Press.

Muter, P. (1980). Very rapid forgetting. *Memory and Cognition, 8,* 174–179.

Nash, M. (1987). What, if anything, is regressed about hypnotic age regression? A review of the empirical literature. *Psychological Bulletin, 102,* 42–52.

Nass, R. (1984). Case report: Recovery and reorganization after congenital unilateral brain damage. *Perceptual and Motor Skills, 59,* 867–874.

Nass, R., Peterson, H. DeC., & Koch, D. (1989). Differential effects of congenital left and right brain injury on intelligence. *Brain & Cognition, 9,* 258–266.

Nathan, P. E., & Skinstad, A. H. (1987). Outcomes of treatment for alcohol problems: Current methods, problems, and results. *Journal of Consulting and Clinical Psychology, 55*(3), 332–340.

Nathans, J., Thomas, D., & Hogness, D. S. (1986). Molecular genetics of human color vision: The genes encoding blue, green and red pigments. *Science, 232,* 193–202.

National Coalition on Television Violence. (1984). Shocking findings confirm TV violence causes adult crime. *NCTV Newsletter, 5,* 1.

National Council on Aging (1976). *The myth and reality of aging in America.* Washington, DC.

Neisser, U. (1979). The concept of intelligence. In R. J. Sternberg & D. K. Detterman (Eds.), *Human intelligence: Perspectives on its theory and measurement* (pp. 179–189). Norwood, NJ: Ablex.

Neisser, U. (1979). The control of information pickup in selective looking. In A. D. Pick (Ed.), *Perception and development: A tribute to Eleanor J. Gibson.* Hillsdale, NJ: Erlbaum.

Neisser, U. (Ed.). (1982). *Memory observed: Remembering in natural contexts.* New York: W. H. Freeman.

Nemeth, C. (1986). Differential contributions of majority and minority influence. *Psychological Review, 93,* 23–32.

Nemeth, C., & Chiles, C. (1988). Modelling courage: The role of dissent in fostering independence. *European Journal of Social Psychology, 18,* 275–280.

Nestoros, J. N. (1980). Ethanol specifically potentiates GABA-mediated neurotransmission in feline cerebral cortex. *Science, 209,* 708–710.

Neuberg, S. L. (1989). The goal of forming accurate impressions during social interactions: Attenuating the impact of negative expectancies. *Journal of Personality and Social Psychology, 56,* 374–386.

Neuchterlein, K. H., & Dawson, M. E. (1984). Information processing and attentional functioning in the developmental course of schizophrenic disorders. *Schizophrenia Bulletin, 10,* 160–203.

Neuman, O. (1987). Beyond capacity: A functional view of attention. In H. Heuer & A. F. Sanders (Eds.), *Perspectives on perception and action* (pp. 361–394). Hillsdale, NJ: Erlbaum.

Newcomb, M. D., & Bentler, P. M. (1989). Substance use and abuse among children and teenagers. *American Psychologist, 44,* 242–248.

Newcomb, T. (1961). *The acquaintance process.* New York: Holt, Rinehart & Winston.

Newcomb, T. M. (1943). *Personality and Social Change: Attitude Formation in a Student Community.* New York: Dryden Press.

Newell, A., & Simon, H. A. (1972). *Human problem solving.* Englewood Cliffs, NJ: Prentice-Hall.

Nezu, A. M., Nezu, C. M., & Blissett, S. E. (1988). Sense of humor as a moderator of the relation between stressful events and psychological distress: A prospective analysis. *Journal of Personality and Social Psychology, 54,* 520–525.

Nichols, D. G. (1979). Brown adipose tissue mitochondria. *Biochimica et Biophysica Acta, 549,* 1–29.

Nicoll, R. A., & Madison, D. V. (1982). General anesthetics hyperpolarize neurons in the vertebrate central nervous system. *Science, 217,* 1055–1057.

Nielson Media, (1990). *1990 Report on Television.* New York.

Nisbett, R. E. (1972). Hunger, obesity, and the ventromedial hypothalamus. *Psychological Review, 79,* 433–453.

Nisbett, R. E., & Ross, L. (1980). *Human inference: Strategies and shortcoming of social judgment.* Englewood Cliffs, NJ: Prentice-Hall.

Novin, D., VanderWeele, D. A., & Rezek, M. (1973).

Hepatic-portal 2-deoxy-D-glucose infusion causes eating: Evidence for peripheral glucoreceptors. *Science, 181,* 858–860.

Novin, D., Robinson, B. A., Culbreth, L. A., & Tordoff, M. G. (1983). Is there a role for the liver in the control of food intake? *American Journal of Clinical Nutrition, 9,* 233–246.

Noyes, R., Jr., Clarkson, C., Crowe, R. R., Yates, W. R., & McChesney, C. M. (1987). A family study of generalized anxiety disorder. *American Journal of Psychiatry, 144,* 1019–1024.

O'Connell, D. N., Shore, R. E., & Orne, M. T. (1970). Hypnotic age regression: An empirical and methodological analysis. *Journal of Abnormal Psychology Monograph, 76*(3, Pt. 2).

O'Donohue, T. L., Millington, W. R., Handelmann, G. E., Contreras, P. C., & Chronwall, B. M. (1985). On the 50th anniversary of Dale's law: Multiple neurotransmitter neurons. *Trends in Pharmacological Sciences, 6,* 305–308.

O'Hara, M. W., Behm, L. P., & Campbell, S. B. (1982). Predicting depressive symptomatology: Cognitive-behavioral models and post-partum depression. *Journal of Abnormal Psychology, 91,* 457–461.

O'Leary, A. (1990). Stress, emotion and immune function. *Psychological Bulletin, 108,* 363–382.

O'Sullivan, C. S., & Durso F. T. (1984). Effects of schema-incongruent information on memory for stereotypical attributes. *Journal of Personality and Social Psychology, 47,* 55–70.

Oatley, K., & Johnson-Laird, P. N. (1987). Towards a cognitive theory of emotions. *Cognition and Emotion, 1,* 29–50.

Ojemann, G. (1983). The intrahemispheric organization of human language, derived with electrical stimulation techniques. *Trends in Neurosciences, 6,* 184–189.

Oldfield, S. R., & Parker, S. P. (1984). Acuity of sound localization: A topography of auditory space: II. Pinna cues absent. *Perception, 13,* 601–617.

Olds, J., & Milner, P. (1954). Positive reinforcement produced by electrical stimulation of septal areas and other regions of rat brains. *Journal of Comparative and Physiological Psychology, 47,* 419–427.

Olson, R. R., & Attneave, F. (1970). What variables produce similarity grouping? *American Journal of Psychology, 83,* 1–21.

Ono, M. E., Rivest, J., & Ono, H. (1986). Depth perception as a function of motion parallax and absolute-distance information. *Journal of Experimental Psychology: Human Perception and Performance, 12,* 331–337.

Orbell, J. M., van de Kragt, A. J. C., & Dawes, R. M. (1988). Explaining discussion-induced cooperation. *Journal of Personality and Social Psychology, 54,* 811–819.

Orlinsky, D. E., & Howard, K. I. (1986). Process and outcome in psychotherapy. In S. L. Garfield & A. E. Bergin (Eds.), *Handbook of psychotherapy and behavior change* (3rd ed., pp. 311–381) New York: Wiley.

Orne, M. (1962). On the social psychology of the psychological experiment: With particular reference to demand characteristics. *American Psychologist, 17,* 776–783.

Orne, M., & Holland, C. C. (1968). On the ecological validity of laboratory deceptions. *International Journal of Psychiatry, 6,* 282–293.

Ortony, G. L., Clore, A., & Foss, M. A. (1987). The psychological foundations of the affective lexicon. *Journal of Personality and Social Psychology, 53,* 751–766.

Osgood, C. E. (1962). *An alternative to war or surrender.* Urbana: University of Illinois Press.

Over, R. (1987). Can human neonates imitate facial gestures? In B. E. McKenzie & R. H. Day (Eds.), *Perceptual development in early infancy: Problems and issues* (pp. 219–233). Hillsdale, NJ: Erlbaum.

Paivio, A. (1971). *Imagery and verbal processes.* New York: Holt.

Palo, J. (1989). Sleep researchers awake to possibilities. *Science, 121,* 351–352.

Panksepp, J. (1986). The neurochemistry of behavior. *Annual Review of Psychology, 37,* 77–107.

Parke, R. D., & Slaby, R. G. (1983). The development of aggression. In P. H. Mussen (Ed.), *Handbook of child psychology: Vol 4. Socialization, personality, and social development.* New York: Wiley.

Parker, K. C. H., Hanson, R. K., & Hunsley, J. (1988). MMPI, Rorschach, and WAIS: A meta-analytic comparison of reliability, stability, and validity. *Psychological Bulletin, 103,* 367–373.

Parten, M. (1933). Social play among preschool children. *Journal of Abnormal and Social Psychology, 28,* 136–147.

Patterson, F. G., Patterson, C. H., & Brentari, D. K. (1987). Language in child, chimp, and gorilla. *American Psychologist, 42,* 270–272.

Patterson, G. R. (1982). *Coercive family processes.* Eugene, OR: Castilia Press.

Paul, G. L., & Lentz, R. J. (1977). *Psychosocial treatment of chronic mental patients: Milieu versus social learning programs.* Cambridge, MA: Harvard University Press.

Pavlov, I. P. (1927). *Conditioned reflexes.* Oxford: Oxford University Press.

Pekkanen, J. (1982). Why do we sleep? *Science, 82,* 86.

Penfield, W., & Rasmussen, T. (1957). *The cerebral cortex of man: Clinical study of localization of function.* New York: Macmillan.

Pennebaker, J. W. (1989). Stream of consciousness and stress: Levels of thinking. In J. S. Uleman & J. A. Bargh (Eds.), *Unintended thought.* New York: Guilford.

Perkins, D. V. (1982). The assessment of stress using life events scales. In L. Goldberger & S. Breznitz (Eds.), *Handbook of stress: Theoretical and clinical aspects.* New York: Free Press.

Perls, F. (1973). *The Gestalt approach and eyewitness to therapy.* Palo Alto, CA: Science and Behavior Books.

Persky, H., Lief, H. I., Strauss, D., Miller, W. R., & O'Brien, C. P. (1978). Plasma testosterone level and sexual behavior of couples. *Archives of Sexual Behavior, 7,* 157–173.

Peters, R. S., & Mace, C. A. (1967). Psychology. In P. Edwards (Ed.), *The encyclopedia of philosophy* (Vol. 7, pp. 1–27). New York: Macmillan.

Peterson, C., & Seligman, M. E. P. (1984). Causal explanations as a risk factor for depression: Theory and evidence. *Psychological Review, 91,* 347–374.

Peterson, C., Seligman, M. E. P., & Vaillant, G. E. (1988). Pessimistic explanatory style is a risk factor for physical illness: A thirty-five-year longitudinal study. *Journal of Personality and Social Psychology, 55,* 23–27.

Peterson, L. R., & Peterson, M. (1959). Short-term retention of individual verbal items. *Journal of Experimental Psychology, 58,* 193–198.

Petty, R. E., & Cacioppo, J. T. (1981). *Attitudes and persuasion: Classic and contemporary approaches.* Dubuque, IA: Brown.

Petty, R. E., & Cacioppo, J. T. (1986). The elaboration likelihood model of persuasion. In L. Berkowitz (Ed.), *Advances in experimental social psychology* (Vol. 19, pp. 123–205). New York: Academic Press.

Phares, E. J. (1976). *Locus of control in personality.* Morristown, NJ: General Learning Press.

Phelps, M. E., & Mazziota, J. C. (1985). Positron emission tomography: Human brain function and biochemistry. *Science, 228,* 799–809.

Phillips, D. P., & Brugge, J. F. (1985). Progress in neurophysiology of sound localization. *Annual Review of Psychology, 36,* 245–274.

Piaget, J. (1936/1977). Experimental psychology: Its scope and method. Reprinted in H. E. Gruber & J. J. Voneche (Eds.), *The essential Piaget.* New York: Harper.

Piaget, J. (1952). *The origins of intelligence in children.* New York: International Universities Press.

Piaget, J. (1971). *Biology and knowledge.* Chicago: University of Chicago Press.

Piaget, J. (1978). *Behavior and evolution.* (D. Nicholson-Smith, Trans.) New York: Random House.

Piliavin, I. M., Rodin, J., & Piliavin, J. A. (1969). Good samaritanism: An underground phenomenon. *Journal of Personality and Social Psychology, 13,* 289–299.

Piliavin, J. A., Dovidio, J. F., Gaertner, S. S., & Clark, R. D. (1981). *Emergency intervention.* New York: Academic Press.

Pines, A., & Gal, R. (1977). The effect of food on test anxiety. *Journal of Applied and Social Psychology, 7,* 348–358.

Pitcher, E. G., & Schultz, L. H. (1983). *Boys and girls at play: The development of sex roles.* New York: Praeger.

Plutchik, R. (1980). *Emotion: A psychoevolutionary synthesis.* New York: Harper & Row.

Poulos, C. X., Hinson, R. E., & Siegel, S. (1981). The role of Pavlovian processes in drug tolerance and dependence: Implications for treatment. *Addictive Behaviors, 6,* 205–211.

Prechtl, H. F. R. (1982). Regression and transformations during neurological development. In T. G. Bever (Ed.), *Regressions in mental development: Basic phenomena and theories.* Hillsdale, NJ: Erlbaum.

Premack, D. (1986). *Gavagai! On the future history of the animal language controversy.* Cambridge, MA: MIT Press.

Premack, D. (1976). *Language and intelligence in ape and man.* Hillsdale, NJ: Erlbaum.

Prentice-Dunn, S., & Rogers, R. W. (1989). Deindividuation: The absence of awareness and self-regulation in group members. In P. B. Paulus (Ed.), *Psychology of group influence* (2nd ed., pp. 209–242). Hillsdale, NJ: Erlbaum.

Prinzmetal, W. (1981). Principles of feature integration in visual perception. *Perception and Psychophysics, 30,* 330–340.

Purdy, J. E., & Olmstead, K. M. (1984). New estimate for storage time in sensory memory. *Perceptual and Motor Skills, 59,* 683–686.

Pye, C., Ingram, D., & List, H. (1987). A comparison of initial consonant acquisition in English and Quiche. In K. E. Nelson & A. van Kleeck (Eds.), *Children's language* (Vol. 6, pp. 175–190). Hillsdale, NJ: Erlbaum.

Rachman, S. (1971). *The effects of psychotherapy.* New York: Pergamon.

Radecki, T. (1984). Deer hunter continues to kill, 35th victim—31 dead. *NCTV News, 5,* 3.

Ravussin, E., Lillioja, S., Knowler, W. C., [et al.] (1988). Reduced rate of energy expenditure as a risk factor for body weight gain. *New England Journal of Medicine, 318,* 467–472.

Raymond, C. (1989). A miracle goes sour. *Discover, 10,* 72.

Reisenzein, R. (1983). The Schachter theory of emotion: Two decades later. *Psychological Bulletin, 94,* 239–264.

Rescorla, R. A. (1988). Pavlovian conditioning: It's not what you think it is. *American Psychologist, 43,* 151–160.

Rescorla, R. A. (1968). Probability of shock in the presence and absence of CS in fear conditioning. *Journal of Comparative and Physiological Psychology, 66,* 1–5.

Reznikoff, M., Aronow, E., & Rauchway, A. (1982). The reliability of inkblot content scales. In C. D. Spielberger & J. N. Butcher (Eds.), *Advances in personality assessment* (Vol. 1). Hillsdale, NJ: Erlbaum.

Rhodewalt, F., & Agustsdottir, S. (1984). On the relationship of hardiness to the Type A behavior pattern: Perception of life events versus coping with life events. *Journal of Research in Personality, 18,* 212–223.

Ribble, M. A. (1943/1965). *The rights of infants.* New York: Columbia University Press.

Rich, D. L., Fowler, R. C., Fogarty, L. A., & Young, D. (1988). San Diego suicide study: III Relationships. *Archives of General Psychiatry, 45,* 533–541.

Richardson, J. T., & Zucco, G. M. (1989). Cognition and olfaction: A review. *Psychological Bulletin, 105,* 352–360.

Ridley, M. (1987). Pavlov, Ivan Petrovich. In R. Gregory (Ed.), *The Oxford companion to the mind* (pp. 594–596). New York: Oxford University Press.

Riegel, K. (1973). Dialectical operations: The final period of cognitive development. *Human Development, 16,* 346–370.

Robberson, M. R., & Rogers, R. W. (1988). Beyond fear appeals: Negative and positive persuasive appeals to health and self-esteem. *Journal of Applied Social Psychology, 18,* 277–287.

Roberts, S. B., Savage, J., Coward, W. A., Chew, B., & Lucas, A. (1988). Energy expenditure and intake in infants born to lean and overweight mothers. *New England Journal of Medicine, 318,* 461–466.

Robins, L. N., & Helzer, J. E. (1986). Diagnosis and clinical assessment: The current state of psychiatric diagnosis. *Annual Review of Psychology, 37,* 409–432.

Robins, L. N., Helzer, J. E., Weissman, M. M., Orvaschel, H., Gruenberg, E., Burke, J. D., Jr., & Regier, D. A. (1984). Lifetime prevalence of specific psychiatric disorders in three sites. *Archives of General Psychiatry, 41,* 949–958.

Robinson, F. P. (1970). *Effective study.* New York: Harper & Row.

Robles, R., Smith, R., Carver, C. S., & Wellens, A. R. (1987). Influence of subliminal: Visual images on the experience of anxiety. *Personality and Social Psychology Bulletin, 13*(3), 399–410.

Rodin, E. (1987). Psychosurgery: A rebuttal. *New England Journal of Medicine, 317*(2), 120.

Rodin, J. (1981). Current status of the internal-external hypothesis for obesity: What went wrong? *American Psychologist, 36,* 361–372.

Rodin, J. (1985). Insulin levels, hunger and food intake: An example of feedback loops in body weight regulation. *Health Psychology, 4,* 1–18.

Roediger, H. L., Weldon, M. S., & Challis, B. H. (1989). Explaining dissociations between implicit and explicit measures of retention: A processing account. In H. L. Roediger & F. I. M. Craik (Eds.), *Varieties of memory and consciousness: Essays in honor of Endel Tulving* (pp. 3–41). Hillsdale, NJ: Erlbaum.

Roffwarg, H. P., Munzio, J. N., & Dement, W. C. (1966). Ontogenic development of the human sleep-dream cycle. *Science, 152,* 604–619.

Rogers, C. R. (1951). *Client-centered therapy: Its current practice, implication and theory.* Boston: Houghton Mifflin.

Rogers, C. R. (1959). A theory of therapy, personality, and interpersonal relationships, as developed in the client-centered framework. In S. Koch (Ed.), *Psychology: A study of a science* (Vol. 3, pp. 184–256). New York: McGraw-Hill.

Rogers, C. R. (1961). *On becoming a person*. Boston: Houghton Mifflin.

Rogers, C. R. (1985). Client-centered psychotherapy. In H. I. Kaplan & B. J. Saddock (Eds.), *Comprehensive textbook of psychiatry* (4th ed., pp. 1563–1568). Baltimore: Williams & Wilkins.

Rogers, C. R., Gendlin, E. T., Kiesler, D. J., & Truax, C. B. (Eds.). (1967). *The therapeutic relationship and its impact: A study of psychotherapy with schizophrenics*. Madison, WI: University of Wisconsin Press.

Rolls, E. T. (1986). Neuronal activity related to the control of feeding. In R. Ritter & S. Ritter (Eds.), *Neural and humoral controls of food intake*. New York: Academic Press.

Rolls, E. T., Baylis, G. C., Hasselmo, M. E., & Nalwa, V. (1989). The effect of learning on the face-selective responses of neurons in the cortex in the superior temporal sulcus of the monkey. *Experimental Brain Research, 76*, 153–164.

Rosch, E. (1973). On the internal structure of perceptual and semantic categories. In T. E. Moore (Ed.), *Cognitive development and the acquisition of language* (pp. 111–144). New York: Academic Press.

Rosch, E. (1978). Principles of categorization. In E. Rosch & B. B. Lloyd (Eds.), *Cognition and categorization* (pp. 27–48). New York: Wiley.

Rose, R. J., Koskenvuo, M., Kaprio, J., Sarna, S., & Langinvainio, H. (1988). Shared genes, shared experiences, and similarity of personality. Data from 14,228 adult Finnish co-twins. *Journal of Personality and Social Psychology, 54*, 161–171.

Rosen, B. C., & D'Andrade, R. G. (1959). The psychological origins of achievement motivation. *Sociometry, 22*, 185–218.

Rosenblith, J. F., & Sims-Knight, J. E. (1985). *In the beginning: Development in the first two years of life*. Monterey, CA: Brooks/Cole.

Rosenhan, D. (1973). On being sane in insane places. *Science, 179*, 250–258.

Rosenman, R. H. (1986). Current and past history of Type A behavior pattern. In T. H. Schmidt, T. M. Dembrowski, & G. Blumchen (Eds.), *Biological and psychological factors in cardiovascular disease* (pp. 15–40). New York: Springer-Verlag.

Rosenthal, R., & Jacobson, L. (1968). *Pygmalion in the classroom: Teacher expectation and pupils' intellectual development*. New York: Holt, Rinehart & Winston.

Rosenzweig, M. R. (1984). Experience, memory and the brain. *American Psychologist, 39*, 365–376.

Rosenzweig, M. R. (1984). U.S. psychology and world psychology. *American Psychologist, 39*, 1389–1407.

Ross, E. D. (1981). The aprodosias: Functional-anatomical organization of the affective components of language in the right hemisphere. *Archives of Neurology, 38*, 561–569.

Ross, E. D. (1984). Right hemisphere's role in language, affective behavior and emotion. *Trends in Neurosciences, 7*, 342–346.

Ross, L. (1977). The intuitive psychologist and his shortcomings: Distortions in the attribution process. In L. Berkowitz (Ed.), *Advances in experimental social psychology* (Vol. 10, pp. 173–220). New York: Academic Press.

Rotter, J. B. (1966). Generalized expectancies for internal versus external control of reinforcement. *Psychological Monographs, 80* (Whole No. 609). American Psychological Association.

Rotter, J. B. (1954). *Social learning and clinical psychology*. Englewood Cliffs, NJ: Prentice-Hall.

Rubinstein, E. A. (1983). Television and behavior: Research conclusions of the 1982 NMIH report and their policy implications. *American Psychologist, 38*, 820–825.

Rule, B. G., & Ferguson, T. J. (1986). The effects of media violence on attitudes, emotions and cognitions. *Journal of Social Issues, 42*, 29–50.

Rumbaugh, D. (1977). *Language learning by a chimpanzee: The Lana project*. New York: Academic Press.

Rushton, J. P. (1979). Effects of prosocial television and film material on the behavior of viewers. In L. Berkowitz (Ed.), *Advances in experimental social psychology* (Vol. 12, pp. 321–351). New York: Academic Press.

Rushton, J. P., & Campbell, A. C. (1977). Modeling, vicarious reinforcement and extraversion on blood donating in adults: Immediate and long-term effects. *European Journal of Social Psychology, 7*, 297–306.

Russel, M. J. (1976). Human olfactory communication. *Nature, 260*, 520–522.

Rutte, C. G., Wilke, H. A. M., & Messick, D. M. (1987). Scarcity or abundance caused by people or the environment as determinants of behavior in the resource dilemma. *Journal of Experimental Social Psychology, 23*, 208–216.

Ryan, W. (1971). *Blaming the victim*. New York: Random House.

Salapatek, P., & Cohen, L. (Eds.). (1987). *Handbook of infant perception, 2: From perception to cognition*. New York: Academic Press.

Salholz, E. (1987, December 1). Behavior pills: Disciplining unruly kids with a potent drug. *Newsweek, 109*, 76.

Salthouse, T. A. (1985a). *A theory of cognitive aging*. Amsterdam: North-Holland.

Salthouse, T. A. (1985b). Speed of behavior and its implications for cognition. In J. E. Birren & K. W. Schaie (Eds.), *Handbook of the psychology of aging* (2nd ed.). New York: Van Nostrand Rheinhold.

Santos-Sacchi, J. (1988). Cochlear physiology. In A. F. Jahn & J. Santos-Sacchi (Eds.), *Physiology of the ear*. New York: Raven Press.

Sarbin, T. R., & Coe, W. C. (1972). *Hypnosis: A social psychological analysis of influence communication*. New York: Holt, Rinehart & Winston.

Sarbin, T. R., & Coe, W. C. (1979). Hypnosis and psychopathology: Replacing old myths with fresh metaphors. *Journal of Abnormal Psychology, 88*, 506–526.

Sartorius, N., Jablensky, A., Korten, A., Ernberg, G., Anker, M., Cooper, J. E., & Day, R. (1986). Early manifestations and first-contact incidence of schizophrenia in different cultures. *Psychological Medicine, 16*, 909–928.

Sato, K. (1987). Distribution of the cost of maintaining common resources. *Journal of Experimental Social Psychology, 23*, 19–31.

Sato, T. (1986). Receptor potential in rat taste cells. *Progress in Sensory Physiology, 6*, 1–38.

Savin-Williams, R. C., & Demo, D. H. (1984). Developmental change and stability in adolescent self-concept. *Developmental Psychology, 20*, 1100–1110.

Sawyer, J. (1966). Measurement and prediction, clinical and statistical. *Psychological Bulletin, 66*, 178–200.

Scarr, S., & Carter-Saltzman, L. (1982). Genetics and intelligence. In R. J. Sternberg (Ed.), *Handbook of human intelligence* (pp. 792–896). New York: Cambridge University Press.

Scarr, S., Pakstis, A. J., Katz, S. H., & Barker, W. B. (1977). The absence of a relationship between degree of white ancestry and intellectual skills within a black population. *Human Genetics, 39*, 69–86.

Scarr, S., Phillips, D., & McCartney, K. (1989). Working mothers and their families. *American Psychologist, 44*, 1402–1409.

Scarr, S., Phillips, D., & McCartney, K. (1990). Facts, fantasies and the future of child care in the United States. *Psychological Science, 1,* 26–35.

Scarr, S., & Weinberg, R. A. (1983). The Minnesota adoption studies: Genetic differences and malleability. *Child Development, 54,* 266–267.

Schacht, T. E. (1985). DSM-III and the politics of truth. *American Psychologist, 40,* 513–521.

Schacter, D. L. (1989). On the relation between memory and consciousness: Dissociable interactions and conscious experience. In H. L. Roediger & F. I. M. Craik (Eds.), *Varieties of memory and consciousness: Essays in honor of Endel Tulving.* Hillsdale, NJ: Erlbaum.

Schachter, S. (1968). Obesity and internal and external cues differentially affect the eating behaviors of obese and normal subjects. *Science, 161,* 751–756.

Schachter, S., & Singer, J. E. (1962). Cognitive, social and physiological determinants of emotional state. *Psychological Review, 69,* 379–399.

Schachter, S., & Wheeler, L. (1962). Epinephrine, chlorpromazine, and amusement. *Journal of Abnormal and Social Psychology, 65,* 121–128.

Schaie, K., & Herzog, C. (1983). Fourteen-year cohort-sequential studies of adult intelligence. *Developmental Psychology, 19,* 531–543.

Scheier, M. F., & Carver, C. S. (1985). Optimism, coping and health: Assessment and implications of generalized outcome expectancies. *Health Psychology, 4,* 219–247.

Scheier, M. F., & Carver, C. S. (1987). Dispositional optimism and physical well-being: The influence of generalized outcome expectancies on health. *Journal of Personality, 55,* 169–209.

Scheier, M. R., Weintraub, J. K., & Carver, C. S. (1986). Coping with stress: Divergent strategies of optimists and pessimists. *Journal of Personality and Social Psychology, 51,* 1257–1264.

Schlenker, B. R., & Forsyth, D. R. (1977). On the ethics of psychological research. *Journal of Experimental Social Psychology, 13,* 369–396.

Schmidt, F. E., & Hunter, J. E. (1981). Employment testing: Old theories and new research findings. *American Psychologist, 36,* 1128–1137.

Schneider, J. W., & Hacker, S. L. (1973). Sex-role imagery and the use of generic "man" in introductory texts. *American Sociologist, 8,* 12–18.

Schooler, J. W., Gerhard, D., & Loftus, E. F. (1986). Qualities of the unreal. *Journal of Experimental Psychology: Learning, Memory and Cognition, 12,* 171–181.

Schranger, J. S., & Osberg, T. M. (1981). The relative accuracy of self-predictions and judgments by others in psychological assessment. *Psychological Bulletin, 96,* 322–351.

Schull, J. (1979). A conditioned opponent theory of Pavlovian conditioning and habituation. In G. H. Bower (Ed.), *The psychology of learning and motivation* (Vol. 13, pp. 57–90). New York: Academic Press.

Schwartz, B. (1984). *Psychology of learning and behavior.* New York: Norton.

Schweickert, W., & Boggs, G. J. (1984). Models of central capacity and concurrency. *Journal of Mathematical Psychology, 28,* 223–281.

Segal, M. (1985). Mechanisms of action of noradrenaline in the brain. *Physiological Psychology, 13,* 172–178.

Segall, M. H., Campbell, D. T, & Herskovits, M. J. (1966). *The influence of culture on visual perception.* Indianapolis: Bobbs Merrill.

Seligman, M. E. P. (1971). Phobias and preparedness. *Behavior Therapy, 2,* 307–320.

Seligman, M. E. P. (1975). *Helplessness: On depression, development, and death.* San Francisco: Freeman.

Selye, H. (1976). *The stress of life.* New York: McGraw-Hill.

Sergent, J. (1987). A new look at the human split brain. *Brain, 1190,* 1375–1392.

Shapiro, C. M., Bortz, R., Mitchell, D., Bartel, P., & Jooste, P. (1981). Slow-wave sleep: A recovery period after exercise. *Science, 214,* 1253 -1254.

Shapiro, S., Ross, L. J., & Levine, H. S. (1965). Relationship of selected prenatal factors to pregnancy outcome and congenital anomalies. *American Journal of Public Health, 55,* 268–282.

Sheehan, P. W. (1982). Imagery and hypnosis—forging a link, at least in part. *Research in Community Psychology, Psychiatry and Behavior, 7,* 257–272.

Sheldon, W. H. (1942). *The varieties of temperament: A psychology of constitutional differences.* New York: Harper.

Shelton, R. C., & Weinberger, D. R. (1986). Computerized tomography in schizophrenia: A review and synthesis. In H. A. Nasrallah & D. R. Weinberger (Eds.), *Handbook of Schizophrenia* (Vol. 1). Amsterdam: Elsevier.

Shepard, G. M. (1987). *Neurobiology.* New York: Oxford University Press.

Shepard, R. N. (1978). Externalization of mental images and the act of creation. In B. S. Randhawa & W. E. Coffman (Eds.), *Visual learning, thinking and communicating.* New York: Academic Press.

Shepard, R. N., & Cooper, L. A. (1982). *Mental images and their transformations.* Cambridge, MA: MIT Press.

Sherif, M. (1936). *The psychology of social norms.* New York and London: Harper & Brothers.

Sherif, M., Harvey, L. J., White, B. J., Hood, W. R., & Sherif, C. W. (1988). *The Robbers Cave experiment: Intergroup conflict and cooperation* (rev. ed.). Middletown, CT: Wesleyan University Press. (Original work published 1961)

Shiffrin, R. M. (1985). Attention. In R. C. Atkinson, R. J. Herrnstein, G. Lindsey, & R. D. Luce (Eds.), *Stevens' handbook of experimental psychology* (Vol. 2, pp. 739–811). New York: Wiley.

Shiffrin, R. M., & Schneider, W. (1977). Controlled and automatic human information processing: II. Perceptual learning, automatic attending and a general theory. *Psychological Review, 84,* 127–190.

Shneidman, E. S. (1987). A psychological approach to suicide. In G. R. VandenBos & B. K. Bryant (Eds.), *Cataclysms, crises, and catastrophies: Psychology in action* (pp. 147–183). Washington, DC: American Psychological Association.

Siegel, S. (1983). Classical conditioning, drug tolerance, and drug dependence. In Y. Israel, F. B. Glaser, H. Kalant, R. E. Popham, W. Schmidt, & R. G. Smart (Eds.), *Research advances in alcohol and drug problems* (Vol. 7). New York: Plenum.

Siffre, M. (1975). Six months alone in a cave. *National Geographic, 147,* 426–435.

Sigall, H., & Landy, D. (1973). Radiating beauty: The effects of having a physically attractive partner on person perception. *Journal of Personality and Social Psychology, 51,* 615–621.

Sigall, H., & Landy, D. (1973). Radiating beauty: Effects of having a physically attractive partner on person perception. *Journal of Personality and Social Psychology, 28,* 218–224.

Silberglied, R. E. (1979). Communication in the ultraviolet. *Annual Review of Ecology and Systematics, 10,* 373–398.

Silveira, J. M. (1971). *Incubation: The effect of interruption timing and length on problem solution and quality of problem processing.* Unpublished doctoral dissertation. University of Oregon, Eugene.

Simpson, J. A., Campbell, B., & Berscheid, E. (1986). The association between romantic love and marriage: Kephart (1967) twice revisited. *Personality and Social Psychology Bulletin, 12,* 363–372.

Singer, J. (1976). *The inner world of daydreaming.* New York: Harper & Row.

Singer, J. L., & Singer, D. G. (1983a). Implications of childhood television viewing for cognition, imagination, and emotion. In J. Bryant and D. R. Anderson (Eds.), *Children's understanding of television: Research on attention and comprehension.* New York: Academic Press.

Singer, J. L., & Singer, D. G. (1983b). Psychologists look at television: Cognitive, developmental, personality, and social policy implications. *American Psychologist, 38,* 826–834.

Sirignano, S. W., & Lachman, M. E. (1985). Personality change during the transition to parenthood: The role of perceived infant temperament. *Developmental Psychology, 21,* 558–567.

Skinner, B. F. (1938). *The behavior of organisms: An experimental analysis.* New York: Appleton-Century-Crofts.

Skinner, B. F. (1948). *Walden two.* New York: Macmillan.

Skinner, B. F. (1953). *Science and human behavior.* New York: Macmillan.

Skinner, B. F. (1961). *Cumulative record* (3rd ed.). Englewood Cliffs, NJ: Prentice-Hall.

Skinner, B. F. (1971). *Beyond freedom and dignity.* New York: Knopf.

Slovic, P., Fischhoff, B., & Lichtenstein, S. (1976). Regulation of risk: A psychological perspective. In R. Noll (Ed.), *Social science and regulatory policy* (p. 292). Berkeley, CA: University of California Press.

Smelser, N., & Erikson, E. H. (Eds.), (1980). *Themes of work and love in adulthood.* Cambridge, MA: Harvard University Press.

Smith, C. (1985). Sleep states and learning: A review of the animal literature. *Neuroscience and Biobehavioral Reviews, 9,* 162–163.

Smith, E. E., & Medin, D. L. (1981). *Categories and concepts.* Cambridge, MA: Harvard University Press.

Smith, M. C. (1983). Hypnotic memory enhancement of witnesses: Does it work? *Psychological Bulletin, 81,* 178–195.

Smith, M. L., Glass, G. V., & Miller, T. I. (1980). *The benefits of psychotherapy.* Baltimore: Johns Hopkins University Press.

Snyder, C. R., & Fromkin, H. L. (1980). *Uniqueness: The human pursuit of difference.* New York: Plenum.

Snyder, M. (1974). Self-monitoring of expressive behavior. *Journal of Personality and Social Psychology, 30,* 526–537.

Snyder, M., & Gangestad, S. (1986). On the nature of self-monitoring: Matters of assessment, matters of validity. *Journal of Personality and Social Psychology, 51,* 125–139.

Snyder, M., & Ickes, W. (1985). Personality and social behavior. In G. Lindzey & E. Aronson (Eds.), *Handbook of social psychology* (3rd ed., pp. 883–947). New York: Random House.

Snyder, M., & Swann, W. B., Jr. (1978). Behavioral confirmation in social interaction: From social perception to social reality. *Journal of Personality and Social Psychology, 36,* 1202–1212.

Snyder, M., Tanke, E. D., & Berscheid, E. (1977). Social perception and interpersonal behavior: On the self-fulfilling nature of social stereotypes. *Journal of Personality and Social Psychology, 35,* 656–666.

Snyder, S. H. (1984). Drug and neurotransmitter receptors in the brain. *Science, 224,* 22–31.

Solomon, R. L. (1980). The opponent-process theory of acquired motivation: The costs of pleasure and the benefits of pain. *American Psychologist, 35,* 691–712.

Sommer, R. (1969). *Personal space.* Englewood Cliffs, NJ: Prentice-Hall.

Spanos, N. P. (1986). Hypnotic behavior: A social-psychological interpretation of amnesia, analgesia, and "trance logic." *The Behavioral and Brain Sciences, 9,* 449–467.

Spanos, N. P., Gwynn, M. I., & Stam, H. J. (1983). Instructional demands and ratings of overt and hidden pain during hypnotic analgesia. *Journal of Abnormal Psychology, 92,* 479–488.

Spanos, N. P., & Hewitt, E. C. (1980). The hidden observer in hypnotic amnesia: Discovery or experimental creation? *Journal of Personality and Social Psychology, 39,* 1201–1214.

Spanos, N. P., Lush, N. I., & Gwynn, M. I. (1989). Cognitive skill-training enhancement of hypnotizability: Generalization effects and trance logic responding. *Journal of Personality and Social Psychology, 56,* 795–804.

Spanos, N. P., Weekes, J. R., & Bertrand, L. D. (1985). Multiple personality: A social psychological perspective. *Journal of Abnormal Psychology, 94,* 362–376.

Spearman, C. (1927). *The abilities of man.* London: Macmillan.

Sperling, G. (1960). The information available in brief visual presentations. *Psychological Monographs, 74* (11, Whole No. 498). American Psychological Association.

Sperry, R. W. (1968). Hemisphere deconnection and unity in conscious awareness. *American Psychologist, 23,* 723–733.

Spitz, R. (1945). Hospitalism: An inquiry into the genesis of psychiatric conditions in early childhood. In R. S. Eissler (Ed.), *Psychoanalytic study of the child.* New Haven: Yale University Press.

Squire, L. R. (1986). Mechanisms of memory. *Science, 232,* 1612–1619.

Stark, E. (1986, May). Mom and dad: The great American heroes. *Psychology Today,* pp. 12–13.

Steele, C. M., Critchlow, B., & Liu, T. J. (1985). Alcohol and social behavior: II. The helpful drunkard. *Journal of Personality and Social Psychology, 48,* 35–46.

Steele, C. M., & Southwick, L. (1985). Alcohol and social behavior: I. The psychology of drunken excess. *Journal of Personality and Social Psychology, 48,* 18–34.

Steinbruek, S. M., Maxwell, S. E., & Howard, G. S. (1983). A meta-analysis of psychotherapy and drug therapy in the treatment of unipolar depression with adults. *Journal of Consulting and Clinical Psychology, 51,* 542–549.

Steiner, J. E. (1977). Facial expressions of the neonate infant indicating the hedonics of food-related chemical stimuli. In J. M. Weiffenbach (Ed.), *Taste and development: The genesis of sweet preference* (DHEW Publication [NIH] 77–1068). Rockville, MD: National Institutes of Health.

Stellar, E. (1954). The physiology of motivation. *Psychological Review, 61,* 5–22.

Stengel, R. (1987, September 14). At issue: Freedom for the irrational. *Time, 130,* 88.

Stern, D. (1977). *The first relationship: Mother and infant.* Cambridge, MA: Harvard University Press.

Stern, D. B., Brown, M., Ulett, G. A., & Sletten, I. (1981). A comparison of hypnosis, acupuncture, morphine, Valium, aspirin, and placebo in the management of experimentally induced pain. In W. E. Edmonston (Ed.), *Hypnosis and relaxation: Modern verification of an old equation.* New York: Wiley-Interscience.

Sternberg, R. J. (1985). *Beyond IQ.* Cambridge, Eng.: Cambridge University Press.

Sternberg, R. J. (1986). *Intelligence applied.* New York: Harcourt Brace Jovanovich.

Stevenson, H. W., Lee, S. Y., & Stigler, J. W. (1986). Mathematics achievement of Chinese, Japanese, and American children. *Science, 231,* 693–699.

Stewart, A. J., Sokol, M., Healy, J. M., Jr., & Chester, N. L. (1986). Longitudinal studies of psychological consequences of life changes in children and adults. *Journal of Personality and Social Psychology, 50,* 143–151.

Stine, E. L., Wingfield, A., & Poon, L. W. (1988). How much and how fast? Rapid processing of spoken language in later adulthood. *Psychology and Aging, 1,* 303–311.

Stone, A. A., & Neale, J. M. (1984). New measure of daily coping: Development and preliminary results. *Journal of Personality and Social Psychology, 46,* 892–906.

Stoner, J. (1961). *A comparison of individual and group decisions involving risk.* Unpublished Master's Thesis, Massachusetts Institute of Technology. Cited in R. Brown (1965), *Social psychology.* New York: Free Press.

Storms, C., & Storms, T. (1987). A taxonomic study of the vocabulary of emotions. *Journal of Personality and Social Psychology, 53,* 805–816.

Storms, M. (1973). Videotape and the attribution process: Reversing actors' and observers' points of view. *Journal of Personality and Social Psychology, 27,* 165–175.

Strack, F., Martin, L. L., & Stepper, S. (1988). Inhibiting and facilitating conditions of facial expressions: A nonobtrusive test of the facial feedback hypothesis. *Journal of Personality and Social Psychology, 54,* 768–776.

Strack, S., & Coyne, J. C. (1983). Social confirmation of dysphoria: Shared and private reactions to depression. *Journal of Personality and Social Psychology, 44,* 798–806.

Straus, M. (1979). Family patterns and child abuse in a nationally representative sample. *International Journal of Child Abuse and Neglect, 3,* 213–225.

Striegel-Moore, R. H., Silberstein, L. R., & Rodin, J. (1986). Toward an understanding of risk factors for bulimia. *American Psychologist, 41,* 246–263.

Stromeyer, C. F., III. (1970). Eidetikers. *Psychology Today,* 76–80.

Stroop, J. R. (1935). Studies of interference in serial verbal reactions. *Journal of Experimental Psychology, 18,* 643–662.

Sue, D., Sue, D., & Sue, S. (1990). *Understanding abnormal behavior.* Boston: Houghton Mifflin.

Sue, S. (1988). Psychotherapeutic services for ethnic minorities: Two decades of research findings. *American Psychologist, 43,* 301–308.

Suls, J., & Fletcher, B. (1985). The relative efficacy of avoidant and nonavoidant coping strategies: A meta-analysis. *Health Psychology, 4,* 249–288.

Summers, W. V., Horton, D. L., & Diehl, V. A. (1985). Contextual knowledge during encoding influences sentence recognition. *Journal of Experimental Psychology: Learning, Memory and Cognition, 11,* 771–779.

Szapocnik, J., Kurtines, W. M., Foote, F., Perez-Vidal, A., & Harris, O. (1986). Conjoint versus one-person family therapy: Further evidence for the effectiveness of conducting family therapy through one person with drug-abusing adolescents. *Journal of Consulting and Clinical Psychology, 54,* 395–397.

Szymanski, K., & Harkins, S. G. (1987). Social loafing and self-evaluation with a social standard. *Journal of Personality and Social Psychology, 53,* 891–897.

Tajfel, H. (1982). Social psychology of intergroup relations. *Annual Review of Psychology, 33,* 1–39.

Tallent, N. (1976). *Psychological report writing.* Englewood Cliffs, NJ: Prentice-Hall.

Taube, C. A., & Barrett, S. A. (Eds.). (1985). *Mental health, United States 1985* (DHHS Publication No. IADM 85–1378). Washington, DC: National Institute of Mental Health.

Tavris, C. (1984). On the wisdom of counting to ten: Personal and social dangers of anger expression. In P. Shaver (Ed.), *Review of personality and social psychology* (Vol. 5). Beverly Hills, CA: Sage.

Taylor, J. R., & Carroll, J. L. (1987). Current issues in electroconvulsive therapy. *Psychological Reports, 60,* 747–758.

Taylor, S. E., & Brown, J. D. (1988). Illusion and well-being: A social psychological perspective on mental health. *Psychological Bulletin, 103,* 193–210.

Taylor, S. E., & Crocker, J. (1981). Schematic bases of social information processing. In E. T. Higgins, C. P. Herman, & M. P. Zanna (Eds.), *Social cognition: The Ontario symposium.* Hillsdale, NJ: Erlbaum.

Teeter, J. H., & Brand, J. G. (1987). Peripheral mechanisms of gustation: Physiology and biochemistry. In T. E. Finger & W. L. Silver (Eds.), *Neurobiology of taste and smell.* New York: Wiley.

Tellegen, A., Lykken, D. T., Bouchard, T. J., Jr., Wilcox, K. J., Segal, N. L., & Rich, S. (1988). Personality similarity of twins reared apart and together. *Journal of Personality and Social Psychology, 54,* 1031–1039.

Teller, D. Y., & Bornstein, M. H. (1987). Infant color vision and color perception. In P. Salapatek & L. Cohen (Eds.), *Handbook of infant perception, 1: From sensation to perception.* New York: Academic Press.

Terman, G. W., Shavit, Y., Lewis, J. W., Cannon, J. T., & Liebeskind, J. C. (1984). Intrinsic mechanisms of pain inhibition: Activation by stress. *Science, 226,* 1270–1277.

Terman, L. M. (1916). *The measurement of intelligence.* Boston: Houghton Mifflin.

Terrace, H. S., Pettito, L. A., Sanders, R. J., & Bever, T. G. (1979). Can an ape create a sentence? *Science, 206,* 891–902.

Tesser, A., & Shaffer, D. R. (1990). Attitudes and attitude change. *Annual Review of Psychology, 41,* 479–523.

Thigpen, C. H., & Cleckley, H. (1954). *The three faces of Eve.* Kingsport, TN: Kingsport Press.

Thoits, P. (1983). Dimensions of life events that influence psychological distress: An evaluation and synthesis of the literature. In H. B. Kaplan (Ed.), *Psychosocial stress: Trends in theory and research.* New York: Academic Press.

Thoits, P. A. (1983). Dimensions of life events as influences upon the genesis of psychological distress and associated conditions: An evaluation and synthesis of the literature. In H. B. Kaplan (Ed.), *Psychosocial stress: Trends in theory and research.* New York: Academic Press.

Thomas, A., & Chess, S. (1977). *Temperament and development.* New York: Brunner-Mazel.

Thompson, J. K., Jarvie, G. J., Lakey, B. B., & Cureton, J. J. (1982). Exercise and obesity: Etiology, physiology and intervention. *Psychological Bulletin, 91,* 55–79.

Thompson, N. S. (1987, May-June). Rare sighting. *Harvard Magazine,* p. 9.

Thorndike, E. L. (1911). *Animal intelligence.* New York: Macmillan.

Thorndike, E. L. (1931). *Human learning.* Cambridge, MA: MIT Press.

Thorne, A. (1987). The press of personality: A study of conversations between introverts and extroverts. *Journal of Personality and Social Psychology, 53,* 718–726.

Thurstone, L. L. (1938). *Primary mental abilities.* Chicago: University of Chicago Press.

Tiffany, S. T., Martin, E. M., & Baker, T. B. (1986). Treatments for cigarette smoking: An evaluation of the contributions of aversion and counseling procedures. *Behavior Research and Therapy, 24,* 437–452.

Tilley, A. J. (1981). Retention over a period of REM or non-REM sleep. *British Journal of Psychology, 72,* 241–248.

Tolman, E. C. (1932). *Purposive behavior in men and animals.* New York: Century Co.

Tolman, E. C., & Honzik, C. H. (1930a). "Insight" in rats. *University of California Publications in Psychology, 4,* 215–232.

Tolman, E. C., & Honzik, C. H. (1930b). Introduction and removal of reward, and maze performance in rats. *University of California Publications in Psychology, 4,* 257–275.

Tong, Y. C., Clark, G. M., Blamey, P. J., Busby, P. A., & Dowell, R. C. (1982). Psychophysical studies for two multiple-channel cochlear implant patients. *Journal of the Acoustical Society of America, 71,* 153–160.

Trevarthen, C. (1979). Descriptive analyses of infant communicative behavior. In H. R. Schaffer (Ed.), *Studies in mother-infant interaction.* New York: Academic Press.

Triplett, N. (1898). The dynamogenic factors in pacemaking and competition. *American Journal of Psychology, 9,* 507–533.

Trope, Y. (1975). Seeking information about one's ability as a determinant of choice among tasks. *Journal of Personality and Social Psychology, 32,* 1004–1013.

Truax, C. B., & Carkhuff, R. R. (1967). *Toward effective counseling and psychotherapy.* Chicago: Aldine.

Tucker, D. M., Watson, R. T., & Heilman, K. M. (1977). Affective discrimination and evocation in patients with right parietal disease. *Neurology, 27,* 947–950.

Tufte, E. R. (1990). *Envisionary information.* Cheshire, CN: Graphics Press.

Tulving, E. (1982). *Elements of episodic memory.* New York: Oxford University Press.

Tulving, E. (1985). How many memory systems are there? *American Psychologist, 40,* 385–398.

Turner, S. M., Beidel, D. C., & Nathan, R. S. (1985). Biological factors in obsessive-compulsive disorders. *Psychological Bulletin, 97,* 430–450.

Tversky, A., & Kahneman, D. (1980). Causal schemas in judgments under uncertainty. In M. Fishbein (Ed.), *Progress in social psychology.* Hillsdale, NJ: Erlbaum.

Tversky, A., & Kahneman, D. (1983). Extensional versus intuitive reasoning: The conjunction fallacy in probability judgment. *Psychological Review, 90,* 293–315.

Uleman, J. S. (1989). A framework for thinking intentionally about unintended thoughts. In J. S. Uleman & J. A. Bargh (Eds.), *Unintended thought: The limits of awareness, intention and control.* New York: Guilford.

Underwood, B. J. (1957). Interference and forgetting. *Psychological Review, 64,* 49–60.

U.S. Bureau of the Census. (1990). *Statistical abstract of the United States.* Washington, DC: U.S. Government Printing Office.

Vallerand, R. J., & Richer, F. (1988). On the use of the Causal Dimension Scale in a field setting: A test with confirmatory factor analysis in success and failure situations. *Journal of Personality and Social Psychology, 54,* 704–712.

Valliant, G. E. (1977). *Adaptation to life: How the best and brightest came of age.* Boston: Little, Brown.

Van Putten, T., May, P. R. A., Marder, S. R., & Wittman, L. A. (1981). Subjective response to antipsychotic drugs. *Archives of General Psychiatry, 38,* 187–190.

Venter, J. C., Di Porzio, U., Robinson, D. A., Shreeve, S. A., Lai, J., Kerlavage, A. R, Fracek, S. P., Jr., Lentes, K.-U., & Fraser, C. M. (1988). Evolution of neurotransmitter receptor systems. *Progress in Neurobiology, 30,* 105–169.

Vogel, G. W. (1975). A review of REM sleep deprivation. *Archives of General Psychiatry, 32,* 749–761.

Vogel, G. W., Vogel, F., McAbee, R. S., & Thurmond, A. J. (1980). Improvement of depression by REM sleep deprivation. *Archives of General Psychiatry, 37,* 247–253.

von Békésy, G. (1960). *Experiments in hearing.* New York: McGraw-Hill.

von Békésy, G. (1967). *Sensory inhibition.* Princeton: Princeton University Press.

von Békésy, G., & Rosenblith, W. A. (1951). The mechanical properties of the ear. In S. S. Stevens (Ed.), *Handbook of experimental psychology* (pp. 1075–1115). New York: Wiley.

von Frisch, K. (1974). Decoding the language of the bee. *Science, 185,* 663–668.

Vygotsky, L. S. (1962). *Thought and language.* Cambridge, MA: MIT Press.

Wagner, G. A., & Morris, E. K. (1987). "Superstitious" behavior in children. *Psychological Record, 37,* 471–488.

Walk, R. D. (1981). *Perceptual development.* Monterey, CA: Brooks/Cole.

Wallace, P. (1977). Individual discrimination of humans by odor. *Physiology and Behavior, 19,* 577–579.

Wallace, R. K. (1970). The physiological effects of transcendental meditation. *Science, 167,* 1751–1754.

Wallach, H., Newman, E. B., & Rosenzweig, M. R. (1949). The precedence effect in sound localization. *American Journal of Psychology, 62,* 315–336.

Walsh, G., Charman, W. N., & Howland, H. C. (1984). Objective technique for the determination of monochromatic aberrations of the human eye. *Journal of the Optical Society of America, 1,* 987–992.

Warner, R. (1985). *Recovery from schizophrenia.* London: Routledge & Kegan Paul.

Warren, R. M., & Warren, R. P. (1968). *Helmholtz on perception: Its physiology and development.* New York: Wiley. (Original work published 1866)

Wason, P. C., & Johnson-Laird, P. N. (1972). *Psychology of reasoning: Structure and content.* Cambridge, MA: Harvard University Press.

Watkins, L. R., & Mayer, D. J. (1982). Organization of endogenous opiate and nonopiate pain control systems. *Science, 216,* 1185–1192.

Watson, D., & Pennebaker, J. W. (1989). Health complaints, stress, and distress: Exploring the central role of negative affectivity. *Psychological Review, 96,* 234–254.

Watson, J. B. (1928). *Psychological care of infant and child.* New York: Norton.

Watson, J. B., & Rayner, R. (1920). Conditioned emotional reactions. *Journal of Experimental Psychology, 3,* 1–14.

Watson, J. B., & Rayner, R. (1920). Conditioned emotional reactions. *Journal of Experimental Psychology, 10,* 421–428.

Watson, R. I., Jr. (1973). Investigation into deindividuation using a cross-cultural survey technique. *Journal of Personality and Social Psychology, 25,* 342–345.

Watzlawick, P., Beavin, J. H., & Jackson, D. D. (1967). *Pragmatics of human communication: A study of interactional patterns, pathologies, and paradoxes.* New York: Norton.

Webb, E. J., Campbell, D. T., Schwartz, R. D., & Sechrest,

L. (1966). *Unobtrusive measures: Nonreactive research in the social sciences*. Chicago: Rand McNally.

Webb, W. B., & Cartwright, R. D. (1978). Sleep and dreams. *Annual Review of Psychology, 29,* 223–252.

Wechsler, D. (1958). *The measurement and appraisal of adult intelligence.* (4th ed.) Baltimore: Williams & Wilkins.

Weiner, B. (1986). *An attributional theory of emotion and motivation.* New York: Springer-Verlag.

Weiner, B., Frieze, I., Kukla, A., Reed, W., Rest, S., & Rosenbaum, R. M. (1972). *Perceiving the causes of success and failure.* Morristown, NJ: General Learning Press.

Weiner, R. D. (1985). Convulsive therapies. In H. I. Kaplan & B. J. Saddock (Eds.), *Comprehensive textbook of psychiatry* (4th ed., pp. 1558–1563). Baltimore: Williams & Wilkins.

Weingartner, H., Adefris, W., Eich, J. E., & Murphy, D. L. (1975). Encoding-imagery specificity in alcohol state-dependent learning. *Journal of Experimental Psychology: Human Learning and Memory, 2,* 83–87.

Weiskrantz, L. (1987). Neuroanatomy of memory and amnesia: A case for multiple memory systems. *Human Neurobiology, 6,* 93–105.

Weisz, J. R., Weiss, B., Alike, M. D., & Kloltz, M. L. (1987). Effectiveness of psychotherapy with children and adolescents: A meta-analysis for clinicians. *Journal of Consulting and Clinical Psychology, 55,* 542–549.

Weitzenhoffer, A. M., & Hilgard, E. R. (1962). *The Stanford Hypnotic Susceptibility Scale, Form C.* Palo Alto, CA: Consulting Psychology Press.

Weitzman, E. D. (1981). Sleep and its disorders. *Annual Review of Neurosciences, 4,* 381–417.

Wender, P. H., Rosenthal, D., Kety, S. S., Schulsinger, F., & Welner, J. (1974). *Archives of General Psychiatry, 36,* 121–128.

Werker, J. F., & Tees, R. C. (1984). Cross-language speech perception: Evidence for perceptual reorganization during the first year of life. *Infant Behavior and Development, 7,* 49–63.

Wever, E. J. (1949). *Theory of hearing.* New York: Wiley.

Whalen, C. K., & Henker, B. (Eds.). (1980). *Hyperactive children.* New York: Academic Press.

Whitehouse, P. J., Price, D. L., Struble, R. G., Clark, A. W., Coyle, J. T., & DeLong, M. R. (1982). Alzheimer's disease and senile dementia: Loss of neurons in the basal forebrain. *Science, 215,* 1237–1239.

Whorf, B. L. (1956). *Language, thought and reality.* Cambridge, MA: MIT Press.

Wicker, A. W. (1969). Attitudes versus actions: The relationship of verbal and overt behavioral responses to attitude objects. *Journal of Social Issues, 25,* 41–78.

Wickwire, J. (1983). The great Couloir on Everest. *American Alpine Journal,* 8–14.

Wickwire, J. (1991). Personal communication.

Wiesenfeld, A., Malatesta, C., & DeLoach, L. (1981). Differential parental response to familiar and unfamiliar infant distress signals. *Infant Behavior and Development, 4,* 281–295.

Wiggins, J. S., Wiggins, N., & Conger, J. C. (1968). Correlates of heterosexual somatic preference. *Journal of Personality and Social Psychology, 10,* 82–90.

Wilcox, A. J., Weinberg, C. R., O'Connor, J. F., Baird, D. D., Schlatterer, J. P., Canfield, R. E., Armstrong, E. G., & Nisula, B. C. (1988). Incidence of early loss of pregnancy. *New England Journal of Medicine, 319,* 189–194.

Wilder, D. A. (1977). Perception of groups, size of opposition, and social influence. *Journal of Experimental Social Psychology, 13,* 253–268.

Wilder, D. A. (1981). Perceiving person as a group: Categorization and intergroup relations. In D. L. Hamilton (Ed.), *Cognitive processes in stereotyping and intergroup behavior.* Hillsdale, NJ: Erlbaum.

Williams, H. L., Tepas, D. I., & Morlock, H. C. (1962). Evoked responses to clicks and electroencephalographic stages of sleep in man. *Science, 138,* 685–686.

Wilson, E. O. (1975). *Sociobiology: The new synthesis.* Cambridge, MA: Belknap Press of Harvard University Press.

Wilson, E. O. (1978). *On human nature.* Cambridge, MA: Harvard University Press.

Wilson, S. C., & Barber, T. X. (1981). Vivid fantasy and hallucinatory abilities in the life histories of excellent hypnotic subjects ("somnambules"): Preliminary report with female subjects. In E. Klinger (Ed.), *Imagery: Concepts, results, and applications* (Vol. 2, pp. 133–149). New York: Plenum Press.

Winterbottom, M. R. (1958). The relation of need for achievement to learning experiences in independence and mastery. In J. W. Atkinson (Ed.), *Motives in fantasy, action, and society* (pp. 453–478). Princeton, NJ: Van Nostrand.

Wolpe, J. (1958). *Psychotherapy by reciprocal inhibition.* Stanford, CA: Stanford University Press.

Wolpe, J., & Lazarus, A. A. (1966). *Behavior therapy techniques.* New York: Pergamon.

Wong, D. F., Wagner, H. N., Tune, L. E., Dannals, R. F., Pearlson, G. D., & Links, J. M. (1986). Positron emission tomography reveals elevated D2 dopamine receptors in drug-naive schizophrenics. *Science, 234,* 1558–1562.

Wortman, C. B., & Silver, R. C. (1989). The myths of coping with loss. *Journal of Consulting and Clinical Psychology, 57,* 349–357.

Wyatt, J. J. (1988). Some aspects of the mechanisms of accommodation. *Vision Research, 28,* 75–86.

Wyrwicka, W., & Dobrzecka, C. (1960). Relationship between feeding and satiation centers of the hypothalamus. *Science, 132,* 805–806.

Yager, T., Laufer, R., & Gallops, M. (1984). Some problems associated with war experience in men of the Vietnam generation. *Archives of General Psychiatry, 41,* 327–333.

Yamaguchi, S. (1979). The umami taste. In J. C. Boudreau (Ed.), *Food and taste chemistry* (pp. 33–52). Houston: University of Texas Press.

Yeomans, J. (1988). Mechanisms of brain-stimulation reward. *Progress in Psychobiology and Physiological Psychology, 13,* 227–266.

Young, A. W., & Ellis, H. D. (1989). Childhood prosopagnosia. *Brain and Cognition, 9,* 16–47.

Yuille, J. C., & Cutshall, J. L. (1986). A case study of eyewitness memory of a crime. *Journal of Applied Psychology, 71,* 291–301.

Zajonc, R. B. (1965). Social facilitation. *Science, 149,* 269–274.

Zajonc, R. B. (1968). Attitudinal effects of mere exposure. *Journal of Personality and Social Psychology Monographs, 9,* 1–28.

Zajonc, R. B. (1980). Feeling and thinking: Preferences need no inferences. *American Psychologist, 35,* 151–175.

Zajonc, R. B. (1984). On the primacy of affect. *American Psychologist, 39,* 117–123.

Zajonc, R. B., Heingartner, A., & Herman, E. M. (1969). Social enhancement and impairment of performance in the cockroach. *Journal of Personality and Social Psychology, 13,* 82–92.

Zajonc, R. B., Pietromonaco, P., & Bargh, J. (1982). Independence and interaction of affect and cognition. In M. S. Clark & S. T. Fiske (Eds.), *Affect and cognition: The 17th An-*

nual Carnegie Symposium on Cognition (pp. 211–227). Hillsdale, NJ: Erlbaum.

Zanna, M. P., & Cooper, J. (1974). Dissonance and the pill: An attribution approach to studying the arousal properties of dissonance. *Journal of Personality and Social Psychology, 29,* 703–709.

Zelnick, M., & Kantner, J. F. (1980). Sexual activity, contraceptive use and pregnancy among metropolitan-area teenagers: 1971–1979. *Family Planning Perspectives, 12,* 230–237.

Zener, K. (1937). The significance of behavior accompanying conditioned salivary secretion for theories of the conditioned response. *American Journal of Psychology, 50,* 384–403.

Zika, S., & Chamberlain, K. (1987). Relation of hassles and personality to subjective well-being. *Journal of Personality and Social Psychology, 53,* 155–162.

Zilke, J. W. (1988). More voices join medicine in expressing concern over the amount, content of what children see on TV. *Journal of the American Medical Association, 260,* 1831–1832.

Zillman, D. (1983). Transfer of excitation in emotional behavior. In J. T. Cacioppo & R. E. Petty (Eds.), *Social psychophysiology* (pp. 215–242). New York: Guilford.

Zimbardo, P. G. (1970). The human choice: Individuation, reason and order versus deindividuation, impulse, and chaos. In W. J. Arnold & D. Levine (Eds.), *Nebraska symposium on motivation: 1969* (Vol. 17, pp. 237–307). Lincoln: University of Nebraska Press.

Zimbardo, P. G., Banks, W. C., Haney, C., & Jaffe, D. (1973, April 8). The mind is a formidable jailer: A Pirandellian prison. *New York Times Magazine,* 38–60.

Zubec, J. P. (Ed.). (1969). *Sensory deprivation: Fifteen years of research.* New York: Appleton-Century-Crofts.

Zuckerman, M., Koestner, R., DeBoy, T., Garcia, T., Maresca, B. C., & Sartoris, J. M. (1988). To predict some of the people some of the time: A reexamination of the moderator variable approach in personality theory. *Journal of Personality and Social Psychology, 54,* 1006–1019.

Zurek, P. M. (1980). The precedence effect and its possible role in the avoidance of interaural ambiguities. *Journal of the Acoustical Society of America, 67,* 952–964.

Zwislocki, J. J. (1981). Sound analyses in the ear: A history of discoveries. *American Scientist, 69,* 184–192.

Credits

Credits (*Continued from copyright page*)

Chapter 1: **p. 2:** Louis K. Meisel Gallery, New York. **p. 4:** Freidrich Albert Zorn, *Grammar of the Art of Dancing: Theoretical and Practical,* Boston, 1905. **p. 7:** (*top*) Library of Congress. (*bottom*) The Bettmann Archive. **p.8:** (*top*) Clark University Library. **p. 8:** (*left*) Historical Pictures Service. **p.9:** © T. Petersen/The Image Bank. **p. 10:** Louvre, Paris/Scala/Art Resource, New York. **p. 11:** © Yoav Levy/Phototake. **p. 12:** © Yoav Levy/Phototake. **p. 13:** Borrfdon/Explorer/Photo Researchers. **p. 15:** UPI/Bettmann Newsphotos. **p. 19:** © Erica Stone/Peter Arnold. **p. 20:** © Jim Amos/Photo Researchers.

Chapter 2: **p. 24:** Wellesley College Art Museum, Collection of Edward R. Downe, Jr. **p. 25:** © A. Glauberman/Photo Researchers. **p. 27:** © Dr. Jeremy Burgess/Photo Researchers. **p. 28:** (*left*) SIU/Visuals Unlimited. (*right*) SIU/Visuals Unlimited. **p. 29:** (*top, left*) © Dan McCoy/Rainbow. (*top, right*) Science VU/Visuals Unlimited. (*bottom*) © Dan McCoy/Rainbow. **p.41:** (*left*) © Michael Abbey/Science Source/Photo Researchers. (*right*) © Dr. Brian Eyden/Science Photo Library/Photo Researchers. *Figure 2.17* Reprinted with permission of Macmillan Publishing Company from *The Cerebral Cortex of Man* by Wilder Penfield and Theodore Rasmussen. Copyright 1950 Macmillan Publishing Company; copyright renewed © 1978 Theodore Rasmussen. **p. 47:** *Figure 2.22* Reprinted with permission of Macmillan Publishing Company from *The Cerebral Cortex of Man* by Wilder Penfield and Theodore Rasmussen. Copyright 1950 Macmillan Publishing Company; copyright renewed © 1978 Theodore Rasmussen. **p. 51:** Schmitt, Francis and Worden, Frederic, *The Neurosciences: Fourth Study Program,* The MIT Press, Cambridge, Mass. 1979. **p. 52:** © Dan McCoy/Rainbow.

Chapter 3: **p. 58:** Bridgeman/Art Resource, New York. **p. 62:** Lenneberg, Eric H., *Biological Foundations of Language,* Wiley & Sons, New York, 1967. **p. 66:** (*left*) © Dr. G. Bredberg/Photo Researchers. (*right*) Robert E. Preston, courtesy of Prof. Joseph E. Hawkins, Kresge Hearing Research Institute, University of Michigan Medical School, Ann Arbor. **p. 67:** (*left*) N.A.S./M.W.F. Tweedie/Photo Researchers. (*right*) N.A.S./M.W.F. Tweedie/Photo Researchers. **p. 71:** (*left*) © Jawitz/The Image Bank. (*right*) © Ted Russell/The Image Bank. **p. 72:** (*left*) NASA. (*right*) NASA. **p. 76:** Dvorine Color Vision Test © 1944, 1953, 1958 by The Psychological Corporation. Reproduced by permission. All rights reserved. **p. 85:** *Table 3.1* Adapted from Eugene Galanter, "Contemporary Psychophysics," in *New Directions in Psychology,* edited by R. Brown (New York: Holt, Rinehart and Winston, 1962). Used by permission of Dr. Eugene Galanter. **p. 87:** © William Curtsinger/Photo Researchers.

Chapter 4: **p. 88:** © David Hockney, 1985. **p. 92:** (*left and right*) Biederman, Irving et al, Detecting the Unexpected in Photointerpretation, *Human Factors,* 1981, 23 No. 2, The Human Factors Society, Santa Monica, California. **p. 93:** Relativity, © 1953 M. C. Escher/Cordon Art-Baarn-Holland. **p. 100:** © David Madison/Duomo. **p. 102:** Cups 4, Picasso, 1972, Lithograph by Jasper Johns/The Museum of Modern Art, New York. Gift of Celeste Bartos. **p. 104:** (*top*) © Bildarchiv Okapin/Photo Researchers. (*bottom*) © Bill Bachman/Photo Researchers. **p. 107:** (*top*) Both: © Norman Snyder, 1985. (*bottom*) © Walter Wick. **p. 109:** © Enrico Ferorelli. **p. 110:** © Robert Caputo/Stock Boston. **p. 113:** © Brian Palmer. **p. 116:** (*left*) © A. M. Rosario/The Image Bank. (*right*) © Weinberg Clark/The Image Bank.

Chapter 5: **p. 118:** © 1992, Herscovici/Art Resource, New York, The Artists Rights Society. **p. 120:** © Dr. M. Raichle/Peter Arnold. **p. 122:** © Roger Miller/The Image Bank. **p. 125:** *Figure 5.4* Groblewski, Nuñez & Gold, 1980. Used by permission of the authors. **p. 126:** © Michel Siffre. **p. 129:** *Table 5.1* Adapted with permission of Charles Scribner's Sons, an imprint of Macmillan Publishing Company, from *The Psychology of Sleep* by David Foulkes. Copyright © 1966 by David Foulkes. **p. 130:** © Susan Leavines/Photo Researchers. **p. 131:** *Figure 5.8* From "Ontogenetic Development of the Human Sleep-Dream Cycle," by H.P. Roffwarg, J.N. Muzio, and W.C. Dement, *Science,* 152, 1966, pp. 604–619. Copyright 1966 by the AAAS. Used by permission. **p. 133:** *Table 5.2* From *Sleep,* "The Dreams of College Men and Women in 1950 and 1980: A Comparison of Dreams, Contents, and Sex Differences," by C.S. Hall, W. Dornhoff, K.A. Blick, and K.E. Weesner, vol. 5, 1982, pp. 188–194. Reprinted by permission. **p. 137:** Department of Health and Human Services. **p. 139:** *Figure 5.9* By permission of Ernest Hilgard. **p. 140:** Ernest R. Hilgard, Psychology Department/ News and Publications, Stanford University. **p. 145:** UPI/Bettmann Newsphotos. **p. 146:** © Cliff Feulner/The Image Bank.

Chapter 6: **p. 150:** ACA Galleries, New York and the Romare Howard Bearden Foundation. **p. 152:** Culver Pictures. **p. 153:** The Bettmann Archive. **p. 155:** Bank One, Madison, Wisconsin. **p. 160:** UPI/Bettmann Newsphotos. **p. 166:** © Guido A. Rossi/The Image Bank. **p. 174:** Both: © J. Hillis Miller. **p. 176:** Bandura, Ross and Ross, 1963.

Chapter 7: **p. 178:** National Museum of American Art, Smithsonian Institution. **p. 180:** © Paul Loven/Stockphotos. **p. 182:** © Howard Beckerman Animation. **p. 183:** Levine, Michael W., Shefner, Jeremy, *Fundamentals of Sensation and Perception,* Brooks/Cole Publishing Company, Pacific Grove, California, 1988. **p. 185:** The Bettmann Archive. **p. 186:** The Image Works. **p. 200:** (*top, left and right*) Elizabeth F. Loftus, The Malleability of Human Memory, *American Scientist*, vol. 67. no. 3, May–June 1979, © 1979 Sigma xi, The Scientific Research Society of North America, Inc., University of Washington. (*bottom*) © Julie Houck/Stock Boston. **p. 201:** © Phillip Hayson/Photo Researchers. **p. 202:** *Figure 7.5* From "Semantic Memory Content in Permastore: 50 Years of Memory for Spanish Learned in School," by H.P. Bahrick, *Journal of Experimental Psychology; General, 113,* 1984, p. 10. Copyright 1984 by the American Psychological Association. Reprinted by permission.

Chapter 8: **p. 206:** Wildenstein Ltd., Tokyo. **p. 209:** (left) © Lionel Delevingne. (center and left) The Workbench. **p. 210:** (left) © Calvin Larsen/Photo Researchers. (center) © Robert W. Hernandza/Photo Researchers. (right) © Dr. M. P. Kahl/Photo Researchers. **p. 215:** Prints Plus, New York. **p. 220:** Figure 8.10 From Bernstein, D.A., E.J. Roy, T.K. Srull, and C.D. Wickens, Psychology, 2/e. Copyright © 1991 by Houghton Mifflin Company. Used with permission. **p. 229:** Musée d'Orsay, Paris/Giraudon/Art Resource, New York. **p. 234:** Table 8.2 Adapted from E.H. Lenneberg, Biological Foundations of Language. Copyright © 1967 by John Wiley & Sons, Inc. Reprinted by permission of John Wiley & Sons, Inc. **p. 236:** Frank Kiernan/Georgia State University in co-operation with Yerkes Regional Primate Research Center at Emory University. **p. 238:** © David Madison.

Chapter 9: **p. 240:** Private Collection. **p. 241:** © James Wickwire. **p. 242:** (top) © David Madison. (bottom) © Mitch Reardon/Tony Stone Worldwide. **p. 243:** © Lynne Cox/Sygma. **p. 244:** (left) © Mark Boulton/Photo Researchers. (right) © George Holton/Photo Researchers. **p. 246:** © Bernard Heinrich. **p. 247:** Harry F. Harlow, University of Wisconsin, Primate Laboratory. **p. 253:** Neal Miller, Rockefeller University. **p. 258:** © Tom McHugh/Photo Researchers. **p. 259:** Figure 9.11 Masters & Johnson, 1966. Used by permission of the authors. **p. 263:** Figure 9.12 deCharms & Carpenter, 1968. Reprinted by permission of the author.

Chapter 10: **p. 266:** London Transport Museum. **p. 269:** Table 10.1 Adapted from Plutchik (1980). Emotion: A psycho-revolutionary synthesis. New York: Harper & Row. Used by permission. **p. 271:** © Bernard Gottfryd. **p. 272:** All: © Dalia Migdal. **p. 277:** (top) © David Madison. (bottom) both: Dr. Leonard Martin, University of Georgia. **p. 284:** Figure 10.10 Figure from Emotion: A Psychorevolutionary Synthesis by Robert Plutchik. Copyright © 1980 by Robert Plutchik. Reprinted by permission of Harper Collins Publishers Inc. **p. 288:** Table 10.3 Reprinted with permission from Journal of Psychosomatic Research, Vol. 11, No. 2, T.H. Holmes and R.H. Rahe, "The Social Readjustment Scale,", Copyright 1967, Pergamon Press plc. **p. 290:** Haefeli, © Punch, 1990/Rothco. **p. 292:** © Mimi Forsyth/Monkmeyer. Table 10.4 Adapted from Scheier, M.F. & Carver, C.S. (1985). Optimism, coping and health: Assessment and implications of generalized outcome expectancies. Health Psychology, 4, 219–247. **p. 289:** © Freda Leinwand/Monkmeyer. **p. 293:** © Will & Demi McIntyre/Photo Researchers.

Chapter 11: **p. 296:** Collection of Joan Robey, Denver Colorado. **p. 301:** (left) © Biophoto Associates/Science Source/Photo Researchers. (right) Joseph Gall/ Fristrom, J.W, and Clegg, M.T. (1988), Principles of Genetics. W.H. Freeman and Co., N.Y. **p. 303:** © Enrico Ferorelli. **p. 306:** © Lennart Nilsson/Bonnier Fakta. **p. 308:** (left) © Elizabeth Crews/The Image Works. (right) © J. DA Cunha/Petit/Photo Researchers. **p. 309:** Figure 11.8 Cohen & Salapatek, 1975. Used by permission. **p. 310:** Dr. Patricia Kuhl, University of Washington. **p. 311:** Dr. Patricia Kuhl, University of Washington. **p. 313:** Figure 11.9 Haaf & Brown, 1976. Used by permission. **p. 316:** © Anne Martens/The Image Bank. **p. 316:** Figure 11.10 Baillargeon & Graber, 1987. Reprinted with the permission of Ablex Publishing Corporation. **p. 317:** Figure 11.11 Weisenfeld, Malatesta & DeLoach, 1981. Reprinted with the permission of Ablex Publishing Corporation. **p. 318:** Figure 11.12 From T. Berry Brazelton, Neonatal Behavioral Assessment Scale, 2/e. Copyright © 1984. Used by permission of Spastics International Medical

Publications. **p. 320:** © Thomas McAvoy, Life Magazine, © 1955 Time, Inc. **p. 321:** Both: University of Wisconsin, Harlow Primate Laboratory. **p. 324:** © Sybil Shackman/Monkmeyer.

Chapter 12: **p. 326:** Chris Eden. **p. 328:** © Anderson/Monkmeyer. **p. 329:** Harvard University. **p. 330:** UPI/Bettmann Newsphotos. **p. 331:** Table 12.3 Adapted from Childhood and Society by Erik H. Erikson, Second Edition, by permission of W.W. Norton & Company, Inc. Copyright 1950, © 1963 by W.W. Norton & Company, Inc. Copyright renewed 1978 by Erik H. Erikson. **p. 332:** Figure 12.1 Drawing by Joel Ito. **p. 333:** Figure 12.2 Drawing by John Rourke. **p. 335:** Figure 12.4 Reproduced with the kind permission of Educational Review (Carfax Publishing Company, UK). **p. 336:** UPI/Bettmann Newsphotos. **p. 337:** (top) © George Goodwin/Monkmeyer. (bottom left) © Alvis Upitis/The Image Bank. (bottom right) © Joseph Schuyler/Stock Boston. **p. 339:** The Image Works. **p. 341:** (left) © Y. Arthus-Bertrand/Peter Arnold. (right) © J.P. Laffont/Sygma. **p. 344:** Harvard University, Graduate School of Education/Lillian Kemp. **p. 351:** © Bob Daemmrich/The Image Works. **p. 352:** Table 12.5 © by and reprinted with permission of The National Council on the Aging, Inc., 409 Third Street SW, Washington, DC 20024. **p. 354:** Figure 12.9 From The Development of Children by M. Cole and S. Cole. Copyright © 1989 by Michael Cole and Sheila R. Cole, and Judith Boies. Reprinted by permission of W.H. Freeman and Company.

Chapter 13: **p. 358:** Joslyn Art Museum, Omaha. **p. 361:** Table 13.1 From "On the nature of self-monitoring: Matters of assessment, matters of validity," by M. Snyder and S. Gangestad, Journal of Personality and Social Psychology, 51, (1), pp. 125–139. Copyright by the American Psychological Association. Reprinted by permission. **p. 365:** Figure 13.2 © 1990 by Barbara Hustedt Crook. Reprinted by permission. **p. 368:** © Robin Forbes/The Image Bank. **p. 369:** © Stuart Dee/The Image Bank. **p. 372:** The Bettmann Archive. **p. 378:** Figure 13.4 Simulated items similar to those on the Wechsler Intelligence Scale for Children - Revised. Copyright © 1974 by The Psychological Corporation. Reproduced by permission. All rights reserved. **p. 379:** (left) UPI/Bettmann Newsphotos. (center) Reuters/Bettmann. (right) Reuters /Bettmann. **p. 380:** The Bettmann Archive. **p. 384:** Raven Progressive Matrices, J.C. Raven Limited. **p. 386:** Figure 13.8 Duckworth & Anderson, 1986. Used by permission of Accelerated Development Inc., Publishers. **p. 387:** © E. R. Degginger/Bruce Coleman. **p. 388:** Room in New York, 1932. Painting by Edward Hopper, University of Nebraska Art Galleries, F.M. Hall Collection.

Chapter 14: **p. 392:** San Francisco Museum of Modern Art. **p. 397:** Freud, S., New Introductory Lectures on Psycho-analysis, Carlton House, New York, 1933. **p. 399:** © Rhoda Sidney/Photo Edit. **p. 402:** (left) UPI/Bettmann Newsphotos. (right) AP/Wide World Photos. **p. 403:** Paradise of a God, Tibetan painting. Musee Guimet, Paris/Art Resource, New York. **p. 406:** (left) © Mel Digiacomo/The Image Bank. (center) © Dalia Migdal. (right) © Bob Daemmrich/Stock Boston. **p. 407:** UPI/Bettmann Newsphotos. **p. 409:** Table 14.3 From A.H. Maslow, Toward a Psychology of Being, 2/e. Copyright 1968. Reprinted by permission of Van Nostrand Reinhold. **p. 413:** Both: AP/Wide World Photos. **p. 414:** Figure 14.5 "Eysenck's Personality Dimension," from The Causes and Cures of Neurosis; An Introduction to Modern Behavior Therapy Based on Learning Theory and the Principle of

Conditioning, by H.J. Eysenck and S. Rachman, 1965. Reprinted with permission. **p. 417:** *Figure 14.6* From Julian B. Rotter, in *Psychological Monographs* edited by Gregory A. Kimble. Copyright 1966 by the American Psychological Association. Reprinted by permission. **p. 421:** *Figure 14.7* By kind permission of R.B. Cattell.

Chapter 15: **p. 424:** Albright-Knox Art Gallery, Buffalo, New York. Gift of Seymour H. Knox, 1958. **p. 429:** *Table 15.2* From *Archives of General Psychiatry, 41,* pp. 949–958. Copyright 1984, American Medical Association. Used by permission. **p. 433:** *Table 15.3* From Sue, D., Sue, D. and Sue, S., *Understanding Abnormal Behavior,* 3/e. Copyright © 1990 by Houghton Mifflin Company. Used with permission. (*bottom*) Department of Health & Human Services. **p. 434:** UPI/Bettmann Newsphotos. **p. 436:** (*left*) Culver Pictures. (*right*) Superstock. **p. 437:** All: Hans Prinzhorn Collection, Heidelberg. **p. 439:** (*top*) © Grunvitus/Monkmeyer. (*bottom*) Ken Pyne, © Punch/Rothco. **p. 441:** (*top*) The Bettmann Archive. (*bottom left*) Kobal Collection/Superstock. (*bottom, center*) Culver Pictures. (*bottom, right*) Kobal Collection/Superstock. **p. 450:** © Dr. Allan Mirsky. **p. 452:** All: Dr. D. Weinberger /Dept. of Health & Human Services.

Chapter 16: **p. 458:** Ordrupgard Museum, Copenhagen. **p. 461:** Historical Pictures Service. **p. 463:** © Michal Heron/Monkmeyer. **p. 466:** FPG international. **p. 468:** *Figure 16.1* Reprinted with permission from J. Wolfe and A.A. Lazarus, *Behavior Therapy Techniques,* Copyright 1966, Pergamon Press PLC. **p. 472:** Schwadron, © Punch/Rothco. **p. 475:** (*left*) UPI/Bettmann Newsphotos. (*center*) © Lynn McFaren/Photo Researchers. (*right*) UPI/Bettmann Newsphotos. **p. 478:** The Bettmann Archive. **p. 479:** *Table 16.1* Sue, David, Derald Sue, & Stanley Sue, *Understanding Human Behavior,* Third Edition. Copyright © 1990 by Houghton Mifflin Company. Used with permission. **p. 481:** © Will McIntyre, Duke University Medical Center/Photo Researchers. **p. 482:** AP/Wide World Photos. **p. 488:** Historical Pictures Service.

Chapter 17: **p. 490:** Courtauld Institute Galleries, London, Fry Collection. **p. 492:** © Bob Daemmrich/Stock Boston. **p. 495:** *Figure 17.2* From Brehm, S.S. and Kassin, S.M., *Social Psychology.* Copyright © 1990 by Houghton Mifflin Company. Used with permission. **p. 496:** FPG International. **p. 505:** © Julie Houck/Stock Boston. **p. 508:** UPI/Bettmann Newsphotos. **p. 509:** © A. Tannerhawm / Sygma. **p. 519:** (*left*) © Manfred Danegger/Peter Arnold. (*center*) © Manfred Danegger/Peter Arnold. (*right*) © Jack Prelutsky/Stock Boston. **p. 521:** (*left*) AP/Wide World Photos. (*right*) © J.L. Atlan/Sygma. **p. 524:** *Figure 17.12* From Brehm, S.S. and Kassin, S.M., *Social Psychology.* Copyright © 1990 by Houghton Mifflin Company. Used with permission.

Chapter 18: **p. 526:** Musée Leger, Biot/The Bridgeman Art Gallery. **p. 528:** (*left*) © Rick Browne/Stock Boston. (*right*) © Eastcott/Momatiuk/The Image Works. **p. 529:** © Robert Azzi/Woodfin Camp & Associates. **p. 530:** *Figure 18.1* From Brehm, S.S. and Kassin, S.M., *Social Psychology.* Copyright © 1990 by Houghton Mifflin Company. Used with permission. **p. 531:** William Vandivert **p. 537:** AP/Wide World Photos. **p. 541:** Graduate School, University Center of City University of New York. **p. 543:** © Greenlan/The Image Works. **p. 545:** © M. Siluk/The Image Works. **p. 546:** © Eric Pasquier/Sygma. **p. 548:** © Baldev/Sygma. **p. 550:** © Bob Daemmrich/Stock Boston. *Figure 18.9* From "Many Hands Make Light the Work: The Causes and Consequences of Social Loafing," by Latané, K. Williams, and S. Harkins, *Journal of Personality and Social Psychology* 37 (6). Copyright 1979 by the American Psychological Association. Reprinted by permission. **p. 557:** © David Noble/FPG International. **p. 560:** © Erich Hartman/Magnum Photos.

Name Index

Subject Index